ADVANCE PRAISE FOR

Food as Communication/Communication as Food

"Collectively, this book is an assembly prism that disperses light, making transparent food's constitutional force and pervasive influence in most aspects of our daily lives. In addition to being well-organized and well-written, all of the chapters are amazingly free of academic jargon, which make them readily understandable."

Jane Ferry, Webster University

"This fascinating collection of research articles walks the reader through history and space, the ages and the professions to get at the nitty-grittyness of this power.... To make food visible, the authors rightly observe food in very specific ways as each tries to examine the meaning of the particular phenomenon under study, making use of food as the 'communicator' of that meaning."

Toni Liquori, School Food FOCUS and Nutrition Program, Adjunct Full Professor, Teachers College, Columbia University

"This book contributes significantly to food studies by clearly defining one discipline's potential for understanding the subject. In twenty-two chapters of international scope, it outlines theories and methods in the field of communication and demonstrates how they are applicable to understanding food as social, cultural, political, and personal discourse. An excellent resource!"

Lucy Long, Instructor, International Studies & American Culture Studies, University of Pennsylvania

Food as Communication Communication as Food

This book is part of the Peter Lang Media and Communication list.
Every volume is peer reviewed and meets
the highest quality standards for content and production.

PETER LANG
New York • Washington, D.C./Baltimore • Bern
Frankfurt • Berlin • Brussels • Vienna • Oxford

Food as Communication Communication as Food

EDITED BY **Janet M. Cramer, Carlnita P. Greene, Lynn M. Walters**

PETER LANG
New York • Washington, D.C./Baltimore • Bern
Frankfurt • Berlin • Brussels • Vienna • Oxford

Library of Congress Cataloging-in-Publication Data

Food as communication: communication as food /
edited by Janet M. Cramer, Carlnita P. Greene, Lynn M. Walters.
p. cm.
Includes bibliographical references and index.
1. Food habits. 2. Communication and culture.
I. Cramer, Janet M. (Janet Muriel) II. Greene, Carlnita P.
III. Walters, Lynn (Lynn Marie)
GT2850.F663 394.1'2—dc22 2010026815
ISBN 978-1-4331-0963-8 (hardcover)
ISBN 978-1-4331-0962-1 (paperback)

Bibliographic information published by **Die Deutsche Nationalbibliothek**.
Die Deutsche Nationalbibliothek lists this publication in the "Deutsche Nationalbibliografie"; detailed bibliographic data is available on the Internet at http://dnb.d-nb.de/.

The paper in this book meets the guidelines for permanence and durability of the Committee on Production Guidelines for Book Longevity of the Council of Library Resources.

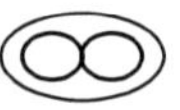

29 Broadway, 18th floor, New York, NY 10006
www.peterlang.com

Printed in the United States of America

Table of Contents

SECTION THREE
CULTURE AND SOCIETY: FOOD AND THE COMMUNICATION OF SOCIAL AND CULTURAL VALUES

SECTION FOUR
ENVIRONMENTAL ISSUES: FOOD COMMUNICATION AND THE NATURAL WORLD

SECTION FIVE
FOOD AND COMMUNICATION IN RELATIONSHIPS: ORGANIZATIONAL AND INTERPERSONAL CONTEXTS

Beyond mere sustenance: Food as communication/ Communication as food

Carlnita P. Greene and Janet M. Cramer

> Now the first and greatest of necessities is food, which is the condition of life and existence—Plato (*The Republic*)

When Williams (1958) identified culture as "ordinary," he was elucidating the potentially transparent nature of those everyday elements that form the very backbone of our existence (p. 4). One example of this "taken for granted" culture of everyday life is food, which while consumed on a daily basis, often is considered as mere sustenance. It is, at once, associated with both a common and an ordinary enterprise. However, food is much more than just a means of survival. It permeates all other aspects of our lives from the most intimate to the most professional practices. It also is a key factor in how we view ourselves and others, is at the center of social and political issues, and is a mainstay of popular media.

From high-tech kitchen gadgets to magazines to the *Food Network*, over the last few decades, we have witnessed a rise in food-focused consumption, media, and culture, such that there has been what we could label a "food explosion." It seems as if food, and the discourses surrounding it, are all over the place from Jaime Oliver's ventures into American school lunchrooms to news stories about urban gardening or buying organic products at the local farmer's market. There is a heightened awareness of food's significance within contemporary society and culture and, as such, there is a further need to explore it.

Although the subject of food has been widely studied within the fields of anthropology, sociology, and cultural history, it has not been addressed very often within the field of communication. In her 1970 essay, Henderson asserted how and why food, and our practices associated with its production and consumption, should be viewed as a form of communication and called for scholars within the field to take up food as a serious form of study (pp. 3–8). Few scholars have answered this call, and while other disciplines have made food a focus, communication largely still lags behind. However, as Lindenfeld and Langellier (2009) suggest, over the last few years there has been a rise in food-related conference panels and presentations within the discipline thus, "marking the growing interest in food studies" (p. 1). Yet, in addition to being an emerging area of study, there are several major reasons why we can view food from the perspective of communication and/or use food as a means for further understanding communication theories and practices.

Broadly defined, communication is the process by which we understand the world and our attempts to convey that understanding to others through both verbal and nonverbal language. In this way, we can view food as a form of communication because it is a nonverbal means by which we share meanings with others. As Roland Barthes has written, food is

> a system of communication, a body of images, a protocol of usages, situations, and behavior. Information about food must be gathered wherever it can be found: by direct observation in the economy, in techniques, usages and advertising; and by indirect observation in the mental life of a given society. (cited in Counihan and Van Esterik, 2008, p. 29)

Paralleling Barthes, scholars such as Claude Levi-Strauss (1983) and Mary Douglas have asserted that we can view food as adhering to the same practices as language because food is a code that can be seen to express patterns about social relationships (cited in Counihan and Van Esterik, 2008, p. 44). Spurlock (2009), in "Performing and Sustaining (Agri)Culture and Place: The Cultivation of Environmental Subjectivity on the Piedmont Farm Tour" also proposes that: "Because of their ability to signify, mediate, contest, and represent 'nature' and 'culture,' foodways are deeply rhetorical and performative" (p. 6).

A primary reason that we should view food as a form of communication is because it is directly linked to both ritual and culture, where ritual is defined as "the voluntary performance of appropriately patterned behavior to symbolically effect or participate in the serious life" (Rothenbuhler, 1998, p. 27). Nowhere can this serious life be viewed more closely than in rituals involving food. It is at the center of our most important events such as birthdays, weddings, funerals, and holidays. Food not only is a part of rituals, but also there are several festivals solely focused on particular food items such as the Gilroy Garlic Festival or the Hilton Apple Fest. Within ritual contexts, food often acts symbolically by representing or "standing in" for expressions such as life, love, grief, or happiness. Even within our daily experiences, the ways that we eat and dine with others can be categorized as ritualistic because they involve repetition, expected behaviors, and roles for both the participants and the food (Rothenbuhler, 1998). Therefore, if food is used ritually, it also can be viewed as a form of culture even in its "ordinary" state.

Following Williams' (1958) work, if we view food as a common facet of our daily lives, and we see culture as "ordinary," then certainly food is a means by which we create cultures. In *Food is Culture*, Montanari (2006) asserts this perspective by claiming: "Food is culture *when it is produced…when it is prepared…when it is eaten…*" (pp. xi-xii, italics in original). That is to say, throughout every step of our encounters with food, we shape it in one way or another whether it is through selections of certain foods versus others, cooking processes, and/or the ways in which we consume it. Spurlock (2009) also maintains: "Through its absences and presences in everyday life, food and foodways highlight the moral, aesthetic, and ethical concerns of a given cultural milieu" (p. 7). Moreover, food acts as a conveyor of culture *precisely because* we use it as means of communication.

In his foundational work, *Communication as Culture: Essays on Media and Society*, Carey (1992) argues: "communication is a symbolic process whereby reality is produced, maintained, repaired, and transformed" (p. 23). If we follow Carey's (1992) argument, then surely food is one of the most readily-available symbols that we have at our disposal, which can be viewed from both the perspectives of communication and culture. In other words, we often use food to communicate with others and as a means of demonstrating personal identity, group affiliation and disassociation, and other social categories, such as socioeconomic class. In this sense, "food is a product and mirror of the organization of society…, a prism that absorbs and reflects a host of cultural phenomena" (Counihan, 1999, p. 6). Food functions symbolically as a communicative practice by which we create, manage, and share meanings with others.

Perhaps one of the most common ways that we utilize food is in the construction of our personal identities. As Brillat-Savarin (2000) claims in *The Physiology of Taste*, "Tell me what kind of food you eat, and I will tell you what kind of man you are" (p. 3). In other words, we regularly define "who we are" according to both the foods that we eat and those that we refrain from consuming. For example, a person may identify as a "vegan," a "carnivore," an "omnivore," or simply as a "foodie." We have a direct, visceral connection to food, and it is often linked to emotion and memory or serves as a source of comfort for some people.

Besides our individual connections to food, we also use it as a means of communicating our identities to others through our processes of preparation and eating. This relationship is situational because we may use food or associated behaviors in different ways depending upon the social situations in which we find ourselves. For example, consider how a person might present his or her identity on a first date, a business luncheon, or at a family gathering. This person may purchase certain foods rather than others in order to reflect a class status or position of authority. Moreover, a person may also abstain from eating too much or may utilize formalized etiquette on the date and at the luncheon, whereas at the family gathering, she or he may not feel the need to prescribe to the rules of etiquette at all.

As well as constituting our own identities, we use food as a means of identifying with others. Food connects people, both physically and symbolically, when we sit down to dine together (Visser, 1991). Similarly speaking, rhetorical scholar Burke (1969) argues that you persuade a person only so far as you align your identity with hers through the use of language (p. 55). Extending this rationale to food, we also identify with others based upon the types of food that we eat such that we may feel a common bond with people who have similar eating habits to ours. Following the previous example, a person may identify himself as a "meat-eater" or "vegetarian" and therefore associate with people who have the same interests and/or views about food consumption. As a result, our selections of food are more complex than simply whether we order wine with dinner or eat a salad instead of a hamburger.

It is through our processes of sharing or discussing food that we can view it as a form of discourse. Much of our notions about food, and its relationship to the natural world, are conveyed and learned through the sharing of narratives and stories. In this sense, we could argue that food serves as a socializing mechanism by which we come to understand our cultures, our societies, and the groups to which we belong. While this aspect occurs on a small scale, discourses about food also are prevalent within larger social structures such as government, media, and popular culture. Often, these discourses come into conflict with each other because they offer myriad perspectives about food and issues related to it.

As discourses, all of these dialogues about food, and its associated practices, operate as "sites of struggle" with significant social and political implications (Fiske, 1997, pp. 5-6). While we consider politics as having an institutionalized center that expounds power, our everyday practices also have political dimensions (De Certeau, as cited in Highmore, 2002, pp. 68–73). In other words, we need to conceptualize politics as located beyond the realms of political campaigns and voting. As Cooks (2009) argues in "You are What You (Don't) Eat? Food, Identity, and Resistance: "For those of us interested in embracing our identities as political and in seeking openings in the tactical moments and performances of everyday life, eating and cooking offer important sites of preservation and imagination" (p. 108). Political struggles also occur over how we make sense of our everyday experiences by using various discourses to describe them (Fiske, 1994).

Within contemporary society, much of the political work that occurs takes place in the practices of our daily lives such as discourses about our relationships with food. For example, in "Unhappy Meals," Pollan (2007) suggests that our relationship to food is simple because all we really need to do is "Eat food. Not too much. Mostly plants," and we will be healthy (p. 38). Similarly, while he parallels Pollan on many food-related issues, Glassner (2007) takes an alternative view of the recent backlash against fast food by claiming: "I come to neither praise fast food nor to bury it, only to question its easy portrayal as the root of all evil" (p. 146).

Aside from conflicting views about our own eating habits, there are also discursive struggles over local versus global food production and consumption. In "The Pride and Prejudice of 'Local,'" Yardley (2010) explains that recently chefs in Portland, Oregon figuratively and literally "came to blows" over a local cooking competition in which one of them used pig from Iowa as the main ingredient for his menu while the other privileged local products only (p. A11). Additionally, while debates continue over the question of genetically-modified foods, "the European Commission will formally propose giving back to national and local governments the freedom to decide whether to grow such crops… which many Europeans derisively call Frankenfoods" (Kanter, 2010, p. B4). Therefore, it is through these multiple discourses that political decisions are made whether they are on individual, local, or global scales. We strongly need to consider the political potential of food because food has the power to influence us and "can condense in themselves a wealth of ideological meanings" (Weismantel, 1988, pp. 7-8).

If food has become increasingly important within our processes of communication as a means of expression, manifestation of identities, form of discourse and ritual, hallmark of social relationships, *and* if food is ubiquitous, then it is for these *very* reasons that we need to more closely consider how food and its practices operate as a means of communication. Furthermore, there is a need for communication scholars to apply our unique methodological and theoretical approaches to the study of food. In this sense, we believe communication studies can offer new insights into how food provides much more than nourishment, or mere sustenance, because food demonstrates a whole host of social, cultural, and political phenomena.

In this edited volume we bring together scholars with diverse research foci and an array of perspectives on food and communication to examine and explore this emerging area of study. Given the various ways that food acts as a form of communication, we propose in the chapters of this book to provide definitive and foundational examples of how food operates as a system of communication and how communication theories can be understood when viewed through the lens of food. In this sense, this book is not only about food but also about communication theories, practices, and effects.

Readers will note that selections in this reader encompass traditional approaches to communication including rhetorical, interpersonal, phenomenological (ethnographic), media and popular culture, environmental, organizational, intercultural, and critical/cultural perspectives. The selections, however, are organized according to an overall consideration of *how* food communicates messages, then focus on *what* those messages communicate related to identities, values, environmental concerns, and overall contexts. This communication focus is traditionally understood as communicator/ message/relationships/culture and society. International and intercultural perspectives are integrated throughout, rather than treated as separate phenomena.

Section One
Food Discourse:
Media, Messages, and Food as a Communicative Practice

Using a variety of approaches including marketing/strategic communication, critical media studies, rhetorical analysis, and cultural/historical studies, the essays in this first section explore how food functions symbolically as a communicative practice. They also address how food, and its surrounding aspects, often function as "sites of struggle" within popular media and wider cultural discourses. By analyzing the ways in which food films engage with and (re)produce discourse while simultaneously erasing the complexities of that discourse, Lindenfeld examines the role of food films in communication studies and offers a rationale for why scholars need to further pursue this course of study. Thomson's essay explores how breakfast cereal companies market themselves to children and the relationship between kids' performativity online to these products. In Chapter 3, Karaosmanoglu addresses cooking and eating practices by way of Istanbul's nostalgic culinary books in relation to the memories of the city. Using the example of home-building practices in an Australian monastery, Wessell and Jones' chapter suggests the ways food can operate as a system of communication and how it can be used to understand different theories and approaches to communication.

Section Two
Communicating Selves:
Food and the Construction/Communication of Social Identities

Increasingly, food has become a means by which we create and manage our identities and how we view the identities of others. The chapters in section two analyze the ways in which food communicates notions of self and the various social categories to which we belong, ranging from socioeconomic class to nationality. It begins with Greene's essay in which she analyzes how the Slow Food Movement uses social style to construct both an identity for the organization and its members. Lucas and Buzzanell, in Chapter 6, consider the role of collective memory of hard times in "Irontown," a small mining community in the U.S. Rust Belt. Through the analysis of six focus groups, Cosgriff-Hernández, Martinez, Sharf, and Sharkey, in Chapter 7, examine conversations about nutritional beliefs and choices, as well as differences between life in Mexico and the United States. In her essay, German argues that a cookbook created by Mina Pachter and other anonymous women during their camp internment in World War II rhetorically can be viewed as an act of resistance. Parasecoli's essay ends this section by examining how representations of men around food in films can establish, question, reinforce, reproduce or destroy cultural assumptions about masculinity and gender relations.

Section Three
Culture and Society:
Food and the Communication of Social and Cultural Values

Food and our interactions with it communicate, create, and reflect a multiplicity of meanings across a wide spectrum of societies and cultures. As such, the chapters in this section examine the ways in which food often is imbued with social and cultural values as well as how these ideals are established through the use of food and its associated practices. Thompson, in Chapter 10, rhetorically examines how "fast food" and "slow food" operate as tropes in a globalizing world. Through an examination from a cross-cultural/inter-cultural communication perspective of both *what* and *how* people eat at Chinese restaurants in New York City, Cheng's essay demonstrates that, contrary to what many U.S. citizens might believe, Chinese restaurant culture in the United States is actually quintessentially "American." Drawing on 18 months of ethnographic research, McCullen, in Chapter 12, explains the process through which an attempt to defetishize food production fails by excluding the story of labor relations on farms and, through market interactions and narratives, makes Latino farm workers invisible. In Chapter 13, Mudry describes how discourses of science and quantification were integrated into American nutrition policy, how this integration was abetted by technologies, and how these discourses aligned the USDA nutrition policy with the goals of Progressive reformers.

Section Four
Environmental Issues:
Food Communication and the Natural World

Food is nature's bounty in peril. In this period of abundant food, especially in the United States, millions of people still starve, suffering hunger and deprivation that some may think is experienced only in developing nations. The chapters in section four regard human action and impact on food in the environment by considering the relationships among humans, food, and the natural world, including food activism, environmental justice, and media discourses about food. In the opening chapter, Brummett uses a homological analysis to make some observations and suggestions about the current state of political discourse using the examples of hunting and gardening. In Chapter 15, Bruner and Meek explore contemporary public discourse surrounding seafood with a focus on the complicated environmental-demands and nutrition-demands faced by seafood consumers. Todd's essay uses rhetorical analysis to reveal why the "Eat the View" campaign successfully persuaded the Obamas to plant a vegetable garden on the White House lawn. Cramer, in Chapter 17, analyzes discourses of food on the Food Network from a framework that assumes that human relationships with food and, especially, the process of producing and preparing one's own food, is key to understanding or reconceptualizing a relationship between humans and the earth that is more sustainable.

Section Five
Food and Communication in Relationships: Organizational and Interpersonal Contexts

We communicate about food and food choices in various personal and societal contexts, such as family relationships, educational institutions, and organizations. The chapters in this final section emphasize that while interpersonal influences on food choices are often initiated within the family, they also develop in the context of societal values and market structure. Through the use of a focus-group study, Kaplan, James, Alloway, and Kiernan explore how a framework for understanding child involvement and empowerment can be used to develop two family-based nutrition education programs. LeGreco, in Chapter 19, demonstrates how a variety of school meal stakeholders in Arizona use food as a means to communicate agency through three dominant discourses that organize eating. Schuwerk's essay employs qualitative research, conducted in the Southwestern United States, to provide valuable information in relation to organizational culture and its implications on food banking and the community. Singer offers a case study on Monsanto, the U.S.-based multinational firm, to detail some of the ways by which corporate agriscience strategically positions itself in relation to stakeholders on issues of hunger and agricultural development. Finally, in Chapter 22, Walters uses an interpretive approach to examine how high school students construct meaning through interaction with food and the environment to further understand influences on the dietary patterns of youth.

As stated earlier, food provides a rich vehicle by and through which communication occurs. Food is both constituted by a people or culture and it is constitutive of people and cultures. It transcends nation, race, class, and gender, even as it defines them. The possibilities for communication scholars seem endless when food is conceptualized in this way. One fruitful area to consider is the very definition of communication itself. For some, communication is a process that attempts to create—and sometimes, perhaps frequently, achieves—shared meaning, a process that is influenced by myriad factors such as social and cultural context, participants, motivations, purposes, and goals (or the lack thereof). But as other communication scholars have rightly observed, communication is also the process by which a society or culture comes into being. In this sense, communication has constitutive power and is not merely a process of creating something external—or ancillary to—the makeup of a society or culture. Considered semiotically, communication could also be construed as the process by which objects are infused with meaning or the arena in and through which symbols function. And, for some, communication is its technology—the media through which the process occurs and through which we connect with others. Finally, communication may be understood in its simplest expression, as a conversation. The chapters in this book have considered both food and communication in varied ways, leading us to conclude that whatever definition or perspective of communication is privileged, food remains one of its most flexible and useful models.

It is hoped that this edited volume not only will contribute to studies of food in communication but also will serve as a means for spurring future dialogues on this subject due to its vast array of ideas about food and its relationship to our communication practices. We hope, too, that scholars will reconsider models of communication based on the insights that food and its discourses provide.

References

Barthes, R. (2008). Toward a psychosociology of contemporary food consumption. In C. Counihan & P. Van Esterik (Eds.), *Food and culture: a reader* (2nd ed.) (pp. 28-35). New York: Routledge.

Brillat-Savarin, J. (2000). *The physiology of taste: Or, meditations on transcendental gastronomy.* (M.F.K. Fisher, Trans.). Washington, DC: Counterpoint.

Burke, K. (1969). *A rhetoric of motives.* Berkeley, CA: The University of California Press.

Carey, J. (1992). *Communication as culture: Essays on media and society.* New York: Routledge.

Cooks, L. (2009). You are what you (don't) eat? Food, identity, and resistance. *Text and Performance Quarterly, 29,* 1, 94-110.

Counihan, C. (1999). *The anthropology of food and body: Gender, meaning, and power.* New York, Routledge.

DeCerteau, M. (2002). General introduction to the practice of everyday life. In B. Highmore (Ed.). *The everyday life reader* (pp. 63-75). London: Routledge.

Douglas, M. (2008). Deciphering a meal. In C. Counihan & P. Van Esterik (Eds.), *Food and culture: a reader* (2nd ed.) (pp. 44-53). New York: Routledge.

Fiske, J. (1994). *Media matters: Everyday culture and political change.* Minnesota, MN: University of Minnesota Press.

Fiske, J. (1997). *Reading the popular.* London: Routledge.

Glassner, B. (2007). *The gospel of food: Everything you think you know about food is wrong.* New York: HarperCollins Publishers.

Henderson, M. (1970). Food as communication in American culture. *Today's Speech, 18,* 3, 3-8.

Kanter, J. (2010, July 8). In Europe, a move to ease curbs on growing biotech crops. *New York Times* p. B4.

Levi-Strauss, C. (1983). *The raw and the cooked: Mythologiques volume one.* Chicago: University of Chicago Press.

Lindenfeld, L. and Langellier, K. (2009). Introduction. *Text and Performance Quarterly, 29,* 1, 1-4.

Montanari, M. (2006). *Food is culture.* New York: Columbia University Press.

Plato. (2006). *The republic.* Sioux Falls, SD: NuVision Publications.

Pollan, M. (2007, January 28). Unhappy meals. *New York Times* p. 38.

Rothenbuhler, E. (1998). *Ritual communication: From everyday conversation to mediated ceremony.* Thousand Oaks, CA: Sage Publications.

Spurlock, C. (2009). Performing and sustaining (agri)culture and place: The cultivation of environmental subjectivity on the piedmont farm tour. *Text and Performance Quarterly, 29,* 1, 5-21.

Visser, M. (1991). *The rituals of dinner: The origins, evolution, eccentricities, and meaning of table manners.* New York: Penguin Books.

Weismantel, M.J. (1988). *Food, gender and poverty in the Ecuadorian Andes.* Philadelphia, PA: University of Pennsylvania Press.

Williams, R. (1958). *Resources of hope: Culture, democracy, socialism.* London: Verso.

Yardley, W. (2010, July 9). The pride and prejudice of 'local.' *Portland Journal* p. A11.

Section One

Food Discourse: Media, Messages, and Food as a Communicative Practice

1

Feasts for our eyes: Viewing films on food through new lenses

Laura A. Lindenfeld

Food media constitute a ubiquitous presence in daily U.S. life. Millions of U.S. viewers tune in daily to watch the *Food Network;* representations of food in magazines and on web sites abound; and the number of food films has increased significantly over the past decades. Box office hits like *Ratatoullie* (Bird et al., 2007) and *Julie and Julia* (Ephron, 2009) demonstrate the establishment of the food film as a genre and its move into the eyes of the broader U.S. public. The *New York Times* goes so far as to state that we are "in the midst of a feeding frenzy" when it comes to food media (Chagollan, 2009). Food media have become a part of the fabric of our daily lives.

Probyn (2000) expresses concerns about the kinds of messages that food media communicate in their pervasiveness by explaining: "it is seemingly impossible to avoid the television programmes and the food pages of newspapers or glossy magazines that promise a return to the real things of life through eating" (Probyn, 2000, p. 3). Simultaneous with the increased production and consumption of food media, the time spent preparing food at home has dropped in the United States and Europe, and the number of meals consumed outside of the home has steadily increased (Miller, 2007). The overconsumption of food poses significant health risks to the U.S. populace and other post-industrial societies. Increases in obesity, eating disorders, and other food-related health problems parallel the growth in markets of supposedly newer and better products. At the same time, food insecurity and malnutrition continue to plague populations across the globe. The marketability of food, its pervasive and lucrative representations on television and in magazines, advertising, film, literature, and a plethora of self-help and cooking books suggest that narratives about eating constitute a highly contested arena in which cultural, social, economic, and political tensions converge.

Discourse on food occurs in a complex web of communication in which debates about citizenship, culture, identity, economics, and politics intertwine. Food, as a liminal substance, slips across diverse kinds of boundaries, and narrative shapes food's preparation and consumption. As Mintz (1996) reminds us, food is "always conditioned by meaning" (p. 7). Food media play important roles in cultivating and assuaging anxieties about diversity, health, gender, national identity, social class, sexuality, and other arenas. Dominant U.S. media offer the seeming pleasure of celebrating diversity while simultaneously positioning gendered, racialized, and sexualized bodies as objects of consumption. Food films provide an intensified version of this trend in that they mask themselves as embracing progressive politics. The film industry, in particular, tends to present ethnic Otherness as safe for mass consumption, while leaving hierarchies of race, class, and gender intact (Dávila, 2001, p. 124).

Scholars have recognized that food discourse is critical to the negotiation of U.S. cultural politics. As such, communication brings unique and important vantage points from which to study food. Communication offers important tool sets for unpacking these discourses and considering the contexts within which food appears and comes to matter. Part of our work in communication is to help unravel what Barthes describes as the "veritable grammar of food" (Counihan & Van Esterik, 1997, p. 22). This chapter aims to unravel three ways in which food films engage with and (re)produce discourse while simultaneously erasing the complexities of that discourse. I do not mean to imply that these are the only or even the most important strands of discourse that cut across food media, but rather that they are significant ones that appear in the larger body of food films. Similarly, they are strands, or "courses," of discourse that have significant implications for U.S. society and the United States' impact beyond its own borders. The first course asks how food films collectively promote consumption through the privileging of certain social class values. The second course considers how food films gender, sexualize, and racialize consumption and lifestyle. The third course investigates how food films interpellate viewers as white citizens invited to visit vicariously the homes and lives of ethnic Others. These films encourage non-white people to view themselves as Others and to participate in defining whiteness as normative. These courses allow us to explore new ways of thinking about food as communication and communication as food and to shed light on communication theory and practice.

Food Films as Cultural Citizenship

In asking what kind of *work* these films do, I deliberately shift from the language of what they represent to the question of how they participate in the construction of culture and, in particular, of cultural citizenship. Thus, I seek to examine the dynamic processes of which food films are a part. Discourses on food map cultural hierarchies and power structures, while providing a lens into experiences of marginalization and disenfranchisement. Cultural citizenship, the kind of citizenship that appears in daily culture—that is in leisure, entertainment, and in consumption of goods, services—marks an important vantage point for approaching food films. Food films, like other forms of media, help to co-construct identity, citizenship, and belonging. As such, they operate from the vantage point of culture, even though they have important implications for economic and political citizenship. Similar to other forms of food media, they "actively *produce* cultural sensibilities and the possibility of transgression" (LeBesco & Naccarato, 2008, p. 2). Like Miller (2007), I understand cultural citizenship as the "uneasy interdependence of citizenship, consumption, and politics" (p. 28). Media have increasingly become part of the fabric of everyday life. The entertainment industries play a critical role in the production and contestation of cultural citizenship as part of our lived rituals and practices. Cultural citizenship, in turn, is also political. As Burgess, Foth, and Klaebe (2006) write, "bona fide citizenship is practiced as much through everyday life, leisure, critical consumption, and popular entertainment as it is through debate and engagement with capital 'P' politics" (p. 1). Studying the intersection of food and media becomes especially important as it provides insight into both ritualized, quotidian practices and commercially based popular entertainment industries. Together these two foci that converge in the genre of the food film provide diverse angles from which to think about practices of citizenship, the role of aesthetics—especially of food and the sublime—and of pleasure and affect.

Finkelstein (1999) argues that the consumption of food has become "more deeply located within the entertainment industries," a phenomenon she labels "foodatainment" (p. 130). Adema (2000) produces a similar argument about food TV when she writes that it "is not about eating: It is about watching food and being entertained by the personality" (p. 116). Food and media condition the consumption of each other and thus form a locus of struggle and contestation where various kinds of cultural work get done. This body of films emerged beginning in the early 1990s and engaged in the culture wars and concurrent debates on multiculturalism, political correctness, difference, power, and disenfranchisement. It is precisely within cultural production that we find remarkable opportunities to unpack conflicting and sometimes contradictory discourses. Likewise, this approach allows us to understand how the world of food media engages citizens/consumers from the vantage point of culture. As such, an overarching question that guides this chapter is the consideration of how the study of food media might push us as communication scholars to reconfigure how we think about communication, identity, and power. Studying the interplay between media and the seemingly mundane practice pushes us to think about the relationship of narrative and image to broader sets of discourse and to examine how these come to matter in people's lives.

The method I employ to study these films specifically pushes the question of how identity, power, and communication intersect. Addressing these texts as ideological markers and sites of tension and rupture requires a kind of mapping that links the individual media texts with the broader contexts in which they are produced, consumed, and reproduced. It assumes that these texts exist within various kinds of relationships with each other and with other food media. This form of ideological criticism falls within the larger terrain of critical/cultural approaches to media studies and seeks to understand how "practices and discourse dialectically construct each other, engaging in acts of marking and erasure that constitute culture rather than reveal it" (Mason, 2008, p. 108). Methodologically, it seeks to identify discourses and the degree to which they dissent with and transgress from or even modulate dominant ideologies. Likewise, I ask which conflicts and contexts the collective body of films avoids or represses. This allows me to talk about threads that food films take up and theorize why and how they do that. Undergirding this approach lays a detailed, close analysis of each individual film that evaluates the work of narrative, visual, and aural culture. At the same time, this approach sees individual representations not as an effect of a single apparatus, for example, film, but as part of an overall media culture (Kellner, 1995) and as part of a broader landscape that considers the intersection of the socio-cultural, political, and economic realms.

A Brief Overview and History of the Food Film

This analysis focuses specifically on food films, rather than on the treatment of food in film more generally. While food has appeared in film since the very inception of this medium, scholars and food film aficionados point to the notorious food/sex scene in *Tom Jones* (Richardson, 1963) as the first actual "foodie" scene. Since then, a growing body of films has appeared that place eating and cooking in the center. The initial films that focus on food and eating often demonstrate a conspicuous *absence* of food or treat food with disgust. Bunuel's *La Charme Discret de la Bourgeoisie* (Bunuel, 1972) consistently postpones the meal to the point where food never actually appears. *La Grande Bouffe* (Ferreri, 1973) depicts four friends who spend the weekend in a villa with the goal of gorging themselves to death. This earlier body of food films tends to treat the subject of food and eating as a pathway for expressing social criticism. Starting with films like *Babette's Feast* (Axel, 1987) and *Tampopo* (Itami, 1986) food appears as exotic, idealized, and sexualized. Generally, there is a trend toward food as utopian in this emerging body of films. While there are certainly films that represent food as disgusting (for example, *The Cook, the Thief, His Wife, Her Lover* (Greeneway, 1989)), food appears as sublime in the growing genre of the food film. Until the early 1990s, most of these films were produced outside of the United States (*Babette's Feast, Tampopo, Like Water for Chocolate* (Arau, 1989). U.S. arthouse and foreign film aficionados followed these films at small independent theaters in metropolitan centers. With the appearance of *Babette's Feast* (Axel, 1987), film critics begin to use the term "food film," and we begin to see an increasing number of films appear on the market.

In the latter part of the 1990s, U.S. independent film producers began to make feature length, narrative U.S. food films, with *Big Night* (Scott/Tucci, 1996) representing the first film in this group. *Big Night* opened on arthouse screens and eventually made its way to mainstream theaters across the country. While the first food films produced in the United States tended to target the arthouse cinema crowd, as the genre became more popular, larger-scale independent and Hollywood productions emerged, such as *Woman on Top* (Torres, 2000), *Tortilla Soup*, and *Chocolat* (Hallstroem, 2000).

This is not to suggest that food did not appear as an important theme in earlier films in the United States. *The Joy Luck Club* (Wang, 1993), *The Age of Innocence* (Scorsese, 1993), and *Fried Green Tomatoes* (Avnet, 1991) place food in important positions and display highly stylized imagery of food, but they do not position food as a character as do films like *Big Night* or *Chocolat,* and food does not serve as the central driving force of the films' narratives. These representations of food deserve a thorough academic analysis in and of themselves, but they extend beyond the parameters of this analysis.

These films share qualities with each other that justify the designation of a genre, the food film. In each of these films, food, meal preparation, and eating provide the central driving force for the film's narrative structure. It connects the characters, and food itself often becomes a character in its own right. Food and cooking take center stage and are often shot in close-up and appear beautiful and enticing. Food becomes sexualized and intertwined with desires for an idealized utopian state. It serves as the vehicle through which the characters achieve a utopic happy ending. These films all contain pivotal scenes in which food changes the course of the narrative build-up: food continually instigates the narrative turning point which frequently occurs at a point in the narrative when the characters collectively consume a large, elaborate meal.

Conceptualizing these films as a genre is important in a second way. Viewers and critics tend to group them together and call them food films. Customers of amazon.com, for example, have created lists of their favorite "food films." Marketing and distribution of new food films link these to older films within the genre. Full page ads in *Gourmet* and *Bon Appetit* magazines often feature ads for up and coming food films. The use of the term food film is appropriate in yet a third sense. Many food films (*Woman on Top, Simply Irresistible, Chocolat, Mostly Martha* (Nettelbeck, 2001), *No Reservations* (Hicks, 2007) tend to cite each other (*Mostly Martha,* for example, uses some of *Big Night*'s well known soundtrack). Often, the newer films cite narrative elements, dialog, visual tropes, or the use of sound from earlier films such as *Babette's Feast* and *Like Water for Chocolate.* In the past few years, food films like *Sideways* (Taylor & Payne, 2004), *Volver* (Almodóvar, 2006), *No Reservations*, *Ratatouille* (Bird & Pinkava, 2007), and the blockbuster *Julie & Julia* (Ephron, 2009) have increasingly appeared before U.S. mainstream audiences.

It would be shortsighted to neglect mentioning the body of documentary films that has emerged over the past decade. These series of films collectively critique mainstream foodways and the food system. They take on aspects that the narrative food films described above collectively ignore by dealing with food policy, industrial food production, issues of food and health, the erosion of traditional farming culture and communities, and issues of labor. This group includes films such as: *The Future of Food*, 2004, dir. Koons; *Super Size Me*, 2004, dir. Spurlock; *The Real Dirt on Farmer John*, 2005, dir. Siegel; *Our Daily Bread,* 2006, dir. Geyrhalter); *How to Cook your Life*, 2007, dir. Doerrie; *King Corn*, 2007, dir. Wolff; and most recently *Food Inc.,* 2009, dir. Kenner. These films provide a stark contrast to the utopian images of food that the narrative food films construct. The absence of environmental discourse in the body of narrative food films is conspicuous and troubling. Both narrative and documentary food films can provide important vantage points from which to study culture and communication processes. The following sections explore three strands, or courses, of discourse that have continually emerged in the collective body of narrative food films.

First Course: Food Films, Consumption, and Class

When the purchase and consumption of goods serve as a driving force for the formation of individual, group, and national identity, the consumption of food and the food narratives in particular provide links to understanding how identity and citizenship constitute, maintain, and reestablish themselves. Mediated narratives of food are especially important objects of analysis because they offer insight into food's signifying power, the interconnected and interdependent pleasure of consuming food via media, and the commercialization of basic necessities. While food belongs to the category of goods required for basic subsistence, food consumers have become increasingly removed from food production. Consequently, in late capitalist western society food tends to slip "into image, into the imaginary, it becomes necessary for lifestyle, rather than sustaining life" (Cooks, 2009, p. 95). With its slippage into image, food becomes "more available for signification" (Cooks, 2009, p. 95). It therefore behooves us as scholars of communication to think about how food functions as style while promoting certain types of social class values and mores.

Food films tend to underscore how closely woven our patterns of consumption are with our sense of belonging in the nation. The U.S. food films as a group promote consumption, even while they appear to critique habits of consumption. In doing so, the films also affirm and concretize certain social class norms through an appeal to middle-class ideologies of what constitutes style and good taste. In this section, I demonstrate how food films participate in this discourse. I then point to some examples of how these films have encouraged communities and individuals to engage in further practices of consumption.

Food films seem to offer a critique of dominant models of consumption. Analysis of food films can lay bare and provide insight into some of the mechanisms of consumption. *Big Night*, the first U.S. produced food film, serves as an especially good example of this phenomenon. *Big Night* focuses on the experience of two Italian immigrant brothers and considers how mainstream culture engulfs and consumes Otherness, both on the screen and on our plates. We see how brothers Primo and Secondo struggle to realize their vision of the American dream by running a restaurant that refuses to pander to mainstream tastes. Brought to failure by the entrepreneurial Pascal, a competitor down the street who serves mediocre food in a flashy pseudo-Italian restaurant, the brothers face the choice of capitulating by returning home to Italy or working for Pascal. The film resists closure and allows us to guess what the brothers will choose. Throughout *Big Night* there is a constant tension between "giving the people what they want," that is, carelessly produced bulk food designed to turn a profit, and the production of art for art's sake.

Other food films play with this theme as well. *Chocolat* offers communal cooking and eating as a collective way of overcoming marginalization and hierarchies among diverse groups. *Chocolat* follows the change that transpires in a conservative French town when Vianne and her daughter Anouk arrive to open a new shop, "Chocolaterie Maya." The chocolate shop causes a big stir, and the town's mayor and moral leader takes it upon himself to ruin Vianne's business and run her out of town. Throughout the course of the film, her chocolates—which have magical qualities—help to unite the community. When a group of gypsies arrive in Lansquenet, Vianne fights to have the group accepted by the townspeople, and Vianne falls in love with one the dashing gypsy Roux. The film ends with the townspeople embracing Vianne and her chocolatrie, a solidified romance between Vianne and Roux, and the town in a happy, much improved condition. Like *Big Night,* on the surface *Chocolat* seems to support a model of consumption that privileges community building and the collective good over corporate earnings.

Collectively as a genre food films try to remind us of the beauty of food, how it can make us connect with each other, and how it can help us to overcome differences. In both of the above mentioned films, food appears as beautiful, sensuous, and sensual. It receives heavy coverage, erotic lighting, and elaborate musical scores. The camera devotes much of its time to images of strikingly beautiful edibles, reproducing normativity through aestheticization (Bower, 2004). *Big Night* contains some of the most explicit examples of this tendency. The film's turning point takes place at a dinner prepared by the two brothers. In close-up, we see detailed presentations of dinner guests consuming luscious dishes with passion and fervor. As we watch a woman bite and then suck a piece of risotto that has fallen down off the side of her hand, we are drawn into an erotic, sensuous world of food as an intimate participant. We continually see shots like this in various food films. The films' foregrounding of food as object of consumption frequently overshadows their depiction of food as a source of community.

While food films appear to support a sense of community and to critique mainstream U.S. consumption, they ultimately privilege consumption in a number of ways. Similar to the culture of dining out, food films privilege the spectacular. As Finkelstein (1998) argues "the aura of the restaurant becomes integral to the pleasures of dining out. The event comes to be enjoyed as a form of entertainment and a part of the modern spectacle in which social relations are mediated through visual images and imagined atmosphere" (p. 2). The pleasure in watching food films parallels and complements the restaurant experience in that it creates an imagined experience. Collectively, these films promote certain kinds of social class norms that tend to privilege white, middle class, Eurocentric values and cultural norms. Even the films that focus on communities of color tend to gloss over cultural differences and make Otherness a safely consumable commodity for white audiences. Films often focus on those minority groups who can assimilate with greater ease than others as a way of suggesting a cultural openness to difference. *Mostly Martha,* for example, positions an Italian man as the Other and thereby avoids more difficult conversations about the lives of Turks and other immigrants in Germany who have had a more difficult time adjusting to and being accepted by German culture (Hoecherl-Alden & Lindenfeld, 2010). *Big Night* deals with the difficulty of assimilating to the United States and employs erotic and nostalgic tropes to represent Italian identity cooking. The film's ability to suture the spectator into the subject positions of Primo and Secondo depends on the social position of Italian-Americans, a group that has enjoyed the privileges of whiteness.

Furthermore, all the films gloss over the traces of food production, never showing us the process by which food enters restaurants and supermarkets. Instead, they focus on characters in clean beautiful environments who have time to gather around tables and bond with each other. It is not uncommon to see a softly lit scene in each of these films where a group of people consume a handsomely prepared meal in an inviting space. Significant about this in terms of consumption is that we are not seeing in these films how most people *actually* eat. We never see people eating in cars, wolfing down fast food, or making dinner in a rush out of pre-prepared packages, and we certainly do not see where food comes from and how it is handled before it reaches our fork.

Instead, the films reinforce classist foodie culture that builds on preconceived notions of what constitutes style and taste. Style, as Ewen (1999) observes, is "linked to consumption, and to the power of the mass media to convey, magnify, refract, and influence popular notions of style" (p. 10). An "official idiom of the marketplace," Ewen writes, style possesses the "power of provocative surfaces (to speak) to the eye's mind, overshadowing matters of quality or substance" (p. 10). Food films produce a filmic style that emulates the type of design that we find in much of hegemonic corporate culture. Like the Olive Garden, Starbucks, and the Pottery Barn, films like *Tortilla Soup, Big Night, No Reservations, Julie & Julia, Sideways*, and others possess the glossy veneer of commercial culture that appeals to supposed Europeanized tastes. The European aura that these films invoke plays into contemporary U.S. hegemonic understandings of what constitutes class and tastefulness with décor, design, and style that appeal to the food film audience and consumers of *The Food Network* and other forms of food television. As much as these films might appear to offer a different view of the world, they collectively reiterate and contribute to culture in ways that underscore social class privilege.

Even though some of these films might appear to critique consumption, they ultimately promote it. We see evidence of this in the numerous marketing tie-ins associated with these films (novelizations, movie sound tracks, DVDs with extra features, cookbooks, and in the case of *Soul Food* (Tillman, 1997), there was even a spin-off television series on *Showtime).* Web sites like amazon.com promote the purchase of films by genre and contain lists of "favorite" and "best food films." Some of the films have direct marketing tie-ins to cooking products. *Tortilla Soup,* for example, marketed Mexican cooking products on surlatable.com as part of a "*Tortilla soup* shop."

Food marketing takes place across a range of media of which the films are part, and it is thus important to consider them within the context of broader media culture. Food magazines market food films; commercial food television shows function as vehicles to expose target consumer groups to specific advertisements an optimum number of times. As part of a broader media culture, food films are inseparable from broader discourses of food. There is significant overlap between audiences and consumers of these media, and we must think of them as being in conversation with each other.

The discrepancy between food films' attempts to situate food as a form of community and the films' tendency to support commercialization manifests itself as well in what viewers do with these films. After the release of *Big Night*, restaurants across the United States began cooking *Big Night* meals, some of them with optional conga lines. Other restaurants even recreate the meal in *Babette's Feast.* This is deeply ironic in that the meals in these films functioned as so exceptional and extraordinary that they could change the basic life circumstances of the people eating together. This phenomenon foregrounds the commercialization of food and culture rather than strengthening fragile communities.

The treatment of both *Big Night* and *Babette's Feast* reflect the tendency of hegemonic U.S. culture, in particular eating culture, to depoliticize consumption and focus on utopian elements devoid of their political implications. This escapism involves a further commercialization of the films. We see this as well in the numerous food film festivals that have popped up in the United States and other countries. The New York City Food Film Festival, the London Food Film Fiesta, and numerous other food film festivals further promote these films as objects of consumption. Likewise, this consumption is deeply gendered and sexualized, as the next section discusses.

Second Course: Consuming Sex

When we feast our eyes on these films, what else is it that we are invited to consume? Above and beyond any social class values that these films communicate, they also help, along with other kinds of media, to re(inscribe), perpetuate, and even change our participation in civil society as gendered, sexualized, racialized beings. Food films engage in a kind of "lifestyle" marketing, as do food television and other forms of lifestyle media, and this participation is gendered, sexualized, and racialized in particular ways. In this section, I focus on the intersectionality of gender, sexuality, and race in food films. I discuss how these films configure women and femininity either as fetishized objects of consumption and or as actors whose power, although significant, is always limited to the domestic sphere.

Media representations often stylistically code food with an erotic aura. Food films feature endless close-ups of beautiful glistening dishes that are often consumed in a state of semi-arousal. The sexualization and eroticization of food across a range of U.S. media is pervasive enough that one could comfortably call it food porn. Some representations allow food to stand in as a sexualized, eroticized object of desire. The food can be sexy and erotic in and of its own right without the display of a sexualized body in conjunction with it. Sexualized images of food, one might argue, appear discursively much in the way that we are used to seeing female bodies: as objects to be desired and consumed.

Citing the tradition of the Mexican food film *Like Water for Chocolate,* a number of food films depict female characters as capable of imbuing food with magical qualities. In the U.S. food films, magic functions as a prop leading to romance rather than as a tool to establish a sense of self in an otherwise restricting world. In *Simply Irresistible,* for example, Amanda, an untalented chef who must pull her restaurant together quickly or face bankruptcy, acquires a magical crab at a farmers' market. Each time Amanda cooks, the "little guy" waves his magic claw and the magical plinking of the soundtrack reminds us that male crustacean has saved her from being the "shitty cook" that she was until he appeared in her life. Suddenly, beautiful, seductive, amazing entrees appear on plates, and Amanda is stunned at her own capacity. The editing underlines the passive role that Amanda plays in the creation of this food. We see the layers of food added to the plate in one quick shot after another, but we never see Amanda actually placing it there. The food simply appears in front of the camera, much in the way some women have appeared as objects of desire in mainstream U.S. cinema.

Films like *Woman on Top* and *Tortilla Soup* complicate this trend by imbuing women of Latin descent with particularly racialized characteristics. In *Woman on Top,* lead character Isabella, played by Penelope Cruz, possesses the ability to revive a half-dead flower. When her sweat drops onto a rose she is wearing, the rosebud suddenly blossoms into a magnificent flower. Her scent has a similar effect, and the food she makes creates an intoxicating aroma that appears only to affect heterosexual men who follow her through the streets of San Francisco like obedient dogs. Perhaps one of the most disturbing and problematic issues in this film's representation of femininity and food is the representation of Isabella as a hot pepper, a correlation that is simultaneously gendered and racialized. The association of food with women's bodies is a long-standing trope in western culture that manifests itself in popular culture items such as the Strawberry Shortcake dolls that smell like different kinds of fruit (Varney, 1996). Here, Isabella is food, and food is Isabella. Isabella has a magical effect on men that literally heats them up, and we often see her dressed in tight red dresses that match the color of the chili peppers she uses in her cooking.

The film's marketing reinforces this association. On the lower left side of the film's poster there are two chili peppers shaped like a woman's lips. The text on one of the posters reads "Spice up your life," clearly a double entendre aimed at correlating actress Penelope Cruz's hotness and the spiciness of character Isabella's cooking. The Latina body and food become interchangeable as objects of desire. Colonialist tropes that position bodies of people of color as particularly animalistic tend to "associate Latin America, and especially Latin American women, with verbal epithets evoking tropical heat, violence, passion, and spice" (Shohat & Stam, 1994, p. 138). As a stark contrast, Amanda in *Simply Irresistible* tastes like vanilla, a move that underscores her whiteness and the safe nature of her sexuality compared to characters like Isabella. That food and the Latina body receive this same treatment alongside and in conjunction with each other is indicative of a culture based on consumption, one that neatly packages "diversity through digestion" and appeals to desires for supposed "authenticity."

These films often represent women as passive, hypersexualized, and dependent on men. *Chocolat, Fried Green Tomatoes,* and *Waitress* (Shelly, 2007) depict the kitchen as a space that protects women from domestic violence. This return to the kitchen as a site of individuation is, however, problematic in that it often results in the establishment of a new or improved heterosexual romantic liaison (*Mostly Martha, Simply Irresistible, Woman on Top,* and *Julie and Julia* all follow this pattern). Any moments of power that appear to occur do not result in actual social, economic, or political empowerment. Explicit political discourse is strikingly absent across this entire body of films. *Waitress* provides a contrast to this tendency in that the final scenes show us lead character Jenna running her own pie shop and raising her toddler-aged daughter on her own after leaving her abusive spouse.

Even films like *No Reservations* and *Mostly Martha* that depict female characters as seemingly strong and autonomous adhere to a pattern of quasi-liberation in the kitchen. Probyn takes this trope to task when she writes: "beyond the now tattered dream of liberation in the bedroom, and freed from the obligations of cooking, the kitchen is now sold to women as the new sphere of sensual liberation" (Probyn, 2000, p. 4). Thus, films like *Chocolat* and *Fried Green Tomatoes* that present themselves as feminist texts tend to limit women's realm of authority to the kitchen and to reinforce women's roles as domestic. Both *Mostly Martha* and *No Reservations* end with weddings, and *Julie & Julia* concludes with a separated couple reuniting.

The collective body of films develops a troubling equation between women and food. In positioning women and food as consumable objects alongside each other, food films essentialize women's bodies in ways that simultaneously give, but then take back, their power. Particularly troubling is the repeated trope that food, a realm traditionally designated to women, takes on essentialized qualities that treat women's bodies as consumable objects. Coopting feminist ideas that posit the sexualization of women cooking and doing kitchen work as a form of empowerment without granting actual political or economic power to women is deeply troubling. The glistening, beautiful food that appears across a range of media links women and food in dangerous proximity and association with each other.

Third Course: Consuming Otherness via Food Films

As Probyn (2000) states, U.S. culture possesses a "hearty enthusiasm for 'foreign food' that is supposed to hide the taste of racism" (p. 2). American television and films are inundated with scenes of the "ethnic" food experience. Food films continually parade groups of assimilated ethnic people, whether they are African-Americans, Latinos, or Asian-Americans, that appear readily palatable for mainstream white audiences. The third and final strand of discourse that I examine in this chapter is one that positions viewers as visitors in the homes and lives of characters of color. Food films like *The Joy Luck Club, Tortilla Soup, Woman on Top, Soul Food, What's Cooking* and numerous others invite the viewer to the tables and lives of U.S. American ethnic families providing a kind of culinary tourism that functions as an especially comfortable way to contain Otherness while rendering it a marketable commodity (Lindenfeld, 2007). As Shugart (2008) expresses this, "via a motif of controlled mobility," food "rhetorically manages contemporary anxieties around ambiguity and permeability as relevant to cultural identities prompted by desire for and consumption of Otherness" (p. 72).

Numerous food films focus on ethnic families in the contemporary United States, and the family becomes the specific site where the viewer can supposedly experience diversity and difference vicariously through the images on the screen. These films are ambivalent in their self-positioning in that they seek to appeal to ethnic/non-white audiences (*Soul Food,* for example, was heavily marketed to African Americans) while carefully navigating their spectatorial positioning so that they can target and appeal to mainstream white audiences. These films position themselves in such a way that the white spectator can safely visit the world of the ethnic Other and consume images of food and family in a comforting, inviting, vicarious environment without the threat of getting to close to difference that might be threatening. Thus, these films function in part as ideologically problematic pedagogies of whiteness and Otherness.

Food films serve as a platform for experiencing Otherness. Hooks (1998) writes, "It is within the commercial realm of advertising that the drama of Otherness finds expression. Encounters with Otherness are clearly marked as more exciting, more intense, and more threatening" (p. 186). In inviting tourists to a virtual table, *Tortilla Soup, Woman on Top, Soul Food,* and *What's Cooking,* just to mention a few of the more significant films that operate in this rhetorical fashion, demonstrate how easy it is to commodify ethnic difference at a time when ethnic groups are so often positioned problematically within U.S. visions of multiculturalism.

As an example, Chadha's film *What's Cooking* is an ensemble film that portrays four ethnic families living in LA's Fairfax neighborhood as they prepare for and celebrate Thanksgiving. We visit the homes of a Latino family, a more recently immigrated Vietnamese family, an African-American family, and a Jewish family. Crosscutting among the four families, the film depicts their respective processes of preparing and eating a Thanksgiving meal together and the tensions that arise on this day. From the outset, the film presents Los Angeles (and by extension the United States) as a hybrid culture. The notion of the all-American family as a white family emerges as a myth as the final shot of the opening credits lands on a park bench with the words "Feliz Dia de Gracias" and an image of a happy Latino family on it. The soundtrack transitions back to the Star Spangled Banner to confirm the film's adherence to a liberal, multicultural interpretation of American citizenship.

Ultimately, the film devolves into sitcom-like stereotypes. The Vietnamese family faces the threat of their son having a gun and being part of a gang. The African-American family faces tension between the father's adherence to white, upper-middle class social values and the son's desire to connect with his African-American heritage and critique his father's adherence to dominant white cultural values. The Latino family must deal with a group of patriarchal males angry at a mother for starting a new relationship after a divorce. The Jewish family deals with the fact that their daughter is a lesbian who is expecting her first child with her partner. Rather than challenging the complex ways that race and ethnicity function in mainstream U.S. society, *What's Cooking* uses food as a metaphor to bridge the four families, who we learn at the end of the film, live across from each other. *What's Cooking* and numerous other food films deploy food as a means of celebrating difference. Yet, this celebration hovers at a superficial level that fails to interrogate how race and ethnicity actually impact people's lived experiences. As such, these films tend to participate in discourses that sometimes treat ethnic difference as racial stereotypes, sometimes as post-ethnic and assimilated.

In this post-ethnic framework, ethnicity and race appear as a configuration that "favors voluntary over involuntary affiliations, balances an appreciation for communities of descent with a determination to make room for new communities, and promotes solidarities of wide scope that incorporate people with different ethnic and racial backgrounds" (Hollinger, 1995, p. 3). What is problematic is that ethnicity becomes something that one can choose to be or have, rather than something that society ascribes and that impacts one on a daily basis. These films tend to position ethnicity as a propensity or an inclination, relegating race and ethnicity to issues of style and choice that ultimately privilege whiteness. As such, this discourse helps to "obscure the very real economic and social inequalities based on racial identity that still persist in American society" (Halter, 2000, p. 183).

At the same time, the films often engage in the contradictory act of essentializing race so that characters like Isabella in *Woman on Top* and Hortensia in *Tortilla Soup* appear hypersexualized because it is within their nature as Latinas. Similarly, *The Joy Luck Club* straddles the task of representing the lives of four Chinese immigrant women and their American born daughters and falls prey to representing these characters in such a way that they strike appeal with white American audiences while stereotyping Chinese women and representing China as a mythic construct (Chin, 2005; Jing, 2005; Tseo, 1996). *Soul Food* carefully navigates its spectator positioning in order to market itself toward black and white audiences by reiterating some stereotypes and providing a seemingly "safe" vicarious, mediated space to "experience" the Other. The film dehistoricizes soul food, unilaterally relegating it to the stereotypified domain of "finger-licking" home-cooking. A number of women in the film appear as animalistic seductresses, a move that reaffirms stereotypes about African American women and sexuality rather than calling them into question.

Consumption and commodification reify ethnic and racial difference, homogenizing and subordinating "Otherness." Food films carefully navigate the experience of ethnic Otherness by ensuring that we never come too close to difference. Food itself is rendered palatable for mainstream audiences so that some styles of African-American cooking in *Soul Food* contain items like macaroni and cheese and fried chicken, but never dishes like chitterlings that might invoke a sense of disgust in mainstream spectators. *Tortilla Soup* and *What's Cooking* dish up beautiful Mexican food that carefully avoids items that some U.S. Americans would generally not eat such as barbecued beef head *(barbacoa de cabeza)*, entrails, or goat. *The Joy Luck Club* never shows dishes like chicken feet or foods that are displeasing in texture to some Americans, but rather presents only foods that mainstream Americans would find appealing (and available to them in U.S. Chinese restaurants). The food in these films presents assimilated versions of traditional cuisines that appear in overtly romanticized, beautified imagery like one might find in *Gourmet* food magazine.

U.S. food films offer safe, commodifiable experiences of Otherness that lack nuanced, self-reflexive representations. Food media maintains these differences, encouraging the consumption of Otherness without promoting understanding of the ways in which U.S. culture politically positions ethnicity and race. Beautified ethnic food creates a sense of safety and acceptability that leaves whiteness and the privileges with it intact.

A Sobering Digestif

When we feast our eyes on food films, we do so in deeply complex ways that interpolate and engage us simultaneously as citizens and consumers. From the perspective of communication research, food films offer the opportunity to conceptualize how we as citizens participate in convoluted infrastructures that situate us both consciously and unconsciously, willingly and unwillingly within multifarious discourses. The study of food media reminds us that we cannot so easily separate our behavior as consumers—purchasing meals at *The Olive Garden* and jars of chutney at *Trader Joe's*—from our participation in media culture and our decision making processes as political citizens. These arenas are interwoven with each other in deeply complicated and layered ways. Studying food films and other forms of food media as communication scholars and/or as the general public pushes us to move beyond documenting what appears as representations to ask how these representations *matter* in our daily lives and in the choices we make.

From the vantage point of food, we as communication scholars find ourselves challenged to move outside of our comfort zones. Food asks us to think on multiple levels simultaneously. We can never simply take a meal at face value, but rather we must continually unravel food's grammar. Food, in its everydayness, runs the risk of appearing so normal and uncomplicated. For this reason, it has taken decades for food studies to establish itself as an important and legitimate arena of scholarly discourse. Yet it is precisely this seeming normality that provides communication scholarship with an important push to unravel the socio-economic, political, and cultural complexities of lived experience and the ramifications of our everyday choices as citizens. For me personally, studying food has meant becoming involved in increasingly large interdisciplinary collaborations that involve research activities with scholars from a wide range of disciplines ranging from hydrological engineering to economics to stream ecology. Food, in this case, has pushed me to stand both inside and outside the world of communication scholarship to think about how we can actually change the way that we consume to create more sustainable futures for ourselves and the planet.

This chapter has focused on three courses of discourse that cut across food films. There are certainly others that bear deep significance and deserve attention in another time and space. Discourses of health, sexuality, and masculinity have received attention in communication scholarship, but there is more work to be done. Environmental discourse and the lack thereof in certain types of media provide fertile ground for communication scholars. Food films themselves have not received nearly as much attention as food television has, and even food television would benefit from increased scholarly attention. There are tremendous opportunities to study the production contexts of these media and to understand more details about the historical contexts in which food media appear.

Empirical communication scholarship offers opportunities to investigate how food media impact our eating habits and worldviews. Interdisciplinary approaches that consider media effects in conjunction with ideological analysis might help us to achieve greater sustainability or achieve a stronger sense of social justice among diverse groups of people with competing interests. Critical/cultural studies has the overarching goal of changing things, of not being satisfied with the status quo, and of repairing inequities and helping us to protect each other. Food studies issues a call to action for communication scholarship, and communication scholars bring to the table unique and important tools for this work.

References

Adema, P. (2000). Vicarious consumption: Food, television and the ambiguity of modernity. *Journal of American & Comparative Cultures, 23*(3), 113.

Burgess, J. E., Foth, M., & Klaebe, H. G. (2006). *Everyday creativity as civic engagement: A cultural citizenship view of new media.* Paper presented at the Communications Policy & Research Forum.

Chagollan, S. (2009, July 9). Eat drink make movie: Hollywood's next course. *New York Times.* Retrieved December 3, 2009, from http://www.nytimes.com/2006/07/09/movies/09chago.html

Chin, F. (2005). Come all ye Asian American writers of the real and the fake. In K. A. Ono (Ed.), *A companion to Asian American studies. Blackwell companions in cultural studies* (pp. 133–156). Malden, MA: Blackwell Pub.

Cooks, L. (2009). You are what you (don't) eat? Food, identity, and resistance. In *Text & Performance Quarterly* (Vol. 29, pp. 94–110).

Counihan, C., & Van Esterik, P. (1997). *Food and culture: A reader.* New York: Routledge.

Dávila, A. M. (2001). *Latinos, Inc.: The marketing and making of a people.* Berkeley, CA: University of California Press.

Ewen, S. (1999). *All consuming images: The politics of style in contemporary culture* (Rev. ed.). New York: Basic Books.

Finkelstein, J. (1998). Dining out: The hyperreality of appetite. In R. Scapp & B. Seitz (Eds.), *Eating culture* (pp. 201–215). Albany: State University of New York Press.

Finkelstein, J. (1999). Foodatainment. *Performance Research, 4*(1), 130.

Halter, M. (2000). *Shopping for identity: The marketing of ethnicity* (1st ed.). New York: Schocken Books.

Hoecherl-Alden, G., & Lindenfeld, L. (2010). Thawing the north: *Mostly Martha* as a German-Italian eatopia. *Journal of International and Intercultural Communication, 3,* 2, 114–135.

Hollinger, D. A. (1995). *Postethnic America: beyond multiculturalism.* New York: BasicBooks.

hooks, b. (1998). Eating the Other: Desire and resistance. In R. Scapp & B. Seitz (Eds.), *Eating culture* (pp. 181–200). Albany: State University of New York Press.

Jing, Y. (2005). Constructing the Other: A critical reading of *The Joy Luck Club. Howard Journal of Communications, 16,* 3, 149–175.

Kellner, D. (1995). *Media culture: cultural studies, identity, and politics between the modern and the postmodern.* London; New York: Routledge.

LeBesco, K., & Naccarato, P. (2008). *Edible ideologies: Representing food and meaning.* Albany: State University of New York Press.

Lindenfeld, L. (2007). Visiting the Mexican American family: *Tortilla Soup* as culinary tourism. *Communication & Critical/Cultural Studies, 4,* 3, 303–320.

Mason, E. (2008). Cooking the books. Jewish cuisine and the commodification of difference. In K. LeBesco & P. Naccarato (Eds.), *Edible ideologies: Representing food and meaning* (pp. 105–125). Albany: State University of New York Press.

Miller, T. (2007). *Cultural citizenship: Cosmopolitanism, consumerism, and television in a neoliberal age.* Philadelphia: Temple University Press.

Mintz, S. W. (1996). *Tasting food, tasting freedom: Excursions into eating, culture, and the past.* Boston: Beacon Press.

Probyn, E. (2000). *Carnal appetites: Foodsexidentities.* London; New York: Routledge.

Shohat, E., & Stam, R. (1994). *Unthinking Eurocentrism: Multiculturalism and the media.* London; New York: Routledge.

Shugart, H. A. (2008). Sumptuous texts: Consuming "Otherness" in the food film genre. *Critical Studies in Media Communication, 25,* 1, 68–90.

Tseo, G. K. Y. (1996). Joy Luck: The perils of transcultural 'translation'. *Literature Film Quarterly, 24,* 4, 338.

Varney, W. (1996, May, June). The briar around the strawberry patch. *Women's Studies International Forum,19,* 267–272.

2

Play with your food: The performativity of online breakfast cereal marketing

Deborah Morrison Thomson

Flipping through my 8-year-old daughter Dana's *National Geographic Kids* magazine, I find a treasure hunt. I loved treasure hunts when I was a kid. This one is hosted by a toucan pirate named "Black Beak." *So ye want to find me next Fruity Treasure,* he beckons. I do. *First ye should count the red Froot Loops pieces and then the purple ones. The answer be the page number of the next clue.* I cannot resist, dutifully counting loops to pursue the promised treasure. I crack the code and jump forward 39 pages to find Black Beak again. *Arrgh! Ye be a clever one. But can ye make it to Star Fruit Atoll?* More loops to count. 7 times 7. 49! Page 49! *Congratulations! You've discovered Starberries! The oh-so fruity part of NEW STARBERRIES FROOT LOOPS CEREAL!*

In the grocery store I encounter Black Beak again, this time on a box of Froot Loops cereal. He has another puzzle to be solved and another prize to be won. The unscrambled code answers the question: "What's the difference between Starberries and Froot Loops?" The answer is two words. First word: four letters. Second word: six letters. FIVE POINTS! The answer, it turns out, is the prize. It is a secret code that promises to "boost my game experience at Frootloops.com." I go online. The front page of Frootloops.com is an interactive treasure map with circling sharks and the sound of blowing winds on the high seas. With one click I arrive in the mythical moors of "Star Fruit Atoll," with its magical snow globe twinkling with Froot Loops and Starberries. One click later, I am Toucan Sam, hopping on the loop globe as it launches into the air, taking me to a tropical jungle laden with Froot Loops waiting to be gobbled up. I run, jump, and fly, disappearing Froot Loops and Starberries as I go, upping my score the more I consume. I hop on a cloud beckoning "Bonus"; it lifts me to an upper realm where the game stops. I must enter a secret code, attained—the game reminds me—"by solving the puzzle on boxes of Froot Loops Starberries or in National Geographic for Kids." I enter the code and unlock the secret upper realm. No longer in the jungle, I am now rolling through the clouds on a snow globe filled with Froot Loops and Starberries, gobbling up extra loops and stars for so many bonus points that I am now on the High Score leader board.

From a marketer's perspective, the Black Beak campaign described above is brilliant. It effectively entices the potential consumer to move from one piece of marketing to another, prolonging engagement with the Froot Loops brand across media (from print to box to Web), as players solve cereal-themed puzzles and play cereal-related games, interacting with Black Beak and Toucan Sam and simulating consumption of those virtual loops. The length and depth of such brand immersion far exceeds anything that can be hoped for in a Saturday morning commercial. But to view this encounter from the perspective of the child advocate, such marketing is highly problematic, particularly during what has been described as an "epidemic of childhood obesity" (Institute of Medicine, 2007). The first ingredient in Froot Loops, after all, is sugar, making it one of those cereals nutritionists tell us to avoid (Nestle, 2006).

Online food advergaming functions symbolically as a communicative and persuasive practice, one rich with codes of meaning surrounding the food item, which in game play becomes "much more than mere sustenance" (Greene, 2008, p. 31). It also has become a site of struggle between food corporations and their allies, on the one hand, and public health and child advocates, on the other. In this chapter, I argue that online interactive marketing of breakfast cereals is, at its core, performative; it calls upon a host of imagined narratives, characters, and symbols, locating them in an environment in which food is entertainment—something to be played with. Consider: playing with your food is something your parents told you *not to do* at the dinner table as you stirred your cranberry sauce into your peas and potatoes (or in this case at the breakfast table as you floated your cereal box prize in your bowl of Rice Krispies). Yet contemporary marketing seems to undermine this parental imperative, positioning the child as player/consumer, engendering a host of actions/behaviors that are designed as "fun"—and seemingly innocuous—yet are involved in the serious business of cultivating food desire and branding young consumers. As this marketing does its work through performance processes and performative discourses, it functions as a rehearsal for cereal purchase and consumption. In so doing, online cereal marketing creates a space to "play with your food" in a virtual world beyond (and potentially undermining) parental authority.

It makes sense, then, to attempt an understanding of digital games in terms of performance. In this chapter, I undertake such a project in the mixed mode of performative writing evoking cereal game-play and critical analysis of cereal play performativity. Before I begin, let me say a few words about how I am using "performativity" to each of these ends. I write following Pollock's (1998) call to use language "like paint to create what is self-evidently a *version* of what was, what is, and/or what might be" (p. 80). Performative writing can transport the reader. According to Pollock (1998):

> Performative writing is *evocative*. It operates metaphorically to render absence present—to bring the reader into contact with "other-worlds," to those aspects and dimensions of our world that are other to the text as such by re-marking them. Performative writing evokes worlds that are other-wise intangible, unlocatable: worlds of memory, pleasure, sensation, imagination, affect, and in-sight. (p. 80)

Pollock (2007) conjures what she identifies as the "performative 'I'": a messy, at times improvisational, way of resisting the dangers of sterile third person writing on the one hand and self-indulgent first person writing on the other. Instead, she calls for "the passionate, excessive, errant, collective, and often exuberantly irregular "I" excluded by the systematic reproduction of sameness" (2007, p. 240). Following Pollock's call to write performatively, I attempt to *play* the games I discuss below through my *writing* of them, evoking the experience of the player by calling attention to the landscapes, actions, personas and other elements involved in online cereal play.

I also use the concept of "performativity" in my critical analysis, paying close attention to those elements of online cereal play in terms of discursive enactment or anticipated action. Notions of performativity originate from the work of linguist J. L. Austin (1962), who conceived of performatives as those enunciations that are both a saying and a doing, in effect a calling into being of that which they name. Although Austin's early work limited performativity to a highly delineated speech act, his theory quickly evolved beyond those limits in the work of Derrida (1977/1988), Butler (1993), and others. In particular, Butler's work on gender performativity has led to an ongoing discussion of the social structures, norms and values entailed and cited, reiteratively or subversively, within the performative act. More recently, digital game theorists have been speaking of performativity in the sense of "taking on and acting out specific roles" (Crawford, 2006, p. 500), a central defining pleasure in digital games (Rehak, 2003). Online digital advergaming is performative in a number of ways. It positions the child player in doubled role: that of avatar/character within the game world and that of branded consumer within the life world. It does so through a performative citationality of brand symbols and icons, creating a discourse in which cereal becomes much more than just what is for breakfast.

Below I look at cereal marketing on General Mills' web site Millsberry.com. The site promotes such cereal brands as Lucky Charms, Trix, Cheerios, and Cinnamon Toast Crunch. To play in the site's fictional town of "Millsberry," players create a "Buddy" (an avatar) and are given a virtual home to fill with items purchased in downtown shops using Millsbucks, the town's virtual currency. Players earn this money by playing video games in the Millsberry arcade, a fantastic reversal of the pay-to-play of "real world" arcades. Below I discuss play on the Millsberry site from a number of angles. I look at three types of play on Millsberry: avatarial play, exploratory play, and game play. I conclude by reflecting on the implications of these findings for communication researchers and policymakers.

Enter the Player

I enter the cereal-themed virtual town of Millsberry without a body. My first task is to create one.

Step 1. Choose Gender. Two faceless cartoon child figures appear before me, one male, one female. Other than differences in hairstyle, they are identical: bare arms and shoulders, bare legs, clothed in a black towel of sorts. They both have the prepubescent flat-chested linear body that makes so many people mistake my own short-haired daughter for a boy. I choose "female." *Step 2. Choose a Name.* I type "Researchkid," hit enter, and she appears before me standing in what looks like a child's bedroom complete with messy dresser, drawers overspilling with "cleaned up" clothes. Now I can alter her physical features: skin tone, nose, eyes, and hair. I am warned that my choices are permanent, give my assent by clicking "OK," and my Buddy appears with a white t-shirt and jeans, ready to start playing.

Like every Buddy created in Millsberry, Researchkid comes with a set of "Buddy Stats," her vital statistics: fitness, civics, health, intelligence, and hunger. All are at 50%, except her hunger level, which shows her to have arrived on the scene completely full. The other measures—fitness, civics, health, intelligence—have room for improvement, a reason to play. But over time this Buddy will get hungry and need to be fed. This will require a trip to the grocery store.

In the virtual world of digital games, an avatar—or virtual self—stands in place of the absent physical body of the player. As Rehak (2003) notes, player and avatar are one and not one: "Appearing on screen in place of the player, the avatar does double duty as self and other, symbol and index" (p. 106). For Boulter (2005) the avatar is a "prosthetic sublime" and transport vehicle for exploring other worlds:

> The avatar, a fractal version of the self, serves as a prosthesis-self, transporting the subject elsewhere. The fascination of the game lies in its ability to *transport* the self; the sublime ecstasy of the player-cyborg lies in her ability to *project* the self beyond space and time limits. (p. 60)

Your "prosthetic sublime" in Millsberry, your Buddy, is not you the player, per se. It is the character you take on. Or to use Schechner's (1985) formulation of what happens when you perform, you are *both* not Buddy and not *not* Buddy. In this uneasy intimacy there is pleasure—the pleasure of experimenting with an alternate identity, an expendable body.

In Millsberry, the avatarial body of the Buddy, once created, stands erect, motionless, and gestureless under its name whenever the player is logged on. The rigid paralysis of the Millsberry Buddy, however, belies its bodily needs. The Buddy's bodily and social statistics are measured and published for all other players to see. The last of these measures, hunger, is represented as a cereal bowl. And while the Buddy gets hungry and full, s/he never becomes overweight or insulin-resistant. With the prominent display of General Mills cereals, and the cereal bowl icon representing hunger, it seems clear what your Buddy should be eating, at least for breakfast. To eat breakfast, a Buddy will need to buy food. To buy food a Buddy will need Millsbucks. To earn Millsbucks a Buddy will need to play video games. This trinity sets up an insidious symbiosis between bodily need, purchase/consumption, and digital game play.

The Simulated City (of Cereal)

Schechner (1988) distinguishes play from other types of performance activity such as games, sports, theatre, and ritual, noting: "Play is a 'free activity' where one makes one's own rules. In Freudian terms play expresses the pleasure principle, the *private* fantasy world" (Schechner, 1988, p. 13) As game theorists have pointed out, digital games present unique performance spaces. According to Whitlock (2005), "the video game player of today is a performer. He/she is actively engaged in an interactive state that is both physical and mental, playing a character" (p. 189). As suggested by the title of her landmark book *Computers as Theatre,* Laurel (1991) makes the case that theatre is the best metaphor to apply to the human-computer interface. The game designer is like the scene designer: "both create representations of objects and environments that provide a context for action" (p. 9). Likewise, when the audience is engrossed in the play or the game, they forget about, ignore, or are simply oblivious to, what is happening backstage and in the wings (p. 15).

Part of the fun of playing in the fantasy world of Millsberry is what King and Krzywinska (2006) describe as the "pleasure of exploration" in digital games (p. 95). Destinations within the digital game world offer "possibility spaces" (Jenkins & Squire, 2002) which link "the embedded 'overarching narrative' of a game to the emergent actions and outcomes of moment-to-moment play" (Salen & Zimmerman, 2003, p. 390). Millsberry is laid out as a city waiting to be explored, with a downtown encircled by neighborhoods and parks. On the outskirts of town you will find neighborhoods such as Ravenwood, Lakeview, and Golden Valley. Within each neighborhood are houses and their Buddies, who stand motionless outside on the front lawn as if preparing to greet an expected visitor. We see just the faces of the houses, each with its one window and front door. The houses differ, however, in style. Buddies can upgrade the look of their doors, windows, or house skins, by purchasing more novel or stylish ones downtown in Peterson's Construction and Hardware Emporium.

Click on "Downtown," and you are presented with what de Certeau (1984) called "the pleasure of seeing the whole" in terms of the voyeur's view of the city from above (p. 92). This view allows the player "to read it, to be a solar Eye, looking down like a god" (p. 92). And yet, "down below" this downtown is not the chaotic, organic, cityscape of urban excesses described by de Certeau. It is more like Baudrillard's (2001) Disneyland, "embalmed and pacified" (p. 174) or Eco's (1986) "city of robots" (p. 39).

In the heart of downtown is the Millsberry Academy: the town's school, complete with classrooms, gym, and school cafeteria. Across the street is Town Hall housing the Millsberry Historical Society and a Post Office where Buddies can mail packages to each other. This civic-minded town also has a Community Center with art classes and a swimming pool and a Museum featuring travelling exhibitions of various sorts. In the Millsberry Bank Buddies can deposit their hard-earned Millsbucks and earn anywhere from 4.4% to 11% interest, depending on the type of account. The Millsberry Police Department offers safety tips, with a Sherriff who is there to help "anyone who gets a little lost." And, of course, there are a number of stores in Millsberry, with items to purchase for a Buddy, from groceries, to furniture, to electronics, to toys, to pets, and beyond. When Buddies feel a need to change their looks, they can stop in at the Millsberry Clothing Store for new duds, or pop over to Tania's Hair Salon for that green mohawk they have always wanted. For entertainment, a Buddy can visit the Downtown Entertainment Complex, or if feeling more creatively inclined, stop in at the Millsberry Recording Studio to mix up a new tune. If your Buddy is feeling particularly altruistic, visit the latest addition to Millsberry, the Cause Tour Bus, where this month's effort in goodwill is "pet awareness."

Millsberry offers a kind of idealized American downtown, with its mix of shops and civic buildings. In fact, the town seems to be working hard to perform "good." There are good schools with "computers, microscopes, beakers, chemicals, books, and telescopes—all ready for exploration and discovery!" The community center with its free activities is a "great place to meet, interact and participate in various programs available to all in the community." There are opportunities for being good (visit the museum for an art class) and doing good (take up a "cause"). In part, this performed goodness is a rhetorical strategy for communicating to parents that the site is "safe" and even "educational"—you can learn about saving money in the bank, and check out books in the library. As utopian as this reading of Millsberry might make it seem, its Stepford-esque perfection is the hyperreal container for the all too real advertisement. It makes sense, then, to read Millsberry as the city of cereal.

General Mills cereals are strangely omnipresent in this fictional town. For example, upon entering the Recording Studio, you learn that the studio is "a collaboration between musician/producer Tony 'Tee-Ray' Rayford and the folks at Cinnamon Toast Crunch." Within the image of the recording studio, resting there on the mixing board console, are a box and bowl of Cinnamon Toast Crunch ready to be eaten. Tee-Ray's sound tracks—the ones players can mix to create their own groove—have names like "Crunchy," "Cinnamon," and "Swirl." These more subtle insertions of the General Mills brand stand in contrast to the more blatant use of commercials, which happen to be the only cinematic works "now showing" at the Downtown Entertainment Complex.

These "films" advertise cereal or other cereal-themed web sites, such as the ad for Cuckooshow.com, a Cocoa Puffs advergaming site.

As one would expect, the Millsberry grocery store is full of General Mills items. Indeed, it offers a strange mix of generic and branded items: fried egg, Count Chocula cereal, cucumber, Franeknberry cereal, and so on. General Mills' branded items currently make up only one quarter of all available foods in the store, but 36 of the first 37 items listed in the store are General Mills products, so players have to dig a bit deeper to get to the generic items. Once a player purchases a food item, it gets automatically deposited in a player's refrigerator or pantry, depending on the type of item. The image of a player's pantry—which does not change regardless of a player's actual pantry items—is also a mix of branded and unbranded items. Alongside raisins, tomato sauce, and the unappetizingly generic "fish" are General Mills items such as Lucky Charms and Trix cereals and Fruit Roll Ups.

Perhaps most intriguingly, branded cereal items adorn the homes of Millsberry's residents. Say you wanted to spruce up your home with some Millsberry flair. You could purchase a Honey Nut Cheerios beehive-shaped front door with Buzz the bee on it. Or, perhaps you would like a Honey Nut Cheerios cereal-shaped window. They cost 125 Millsbucks and 200 Millsbucks, respectively. Branded items can also be won. For example, in February of 2008, Millsberry residents were invited to help solve the mystery of the "missing Cinnamon Toast Crunch" by searching the town for "clues." These clues appeared in various locations around town for players to click on and receive a prize. During the period of this game, my daughter won the following items, which now adorn her bedroom in Millsberry: a Cinnamon Toast Crunch poster, a Cinnamon Toast Crunch bedspread, a Cinnamon Toast Crunch microscope, a Cinnamon Toast Crunch walkie talkie, and even a Cinnamon Toast Crunch houseplant blooming with Cinnamon Toast Crunch cereal pieces.

Cereal Play: Food as Fun

At the arcade I click on "Lucky Charms Charmed Life" and I am Researchkid playing Lucky the leprechaun, the branded spokescharacter of Lucky Charms cereal. My task is to "guide Lucky past the kids who are after his Lucky Charms." I launch the game and am now looking down on a heart-shaped maze of squares. Spread out across these squares are small cereal bowls and marshmallow charms. My goal is to eat all of the bowls of cereal and then exit to the next level before being caught by one of the kids who are running after me. To thwart the kids I can use the different types of magic offered by the "lucky charms" that appear in the maze.

The game begins and I am Lucky, running toward cereal. I move over a bowl of cereal, and it disappears. I get 10 points. I have to move quickly: the kids are trying to catch me. I collect the balloon charm and use its magic to make the kids float in place. It is easy now to get the other cereal bowls and charms. I head toward the exit. Level 2 is much harder: there are more kids now and they are nearly impossible to avoid. I use the moon charm to make myself momentarily invisible to them, but it wears off before I can gather the last cereal bowl, located on the other side of a wall of short trees. I use the rainbow charm to fly over the wall and I race toward the cereal bowl, a kid catches me. The game ends, but my Buddy Researchkid has earned 377 Millsbucks and 5 Intelligence Points for playing. These rewards instantly show up in my account.

When Huzinga (1938/1955) described our species as *homo ludens*, he imagined play as a "magic circle," one given to "absorbing the player intensely and utterly" (p. 13). What Sutton-Smith (1997) calls the "ambiguity of play"—simultaneously real and not real—positions it as what Turner (1982) calls a "liminal" space, one with transformative potential (p. 27). Gadamer (1960/2000) echoes this notion, writing "play itself is a transformation of such a kind that the identity of the player does not continue to exist for anybody" (p. 112). Online food marketing sites are, in essence, "colorful, interactive online playgrounds [...] encouraging young consumers to engage playfully with products over long periods" (Chester & Montgomery, 2007, p. 42). In Millsberry, food is depicted in a number of ways, but perhaps most interestingly as something to be "played with." This can be observed in the use of food in many of the digital games found in the Millsberry Arcade. It can also be seen in the fictional "goings on" documented in the *Millsberry Gazette.* I treat each of these below.

The arcade games displace the Millsberry character and location momentarily, as the Buddy turns into Lucky or some other character within the new fiction of the video game. In this alternate world, food is no longer what a Buddy must eat. It is now an object for play. In "Lucky Charms Charmed Life," food is what Lucky must gather for points (e.g., the cereal bowls). But it is also imbued with magical properties. The marshmallow charms make the kids float or Lucky fly. In this, the food item becomes more than something to eat. It is something with the added value of fun or even magic.

Play *Fruity Cheerios Bumper Boat*s and you will be one of Millsberry's residents (Coach Danner, for example) sitting inside a fruit-flavored Cheerio trying to bump another player out of a water ring. Not only is your "boat" a giant cereal piece, other Fruity Cheerios appear in the water to be collected for added power. Play *Sudoku* and instead of trying to match up numbers in your three by three grid, you are matching up the "charms" from Lucky Charms cereal. In "Honey Nut Cheerios Save the Honey," you are out on a golden sea, with floating beehives that must be lassoed in order to "save the honey" from a pirate ship. And if a game of skill is not appealing, try a game of chance. In *Cinnamon Toast Crunch Swirl* you need only drop a cereal piece from the top of your screen and then see if you have won or lost points. As the pieces fall, cinnamon and sugar get sprinkled on them, making this a strange hybrid of a gambling game and simulated cereal factory. This game mixes the food as play-object/food as consumable-object paradigms in one other way. High scorers of this game receive a "prize": a virtual box of Cinnamon Toast Crunch delivered straight to Buddy's pantry.

Cereal also features prominently in the goings-on in and about town. Each time you log in to Millsberry, you are greeted by *The Millsberry Gazette*, the town newspaper. However, these goings-on actually *never go on* outside of their reportage. With only a few exceptions—such as the hunt for the Cinnamon Toast Crunch mystery clues—the events documented in the *Millsberry Gazette* are a kind of pure fiction, creating the illusion of a live town in which newsworthy (though never bad) *things happen.* All of the back issues of the *Millsberry Gazette* are archived in the Millsberry Historical Society, so players can read a history of the town over time. News stories refer to characters that ostensibly "live" in town. Apart from the player-generated Buddies who reside in Millsberry by virtue of having registered to play on the site and creating homes there, there are a handful of (adult) non-player characters to support this town fiction. There is Coach Danner, coach for the local baseball team and gym teacher at the Millsberry Academy. Or Pete Peterson, owner of Peterson's Construction and Hardware Emporium. These characters are referred to in the *Millsberry Gazette* as though they lived in Millsberry. Yet they exist only in what is written about them. But their job is an important one; the fiction that is Millsberry depends upon these characters creating the illusion that a town—a community even—exists.

In the *Millsberry Gazette*, it becomes clear that excitement over cereal is common in this town, as branded spokescharacters such as Lucky the leprechaun and the Trix rabbit appear from time to time. For example, in an incident in 2005, a mysterious breakfast cereal was found in a crate by

Millsberry Academy students on a nature walk in Peabody Park. The *Gazette* was on the case:

> *The Millsberry Gazette* was also allowed to examine the contents of the chest, and it appears that the students are quite correct. The chest is filled to the top with what looks and tastes like a great chocolatey cereal; however, it also contains marshmallow bits in differing colors and shapes! Whatever it is, it is certainly new and different, and will likely be very popular with kids and adults alike! (News Update, 2005)

The next week the mystery was solved, with mayor Trumble presenting the cereal-finding students with civic awards in a special presentation that took place in the breakfast cereal aisle of the Millsberry Grocery Store. According to the story, student Rand Allen had solved the mystery by taking some of the cereal from the crate into the grocery to compare it to items on the shelves. After it was identified as new Chocolate Lucky Charms, Grocer Harold Ettin reported a shortage as everyone in Millsberry wanted to try this new "delicious and nutritious new product." The article ends by insinuating that Lucky the leprechaun must have left the cereal in the woods, because of the four leaf clover found on top of the crate.

The above story, first and foremost, connects cereal to fun. The child characters find a mysterious item in a treasure chest and then have the fun of trying to figure out (Hardy Boys style) where it came from and what it is. Much of the story takes place in the cereal aisle, where the mystery gets solved, and the protagonists later get rewarded for their "heroic" efforts. This story also functions as a rehearsal for a future performance, one anticipated by the folks at General Mills. In essence, this game of finding the new Chocolate Lucky Charms is one that General Mills hopes the Millsberry player will repeat the next time s/he is in the cereal aisle of a real grocery store.

Conclusion

In Millsberry, the performativity of the avatar's consumption stands in place of the player's, rehearsing it in anticipation of decisions to be made in the real grocery store. As such, online cereal marketing rehearses cereal purchase and consumption in a way that commingles the pleasures of play, of purchase, and of consumption, pleasures that are intimately connected with issues of power and control.

Video games afford what Grodal (2000) has termed the "pleasures of control," as players sense their own agency by manipulating events and outcomes, a notion particularly salient in the case of children, who have only limited control over the choices made in their everyday lives. One of the pleasures of Millsberry, for children, is this pleasure of control, as the Buddies of Millsberry live in a world without parents, where they can choose their own clothes, decorate their own houses, and buy whatever they want with their own "money." This appeal of control is made blatant by the advertisement for Millsberry on the side panel of a box of Lucky Charms cereal, which states: "Kids Rule in Millsberry! Create your character, design your house then explore the town of Millsberry to find fun games and earn Millsbucks." In other words, in Millsberry kids can go where they want, do what they want, and when they want.

In addition to cultivating the branded child consumer, online food marketing creates a new version of Foucault's (1977/1995) docile body: the body of the disciplined subject who has undergone "the means of correct training" for cereal play/consumption, a training that in addition to producing consumptive desire has produced a materially docile body that (ironically) threatens that desire. Indeed, the body of the game player is docile in the extreme: needing only to click a mouse or press a key, and performing these mechanized movements over and again, held captive by the desire to improve a score, to gain more currency, or to attain the proper knowledge. Online food marketing presents a double threat to the child player as it simultaneously produces consumptive desire and a sedentary body: a disastrously perfect example of the "toxic environment" giving rise to childhood overweight and obesity (Brownell & Horgen, 2004).

Recently the material realities of the docile child body have been seeping into Millsberry, with Coach Danner now periodically telling online players to take a break and get some exercise. In such a call-to-exercise General Mills is implicitly acknowledging that online play contributes to the problem of childhood obesity, all the while ignoring (dismissing, hiding) the role that food marketing plays in getting kids to eat poorly. According to Brownell & Horgen (2004), this is a classic food industry tactic in response to obesity: promote exercise to divert attention away from food choice. Indeed, kids who burn off the calories they consume present fewer liabilities for companies who sell high-calorie processed foods.

Nutrition scholar Marion Nestle (2006) claims the power of the breakfast cereal industry can be read all over the cereal aisle in your local grocery store. Cereal boxes, claims Nestle, "represent the best thinking of marketers about how to get you to eat processed cereals, to believe that they are good for you, and to insist that nothing else will do for breakfast" (p. 349). Not surprisingly,

Nestle is not convinced that breakfast cereals are good for you, especially what she calls the "sugary cereals" that are intensely marketed to children and which Nestle identifies as "so thoroughly processed and sugared and filled with additives that they might as well be cookies" (p. 339). Cookies are easier for parents to say "no" to, however, because they are easily recognized as a junk food. To discern the nutritional benefits of one breakfast cereal over another, a parent must be versed in ratios of sugars and fiber to overall calories, and—as Nestle tells us—have a calculator at the ready in the cereal aisle. The "Big 4" cereal companies—General Mills, Kellogg, Post, and Quaker—spend a combined $2 billion annually marketing breakfast cereals, and if your cereal aisle is any indication, a sizable portion of those marketing dollars is spent getting children to influence family purchases (p. 339).

Child advocates have long argued that marketing to children is "unfair" because children cannot fully understand the persuasive intent and impact of the marketing messages they encounter (John, 1999). If marketing to children in the traditional television commercial is "unfair," then online food marketing to kids should be viewed as infinitely more so. On the Web there are rarely such markers as one might find separating commercials from television programming, as content and marketing is increasingly merging into a seamless "flow." Writing about the ethics of interactive food marketing, Chester & Montgomery (2007) declare: "On the face of it, a number of these practices are exploitive and unfair. Some may well be deceptive. For adults, they are problematic enough. For children and teens, they are even more serious" (p. 62). Many agencies and individuals have raised concerns about the levels of marketing targeting children and youth, particularly when it comes to food advertising. But the federal government has so far declined to get involved, preferring instead to have the food and marketing industries self-regulate (Mayer, 2006). Because food advergaming is only increasing in its use and scope (Moore, 2006), it is urgent that communication scholars investigate the discourses and performances that such food advergaming sites present.

As I have argued here, online food advergaming such as that found on Millsberry creates a different relationship with its "audience members" (kids) who turn into performers in virtual worlds. Online cereal marketing to kids rehearses cereal purchase and consumption in a number of ways. Some of these ways are symbolic (Toucan Sam gobbling up Froot Loops for points), and others enact a more realistic purchase (buying Lucky Charms in the Millsberry grocery store). All of them anticipate that moment in the cereal aisle when little hands will reach out for a brightly colored box.

References

Austin, J. L. (1962). *How to do things with words.* Oxford: Clarendon Press.

Baudrillard, J. (2001). *Selected writings.* M. Poster (Ed.), Stanford, CA: Stanford University Press.

Boulter, J. (2005). Virtual bodies, or cyborgs are people too. In N. Garrelts (Ed.), *Digital gameplay* (pp. 52–68). Jefferson, NC: McFarland and Co.

Brownell, K. D. & Horgen, K. B. (2004). *Food fight: The inside story of the food industry, America's obesity crisis, and what we can do about it.* Chicago: Contemporary Books.

Butler, J. (1993). *Bodies that matter.* New York: Routledge.

Chester, J. & Montgomery K. (2007). *Interactive food & beverage marketing: Targeting children and youth in the digital age.* Berkeley, CA: Berkeley Media Studies Group.

Crawford, G. (2006). The cult of champ man: The culture and pleasures of championship manager/football manager gamers. *Information, Communication & Society, 9,* 496–514.

de Certeau, M. (1984). *The practice of everyday life.* Berkeley: University of California Press.

Derrida, J. (1988). *Limited Inc* (S. Weber, Trans.). Evanston, IL: Northwestern University Press. (Original work published 1977)

Eco, U. (1986). *Travels in hyperreality* (W. Weaver, Trans.). San Diego: Harcourt Brace.

Foucault, M. (1995). *Discipline and punish: The birth of the prison* (A. Sheridan, Trans.). New York: Vintage Books. (Original work published 1977)

Gadamer, H.-G. (2000). *Truth and method.* (J. Weinsheimer & D.G. Marshall, Trans.) New York: Continuum. (Original work published 1960)

Greene, C. P. (2008). Shopping for what never was: The rhetoric of food, social style, and nostalgia. In L. Rubin (Ed.), *Food for thought: Essays on eating and culture* (pp. 31–47). Jefferson, NC: McFarland & Co.

Grodal, T. (2000). Video games and the pleasures of control. In D. Zillman (Ed.), *Media entertainment: The psychology of its appeal* (pp. 197–214). Mahwah, NJ: Lawrence Erlbaum Associates.

Huzinga, J. (1955). *Homo ludens* (Uncredited Trans.). Boston: Beacon Press. (Original work published 1938)

Institute of Medicine. (2007). Focus on childhood obesity. Retrieved May 21, 2009, from http://www.iom.edu/CMS/22593.aspx

Jenkins, H. & Squire, K. (2002). Art of contested spaces. In King, L. (Ed.), *Game on: The history and culture of video games* (pp. 64–75). New York: Universe Publishing.

John, D. R. (1999). Through the eyes of a child: Children's knowledge and understanding of advertising. In M. C. Macklin & L. Carlson (Eds.), *Advertising to children: Concepts and controversies* (pp. 3–26). Thousand Oaks, CA: Sage Publications.

King, G. & Krzywinska, T. (2006). *Tomb raiders and space invaders: Videogame forms and contexts.* London: I.B. Tauris.

Laurel, B. (1991). *Computers as theatre.* Reading, MA: Addison-Wesley Publishing Company.

Mayer, C. E. (2006, May 3). Restraint urged in junk-food ads aimed at kids. *The Washington Post*, p. D1.

Moore, E. (2006). *It's child's play: Advergaming and the online marketing of food to children.* Retrieved July 16, 2007, from http://www.kff.org/entmedia/7536.cfm

Nestle, M. (2006). *What to eat.* New York: North Point Press.

News update: Mysterious breakfast cereal found in crate. (2005, January 14). Retrieved June 1, 2009, from http://www.millsberry.com/town_hall/historical_society.phtml

Pollock, D. (2007). The performative "I". *Cultural Studies <=> Critical Methodologies*, *7*, 239–255.

Pollock, D. (1998). Performing writing. In P. Phelan & J. Lane (Eds.), *The ends of performance* (pp. 73–103). New York: New York University Press.

Rehak, B. (2003). Playing at being: Psychoanalysis and the avatar. In M. J. P. Wolf & B. Perron (Eds.), *The video game theory reader* (pp. 103–127). New York: Routledge.

Salen, K. & Zimmerman, E. (2003). *Rules of play: Game design fundamentals*. Cambridge, MA: Massachusetts Institute of Technology Press.

Schechner, R. (1985). *Between theater and anthropology*. Philadelphia: University of Pennsylvania Press.

Schechner, R. (1988). *Performance theory*. New York: Routledge.

Sutton-Smith, B. (1997). *The ambiguity of play*. Cambridge: Harvard University Press.

Turner, V. (1982). *From ritual to theatre: The human seriousness of play*. New York: PAJ Publications.

Whitlock, K. (2005). Beyond linear narrative: Augusto Boal enters Norrath. In N. Garrelts (Ed.), *Digital gameplay* (pp. 189–207). Jefferson, NC: McFarland and Co.

3

Remembering past(s): The construction of cosmopolitan Istanbul through nostalgic flavors

Defne Karaosmanoglu

Culinary issues give us numerous entry points into the question of how identities and experiences are reconfigured among and within societies. When taken as a communicative practice, food becomes an important site for identity claims, for identifications, and of solidarity and struggle within cultural and historical studies. In this chapter, I analyze the representations of the past by way of food to see what kinds of everyday spaces and identifications food marks out. Nostalgic culinary books attempt to bring back or re-create a world we have already lost through cooking and eating. They develop a dynamic connection between food, nostalgia, memory, and identity. In those books, food becomes a medium of communication that establishes relationships and social barriers. In other words, food is used as a means to communicate sameness and difference, selfness and Otherness, within a broader social field. It becomes a tool in building relationships, (dis)connecting people, and expressing cultural differences. It is also a means of separating the past from the present and of connecting different pasts.

According to Ferguson (2004), "cuisine constructs and upholds a community of discourse, a collectivity held together by words, by language, by interpretations of the world in which we live" (p. 8). Therefore, cuisine is the foundation of culinary discourse and a discipline which "allows us to discuss and to represent taste" (p. 18). Krögel (2009) also discusses the role food plays as a communicator of meaning especially in the construction and reinforcement of group identities. She argues that representations of foodways in oral narratives provide an important symbolic locus for the transmission and strengthening of identities (pp. 105–107). It is also important to note that cuisine and culinary activities not only express existing community feelings but also create community. People use food to cultivate relationships and transcend social barriers. In this respect, cuisine can be viewed as a means of connecting; not only does it articulate nostalgia for a homeland, but it also helps to compose and recompose cultural and historical boundaries. Culinary products offer a powerful way of imagining connectedness and symbolizing and mobilizing community actions (Valentine, 1999).

Analyzing the representation of food cultures of a particular community helps us to understand how that community connects to the past, lives in the present, and imagines the future. In this case, culinary nostalgia within food references should be analyzed to see how food becomes a vehicle for constructing a sense of home and imagining an ideal society (Swislocki, 2009, pp. 2–4). Over the last decade, culinary memoirs and autobiographies in Turkey have been tripled in number. They are also called "cookbook-memoirs," "memoirs with recipes" (Bardenstein, 2002, p. 357), or "nostalgia cookbooks" (Sutton, 2001, p. 142). This chapter looks at this subgenre of books, which capture old Istanbul through personal memories and oral histories. Bardenstein (2002) urges us to look for multiple genres or subgenres, since culinary books differ considerably in terms of their emphasis on individual or collective memory. They are also divided as narrative and recipe-based books. Sutton (2001) argues that "even within cultures, the past comes in many different containers bearing different labels—from 'history' to 'tradition,' from 'custom' to 'heritage'" (p. 3). In Turkey, culinary memoirs or nostalgia books range from highly personal memories to less personal oral histories. Recipes in these books play either a central or a supportive role. I choose to call them "nostalgic culinary books" because they cannot be classified as cookbooks per se; some are composed mainly of the descriptions of culinary traditions with few recipes, and all of them, in one way or another, circle around the notion of "nostalgia."

In nostalgic culinary books, Istanbul is perceived as an extension of the Ottoman imperial city with its highly multicultural character. Rather than a coherent national identity, individual and family identities are reconstructed as a part of Istanbul's fragmented nature. The city is a Greek Orthodox Byzantine city, as well as being an Ottoman, Muslim, and Turkish city. It is Armenian and also Jewish. In this study, I analyze the nostalgic culinary books considering the following questions: What are the ways in which nostalgic culinary books reformulate identities through food in the city? Which past(s) are significant for different identifications? How do those books define pasts and presents in relation to one another? What are the ways in which we consider the past as a spatial representation? In what respect does the past function as an open space, that is, open to flows, movements and changes, and a prison where traditions are untouched by internal and external flows? Finally, what kind of an image of Istanbul do those books portray? And in this picture, how do they construct the notion of cosmopolitanism or multiculturalism?

Impulses of Memory: Personal Experiences and Everyday Lives

The city is a place where cultural memory of various kinds is contested and the impulses of nostalgia and heritage are fully expressed. The histories and their different representations and meanings shape the present debates over cultural heritage in Istanbul. Heritage could be used in multiple ways in order to sell the city as well as to construct and deconstruct its sense of place (Bartu, 1997, p. 139). As Boym (2001) claims, the city is a junction for "longing and estrangement, memory and freedom, nostalgia and modernity" (p. 76). Thus, there is a "longing for the visible and invisible cities of the past" (p. 75). For Boym, "the city becomes an alternative cosmos for collective identification, recovery of other temporalities and reinvention of tradition" (pp. 75–76). Nostalgic culinary books, which are the concern of this study, represent the city by way of diverse identifications and various temporal and spatial representations. This chapter analyzes four books in relation to the representations of personal experiences and everyday lives in the city.

İstanbul Lezzetleri: Istanbullu Rumların Mutfak Kültürü (Istanbul Tastes: Culinary Culture of Istanbulian Greeks) (2000) is written by an Istanbulian Greek, Sula Bozıs, who lives in Athens, Greece. The original Greek version of this book, *Politiki Kuzina*, was first published in Greece in 1994. Bozıs collected data from interviews with Greek women over 50 years of age who were born in Istanbul. She also writes about her own childhood experiences, describing scenes of old Istanbul streets, bazaars and homes from Byzantine and Ottoman times. As well as presenting an account of personal stories and past experiences, Bozıs presents a history of culinary traditions and trade relations from this same time span. Also, she gathers information on the eighteenth and nineteenth centuries from the historical sources and archives; in this respect, the past is not constructed by lived experience. *İstanbul Lezzetleri* may be considered both a personal history and a general history book.

Çok Kültürlü İstanbul Mutfağı (Multicultural Istanbul Cuisine) (Eksen 2001) is an oral history, which is based on the personal and everyday experiences of past generations. Eksen (2001) compiles recipes from the interviews he made with Istanbulians, ages 45 to 85, who come from various ethnic and religious backgrounds. Therefore, in this book, "the past" is captured in 20th-century Istanbul.

In her book, *Bizanslı Yemekler (Byzantine Cuisine)*, Temizkan (2002) draws a picture of Istanbul through her own personal memories, through the recipes of her Greek grandmother (Madam Tyopulo), and through interviews with the older generation of Armenians, Greeks, and Jews. She provides scenes from the everyday lives of her family, relatives, and neighbors who have different ethnic and religious backgrounds.

Sofranız Şen Olsun (Cheer to Your Table) (2004) is written by a Turkish Armenian, Takuhi Tovmasyan. It is a culinary autobiography that captures the past through the family stories of Tovmasyan. The stories and recipes are mainly based on the daily cooking practices of the author's two grandmothers, who moved to Istanbul from their hometown of Çorlu during World War I. Each section of the book is named after a dish such as *Topik, Midye Dolması* (Stuffed Mussels), *Uskumru Dolması* (Stuffed Mackerel), Potato Salad, Bean *Pilaki,* and *Havidz*. Sections start with personal stories and continue with the cooking details. Anecdotes are used to describe the preparations of the dishes.

Different Past(s), Different Identities: Constructing Cuisines

In *Istanbul Lezzetleri*, Bozıs (2000) constructs her Greek identity through an Orthodox Byzantine connection. She longs for a past she never lived, the Byzantine and Ottoman times when religious festivities were fully celebrated. The dishes she introduces support the construction of her Orthodox Byzantine identity. She introduces *Vasilopita* as the traditional dish of Christmas, New Year's Eve and *Teofania* (the day Jesus was believed to be baptized). Here, she presumes historical continuity between the Byzantine culinary cultures and the Istanbul (Greek) cuisine of the nineteenth and twentieth centuries. Therefore, Bozıs describes Istanbul through many layers of history. She uses diaries and life experiences of both travelers and dwellers from the fifteenth century onwards as historical sources of culinary cultures.

In *Bizanslı Yemekler,* Temizkan, as well, develops a strong sense of Greek identity through her grandmother. However, she presents a blend of ethnic identities associated with her family and her neighbors. Jewish, Armenian and Greek identities have equal importance in her book. On the other hand, not only commonalities and sameness in cuisine, but also dishes that are unique to a community are emphasized in *Bizanslı Yemekler.* In this case, cultures preserve their distinct features within Istanbul. Temizkan presents Mario Levi's recipes of *çiroz salad, leek köfte, fish with plum* as uniquely Jewish. Temizkan also provides the story of a forgotten Armenian dessert, *Khavidz* (Temizkan, 2002, p. 143), a special recipe of *paskalya çöreği* (Easter pastry) by Istanbulian Greeks (Temizkan, 2002, p. 100), and details about the unique serving style of *Arap aşı çorbası* (Arabic soup) (Temizkan, 2002, p. 95). Temizkan refers to a multiplicity of identities in Istanbul where each culture prisons itself in a space untouched by any kind of flows and cultural interactions. Cooking, in this case, becomes a tool in expressing cultural differences and building imaginary boundaries between cultures.

Two layers of history are evident in *Byzantine Cuisine*; one period is 1940s and 1950s Istanbul, that is the childhood of Temizkan, and the other period is prior to the fifteenth century, in other words, Byzantine times. The first historical period is based on the personal pasts and everyday lives of the past generation. The second period is about the myths and tales of the Byzantine. For example, Temizkan refers to an old poem which confirms the existence of *hamsi* (anchovy, a fish of the Black Sea) during Byzantine times (Temizkan, 2002, p. 25). *Tarator* (a kind of dip made with bread, garlic, lemon, and walnuts) and *Labaneh* (a kind of yogurt) are other examples of common Byzantine cuisine (Temizkan, 2002, pp. 112, 140). Moreover, she traces the Byzantine roots of some legumes, such as lentils, which, we are told, symbolize the tears of the Virgin Mary (Temizkan, 2002, p. 78) and peas, which date back to the time of the Early Romans (Temizkan, 2002, p. 82). In other words, Temizkan looks for her Greek identity in Byzantine history and Christian traditions, beliefs, and pre-Christian mythologies. In a way, Istanbul's geography is reconstructed through the stories of everyday lives of the previous generation of non-Muslims who were assumed to have a connection with the Byzantine past. Temizkan identifies her childhood with an imagined Byzantine of the thirteenth and fourteenth centuries. Therefore, she has a longing not only for the times and spaces of her childhood, but also for an imagined Byzantine culture.

In *Sofranız Şen Olsun,* nostalgia and identity are captured in the personal family memories and lived experiences of the author's grandparents. In search of her identity, Takuhi Tovmasyan takes a very personal journey. Instead of searching the Armenian identity in history in general, she looks for it in her own personal past. In this respect, the past is rewritten and represented by the memories of the Tovmasyan family wherein Armenianness plays the most dominant role in the discourses of memory and nostalgia. That is, the culinary culture and identity of the Tovmasyan family are mainly characterized by Armenianness. Most of the dishes are introduced through Christian Armenian traditions and most of the time Tovmasyan uses Armenian words to refer to her family members, such as *yaya* (grandmother), *dayday* (uncle), *mayrik* (mom), and *ahpar* (brother). She compiles these Armenian words in a separate section at the end of the book. She also emphasizes some distinct features of her Armenian family cuisine. As well as general Armenian dishes, she introduces dishes which are particular to the Tovmasyan family. For example, *Akabi Yaya Böreği* is a dish that takes its name from the author's grandmother, Akabi (Tovmasyan, 2004, p. 80).

Besides Armenian identity (in ethnic and religious terms), regional identities are also crucial in *Sofranız Şen Olsun*. Together with being Armenian, being *Çorlulu*, that is being from Çorlu (a county in the city of Tekirdağ) is essential to the construction of Tovmasyan's identity and culture in Istanbul. Thus, dishes that are considered uniquely Armenian, such as *topik, havidz, anuşabur* play an important role for her, but equally important are *Çorlulu Armenian* dishes like *jamkapısı* that were introduced as part of her family's cooking. Tovmasyan indicates that the dishes of her childhood, as cooked by her two grandmothers, are not necessarily Armenian but are definitely from Çorlu. Being a Çorlu native in Istanbul creates a strong sense of belonging to a diaspora culture, which is a crucial element in the book. Being a *Çorlulu* Armenian in Istanbul creates the sense that the city is a diasporic space for Takuhi Tovmasyan's parents and grandparents. Moreover, the neighborhood of Yedikule in Istanbul is also an important component of Tovmasyan's identity. Tovmasyan mentions that for her father *Yedikulelilik* (being from Yedikule) was associated with being a gentleman (Tovmasyan, 2004). Therefore, not only ethnic and religious, but also regional, identities are used to construct the past in *Sofranız Şen olsun*. Tovmasyan's past and memories in this respect are not limited to Istanbul in general. Instead, Tovmasyan's Armenianness is personalized and mingled with multiple identities associated to multiple places.

Unlike the other authors, Eksen (2001) does not propose to construct an ethnic/religious identity of his own, since neither his religion nor his ethnic origin is revealed in *Çok Kültürlü İstanbul Mutfağı*. Rather, he identifies himself as a multicultural Istanbulian. He portrays early and mid-20th-century Istanbul as highly multicultural with various religious and cultural traditions of feast and fasting. Muslim, Greek, Armenian, and Jewish traditions play equal roles in the multicultural portrayal of the city in *Çok Kültürlü İstanbul Mutfağı*. Eksen defines multiculturalism through the preexisting cultures, religions, and traditions of Istanbul:

> In the Ottoman capital Istanbul, people who were connected to different geographies, different races and different religions had lived in peace for centuries. They did not feel any need to change the names of the dishes that they had learned from one another, such as *aside, papaz yahnisi, rosto*, and so on. (Eksen, 2001, p. 13)

Food reformulates identities in many different ways in nostalgic culinary books. In the construction of identity, religion, ethnicity, family, place, and history play equally important roles. Those diverse identifications and especially Eksen's multicultural approach lead us to the question of how Istanbul's past is portrayed as cosmopolitan through impulses of memory in nostalgic culinary books.

An Image of Istanbul as Cosmopolitan: Past(s)/Present(s) and the Discourse of Loss

> Nostalgic food remembrance often reveals a contrast between a golden past and a present loss, in which psychological comfort is derived from remembering the past. (Chan, 2010, p. 206)

In nostalgic culinary books on Istanbul, notions such as "cultural exchange," "cultural interaction" and "multiculturalism" are widely used, especially in relation to the non-Muslim minority cuisines. However, those notions are not always constructed in the same way. There could be two ways of perceiving cultural relations, which produce discourses of multiculturalism or cosmopolitanism in Istanbul. One has to do with the "internal flows" that move within the city among different communities, and the other has to do with the "external flows" that reach out (principally toward the West).

"Internal flows" concern cultural interactions and mixtures of different religious/ethnic groups for the most part. A common example of this is found in old Istanbul where geography is turned into a space where readers can visualize the dialogues and exchanges that take place among people and families. In this space, Armenian, Albanian, Greek, Jewish, Balkan, and Muslim neighbors meet on a daily basis (Temizkan, 2002). For example, Greek, Armenian and Muslim children play together in the neighborhoods of Istanbul (Eksen, 2001; Tovmasyan, 2004), Armenian and Greek neighbors exchange dishes (Tovmasyan, 2004), people communicate in Greek at the fish bazaar (Tutel, 2001), and so on. Internal cultural flows portray the city as vibrant and dynamic, and, at the same time, as harmonious in human relations. In this case, the present stands in opposition to an imagined conflict-free and "pre-political past" (Sutton, 2001, p. 145). Representations in these nostalgic culinary books offer two perspectives to cultural relations. The first perspective is that cultures exist side by side in harmony but still preserve their culinary traditions. The second is that culinary practices mingle in such a way that it would be impossible to trace the origins of the dishes. What is emphasized is either the "distinctiveness" or the "commonalities" of culinary traditions. While the former approach takes cultures as static and unchanging like a prison untouched by flows, the latter considers them as mixtures and hybrids open to flows and changes. Evidence of both perspectives may be seen in nostalgic culinary books.

With external cultural flows, on the other hand, Istanbul's culinary culture is thought to be revolutionized by a mélange of Eastern and Western culinary traditions. Becoming cosmopolitan here is simply associated with the westernization of the late-Ottomans. This influence is welcomed as it is thought to bring sophistication to the Turkish dishes. For example, with the introduction of béchamel sauce to the Ottoman cuisine, one of the most innovative dishes, *hünkar beğendi,* was invented (Bozıs, 2000). Therefore, in the Ottoman history the influence of the European culinary tradition is appreciated and welcomed as bringing sophistication, while today such influence coming from the West is devalued (see Eksen, 2008, pp. 149–153). An author reveals his unwelcoming thoughts about the newly opened trendy dining places in Istanbul: "Pubs, Snack Bars, and Grill Houses? Don't make me laugh… Those are not for us at all" (Tutel, 2001, p. 58).

In Bozıs' book external flows are taken as highly favorable. Bozıs refers to the late nineteenth century when Istanbul cuisine had one of most crucial developments in its history. For Bozıs, the contribution of Greek cooks, who were working in the embassies at the time, was tremendous. They quickly adapted European dishes and culinary styles (Bozıs, 2000). What Bozıs finds crucial is the blend of Western and Eastern culinary traditions. As she indicates, in the Greek houses, *sarma* (stuffed vine leaves), a traditional dish, and *cutlet pane* (breaded cutlet), a European dish, could be found on the same table. For Bozıs, this is enough to prove the cosmopolitan character of the Greek culture. In this respect, Istanbul cuisine underwent a positive evolution in its history:

> Istanbulian Greeks blended the best products and recipes of the East and the West and created an eclectic gastronomy. Then, in the Greek houses sarma and cutlet pane, pilav and tart, tavukgöğsü and pudding appeared on the same table. (Bozıs, 2000, p. 32)

Bozıs makes a clear distinction between Western and Eastern cultures. For her, what represents "the East" is the Byzantine tradition continued by the

Greeks in Istanbul. "The West," on the other hand, is associated with innovations and civilization:

> Until the early nineteenth century, in the Greek houses people were dining on ground-level tables. There were huge cushion and low stools for the visitors to sit around the table. Hand-knitted serviettes, called *Makrinari,* with two sides crocheted with silk were used to cover the tables. This old Byzantine tradition had continued until the Europeanization of the mid-nineteenth century when it was replaced by European style white linen napkins and tablecloths. (Bozıs, 2000, p. 31)

Bozıs most often quotes Western pilgrims and visitors to reproduce the distinction between the West as "the innovative" and "civilized" and the East as "the traditional." She quotes from historian Fernand Braudel, who wrote about the late Ottoman dinner parties. His writing is crucial toward understanding the ways in which the Greek Byzantine identity is constructed opposite to the so-called civilized West. Braudel referred to the Baron de Tott who was invited to the summerhouse of one of the chief Ottoman governors in 1760. This was the time when the European dining table and eating utensils reached the elite houses of Istanbul. However, there were still obstacles in adjusting to the European civilization. Braudel described the scene as follows:

> Chairs were placed around a round table. Fork, spoon, and all things were in order. The only thing missing was the habit of using them. I saw that a woman guest, while trying to eat in European ways, was taking the olives by hand and sticking it to her fork. (cited in Bozıs, 2000, p. 32)

Moreover, according to Bozıs, early 20th-century dessert notebooks, which reflected the Eastern and Western mixture, are indicators of how urban and cosmopolitan the Istanbulian Greeks were. She examines five handwritten notebooks of dessert recipes, which are written by Domna Ayanoğlu in 1929, by Roksani Çambeci, by Protopapa family before 1922, by Kalyopi Ohanidu in 1941, and finally by Theoğnosia Değirmencioğlu (Bozıs, 2000, p. 36). Those notebooks combined the traditional desserts, such as semolina *helva, Istanbul helva*, and *lokma,* with the European desserts, such as tarts, pies, and cakes (Bozıs, 2000). Cosmopolitanism, for Bozıs, is clearly a blend of the traditional and the European: "desserts contain both Western and Eastern influences and this blend very much reflects the cosmopolitan character of the Istanbulian Greek community" (Bozıs, 2000, p. 36).

Bozıs also talks positively about the *Tanzimat Reforms* in 1839 and the processes of Westernization in the Ottoman Empire at the time. She proudly emphasizes Westernization when the palace chef, the Greek Marko, was sent to France to invite French chefs to the Ottoman palace kitchen in 1866. As she indicates, béchamel sauce was one of the "revolutionary" entries in Istanbul's culinary culture as a result of which many "magnificent" dishes were invented: "With béchamel, eggplant puree was turned into an artwork, *hünkar beğendi*" (Bozıs, 2000, p. 57). Therefore, Bozıs appreciates Western influence for generating cosmopolitanism. She draws a cosmopolitan picture of late 19th-and early 20th-century Istanbul. She refers especially to the Pera area as the heart of entertainment, replete with European style cafés, Russian and French restaurants, German and Austrian beer places (*birahane*), "Brasserie Suisse," Italian stores, and hotels (Bozıs, 2000, pp. 75–79). Being urban and always in touch with Europe define the notion of cosmopolitanism in *İstanbul Lezzetleri*.

On the other hand, Bozıs (2000) focuses specifically on Greek cuisine by differentiating it from the other traditions in Istanbul. She rarely talks about the exchanges and mixtures of culinary cultures of various religious and ethnic groups. Greek culture, in this respect, is imagined to be surrounded by symbolic boundaries that protect it from the internal flows of the city. Bozıs explains this elsewhere:

> The perfection of Istanbul cuisine came from the fact that with the same ingredients different communities used to cook different dishes. In this respect, Greek cuisine was very distinct. (cited in Erevnidis, 2005, p. 75)

Therefore, Greek cuisine in Istanbul is separated as "distinct" even within a space where intense cultural dialogues and interactions were present. Bozıs, in this respect, draws borders around the Greek cuisine (and Istanbul's Greek past, for that matter) in such a way that it is not influenced by other traditions. In this case, Greek culture is considered a prison untouched by flows. It is static and isolated. Istanbul's cuisine is defined by a static Greek past and culture which has been closed to internal flows, and also by a dynamic European and Eastern mixture which has made up the cosmopolitan Istanbul. In this respect, Greek cuisine is regarded as "civilized" as a result of Western cultural flows and consumerist trends that make up the discourses of cosmopolitanism in *İstanbul Lezzetleri*. Istanbul is portrayed as consisting of different geographies in multiple time periods which are then characterized by internal and external cultural flows. The present, however, is totally excluded from this picture.

In *Çok Kültürlü İstanbul Mutfağı*, Eksen (2001) extensively discusses certain dishes to differentiate the cuisine of Istanbul from other regional cuisines, as well as to show culinary variations within multicultural Istanbul. Eksen argues for a single Istanbul cuisine composed of different culinary practices. He presents commonalities in culinary cultures to support the development of a single Istanbul cuisine. *Papaz yahnisi* (Priest's Stew) is a very good example of multicultural Istanbul. He says "call it Greek, Armenian, Georgian or Ottoman, it is one of our common Istanbulian dishes" (Eksen, 2001, p.15). However, he refers to minor differences in its cooking style. Muslims, for instance, cook *papaz yahnisi* with vinegar instead of wine for religious reasons (Eksen, 2001). As well, *aşure* (a pudding-like dessert made with a variety of nuts and fruits) is a common dessert of different traditions. It is Muslim and Jewish as well as Armenian and Greek (Eksen, 2001). Eksen also argues that *dolma* (stuffed vegetable dish with either ground meat or rice) cooking in Istanbul is "distinctive" when compared to the other regions in Turkey. They are sweet and spicy (Eksen, 2001). Even though their cooking styles change, *papaz yahnisi, aşure,* and *dolma* are just a few of the examples that are included in Eksen's Istanbul cuisine. *Keşkek* is another interesting example, which reflects cultural sharing and exchange. Even though it is generally presented as a traditional Armenian dish, it is found in a Turkish cookbook of the nineteenth century, *Aşçıbaşı (The Master Cook)* (Mahmud Nedim bin Tosun 1898). Eksen explains this:

> For centuries, Armenians, Kurds, and Turks had lived together in the same villages side by side. They had cultivated the same wheat and fed the same cow, so what could be more natural than preparing and eating the same dish? (Eksen, 2001, p. 29)

Not only commonalities but also differences in culinary cultures are emphasized in *Çok Kültürlü İstanbul Mutfağı*. In this case, cultural relations and flows within the city do not always cause mixtures. Eksen conceptualizes cultures as existing side by side while they preserve their distinct dishes or cooking styles. Each religious activity brings its own culinary culture. He describes Muslim fasting (*oruç*), Jewish Yom Kippur, and Armenian and Greek fasting (*perhiz*) separately (Eksen, 2001, pp. 36–44). As well, he attributes some recipes to different ethnic/religious communities. Armenian *anuş abur* (Eksen, 2001, p. 28), Greek *basilopide* and *koliva* (Eksen, 2001, pp. 55–56), the "exotic" Ottoman dish *aside* of Arabic origin (Eksen, 2001, p. 15), and the Sephardic *leek köfte* and *eggplant börek* (Eksen, 2001, pp. 21–22) are discussed by Eksen's Istanbulian interviewees. They present traditional Jewish dishes, such as *fish with sour plum* (Eksen, 2001, p. 77), and a dessert called *masapan* as little known among the general Istanbul population. A Sephardic dish, which is called *İstanbul eggs* (also called *Selanik eggs, Jewish eggs* or *Huevos en haminados* in Ladino)

(Eksen, 2001, pp. 102–103), is another example that is kept within the community. Eksen says: "to tell you the truth, this dish is not known among Turks" (Eksen, 2001, p. 102). He also talks about different styles of *dolma* cooked by Armenians, Greeks, Turks and Jews (Eksen, 2001, pp. 86–99). For example, in the Armenian *dolma,* onion is the dominant ingredient (Eksen, 2001, pp. 86–90). As well, Jews have a different way of cooking and eating *dolma*s. According to the rules of the kosher diet, they eat *dolma* with sour tomato paste or lemon juice instead of yogurt, and they eat *zucchini meat dolma* with caramelized sugar (Eksen, 2001, p. 99).

The movement of culinary products and ideas is constructed as an important feature of Eksen's Istanbul. He extensively expresses interactions and conflicts between traditions in order to portray Istanbul as a dynamic and a harmonious city. *Lakerda* (a kind of salted fish, usually made from bonito) is a good example, which reflects culinary cultural flows between Greeks and Armenians. His interviewee Sorkis Seropyan appreciates the Greeks for their expertise in fish dishes and he admits that even though it is common among Armenians, *lakerda* is a Greek dish and is done best by the Greeks (Eksen, 2001, p. 73). Cultural respect as well as cultural sharing is highlighted in the case of *lakerda.*

The multicultural picture of Eksen's Istanbul is dominated by Armenian, Greek, Muslim, and Jewish culinary traditions. However, it is not limited to them. Albanian Necla Canset, who moved to a Circassian family as a bride, talks about Circassian dishes that are barely known in Turkey, such as *metaz* and *haluj.* Muhterem Çalık, whose family migrated from Caucasus in the nineteenth century, also lists the dishes they used to cook, such as *Caucasian pilav, zerde, çığırtma* and *kutab*. Finally, Necla Barın from Bolu who migrated to Istanbul in the early Republican period talks about Bolu-style dishes such as *mantı* and *İstanbul pilavı* (Eksen, 2001, pp. 24–26).

For Eksen (2001), internal and external flows construct multiculturalism in Istanbul. He perceives cultures and traditions both as separate and integrated, and they come together to make up the multicultural Istanbul cuisine. Unlike Bozıs (2000), who focuses only on the Greek culinary traditions in defining Istanbul cuisine, Eksen constructs a single Istanbul cuisine by collecting different culinary practices and emphasizing mixtures of traditions. He highlights multiculturalism as an identity of "his" city and "himself." Eksen's "present" includes traces of the past. Therefore, the present is not a total break from the past. But it is gradually distancing itself since the new generation does not follow the old one.

Tovmasyan (2004), on the other hand, reminds us of the cosmopolitan character of Istanbul through Yedikule. Her father learned to speak Greek from his Greek friends on the streets of Yedikule. As well, Tovmasyan talks about how they exchanged food with their Greek neighbors. They used to send *anuşabur* (an Armenian dessert) and get *Ayvasil pidesi* (a Greek pastry) from the Greeks in return. This is a tradition that is believed to bring wealth (Tovmasyan, 2004, p. 103). Here again food becomes an important means of communication and cultural harmony. Therefore, Yedikule sets up the central picture in the portrayal of multicultural Istanbul and illustrates the cultural and ethnic flows within the city.

Temizkan (2002), as well, draws a highly cosmopolitan portrayal of Istanbul during the 1940s and 1950s, which embraces a diversity of people, such as Armenians, Hungarians, Bulgarians, Greeks, Muslims, and Jews. The quotidian cosmopolitan experience is an important element. In a single page, we are exposed to several acts of cultural exchange. A Hungarian father and his Bulgarian wife, the Greek mother from Bozcaada, Greek tailor Koço, Armenian neighbors, and Albanian aunt Ruhugül are all part of this cosmopolitan scene. As well, cultural interactions and exchange are emphasized extensively. *İrmik helvası* (semolina helva), which exists in different traditions, is a good example of cultural exchange between Greeks, Armenians, Jews, and Muslims (Temizkan, 2002, p. 162).

Like the other authors, in *Bizanslı Yemekler*, Temizkan draws a cosmopolitan time/space to describe "the difference" of old Istanbul from the present one. She often stresses a break between the past and the present in which case the present is always unwelcomed. She associates the past with forgetting, while the present is timeless with no memory and history. While Istanbul of the 1940s and 1950s is conceptualized as a continuation of Byzantine times, present-day Istanbul represents a break from any past described in the book: "In place of uncle Varnelius' *muhallebici* store, which was near the '*Şark muhallebicisi*' on İstiklal Street, a fast-food place which has no memory, no imagination and no history has opened" (Temizkan, 2002, pp. 166–167).

Similarly, Bozıs totally excludes the present from this multicultural picture of Istanbul. She sees the present as a break from the past and defines the present by what it lacks. Therefore, the present is separated from the past as if it has no past, and therefore no memory. As Bozıs claims, "in today's Istanbul, together with the Greeks, all of the small and ordinary things are vanished in history" (2000, p. 6). When describing multicultural Istanbul, Eksen (2001) as well draws a nostalgic picture, even though he claims to escape from nostalgia.

As he says, it is impossible to ignore what was "lost" in terms of culinary traditions and of personal and community relations in Istanbul. The harmony of human and cultural relations, cultural exchange, and sharing characterize the past, whereas he portrays the present as unfriendly, cold, and mechanical in every sense. As with Bozıs, here the present lacks what the past had. For Eksen, globalization and liberalization, which have reorganized the import and export trade relations, have changed the culinary scene of Istanbul. He also emphasizes how eating habits have changed through industrialization: "People who live in the lands that used to be strawberry fields, eat hormonal strawberries and see strawberry jam only in supermarkets in labeled jars" (Eksen, 2001, p. 114).

Moreover, Istanbul's multicultural past, which was replaced by the Anatolian immigrants after the 1950s, is referred to with longing in nostalgic culinary books. The decency, quality of people, their culinary traditions, and family values, which have gradually disappeared from the present scene, are the main concerns (Temizkan, 2002; Eksen, 2001). The authors of these books strive to preserve memories of the city's multicultural past. Therefore, they celebrate the lost Istanbul of old times as highly cosmopolitan, multicultural, and at the same time, harmonious, warm, and friendly in human relations and cultural exchange. Muslims, Jews, Armenians, and Greeks are thought to be the people of the city, cooking and eating common dishes, like *dolma*, *aşure*, and many others (Eksen, 2001).

Spatial Representations of the Past(s)

In nostalgic culinary books, nostalgia and identity are expressed in the daily activities around food, home-cooking, the fresh smell of the vegetables/fruits, and their historical connections (through myths, tales, and symbols). The authors portray the old Istanbul as a sensorial landscape, which is highly cosmopolitan and harmonious. Geographical features are often dominant in the descriptions of old Istanbul. In all layers, history is turned into geography through images of Istanbul streets, houses, restaurants, bakeries, and *meyhane*s (a tavern like place where most commonly *rakı* and *mezes* are served). For example, Bozıs (2000) maps the Pera area of the nineteenth century as a Europeanized geography and a space of nostalgia. She carefully draws spatial features and details in locations while writing about the nineteenth century:

> Across from the Russian embassy there was the café-restaurant Saint Petersburg... Near the Dimitrakopulos grocery store there was Yannis Polihronidis' "Strasbourg"

> beer place where French journalists used to go. A little further there was the German Kuch's bar where they served German specialities. (Bozıs, 2000, p. 77)

Captured as periods, moments, and fractures in history, Istanbul is composed of different geographies of the past. For example, in the "vegetable-fruit" section of her book Bozıs imagines the city through its horticulture. She uses vegetables and fruits to describe places:

> Rumelihisarı and Sarıyer were famous for their cherries. Bosphoros was full of mushrooms and chestnut trees.... Beykoz Village was well-known not only for fishing, but also for its natural spring water and rich plants, and especially for its walnut trees. (Bozıs, 2000, p. 19)

Describing streets and places through aromas is also a way of creating a sensorial geography of the past. Bozıs describes the smell of spices in the Ottoman palace and the aromas of fresh fruits on the streets: "In spring time, Kasımpaşa was invaded by the smell of roses. Those were European roses that were cultivated for 'spoon sweets'" (Bozıs, 2000, p. 18). She continues, "In Spice Bazaar and Bahçekapı, pedestrians were pleased by the smell of *börek* and *poğaça* [a kind of pastry] coming from the street vendors" (Bozıs, 2000, p. 22).

Particular flavors are used to define particular neighborhoods making up the sensorial geography in history. Tovmasyan (2004), as well, draws a spatial and sensorial picture of old Istanbul. In her book, the smell of onions is associated with the Armenian kitchen. As she writes, three or four days before New Year's Eve the heavy smell of onions could be felt on the streets of Yedikule, Istanbul (Tovmasyan, 2004). Again, on Armenian holidays, aromas of onion capture the memories of Tovmasyan's childhood (Tovmasyan, 2004, p. 19). Consequently, in nostalgic culinary books, the past is pictured as a sensorial space. In this respect, nostalgia evokes a spatial longing as well as a temporal one. Difference between the past and the present is produced through various geographies of the past and of today.

Conclusion

Istanbul feeds multiple culinary discourses and memories, and multiple belongings. In nostalgic culinary books, cooking separates "the past" from "the present." Each author reflects both similar and different ways of engaging with memories and myths and reproduces identities of various kinds. In nostalgic culinary books, the past is associated with memory, whereas the present is associated with forgetting. While the past is defined by what it had, the present is described in terms of what it lacks. In this case, the past is attractive, interesting, and lively, but the present is mechanical, artificial, and dull. The lost world those books portray is usually natural, local, and fresh, not urbanized nor industrialized.

Between the past and the present, between remembering and forgetting, the portrayals of old Istanbul show fragments, differences, and frictions. In this respect, nostalgic culinary books that are analyzed in this chapter participate in the fragmentary discourses of multiple traditions in the city of Istanbul. Rather than continuity, they emphasize breaks between the past and the present with a nostalgic look.

In nostalgic culinary books, today's Istanbul is defined by what it lacks. The present-day culinary cultures of Istanbul are dismissed because they are unable to reflect rich cosmopolitan traditions of Istanbul. Moreover, multiculturalism is accepted within certain parameters. Internal flows within the city between several ethnic and religious traditions emphasize both distinctions and communalities. Cultural flows form either a hybrid culinary culture or they form separate and distinctive cultures. Greek, Armenian, Jewish and Muslim cultures are part of internal flows, while "other colors" of Istanbul, such as Kurds, Anatolian immigrants, and Romanians are excluded. External flows, on the other hand, are described through Westernization, transnational migration flows from the West (and North) and the new look of Pera with European cafés and restaurants. This constitutes the notion of cosmopolitanism in late-Ottoman Istanbul.

However, the cosmopolitan picture of Istanbul's culinary culture in nostalgic culinary books does not include such present-day characteristics as the cuisines of the Black Sea and Southeast regions, whose contribution to Istanbul's culinary culture is unquestionable. Present-day cosmopolitanism is excluded as being beyond consideration from the perspective of the nostalgic culinary books. Today's multiculturalism is not only unappreciated, but also devalued, and it is assumed that it has spoiled the richness of the old culinary practices. While the Western (European) influence in the nineteenth century is appreciated and celebrated as "progressive," globalization in the present day is not welcomed. Fast-food traditions, global cuisines and dining places are seen as threats to the traditional culinary cultures of Istanbul.

Finally, the authors of nostalgic culinary books represent the past as a space where everyday lives are portrayed through cooking and eating. However, the borders of that space are drawn in different ways in each book. While the past is portrayed as an open space where traditions and cultures flow freely, it could also be perceived as a prison, where traditions are stabilized and fixed for certain groups.

References

Bardenstein, C. (2002). The Gender of Nostalgia. *Signs: Journal of Women in Culture and Society, 28,* 11, 353–61.

Bartu, A. (1997). *Reading the past: The politics of cultural heritage in contemporary Istanbul.* Berkeley: University of California. (Unpublished Ph.D. dissertation).

Boym, S. (2001). *The Future of Nostalgia.* New York: Basic Books.

Bozıs, S. (2000). *İstanbul Lezzeti: İstanbullu Rumların Mutfak Kültürü.* (F. Benlisoy and S. Benlisoy, Trans.). İstanbul: Tarih Vakfı Yurt Yayınları. (Original work published 1994).

Chan, S. C. (2010). Food, Memories, and Identities in Hong Kong. *Identities, 17,* 2, 204–227.

Eksen, İ. (2001). *Çok Kültürlü İstanbul Mutfağı.* İstanbul: Sel Yayıncılık.

Eksen, İ. (2008). *İstanbul'un Tadı Tuzu: Saray Sofralarından Sokak Yemeklerine.* İstanbul: Everest.

Erevnidis, P. (2005). Politika Mutfağında Tavuk Göğsü. *Yemek ve Kültür,* 1(Winter), 66–86.

Ferguson, P. P. (2004). *Accounting for Taste: The Triumph of French Cuisine.* Chicago: The University of Chicago Press.

Krögel, A. (2009). Dangerous Repasts: Food and the Supernatural in the Quechua Oral Tradition. *Food and Foodways, 17,* 2, 104–132.

Mahmud Nedim bin Tosun (1898) [1998]. *Aşçıbaşı.* Istanbul: Yapi Kredi Yayinlari.

Sutton, D. E. (2001). *Remembrance of Repasts: An Anthropology of Food and Memory.* Oxford: Berg.

Swislocki, M. (2009). *Culinary Nostalgia: Regional Food Culture and the Urban Experience in Shanghai.* California: Stanford University Press.

Temizkan, S. (2002). *Bizanslı Yemekler.* İstanbul: Özgür Yayınları.

Tovmasyan, T. (2004). *Sofranız Şen Olsun: Ninelerimin mutfağından damağımda, aklımda kalanlar.* İstanbul: Aras Yayıncılık.

Tutel, E. (2001). *Şükür ki gurme dediklerinden değilim.* İstanbul: Oğlak Yayınları.

Valentine, G. (1999). Imagined Geographies: Geographical Knowledge of Self and Other in Everyday Life. In D. Massey, J. Allen, P. Sarre (Eds.), *Human Geography Today* (pp. 47–61). Cambridge: Polity Press.

4

Faith-based homespace: Decoding good taste in a monastery

Adele Wessell and Andrew Jones

Food is a crucial ingredient in defining historical identity. It plays a distinctive role in everyday life and is inextricably linked to the economic, social and political circuits of culture. Food and its traditions can be examined as historical texts in order to represent or communicate the narratives that communities tell about themselves. As such, food can be seen as a receptacle of cultural memory, a sign system capable of revealing official and hidden transcripts alike. Food comforts as well as nourishes, it provides an embodied experience of the past as well as a physical one. It "is symbolically associated with the most deeply felt human experiences, and thus expresses things that are sometimes difficult to articulate in everyday language" (Farb & Armelagos, 1982, p. 9).

Impressions of home and faith, concepts that are both everyday and profound, loom large in this chapter. Using the example of home-building practices in an Australian monastery, we hope to illustrate the way food can operate as a system of communication, and can be used to understand different theories and approaches to communication. This work is a joint effort; Andrew has an interest in religion and colonialism and teaches media studies, while Adele has been working in food history. Our interests collided fruitfully in New Norcia, a small monastic town outside Perth in Western Australia. By looking at the history of this place where the monastery was founded in 1846, and where the first substantial introduction of Mediterranean food was made, we will discuss national cuisine as a discursive construction that can operate to conceal the histories of colonialism and its legacies.

Home is a repository of memory, inscribed with the associations between people, sites, and time. The colonial project was carried out, however, by people who were displaced from these very associations that might have articulated such deep roots to them. In the Australian context, acts of remembering took on a performative meaning within a charged field of contested moral and political claims to home. Our concern is with home-building practices centered on the production and consumption of food, the encoding and decoding of food, in terms of how Mediterranean meals were maintained and transformed in colonial Australia in the domestic space of a monastery. Following Stuart Hall, our emphasis is on the interpretation of the monastic code as a process of reproduction expressed through the consumption of food.

Stuart Hall's essay "Encoding Decoding" (1980) was influential in opening the field of communications to new theoretical directions as a reformulation of Aristotle's three-part approach to rhetoric (Jasper, 2007, p. 388). Underscoring the active role of decoding in the process of cultural signification, Hall's work is pivotal in the development of British cultural studies. Hall's model represented a turn toward textual analysis as part of a three-pronged investigation of meaning construction. Focusing on communications media, Hall insisted that media institutions and their practices needed to be considered at the level of production, a close analysis should be applied to the text, and a variety of methods utilized for observing and recording the audience's interpretations and uses of those same texts. Hall acknowledged that texts were encoded to promote preferred readings in line with institutions and dominant ideologies. However, meaning is not fixed here in the text but forged at the moment of reception. Audiences were therefore appreciated as active, interpretive communities who would decode, negotiate and sometimes utterly reject a text"s dominant meaning (Hall, 1980, p. 136). This turn toward the text and the creative activity of interpretation was accompanied by an insistence on contextualization. Hall was interested in how the various stages of meaning construction interacted, and under what circumstances and cultural frameworks positions were struggled for. The model has been applied for instance to discursive constructions of climate change, which has generated significant political attention worldwide (Carvalho & Peterson, 2009).

Hall (1980) referred to several "linked but distinctive moments—production, circulation, distribution/consumption, reproduction" (p. 128) as part of a "circuit of communication" that could also be applied in food studies. The production and consumption of food are socially contingent practices that may be directly aligned in relation to each other, but that is not the exclusive vehicle of meaning. Our intention is to explore the Rule of St Benedict and its application in Australia, far removed from the Italy of the sixth century where it was first conceptualized and practiced. The monastic narratives of New Norcia demonstrate that interpretation and meaning are by no means fixed; rather, they are forged from the encounter between people and food, community and their environments, and cooks and eaters. All of these relations articulate constant and critical issues in everyday life that go well beyond our nutritional needs. While food is a cornerstone of religious practice and ritual, the discussion departs from previous work focusing on the spiritual significance of food to consider how such practices are used as a form of communication (for example, Shannon, 2004).

Tastes are subjective but they are also relative to culture—individual, yet shared. Food can be understood as encoded, organized into systems that provide the rules, explicit or implicit, and agreed upon by members of a culture or society. Foods carry meanings that can be read by people who understand the codes and it is used to disseminate those codes. While food is encoded with different layers or levels of meaning, it can also be read for different levels of meaning. The meaning depends on the context as well as the audience. People do not consume culture mindlessly and passively. Instead, as Nadine Dolby puts it, "they use it in their lives in innovative ways—much as an artist uses paint or a musician uses notes and chords—to create and express identity" (2006, p. 33).

In colonial migration people took their food preferences with them when they left home, but maintaining their cooking and eating habits expressed cultural boundaries as well as individual subjectivities, and the production and consumption of food was a home-building practice. Historical factors are critical to food preferences and these can change over time, according to the way existing conditions converge with tradition to shape how foods are used. The availability of traditional foodstuffs, differences in the level of practical cooking knowledge, forms of cultural contact all have an important role to play in the development of what Falk (1994) calls a "tastescape" (p. 68). Our use of tastescape links time and space, the actual foodstuffs that are consumed, and the experiences, imaginings, and beliefs we bring to the table. The early colonists were faced with a landscape and social setting devoid of familiar networks of meaning. Unhinged from the architecture of life at home; the streetscapes in which the family home is located, social organization of village and town life, habits of behaviour that are located over time and space in larger places called "home": familiar food may have been one of the few comforts colonists could look forward to which communicated a sense of home. In the absence of these material, physical effects, and locations of home, the kitchen works metonymically as the "mother country," and represents a retreat to the interior effects of home. Kitchen space is free of some of the striking and obvious differences that the colonial subject encounters outside: landscape, social organization. Food could, therefore, provide a practice by which members of the empire could make themselves feel "at home."

Consuming food is an embodied, concrete, practical experience of the past. A dish invokes its own history, bringing it into the present moment. It resonates with the history of its creator, and how it is ingested is dependent on and enhances the diner's sense of his or her past. In this way, food traverses the boundaries between producer and consumer, encoding and decoding, between present and past, and in these interstitial spaces establishes new relations of meaning between the subject and cultural, social locations. Moreover, the rituals which meals perform invoke the past, bringing it into the present moment. Far from being bound by geography and material resources, culinary cultures can inhabit multiple times and places that mutually constitute each other. Thus, food can play a mediating role in the translation from one spatio-temporality to another (Harvey, 1996, p. 233). Colonial tastescapes were constructed in Europe *and* Australia through the consumption of food; they were both socially and personally subjective and created new subjectivities.

The consumption of food in the colonies can be considered as a home-building practice centred on the maintenance and transformation of meals. Colonists were displaced from the sites where they could articulate deep roots. As Penelope Lively writes,

> Displaced persons are displaced, not just in space but in time; they have been cut off from their own pasts.... If you cannot revisit your own origins—reach out and touch them from time to time—you are forever in some crucial sense untethered. (as cited in Lowenthal, 1998, p. 9)

This invokes the importance of material sites of memory, and food provided this tangible link with the past. In simultaneously historicizing the everyday and evoking the past, the preparation and consumption of food plays an essential role in defining historical identity and constructing a sense of the past.

The food consumed by colonists in Australia was not simply the residue of old food habits, or traces of colonial history, but a device to reaffirm cultural and historical bonds and sustain a shared sense of identity. Gabaccia (1998) describes the link between food and identity:

> It is easiest to see how food choices reflect the eaters identity... humans cling tenaciously to familiar foods because they become associated with nearly every dimension of human social and cultural life... food thus entwines intimately with much

> that makes a culture unique, binding taste and satiety to group loyalties. Eating habits both symbolize and mark the boundaries of cultures. (p. 8)

Food preferences then are not incidental to the formation of identity, merely reflecting the location of a cultural effect. Eating is the primary way in which we initiate and maintain human relationships. It therefore becomes a means of creating and embracing social memories as well as private experiences, since we eat communally as well as alone. The world is not exclusively experienced by any individual; rather it is a shared world. In Dussel's (1969) words, "the world of *nosotros*, our world, (of our culture, of our region, our house, our life) is the place of shared existence" (p. 105).

Sacramental foods are central to many religions, and the Catholicism practiced at New Norcia is no exception. Here such holy edibles extend food's nourishing function to the soul. Eating exposes the fallacy of self-sufficiency or autonomy by traversing the boundary lines between ourselves and the world. Indeed, the root of the word incorporation is in the body; it is a process concerned with embodiment and the bringing of bodies together (Kilgour, 1990, p. 9, 5–6). In the Catholic faith the mystery of the Eucharist plays out this identity complex in a fascinating way. At the moment of transubstantiation nutritional substances (the *sacramental* foods) are transformed into the blood and body of Christ, they do not change in essence; rather their consumption is intended to change those who partake of it. As Camporesi (1989) contends, God gives himself

> to us as food. Since nothing merges with us more intimately than food which, by means of natural heat, transforms itself into our own substance, and becomes one with us… "He who eats of my flesh and drinks of my blood shall remain in me and I in him [*Qui manducat meam carnem et bibit meum sanguinem, in me manet, et ego in eo*]." But there is a difference between other food and this one: whereas the former transforms itself into us and becomes our own substance, the latter transforms us into itself. (Diotallevi, as cited in Camporesi, 1989, p. 227)

Communion is an act of ritual incorporation where the boundary between inside and outside, eater and eaten is problematized by the consumption of the Host (the *holy morsel* is so aptly named).

There are only a handful of monasteries in Australia, and New Norcia, located in Badimaya Country, 120km from Perth, is the only monastic town. New Norcia is a Benedictine community; the cornerstone of its monastic life is comprised of prayer, contemplation, and labour—all underpinned by the ideals and practices of its 6th-century patron, St. Benedict. Monasticism preceded

Benedict of Nursia by some centuries, but he is widely considered the father of Western monasticism. His enduring influence on religious community life was his Rule, which he penned as a guide to the daily practicalities of life in a monastery. St. Benedict developed a guide for those wanting to live a communal life of disciplined devotion to God. A departure from the extreme austerities that had evolved in monastic traditions, St. Benedict's Rule is characterised by its elasticity, moderation, and practical nature. Such a blueprint gave to religious life the malleability necessary to adapt to different locales and circumstances. St. Benedict developed his Rule from his own experiences. It is by no means merely a timetable for daily liturgical practice; rather it covers a range of daily concerns including the dispensation of food and drink and an appreciation for the importance of hospitality.

The Prologue and seventy-three chapters of St. Benedict's Rule provide detailed instruction on the practices of everyday monastic life and conduct. This coda addresses all aspects of monastic life, but many chapters specifically relate to food, suggesting its significance in faith, home building, and the stability of a community. The Rule of St. Benedict demonstrates literally the complex ways in which meals can be read as a text that signifies a host of intersecting activities, values, and traditions. In its production, preparation, and modes of consumption, food articulates aspects of our needs and desires. Food can be a vehicle for an intimate expression of ourselves; our ideals, and who and how we love. Food is a constant reminder that we are social beings. The notion of service to one's community is a thread through St. Benedict's Rule. This is clearly stated in Chapter 35 where it is decreed that all monks engage in kitchen duties, " Let the brethren serve one another, and let no one be excused from the kitchen service except by reason of sickness or occupation in some important work. For this service brings increase of reward and of charity" (as cited in *Holy Rule of St. Benedict*, n.d.).

Compassion is at the heart of Chapters 36 and 37, which puts a caveat on dietary restrictions for the aged and infirm:

> Let their weakness be always taken into account, and let them by no means be held to the rigor of the Rule with regard to food. On the contrary, let a kind consideration be shown to them, and let them eat before the regular hours. (as cited in *Holy Rule of St. Benedict*, n.d.)

The dynamics of a mealtime reading are discussed in Chapter 38. Readers are permitted a light repast to sustain them through their performance, and they take their seat again at the table once their chosen passage is complete.

Restricting the spoken word at the dining table facilitates listening, though gesturing for necessities is permitted. Both the quality and quantity of food is prescribed in Chapters 39 and 40:

> Let two kinds of cooked food, therefore, be sufficient for all the brethren. And if there be fruit or fresh vegetables, a third may be added. Let a pound of bread be sufficient for the day, whether there be only one meal or both dinner and supper. If they are to eat supper, let a third part of the pound be reserved by the Cellarer and be given at supper. If, however, the work hath been especially hard, it is left to the discretion and power of the Abbot to add something, if he think fit, barring above all things every excess, that a monk be not overtaken by indigestion. For nothing is so contrary to Christians as excess, as our Lord saith: "See that your hearts be not overcharged with surfeiting" (Lk 21:34). Let the same quantity of food, however, not be served out to young children but less than to older ones, observing measure in all things. But let all except the very weak and the sick abstain altogether from eating the flesh of four-footed animals. (as cited in *Holy Rule of St. Benedict*, n.d.)

Mealtimes are set down in Chapter 41. "And let no one presume to take food or drink before or after the appointed time." Hospitality toward guests is outlined in Chapter 53:

> Let all guests who arrive be received like Christ, for He is going to say, "I came as a guest, and you received Me" (Matt. 25:35). And to all let due honor be shown, especially to the domestics of the faith and to pilgrims. (as cited in *Holy Rule of St. Benedict*, n.d.)

For those that stray from the Benedictine communal path, punishments are issued and one of these is to be deprived the companionship of one's brethren at mealtimes, "Let him get his food alone in such quantity and at such a time as the Abbot shall deem fit; and let him not be blessed by anyone passing by, nor the food that is given him" (as cited in *Holy Rule of St. Benedict*, n.d.).

St. Benedict fashioned his Holy Rule so that it could be applied beyond the monastery walls in the homes of religiously inclined lay folk. The Rule thus communicates a pathway to grace embedded in everyday practices, which reiterates the intimate and fundamental relationship between food and home. In contemporary terms, a "proper meal" is generally defined by a meal eaten with family and its preparation contributes to the production of both "family" and "home" (Bell & Valentine, 1997, p. 60). The titles used in monasteries give the space emotional legitimacy as home; a group of brothers are brethren. Indeed, the title "Dom" given to monks, especially Benedictines, links God, Domino with domestic and domicile. The use of such titles has the power to create a sense of family and a discursive right to home; a place to live and work. The concept of home has often conjured up an image of a settled community, a sense of stability, and familiarity. In settler societies, such as Australia, the colonisers did not go home, problematicising and fracturing the relationship between home and colony.

Travel, colonialism, and migration have provided the conditions for an exchange of foods but colonising Australia was never intended as a gastronomic adventure. From the outset, native foods were largely overlooked or translated as inedible. In his journal, James Cook wrote, "The Land naturally produces hardly anything fit for Man to eat, and the Natives know nothing of Cultivation" (Cook & Wharton & Libraries Board of South Australia, 1893). A similar indifference infuses Dampier's observations; "There is neither herb, root, pulse, nor any sort of grain for them to eat that we saw, nor any sort of bird or beast that they can catch, having no instruments" (Dampier, 1967, p. 8). A strong correspondence, then, is exposed between cultural representations and the sensual experience of foods. Kalcik suggests a formula "not-so-strange food equals not-so-strange people" (cited in Sutton, 2001, p. 6). What is edible is determined by the symbolic function of different foodstuffs; how the food is positioned within broader cultural differentiations. As Lévi Strauss (1963) wrote, "food has to be good to think as well as to eat" (p.128).

The Benedictine monks Rosendo Salvado and Joseph Serra led the initial missionary party to the area they called New Norcia, named in deference after the Italian birthplace of their patron. The act of naming and possessing a land already occupied, and ignoring, subverting, or appropriating indigenous names and histories of the land is a primary colonising process. Because language is productive, rather than merely representational, it also serves to create histories and identities. As Birch (1996) argues, "To name spaces is to 'name histories' and also to create them" (p. 177). In the act of naming the new settlement after the birthplace of their patron in Italy the two monks produced and defined a sense of place that spoke to their own history. Dom Salvado and Dom Serra had met at the monastery of St Martin in Santiago de Compostella, which they fled together in the wake of the Spanish anti-clerical revolution of 1835. In Italy the two monks found themselves in the midst of a monastic revival led by Benedictine Pope Gregory XVI. Pope Gregory was keen to revitalise the foreign missionary work of previous centuries. At a farewell audience in June 1845 the Pope appealed:

> Remember, my sons, that you belong to the great family of our glorious patriarch, St. Benedict, your father and mine. You are about to enter on the path trodden by the illustrious apostles, who were our brethren. They converted a great part of the peoples of Europe to the Christian faith and procured for them the blessings of civilisation, whilst by their preaching and labours savage peoples were transformed into cultured nations. Go then and do honour to the habit you wear and may heaven bless your zeal and render your apostolate fruitful. (as cited in Lennon, 1991)

Initial contact with the Nyungar Aborigines in the New Norcia district had the fundamental motivations of survival and the building of a rapport with the local inhabitants. Salvado's party made first contact with the Aborigines of the district at the beginning of March 1846. Tensions were allayed when the missionaries made offerings of sugar, tea, and bread—a rather motley cross-continental repast facilitated by the intersections of colonial encounters from elsewhere. These foodstuffs, nevertheless, conveyed a message of companionship and a strategy of survival. Likewise, Dom Salvado's desire to learn the local Aboriginal languages demonstrated respect for the Spaniard's hosts, and simultaneously a medium to acquire vital information. After a couple of months the Benedictine's food supplies reached exhaustion, Aboriginal knowledge of food sources became essential. Returning to Perth and travelling with a Badimaya guide who introduced him to the bush foods necessary to survive the trip, Salvado wrote of the unfamiliar fare: "Kangaroo or possum sometimes made up our meal, but for supper I used to prefer roasted lizard, which under the circumstances, was a delicacy" (as cited in Lennon, 1991). It is important to note that it has only been recently that kangaroo meat has been widely available for purchase in Australia, despite its abundance and the environmental costs of livestock production.

Native produce was, by necessity, an important part of the diet for many colonialists during the nineteenth century; nevertheless, few differences in food preparation show up in early Australian recipes; instead new ingredients were adapted to fit in with familiar culinary expectations in a new setting. Cookbooks functioned to normalise Anglocentric discourses and to marginalise the exploration of ethnic identity in many historical narratives. In the first book of recipes published in Australia, *The English and Australian Cookery Book*, which appeared in 1864, Edward Abbot evoked "the roast beef of old England, oh!" (1864). The use of such a potent symbol of English identity in the nineteenth century may seem likely, and colonists (who could afford them) continued to rely on English cookbooks for many years after Abbot's publication. Abbot often drew on native and exotic ingredients to produce very familiar dishes using English methods and principles, such as kangaroo stuffed with beef suet, bread crumbs, parsley, shallots, marjoram, thyme, nutmeg, pepper, salt, cayenne, and egg. It was not until the 1890s that a large body of locally written books became available but by this time food supply was widely held to be abundant; the cultivation of exotic foods in Australia, like wheat, sheep and cattle, had established a familiar and long-term food supply for English colonists. *Mrs. Beeton's Cookery Book and Household Guide*, published in 1892, gave a selection of "Australian" recipes for the English: Kangaroo Tail Soup (ox tail soup), Roast Wallaby, compared to hare, Parrot Pie ("not unlike one made of pigeons") (Beeton, 1892). Recipes included in the new edition would land a modern cook in jail: Bandicoot and Tomatoes, Black Swan, roasted or boiled and Jugged Wallaby (Beeton, 1909). Mediterranean foods and ingredients, with few exceptions, do not make it into Australian cookbooks until many years later.

The reality of postcolonial experiences throughout the world is a history of migrations, displacements, and exile that tells different stories, all of which have a role in the production of culinary culture and the different types of cultural politics that envelop them. The taste for curry in England was in striking contrast to the attitudes of the British *in* India. As Chaudhuri argues,

> To protect their status as rulers and defend British culture in India, the Anglo-Indians during the nineteenth century chose racial exclusiveness and rejected Indian goods and dishes…Thus, even when the Victorians at home decorated their homes with Indian decorative objects and started to eat curry, nineteenth century memsahibs, to create a British lifestyle in the sub-continent, seem to have collectively rejected Indian objects in their colonial homes, and refused Indian dishes in their diet. (as cited in Narayan, 1995, p. 66)

As Narayan (1995) notes, the appropriation of Indian cultural artifacts was easier for those in England who did not have to distinguish themselves from their colonial subjects. This practice is not exclusive to those groups trying to maintain an elevated status and defend British culture. Research on immigrant cuisines in the social sciences suggests that immigrants and ethnic minorities try to maintain their own cooking and eating habits as long as possible, even against strong pressures to change them (Mennell, Murcott & van Otterloo, 1992). In Australia, colonists ate Indigenous foods, but they concealed their consumption in familiar flavours, in the absence of references in cookbooks and by focusing their agricultural and livestock production on exotic foods imported from "home."

The consumption of Mediterranean foods in Australia was important to the practice of self-identification. This relates to the context in which it is consumed. But it is important to recognize that this is dependent on the connections made within that place—the provision of food supplies, the knowledge about how to prepare them, and what they symbolise. Massey (1995) argues that "places, in fact, are always constructed out of articulations of social relations...which are not only internal to that locale but which link them to elsewhere" (p. 183). Traditions, therefore, do not have to be "place-bound"—they are a mass of interconnecting cultures, ideas, histories, and so on. Traditions do not only belong in the past, they can be "actively built in the present also" (Massey, 1995, p. 184). In New Norcia, such traditions provide an alternative to the narratives of Anglo food and the dominance of Protestant traditions in Australia, as well as the rejection of indigenous foods. The survival of colonists was dependent upon the knowledge and experience of Aboriginal people, thus complicating the history of eating in Australia.

The integration of radically different political and cultural systems that characterises the encounter between Christianity and other faith systems raises fundamental questions about notions of alterity, and the dynamics of exclusion in colonial and postcolonial societies. Dom Salvado's vision was to establish an Aboriginal mission as a self-sufficient agricultural village centered on the Monastery. The community would be based around agriculture, with an emphasis on practical farming and artisan skills. In the twentieth century, the emphasis of the mission shifted on to the orphanage and industrial school, but in the early period Badimaya people helped establish the mission's agricultural enterprises. Salvado's charismatic figure looms large over the early formative years of New Norcia. In accord with missionary discourses of the nineteenth century, his purpose was to "civilise" and evangelise according to the European ideals of the time; despite this common colonial conceit he did so with a consideration of Indigenous culture that was rare at the time (Spearritt, 1997, p. 3). Salvado's attempts to "Aboriginalise" the Catholic Church, however, by training young Aboriginal men for the priesthood to evangelise their own people resulted in great tragedy. Salvado took two Aboriginal boys, eleven-year-old Joannes Maria Dirimera and seven-year-old Francis Xavier Conaci to Rome in 1849 (Ride, 2007). Both boys died, as did other boys dispatched to Europe and the girls sent to the Mercy Convent in Perth. Bob Reece suggests that the children lost their will to live being completely separated from their familial and familiar environment and subjected to a strict discipline (Reece, 2008, p. 113).

Western Australia was the most isolated of all the colonies and the project of acclimatisation had cultural and economic dimensions. The colony needed agricultural products to sustain itself and advance its economy, but the choices made by the Benedictine monks related to their vocation and to where they had come from. Food emerges clearly in this case as a form of communication which can be likened to other processes as humans translate an aspect of their interior life into a form that can be transmitted across space to another person and adjusted through feedback (Axel, 2006, p. 359). Vines and grain were cultivated with a religious dedication or passion, but they had to grow in West Australia and be consumed by people less familiar with the meanings they held. Of their early agricultural labours Salvado (as cited in Lennon, 1991) commented, "Father Serra directed the bullocks, and I guided the plough. Indeed I can say that I have watered the Australian soil with the sweat of my brow and with the blood of my lacerated feet." By the time of Salvado's death in 1900, New Norcia was producing a variety of products including wine, olive oil, silk, soap, and tobacco. A flourmill was constructed in 1879; by-products included breads, macaroni, and spaghetti. Oil and bread and wine were also central to the history of settled agriculture and the first manufactured foodstuffs in Europe. All three have a role in Christian sacraments; religious ceremonies or acts regarded as imparting spiritual grace. This passage from the Gospel of Matthew brings together bread, wine, and oil in what Maguelonne Toussaint-Samat (1994) terms "the fundamental trinity" (p. 203):

> And as they were eating, Jesus took the bread, and blessed it, and broke it, and gave it to the disciples, and said, Take, eat; this is my body. And he took the cup, and gave thanks, and gave it to them saying, Drink ye all of it; For this is my blood of the new testament, which is shed for many for the remission of sins. But I say unto you, I will not drink henceforth of this fruit of the vine, until that day when I drink it new with you in my Father's kingdom. And when they had sung a hymn, they went out into the Mount of Olives. (Mathew 26:26–30)

Food is at the heart of our cultural imaginary; at a corporeal level it forms part of our common lexicon. The rituals of both sacrament and sacrifice are symbolically bound to the use of food and the Spanish word *salud* refers to both health and salvation. By assuming the shape of food and drink the Eucharist alone among the sacraments is received internally. Receiving the Host is fundamental to achieving the fullness of grace. Brillat-Savarin's aphorism "Tell me what you eat; I will tell you who you are," has particular substance here, the wonder and distinction of the eucharistic event was, as Camporesi (1989) points out, "the assimilation of the divine into the human, and then to the passage and the fusion of the human into the divine—the crucible where the swallowed food becomes one with the swallower. There is, however, one fundamental difference" (p. 230). As Cuniliati theologised in the 18th century, "in the Eucharist … it is not the food that turns into the person who has received it, but rather the person who spiritually turns into the received food" (as cited in Camporesi, 1989, p. 230). In this sense food is not merely a reflection of, but is rather constitutive of, identities. These identifications may be religious as well as ethnic, where the focus has largely been in colonial food studies. Through food we simultaneously incorporate our cultural identity and we communicate ourselves. We play with the menu to inflect it with our own experiences and tastes. The resulting melange of ingredients communicates a history of tradition, encounters, and change.

The Benedictines did not introduce olives, wheat, and grape vines to Australia, but New Norcia is identified as the site of the first significant cultivation of Mediterranean food. An annual banquet in the town celebrates its Mediterranean food culture—namely bread, wine, and oil. Olive oil is rich with cultural symbolism and varied in its social applications. As well as being a culinary staple, the "good oil" is used liberally as a medicinal agent, and is a ritual feature in many religious rites—Christenings, baptisms, consecrations, offerings, and burials, to name a few. New Norcia produces cold-pressed virgin olive oil for use as religious holy oils (Kailis, 1997). The monastery's vineyard still produces wine, which also has both sacramental and general uses. Ironically, the monastery's main oven is now used to produce Nut Cake, Pan Chocolatti, and Almond Biscotti, which are available at Harvey Nichols and Selfridges—department stores in London.

Food traditions are born from exchange. Food played a prominent role in the processes of enculturation in the colonies by passing on certain types of memories and histories. As long as the present is constructed as the exclusive site of multiculturalism in Australia and English traditions themselves are essentialised, Australian history will be rendered as an unbroken line back to the British Empire. The discourse of home can be called upon to create and sustain empire. Alternatively, the complexity and ambivalence of the concept can be restored.

The privileging of written and visual texts in postcolonial studies has meant other senses—taste and smell—are frequently neglected. Yet the consumption of olive oil and wine in the bush provide an embodied, sensorial image of the past—a memory Connerton (1989) would locate as "sedimented in the body," so always there, always remembered (pp. 70–71). The bodily sense of memory is captured by the word *recordan*—to remember–which, via the Latin, means to pass back through the heart. Memory's rich etymology hints at the somatic influences of food and reminds us that the heart bears witness to sorrow and longing—a locale of memory's incarnation, a sensual remembrance. At the monastery in New Norcia, the moments of production, consumption, taste, and faith come together, where food communicates a remembrance of home, of kitchen, of being on the inside of culture, which St. Benedict understood as so central to a communal life. Much has been written on the challenges of communication inherent in the colonial project. This scholarship needs to be extended to food as such a significant means of communicating. Hall (1980) provides one method for understanding how this worked. Food may be encoded with particular meanings by those engaged in its production or preparation, and these are central to the maintenance of eating patterns in new circumstances. However, Aboriginal people in New Norcia would have understood Mediterranean foods very differently and certainly attached different meanings than the Spanish would have to their own foodways. A shift to understanding how meaning is constructed through the decoding or consumption of texts or foods reveals the importance of reception. Not talking while you are eating may not just be a rule of good manners that Benedictines would embrace; it may also be unnecessary given the richness of food as another form of communication.

References

Abbot, E. (1864). *The English and Australian Cookery Book.* London: Sampson Low, Son and Marsden.

Axel, B. K. (2006). Anthropology and the New Technologies of Communication. *Cultural Anthropology* 21(3), pp. 354–384.

Beeton, I. (1892). *Mrs Beeton's Cookery Book and Household Guide.* London: Ward.

Beeton, I. (nd c. 1909). *Mrs Beeton's Book of Household Management New Edition.* London and Melbourne: Ward, Lock and Co. Ltd.

Bell, D. & Valentine, G. (1997). *Consuming Geographies: We are where we eat.* London: Routledge.

Birch, T. (1996). A land so inviting and still without inhabitants: Erasing Koori culture from (post-) colonial landscapes. In K. Darian-Smith, E. Gunner & S. Nuttall (Eds.) *Text, Theory, Space: Land, literature and history in South Africa and Australia* (pp.173–88). London: Routledge.

Camporesi, P. (1989). The consecrated host: A wondrous excess, trans. A. Cancogne. In M. Feher (Ed.) *Fragments for a History of the Human Body Part One* (pp. 221–38). New York: Zone.

Carvalho, A. & Peterson, T. R. (2009). Discursive Constructions of Climate Change: Practices of Encoding and Decoding. *Environmental Communication: A Journal of Nature and Culture.* 3(2), pp. 131–133.

Cook, James, & Wharton, W. J. L. & Libraries Board of South Australia. (1893). *Captain Cook's journal during his first voyage round the world made in H.M. Bark Endeavour, 1768–71: a literal transcription of the original mss.* With notes and introduction edited by Captain W. J. L. Wharton Elliot Stock, Libraries Board of South Australia, London: [Adelaide: Libraries Board of South Australia, 1968].

Connerton, P. (1989). *How Societies Remember.* Cambridge: Cambridge University Press.

Dampier, W. (1697). *A new voyage round the world.* St. Paul's Churchyard, London. Retrieved from http://sacred-texts.com/aus/awa/awa04.htm

Dussel, E. (1969). *Catholicismo populare en Argentina,* Volume. 4 Buenos Aires: Editorial Bonum.

Dolby, N. (2006). Popular Culture and Public Space in Africa: The Possibilities of Cultural Citizenship. *African Studies Review* 49(3), pp. 31–47.

Falk, P. (1994). *The Consuming Body.* London: Sage.

Farb, P. & Armelago, G. (1982). Consuming passions: The anthropology of eating. In D. Kirk & E. K. Eliason (Eds.), *Food and People* (pp. 6–11). San Francisco: Boyd and Fraser Publishers.

Gabaccia, D. R. (1998). *We are what we eat: Ethnic food and the making of Americans.* Cambridge: Harvard University Press.

Hall, S. (1980). Encoding/decoding. In Centre for Contemporary Cultural Studies (Ed.), *Culture, Media, Language: Working Papers in Cultural Studies, 1972–79* (pp. 128–38). London: Hutchinson.

Harvey, D. (1996). *Justice, Nature and the Geography of Difference.* Oxford: Blackwell.

Holy Rule of St. Benedict|Christian Classics Ethereal Library. (n.d.). Retrieved from http://www.ccel.org/ccel/benedict/rule.xli.html

Jasper, James M. (2007). What Do We Do with Meanings?. *Sociological Forum,* 22(3), 387–395.

Kailis, G. S. (1997). Bread and Olives: New Norcia Style. *New Norcia Studies, 5,* (October). pp. 28–43.

Kilgour, M. (1990). *From Communion to Cannibalism: An Anatomy of Metaphors of Incorporation.* Princetown: Princetown University Press.

Lennon, S. (1991). *The Story of New Norcia prepared and published by the Benedictine community of New Norcia, Western Australia.* 7th edition. New Norcia: Frank Daniels Pty Ltd. W.A.

Lévi-Strauss, C. (1963). *Totemism.* Boston, Beacon Press.

Lowenthal, D. (1998). *The Heritage Crusade and the Spoils of History* Cambridge: Cambridge University Press.

Massey, D. (1995). Places and their pasts. *History Workshop Journal, 39*(1):182–192.

Matthew 26:26–28 Passage Lookup King James Version (n.d.). Retrieved from http://www.biblegateway.com/passage/?search=Matthew+26%3A26-28&version=KJV

Mennell, S. Murcott, A. & van Otterloo, A. H. (1992). *Sociology of Food: eating, diet and culture.* London: Sage.

Narayan, U. (1995). Eating cultures: Incorporation, identity and Indian food. *Social Identities, 1,* 63–82.

Reece, B. (2008). The Grand Experiment: Two boys, two cultures. *Australian Aboriginal Studies* 2(Fall), pp. 112–114.

Ride, A. (2007). *The Grand Experiment: Two boys, two cultures.* Sydney: Hachette.

Shannon, J. L. (2004). *Food for Life: the Spirituality and Ethics of Eating.* Minneapolise: Fortress Press.

Spearritt, P. (1997). Background to New Norcia. *New Norcia Studies, 5* (October).

Sutton, D. E. (2001). *Remembrance of Repasts: An Anthropology of Food and Memory.* Berg, Oxford, United Kingdom.

Toussaint-Samat, M. (1993). *A History of Food.* Trans. Anthea Bell. Oxford: Blackwell.

Section Two

Communicating Selves: Food and the Construction/ Communication of Social Identities

5

Competing identities at the table: Slow food, consumption, and the performance of social style

Carlnita P. Greene

> Food reveals our souls. Like Marcel Proust reminiscing about a madeleine or Calvin Trillin astonished at a plate of ribs, we are entangled in our meals. The connection between identity and consumption gives food a central role in the creation of community, and we use our diet to convey images of public identity.
>
> –Gary Alan Fine, *Kitchens: The Culture of Restaurant Work* (1996)

Within contemporary, postmodern society, food has moved out of the realm of "mere sustenance" and taken on an increased significance as people are concerned with its health effects, issues surrounding its production and consumption, and its global distribution. There has been such an outpouring of food-focused television programming, magazines, films, and other aspects of popular culture that one could argue we are currently experiencing a "food explosion." Simultaneously, at the epicenter of these concerns with food, is a growing movement that seeks to bring taste and pleasure back to the forefront of our dining experiences. However, I propose that in addition to the food itself, it is a movement creating meanings through the use of style and performances.

Launched in 1986, the Slow Food Movement not only operates as a means of resisting the ubiquity of fast foods, I claim that it creates a *social style* for its members that allows them to create polycategorical and fluid identities. Yet, I assert that because the movement is rooted within two competing rhetorical homologies of personae, the "Utopian Foodie" and the "Grand Gourmand," ultimately these identities are contradictory in nature due to their divergent underlying ideologies. As such, I maintain that these identities also have disparate rhetorical, social, and political implications, which reflect how identity functions within contemporary society.

Therefore, in this chapter I begin by providing a brief overview of the theoretical and methodological framework of *rhetorical personae*. Next, I trace the origins of the Slow Food Movement and analyze it as a text by moving from the performance of social style to rhetorical homologies of personae. Arguing that the movement is situated within two competing personae, finally I discuss the rhetorical, social, and political implications of the Slow Food Movement in the context of contemporary society.

Rhetorical Personae: A Framework for Understanding Identities Today

In an earlier study, I argued that style has taken on an increased significance within contemporary culture and that style is a key way that we create and manage meanings about our identities today (Greene, 2006, pp. 38–40). To understand how these identities are both communicative and rhetorical, and managed through the use of style, I offered the theoretical and methodological framework of *rhetorical personae* (Greene, 2006, pp. 84–104). This method is a combination of my notion of *social style* coupled with Barry Brummett's (2004) theory of rhetorical homology. Because I have outlined this method in great detail in the previous work, here I will summarize its central tenets such that it is easier to understand how they apply within the context of the Slow Food Movement.

Social style is a combination of four dimensions—performance, language, commodities, and aesthetics—that we use to create our identities (Greene, 2006, pp. 60–71). That is to say, our identities are rhetorical performances in which we utilize language, commodities, and aesthetics in order to present ourselves to others depending upon the social situations in which we find ourselves (Greene, 2006, p. 71). However, in conjunction with our use of social styles, I assert that people create their identities by drawing upon rhetorical homologies in the form of larger cultural personae or stock characters that exist within popular media or everyday life (Greene, 2006, pp. 84–104). In using the method of rhetorical personae, one can proceed by analyzing the social style of a person to see if it resembles a particular rhetorical homology or one can use a rhetorical homology to determine the elements of social style that create a particular persona (Greene, 2006, p. 94). Therefore, I begin with an overview of the movement's origins to demonstrate how it creates an identity for both group members and the organization itself.

A Return to the Table: The Origins of the Slow Food Movement

The Slow Food Movement began as a response to concerns over fast food's impact within the global arena. According to Gaytán (2004) in "Globalizing Resistance: Slow Food and New Local Imaginaries," the movement started in 1986 and was sparked by the opening of a McDonald's in Rome which its founders viewed as anathema to cultural diversity and taste (p. 98). Petrini (2001a), Slow Food's founder and leader, asserts in *Slow Food: The Case for Taste*: "The Slow Food project was born in Italy in opposition to the fast food that landed on our shores and tried to take over" (p. 17). That is to say, the founders of Slow Food were disturbed by the global proliferation of fast foods as mass-produced, homogenized products that lack quality and cause health-related issues such as obesity.

As Ritzer claims in "Slow Food versus McDonalds," "McDonaldization has led to a trade-off in which we are able to obtain things faster and faster, but the quality of goods and services we receive suffers with every increase in speed and efficiency" (in Petrini, 2001b, p. 20). Petrini (2001a) states that on December 9, 1989, Slow Food became an international movement "when delegates from fifteen countries signed a founding protocol signifying their adhesion to the ideological principles contained in the *Manifesto*" (p.16). Adopting the snail as its symbol, the *Manifesto* calls for a resistance to "fast life" and speed, "a firm defense of quiet material pleasure," and a defense that "should begin at the table with Slow Food" (Petrini, 2001a, xxiii–xxiv). Therefore, the Slow Food Movement is not just a response to fast food, but also to "fast life" or what they view as our increased drive for speed within culture.

Since 1989, the movement has grown exponentially, and today, Slow Food has "over 85,000 members in 132 countries" with Slow Food USA being the second largest chapter (Slow Food International Website; Andrews, 2008, p. 12). Slow Food's philosophy has expanded such that today it focuses on "good, clean, and fair food" by declaring:

> We believe that everyone has a fundamental right to pleasure and consequently the responsibility to protect the heritage of food, tradition and culture that make this pleasure possible. Our movement is founded upon this concept of eco-gastronomy—a recognition of the strong connections between plate and planet. (Slow Food International Website)

Paralleling its mission, the movement currently includes projects that aim at "a defense of biodiversity," "taste education," and "linking producers and co-producers" (Slow Food International Website). However, while it has broadened its philosophy and mission, the Slow Food Movement still retains the ideals found within the original Manifesto at its core, which are related to both pleasure and taste.

As a new social movement, Slow Food has not been without its fans or critics. Some scholars argue that the movement is a beneficial one that has the potential to revolutionize our views on our food production, consumption, and distribution (Weismantel, 2002, pp. 3–6; Andrews, 2008, pp. 22, 86–87; Schneider, 2008, pp. 391–395). Others criticize the movement's elitist leanings, are more skeptical of it, and question the extent to which it can actually challenge the dominant hegemonic forces of the fast food industries (Leitch, 2003, p. 448; Peace, 2008, p. 39; Jones et al., 2003, pp. 303–304). Yet, I argue that another key reason for Slow Food's successes and failures is because it uses social style to create rhetorical performances of self for its members and organization. Therefore, to further understand how the Slow Food Movement draws upon rhetorical homologies of personae, I will now outline its social style.

A Snail's Social Style: An Analysis of the Slow Food Movement as a Text

To examine the Slow Food Movement's social style, I utilize a number of scholarly and popular articles that were written about its development, the Slow Food International Website, and the Slow Food USA Website. Due to the sheer volume of information, I limit my analysis to those aspects of its social style that I believe capture its key characteristics by beginning with its performances.

Performance

The main performances of the Slow Food Movement are directly linked to the purchasing, preparation, and consumption of food—all of which are permeated by an emphasis on slowness at the table. First, arguing against fast food's mass-produced, homogenized meals, Slow Food members believe that people should purchase goods that are both locally based and reflect the diversity of the regions in which they live (Slow Food International Website). They assert that by buying organic foods and visiting farmer's markets, they not only support their local economies, but also will help to ensure that they consume high-quality goods that reflect cultural diversities of taste. Yet, they also advance that people should take the time necessary to prepare these foods.

Instead of foods that are quickly ready without much effort, like convenience foods, participants opt for home cooked meals prepared according to "slow methods" (Schepers, 2002, p. 2). Or, when dining out, they choose meals that are traditionally prepared and reflect the regional cuisines of an area (Slow Food International Website). Members believe that these meals should be prepared with thought, knowledge, and expertise while keeping the goals of pleasure and taste at the center of the process. Therefore, a considerable dimension of member gatherings revolves around learning how to prepare foods according to traditional methods (Jones et al., 2003, p. 298).

Perhaps the most important aspect related to performance for Slow Food members is the act of eating itself. This process of eating has a performative dimension because people often use performances associated with food and eating, and the food itself, to create their identities paralleling the well-known phrase "You are what you eat." However, we could amend this statement even further in the case of Slow Food members to say that you are not only *what* you eat, but also *how* you eat it. As such, they view the art of dining as one that should be "slow," preferably hours on end, with a number of courses, and interspersed with jovial conversations.

These ideals related to performance are reflected in Slow Food events internationally, but are particularly a hallmark of the organization's "Convivia" or local chapter meetings. As Jones et al. (2003) reveal in "Return to Traditional Values?: A Case Study of Slow Food": "...the backbone of the organization is said to be its 'Convivia'—groups of members who meet regularly to promote local products and traditions, to participate in simple rituals of traditional cooking and eating, to spread the Slow Food message and to have fun" (p. 298). As such, these events are a chance for Slow Food members to come together as a community and serve to reinforce their identities within the group both figuratively through conversation and viscerally through eating.

The members' performances also contribute to the creation of Slow Food's organizational identity. For example, as Peace (2006) argues in "Barossa Slow: The Representation & Rhetoric of Slow Food's Regional Cooking": "Taken as a whole, Barossa Slow was a great success. Attendees especially enjoyed the performative nature of many of the encounters, their theatrical dimension..." (p. 56). Yet, because these events help to reinforce both individual and group identities through performances, Peace (2006) suggests: "arguably the most important property of Barossa Slow was its providing a substantive context for the expression and pursuit of cultural capital, which customarily informed the everyday lives of the attendees" (pp. 56–57). That is to say, through their performances at organizational events Slow Food members learn and participate in "slow" ideals that can inform their creations of identity in other aspects of their lives such as when they are shopping for food or eating at home.

Therefore, a significant portion of the movement accentuates those aspects of performance that occur *at the table itself* in terms of educational opportunities, taste, pleasure, conversation, and community-building. In "Good, Clean, Fair: The Rhetoric of the Slow Food Movement" Schneider (2008) explains: "The dinner table, then, is understood as the critical space that the Slow Food movement advocates, a site where slow philosophy can be immediately and effectively practiced" (p. 398). These performances at the table directly relate back to Slow Food's manifesto and parallel Slow Food's use of language.

Use of Language

Corresponding to the performances at the table, the Slow Food Movement also uses the notion of "the table" metaphorically to indicate its inclusiveness. In *The Rituals of Dinner: The Origins, Evolution, Eccentricities, and Meaning of Table Manners*, Visser (1991) explains that the table signifies "the embodiment not only of togetherness," but also is "a space…where people can meet on equal terms freed for a time from social structures" (pp. 82, 123). In this way, the metaphorical table of the Slow Food Movement is one in which anyone can participate regardless of class, race, gender, sexual orientation, age, geographic location, and/or a host of other demographics.

Petrini (2001a) expresses this view of membership diversity and inclusion claiming: "…the spread of the movement means receiving new input, mingling countless voices…such a variety of people have joined or expressed support that Slow Food has become like a nerve center…slow culture is growing, it is heterogeneous but strongly cohesive, and it creates an elite without excluding anyone" (p. 19). Not only does the table metaphor encourage participation from around the world, it also creates a language of openness and equality, which is expressed by the Slow Food *Manifesto* and its organizational philosophy.

Following this language of equality and inclusion, a main ideology underlying the movement suggests that "Fast Life" negatively affects *everyone* "has changed our way of being and threatens our environment and our landscapes" (Petrini, 2001a, p. xxiv). Providing Slow Food as the solution, the organization uses ideas associated with "slow" both epistemologically and practically as a means of resisting our fast paced lives within contemporary society (Schneider, 2008, p. 391). Schneider (2008) captures this notion of resistance in Slow Food's use of language maintaining: "Understood as a cultural and symbolic form of resistance, slowness becomes an important rhetorical strategy. Insofar as slowness is understood as a more thoughtful and intense way of living, it also encourages critical engagement on a number of levels" (p. 398). With themes such as "Go Slow," this idea of "slow" has expanded to other areas, both within and outside of the movement, such that now there is even a movement for slow cities (Jones et al., 2003, p. 301).

In its latest campaign, "good, clean, and fair food," Slow Food has broadened its mission of equality to further highlight not just good food, but also environmental issues and the rights of local producers by stating: "Slow Food is good, clean and fair food. We believe that the food we eat should taste good; that it should be produced in a clean way that does not harm the environment, animal welfare or our health; and that food producers should receive fair compensation for their work" (Slow Food International Website). This restructured campaign, therefore, expands its philosophy and mission such that the language of Slow Food is steeped in the ideals of knowledge and education.

Members believe that people should know where their food comes from, be informed about environmental issues surrounding its production and consumption, know the means of preparing food, and learn how to taste it. Each of these aspects is expressed in the self-label of "eco-gastronomes" (Slow Food International Website; Gaytán, 2004, p. 2; Andrews, 2008, pp. 18–21). Andrews (2008) explains in *The Slow Food Story: Politics and Pleasure*: "Eco-gastronomy, then, presents a challenge to mainstream ideological traditions…it incorporates a systematic critique of the current world order ('fast life'), embodies alternative values, and envisages a different way of 'slow living'"(p. 21). As "eco-gastronomes," members view themselves as different than "regular" consumers because their consumption habits are imbued with Slow Food principles such as becoming co-producers, acting responsibly in terms of their food purchases, and striving for slow living. Not only can members learn about these principles, now Slow Food has its own university, the University of Gastronomic Sciences, where one can study courses such as food history, sensory analysis, and aesthetics earning a degree in Gastronomic Sciences (University of Gastronomic Sciences Website).

However, perhaps the central tenet of the movement, and its driving force, is that everyone has the right to both taste and pleasure (Slow Food International Website). As Donati (2005) argues, in "The Pleasure of Diversity in Slow Food's Ethics of Taste": "Slow Food's philosophy is underpinned by an understanding of pleasure as a right rather than a privilege which places cultural and ecological diversity at the center of its ethics of taste" (p. 228). That is to say, Slow Food members advocate that people should enjoy, not just preparing their foods, but also eating them. They should train their palates to maximize their abilities to discern good foods and to hone their tastes. Finally, in applying their Slow Food educations they should derive pleasure from the authentic tastes of regional cuisines in contrast to the homogenized, mass-produced fast foods that are sold as global commodities.

Commodities

As its name suggests, the main commodity associated with Slow Food's creation of social style is food. However, as Pietrykowski (2004) reveals in "You Are What You Eat: The Social Economy of the Slow Food Movement," "Slow Food seeks to position food as a key constituent in the development and maintenance of community. It seeks to de-center the identification of food with its status as a commodity" (p. 311). In this way, Slow Food wants to change the nature of our consumption habits by opposing the conspicuous consumption that is so prevalent today.

The Slow Food organization claims that it is not focused on consumption in a traditional sense and members view themselves as co-producers instead of consumers because: "Slow Food rejects a life reduced to capitalist consumption" (Schneider, 2008, p. 392). Paralleling this perspective, Andrews (2008) believes that the Slow Food Movement can be viewed as an alternative form of consumption suggesting: "This is reflected in the description of the enlightened consumer as a 'co-producer' and by the emphasis on 'food communities,' in which consumers and producers are brought together and benefit from mutual exchange…to take a further step, to overcome the widening divisions between producer and consumer, indeed to go beyond 'consumerism. Only then would we be able to 'eat responsibly'…" (pp. 87–89).

Yet, as stated earlier, the focus is on high-quality, regionally based foods as opposed to mass-produced, fast, or convenience foods. Slow Food members recommend buying organic, locally grown or raised foods instead of foods that have to travel over long distances in the global marketplace (Andrews, 2008, pp. 33–39). While these locally based products do not have to travel too far before they are consumed, these kinds of foods sometimes tend to be more expensive than fast and/or convenience foods. In this way, the purchase of high-quality foods as commodities also might indicate the class status of group members.

Although not explicitly stated by the movement, it seems likely that members who purchase high-quality foods would also buy those products associated with its preparation and consumption paralleling other recent "foodie" trends. For example, some members may purchase cutlery, appliances, pots and pans, and dishes to complement and/or to enhance food preparation and dining experiences. Going even further, some may expand their purchases to include primarily aesthetic aspects such as kitchen or dining room furniture or complete renovations of these eating areas, which parallels recent trends that place an importance on food and aesthetics in the creation of lifestyles. That is to say, it is likely that some Slow Food members may purchase additional food-related commodities to support and/or to augment their Slow Food cultures.

Aside from the food being used as a commodity to create Slow Food's social style, the organization sells educational materials, like guidebooks to Slow Food restaurants, writings on the movement itself, and Slow Food-related paraphernalia such as a snail pin costing $10.00, a T-shirt for $25.00, a tote bag at $20.00, and stickers featuring the slogan "Go Slow" which cost $2.50 each (Slow Food USA Website). People interested in becoming members can join Slow Food USA for around $60.00 per individual although there are additional costs associated with locally, nationally, and/or globally-sponsored Slow Food events (Slow Food USA Website).

As such, one could view the Slow Food events, like the "Convivia," Slow Food Nation, and Terre Madre as further commodities associated with the group membership. These events range in price from potlucks costing $5 to $500.00 per person for the 2008 Slow Food Nation dinner at San Francisco City Hall (Slow Food USA Website). Thus, it seems that the organization's name also is commodified as an indicator of restaurant quality and as a branding strategy although the organization is a not for profit with a budget of around 39 million (Severson, 2008). Yet, another aspect that distinguishes the Slow Food Movement from other social movements is its focus on aesthetics.

Aesthetics

As Miele and Murdoch (2002) argue in "The Practical Aesthetics of Traditional Cuisines: Slow Food in Tuscany," instead of being focused only on the experiences related to dining, such as entertainment or the atmosphere, they claim that the main focus of the Slow Food Movement directly connects to eating (p. 313). In this way, they believe that the movement could be labeled as being rooted within a "practical aesthetics," which focuses on the quality of foods, has an ethical core, and is connected to environmentalism and the local economy (Miele and Murdoch, 2002, p. 313). Similarly, another key way that the Slow Food Movement creates its social style is through the aesthetics of taste.

This aesthetics of taste is the driving force behind the movement as Skidelsky (2003) in "Slow Food's Rallying Cry in the Global War Against Big Mac and Large Fries" claims: "The bedrock of Slow Food's case against fast food, however, is aesthetic: it fears for the taste buds of a generation raised on hamburgers and pizzas. The movement's primary motivation, in other words, is hedonistic: it wants to prevent a set of traditional pleasures–those of the table–from being comprehensively destroyed" (p. 40). In other words, not only does the Slow Food Movement promote food that tastes good, it also emphasizes striving for a diversity of the palate with local and regional cuisines. Slow Food members believe that people can find pleasure in eating locally because each region has its own unique foods, traditional methods of preparation, and flavors which suggests: "…to Slow Food supporters that which is truly 'good' is that which embodies taste" (Miele and Murdoch, 2002, p. 323).

However, for Slow Food members, taste is an aspect that has to be developed and refined. As stated earlier, participants argue that people have to be properly trained in the aesthetics of taste. This aspect especially is important for children so that they can move out of the fast food humdrum, learn to eat healthier foods, and learn to appreciate regional flavors (Slow Food International Website). Therefore, one of the main projects related to taste that the Slow Food organization sponsors is the "Ark of Taste," in which it tries to save regionally based products. According to the Slow Food International Website: "The Ark of Taste aims to rediscover, catalog, describe and publicize forgotten flavors. It is a metaphorical recipient of excellent gastronomic products that are threatened by industrial standardization, hygiene laws, the regulations of large-scale distribution and environmental damage." In this way, it is hoped that members will be able to save and pass on local cuisines for future generations.

However, Slow Food's social style is not just related to taste as it uses the *visual* appeal of appetizing foods in its own promotional materials and events. For example, the Website includes images of foods from all over the world such as mouth-watering fresh bread from the UK, fresh fish, and Jamtland cellar matured goat cheese from Sweden (Slow Food International Website). Not only is the food itself enticing, the picturesque locations in which it is being produced or consumed also heightens its appeal. These aesthetically pleasing foods and settings not only serve as models for what Slow Food members can strive for in their own eating experiences, they moreover serve as a visual reinforcement of the organization's underlying philosophy about food's role in society.

In turn, these aesthetically pleasing images also serve as a further promotion for the organization as having a potentially positive global impact. Finally, the images of the food combined with the overall style of the organization's Web site and its use of bold colors, like orange, blue and red, coupled with its stylized snail logo work together to create the Slow Food brand. As such, the Slow Food Movement relies on a multifaceted use of aesthetics to create its social style and identity.

As stated previously, each of these aspects—performance, language, commodities, and aesthetics—combines to create Slow Food's social style. This social style is one that operates both for the organization as a whole and is also employed by individual members of the movement. Yet, I assert that this use of social style also is rooted within two rhetorical homologies of personae, the "Utopian Foodie" and the "Grand Gourmand" to which I now turn.

The Utopian Foodie versus the Grand Gourmand: Competing Rhetorical Homologies of the Slow Food Movement

Although the Slow Food Movement is an organization and not an individual, I claim that nevertheless it draws upon two rhetorical homologies personae to create both its social style and identity. I suggest that individual members attempting to create their identities steeped within the Slow Food lifestyle also employ these two personae. Yet, while there are some parallels between the "Utopian Foodie" and the "Grand Gourmand," ultimately they are competing personae that are sometimes contradictory in nature. Therefore, I begin by discussing the first persona that emerges from the Slow Food Movement, the "Utopian Foodie."

The Utopian Foodie

The first persona that pervades the Slow Food Movement's employment of social style is one which I label as "The Utopian Foodie." According to Levitas (2007) in "Looking for the Blue: The Necessity of Utopia," "…utopia, is at root, the expression of the desire for a better way of being" (p. 290). She further explains that utopia "occurs as an embedded element in a vast range of human practices and culture" (Levitas, 2007, p. 291). Following Levitas' argument, I claim that a central component of Slow Food's creation of identity is rooted within this rhetorical homology of persona because, as can be assumed by its name, it reflects the qualities associated with utopianism. In other words, the Utopian Foodie embodies and reflects the desire that Slow Food members have to change the ways that we engage in our food practices including its production, distribution, and consumption.

The notion of utopia is certainly not new to how people envision food's purpose as Sack (2007) argues that in the past many groups "...believed that food practices not only reflected social structures, but could also change those structures. Most of these groups developed new foodways with the goal of bringing about Utopia through changing practices in the larger culture" (p. 457). Given the leftist Italian roots of the movement coupled with the influences of Marxism, 1960s American counter-culture, and environmentalism, it is not surprising that the persona created by Slow Food is the Utopian Foodie (Andrews, 2008, pp. 5–7, 12, 22). As most social movements seek to enact change in the world, because they see the contemporary state as problematic, it makes sense that The Utopian Foodie would be a part of Slow Food's creation of both its organizational identity and the identities of its members.

The Utopian Foodie also arises in the Slow Food Movement as a reflection of "Everyman" because anyone can participate in and/or become a part of the movement. In this sense, the Utopian Foodie is anyone who wants to enact change in the world's food practices and foresees a better future. It is for this *very* reason that this persona is created within a movement that strives to combat forces that members see as destructive in terms of our global society. Therefore, the Utopian Foodie seeks to change our current eating habits, which she views as detrimental, through the use of education.

Yet, I am not arguing that the Slow Food Movement is utopian in the sense that its members are naïve about or unaware of economic, material, social, cultural, and/or political issues or the complexities involved in solving the world's food problems. In fact, Slow Food has made an even greater attempt to deal with and discuss problems such as world hunger and biodiversity through its expanded philosophy and mission.

However, at their core these ideals are rooted in utopian fantasies suggesting that *everyone* has the right to pleasure and moreover that *all* people can obtain it regardless of class status. The Utopian Foodie strives for a perfect world in which everyone is equal and has equal access to quality foods. She also believes that there can be equal participation and voice given to all members, including producers, which is most reflected in the original goals of the movement and its new shift to the ideologies of "good, clean, and fair." That is to say, the Utopian Foodie views her relationship with local food producers as mutually beneficial and cooperative. Further, she sees her involvement with food becoming more directly that of a co-producer or producer as she can "go even slower" by purchasing locally grown organic products or by growing her own food.

Finally, some argue that the Utopian Foodie is a fantasy that never can be achieved because one movement cannot have such a significant impact on global society or combat the multi-national fast-food conglomerates. As Jones et al. (2003) argue: "The extent to which the Slow Food Movement can genuinely challenge and confront the modern world of fast food has to be seriously questioned…[its ability]…to provide a realistic challenge to a massive corporate power of the global fast food operators, seems at best unrealistic and at worst ridiculous" (p. 302). Thus, the movement's Utopian Foodie persona remains an idealized one. Yet, there is another competing persona created by the Slow Food Movement's use of social style, the "Grand Gourmand," to which I now turn.

The Grand Gourmand

Schneider (2008) argues that we can consider the Slow Food Movement as creating a *new* gastronomy (emphasis added, p. 392). However, I argue that the movement's social style is rooted in a much older cultural persona, the gourmand. According to *Gusto: Essential Writings in 19th Century Gastronomy*, the gourmand was a figure that arose within 19th century society along with the development of gastronomy as a result of a "serious philosophical effort, expressed in a lively tongue-in-cheek manner, to define a new cultural arena for the practice of aesthetics" that was directly related to a "transformation in taste" (Gigante, 2005, pp. xvi–xviii). It is because of its focus on the aesthetics of food, taste, and pleasure that I believe the Slow Food Movement's social style creates a persona that I label the "Grand Gourmand."

Describing the key characteristics of a gourmand, "The Gourmand's Almanac" states: "The Gourmand is more than just a creature whom Nature has graced with an excellent stomach and vast appetite…rather he also possesses an enlightened sense of taste, the first principle of which lies in an exceptionally delicate palate, developed through extensive experience" (Grimod in Gigante, 2005, p. 12). In this sense, the Gourmand is a person who considers all matters related to food to be important. He not only is a person who takes pleasure in eating, moreover he educates his palate such that he can derive the most pleasure from taste, which is a key hallmark of the Slow Food Movement.

The Grand Gourmand's obsession with taste embodies the ideals set forth by food writer Jean-Anthelme Brillat-Savarin in his *Physiology of Taste*. That is to say, the Grand Gourmand takes pride in his ability to "properly" taste foods and believes that this skill makes him different from others because: "… there is a privileged class whom a material and organic predisposition summons to the enjoyments of taste" (Brillat-Savarin in Gigante, 2005, p.167). However, Slow Food members also believe that people can become Grand Gourmands by training their palates paralleling the notion that: "If there are gourmands by predestination, there are others who become so by their calling" (Brillat-Savarin in Gigante, 2005, p. 169). In other words, a Grand Gourmand not only has a predisposition toward the pleasures of the table, but also is called forth to hone his ideals of taste through the "slow eating" of long lunches or multiple course dinners.

Therefore, this focus on pleasure and taste are the very foundations upon which the Grand Gourmand thrives and it is most apparent in the Slow Food Movement's "Convivia," which harken back to the ancient Roman "convivial," in which guests enjoyed foods, wine, and entertainment on a grand scale (Strong, 2002, pp. 24–36). In *Feast: A History of Grand Eating*, Strong (2002) reveals, "Conviviality, to both the Greeks and the Romans, was seen as one of the cornerstones of civilization…The table and those bidden to gather round it and share its pleasure could be a vehicle for social aggregation and unity…" (p. 7). Paralleling this perspective, Gigante (2005) explains that the 19th century gourmand was expected to be excellent in conversation since: "Crucial to the gastronomer's stance as post revolutionary Man of Taste was his capacity for eloquent self-expression. One needed not merely to grasp the rational principles upon which one's pleasure was based, but to discourse gracefully upon them" (p. xxi). Following this argument, I believe that the 21st century Grand Gourmand also has this expectation placed upon him. Therefore, the Grand Gourmand of the Slow Food Movement participates in "Convivia" where he can learn about traditional cooking methods, eat regional cuisine, and enjoy the company of others.

I claim that Slow Food's Gourmand persona is "grand," not only because it promotes a way of living that is steeped within diverse pleasures, but also because it directly relates back to an ideal of taste that is steeped in class assumptions. As Pietrykowski (2004) argues we can view the Slow Food Movement as creating a habitus for its members because: "The cultural capital acquired by participants in the Slow Food movement signals that one has a rather sophisticated palate, a love of food, and a respect for local cultures and farming techniques that are light on the earth…" (p. 314). However, he further believes that the Slow Food's cultural capital and habitus are class-based suggesting: "Yet…adopting cultural capital normally associated with upper-income or highly educated individuals conveys elitism and an aesthetic sensibility that privileges symbolic use value over material use value…" (Pietrykowski, 2004, p. 314). As such, the Slow Food Movement promotes an upper class lifestyle that places an emphasis on high quality foods.

Yet, these foods, such as organic meats and vegetables often are more expensive, which means that not everyone can adopt this lifestyle. Similarly, the notion that one's taste has to be refined and trained is steeped in upper class assumptions. Finally, the suggestion offered by the Slow Food Movement for training one's palate is through eating numerous foods from around the world, which entails travel. As Petrini (2001a) says: "In order to find slow pleasure, one has to travel" (p. 18). Therefore, one has to have a certain income and the leisure time to be able to experience foodways in other countries.

The class assumptions of the Grand Gourmand also are indicated by critics of the movement as Donati (2005) reveals: "With Slow Food's membership comprised predominately of upper middle-class members, I question the extent to which Slow Food is truly subverting the industrialized food supply and suggest that there is a tendency to fetishize cultural diversity in order to satisfy the appetites of a privileged minority" (p. 229). As such, the Grand Gourmand is unattainable for many potential members and even some of the current members. Nevertheless, its appeal lies in the fantasy and desire to live well, to eat well, and to experience pleasure.

Overall, the Grand Gourmand and the Utopian Foodie could be viewed as mirror images of each other since both stress high quality foods and view education as the key to changing our dining habits. They aspire to raise our levels of consciousness about the power of food and the pleasures of the palate. Finally, these two rhetorical homologies of personae provide Slow Food members with self-gratification, both consciously and subconsciously, whether it is through feeling better about their food purchases or by being fully immersed within the aesthetics of taste. However, there are some key differences between these two rhetorical homologies of personae.

The Utopian Foodie persona is more egalitarian because it does not exclude or offend people based on class assumptions and seems more altruistic in terms of its relationship to food producers. In contrast, the Grand Gourmand persona is more elitist since many working-class people cannot afford to participate in the movement and often do not attend Slow Food events. Similarly within the Grand Gourmand persona there is an underlying pretension to the issue of having the "right kind" of taste, which is steeped in class assumptions and reflects a highbrow (i.e. Slow Food) versus lowbrow (i.e. Fast Food) distinction. Nevertheless, these two rhetorical homologies of personae coupled with its social style create the Slow Food Movement's organizational identity.

Following Gaytán's (2004) argument, I believe that the Slow Food Movement helps its participants to create identities that are multiple and rooted within the imagined community of Slow Food (pp. 100–101). In "Globalizing Resistance: Slow Food and New Local Imaginaries," she states: "…Through new local imaginaries, members of Slow Food situate the local as an imaginative site where multiple identities come together as a fusion of social and political mobilization…" (Gaytán, 2004, p. 100). In this sense, I maintain that the Slow Food Movement, as rooted with rhetorical homologies of personae, allows its members to create polycategorical and fluid identities, which are sometimes contradictory, because they are rooted in personae with opposing underlying ideologies.

As such, I propose that Slow Food Movement allows its participants to maneuver back and forth *between* the two rhetorical homologies of personae on a continuum. For example, the Grand Gourmand persona may be appealing to wealthier individuals, but the Utopian Foodie persona also allows them to feel good about themselves because they seem more selfless since they are buying locally. Similarly, a person who is concerned with the Utopian Foodie persona does not have to feel guilty about enjoying himself in the process of eating.

Further, the Utopian Foodie and Grand Gourmand allow a person to participate more or less fully in the movement depending upon his budget, lifestyle, and/or time constraints. For example, he may only be able to afford going "slow" by dining at home once a week or as Jones et al. (2003) argue he may combine both fast and slow eating (pp. 303–304). Yet, as these two competing rhetorical homologies of personae create multiple identities that are sometimes contradictory, they also have significant social and political implications.

Social and Political Implications of the Slow Food Movement as a Text

Because the Slow Food Movement contains within it two competing rhetorical homologies of personae, it also therefore has contradictory social and political implications. As Peace (2008) asserts in "Terra Madre 2006: Political Theater and Ritual Rhetoric": "What is particularly challenging about this movement is that it strives to establish a critical analysis of the power exercised by global forces…[yet] essentially reflects the power and mirrors the contradictions of the system against which Slow Food pitches its political and symbolic resources" (p. 39). That is to say, it contains within it both counter-hegemonic and hegemonic forces that I believe contribute to the mixed responses and ambivalence that some audiences and critics have toward it.

On the one hand, it is a movement that ideally would have a positive impact on global society as it ties in with environmentalism, tries to ensure that everyone can obtain healthy, safe food, and promotes a less hectic lifestyle. The idea of education, especially in terms of youth and children, as a means of promoting a healthier lifestyle can act as a counter to a fast food nation. Many people feel that that they can participate in the movement and it allows its members flexibility in terms of identity creation and management. It also parallels other activities that some people already undertake such as cooking at home or shopping locally. Therefore, it seems as if it could be a viable solution or counter-hegemonic force to globalization because it provides an alternative view of consumption and combats the trend of conspicuous consumption that has come to dominate our consumer society. Finally, in striving for equality between farmers and consumers the movement also seems economically, socially, and culturally beneficial.

Yet, ironically the movement also contains within it the *very same* hegemonic forces linked to capitalist consumption in the ideal of pleasure. As Williamson (1988) argues in *Consuming Passions: The Dynamics of Popular Culture* within our consumer culture, people are driven by their passions or emotions for objects and are motivated by pleasure, desire, and the notion of individuality (p. 12). In this way, the movement may be seen to reproduce the very system of consumption it is fighting against. In other words, it could be viewed simply as a *different* way to consume, but one that is still rooted in consumption. Further, some skeptics of the movement may view this pursuit of pleasure as less important than other issues such as a hunger or environmental destruction.

As the movement continues to grow, it also may move further away from its utopian roots to become more entrenched within the realm of consumption. Thereby, it could become co-opted by the marketplace because of its appeal. Andrews (2008) explains this popularity of the term "Slow Food": asserting: "The phrase 'Slow Food', which would appear increasingly in restaurant reviews, newspaper articles about farmers' markets, and TV programmes about the quality of life, would come to be used as a counter to these trends— [of fast food consumption] an offer of something different, which questioned the pace of modern life while restating the importance of aesthetic pleasure" (p. vii). Therefore, another social, political, and rhetorical implication is the fact that the use of "Slow Food" and "slow" have moved beyond the movement itself and are now being used in a number of ways that may or may not reflect the original ideals of the movement.

Like many new social movements, Slow Food is steeped in a politics of identity. However, it is a politics of identity that is based upon social style and situated within two competing rhetorical homologies of personae. The movement both embodies the uncertainty of the present and the promises of the future, which also reflects how identities operate in contemporary, postmodern society. Thus, Slow Food allows for the creation of identities that are polycategorical and fluid, yet strongly rooted in one of life's most basic necessities, food.

References

Andrews, G. (2008). *The slow food story: Politics and pleasure.* Montreal: McGill-Queen's University Press.

Brummett, B. (2004). *Rhetorical homologies: Form, culture, experience.* Tuscaloosa, AL: The University of Alabama Press.

Donati, K. (2005). The pleasure of diversity in slow food's ethics of taste. *Food, Culture, & Society* 8(2) 227–242.

Fine, G.A. (1996). *Kitchens: The culture of restaurant work.* Berkeley, CA: University of California Press.

Gaytán, M.S. (2004). Globalizing resistance: Slow food and new local imaginaries. *Food, Culture, and Society, 7,* 2, 97–116.

Gigante, D. (Ed.) (2005). *Gusto: Essential writings in nineteenth-century gastronomy.* New York: Routledge.

Greene, C.P. (2006). Beyond the binaries to self-fashioning: Identity as the rhetoric of social style. (Doctoral Dissertation, University of Texas at Austin, 2006). Dissertation Abstracts International, 68(06A) 2242.

Jones, P., Shears, P., Hillier, D., Comfort, D. & Lowell, J. (2003). Return to traditional values?: A case study of slow food. *British Food Journal 105,* 4/5, 297–304.

Leitch, A. (2003). Slow food and the politics of pork Fat: Italian food and European identity. *Ethno, 68,* 4, 437–462.

Levitas, R. (2007). Looking for the blue: The necessity of utopia. *Journal of Political Ideologies, 12,* 3, 289–306.

Miele, M. and Murdoch, J. (2002). The practical aesthetics of traditional cuisines: Slow food in Tuscany. *Sociologia Ruralis, 42,* 4, 312–328.

Peace, A. (2006). Barossa slow: The representation and rhetoric of slow food's regional cooking. *Gastronomica: The Journal of Food and Culture, 6,* 1, 51–59.

Peace, A. (2008). Terre madre 2006: Political theater and ritual rhetoric in the slow food movement. *Gastronomica: The Journal of Food and Culture, 8,* 2, 31–39.

Petrini, C. (2001a). *Slow Food: The Case for Taste.* New York: Columbia University Press.

Petrini, C. (Ed.) (2001b). *Slow food: Collected thoughts on taste, tradition, and the honest pleasures of food.* White River Junction, VT: Chelsea Green Publishing Company.

Pietrykowski, B. (2004). You are what you eat: The social economy of the slow food movement. *Review of Social Economy, 62,* 3, 307–321.

Sack, D. (2007). Eating in eden: Food and American utopias. *Church History, 76,* 2, 456–458.

Schepers, A. (2002, July). Slow food movement counters fast food culture. *Environmental Nutrition* p. 2.

Schneider, S. (2008). Good, clean, fair: The rhetoric of the slow food movement. *College English* 70(4) 384–402.

Severson, K. (2008, July 23). Slow food savors its big moment. *New York Times* p. F1.

Skidelsky, W. (2003, August 11). Slow food's rallying cry in the global war against Big Mac and large fries. *New Statesman* p. 40.

Slow Food International. Retrieved September 1, 2008, from http://www.slowfood.com/

Slow Food USA. Retrieved September 1, 2008, from http://www.slowfoodusa.org/

Strong, R. (2002). *Feast: A history of grand eating.* Orlando, FL: Hartcourt, Inc. University of Gastronomic Sciences. Retrieved September 1, 2008, from http://www.unisg.it/welcome_eng.lasso

Visser, M.(1991). *The rituals of dinner: The origins, evolution, eccentricies, and meaning of table manners.* New York: Penguin Books.

Weismantel, A. (2002). Slow food. *Journal of Agricultural and Food Information, 4,* 4, 3–6.

Williamson, J. (1988). *Consuming passions: The dynamics of popular culture.* London: Marion Boyers.

6

It's the cheese: Collective memory of hard times during deindustrialization

Kristen Lucas and Patrice M. Buzzanell

Unquestionably, food and the way we communicate about it are important markers of identity. Like other chapters in this volume that illuminate connections to cultural, social, and gendered identities, food also is inherently linked to social class. Dougherty, Dixon, and Chou (2009) explain that people from different social classes have distinct relationships with food. From the security and taken-for-grantedness of food in middle and upper classes to the insecurity of food in lower socioeconomic classes, people's relationships to food structure everyday practices and discourses. Particularly for working class people (because "food on the table" is not always a taken-for-granted assumption), food is a highly salient issue that affects a number of behaviors, including not only how they talk about food but also how they prepare meals (Calnan, 1990) and make risk-benefit assessments in occupational settings (Lucas, 2007). In this chapter, we focus our attention on a context in which temporary economic upheaval highlights the importance of food in understanding the material complexities of social class and financial insecurity.

In the current global recession, researchers and popular media have traced economic indicators such as unemployment figures and consumer indices. They have also followed how people have been dealing with massive and long-term job loss, stretched social services, uncertainties about fulfillment of basic needs, and the potential collapse of major industries. For many people reading today's headlines, this is not a new story. In the early 1980s, the United States' "Rust Belt"—the manufacturing region that spans from the Northeast to the Upper Midwest—and other industrial centers throughout the world suffered massive economic downturn and the failure of core industries (Bluestone & Harrison, 1982; Bradley, 2008; Newman, 1999; Wilson, 2004; Worley, 2007). During that period, the United States "deindustrialized," as the core of its economy shifted from heavy industry (e.g., steel, auto making) to more knowledge and service-based work (e.g., financial investment, real estate; see Bluestone & Harrison, 1982). Although many economic shifts have occurred throughout U.S. history (Cowie, 1999; Hareven & Langenbach, 1978), deindustrialization reached epidemic proportions in the late 1970s and ran rampant throughout the 1980s.

In the wake of deindustrialization, individuals, families, and communities struggled to get by. Layoffs were mounting, blue-collar jobs were being eliminated permanently, homes were being foreclosed, businesses were locking their doors, factories were shutting down their assembly lines, and small towns were all but disappearing as residents left in droves due to lack of gainful employment opportunities. By the early 1980s, Bluestone and Harrison (1982) calculated that between 32 and 38 million people lost jobs as a direct result of deindustrialization. The financial devastation and hard times faced by people living in that period cannot be overstated. Many breadwinners from middle-class working families—especially those who worked in heavy industry—experienced extended periods of unemployment that led to missed mortgage payments, depleted saving accounts, and the need to accept government assistance.

In this study, we take a retrospective observer-participant stance to gain insight into accounts of hard times by individuals who were coming of age during the early 1980s recession. Our communicative lens focuses attention on the content and processes whereby people construct messages, tell stories, rework identities, and talk into being those revised realities that incorporate the consequences of negative life events (Buzzanell, in press; Buzzanell, Shenoy, Remke, & Lucas, 2009; Marin, Bohanek, & Fivush, 2008; Shellenbarger, 2009). While the individuals' parents recalled particular strategies enabling resilience, such as talk and material practices associated with "tightening one's belt," preparing for anticipated hard times by saving money and stocking up, and seeking alternative sources of income (Lucas & Buzzanell, 2010), individuals who were children or adolescents during the 1980s commented on a different event—government giveaways of surplus cheese—and its significance for them. Nearly 30 years later, these kids, who are now mid-life adults, spontaneously and consistently brought up "the cheese" during interviews about life during the 1980 recession. Our research project examines why "the cheese" is so important to them and how it played a central role in this cohort's collective memory of hard times in "Irontown," a small mining community in the Rust Belt.

To begin this chapter, we provide the historical context for this study by describing Irontown and how it was affected by the 1980s recession. Next, we describe the authors' positionality in this study. From there, we bring in the newspaper accounts of a community-wide cheese distribution and personal accounts of individuals who grew up in Irontown during the 1980s and whose parents were employed or, more often, laid-off by Irontown Mining Inc. (IMI) during that recession. Finally, we explain how their story of the cheese serves as the centerpiece for their collective memory and why collective memory offers a different, but significant, theoretical lens for organizational communication scholars interested in human resilience during detrimental organizing and economic processes (Lutgen-Sandvik & Sypher, 2009).

Hard Times in Irontown

Irontown is a small, remote town (pop. 12,000) located in the upper Midwestern United States. Its heritage and identity are steeped in the iron ore mining industry. Its streets, businesses, community organizations, and physical environment bear outward signs of this heritage. Cars and pickup trucks drive daily along streets named after ores, mines, and prospectors. The businesses, schools, and community organizations along those streets carry similar names. The most prominent and recognizable images along the horizon are numerous mining shaft houses, tall housing structures that sit above old mine shafts. Almost all past and present residents of the community have had a parent and/or grandparents who have been employed by IMI.

The mid- to late-1970s was a major boom period for the mines in Irontown. Employment figures steadily rose from 2,400 hourly employees in 1972 to 3,600 in 1978. IMI even had a trailer set up in its main office parking lot to handle the surge of applicants. In addition, more than 1,800 construction workers, many of them from out of the area, found work at two major expansion projects at mines ("IMI operations undergo," 1979). However, this boom period, typical of the "resource roller coaster" experience of mining towns (Wilson, 2004), did not last. The once vibrant mining industry faced waves of severe and progressive deindustrialization, not the least of which was the 1980s recession.

By May 1980, the top headline of the local daily newspaper read what people had known and lived for more than a year: "Recession here, U.S. admits" (1980). In addition to consumer woes (e.g., steep inflation, skyrocketing interest rates), heavy industry took heavy hits. With the surge in gas prices, U.S.-manufactured gas-guzzling vehicles sat in sales lots while smaller, more fuel-efficient Japanese imports sold. The downturn in the auto making industry was felt by the steel industry, whose outdated equipment could no longer keep up with foreign competitors. This downturn eventually reached the mining industry, whose product was no longer needed to fill the orders for steel mills. Within a month of the official announcement of the recession, it became clear how hard the United States iron ore industry would be hit. Of the 13,900 people who were employed by this industry in manual labor positions in 1977, only 7,000 remained by 1982 (U.S. Census Bureau, 1979; 1985). The number of operating companies and mine properties also decreased by more than one-third.

When demand for iron ore came to a near halt because of mounting troubles in the partner industries of auto making and steel, Irontown's mining properties were idled. Some properties were put on partial production schedules, while other mines closed permanently. IMI's number of hourly workers dropped to 2,600 in 1980 and 1,600 in 1981. The overall employment figures hid the day-to-day struggles faced by miners and their families, including temporary layoffs for seasoned employees. By mid-1982, nearly one-third of the reduced workforce was laid off. The jobless rate in the county ranged from a low of 14.3%, to a high of 29.7% for the year (Bureau of Labor Statistics, 2006; Lucas, 2006). These shutdowns and slowdowns resulted in dramatic financial hardship in the local community. Thousands of idled miners in the community bided their time while nervously waiting to be called back to work. They stood in line at makeshift unemployment offices that were established to meet the overwhelming demand for social services. They filled out eligibility cards for government food stamps and union-distributed relief boxes.

The costs of these economic downturns were more than monetary. In its 1981 annual report, the state's Public Health Department linked several health problems to economic hardship ("Economy implicated," 1982). First, an unknown number of families lost medical coverage due to layoffs, which resulted in many people postponing (or not seeking) needed medical care. Second, suicide became the tenth leading cause of death in the state by 1980. Third, drug and alcohol abuse increased. Admissions to drug and alcohol abuse programs increased by 12% during the 1979–1980 fiscal year and more than half of these patients were unemployed.

While the above account of the deindustrialization era of 30 years ago may appear to be simply an historical overview, we note that the characteristics of the economic downturn in the 1980s closely mirror the current global recession: widespread unemployment, plant closings, industries teetering on the brink of bankruptcy, entire families without income except for unemployment funds or payment for pick-up jobs, housing industry slumps and foreclosures. As such, this chapter is more than just a history lesson. The insights gained about how people have retrospectively found meaning in similar set of circumstances may be able to shed light on how families and communities can best make sense of the current recession.

By examining the discourse of a generation growing up in Irontown during the 1980s recession, we delve into the collective memory construction—not of a particular commemorative monument or site, as often is examined in collective memory studies (e.g., Ehrenhaus, 2009; Zelizer, 1985)—but of an event etched into and evocative of generational identities, thinking, feelings, and understandings about hard times. As Zelizer (1985) notes, it is through collective memory that people connect the past with the present, their inner thoughts with the external environment, and their individual selves with a particular collective. The group shapes and is shaped by memory; the group reconstructs the past to say something that resonates with the present. The significance of the memory is in its connections of material and symbolic, its impact on how people value certain events, and its place in "stake[ing] out a claim on how we should (or should not) stand in relationship to that past" (Ehrenhaus, 2009, p. 234).

Author Positionality

I (Kristen) was born and raised in Irontown. My grandfathers made life-long careers of mining. My older grandfather was retired by the time of my earliest memories. However, my younger grandfather worked swing shift in the mines until I was 20 years old. It was he who was my window to that occupation. Strangely, what I remember most about my grandfather being a miner is tied up in memories of my grandmother. It seemed that every time I visited (which was usually a few times a week), she was packing his lunch pail. Sometimes it was in the morning, but more often than not it was in the afternoon or late evening for his shifts that rotated between 8 a.m., 4 p.m., and midnight starts. I can still hear the clacking sound of his metal lunch bucket and picture its typical contents: three sandwiches, a piece of fruit, a plastic-wrapped Hostess™ cupcake of some sort, and a full thermos of coffee sweetened with cream and sugar. During the times when he was out of work and there was no lunch pail to pack, he brought home relief boxes filled with nonperishable food items. I can still see, from my vantage spot perched on the counter in their tiny kitchen, my grandmother quickly unpacking and putting away the food in the cupboards. Logically I know that there were a variety of items, but somehow the only thing I can remember with any clarity is the cheese.

Maybe it is because the bright yellow-orange color stood in such sharp contrast to the plain box. Maybe it is because it was the only item that went into the refrigerator instead of the cupboard. Maybe it was because the cheese was a much bigger conversation starter than the other items. Several of the adults condemned it, groaning "Oh no, not government cheese." Another, who regularly received cheese through state welfare rolls, defended it, saying "Hey, that's good stuff!" My own memory of one particular day is that my grandparents—who were empty nesters by this point—made grilled cheese sandwiches for the large group of extended family and friends who regularly gathered around their kitchen table on weekends to drink coffee, smoke cigarettes, and converse for hours on end about everything and nothing at all.

I grew up in Irontown, had family who worked in the mines, and ate the cheese. Experiences such as these make me an insider. But for other reasons, I am more of an outsider. Although both of my grandfathers had life-long careers in the mines, my father never worked in one. Instead, he had had steady employment in the maximum security prison about 20 miles down the road. His career provided a modest and, most importantly, *stable* lifestyle. My family was never subjected to the financial volatility brought on by the layoffs, strikes, and seasonal slowdowns that plagued mining families in Irontown. When my peers' parents were collecting unemployment checks, leaving town to seek temporary hold-over money-making opportunities, and worrying about making their next mortgage payment, my life went along relatively uninterrupted. I knew even as a preteen that my experiences during the recession were markedly different from most of my classmates' experiences. Therefore, because of my positionality as *outsider*-insider, I take a stance of observer-participant, one who observes more than she participates, one who is more familiar than fully knowing, and one who listens more than she speaks in the telling of this story.

I (Patrice) didn't grow up with government cheese. But I had family members who did. My dad had working class roots, having worked as a steelworker before pursuing an executive career in the federal government. His father was a railroad engineer. Many of my cousins, aunts, and uncles remain connected to the steel industry, unions, and blue-collar work. Although I never experienced deindustrialization in the same way as the kids who grew up in Irontown, I did gain understanding of the hardship associated with deindustrialization through my own vantage point. I was aware of economic and lifestyle differences between my immediate and extended family. I recognized the gratitude my father had in his ability to help his parents and his many siblings and their families during hard times. I was cognizant that we were fortunate to have economic stability whereas others did not. Because I was never a recipient of government cheese, nor do I have any personal ties to Irontown, I am largely an outsider. However, my extended family ties, which allowed me a glimpse into the need for government cheese and other assistance during hard times, make me empathetic to the situation. Therefore, my positionality is that of an empathetic outsider: one who stands back and provides a perspective that is not swayed by personal recollections, yet one who remains committed to the story of the cheese and sensitive to the lived experiences of the people who tell it.

The Story of the Cheese

In the summer of 1982, the United States government opened its storehouse of food surpluses to distribute blocks of yellow cheese to millions of citizens hard hit by deindustrialization. The cheese giveaway government program was signed into effect by President Ronald Reagan to the tune of 30 million pounds because, as Reagan noted, "At a time when American families are under increasing financial pressure, their Government cannot sit by and watch millions of pounds of food turn to waste" ("A mess however," 1982, para. 1).

The five-pound blocks of "American cheese," a processed cheese with a texture and flavor that lay between cheddar and Velveeta™, had been stored for upwards of 18 months in government warehouses and had "USDA" (United States Department of Agriculture) stamped on the outside of its plain cardboard box. The surplus cheese was acquired as a result of government purchases to subsidize American dairy farmers and maintain productivity and prices. Cheese and other food items regularly were given to families on welfare through charitable organizations. Reagan's move lifted the restriction that limited cheese distribution to permanently displaced workers and families below the poverty line. The cheese's association with socioeconomic status provoked mixed recollections during fairly recent blogs and chatroom postings (Democratic Underground, 2005; Roadfood.com, 2004). While some comments in online forums indicate that young recipients whose families were enrolled in welfare programs for long periods of time expressed gratitude and fondness for the cheese, others resented the receipt of old cheese and its part in signaling their families' poverty to others.

Irontown and surrounding communities received surplus cheese as part of a federal relief program for blue-collar workers and their families who were displaced due to the recession. The first cheese distributions were in California, Nevada, and Texas. Irontown miners and their families received their cheese in August 1982. During the peak of IMI layoffs in August 1982, the local newspaper ran a front-page story that announced that a joint effort of the mine union and the county would make 30,000 pounds of cheese available for distribution to temporarily laid-off iron ore workers ("Surplus cheese giveaway," 1982). The assistant director of the county office said, "We feel that with the economy the way it is now and with so many people unemployed in our area that the cheese will be greatly appreciated by those eligible to receive it" ("Surplus cheese giveaway," 1982, p. 1A).

Indeed, the cheese was big news in the region. One week after the announcement, the local union ran a large advertisement and a full distribution schedule. It boldly announced, "STEELWORKERS! SURPLUS CHEESE AVAILABLE" (United Steelworkers, 1982). Droves of unemployed miners lined up at the Union Hall and other distribution points throughout the county to pick up blocks of cheese encased in plain brown cardboard boxes ("Cheese giveaway," 1982). As inconspicuous as its wrapper was, the cheese left a lasting and vivid impression on the children and adolescents who ate it on their grilled cheese sandwiches and in macaroni and cheese casseroles.

Collective Memories of the Cheese

This chapter emerged from a larger study about family-based socialization messages in working class families. A total of 62 interviews were conducted with families from a blue-collar mining town: a cohort of 23 men and women who were between 8 and 17 years old during the 1980s recession, 20 fathers (who worked in the mines), and 16 mothers. The interview protocol included two questions that specifically queried people's recollections of the economic downturn in the 1980s. The first asked what they remembered about that period and the second asked if and/or how they talked about it with their family. However, talk about this period surfaced throughout the entirety of the interviews and was not limited to responses to these two questions. The interviews resulted in more than 60 hours of talk and 1,000 pages of single-spaced transcriptions. These data were supplemented by analyses of community and company documents available from the local labor archives, the *Irontown Daily News* (a pseudonym), a local mining museum, and IMI's administrative office.

For the cohort of "kids," who were in their 30s and early 40s at the time of the interviews, the food was a central element of their discourse. They brought up the work in which their parents and extended family members engaged to put "food on the table," shared memories of purchasing groceries with food stamps, and described changes to family meals during layoffs. Approximately half spoke specifically and at length about government cheese. Because no specific questions about food or government cheese were part of the interview protocol, their spontaneous talk indicates the relevance of food for participants in making sense of hard times.

Their recollections of the cheese are deemed collective memories because of the consistency of the memory structures, the focus on a particular contested site (i.e., the cheese itself and its meaning), and the ways in which recall of cheese—whether factual or not—arose unannounced in interviews. The recollections sealed one's identity as an insider in a community bounded not by geographic location but by working class values and promise (Lucas, 2009). Through a thematic approach (see Owen, 1984) oriented toward a particular entity (cheese) and grounded within and across entire interviews and archival documents, two primary interpretations of the cheese as collective memory emerged: (a) cheese as symbol of daily struggle; and (b) cheese as symbol of camaraderie.

Cheese as Symbol of Daily Struggle

More than a third of the younger cohort of participants explicitly talked about the cheese when recalling what it meant for them to have their fathers work at the mines or live through the layoffs of the 1980s. It was a shorthand marker that indicated the daily struggle associated with making ends meet during hard times. For example, within the first few minutes of her interview, Tracy (all names are pseudonyms) alluded several times to the depressed economic conditions of Irontown. For her, her father's job and her childhood were characterized by the volatility of the mines. When asked what she remembered about the layoffs of the 1980s, she said:

> I lived it. I was there. I was aware. I think a part of it is too that I am the oldest of five. I mean, I was only 9 years old in 1981. But I mean, it's government cheese, you know? And then when the government cheese was gone, my brothers would use the boxes for their baseball cards. So just, I remember the food of that type and, you know, my Mom or Dad going to pick it up. And my Dad being gone for a certain amount of time and not seeing him when he was at other places. And just, you know, I guess maybe the uncertainties and the worries.

Lisa used the cheese as a comparison point between the good times and bad times of her father's career. She remarked:

> Well, it was kind of funny because it was either feast or famine, you know. When I was growing up in the '70s and '80s, my dad was laid off a lot. So when the times were good, they were really good. But when they were bad, we were eating government cheese.

Kim also noted the connection between the cheese and financial hardship.

> I remember my friends having to move away because of the layoffs. And I remember getting the free cheese. [laugh] That was good cheese. We talked about that the other day. But I do remember lots of people having to leave. And you're wondering if they're ever going to come back. But yeah, I remember it was very. . . . Lots of people not knowing where they were going to be. Or lots of people having to leave.

Other individuals talked about the cheese in less direct ways. Several people discussed the need relief packages or food stamps along with the way that meals changed at home. When talking about tough financial times, Frank said,

> Macaroni and cheese was used a lot more. [laugh] and the funny thing when you say that, believe it or not, you can tell our economy based on the sale of macaroni and cheese. But just hard times, guys looking for jobs, sweating it out.

Matthew echoed some of Frank's sentiment that the quality of meals declined:

> Oh yeah, IMI, yeah. There was layoffs, strikes, all that stuff. Yeah, the beef roast went to half size, the pot of potatoes went to twice the size, and there was lots of gravy. Yeah, when things were tight, it was tight.

For these individuals, the government cheese was embedded within webs of stories marking changes in their lives: their fathers going out of town to find work and returning home only on weekends or for a few days once a month, standing in line at unemployment offices, the worry associated with overhearing their parents talking of financial matters, friends and family members moving away permanently, and, especially for the older members of the cohort, concern about their own future career prospects.

Through their memories of uncertainties and changes in family rhythms, the cheese offered a site for emotional reconstruction and a point of departure.

For the children of deindustrialization, it is the cheese that captures collective memory: a symbol of an era and a people.

Cheese as a Symbol of Camaraderie

Although the cheese distribution occurred precisely because of financial hardship, a situation that certainly was not pleasant, participants became very animated when they talked about it. Many of them laughed about how much they enjoyed eating the cheese and said that they still reminisce about it with friends. Their seemingly counterintuitive positive response raises the question as to why they recollect this event so fondly. The answer is in that the cheese was not solely a marker of hard times. It also was a stability point for communal identity and camaraderie among family, friends, and neighbors who were in the same precarious position.

Eric discussed the fact that "everyone was getting Reagan cheese" and was receiving other forms of assistance. For Eric, then, there was no shame because, in his world, everyone was in the same situation. He accepted the cheese in the same way he accepted blue lunch tickets:

> Yeah. I remember like, well, everyone was getting Reagan cheese. And we all had the blue-colored lunch tickets. Those were like the people who didn't have a lot of money. But it really didn't faze me too much back then because, like I said, all your friends' dad worked at the mine, you know, 90 percent of them, so it's not like you were some. . . . If, like calling yourself a destitute, we all were. Because none of our parents were working at the time, you know.
>
> Interviewer: So you weren't the only kid with a blue lunch ticket?
>
> Far from it. I mean we were all, everyone knew everybody else was broke, basically. The group I hung around with, it wasn't that big of a deal.

For Eric, the cheese and lunch tickets signaled membership in a community for which government assistance and free lunch were pragmatic options. Similarly, David stated that "everyone" received surplus cheese. David remembered the distribution of surplus cheese as happening more than once and as being the impetus for people getting together at the Union Hall:

> They used to go on strike every three or four years. And we had to get, you know, the government cheese and the government peanut butter. So we'd be living on food stamps and stuff for two, three months, waiting for them to settle the contract.

Interviewer: Did you and your parents ever talk about layoffs and strikes when they were going on?

No, not really. You know, we just knew they were on strike because we had to go. It was like a fact of life, you know. Every few years, you had to go down to the Union Hall and pick up your basket of government cheese and food stamps and all that fun stuff. So you knew there was a strike. But I mean, it wasn't like it was just one family. You knew it because like everyone in the whole area, of course, was employed that way. So it was pretty common.

Interviewer: The Union Hall was probably the most happening place in town.

Oh, it sure was. You'd see everybody. [laugh]

The conversation surrounding the distribution of food boxes was not limited only to the Union Hall. It also was a topic of conversation within the schools. For Rachel, getting government cheese and free boxes of groceries was a sign of fitting in:

I can remember, I was a senior in high school, and my dad was on strike. And I think it was once a week or twice a week, or every other week, we got a box of food from the Union. And that was the big conversation in our classes. "What did you get in your begging box?" Well we got this, this, and this. And then you got some classmates whose parents didn't work at the mine were saying how they wished their parents did so they could be involved in these conversations. But it was just a way of life for everybody, for most everybody up here. It was just, I don't know, normal.

Rachel's mother (in a separate interview) also recalled school-based talk about food boxes:

I didn't realize until years later, like when you were on strike and you'd get those food boxes that the kids in school would go to school and compare. And they called them begging boxes. And you know, because sometimes there'd be Girl Scout cookies in them or sometimes there'd be different kinds of cereal. And after the begging boxes came, the kids would go to school, "What did you get in your box?" I mean, it was a *thing* for these kids. They made it kind of funny. Yeah, it's cool.

The camaraderie that Eric, David, and Rachel recall is imbued with emotion, friendliness, and commonalities in life experience fine-tuned by in-group solidarity. Further, these memories also are whitewashed of the ugliness, fear, and raw emotion found in job loss literature by individuals who lose their jobs and by their family members (Buzzanell & Turner, 2003; Gunn, 2008). In blue-collar industries, job loss is often faced by entire communities, and does not have the selective nature or isolation of grey- and white-collar sector job loss (Ehrenreich, 2005; Newman, 1999). Knowing that there are other people in the same dire straits can be a source of comfort while locating and transitioning to new employment and new residences.

Collective Memory and Symbolic Value of Food

In explaining the importance of "the cheese," we draw upon two bodies of literature: the linkage of memorable moments with collective memories, and the symbolic value of food. Memorable message or moments focus on individual recollections about past events that carry import and may even mark turning points for work and/or family relationships and career development. While they often occur in the context of organizational (Bullis & Bach, 1989; Dallimore, 2003; Lucas, in press) or family socialization (Marin et al., 2008; Medved, Brogan, McClanahan, Morris, & Shepherd, 2006), memorable moments also can occur as a result of critical media accounts of specific events (Greenberg, 1988).

Although originally considered to consist of direct socialization prescriptions, the concept of memorable messages has been enlarged to consider ambient (implicit and indirect) socialization that might result from observing others or through personal experiences (Dallimore, 2003; Lucas, in press). Memorable messages are remembered for a long period of time, are perceived as influential in the message recipients' lives, and often occur early in people's lives or work experiences. These messages may be single but life-altering statements or may be oft-repeated family sayings, stories, or mantras. The influences of memorable messages and, by extension, collective memory both assist in sensemaking and in socializing individuals about important life realms or processes (Knapp, Stohl & Reardon, 1981; Stohl, 1986).

In this study, the cheese was recalled spontaneously and easily amidst layers of hardships and personal recollections of that time, marking its vivid memorability for this cohort. Archival research sheds some light as to possible reasons why. The original cheese distribution schedule was published in the *Irontown Daily News* on August 25, 1982 (United Steelworkers). The very next day, IMI announced that workers would be recalled to work over the next few months (Owens, 1982). It is possible that some of the warm affect that people conjure up when talking about the cheese is that by the time the first slices were cut from the block and grilled between pieces of Bunny™ bread, their families' spirits had been boosted with the good news that they would soon be returning to work. So the cheese is tied to a low point, but also to a turning point when things became markedly better. It symbolized good after a long stretch of hardship.

Surprisingly, archival research also revealed that the cheese distribution to families was a one-time occurrence during the 1980s IMI layoffs. Granted, some families in the community who were on welfare rolls received surplus cheese regularly. Additionally, union-provided food boxes were a mainstay during strikes and layoffs. However, there was only one box that included "government cheese." Yet, in the case of the cheese, the memories of cheese distribution were so common and vivid among participants that their discourses made it seem as though the cheese distribution happened frequently.

Characteristics of memorable messages on an individual level are consistent with those of collective memory. In both, the memories need not be factual, but may be absorbed into individual or collective consciousness through repeated tellings and importance of the "memory" to the individual, family, or community (Neath & Surprenant, 2003; Zelizer, 1985). Therefore, what is important about the collective memory of the cheese is not its verifiable truth, but instead "why one construction has more staying power than its rivals" (Zelizer, 1985, p. 217).

Although we noted that it might be the co-occurrence of cheese distribution with uncertainty (negative economic times) and hope (call for return to work the next day), we also believe that the collective memory of cheese distribution as mostly positive suggests ideological work. Parents attempted to shield their children. They did this through focusing on family talk that foregrounded a realistic, but confident, financial outlook and deemphasized the emotionality of job loss (Lucas & Buzzanell, 2010). For example, one mother prepared her children by telling them, "We'll cut back on many things. There won't be as much luxury. There won't be as much ice cream and pop and that kind of stuff. We'll have mainly meals. But there won't be any luxuries."

This kind of talk, combined with financial stretching, stocking up, and location of other income and resources enabled working class families to engage in ideological control that focused on providing for and protecting their individual families without overtly resisting and embracing departures from class values. The lifelong lessons that one can "make do," figure out strategies to stretch food budgets and earn money, anticipate the end of strikes, layoffs, and changes in the economy are strategies of resilience that enabled families to bounce back and reintegrate into new realities (Buzzanell, in press; Lucas & Buzzanell, 2010).

With regard to families, communication about the talk during prior economic hard times and strategies used by family members can build self-confidence and hope for getting by, and even ahead, during current difficulties. Much like the research on family stories cited earlier, everyday talk about past family events, values, and traditions can prepare children for the increasing volatility of today's labor market and recession. Therefore, we do not believe that the mostly positive collective recollections of cheese are accidental.

Moreover, we do not believe that sons' and daughters' recall of food—for sustenance, comfort, and warmth in casseroles, soups, or grilled cheese sandwiches—is accidental either. Food has long served to bind communities together in religious or neighborhood celebrations and tragedies and to pass along family, community, and national or ethnic values (e.g., Beoku-Betts, 1995; DeVault, 1995; Meyers, 2001). For instance, DeVault's (1995) work with dietary food and nutrition practitioners dealt, in part, with how female African American nutritionists were sensitive to different groups' dietary preferences and vocabulary. Sensitivity to ethnicity (e.g., the inadequacy of grouping Caribbean, Puerto Rican, Cuban, Mexican American, clients' foods together) enabled these minority women to see how attitudes and beliefs toward food and eating were linked with ethnic backgrounds. The food preserved core parts of themselves and their social identity group. Similarly, Beoku-Betts (1995) described the Gullah community, direct descendants of slaves from West African rice communities, who maintained their African heritage while living on the Sea Islands and on the coastal regions of Georgia and South Carolina in the United States. They preserved their links with their past and with each other through elaborate rice preparation for their main meal, storytelling about traditional ceremonies, making unique handicrafts, and attending religious services. The Gullah organizational system centered around harmony and social exchange influenced by African spiritual beliefs. These beliefs prioritized the whole community by weaving together individual existence and relationships among God, ancestors, other humans (including the unborn), extended family members, and living/nonliving beings. Residents were able to bounce back from hard times and retain community values through their food, its preparation, its consumption, and its accompanying talk of the past and future.

In Irontown, the cheese—ordinary, low cost, yellow American cheese—seems to have symbolized and renewed working class values of community, endurance, plain and wholesome food, ethics of providing and protecting, efforts to "make do" or handle life crises as they occur, and the inventiveness required to survive and even thrive during hard times. As such, the cheese is a collective memory about the individuals' identification with their community of origin's values, lifestyles, and time-honored traditions. The cheese represents a time of hope and resilience, even as America's Rust Belt has continued to decline and today faces yet another economic crisis (Bradley, 2008).

Conclusion

The cheese is a simple image that encapsulates and represents a variety of complex issues that children of the 1980s deindustrialization were negotiating at the time and are still of concern. First, it symbolizes that parents were out of work and unable to provide for the same lifestyle as they had in the past. The children used the cheese as a type of shorthand to identify that there were significant financial struggles at home without having to describe them in-depth. Second, and perhaps more importantly, it normalized the experience of family job loss for the kids. Rather than feeling like a stigmatized "Other," they felt normal because they were not alone. Moreover, the cheese gained salience as a collective memory because of its original distribution during a turning point between rough financial times and the hopefulness engendered by industry call-backs to work. The cheese also gained prominence because of the fact that it is a food that comforts, gives sustenance, and was part of parents' attempts to shield their children from full recognition of economic hardship. As a result, the cheese serves as the centerpiece for these individuals' collective memory of family and community resilience. They may have moved away from Irontown and out of the working class but they retain a sense of community and an appreciation for working class values. As the cheese became a collective memory for the children of the 1980s deindustrialization, we ask, what will be the collective memory of today's recession for our children?

References

A mess however it's sliced. (1982, January 4). *Time*. Retrieved August 28, 2009, from http://www.time.com/time/magazine/article/0,9171,953288,00.html

Beoku-Betts, J. A. (1995). We got our way of cooking things: Women, food, and preservation of cultural identity among the Gullah. *Gender & Society, 9*, 535–555.

Bluestone, B., & Harrison, B. (1982). *The deindustrialization of America: Plant closings, community abandonment, and the dismantling of basic industry*. New York: Basic Books.

Bradley, H. (2008). No more heroes? Reflections on the 20th anniversary of the miners' strike and the culture of opposition. *Work, Employment and Society, 22*, 337–349.

Bullis, C., & Bach, B. W. (1989). Socialization turning points: An examination of change in organizational identification. *Western Journal of Speech Communication, 53*, 273–293.

Bureau of Labor Statistics. (2006). Labor force statistics from the current population survey (1979–1983). Retrieved May 25, 2006, from http://www.bls.gov/data/home.htm

Buzzanell, P. M. (in press). Resilience: Talking, resisting, and imagining new normalcies into being. *Journal of Communication.*

Buzzanell, P. M., Shenoy, S., Remke, R. V., & Lucas, K. (2009). Intersubjectively creating resilience: Responding to and rebounding from potentially destructive organizational experiences. In P. Lutgen-Sandvik & B. D. Sypher (Eds.), *The destructive side of organizational communication: Processes, consequences and constructive ways of organizing* (pp. 293–315). New York: Routledge.

Buzzanell, P. M., & Turner, L. H. (2003). Emotion work revealed by job loss discourse: Backgrounding-foregrounding of feelings, construction of normalcy, and (re)instituting of traditional masculinities. *Journal of Applied Communication Research, 31,* 27–57.

Calnan, M. (1990). Food and health: A comparison of beliefs and practices in middle-class and working-class households. In S. Cunningham-Burley & M. McKegney (Eds.), *Readings in medical sociology* (pp. 9–36). London: Tavistock/Routledge.

Cheese giveaway [Photo with caption]. (1982, August 28). *Irontown Daily News,* p. 2A.

Cowie, J. R. (1999). *Capital moves: RCA's seventy-year quest for cheap labor.* New York: New Press.

Dallimore, E. (2003). Memorable messages as discursive formations: The gendered socialization of new university faculty. *Women's Studies in Communication, 26,* 214–265.

Democratic Underground. (2005, February 11). Middle class woman gets government cheese, and lives to tell the tale [Web log forum]. Retrieved August 28, 2009, from http://www.democraticunderground.com/discuss/duboard.php?az=view_all&address=105x2619018

DeVault, M. L. (1995). Ethnicity and expertise: Racial-ethnic knowledge in sociological research. *Gender & Society, 9*, 612–631.

Dougherty, D., Dixon, J., & Chou, C. (2009, November). *The communication problematics of social class.* Paper presented at annual meeting of the National Communication Association, Chicago, IL.

Economy implicated in health problems. (1982, February 3). *Irontown Daily News,* p. 2A.

Ehrenhaus, P. (2009). Memorials and other forms of collective memory. In W. F. Eadie (Ed.), *21st century communication: A reference handbook* (vol. 1, pp. 228–236). Los Angeles: Sage.

Ehrenreich, B. (2005). *Bait and switch: The (futile) pursuit of the American Dream.* New York: Metropolitan Books.

Greenberg, B. S. (1988). Some uncommon television images and the drench hypothesis. In S. Oskamp (Ed.), *Applied social psychology annual: Television as a social issue* (vol. 8, pp. 88–102). Newbury Park, CA: Sage.

Gunn, A. (2008). "People's lives are hanging here": Low wage workers share their experience of job loss. *Journal of Contemporary Ethnography, 37*, 679–693.

Hareven, T. K., & Langenbach, R. (1978). *Amoskeag: Life and work in an American factory-city.* New York: Pantheon Books.

IMI operations undergo significant changes. (1979, April 23). *Irontown Daily News*, pp. 1A–2A.

Knapp, M. L., Stohl, C., & Reardon, K. K. (1981). "Memorable" messages. *Journal of Communication, 31,* 27–42.

Lucas, K. (2006). *No footsteps to follow: How blue-collar kids navigate postindustrial careers.* Unpublished dissertation, Purdue University, West Lafayette, IN.

Lucas, K. (2007). Problematized providing and protecting: The occupational narrative of the working class. In W. DeGenaro (Ed.), *Who says? Working-class rhetoric, class consciousness, and community* (pp. 180–199). Pittsburgh, PA: University of Pittsburgh Press.

Lucas, K. (2009, May). *When the dream and promise collide: Accounting for class mobility-based ambivalences.* Paper presented at annual meeting of the International Communication Association, Chicago, IL.

Lucas, K. (in press). Anticipatory socialization in blue-collar families: The negotiation of contradictory messages of social mobility and reproduction. *Western Journal of Communication.*

Lucas, K., & Buzzanell, P. M. (2010, April). *Communicating during economic downturns: Construction of family resilience through intergenerational processes.* Paper presented at annual meeting of the Central States Communication Association, Cincinnati, OH.

Lutgen-Sandvik, P., & Sypher, B. D. (Eds.). (2009). *The destructive side of organizational communication: Processes, consequences and constructive ways of organizing.* New York: Routledge.

Marin, K., Bohanek, J., & Fivush, R. (2008). Positive effects of talking about the negative: Family narratives of negative experiences and preadolescents' perceived competence. *Journal of Research on Adolescence, 18*, 573–593.

Medved, C., Brogan, S., McClanahan, A., Morris, J., & Shepherd, G. (2006). Family and work socializing communication: Messages, gender, and ideological implications. *Journal of Family Communication, 6*, 161–180.

Meyers, M. (2001). *A bite off mama's plate: Mothers' and daughters' connections through food.* Westport, CT: Bergin & Garvey.

Neath, I., & Surprenant, A. M. (2003). *Human memory: An introduction to research, data, and theory* (2nd ed.). Belmont, CA: Wadsworth.

Newman, K. S. (1999). *Falling from grace: Downward mobility in the age of affluence*. Berkeley: University of California Press.

Owen, W. F. (1984). Interpretive themes in relational communication. *Quarterly Journal of Speech, 70*, 274–287.

Owens, S. (1982, August 26). First mine to start up next month: Second to reopen in November. *Irontown Daily News,* p. 1A.

Recession here, U.S. admits. (1980, May 1). *Irontown Daily News,* p. 1A.

Roadfood.com. (2004, November 20). Government cheese [Web log forum]. Retrieved August 28, 2009 from http://www.roadfood.com/Forums/tm.aspx?m=110800&mpage=

Shellenbarger, S. (2009, March 11). Life stories: Children find meaning in old family tales. *Wall Street Journal.* Retrieved August 1, 2009, from http://online.wsj.com/article/SB123673699703791017.html

Stohl, C. (1986). The role of memorable messages in the process of organizational socialization. *Communication Quarterly, 34,* 231–249.

Surplus cheese giveaway is aimed at idle workers. (1982, August 18). *Irontown Daily News,* p. 1A.

U.S. Census Bureau. (1979). *1977 census of mineral industries: Subject, industry, and area statistics.* Washington, DC: U.S. Government Printing Office.

U.S. Census Bureau. (1985). *1982 census of mineral industries: General summary.* Washington, DC: U.S. Government Printing Office.

United Steelworkers. (1982, August 25). Steelworkers! Surplus cheese available [Advertisement]. *Irontown Daily News,* p. 5A.

Wilson, L. J. (2004). Riding the resource roller coaster: Understanding socioeconomic differences between mining communities. *Rural Sociology, 69,* 261–281.

Worley, J. L. (2007). "Fighting for our share of the American pie": The 1985 Wheeling-Pittsburgh Steel strike. *Labor Studies Journal, 32,* 82–95.

Zelizer, B. (1985). Reading the past against the grain: The shape of memory studies. *Critical Studies in Mass Communication, 12,* 214–239.

7

"We still had to have tortillas": Negotiating health, culture, and change in the Mexican American diet

Kevin-Khristián Cosgriff-Hernández, Amanda R. Martinez, Barbara F. Sharf, and Joseph R. Sharkey

In this chapter we examine how participants communicate about the selection, production, and consumption of food in relation to their nationality. Analysis of several conversations with participants about their beliefs and choices about food provide insights into the differences in their lives in Mexico and the United States. In the process, we expand our understanding about the relationship between food and communication, and its significance as an expression of identity.

As obesity, diabetes, and cardiovascular disease continue to escalate throughout the United States, Americans of all races and ethnicities, and within all income levels, grapple with issues of diet and nutrition. For the poorest in this country, food scarcity remains a grave problem, but for millions of others for whom food is available, the issue is more one of making good choices. Although health promotion information about nutrition abounds—eat more fruits and vegetables, limit meat and animal-based fat intake, increase whole and multi-grains and other complex carbohydrates, substitute olive and canola oils for other types of fats—other factors frequently determine what people end up eating.

Mexican Americans are disproportionately affected by many diseases and health problems. As a largely immigrant population often stigmatized by language differences, skin color and appearance, and suspicions about legal status in residency and citizenship, Mexican Americans are frequently at a disadvantage occupationally, financially, socially, and politically (for several measures of these assertions, see Pew Hispanic Center). Thus, the dietary dilemmas that face the American population at large are of particular concern to this sub-population:

In early 1999, data released by the Centers for Disease Control and Prevention (CDC) indicated that six percent of Hispanic adults in the United States and Puerto Rico had been diagnosed with diabetes—twice the rate of Caucasian Americans—while another six percent had undiagnosed diabetes. . . . Approximately one out of every ten Mexican Americans aged twenty years and older had diabetes (National Alliance for Hispanic Health).

Hispanic children, along with Native American and African-American children, are disproportionately at risk for obesity (Park, 2009), a fact attributed to lack of exercise (Cooper, 2005) and poor but cheap dietary choices made by immigrants, plus a cultural belief that "bigger is better," stemming from prior experiences of malnutrition. Though Hispanic men are actually at less risk for cardiovascular-related ailments than non-Hispanic whites (Office of Minority Health, 2009), it is a different story for Hispanic women where "heart disease is the #1 killer of Latinas in the United States. Thirty-four percent of Mexican American women have cardiovascular disease. Together with stroke, heart disease accounts for a third of all deaths among Latinas" (Aetna.com. July 18, 2008). Furthermore, "Hispanic women's heart disease risk is comparable to the heart disease risk level of Caucasian women who are about a decade older" (Velarde, Pacos, Hume, Petit & Huntress, 2007). In short, in so far as these health conditions are related to eating patterns, the health disparities literature is a testament to a struggle that Hispanics in the United States, and in particular Mexican Americans, have with healthy nutritional decision-making, possibly due to a related inequality in accessing and understanding nutritional information. This study examines conversations about nutritional beliefs and choices, as well as differences between life in Mexico and the United States, which occurred in six focus groups with Mexican American adults living in central Texas.

Dutta's (2008) culture-centered model of health communication posits interrelationships among the three major elements of *culture*, *structure*, and *agency* to create "openings for listening to the voices of marginalized communities… [and] engaging them in dialogue" (p. 5). From this perspective, culture entails intrinsic ways of living and webs of meaning from which understanding of health emerge, which include beliefs about nutrition, patterns of eating, and traditional ways of food preparation. Food is a major expression of cultural solidarity, identity, and enjoyment. Structure refers to constraining and enabling aspects of social organization and material resources. For participants in this study, the social organization of sizeable communities of Spanish-speaking Mexican Americans may be considered by many as an enabling factor, though lack of facility with English is likely a constraint to obtaining and understanding health information. To a group of people already experiencing severe financial constraints, the recent national economic downturn is an especially large burden. Agency is the capacity of community members to enact choices and negotiate structural impediments, and that is the ultimate concern of this work—to find ways to bolster people's agency to make good dietary choices, even in light of constraining factors such as economic limitations and traditional ways of knowing and doing, that lead to improved health outcomes for Hispanic families.

In the following analysis, we see dynamic tensions being articulated around the issue of maintaining cultural identity while working toward healthier lifestyle choices. There is a temporal aspect to these discussions, namely: Who we (i.e., Mexican Americans) were in the past, who we are now, and who do I (as a Mexican American and unique individual) hope to become in terms of my food choices? We also perceive two concurrent yet conflicting master narratives unfolding. In one narrative, cultural food preparation that connotes strong ethnocultural identity and personal enjoyment is in tension with new knowledge about what is entailed in healthier food choices. From this perspective, the traditions of Mexican meals are found to be faulty and in need of change. The other narrative has to do with remembrance of natural, home-grown food products in Mexico, in contrast to the highly processed food products and junk foods ubiquitous in the contemporary United States. In this story, American culture is the culprit. It is in the context of these tensions that this research project strives to identify: How do changes in nutritional decision-making occur and what gets in the way of such changes?

Food as Cultural Expression

Food is an avenue by which we can examine culture, group affiliations and identity. Anthropologists have long been concerned with intersections of culture and food (Mintz & Du Bois, 2002). In particular, the works of Barthes (1961), Levi-Strauss (1966), and Douglas (1974) provided theoretical foundations for subsequent scholarship about food and culture. The culinary triangle presents a traditional structuralist framework from which we can begin to recognize how the natural state of food (raw) is altered through cooking, boiling and grilling (Levi-Strauss, 1966). Douglas' (1974) examination of the rites of meals delved into how the rules we create to distinguish what is and is not acceptable creates a system of symbolism and understanding of how taboo is created. Barthes (1961) recognizes the importance of structure, but extends this idea to highlight how "substances, techniques of preparation, habits, all become part of a system of differences in signification; and as soon as this happens we have communication by way of food" (p. 30). Put another way, food is "not only a collection of products that can be used for statistical or nutritional studies. It is also, and at the same time, a system of communication, a body of images, a protocol of usages, situations, and behavior" (Barthes, 1961, p. 29). From these earlier works, it is apparent that food may be examined as communicative expressions and performances of social identity.

Within this framework, it is important to recognize the role of structure, agency and group affiliation. Food is altered by individuals or groups of people according to certain norms or recipes. When this is done, food "takes on the characteristics of an institution, its function can no longer be dissociated from the sign of that function" (Barthes, 1961, p. 29). Recipes serve as symbolic references to a structure that connects groups of people. However, cultural communicative expressions are not limited to recipes. Preparation of food (cooking) and eating are "expressive behavior, relatively easy to observe, and heavily laden with symbolic meaning" (Lockwood & Lockwood, 2000, p. 516). The examination of food is not just about how we alter food, but also how we produce and consume it, as well as the patterns associated with each of these categories.

Food uniquely communicates to in- and out-group members since it "serves both to solidify group membership and to set groups apart" (Mintz & Dubois, 2002, p. 109). Classifying food as *ethnic* communicates a classification and creates a group identity. Our understanding of what constitutes a cultural group is communicatively constructed and expressed via food. Examinations of food that have focused on structure, symbolism, and semiotics help to generate a deeper understanding for the nuances that differentiate groups, culminating in a greater cultural appreciation. However, a limitation of these approaches is that they rarely delve into the power dynamics of control, resistance, and change.

Many scholars have investigated the concepts and dynamics of power, group identity, and creolization (Brown & Mussell, 1984; Counihan, 1999, 2008; Lockwood & Lockwood, 2000). Creolization is a process of creating ethnic culture that "takes place within the particular constraints of minority life: the homesickness, the prejudice, the sense of being different, the urge to assimilate or to resist assimilation, the need to recreate the Old World in the New or reject all possible reminders of the life that was" (Lockwood & Lockwood, 2000, p. 516). Ethnic groups create an identity via the food they grow, gather, prepare, cook and eat. These challenges are not limited to one generation. Kalčik (1984) recognizes the "struggle to keep or give up ethnic food habits continues into the succeeding generations as they struggle to adjust their sense of ethnic identity and their relationship to the larger unit of American society" (p. 41). The tensions between old and new expectations are critical to understanding how culture is communicated.

In this context, Williams (1984) argues that "families and family foodways must be worked at, and among migrants it is women who most vigorously do so" (p. 123). Women are in a particularly powerful position in relation to what is communicated and the identity that is formed via food. The works of Counihan (1999, 2008), and Abarca (2006) utilize a feminist approach that brings the voices of women to center stage. These discussions made space for critical questioning pertaining to issues of gender through closer attention to what and how culture is communicated and by whom. Examining food from this perspective emphasizes the role of women in relation to culture where cuisine contributes to an identity that binds not only the family, but also the community.

Other scholarship has focused less on the group dynamic of food and communication and argued for more individualized investigations that examine the relationship of food, communication and individuality (Adler, 1981; Abarca, 2004). Of note is the idea of creative eating which focuses on the eating habits of the individual in contrast to the norms and rituals of standardized eating. Adler (1981) suggests that creative eating "involves a number of ideas which are in opposition to each other yet somehow complementary" (p. 6). Abarca (2004) argues for a paradigm shift that concentrates on changes that "speak to a person's creative growth," as opposed to the authenticity of food (p. 3). In other words, individuality and agency are brought to the forefront. These arguments for a paradigmatic shift emphasize a need to explore the tensions between individuality (agency), norms and expectations of the group (ethnicity), and how those are communicated via food. Communication scholars are uniquely positioned to explore tensions that emerge between the desire to express individuality and the need to connect with others.

Methodology

Study Context and Participants

The current study included a total of six focus groups with a total of 65 participants, each comprised of 8 to 14 participants from Bryan, Texas. Participants were recruited with the assistance of health educators from a local community health center, which provides health care for a large Hispanic/Latino Spanish-speaking population. The participants from the health center consisted of two groups of health center employees. Other focus group participants were recruited from two local churches and an adult learning center.

All of the participants were of Hispanic descent. An overwhelming percent (95.4) of the participants were women. Just over seventy percent (70.7%) of the participants reported as being married or living with a partner. Participants ranged in age from 16 to 64, with a strong majority (78.5%) falling within the range of 21 to 49 years of age. The largest segment (38.5%) completed high school, with 21.5% having less than an eighth grade education and 18.5% completed somewhere between an eighth to eleventh grades. From an economic perspective, a majority of the participants come from households that are economically challenged. Over half (58.8%) live in households that make less than $25,000 a year, and 13.8% reported earning more than $35,000. Participants reported taking part in nutritional aid programs including WIC (32.3%), School Breakfast Program for children (29.2%), National School Lunch Program (reduced or free lunch) for children (24.6.%), and Supplemental Nutrition Assistance Program (18.5%). Finally, of note is the percentage of participants who live in households with someone who has a chronic health condition, such as diabetes (47.7%), obesity (26.1%), or heart problems (15.4%).

Each focus group lasted approximately one hour. Participants received a $20 gift card from a local fresh produce store for their time. The majority of the focus groups were conducted in Spanish, with native Spanish-speaking facilitators guiding discussions; at their discretion, group members used a mix of Spanish and English.

Analysis of Focus Group Data

Audio-taped focus group sessions were transcribed verbatim and translated by a bi-lingual/bi-cultural team member, resulting in a total of 109 pages for analysis. English language transcripts were then analyzed by three team members who had not been involved in facilitating or transcribing focus group data. Due to the time-consuming nature of the translation/transcription process, the analysis team received the transcripts in batches. Transcripts of focus groups 1 to 4 were each read by all three team members and separately coded by two analysts. Coding was facilitated by use of Atlas.ti 5.5 software for data storage, sorting, and retrieval. Individual code lists were compared and discussed among all three analysts. Disagreements, discrepancies, and overlaps were discussed until agreement was reached. Definitions were agreed upon and written for each code. Coded material from the transcripts was reviewed to ensure that supporting quotations fit with the consensus definition. As a result of this procedure, definitions were clarified or expanded, as needed. Our objective was to develop code categories that were distinct from one another and which conveyed specific qualities of the focus group discussion.

In essence, this process of team coding followed a constructivist grounded theory process (Charmaz, 2006). In lieu of codes derived from *a priori* categories or theoretical constructs, open coding of the transcribed discussions were grounded in the discourse itself with the goal of constructing overall meanings across and within the focus group discussions. A code list began with Focus Group 1 and was carried into the analysis of the second transcript, at which point new codes were added; old codes were modified as necessary in light of new data. This process was repeated with each additional transcript.

At the juncture in which focus groups 1 to 4 had been analyzed, the analysis team developed a superordinate list of code families. Each code family represents a code cluster in which individual items are related conceptually. This part of the process resulted in the six supra codes detailed in the next section of this chapter.

The third step in this analysis was to review transcripts from focus groups five and six. Each of these transcripts was read by one analyst, who noted and defined new codes that emerged from these groups. At this point, fewer new codes were identified, thus cueing the analysis team that we were nearing data saturation. New codes and their definitions were discussed by all three team members, again until agreement could be reached. Previous codes were also revisited and revised, when appropriate. The chief reason for having a three-person analysis team was for triangulation, that is, to bring different perspectives and interpretive sensibilities to bear on the data.

Data Analysis and Discussion

Six code families were generated from our grounded theory analysis of the focus group transcripts. The focus group discussion guide led to participants' elaborations of remembrances of eating patterns while growing up, distinctions between Mexican and American culture, ideas about what defines healthy eating, and identifying and enacting healthful nutrition practices. In this section, five of the six code families will be explored, while the sixth provides the basis for our concluding remarks on the process of changing to a better diet.

Perceptions of "what's healthy." In the course of discussing food choices, patterns, and opinions, focus group participants expressed very clear opinions about what is healthy and what is not in terms of food preparation and nutrition. In several instances, the perception of healthy foods was depicted in contrast to what is not: "For example, when we have an activity, we do not serve cokes. We put natural water or fruit waters and we don't bring all of those foods that have a lot of condiments and with too much grease. Now, there is more vegetables, fruits, and lighter things" (Focus Group 1: Participant 3, otherwise noted as FG1:3). Two qualities, in particular, serve as markers of healthy food. The first is the perception of being natural, that is, unprocessed or organic and was a quality frequently associated with memories of growing up in Mexico:

> I like natural things. Like in Mexico, the cheeses were freshly made and the meat was fresh. They would kill the cows and the chickens and they will sell the meat that same day. You don't find that here. I don't like the meat or the cheeses from here that much. I eat them but I don't like them as much. (FG6:8)

> We would eat cactus, beans, eggs…because we had chickens. In regards to fruits in the home, we had limes, oranges, and then we had pears and apples. There whenever we wanted some, we would just go and climb the trees and we would eat. (FG1:6)

In contrast, modern life in the United States is fraught with an overabundance of processed foods that preclude the natural:

> The only thing that I used to have was fruit, back in the day. So now my grandkids have the fruit and the cupcakes and the Twinkies and all those things. Donuts from Wal-Mart and all of these string cheese, just because it has Spiderman on the thing. (FG3:5)

A second quality that was emphasized by one group of participants (FG1) as being healthy is cleanliness: "They teach you that you have to wash your hands for at least 5–10 seconds and leave them in water and you have to sterilize everything and you can't cut meat and then cut limes with the same knife" (FG1:6).

Third, many of the focus group participants demonstrated an awareness of basic nutrition. For instance, when an all female group was asked what foods were important to include in their family's diet, FG6:2 replied,

> Fiber, calcium, and the protein…calcium for my kids, in yogurt, milk and cheese. Protein, usually from meats and beans. It's better from the meat but they don't like meat that much. It's more beans. Peanut Butter as well. For fiber, well, cereals that have wheat grains.

FG6:6 added, "Lentils, kidney beans and broccoli all have iron as well. It's recommended to eat a lot of those things for a healthy diet."

In sum, focus group participants were well aware of what foods are healthy and what are not, mentioning sources from whom or which they received such information. Respondents referred to information received from health professionals, mass media, other people, and public education. The majority of references to a professional source were to lessons taught by the clinic's health educators. These responses tended to be enthusiastic: "Me and Norma have been here for the last five years and we always get health education classes from [the health educators] especially so we know where to start from and know what to look out for and how to feed our family more healthy foods" (FG4:7). There were also allusions to advice from doctors, though not necessarily heeded: "The kids drink a lot of coke because it's a party, and the dentists say not to give them coke nor candy. They advise to put vegetables and fruits in the piñatas but no one is going to want them with that. [laughs]" (FG6:8). Various media formats, including radio, magazines, books, and the Internet, were also identified as information sources. Overwhelmingly, however, media references were to television, including news, education, cooking shows, and entertainment: "We are trying through TV because normally, TV is not all about soap operas because there are many informative programs. Many programs of people cooking and preparing everything healthy. They tell you how to cook it" (FG2:4). The third information source was other people, with the majority of references to extended family members, friends, and neighbors: "Friends and family. My aunt when she makes something, I will ask her where she made it from or where she get the recipe and just ask questions…. I would hear her say she is going to make some certain dish and I ask her how is she going to make that" (FG4:9). A few mentioned non-familiar sources that brought new information to their attention:

> I used to go to the house of an American family and it was really funny because one is used to having the refrigerator full of sodas, fruit waters, juices and in that house it was not like that. They only had bottled water. They had lettuce, they were vegetarians…I would eat it and I did learn a lot of things about organic foods because they are good for the health. She would tell me what was organic and what was healthy and that did not pollute the environment. She would tell me how it was cultivated. In other words, I was learning from her and you learn to know more about what you are putting into your body because sometimes one just does not know. (FG1:6)

In addition to information from the health clinic, participants mentioned the government-sponsored program WIC supplemental nutrition (Women, Infants and Children) as an important information source:

> When I went to WIC, they gave my baby a cup with the exact measure of juice he should get. When he would ask me, I would give him a large cup and fill it up to the top and I would tell him to drink it all. I thought that was the right thing but they told me that it is not because the teeth get bad. (FG5:5)

> I was enrolled in some cooking classes in WIC. They gave me a book with recipes on healthy cooking and using less fat and more fruits and vegetable…and I made some things and it was good. (FG6:8)

Responses to information from other forms of public information were much more mixed. Some were critical of cooking demonstrations and recipes distributed at a popular local market: "At H-E-B now they have that person that will teach you how to cook the dishes and the meats. It would be nice if they could extend that maybe to show to make the vegetables" (FG4:2). Another participant observed: "There are signs in McDonalds, for example, that they give you the tray and the paper is there too, but who looks at it?" (FG2:11). A few participants noted that their children learned helpful nutritional information at school. One individual suggested:

> If they had little things for kids during school time. Like part of their classes to be a nutrition class, where they learn how to prepare little things with vegetables and tell them to try it that it can be good. It will be part of the classroom and they would go home and show their parents. This should be a subject for them because we have trouble with our kids because they are obese. (FG4:7)

With such awareness and knowledge of the importance of good nutrition, what then are specific issues for this population that may mitigate enacting healthy eating behaviors? Negotiating food preparation methods and ritualistic consumption patterns influence the incorporation of American and Mexican cultures simultaneously. Many participants noted the challenge of striking a balance between two cultures and ways of eating.

Cultural practices. Adjustment to different types of food is one of the challenges in healthy preparation and taste of meals. Focus group participants discussed food habits influenced by their Mexican heritage which inform cooking methods, foods used in specific dishes, and use of condiments and spices. Among consideration of preparation methods is whether to cook the traditional way, using lard, or healthier methods, such as using oil or less fat for a balance of healthiness and tastiness. Some participants recognized traditional ways of preparing Mexican food as unhealthy and in need of change: "We got to understand some of the bad foods in the Hispanic diet. Rice, beans and then the making of the tortillas. A glob of lard thrown in there. When my wife saw the way it was made, she almost fainted [laughs]" (FG3:1). Similarly, another participant (FG2:11) notes a change in her cooking style: "I cook with oil. I have always cooked with oil but before, I used to cook with a lot of grease and lard."

The participants highlight dishes specific to Mexican culture, such as *menudo*, *tamales*, and *sopas* as well as staple ingredients in preparation, including chile, cactus, beef, and chicken. This participant (FG4:9) notes the importance of one such ingredient: "Chile of course. That is a big thing because everything has chile in it." Other additions are important to taste, as one participant (FG3:5) explained, "I still buy the salt and the black peppers and I still buy my condiments and the garlic and the season-all and all of that. I can only cut corners as much as possible or at least I try to." Many participants readily described staple foods. One participant (FG5:3) noted, "Beans and tortillas are always present at my house." Another participant (FG5:6) added, "Also, tacos and beans because in all of the states of Mexico, they are used to the beans, even though they make them in several different ways such as charros, black or pintos." The participants simultaneously occupy a cultural space between the larger American culture and Mexican heritage, which leads to negotiating mixed cultural identities in food preparation and consumption within the family and community contexts.

In negotiating mixed identities, participants often made cultural comparisons between their home country and the United States in reference to schedules and eating more meals alone, due to time constraints. Schedules also influence modes of preparation, for example, not having time to prepare food from scratch, a common practice in Mexico. Participants also discussed how they integrate these two cultural practices. For example, many participants noted that tortillas are still eaten with most meals, as one participant (FG3:7) stated: "You could not be without tortillas. Even if it was American food, we still had to have tortillas." Many participants elaborated on their own evolving style by cooking a variety of Mexican, American, or Tex-Mex cuisine. As one participant (FG4:6) pointed out, "She [participant's mother] was more Tex-Mex style because my mom came [to the U.S.] when she was two years old, so she would cook Mexican food but more Americanized. I have more [of] that Tex-Mex style with my husband but I do cook lasagna and chicken Alfredo but I will still cook chicken and rice. Just having a mixture."

Ritualistic consumption based on scheduling and special days is described in terms of family gatherings, parties, special occasions, holidays, and the traditional importance of eating meals together. Eating meat on Sundays, usually a day reserved for the family, was one practice. Participant (FG1:5) stated, "Sunday's the day where we dedicate it to the family." Other specific rituals tied to time frames include eating out at restaurants on a specific day (either as a whole family, or with co-workers), and preparing special foods coinciding with holidays, such as tamales for Christmas and New Year's Day.

Developing a cooking style that considers elements of both American and Mexican culture is an endeavor undertaken by many participants. Discussion also brought to light the ways in which economic and time factors influence the food choices made by participants for themselves and their families.

Economic and temporal influences on consumption. Economic limitations lead to using coupons and purchasing inexpensive foods that are satisfying and provide an adequate food source for the family. While grocery shopping, many make conscious decisions, as this participant (FG2:5) noted: "If we do not have enough [money], you choose what is the cheapest. Beans and potatoes, eggs." Strategic grocery shopping is common practice, as another participant (FG1:6) states:

> One is always after the coupons, even if it is just fifty cents because everything is so expensive. I look at the potatoes because I like the yellow ones because they are better and I say, well, this packet here costs about the same to the ones that I want so I take the ones that are the cheapest and the biggest.

Another shopping strategy is revealed by this participant (FG2:8):

> When I go grocery shopping, I don't just go and grab and sack, grab and sack. I go and already know how much and what I am going to get. I weigh it and if I don't need any more, then I don't get it.

Attempts to stretch money often result in frustration. One participant (FG4:9) stated, "We come home with $150 worth of groceries, and these days [that] is really not that much, and it can be gone in two or three days." This sentiment resonates with others, as another participant (FG1:3) said, "I am very angry because the food is so expensive… you go to the store and three little things amount to $50 and if you take groceries for the whole week, it does not last." Household size and economic constraints remain relevant factors in consumption patterns.

In addition to finances, work schedules and time of day influence food decisions. Participants talked about having limited time for lunch while working, so they opt for fast food or available cheap snacks because they may lack adequate time to prepare food in the home, which seems a constant negotiation. As this participant (FG2:3) points out, "Time is also an issue...Like at work, one eats fast so one can get back to work as fast as possible." At times, eating the first available option is convenient and the choice is between achieving nutritional value weighed against cheap, fast options. One participant (FG2:10) echoes this theme: "The most nutritional, but the cheapest. McDonald's and all of that." However, foods that are familiar and accommodate preferred tastes are, when conveniently available, mostly cooked at home. One participant (FG2:9) said,

> On the weekends, that's when I take more time to cook and I cook the dishes that are healthiest because that is when I have more time…[during the work week] I make a sandwich with turkey for them [children] and it is fast because I want to make sure they have eaten before I go off to my next job.

Regular weekly food planning takes place among participants, as does longer-term planning. Buying in bulk or preparing food at home for long-term storage and consumption are common practices, in addition to making food stretch by preparing various dishes out of few ingredients. One participant (FG3:6) revealed,

> What we do is we go and buy a [lot] of ground beef and just cook off of that. Ground beef you can make meatloaf…beef with potatoes…or tacos, *fideos* or soups…spaghetti…hamburger steaks and all. I can make so much out of one package of ground meat.

Similarly, another participant (FG3:5) notes, "Big chunks of steak cut up in three parts and frozen and that was three meals." Other determinant factors include what ingredients and foods are available at home, as well as habitual consumption and health concerns.

Habits and health. While inquiring about consumption patterns, preferences for certain foods emerge. Participants describe being mindful of the amount of soda and sweets consumed. One participant (FG2:4) noted, "I used to like chocolates too much. Snickers, I used to eat them a lot, but I stopped already." Many participants relay their conscious eating habits often indicative of patterns which largely revolve around individual work schedules and an "on-the-go" lifestyle. Changing routines spur changes in eating habits, too. One participant (FG1:1) states, "I used to have that routine there [eating late] but when I got here, I could not do it anymore because I could not sleep if I ate too much." Further, another participant (FG3:6) notes, "It is not what we eat, [but] the amount that we eat. Portion sizes. Sometimes people think that they are bored, that they are hungry. Sometimes, that is not the answer." The desire to change unhealthy eating habits also arose in discussion, as this participant (FG3:3) noted: "Well, again, the weight. That is one of the main things that makes me want to eat healthy, and the other one is health."

Eating habits are further complicated with serious changes in health, such as onset of diabetes. Diabetes led some participants to reconsider their cooking habits: "I also used to cook a lot with grease. I used to like cooking with it a lot. But since then, I was prone to diabetes. So I was put in a diet and learned to cook better" (FG2:1). Another participant referenced that "[s]ince I got diabetes, I don't eat things that are too greasy. I have also avoided coke because it has a lot of sugar and I do not go over that now" (FG2:11). Family members with diabetes also impact how meals are negotiated:

> I taught myself how to cook here because my husband is diabetic. They told me to eat less fats and to eat more vegetables, but he likes the fats too much and does not listen. That is why I'm here too. To listen. He does not listen because he likes it and he does not make changes. (FG2:2)

What emerges from these comments is that diabetes, and those that are struggling with it in the context of the family, influence what is selected, and how it is prepared. Striking a balance between consumption of preferred foods and receiving healthful nutritional value is a daily struggle for individuals and families. To better understand this negotiation, it is useful to delve into familial influences that impact nutritional decisions.

Family influence on diets. Family is an important consideration when it comes to negotiating food choices. As families merge, many of the female participants noted how meals were negotiated:

> My mom, she would never prepare anything with chile. She would make a salsa on the side for my dad. She did not grow up eating chile so she would just put it on the side. When we wanted some, we would get some so I grew up not eating chile. But when I married, and I went to my husband's family, everything had chile in it. (FG4:2)

> I made tortillas everyday for a whole year and a half. Without any rest because in my husband's family, they eat the flour tortillas a lot and I had to learn. They don't eat them that much now, but then, they did. I tell my husband that is why we are the way we are (laughs). Look at how much weight I have gained since I got married to you (laughs). (FG6: 3)

Another participant who faced a similar merging of cuisines commented how she reacted, stating that, "Later I learned to cook how my husband likes it. Because when I got married, even though we are from the same place, the customs of the two families are very different" (FG1:3). Although not explicitly stated, when it came to merging the tastes and cuisines of families, most participants practiced a strategy of compromise or accommodation.

Other participants note that they negotiate with their children, stating that, "I try to combine it [vegetables] with a little bit of what they like, a little bit of what I like. And if they do not like it, I try to give them a reward so they can eat it and be more healthy" (FG2:1). Most of the parents or guardians made it abundantly clear that when it came to their children that, "One is always thinking what is best for the kids" (FG2:9). As parents or guardians, these participants are influenced by their responsibility to children and their own set of nutritional preferences.

Negotiating the likes and dislikes of the family requires attention to each family member and each meal. In particular, the cook of the family is aware that "we are used to eating one type of food and they [the family] do not go out of that boundary" (FG5:8). One might conclude that negotiating meals emphasizes recognition and understanding of the limits of the family's likes and dislikes.

Within the context of the family, men and women were described as serving specific roles. Participants noted how men influenced what the family selects when involved in the grocery shopping. One female participant highlighted how her husband is the one concerned about what their children eat, stating that he "is the one that goes and does the groceries and everything. When I go home, he is already having the food ready and the vegetables are already eaten" (FG3:6). Women, especially mothers, were named as the primary cook in the household. Mothers were recognized as "the one that cooked and would put us, the women and the girls, to cook as well. I remember she would teach us how to make tortillas, to put the soups and the beans on the stove, because that is what we used more in Mexico" (FG6:1). Similarly, another participant stated that "she (her mother) always prepared the meals" (FG5:6). What is evident from these comments is that mothers are the storytellers of food in that they pass on the information, recipes, ingredients, and ways of preparing food on to their children through cooking. Above all else, participants are aware of how they serve as role models to the younger generation:

> The kids want to do what the parents do. Like us, we wanted to do what our parents did and we got used to what they gave us. I don't eat vegetables that much because we did not have them while growing up. I don't eat them but I try to give them to my daughter, even though she does not like them but I still try to give them to her. (FG6:8)

It is clear that the participants understand their agency, or ability to facilitate change, through self reflective awareness of their functions as parent and role model.

Conclusion: Changing Ways of Eating

Each of the preceding themes leads to an understanding of how change happens for these families in relation to health and nutrition. When referring to changes in diet, participants distinguish between factors that limit their ability to change versus factors that support enacting different ways of eating. Participants were asked to identify "some obstacles that you think might come across in the future" to dietary changes they had proposed. Responses include: "One big obstacle of people is their way of thinking, their mentality" (FG1:3), and that "one cannot change what one has done for the whole life" (FG2:4). Besides personal "mentality" being an obstacle to change, participants also identify family traditions as a contributing factor. This was apparent when probing about particular ways of cooking, stating that "the family has always cooked like that and that is what they do. That is what our grandparents teach us and so that is how we cook. (Laugh) What can you do in that instance? I do not know" (FG1:3). Here, tradition is perceived as something that is not only handed down through the generations, but also as affecting health: "I think that is more what the people are going to like than what is healthy. That's an unfortunate case because we don't like the healthy dishes. I think we look for the traditional dishes instead" (FG6:6). The role of tradition may be understood as a set of rules that help the participants to associate and connect with family, but also serves as an obstacle to changing ways of eating.

Tradition is not the only obstacle to changing healthy habits. Both time and economic status are seen as obstacles to change. "People just don't have that much time. That is what people say that we do not have time…it is time consuming to get from one place to another place and do everything that you have to do and still get home and say: Well I'm going to make a meal" (FG4:6). When time is short, participants note that the quality of the decision in relation to food is poor, noting that, "When they rush to do grocery shopping, for example, my husband, he would just go and get the first thing here and there and would not look at what he got. I make a list of what I need, that is why it takes me longer, and that is what gets him upset. But I am looking at what is better. Because I don't have enough money" (FG5:1). Participants note that time is of the essence and understand how it affects the quality of their decision. However, change does happen. When it does, participants express themselves as being in a position to exercise a sense of *free will* within the moment. These moments might be interpreted as catalysts for transformation, opportunities for experimentation and resistance to existing standards. Of note are moments when the participant expressed a sense of agency via their own self-control which seems to go hand in hand with time to reflect on meals for the day. One participant stated, "I try to eat what I had already in mind before going to work. I tell myself that I was going to eat that, and that is what I eat" (FG1:5). Still another participant frames this self-control as "the body want[ing] something, you can give it to it, but all in measurement and limitations. I have in my mind that is all in limitation" (FG5:6). The participants' comments suggest that there is a mental struggle to eat healthy foods in spite of the pressure to eat unhealthy foods.

Facilitators and Barriers to Change

Besides a sense of free will, what exactly facilitates change? Four themes that facilitate or prohibit change for these participants are experimentation, resistance, responsibility, and education.

Experimentation. Experimentation is a moment of opportunity where participants express breaking away from pre-existing norms of cooking to try new dishes. One participant expressed, "I have been eating Mexican food for I don't know how many years, since I was one year old. I probably tasted beans when I was … you know. I told him I am tired of this so that is why I make meatloaf and I make all of these new things" (FG4:2). Similarly, another participant referenced wanting to try new foods as:

> That is what I would do when I was little. When my mom taught me how to make tortillas since I was eleven. That is what we ate everyday was homemade tortillas. Chicken with rice, potato with hamburger meat, corn with hamburger meat, and then like a few. Well, later on years went by and I was like: 'Man I am tired of eating the same old foods (laughs)'… So, I would have to have dinner ready by the time my mom and dad would come home from work at 3:30pm so I was like, well I already know how to make tortillas and I was like: What can I do in the oven? So, I started making some pig in the blanket. Got the weenies and got the dough and just put it in there. They were good and we ate it. Then, I made homemade cookies because we did not have sweets. I was like: I got to have something, do something. So I started making cookies. So once I started making them my brothers were like: 'Hey, so when are you going to make some more cookies?' (FG3:9)

Resistance. Resistance to change is related to experimentation in that it is a separation from a standard way of cooking from either the perspective of resisting food traditions or resisting notions of what is healthy and then slipping into unhealthy food choices. In discussing separating from tradition, one participant spoke of how she "also cook[s] separately. Other recipes that maybe she [her mother] does not make or have. I like it when I have time and when I feel like it because not all the time do I feel like cooking. But when I do feel like it, I like to make new things, something that I am learning by myself" (FG1:2). Therefore, for experimentation to occur, participants need to have the time to try new recipes and the freedom from pressures of other family members. As for resisting a healthier standard, one participant highlighted "wanting to change" as the point of resistance, "because that happens to me because I have diabetes and I tell myself that this time, I am going to follow the diet. I cannot. I always eat something light but later, I get hungry and I cannot stick to the diet. Then I tell myself that there is no way that I can be eating all the time. I cannot" (FG2:7). Of note, is that these participants know what a healthier choice would entail, but struggle to maintain a healthy diet in light of the tensions between health concerns, convenience, tradition, and economics.

Responsibility. Responsibility is often framed as what one should do for one's health, or for the sake of someone else's health –especially children and spouses. For example, participants seem more likely to read labels on food, paying particular attention to "the carbs, sugar, proteins, calcium and all of that. Things like that because that is what I want to give my kids" (FG4:6). Female participants noted the immense amount of responsibility they feel in regards to the health of the family: "It is difficult for mothers because one is responsible for what the family eats. It is a huge responsibility because what you cook is what your family is going to eat" (FG2:13). Participants recognized that "most of the time, we only think about ourselves and not others. If we think of others, we think about helping the community" (FG1:3). Thus, responsibility is constructed in relation to caring for the health of the family, or the community.

Education. Learning about healthy lifestyles is recognized as important in facilitating positive change. In the words of one participant, "Education is the base for everything" (FG2:4). Participants express a clear desire to "prepare healthy dishes so we can teach our children to do it and give them an example. If we don't fix the adults, then the kids will follow our example as well" (FG5:5). When probed to explain the learning process, one participant stated, "Well maybe one learns from others. Even though we are from different places within the same country. Oh, well not everyone, but the foods are different and the preparation methods as well and so one learns from other places and countries. One learns many other foods" (FG1:8). Besides numerous references to the work of professional health educators at the health center, one participant highlighted the potential for cooking classes or demonstrations as another source for change:

> Maybe classes on how to cook healthy foods. They should put those because sometimes we run out of choices of foods to make. Our world falls apart. You can have the ingredients in front of you but you don't know what to do with them. Maybe if we went to a class, they could tell us what to do with certain things, because if we have not even tried them, then they won't look appealing to us. (FG6:9)

Each of these factors contributes to our understanding of how change happens in relation to diet and nutrition. Change can and does happen despite numerous challenges, obstacles, and constraints that these participants face on a daily basis and from generation to generation. Comments of participants in these focus groups provide insight into how they manage change. This study presents the voices of participants explaining how they manage food choices in relation to shifts in nutrition, health and culture.

Communication scholars are well equipped to contribute to these conversations about food. Rhetorical, organizational, health, media, and cultural communication scholars all bring different perspectives to the discussion. For example, several questions emerged from this study that engaged these different perspectives: What might be the rhetorical significance of the dishes that the participants reference, for example in terms of identification, transcendence, or a unified rhetorical vision? What role do local organizations play in food choice, selection, and preparation? How are concepts such as agency, power and control enacted on a daily basis in relation to food decisions, and by whom? What do the communicative networks that pertain to food look like, and how might they be impacted to improve health? In what ways do media depictions reinforce or help to modify cultural food traditions? How can entertainment-education make a difference in helping people with diabetes learn appetizing ways of eating? Questions such as these challenge communication scholars in new ways and highlight how varied perspectives can contribute to current conversations regarding food, nutrition, and health.

Acknowledgements

This research was supported with funding from the National Institutes of Health/National Center on Minority Health and Health Disparities grant #5P20MD002295 and the Centers for Disease Control and Prevention, Prevention Research Centers Program, through the Center for Community Health Development cooperative agreement #5U48DP000045.

Dr. Julie Ribardo, Carolina Puentes and Raquel Flores contributed to the recruitment and coordination of participants, focus group moderation, and the translation of the focus group protocol and transcripts.

References

Abarca, M. E. (2004). Authentic or not, it's original. *Food and foodways, 12*, 1–25.

Abarca, M. E. (2006). *Voices in the kitchen: Views of food and the world from working-class Mexican and Mexican American women.* College Station, TX: Texas A&M University Press.

Adler, E. M. (1981). Creative eating: The Oreo syndrome. *Foodways and eating habits, 40,* 4–10.

Aetna.com (2008, July, 18). Hispanic women and heart disease. Retrieved May 20, 2009, from http://womenshealth.aetna.com/WH/ihtWH/r.w===23/st.36134/t.36368.html

Barthes, R. (1961). Toward a psychosociology of contemporary food consumption. In C. Counihan & P. Van Esterik (Eds.), *Food and culture: A reader* (2nd ed.), (pp. 28–35). New York: Routledge.

Brown, L. K. & Mussell, K. (Eds.) (1984). *Ethnic and regional foodways in the United States: The performance of group identity*. Knoxville, TN: The University of Tennessee Press.

Charmaz, K. (2006). *Constructing grounded theory: A practical guide through qualitative analysis*. Thousand Oaks, CA: Sage Publications.

Cooper, A. (2005, May 22). Hispanics and obesity—The worrying truth. *EzineArticles.com.* Retrieved May 19, 2009, from http://ezinearticles.com/?Hispanics-and-Obesity—-The-Worrying-Truth&id=37948.

Counihan, C. (1999). *The Anthropology of food and body: Gender, meaning, and power.* New York: Routledge.

Counihan, C. (2008). Mexicans' Food voice and differential consciousness in the San Luis Valley of Colorado. In C. Counihan and P. Van Esterik (Eds.), *Food and culture: A reader* (2nd ed.), (pp. 354–368). New York: Routledge.

Douglas, M. (1974). Deciphering a meal. In C. Geertz (Ed.), *Myth, symbol and culture*, (pp. 61–81). New York: Norton.

Dutta, M. J. (2008). *Communicating health: A culture-centered approach.* Cambridge, UK: Polity Press.

Kalčik, S. (1984). Ethnic foodways in America: Symbol and the performance of identity. In L. K. Brown and K. Mussell (Eds.), *Ethnic and regional foodways in the United States: The performance of group identity* (pp. 37–65). Knoxville, TN: The University of Tennessee Press.

Levi-Strauss, C. (1966). The culinary triangle. In C. Counihan and P. Van Esterik (Eds.), *Food and culture: A reader* (2nd ed.), (pp. 36–43). New York: Routledge.

Lockwood, W. G. & Lockwood, Y. R. (2000). Continuity and adaptation in Arab American foodways. In N. Abraham and A. Shryock (Eds.), *Arab Detroit: From margin to main-stream*, (pp. 515–559). Detroit, MI: Wayne State University Press.

Mintz, S. W. & Du Bois, C. M. (2002). The anthropology of food and eating. *Annual Review of Anthropology, 31,* 99–119.

National Alliance for Hispanic Health (2008, November). Retrieved May 18, 2009 from http://www.hispanichealth.org/diabetes.

Office of Minority Health, U.S. Department of Health & Human Services. Retrived May 20, 2009 from http://www.onhrc.gov/templates/ content.aspx?ID=3325.

Park, M. (2009, April 7). It's not baby fat: Among 4-year-olds, 1 in five is obese. Retrieved May 19, 2009, from http://www.cnn.com/2009/HEALTH/04/07/obesity.preschool.children/ index/html?iref=newssearch.

Pew Hispanic Center. Retrieved May 29, 2009, from http://pewhispanic.org.

Velarde, G. P., Pacos, J., Hume, S., Petit, C., & Huntress, J. (2007, March 7). Hispanic women at higher risk for heart disease. *Medical News Today.* Retrieved May 20, 2009, from http://www.medicalnewstoday.com/articles/64449.php.

Williams, B. (1984). Why migrant women feed their husbands tamales: Foodways as a basis for a revisionist view of Tejano family life. In L. K. Brown and K. Mussell (Eds.), *Ethnic and regional foodways in the United States: The performance of group identity* (pp. 113–126). Knoxville, TN: The University of Tennessee Press.

8

Memory, identity, and resistance: Recipes from the women of Theresienstadt

Kathleen M. German

Acts of resistance to Axis domination during World War II generally call to mind the heroism of the French Resistance fighters, those who fought back from inside the Warsaw ghetto, and others whose physical acts directly countered fascist oppression. At first glance, one would hardly place a cookbook alongside these actions. However, the cookbook written by Mina Pachter and other anonymous women during their internment at Theresienstadt camp, forty miles north of Prague, likewise can be seen as an act of resistance. This chapter examines the circumstances that lead to the creation of the cookbook, its rhetorical functions as resistance rhetoric, and some implications of such acts of resistance.

Although food has been the subject of scholarship in many fields, it has been largely ignored as a means of communication, even though it is an important means of expression, manifestation of identity, and influence in social relationships. An investigation of the function of food as communication of social identity promises to yield new insights into human symbolic interaction.

Circumstances of Survival

The circumstances through which this cookbook survived for decades before surfacing is a testament to the tenacity of its authors. Like many unnamed women who contributed to this cookbook, art historian Wilhelmina (Mina) Pachter (1872–1944) was interned at Theresienstadt camp, also known by its Czech name Terezin, in what is now the Czech Republic. The camp was somewhat unique in the German system of concentration camps. It functioned as a model camp for outside inspectors as well as both a settlement and a staging area for Jews and others on their way to death camps in the East. In the early days of the camp, the elderly, former military heroes World War I, and distinguished members of professional and intellectual society were transported to the camp, especially if their abrupt disappearance would have raised alarms. It was euphemistically referred to in Nazi memos as an old-age camp, a model ghetto for inspectors from the International Committee of the Red Cross, a ghetto for the privileged, and a miniature Jewish state, perhaps because of its Jewish Council of Elders (Rothkirchen, 2005).

Terezin was contradictory in many respects. It was both a well-organized city with its own currency and postage stamps run by a council of peers, but its citizens also witnessed frequent transports of residents for extermination further East (Rothkirchen, 2005). Jews hoped that the camp might survive as a separate Jewish community after the war, but Nazi documents indicate that, following the planned liquidation of its Jewish occupants, its future purpose was as a model German community. Disease and death, resulting from severe overcrowding and lack of food and medical supplies, were rampant. Still, the camp was well known for its artistic and intellectual ferment, producing extensive art works, a children's opera, poetry, literature, and theater (Green, 1978).

This artistic ferment was paradoxical. The camp, like others in the German system, was the site of untenable living conditions and widespread terrors. It is estimated that of the 144,000 Jews deported to the camp, 33,000 died in Terezin and another 88,000 were deported to Auschwitz where most certainly died. In May 1945, only 19,000 people were alive at the liberation of the camp. The death rate for children was astronomical; only 100 of the 15,000 children sent to Terezin were alive at the end of the war (Berenbaum, 1996). It is likely that children were special targets for extermination because they held the promise for the future of the Jewish people.

The elderly suffered similarly high rates of death because they were deemed useless for work and received rations that were generally below the threshold for survival (Lederer, 1983). The diary of a camp guard records their misery: "The sight of these unfortunate people, laboriously picking and eating the scant, downtrodden grass in the park as well as potato peels salvaged from the garbage heap to assuage their hunger…moved me to tears whenever I saw it" (Rothkirchen, 2005, p. 242). Mina Pachter died in 1944 as a result of vitamin deficiency brought on by starvation. This is likely the fate of the other women who contributed to the cookbook that bears her name.

The cookbook itself was written in both German and Czech in an informal style that is reminiscent of a diary or a conversation. It was compiled by several women during their internment, carefully stitched and entrusted to the care of a fellow inmate to be delivered to her daughter, Anny Stern, by Mina Pachter, who feared that she would die. Pachter's fears were well founded, but the manuscript found its way, a quarter of a century later, into the hands of her daughter, Anny Stern, in New York by way of Palestine. As a cookbook, the work contains 82 recipes, some illegible, some written in Czech and others in German, indicating that the contributors were fluent in both languages and probably came from various enclaves in Czechoslovakia and its environs.

Food and the Construction of Identity

The attention of scholars has turned to food as symbolic of the social construction of identity in the past few decades. The work of food scholars has bridged many disciplines, exploring the questions of identity in relation to the specific cultural location of community and family (Valentine, 1999). Their work seeks recognition of the social significance of food and eating, recognizing that food systems are, like myth or other cultural systems, codes wherein the patterns by which a culture operates are embedded (Douglas, 1972). Much of this scholarship has argued that the preparation and consumption of food is more than the processing of material goods, but that human use of food conveys meaning and that the rituals surrounding food mark social relationships of inclusion and exclusion, power and submission (Jones, 2007; Miller, 1987; Padolsky, 2005; Tomlinson, 1990). Food is a primary indicator of social order, often a manifestation of behavior, especially displays of political power in social structure (Douglas, 1984). The location of parents, spouses, children and others within the family unit is often negotiated through the nuances of food preparation and service (Alanen, 1990; Massey, 1992: Morgan, 1996; Waksler, 1986: Young & Wilmott, 1973). There have been numerous cross cultural studies of food as used in ethnic communities to establish their autonomy (Khare & Rao, 1986; Poe, 2001; Soler, 1997).

Food also plays an important part in the negotiation of gender relationships within the family (De Vault, 1991). As Charles and Kerr (1993) conclude in a foundational study: "Food is important to the social reproduction of the family in both its nuclear and extended forms and food practices help to maintain and reinforce a coherent ideology of the family throughout the social structure" (p. 17). Part of the function of producing a meal is to simulate the interrelationships of the family structure, creating a sense of cohesion achieved through shared cultural practice (Fischler, 1988). Food functions much like a linguistic code with its meanings hidden below the surface of the obvious concerns of nutrition and physiognomy (Barthes, 1997; Douglas, 1997; Meigs, 1997). Mealtimes mark continuity within families and in retrospect, induce nostalgia (Valentine, 1999). They provide a temporal rhythm to daily activities and require self-discipline. Across world cultures, eating together at the same table is a particularly important way of incorporating others into the family unit and fostering a sense of unity among disparate groups (Bannen, Dodd, Oakley, & Storey, 1994). For this reason, researchers have attended to the connections between the home and other social spaces in the use of food (Sibley & Lowe, 1992).

The association between identity and food consumption behavior has also been the focus of investigation (Charles & Kerr, 1993; Valentine, 1999). As part of material consumption, food use locates individuals within narratives of identity as they construct and maintain stories of the self (Somers, 1994). Scholars have posited that the consumption of food is a complex social process whereby people relate to food as an artifact on multiple levels, transforming it into symbolic functions as they incorporate the cooking and consumption of food into their lives (West, 2007). Despite the increasing attention to the role of food in the construction of culture, scholars have paid little attention to its uses outside of nuclear families in stable environments.

There have been few analyses of the role of food in terminating or resurrecting relationships or in the longer term cementing of communities. Food has been conceptualized as a marker of physical space or location more often than as a symbolic construction of relationships. The link between food and identity, especially in shifting constellations of human relationships and institutional practices, has been ignored. Food may be a critical component of change as situations of upheaval disrupt the identities of people. It also may be important as they attempt to assemble or reorganize their identities, drawing upon the reassuring practices of food preparation as they define, remember, and retell the stories of their lives. In particular, food may serve as the only window into the lives of people who were swept from history by socio-political forces. This analysis may begin to address these gaps.

It has been confirmed by previous research in psychology that periods of stress or crisis often lead to questioning identity, as C. Margaret Hall (1990) maintains, "Self-discovery and the empowerment of self are more likely to occur in times of crisis than during the course of everyday activity" (p. 118). Obviously, the more severe and sustained the crisis, the greater the challenge to individual identity. It should be noted that during such periods of challenge, the individual seeks to create equilibrium by returning to those everyday activities that were ubiquitous prior to the crisis (Hall, 1990). By maintaining identity in the face of adversity, while oppressors seek to annihilate the individual, a rhetoric of resistance works to confirm human existence.

It is not new to argue that food be included in systems of signification. Barthes (1967), for instance, allows that food, as well as clothing, might be subjected to analysis derived from structural linguistics. As others have argued, cooking can be analyzed as language, as a set of symbolic representations of more complex social relationships (Douglas, 1972; Lehrer, 1969; Levi-Strauss, 1966). As in language, the use of this set of culinary symbols establishes the "speaker" in relationship to the subject by way of the action indicated. Thus the articulation of recipes becomes much more than a mundane routine. It is invested with significance providing a measure whereby one can evaluate one's place in the world. As a result, their place in the story of one's life becomes pivotal.

The importance of the role of food is summed up by Fischler (1988) when he writes, "Food is central to our sense of identity" (p. 275). He explains this claim by arguing that food, unlike other markers of identity, serves to demarcate one's own group from others. It becomes the basis of self-definition and collective identity because it distinguishes those who are familiar, thus trustworthy and safe, from others who may not be so. In some cases, as for example *kosher* food, the rules for the preparation of meals are imbued with spiritual significance as part of the practice of religion (Scholliers, 2001). In such cases, the connections between gender roles in the primary preparation of meals, individual and group identity, and religious practices become multi-layered and reinforce each other (Adler, 1981). On a broader scale, food has a role in the construction of identity at local levels among groups, at regional levels among communities, and at national levels among collectives (Trentmann & Just, 2006).

Food taboos formalize the expression of inclusion and exclusion and ultimately identify those who belong from those who are outsiders (Levi-Strauss, 1970). Food may be such a potent expression of identity because, unlike most other daily activities, it is taken into the body and becomes one with it. It also has the potential, because of its abundant variations, to mirror the complexity of the human relationships that form the foundation of identity. First, we'll examine three ways in which identity is affirmed through the cookbook: recipes as markers of identity, recipes are reminders of relationships, and recipes as connections to community through ritual. Then, we will address the question of how the affirmation of identity can create a rhetoric of resistance.

Recipes as Markers of Identity

In many cultures women have been historically relegated to private spheres of interaction, such as the home, infrequently participating in public arenas. Food and its preparation were among the most concrete markers of the identity of women as wives and mothers in mid-twentieth century Europe. As a result the women of pre-war Europe derived their security and status from the family, often expressed as nurturing values (Baumel, 1999; Hall, 1990). This condition was especially pronounced in the Jewish community where family and family relationships became the primary social structures for defining the role of women, creating for women "the most meaningful relationships," as well as cementing the woman's position and function within the social system (Hall, 1990, p. 182). For these women, cooking was an immense source of personal pride, confirming their importance in the family unit (Farnsworth, 1996). A woman's ability to provide delicious meals for her family was a common source of pride. In addition, the links among family, food, and religion are embedded within the dietary laws of the Old Testament, though perhaps *kosher* practice had lapsed somewhat with the assimilation of Jews into the more dominant German and Czech cultures (Soler, 1997).

Even though the means for preparing meals was unavailable in Terezin camp, it is still likely that women inmates rehearsed their pre-internment roles by fantasizing about the preparation of food. In spite of the fantasy, the preparation of food was a reminder of home and the woman's place in it. As such, the creation of a cookbook was more than a longing for the past, it was an assertion of identity and purpose amid horrific circumstances that denied one's worth at every turn (Burgoyne & Clarke, 1983). As a reminder of their important role in the family, several of the contributors pass judgment on the recipes such as Apple Dumplings served with stewed prunes, about which the contributor adds "It is a good supper" (De Silva, 1996, p. 12). Recipes, such as those for Winter Salad, Fruit Bread, and Rice with Fruits are offered with recommendations for storage to avoid spoilage. As efficient cooks, these contributors understood the practicalities of running a household.

For the women of Terezin, the process of recalling and preserving recipes in desperate circumstances functions to reassure their sense of self and to assist in their struggle to preserve their identity. The sense of pride in their cooking can be gleaned from the recipes, such as the detailed explanation for glazing fruit for which the contributor adds, "If worked in this way, [I] guarantee success" (De Silva, 1996, p. 88). As De Silva (1996) observes, "Food is who we are in the deepest sense, and not because it is transformed into blood and bone. Our personal gastronomic traditions–what we eat, the foods and food ways we associate with the rituals of childhood, marriage, and parenthood, moments around the table, celebrations–are critical components of our identities" (p. xxvi). The range of recipes from the traditional dumplings and goulash to Ice a la Melba and Rye Schnaps, as well as the serving suggestions such as enticing decorations, side dishes, and appropriate temperatures for each dish, suggests the fullness of the identities of the contributors. Their pre-internment circumstances amid the privations of war are also reflected in recipes like the Kriegs Mehlspeise (War Dessert): "7 boiled grated potatoes, 5-6 spoons sugar, 2 spoons flour, 1 spoon cocoa, 2 spoons dry milk, 1 spoon [illegible], 1 knife point [pinch] [illegible]. Bake slowly" (De Silva, 1996, p. 53). This recipe, and others like it, uses limited amounts of scarce ingredients such as sugar and cocoa.

In some ways it is not remarkable that identity took the form of food memories that reflected the individual traditions of women and their families. Schwertfeger (1989) observes that "Food, memories of it, missing it, craving it, dreaming of it, in short, the obsession with food colours all the Theresienstadt memoirs" (p. 38). Especially during periods of extreme physical and emotional stress that were likely prevalent in the camp, the unconscious identification with foods surfaced for the inmates of Terezin (Trentmann & Just, 2006). The recipes in the cookbook hint at some of this fixation with food as, for example, in the suggestion for garnishes that accompany several of the recipes. In Cold Stuffed Eggs Pachter, the contributor advises "Let fantasy run free and the eggs are garnished with ham, [smoked] salmon, caviar, capers. One can put the eggs into paper cuffs and serve them with hot sliced rolls" (De Silva, 1996, p. 52). The inclusion of ham as an ingredient in this recipe reveals the extent of the integration of Czech Jews into mainstream society. In a recipe for Caramels from Baden, the directions include wrapping the caramels in pink paper (De Silva, 1996). The recipes also witness the dementia that accompanied the conditions of extreme deprivation because the contributors omit ingredients, serve dishes before they are cooked, or mix up the steps of their preparation, not things that would likely happen with experienced cooks (Farnsworth, 1996).

Recipes as Reminders of Relationships

It was a common practice to prepare a family cookbook, often handwritten to pass favorite recipes from generation to generation. Across Europe such family cookbooks were a conventional form of literature for women (Brown, 1993; Kaplan, 1990). Most of the women in Terezin were probably acquainted with this tradition. It is likely that they found this form of expression comforting and familiar as a connection to the next generation. It also explains the care that Pachter took in entrusting the manuscript to the safekeeping of another inmate so that her daughter would eventually receive it.

The expression of nurturing values through family and friendship provides the sense of purpose in the lives of women who were raised and formed in a traditional society (Charles & Kerr, 1993). This ethic of care formed the core of women's identity as Hall (1990) explains: "Traditionally nurturing family members is the center of women's morality" (p. 120). The cooked meal was central to this definition of relationships as Murcott (1983) claims, it "symbolizes the home, a husband's relation to it, his wife's place in it and their relationship to one another" (p. 179). But food also allowed the woman to indirectly participate in the public sphere. Outside the home, the meal also serves to encourage connections, constructing positive interrelationships with others. Massey (1992) draws this link: "A large component of the identity of that place called home derived precisely from the fact that it had always in one way or another been open, constructed out of movement, communication, social relations which always stretched beyond it" (p. 44). As the keepers of the hearth, women were continually crossing between private identity and public community as they brought outsiders into the family circle (Sutton, 2008).

Berenbaum (1996) writes that this cookbook "is not to be savored for its culinary offerings but for the insight it gives us in understanding the extraordinary capacity of the human spirit to transcend its surroundings, to defy dehumanization, and to dream of the past and of the future. One can sense a spiritual toughness in the sisterhood forged in these pages" (p. xvi). The bonds of sisterhood add another fragment to understanding how inmates endured deprivation that defies comprehension. The concentration on food and exchange of recipes served to build social alliances and solidarity (Mauss, 1967). As noted, the act of sharing a meal is a way of establishing a physical unity with one's fellow humans, the basis of kinship common in many cultures (Meigs, 1997). Within the walls of the camp, the bonds formed by women living in desperate circumstances served to aid in their survival by mimicking the family units that had previously sustained them. They derived social support and psychological strength by enacting their traditional roles as nurturers. Citing a similar bonding phenomenon documented among Jewish men, Baumel (1999) argues that Jewish women's bonding during the Holocaust "appears…to have been a continuation of similar bonding which was an integral part of Jewish cultural life" (p. 336). The sharing of recipes was an extension of the ethic of care that was central to their lives and identities as Jews and women.

While it might seem incongruous for those who are starving to write recipes, this is a rather common behavior (Shack, 1997). Bondy (1998) writes that "former housewives would 'cook' for hours, telling each other how they use to prepare mushroom sauce with cream or debating the preferred number of eggs for dumplings" (p. 316). Bianca Steiner Brown, a survivor of Terezin, remembers overhearing two women arguing about whether the Viennese or the Czechs baked better cakes (Nathan, 1996). This competition (Pachter called it platonic cooking in a poem) undoubtedly acted as a psychological survival strategy as women asserted their identities through demonstrating their expertise and rejecting Nazi attempts to colonize their spirits (Baumel, 1999; Farnsworth, 1996; Jacobs, 2006).

This cookbook is not alone as a testament to human defiance. A number of recipe books survive from similar horrific situations. At least five other extant cookbooks were created in the conditions of Nazi concentration camp existence. Sabrina Margulies claims that "If we had had paper at Auschwitz we would have written recipes down there, too. And if we had been able to write them down we would have had a cookbook of thousands of pages" (as cited in De Silva, 1996, p. xxix). Similar efforts to record recipes were experienced by male prisoners of war in the Philippines and this phenomenon is also mentioned in other prisoner of war diaries (Beltrone & Beltrone, 1994; Fowler, 1946). Differences exist however; women, probably because of their gender roles, talked about the preparation and serving of food while men discussed the food they would consume after their liberation. In both cases, the uncertainty of the food supply made it the central topic of conversation. Other circumstances of food shortages such as crop failures, population displacement, and even anorexia have led to similar obsessive conversation about food (Shack, 1997).

Recipes as Connections to Community through Ritual

Food consumption rituals are key mechanisms for producing and reproducing ethnic identity (Ashley, Hollows, Jones, & Taylor, 2004; Morley, 1991).

Especially when the ethnic community is isolated or dispersed, these rituals form a link that reminds participants of their common bond:

> Diasporic communities may experience a sense of connection to a wider community through the simultaneous consumption of meals tied to a religious calendar–for example, the Jewish *Seder* brings together a dispersed community through food rituals. Not just the ingredients, but the ceremonial presentation of the food acquires meaning through ritual. (Ashley, et al., 2004, p. 27)

Food functions as ritual in two ways: It performs identity in the act of cooking and it becomes the physical manifestation of familial and community connections in the act of consumption. The woman who prepares the meal thus participates in the construction of her identity first as the cook, then as a member of the celebration of community. It is not surprising, as a result, to find recipes in this cookbook that are specialties for celebrations, for example, goose neck stuffed with farina, groom's cake, linzer torte, and rose hip dessert. Garnishes like fancy cups and pink paper wrapping are additional evidence of the celebratory nature of the recipes. Among the several letters that survived with the cookbook manuscript, Pachter repeatedly refers to her fervent hope of seeing her daughter and grandson again. She inquires after their health and seems especially anxious that they do not get too thin. In one undated letter, she writes "My life right now is not easy but I suffer everything willingly in the hope of seeing you again" (De Silva, 1996, p. 100). Her connections to her family are further evidenced by pleas in other letters that they not forget her.

In Terezin, food prepared in special, albeit limited ways, continued to mark special occasions for inmates. Diarists record birthday cakes, weed salads, and other delicacies featured in special meals (Auerbacher, 1993; Troller, 1991). This use of food reenacts the role of food and memory in Jewish ritual just as the eating of matzah and bitter herbs recreates Judiasm through collective remembrance. As Joseph (1998) describes the symbolic connection:

> In that moment of personalizing history, of making it my own story, it becomes the source of a profound pledge to respond and be responsible.... Memory is called upon to actually shatter historical time, to make present the past, and to make available a mode of experience that...revitalizes a communal heritage. (p. 178)

At this level of identity, the individual is subsumed in the community through historical enactment marked with food rituals. By awakening the past, she can endure the present and hope for a better future. If the individual perishes, the community will endure, preserving the heritage in which she partakes, literally through eating and symbolically in spiritual communion with community.

This cookbook and others like it that survive from the concentration camps can be seen as manifestation of defiance, of spiritual revolt against the harshness of reality. At one level, the contributor to the cookbook enacts "secret resistance to authority and the momentary sense of freedom it provided through bodily ingestion of forbidden substances" (Sutton, 2008, p. 177). While the ingestion of the forbidden is fantasy rather than reality, the act of resistance is nonetheless genuine. The individual can stand against those who exercise the power of life and death by evoking the past in which their identity, both individual and collective, was intact. As a community, Jewish history teaches that life goes on, that even the worst of persecutions will end and the community will survive. To hold on or outlast the enemy, *uberstehen* was a fundamental tenet for many European Jews. It explains their appropriation of food as a symbol of the oppressor in an effort to exert defiance and define themselves in the face of oppression (Brown, 1993).

Another feature of Bohemia was that Jews were culturally well assimilated from the time of Hapsburg Emperor Joseph the Second in 1780 (Berghoff, 2001; Brenner, 1996; Rothkirchen, 2005). This often meant that Jewish identity, while not always practiced in separation from the German and Czech communities, was still maintained through traditions which most often revolved around foods and celebrations (Wechsberg, 1968). Food traditions, even though they were not *kosher*, still functioned to reinforce identity of individual and community by maintaining their traditions. As a result, the surviving manuscript is not just a cookbook, but a memorial—a testament to life—to a life these women have once lived.

Discussion

In some ways the history of the document's survival parallels the lives of the women who wrote it. It was composed in secret, randomly guarded, and almost miraculously preserved by being passed hand to hand. Like the recipes that are intended to bind members of families and communities, this cookbook bound together individuals and generations. It preserves the voices of victims.

So how is a cookbook also a rhetorical document that allows women to resist the conditions of Terezin? As suggested, the cookbook functions to assert personal existence by marking identity; recipes are also reminders of relationships, and they connect individuals to their communities through ritual. While identity formation is a never-ending process of construction, this process is accelerated during periods of extreme crisis when one faces ultimate annihilation (Hall, 1996; Scholliers, 2001). Food rituals are a connection to normalcy. In this case, primary identity is challenged; and that primary identity is often linked to the most stable structure(s) in the life of the individual—usually the family (Scholliers, 2001). To resist the attack requires the reassertion of oneself as an individual. In this way, remembering the daily routines such as cooking that defined one's self in a former life becomes more than nostalgia for the past; rather, it has the function of declaring selfhood in the face of annihilation. Thus, food becomes a key site of memory and identity or, as Sutton (2008) argues, it "is a key mediator of social relationships, a symbol of identity and a marker of difference" (p. 159). And, through food, women symbolically empower themselves as political actors (West, 2007).

Discourses of domination have been well documented through attention to important historical figures and movements that espouse victorious causes, however temporary the victory (Brown, 1993). Such discourses of domination spawn rhetorics of resistance, which thrive by "inverting the master categories and reclassifying them into more embracing conceptions of the human" (Brown, 1993, p. 657). Such rhetoric of resistance asserts humanity in the face of dehumanizing forces. By reacting to the other's attempts to define one's behaviors or attitudes, one can resist through psychological reactance. When that reaction is expressed symbolically, as in recipes, the reactance is rhetorical (Brehm, 1966; Brehm & Brehm, 1981).

As part of the process of identification of "us," there must necessarily be a "them." The assertion that traditions are associated with a community implies that others do not share in the same traditions. In the face of the assimilation of the Jews of Moravia and Bohemia in the mainstream culture, such assertions of separation prior to the rise of Nazi domination are unusual. Following the implementation of Nazi anti-Semitic policies, a gradual but steady shift from a public to a private, family life occurred, probably evidence of the extent of the stress on a community that is ejected from the German/Czech culture that it had adopted (Baumel, 1999). In terms of re-identity formation, the stress of difference is fundamental. Schlesinger (1987) expresses this concept:

> Identity is as much about exclusion as it is about inclusion and the critical factor for defining the ethnic group therefore becomes the social boundary which defines the group with respect to other groups . . . not the cultural reality within those borders. (p. 235)

Schlesinger continues by recognizing that "food is clearly instrumental in the identification of 'other' nations" (p. 235). The function of food as a code—not unlike the structures of language—allows for the binary opposition among people. As Douglas (1997) claims about the subtext of meals, "The message is about different degrees of hierarchy, inclusion and exclusion boundaries and transactions across the boundaries…the taking of food has a social component, as well as a biological one" (p. 36). The processes of preparing and serving food are rich with encoded symbolism (Barthes, 1997).

Because food unifies individuals and their communities against "the other," food also functions as points of fracture or "epochal transformations" that stimulate memory of the past in recognition of the changed present (Sutton, 2008, p. 160). Intrinsically bound up in the recognition of epochal transformation is the understanding that the present builds future memories. Thus, a cookbook functions as the concrete link among memories of the past, the present performance of the past, and the inevitable future. In other words, as a gift from one generation to the next, a cookbook affirms continuity among past, present, and future. When Anny Stern first received the cookbook after its circuitous journey, she did not open it. She said, "I put it away and only much later did I have the courage to look. . . It was something holy. After all these years, it was like her hand was reaching out to me from long ago" (as cited in De Silva, 1996). Instinctively, Stern recognized the transformative nature of the cookbook.

By the time the cookbook reached Stern, there was no doubt that the recipes were not primarily intended as recipes for the preparation of food but as something that had transcended that purpose. As Sutton (2008) discusses the use of special cooking utensils in the preparation of celebratory meals, he recognizes this transcendence: "Another aspect of food memories is the way that the objects associated with cooking become a kind of 'inalienable possession' that is removed from circulation because it represents family or community identity" (p. 166). Thus, the Terezin cookbook is no longer primarily a cookbook, but instead, a cherished heirloom for family members and a historical document for others. The object has acquired a community memory that transcends the original identity formation of its authors but nevertheless retains the values of the community. The memories telescope idealized aspects of the past as they are recalled in the present (Weiner, 1992). Or, put differently, memories of identities are embedded in the shared discourse of the cookbook.

This memorial function associated especially with the preparation of food is elaborated by Atkinson (1983) when he writes that

> food, and the activities of cooking and eating, furnish concrete realizations for the expression of implicit "messages." Food, drinking and associations provide "codes" that is, terms for the working out of "myth-logic," in which cultural oppositions, puzzles and paradoxes may be expressed, and may achieve a symbolic resolution. (p. 10)

What are these paradoxes that must be expressed? Among them is the nature of their existence as individuals confronted with the fragility of life and the precarious relationships that infused their lives with meaning. In the context of the concentration camp, food was equated with human worth, the elderly and disabled receiving less of it because they were deemed worthless and close to death. The absence of food was aligned with the absence of human value, so to regain a sense of humanity, one must fill the absence, even if it is fantasized, with what formerly gave meaning: food. Pachter's awareness of her own mortality and insistence on making the gift of the cookbook to her daughter also concretizes the link to future generations through communal sharing of recipes. Thus, cooking is a vital memory that perpetuates the pre-war tradition of women's identity within the construct of the family and community.

The implicit recognition of mortality in the act of bequeathing the cookbook as a gift to Pachter's daughter is inherent in the process of commemoration. The sacrifice that was necessary for Pachter to preserve her identity and thus heritage for her daughter functions to invest the cookbook with the traits of a memorial. Such sacrifice was made necessary for the survival of the community, symbolized by the cookbook itself. Through future generations, Pachter's sacrifice (and the deaths of the other anonymous contributors) is invested with meaning. As Barthel (1996) summarizes the purpose of sacrifice in the collective construction of historical memory, "It is an unwritten pact between the dead, the living, and the unborn, and it is enacted through social rituals—the acts of commemoration" (p. 80). Like an obelisk or monument to fallen heroes that reminds present viewers of past acts of courage, the cookbook functions to unite individuals, both dead and alive, across temporal divisions in the spiritual concept of communal identity.

Conclusion

Food offered the women of Terezin comfort from the past and hope for the future in the midst of starvation and despair. For them, sharing and recording recipes offered multiple levels of identity that wove together aspects of their private and public lives. As Stanley (1993) argues about the experiences of these women, "Oppression and its struggles should be neither denied nor silenced, nor explained away as momentary" (p. 29). The survival of their spirit through the form that recognizes their core identity adds to our understanding of the patterns of survival utilized in extreme circumstances of the Holocaust. It contributes to the scholarship that has begun to render Jewish women visible, illuminating their experiences and illustrating the richness of their voices that remain in spite of the cataclysm of World War II (Baumel, 1999). This cookbook establishes a largely ignored genre of Holocaust literature, a memoir that is a compilation of traditional dishes created from the fantasies of starving women who were remembering a time when they had families to feed and communities in which to feast and celebrate.

Mina Pachter and the other anonymous women of Terezin who composed the cookbook were victimized by a system that asserted a set of social values that required their deaths and the extinction of their communities. The cookbook serves as a reminder that those social values were contested—not on the battlefield for those women but, nevertheless, in a series of actions no less heroic, as they sought to escape symbolic annihilation by asserting their identity as members of a community. Even though the women did not survive the violence of Terezin, their individual identities and collective memories are anchored in the manuscript that preserves the continuity of humanity for generations to come. The recipes that survived the starvation/cookbook of Terezin hold the past in trust for the future.

In the past and, undoubtedly, in the future, the voices of all people who are oppressed have taken rhetorical forms that exist outside the accepted patterns of expression. It behooves us to examine them with the same sincerity that we accord more mainstream forms, especially when proclamations of identity in the face of the denial of one's humanity become acts of resistance. Like the cookbook that survived Terezin, there are other nontraditional historical texts that capture the spirit of resistance: the spirituals sung by African American slaves, the Black Power salute at the 1980 Olympics in Germany, the American Indian Movement standoff at Wounded Knee, the reclamation of native languages extinguished by the relentless forces of cultural genocide, and even graffiti recorded on the walls of subways. All invite scholarly attention as individuals assert their identity in the face of invisibility.

References

Adler, T. A. (1981). Making pancakes on Sunday; The male cook in family tradition. *Western Folklore, 40,* 45–54.

Alanen, L. (1990). Rethinking socialisation, the family and childhood. *Sociological Studies of Child Development, 3.*

Ashley, B, Hollows, J., Jones, S., & Taylor, B. (2004). *Food and Cultural Studies.* New York: Routledge.

Atkinson, P. (1983). Eating virtue. In Anne Murcott (Ed.), *The sociology of food and eating: Essays on the sociological significance of food* (pp. 9–17). Hants, UK: Gower Publishing Company Limited.

Auerbacher, I. (1993). *I am a star, child of the Holocaust.* New York: Puffin Books.

Bannen, J., Dodd, K., Oakley, A. & Storey, P. (1994). *Young people, health and family life.* Philadelphia: Open University Press.

Barthel, D. (1996*). Historic_preservation: Collective memory and historical identity.* New Brunswick, NJ: Rutgers University Press.

Barthes, R. (1967). *Elements of semiology.* Trans. Annette Lavers & Colin Smith. London: Cape.

Barthes, R. (1997). Toward a psychosociology of contemporary food consumption. In C. Counihan & P. Van Esterik (Eds.), *Food and Culture* (pp. 20–28). New York: Routledge.

Baumel, J. T. (1999). Women's agency and survival strategies during the Holocaust. *Women's Studies International Forum, 22*, 329–347.

Beltrone, A. & Beltrone, L. (1994*). A wartime log.* Charlottesville, SC: Howell.

Berenbaum, M. (1996). Foreward. In C. De Silva, (Ed.), *In memory's kitchen: A legacy from the women of Terezin* (pp. ix–xvi). Northvale, NJ: Jason Aronson Inc.

Berghoff, H. (2001). Enticement and deprivation: The regulation of consumption in pre-war Nazi Germany. In M. Dauton & M. Hilton (Eds.), *The politics of consumption: Material culture and citizenship in Europe and America* (pp. 165–184). New York: Berg.

Bondy, R. (1998). Women in Theresienstadt and the family camp in Birkenau. In D. Ofer & L. J. Weitzman (Eds.), *Women in the Holocaust* (pp. 310–326). New Haven: Yale University Press.

Brehm, S. S. & Brehm, J. W. (1981). *Psychological reactance: A theory of freedom and control.* New York: Academic Press.

Brehm, J. W. (1966). *A theory of psychological reactance.* New York: Academic Press.

Brenner, M. (1996). *The renaissance of Jewish culture in Weimar Germany.* New Haven: Yale University Press.

Brown, R. H. (1993). Cultural representation and ideological domination. *Social Forces, 71,* 657–676.

Burgoyne, J. & Clarke, D. (1983). You are what you eat: Food and family reconstitution. In Anne Murcott (Ed.), *The sociology of food and eating: Essays on the sociological significance of food* (pp. 152–163). Hants, UK: Gower Publishing Company Limited.

Charles, N. & Kerr, M. (1993). Women, food and families. In S. Jackson, et al. (Eds.), *Women's studies* (pp. 188–198). New York: New York University Press.

De Silva, C. (1996*). In memory's kitchen: A legacy from the women of Terezin.* Northvale, NJ: Jason Aronson Inc.

De Vault, D. (1991). *Feeding the family.* Chicago: University of Chicago Press.

Douglas, M. (1972). Structures of gastronomy. *In The future and the past,* Annual Report. New York: Russell Sage Foundation.

Douglas, M. (1984). Standard social uses of food. In M. Douglas (Ed.), *Food in the social order*, (pp. 1–49). New York: Russell Sage Foundation.

Douglas, M. (1997). Deciphering a meal. In C. Counihan & P. Van Esterik (Eds.), *Food and Culture* (pp. 36–54). New York: Routledge.

Farnsworth, E. (1996, December 17). Online newshour: A cookbook from the Holocaust. Transcript available at http://www.pbs.org/newshour/bb/Europe/december96/cook_12–17.html. Retrieved on May 13, 2009.

Fischler, C. (1988). Food, self, and identity. *Social Science Information*, pp. 275–292.

Fowler, C. H. (1946). *Recipes out of Bilibid.* New York: George W. Stewart.

Green, G. (1978). *The artists of Terezin.* New York: Hawthorn Books.

Hall, C. M. (1990). *Women and identity: Values choices in a changing world.* New York: Hemisphere Publishing.

Hall, S. (1996). Introduction: Who needs "identity"? In S. Hall & P. Du Gay (Eds.), *Questions of cultural identity* (pp. 1–17). London: Sage.

Jacobs, J. (2006). The female body as atrocity text: The feminization of the Holocaust at Auschwitz. *English Language Notes, 44*, 243–251.

Jones, M. O. (2007). Food choice, symbolism, and identity: Bread-and-butter issues for folkloristics and nutrition studies. *Journal of American Folklore, 120*, 129–177.

Joseph, N. B. (1998). Zakhor: Memory, ritual, and gender. In Sarah S. Swartz & Margie Wolfe (Eds.), *From memory to transformation: Jewish women's voices* (pp. 177–187). Toronto: Second Story Press.

Kaplan, M. A. (1990). Jewish women in Nazi Germany. *Feminist Studies, 16*, 579–606.

Khare, R. S. & Rao, M. S. A. (1986). *Food, society, and culture: Aspects in South Asian food systems.* Durham, NC: Carolina Academic Press.

Lederer, Z. (1983). *Ghetto Theresienstadt.* New York: Howard Fertig.

Lehrer, A. (1969). Semantic cuisine. *Journal of Linguistics, 3.*

Levi-Strauss, C. (1970). *The raw and the cooked.* London: Cape.

Levi-Strauss, C. (1966, December). The culinary triangle. *New Society, 22*, 166.

Lupton, D. (1994). Food, memory and meaning: The symbolic and social nature of food events. *The Sociological Review, 42*, 664–687.

Massey, D. (1992). A place called home? *New Formations, 3,* 41-57.

Mauss, M. (1967). *The gift.* New York: Norton.

Meigs, A. (1997). Food as a cultural construction. In C. Counihan & P. Van Esterik (Eds.), *Food and Culture* (pp. 95–106). New York: Routledge.

Miller, D. (1987). *Material culture and mass consumption.* Oxford: Blackwell.

Morgan, D. (1996). *Family connections.* Oxford: Blackwell.

Morley, D. (1991). Where the global meets the local: Notes from the sitting room. *Screen, 32*, 1–5.

Murcott, A. (1983). Cooking and the cooked: A note on the domestic preparation of meals. In Anne Murcott (Ed.), *The sociology of food and eating: Essays on the sociological significance of food* (pp. 178–185). Hants, UK: Gower Publishing Company Limited.

Nathan, J. (1996, September 11). At Rosh ha-Shanah, poignant memories of holidays past. Retrieved on May 13, 2009 from http: // www.nytimes.com /1996/09/11/garden/at-rosh-ha-shanah-poigna.

Padolsky, E. (2005). You are where you eat: Ethnicity, food and cross-cultural spaces. *Canadian Ethnic Studies, 37*, 19–31.

Poe, T. N. (2001). The labor and leisure of food production as a mode of ethnic identity building among Italians in Chicago, 1890–1940. *Rethinking History, 5*, 131–148.

Rothkirchen, L. (2005). *The Jews of Bohemia and Moravia.* Lincoln: University of Nebraska Press.

Schlesinger, P. (1987). On national identity. *Social Science Information, 26*, 219-264.

Scholliers, P. (2001). Meals, food narratives, and sentiments of belonging in past and present. In Peter Scholliers (Ed.), *Food, drink and identity: Cooking, eating and drinking in Europe since the Middle Ages* (pp. 3–22). New York: Berg.

Schwertfeger, R. (1989). *Women of Theresienstadt, voices from a concentration camp.* New York: Berg.

Shack, W. A. (1997). Hunger, anxiety, and ritual. In C. Counihan & P. Van Esterik (Eds.), *Food and Culture* (pp. 125–137). New York: Routledge.

Sibley, D. & Lowe, G. (1992). Domestic space, modes of control and problem behaviour. *Geografiska Annala B, 3*, 189–198.

Soler, J. (1997). The semiotics of food in the Bible. In C. Counihan & P. Van Esterik (Eds.*), Food and Culture* (pp. 55–66). New York: Routledge.

Somers, M. (1994). The narrative constitution of identity: A relational and network approach. *Theory and Society, 23*, 605–649.

Stanley, L. (1993). Recovering 'women' in history from historical deconstructionism. In S. Jackson, et al. (Eds.), *Women's Studies* (pp. 29–34). New York: New York University Press.

Sutton, D. (2008). A tale of Easter ovens: Food and collective memory. *Social Research, 75*, 157–180.

Tomlinson, A. (1990). *Consumption, identity and style.* London: Routledge.

Trentmann, F. & Just, F. (2006). Introduction. In F. Trentmann & F. Just (Eds.), *Food and conflict in Europe in the age of the two World Wars* (pp. 1–17). Basingstoke: Palgrave Macmillan.

Troller, N. (1991). *Theresienstadt, Hitler's gift to the Jews.* Chapel Hill: University of North Carolina Press.

Valentine, F. (1999). Eating in: Home, consumption and identity._*The Sociological Review, 47*, 491–524.

Waksler, F. (1986). Studying children: Phenomenological insight. *Human Studies, 8*, 71–82.

Wechsberg, J. (1968). *The cooking of Vienna's empire.* New York: Time-Life.

Weiner, A. (1992). *Inalienable possessions: The paradox of keeping-while-giving.* Berkeley: University of California Press.

West, I. (2007). Performing resistance in/from the kitchen: The practice of maternal pacifist politics and La WISP's cookbooks. *Women's Studies in Communication, 30*, 358–383.

Young, M. & Wilmott, P. (1973) *The symmetrical family.* Harmondsworth: Penguin.

9

Looking at men's tables: Food and masculinities in blockbuster movies

Fabio Parasecoli

As the chapters in this section highlight, the social, economic, and political relevance of food cannot be ignored, as its increasing presence in media seems to point out. Ingestion and incorporation constitute a paramount component of our connections with reality and the world outside our bodies. Food is pervasive and finds itself at the center of frequent and significant social interactions that influence various aspects of subject identity, including gender, functioning as a relevant marker of power, cultural capital, class status, ethnicity, race, and religion (Inness, 2001a and 2001b; Williams-Forson, 2006; LeBesco & Naccarato, 2008; Parasecoli, 2008). These aspects cannot but become evident in many forms of communication that have food as their main focus.

In the past few decades, food has come to the forefront in cinema, to the point of prompting discussions among critics, scholars, and moviegoers about the possible emergence of a "food film" genre. Since the 1980s, women have been especially prominent in movies where food appears conspicuously, such as the classics *Babette's Feast* (1987) and *Like Water for Chocolate* (1992), the crowd pleasers *Chocolat* (2000) and *No Reservations* (2007), and the recent big hit *Julie and Julia* (2009). However, even in these movies, men are always lurking around, ready to steal the scene and make it theirs, as husbands, lovers, or simply as consumers. And recently, the list of movies where men provide food, work in the kitchen, eat, cook, learn how to cook, or gorge themselves, is growing: among the most popular, we can mention *Big Night* (1996), *The Cook, the Thief, His Wife, and Her Lover* (1989), *Eat Drink Man Woman* (1994), *Vatel* (2000) and *Dinner Rush* (2000). Men prepare food in comedies (*Spanglish*, 2004), gangster movies (*Goodfellas*, 1990), and romantic dramas (*Mostly Martha*, 2001). They eat alone and with other men before a killing spree (*The Godfather*, 1972) and after multiple murders (*Pulp Fiction*, 1994). In countless movies, adult and young men share the family table, destroy it, make it into a battlefield, or impose their rule over it.

It would seem that cinematic representations of men's interactions around food tend to become almost as frequent as women's portrayals in film. Is this just a consequence of the renewed—or sometimes brand new—interest in food in all media, reflected for instance in the success of television star chefs—incidentally, mostly male (Adema, 2000; Hansen Rousseau, 2007; Ray, 2007; Swenson, 2009)? Or does it rather constitute an indication of a wider, deep-reaching reflection in popular culture about what makes a man a man? After all, there have been – and there still are – many debates about the crisis of traditional masculinities, from daytime talk shows and self-help books, to activist gatherings and scholarly publications (Bliss, 1987; Moore & Gillette, 1990; Farrell, 1993; MacInnes, 1998; Faludi, 1999; Clare, 2000; Simpson, 2002; Robinson & Spivey, 2007).

Despite the traditional prevalence of men in high-end restaurant cuisines, where cooking is considered as a respectable profession and as a creative endeavor, and the appeal of masculine chefs in TV shows, magazines, and books, daily food procurement and preparation, especially in a domestic setting, are still often perceived as a feminine task, and an inherently emasculating one – arguably with the exception of the occasional outdoors grilling or weekend breakfast (Adler, 1981; DeVault, 1991; Shapiro, 2001 and 2004; Avakian & Haber, 2005). The purpose of this chapter is precisely to examine how representations of men around food in a specific medium – film – can establish, question, reinforce, reproduce or destroy cultural assumptions about masculinity and gender relations. Food-related interactions will be highlighted and analyzed also when they are almost invisible, hidden in plots that exalt and highlight traits of manhood that are far from domesticity and daily life.

Food has become the object of popular concern and of a wide and ever-growing corpus of scholarly research: from marketing to history, from nutrition to anthropology, and more recently in the upcoming discipline of food studies (Ashley, Hollows, Jones & Taylor, 2004; Belasco, 2008; Counihan & Van Esterik, 2008). Yet, many layers of meaning related to food in its connection with masculinity are often left unexplored, although common and mundane objects, attitudes, and practices that revolve around eating play an important role in men's personal development and social interactions. Only recently the relationship between men and food has become the object of scholarly reflection within food studies; despite the interest of the work produced, I believe we have just started scratching the surface (Hollows, 2002; Deutsch, 2003; Bentley, 2005; Parasecoli, 2005; Julier & Lindenfeld, 2005; Roth, 2005; Wilk, 2006; Sellaeg & Chapman, 2008; Buerkle, 2009). This is also the case for film studies, where scholars, although often interested in the role of movies in defining culturally sanctioned gender models and body images, have rarely focused on food as a crucial component of men's identities (Lindenfeld, 2003). Nonetheless, by describing, motivating, and at times defining characters that interact with it, I argue that food on film has the ability to convey messages that would otherwise be lost through speech. Looking at cinema can then help us throw a different light on the connection between food and masculinity.

Eating is a realm of personal and social experience that is usually considered a mere expression of "natural" instincts and mundane needs and, precisely for this reason, is not deemed as politically and culturally sensitive. However, food's neutral and often uncontested character can reveal aspects of cultural and social dynamics that are better concealed in other contexts. In movies, at times, very revealing material is found where we would not necessarily look for it, arguably because scriptwriters, filmmakers, and actors feel freer about performing traits of masculinity that under other circumstances would be erased and made invisible. When the spotlight is not on them, male characters in movies may reveal a lot about themselves while engaged in production, acquisition, and consumption of food, which has the potential to be used to uncover social and power relations that would otherwise not be noticeable. In other words, food-related scenes may provide an apparently neutral and natural space for representations of masculinity to be conveyed. It is possible that precisely for these reasons these scenes tend to be overlooked by viewers, despite their frequency.

Eating Masculinities

In my analysis of the relations between men and food in movies, I have built on the argument, deriving from gender, queer theory, and more specifically masculinities studies, that masculinities are socially and historically constructed, plural, and in constant transformation and, as a consequence, the cultural assumption of a univocal and stable masculinity is an ideological formation (Brod & Kaufmann, 1994; Kimmel 1996; Kimmel, Hearn & Connell, 2005; Whitehead, 2006; Flood, Gardiner, Pease, & Pringle, 2007). In this approach, manhood no longer constitutes a mystical, immutable, and monolithic quality that all males acquire at a certain point in their life, holding on to it as an instrument to affirm their individuality and their role in the world. Most scholars working on gender issues now agree that masculinities, historically and culturally determined, can be analyzed in their formation, development, transformation and, sometimes, demise. At any given time, it is possible to identify a limited set of masculinities that, through different forms of social interactions and ideological dynamics, assume a hegemonic position, in the sense that they are considered as respectable, prestigious, and desirable within the cultures and societies in which they exist (Connell, 1995 and 2000; Connell & Messerschmidt, 2005). These prevalent ideals of manhood, expressed in codified images, practices, and behaviors floating in the increasingly globalized social field of imaginary production, tend to overshadow alternative models that can either disappear or resurface under different forms in various cultural contexts.

To explore the communication potential of food-related images and representations and their impact on cultural constructions of masculinity, I have focused on movies that are usually referred to as "blockbusters," which boast record box office sales all over the world and clearly do not focus on food as their main themes. In them, men are heroes and often superheroes, busy conquering the objects of their affection, saving the world, and even battling the forces of evil, with mixed results.

By looking at food-related representations of men in blockbusters, I aim to identify common elements and themes that are likely to have acquired worldwide visibility, and that as a consequence might arguably play some role in the way masculinities are perceived, constructed, and embodied in the global exchanges and fluxes of communication, media material, visual elements, concepts, values, and practices that constitute contemporary pop culture. Anthropologist Ajun Appadurai noticed in *Modernity at Large* how imagination and fantasy have become a fundamental social practice, playing an important role in shaping everyday life for many people all over the world and interacting with other sphere of cultural, social, and political life (Appadurai, 1996).

Following this line of reasoning, I argue that mass media, and in particular US-made blockbuster movies, offer to many individuals and communities throughout the world new filters through which they can perceive and represent their daily lives. Movies and other forms of visual media are particularly relevant because they provide both visual and aural elements and narrative components (almost like floating pieces of plots, characters, and dialogue) that can be borrowed by individuals, subcultures, and whole communities to make sense of the everyday experience. As a consequence, new narratives, changing identities, and possible practices reflected, created, and made visible by mass media become part of a shared global patrimony that participates in the constitution of contemporary subjectivities. However, it is methodologically imperative to maintain a distinction between the images projected by pop culture, media and commercial entities, in our case mainly based in the USA, and the realities of the everyday lives of men in all walks of life within the USA and in other parts of the world (Hall, 2005: 9). Although the two dimensions are certainly linked, and exert a reciprocal influence, it is important not to take those connections for granted, but rather to examine them in their historical, social, and psychological aspects, analyzing their development and assessing their effects, including unexpected or even aberrant readings (Stam & Spence, 1983, p. 19). Film representations are not mere reflections of reality. Nonetheless, they can play an ideological role in reinforcing power structures and cultural assumptions even when they appear to be critical of the present reality. Under other circumstances, they can constitute subtle provocations and real attacks against social status quo as viewers know it and perceive it.

In this context, food can provide what can be perceived as a universal experience: men all over the world need to get food, prepare it, consume it, maybe share it, and dispose of the leftovers. The dishes and the ingredients might change, the specifics of customs and habits might also differ, the abundance of food or the lack thereof might be apparent, but the whole of humankind shares the fundamental experience of the biological need to eat. The physical necessity of ensuring sufficient nourishment to one's body assumes a cultural dimension that in its naturalness and normality seems to provide stable meanings and social practices. Within this framework, food, its production and its consumption can offer a privileged point of view to look the way various models of masculinity are created, negotiated, questioned and, sometimes, eliminated in the global network of mass media.

Exploring Blockbusters

To examine food-related representations of men in blockbusters, I have further restricted my sample to movies that between 1990 and 2007 have grossed more than 250 million dollars outside of the USA, which happens to be the country of origin for all of them. On July 8, 2008, I accessed the all-time non-USA box office list of movies on the Internet Movie Database. With the exclusion of feature length cartoons, which are a very identifiable kind of movie with their own internal rules that address a specific audience, I ended up with a sample of

58 movies, which I have examined quantitatively and qualitatively by applying content analysis methods.

The films examined are *Titanic* (1997), the movie with the largest box office revenue ever; trilogies such as *The Lord of the Rings* (2001, 2002, 2003), *Spider-Man* (2002, 2004, 2007), *Pirates of the Caribbean* (2003, 2006, 2007), *The Matrix* (1999, 2003, 2003), *Mission Impossible* (1996, 2000, 2006), and the *Star Wars* prequels (1999, 2002, 2005); the *Harry Potter* series (2001, 2002, 2004, 2005, 2007); movies in the James Bond franchise such as *Die Another Day* (2002) and the remake of *Casino Royale* (2006); *Jurassic Park* (1993) and *The Lost World: Jurassic Park* (1997); *Terminator 2: Judgment Day* (1991) and *Terminator 3: Rise of the Machines* (2003); and in order of year of release: *Ghost* (1990), *Pretty Woman* (1990), *The Bodyguard* (1992), *Forrest Gump* (1994), *Die Hard: With a Vengeance* (1995), *Se7en* (1995), *Independence Day* (1996), *Twister* (1996), *Men in Black* (1997), *Armageddon* (1998), *Saving Private Ryan* (1998), *The Sixth Sense* (1999), *The Mummy* (1999), *Gladiator* (2000), *Ocean's Eleven* (2001), *Pearl Harbor* (2001), *The Last Samurai* (2003), *Troy* (2004), *The Day After Tomorrow* (2004), *The Chronicles of Narnia: The Lion, the Witch and the Wardrobe* (2005), *War of the Worlds* (2005), *King Kong* (2005), *Charlie and the Chocolate Factory* (2005), *The Da Vinci Code* (2006), *Night at the Museum* (2006), *Transformers* (2007), *I Am Legend* (2007), and *The Golden Compass* (2007).

The sample constitutes a homogeneous cluster in that, from the chronological point of view, the movies were all produced and distributed in less than 20 years. I explored Hollywood blockbuster cinema as one single "text", whose analysis as such is also justified by the shared cultural background and the political environment in which the movies are conceived, the common social and economic structures of production, distribution, and consumption, and also the widespread awareness and expectations in audiences in terms of actors, directors, plots, editing, development, visual style, production value, etc. Moreover, in terms of long-term transformations and continuity of a cultural concept such as masculinity, it is reasonable to assume that the limited lapse of time between 1990 and 2007 does not present major fractures. The debates in film studies literature (Jeffords, 1989; Cohan & Hark, 1993; Bingham, 1994; Holmlund, 2001; Chopra-Gant, 2005; Baker, 2006; Gauntlett, 2002; Benshoff & Griffin, 2004) suggest that noticeable changes in Hollywood representations of masculinity took place in the 1970s and the1980s, partly as a consequence of the Vietnam war and the following social unrest; however, since then it would appear that the movie industry has been cautious in defying well-established models of manhood, which at any rate are more diverse and complex than in the past, reflecting changes in social perceptions of men and their roles (Clum, 2002; Pfeil, 2002).

By 1990 VCRs were common enough, and rental companies such as Blockbuster established that movies could reach wider and wider sections of potential audiences all over the world. Nowadays, it is easy to have access to 20 year-old movies, especially blockbusters, which circulate in many copies. On the other hand, due to technological innovations like computers, DVDs, DVRs, and iPods, we can safely presume that the newer movies in the sample are likely to have achieved levels of popularity and spectatorship that make them equivalent to the older movies in terms of their impact on viewers and their cultural environments. Moreover, many of the stories and characters represented in the movies I examined were already familiar to large sections of the audiences. For instance, the tragedies of the *Titanic* and Pearl Harbor are events that boast worldwide notoriety. Some movies are adaptations of very famous comic-book series (*Spider-Man*), literary sagas (*The Lord of the Rings* and *Harry Potter*), TV shows (*Mission Impossible*, *Transformers*), or novels (*I Am Legend*, *The Da Vinci Code*). A few are remakes of classics such as *King Kong*, *Willy Wonka*, the *War of the Worlds*, and *Casino Royale*. Others are based on original scripts but, like *Star Wars* or the *Matrix*, have reached cult status in pop culture. Whatever their origin, many characters have become extremely popular all over the world and have appeared in other media.

In order to examine the sample, I have chosen to use content analysis, which I believe could offer solutions to bridge gaps between the humanities and the social sciences, relying on both quantitative and qualitative methodologies. In the *International Encyclopedia of the Social and Behavioral Sciences*, Roberts (2002) points out the quantitative aspects of this methodology explaining:

> Content analysis is a class of techniques for mapping symbolic data into a data matrix suitable for statistical analysis. When the term is used, one refers to the content analysis of cultural artifacts (e.g., books, architectural styles, discourse on prime-time television, etc.). That is, one refers to a mapping of non-numeric artifacts into a matrix of statistically-manipulable symbols. Thus, content-analysis involves measurement, not 'analysis' in the usual sense of the word. (p. 2697)

Of course, for Roberts, analysis only refers to qualitative, non-numeric analysis, as the term is often used in humanities. For Amir Marvasti, "as a qualitative approach, content analysis is widely used by researchers. Its potential to transform large segments of descriptive data into quantified categories is embraced by sociologists who are interested in more 'objective' and formulaic methods of data analysis" (Marvasti, 2003, p. 94).

We can find a fair number of examples of content analysis used to examine visual media such as photography or advertising, also in the case of food-specific elements (Kaufman, 1980; Story & Faulkner, 1990; Sarpavaara, 2007). However, the methodology has not been applied to feature-length movies. The reasons for this absence are various, first and foremost the fact that film criticism has developed under the influence of qualitative approaches such as discourse analysis, semiotics, interpretive criticism, history, and psychoanalysis, while in the social sciences interesting debates have developed in the realm of cognitive research, and very stimulating work has been done in the study of film production structures, distribution mechanisms and audience reception (Carroll, 1993; Bordwell & Carroll, 1996; Hagen & Wasko, 2000; Waller, 2002; Jancovich, Faire, & Stubbings, 2003). The qualms in applying content analysis to movies may also derive from the objective difficulties in segmenting visual materials which, by nature, are not discrete; as a consequence, it is necessary to make arbitrary choices on the level of analysis and on how to determine what kind of signifying units are to be considered.

At first blush, it might appear counterproductive to reduce the rich material of 58 movies, both in terms of variety and depth, to a limited number of coding categories. However, a quantitative approach, introducing a certain amount of measurability, does not preclude or substitute for a qualitative analysis of the films. It does allow, however, discovery of patterns that are too subtle to be visible on casual inspection and protection against an unconscious search for only those which confirm one's initial sense of what the material show (Lutz & Collins, 1993, p. 89). Content analysis can in fact capture elements and regularities that otherwise would stay invisible to the analyst, due to the bulk of the material examined, and that are probably invisible to most viewers.

Applying content analysis, I was able to pinpoint a total of 940 food-related scenes (from now on, "occurrences") involving men and food in the 58 blockbuster movies composing the sample. Furthermore, I coded each occurrence according to recurrent categories, which I defined as "situational scripts," based on theme and content. To ensure the exhaustiveness of my data set as a filtering tool for the movie sample, I decided to create coding categories to classify the food-specific occurrences as I examined the movies, instead of creating them beforehand. I believe this process is the most productive with moving images, where the variables are often subtler and more complex than in the case of static images (pictures, photographs, advertisements and such). In the end, I identified 151 situational scripts, defining recurring narrative elements (interactions among characters, between characters and objects, between characters and environment, between characters and events) that are objectively recognizable independently from the characters involved –who at times are not even human, and from the specific plot development, setting, style, and editing of each movie. Furthermore a single scene, or even a single shot, can present several (and at times simultaneous) food-related situations, each coded under a different situational script, regardless of the relevance or relative visibility of the characters involved.

I decided not to focus on specific foods when defining my coding categories, unlike for instance in Korr's analysis of children's TV shows (Korr, 2008) or in Bell, Berger, Cassady and Townsend's examination of food, alcohol, exercise and sport in popular films (Bell, Berger, Cassady, & Townsend, 2005, p. 30). All kinds of dishes and foods are consumed in the food-specific occurrences in the blockbuster sample because the movies are set in very diverse times and places; focusing on what is actually eaten would have led to a description of the scenes rather than a classificatory taxonomy, which is more useful in terms of analysis. I chose instead to concentrate on eating acts and on other food-related activities, verbal exchanges, and emotional interactions, describing their general characteristics rather than their specific objects or topics. I consider this approach more effective in the analysis of blockbuster movies, where the attention of the audience is often concentrated on dynamic action.

Within this coding framework, I marked each food-specific occurrence according to its narrative weight and diegetic function in the wider economy of the movie plot. These diegetic functions are modeled on Gianpaolo Biasin's analysis of the roles that food can play in literary plots (Biasin, 1993). Each occurrence was marked as "introductory," when a new character is presented; "descriptive," when the food-related interaction is aimed at describing a situation, a place, or a point in time, often as part of the background and of the mise-en-scene; "key," constituting a crucial node where something important for the development of the plot happens; and "narrative," when food is used as a tool to move the plot along or to describe characters.

I have further analyzed each food-specific occurrence—regardless of the situational scripts under which it was coded or its diegetic function—by marking it according to certain traits describing the male characters involved in it. I defined these additional categories of interpretation, which I labeled as "descriptors," at the beginning of the viewing of the sample and remained the same all along. They reflect yes/no (0/1) categories: in other words, the descriptors are turned on or not. They refer to race and/or ethnicity, social status within the movie's diegesis, and age, definition as purely relational to describe the position of male characters in relation to each other.

Most movies in the sample are heroic epics, action-packed adventures, and science-fiction or fantasy sagas. A few are romantic stories, such as the *Bodyguard*, *Ghost*, and *Pretty Woman*. Regardless of the possible genres, it is not surprising that most protagonists are male. More precisely, 56 out of 58 movies in the sample feature a male protagonist. The remaining two do have female lead characters, but they all happen to be children in fantasy tales (*The Chronicles of Narnia: The Lion, the Witch and the Wardrobe* and *The Golden Compass*).

The demographic breakdown of the sample movies shows a clear dominance of male heterosexual protagonists, with a noticeable prevalence of white characters, from a working or middle class social background, in various stages of their adult life. Among all the movies in the sample, there are very few that feature black stars such as Will Smith and Morgan Freeman, and no Asian, Hispanic, or Middle Eastern main characters. It is interesting that in the four movies with a black man in a lead role (*Se7en*, *Men In Black*, *I Am Legend*, and *Independence Day*), the characters are either police officers or soldiers. Both represent careers where black men are traditionally present and that, as a consequence, would not offer challenging representations of African-Americans in unusual occupations. As for their physical appearances, most male leads in the sample show normal or athletic bodies and are accompanied by a cohort of secondary characters and antagonists that present instead more variety in terms of gender and body type.

Food and Male Character Development

Passing from general observations about the protagonists to the actual food-related occurrences, *Charlie and the Chocolate Factory* contains 86 by itself, over 9% of the total in sample. This anomaly is not surprising, since this is the only movie that actually features eating and consumption as its main themes, as the whole story is built around candy. Food constitutes the occasion for the main male characters (both Willy Wonka, the rich owner of a visionary chocolate factory, and Charlie, the poor boy that eventually becomes his heir) to evolve through moral conundrums and emotional trials.

Leaving *Charlie and the Chocolate Factory* aside, since it constitutes an interesting case in itself, the movies with the highest number of food-specific occurrences are *Pretty Woman*, *The Bodyguard*, and *Forrest Gump*, respectively with

38, 32, and 31 occurrences. Interestingly, important aspects of their plots can also be described as romantic. In fact, these three movies are often labeled as "chick-flicks," a definition that usually describes sentimental dramas where women play a relevant role, even if only as romantic interests of the male leads.

In *Pretty Woman*, food plays two main functions. On one hand it is used to underline differences in social status between the high-class male characters and the low class prostitute played by Julia Roberts. For instance, she neither knows how to use the silverware in an upscale restaurant, nor she is familiar with certain foods. These situations turn into occasions for the male lead (Richard Gere) and other male characters to help her acquire good manners in a very protective, almost paternal, way, even when she is apparently making a fool of herself. For example, she famously tries to grab snails with little clamps with the result of causing the snail to fly across the room straight into the hands of an alert waiter. On the other hand, food offers various opportunities to negotiate the relationship between Edward and Vivian, both sexually and emotionally. Special foods (the famous strawberries served with champagne) are used to express physical attraction, but also intimacy between the two characters.

In *The Bodyguard*, Frank Farmer, a professional bodyguard played by Kevin Costner, works for pop star Rachel Marron (Whitney Houston) and saves her from a killer. The two get involved in a very intense relationship that nevertheless ends after Frank finishes his assignment. The bodyguard, although undoubtedly masculine, does not recoil from food preparation. At the beginning of the movie, we see him alone in his kitchen, reading while he cooks and pouring himself a glass of wine while he is having dinner. He likes simple and healthy food, very appropriate for his no-nonsense professional approach (and masculinity). When he first meets the vocalist, she makes fun of him for not drinking alcohol. His attitude clashes with Rachel's, who instead loves the social and spectacular aspect of eating, such as eating out in public. As they get closer, they go for a bite after a movie, but this time we are led to think that Frank chooses the establishment, a simple diner, where they playfully enjoy food. When Frank decides to take Rachel and her family to his father's in the North to protect them, we see both men, from two different generations, very comfortable about cooking, with Frank's father showing a very nurturing ability to use food. However, it is also in kitchens that we see Frank's explosions of rage and tension, first against Rachel's former bodyguard, and later against a Hispanic cook whom he suspects of being involved with the plot against Rachel.

In *Forrest Gump*, the slow-witted but sweet main character resorts to food as a venue to communicate his desires, fears, and emotions. Forrest uses it also as a metaphor of life. At the beginning of the movie, talking with his mouth full, he reminisces: "My mama always said that life was like a box of chocolates; you never know what you gonna get." His desires and appetites often express themselves in terms of food: the box of chocolate we see him hold on his lap at the beginning of the movie ("Do you want a chocolate? I could eat about a million and a half of those"), the buffet at the White House party where he is celebrated as a sports champion ("Now, the real good thing about meeting the president of the United States is the food. They put you in this little room with just about anything you'd want to eat and drink"), or the food in the hospital when he is wounded in battle ("The only thing good about being wounded in the buttocks is the ice cream. They got me all the ice cream I could eat"). Also, his affection for his girlfriend is expressed in edible terms: "From then on, we were like peas and carrots."

Food seems to offer Forrest a venue to establish emotional connections. Its production is at the core of the two male friendships that play a huge role in Forrest's life: a black man first and a burnt-out, handicapped veteran later. The connection with the black man is built on his dream of having his own shrimping business, producing the seafood that the women in his family had to cook for generations for their white employers (and arguably, in the past, masters). The black man goes on and on about the myriad ways to prepare shrimp while he and Forrest are busy with menial tasks, like polishing shoes or cleaning a floor with a toothbrush:

> Shrimp is the food from the sea; you can barbecue it, boil it, broil it, bake it, and sauté it. There is shrimp kebab, shrimp creole, shrimp gumbo, pan fried…deep fried, stir fried. There's pineapple shrimp, coconut shrimp… Shrimp stew, shrimp soup, shrimp salad, shrimp and potatoes, shrimp burger, shrimp sandwich. That's about it.

Food provides the two characters an escape from dire reality, while allowing them to create a bond that Forrest will bring to fruition by buying a shrimping boat, on which he will work with his other male friend, a crippled former lieutenant from his time in the army.

Forrest Gump and the other movies displaying the highest number of occurrences (*Charlie and the Chocolate Factory*, *Pretty Woman*, and *The Bodyguard*) are all built around story lines where the main characters (always males) embark in a path of personal development and discovery of their identities as individuals, or they progressively open up to a relationship with a woman, exploring their more emotional sides. Interestingly, after the four mentioned movies, *Spider-Man 2*, *Spider-Man 3*, and the first and last installments of *The Lord of the Rings* trilogy, which present plots where the protagonists are somehow working on their personal growth and their goals, are the movies with the highest number of food-related occurrences, respectively with 29, 28, and 26. As they become less frequent in the movies, food-related occurrences tend to progressively lose their function of providing characters with venues for self-development and romantic interaction, and they are rather used as the background for the male characters, actions and adventures. For instance, in *The Matrix: Revolutions*, which features only four occurrences, food is presented to a space ship pilot to show gratitude, and it is also passed around during a collective celebration with a cathartic function in the fight against evil machines, while in *Terminator 3* the only three food occurrences offer the setting for the androids to express their calculated and cold violence against the humans, often in gruesome ways.

At the opposite end of the continuum from *Charlie and the Chocolate Factory*, we find *Star Wars: III The Revenge of the Sith*, the last episode of the Star Wars prequel saga and the only movie in the sample without any food scenes at all. Metaphorically speaking, while *Charlie and the Chocolate Factory* is located at the bulimic extreme of the movie sample, *Star Wars III: The Revenge of the Sith* definitely marks its anorexic limit.

In general, aside from *Charlie and the Chocolate Factory* and *Star Wars III: The Revenge of the Sith*, which represent two extremes, the movies in the sample show a noticeable incidence of food-related scenes, which could be surprising due to the fact that most of them fall under genre marketed as "action movie." However, eating and ingestion do not frequently play a primary role but they are often in the background of the main action, used as a tool to move the plot forward, to describe situations, or to suggest personal traits of the characters.

Manly Negotiations around the Table

What are the most common food-related activities in which male characters in blockbuster movies are engaged? Do these specific situations help us outline more precisely the masculinities presented in the movie samples, and the representations of the complex relationship between men and food? To answer these questions, I turned to a closer scrutiny of the 151 "situational scripts" under which all the food-related occurrences are coded. Each situational script, which may repeat itself in the same or in several movies, describes a recognizable circumstance in terms of relationships among the characters, interactions between characters and their environments, actions, verbal exchanges, and emotional undertones. By applying content analysis methods, the most frequent among the 151 situational scripts could arguably allow the identification of relevant traits in the representations of masculinity.

Not surprisingly, most food scenes offer images of strong, determined, and powerful men, ready to assert themselves over other men and over women. The four most frequent situational scripts in the sample are in fact "Men/boys use meal/drinking to share news or information or make plans" (45 occurrences), "Men/boys are served or given food or drink by a woman" (43), "Men/boys drink or eat during an activity/work or as a break during work" (42), and "Men/boys toast or eat/drink together to celebrate or show friendship/respect community" (40). Men are featured while sharing food to communicate and discuss news, to make plans, and to celebrate special events (and reaffirming at the same time their belonging to a specific social group). Also when they are not directly interacting with each other, but often in each other's presence, men eat or drink to take a break during activities or just to relax. In these food-related situations, men seem to need confirmation and reassurance about their masculinity from peers and women through performance and social relations, both confrontational and convivial. Through the experience of a shared sense of community across various networks built on affection, professional ties, or common interests, men's non-violent activities and behaviors reinforce their social standings. However, the possibility for violence to erupt is often lurking behind the apparent lack of tension. After all, meals unite and divide. They connect those who share them, confirm their identities as individuals and as a collectivity, and reinforce their mutual bonds. At the same time, meals exclude those who do not participate in them, threatening and negating their very humanity.

In this attempt to differentiate themselves from their surroundings, men are supposed to build their identities as individuals by affirming their hegemonic positions over other men and over women: in those cases, interactions around food, considered as a source of relaxation and energy, are also used as an arena to assert men's power and their dominant role, in terms of both social and gender relations. So we often see men being served food by women or by other men. The relational nature of masculinity is also revealed in terms of race/ethnicity, social status, and age, with young and adult middle class white men represented as the most acceptable models in assertive positions.

However, the model of hegemonic masculinity apparently prevalent in the sample is less monolithic than it would seem: food can also reveal emotions and fears that contrast with the solid image of themselves that men try to project. In fact, the next most recurrent situational script in the sample is "Men/boys are eaten or in danger of being eaten," with 29 occurrences. On one hand, the frequency of this narrative element can be explained by the fact that in several movies aliens, fantasy and other otherworldly creatures, or even humans turned into monsters threaten the male characters; on the other, it is interesting that this sense of danger, clearly meant to scare and shake the audience, expresses itself in terms of ingestion.

Food is clearly a source of anxiety: in 13 movies of the sample we also have 20 occurrences where men are drugged or poisoned by food, or killed by or around food. In the *Terminator* series, the obviously non-eating androids seem to enjoy killing men when they show their nature as living organisms while drinking milk or sipping coffee; in *Harry Potter*, food can be laced with magical ingredients to make people sleep or to make them change their shapes, while in *Se7en* the serial killer uses poison to carry out his murderous plan based on the seven capital sins (including gluttony). In *Casino Royale*, a woman adds poison to James Bond's drink, almost causing his death. It is also around food that men fight and discuss; food is used to deceive and humiliate, and it is spilled and thrown around in fights and brawls. All these elements suggest that in the movie samples food is represented with a deep ambivalence; it allows men to assert themselves both in their personal traits and in their socio-economical positions, but at the same time it can be used to put them down, to underline their lower social standings, and even to threaten them physically.

Food-related experiences can be fraught with tensions and contradictions also when they involve gender relations between men and women. Female characters are frequently portrayed in relevant roles that are nourishing and caring, aimed at men's emotional and physical well-being, but also clearly as subaltern: as mentioned, one of the four most frequent situational scripts describes women serving food to men (43 occurrences), while other recurrent scripts feature men bringing food into play to get close to women (20), asking for food or drinks from women (13), being called or invited to eat by women (11), using food to humiliate women (10), or to show them their cultural and social superior standing (3). For instance, in *Titanic* the fiancé of the main female character orders food for her in front of other guests, to show how he knows her tastes (and also the extent of his control over her). Women fight back, although much less frequently: we rarely see them spilling food over men, refusing to feed them, scolding them for running out of food, or making fun of them for what they eat or drink, but in the sample these occurrences are rare. We see few scenes where women have a more equal power position: for instance, in four occurrences we see men inviting women to drink or eat with no hidden agenda, and two scenes feature a man toasting with a woman (in *Spider-man 3* and *Mission Impossible 3*, both in romantic situations). However, at times women seem to have the upper hand, with men serving food to them (7 occurrences), or complimenting them about food they prepared or served (5).

All the masculinity models that we identified in the sample, as we noticed, are deeply relational: men need others to affirm themselves, to be acknowledged in their personal and social positions, but also to be reassured. Women also play an important role, but most of the time from a position of less power, even when they are treated with care and respect, allowing the different kind of masculinities to express and to develop themselves. In general, women's presence in the movie sample as a whole and in the food-related scenes, where one would expect to find them, is relatively limited.

These observations seem to support the scholarly literature, inspired by Judith Butler's work and by performance studies, which analyses gender identities in their performative aspects (Butler, 1993; Kirshenblatt-Gimblett, 1999 and 2006; Gough, 1999). For instance, the fact that men embodying hegemonic models of masculinity are not frequently represented while cooking or serving food can be interpreted as an attempt to avoid any trait that could be identified with any feminine or nurturing role. Women, on the other hand, perform and thus reinforce their roles of caregivers since they are responsible with feeding not only their own but also others' bodies. Cooking and serving food are among the most identifiable of these performative feminine traits. They are the result of the reiteration of highly regulated and ritualized practices, norms, and processes that respond to ideals and shared social templates that find their primary materialization in the very body of each individual (Butler, 1993, pp. 1–23). However, performance and practices are not artificial and dispensable, but constitutive necessities for the existence of the individual self, providing the conditions of its emergence and operation, of its boundaries and stability. They mark and reinforce rules and norms, including those related to food. In many ways, movies can be then considered as a performance of a performance, aimed at confirming the cultural validity and the social relevance of food-related actions, attitudes, and values that find visual expression in the actions of the characters on screen. These food-related actions, at the same time, underline what behaviors are gender-appropriate, discretely and unobtrusively offering various models of masculinity to the viewers. The presence and frequency of food-related scenes involving men (and secondarily women) in the movie sample confirm how production, distribution, preparation, and consumption of food are found at the core of recurrent and significant social interactions that mark various aspects of the subject identity, including gender.

However, the analysis of diegetic functions of food-related occurrences showed that, despite their frequency, these scenes seldom play a key role within the larger economy of the movie plots, but they are rather used as narrative or descriptive devices in the mise-en-scene and in the background. Also when they highlight interpersonal dynamics and various traits of the characters (including the protagonists), food-related scenes rarely offer nodal points to the development of the story line or introduce new characters; they rather blend in the narrative flow, just helping to move the action along. The movies in the sample are all Hollywood big-budget blockbusters, and their main goal is to entertain audiences worldwide with plots that, despite the increasingly frequent use of flashbacks and the occasional multiplication of the storylines, remain quite straightforward and easy to follow.

Because of the movies' focus on the succession of events that involve the main characters, food-specific scenes seem to offer an apparently natural and neutral space for representations of masculinity to be conveyed, to the point that viewers often do not notice them. Within this apparently ideological-free space, male characters display various traits, values, and practices through their interactions with food.

Suggestions for Future Menus

The present study suggests several possibilities for future research. The same set of blockbuster movies could be examined by developing a content analysis that focus on the dishes and the ingredient consumed, or on the implements and tools used to produce, prepare, consume, and dispose of food. The resulting data would surely highlight important elements about class, race, age, and gender relations in the movies. However, this analysis should take into account the very different historical and geographical settings. For instance, a thigh of lamb shared among the warriors in *Troy* to celebrate a victory could play the same socio-cultural role as a flute of champagne shared by the engineers and the travelers in *Titanic* to mark their scientific success and technical advancements. On the contrary, the same food could be used in totally different contexts: bread can be a symbol of community when shared by companions in *The Lord of the Rings*, but it could arguably be used to underline class difference if hypothetically a rich person threw a piece of moldy bread to a beggar.

This study also reveals the need for further exploration of the complex relationship between food and masculinity in terms of identity development, social and cultural negotiations, practices, attitudes, and values. Since both masculinity and food studies have begun developing as autonomous fields of research only recently, the topic is still largely unexplored despite its potential from the theoretical and empirical points of view.

Turning to media and communication studies, it would be the task of future research to ascertain how the models of masculinity fabricated by the Hollywood film industry and made available worldwide through capillary distribution and marketing, interact with the actual experiences of men around the globe, both as individuals and in larger social groups. The identification of the main recurring food-related themes constitutes a starting point to subsequently investigate their utilization outside their original environment. The study of audiences worldwide and of the reception of mainstream Hollywood productions could be carried out through interviews, participant observations, surveys, and local media analysis. It is an ambitious program, but clearly an important one not only for media and communication studies, but also for social sciences in general.

References

Adema, P. (2000). Vicarious Consumption: Food, Television, and the Ambiguity of Modernity. *Journal of American & Comparative Cultures, 23,* 3, 113–123.

Adler, T. (1981). Making Pancakes on Sunday: The Male Cook in Family Tradition. *Western Folklore, 40,* 1, 45–54.

Appadurai, A. (1996). *Modernity at Large.* Minneapolis: University of Minnesota Press

Ashley, B., Hollows, J., Jones, S., & Taylor, T. (2004). *Food and Cultural Studies.* London and New York: Routledge.

Avakian, A. & Haber, B. (2005). *From Betty Crocker to Feminist Food Studies: Critical Perspectives on Women and Food.* Amherst: University of Massachusetts Press.

Baker, B. (2006). *Masculinity in Fiction and Film: Representing Men in Popular Genres, 1945–2000.* London and New York: Continuum.

Belasco, W. (2008). *Food: The Key Concepts.* Oxford: Berg.

Bell, R., Berger, C., Cassady, D., Townsend. M. (2005). Portrayals of Food Practices and Exercise Behavior in Popular American Films. *Journal of Nutritional Education and Behavior, 37,* 1, 27–32.

Benshoff, H., & Griffin, S.. (2004). *America on Film: Representing Race, Class, Gender, and Sexuality in the Movies.* Malden, MA: Blackwell Publishing.

Bentley, A. (2005). Men on Atkins: Dieting, Meat and Masculinity. In L. Heldke, K, Mommer, and C. Pineo (Eds.), *The Atkins Diet and Philosophy* (pp. 185–195). Chicago: Open Court.

Biasin, G. (1993). *The Flavors of Modernity: Food and the Novel.* Princeton: Princeton University Press.

Bingham, D. (1994). *Acting Male: Masculinities in the Films of James Stewart, Jack Nicholson, and Clint Eastwood.* New Brunswick NJ: Rutgers University Press.

Bliss, S. (1987). Revisioning Masculinity: A report on the Growing Men's Movement. *Context* 16, 21. Retrieved August 28, 2008 from http://www.context.org/ICLIB/IC16/Bliss.htm.

Bordwell, D. & Carroll, N. (Eds.). (1996). *Post-Theory: Reconstructing Film Studies.* Madison: University of Wisconsin Press.

Brod, H. & Kaufman, M. (1994). *Theorizing Masculinities.* Thousand Oaks, CA: Sage.

Buerkle, W. (2009). Metrosexuality Can Stuff It: Beef Consumption as (Hetero-Masculine) Fortification. *Text and Performance Quarterly, 29,* 1, 77–93.

Butler, J. (1993). *Bodies that matter.* London and New York: Routledge.

Carroll, N. (1993). Towards a Theory of Point of View Editing: Communication, emotion, and the Movies. *Poetics Today, 14,* 1, 123–141.

Chopra-Gant, M. (2005). *Hollywood Genres and Post-war America: Masculinity, Family and Nation in Popular Movies and Film Noir.* London: I.B. Tauris.

Clare, A. (2000). *On Men: Masculinity in Crisis.* London: Chatto & Windus.

Clum, J. (2002). *He's All Man: Learning Masculinity, Gayness, and Love from American Movies.* New York: Palgrave Macmillan.

Cohan, S. & and Hark. I. R. (1993). *Screening the Male: Exploring Masculinities in the Hollywood Cinema.* London and New York: Routledge.

Connell, R.W. (1995). *Masculinities.* Berkeley: University of California Press.

Connell, R.W. (2000). *The Men and the Boys.* Berkeley: University of California Press.

Connell, R. W. & Messerschmidt, J. W. (2005). Hegemonic masculinity: rethinking the concept. *Gender and Society, 19,* 6, 829–859.

Counihan, C. & Van Esterik, P. (Eds.). (2008). *Food and Culture: A Reader.* New York: Routledge.

Deutsch, J. (2003). *Standing the Heat: A Comparative Case Study of Men's Amateur Cooking* (unpublished dissertation). New York: New York University.

DeVault, M. L. (1991). *Feeding the Family: The Social Organization of Caring as Gendered Work.* Chicago: The University of Chicago Press.

Faludi, S. (1999). *Stiffed: The Betrayal of the American Man.* New York: William Morrow.

Farrell, W. (1993). *The Myth of Male Power: Why Men are the Disposable Sex.* New York: Simon & Schuster.

Flood, M., Gardiner, J. K. Pease, B., & Pringle, K. (Eds.). (2007). *International Encyclopedia of Men and Masculinities.* London and New York: Routledge.

Gauntlett, D. (2002). *Gender, Media and Identity.* London: Routledge.

Gough, R. (Ed.) (1999). On Cooking (Special Issue). *Performance Research, 4,* 1.

Hagen, I. & Wasko, J. (Eds.). (2000). *Consuming Audiences? Production and Reception in Media Research.* Cresskill: Hampton Press.

Hall, M. (2005). *Teaching Men and Film.* London: BFI Education.

Hansen Rousseau, S. (2007). *From Chef to Superstar: Food Media from World War 2 to the World Wide Web* (unpublished dissertation). University of Cape Town: Centre for Film & Media Studies.

Hollows, J. (2002). The Bachelor Dinner: Masculinity, class and cooking in *Playboy*, 1953–1961. *Continuum: Journal of Media & Cultural Studies, 16,* 2, 143–155.

Holmlund, C. (2001). *Impossible Bodies: Femininity and Masculinity at the Movies.* London; New York: Routledge.

Inness, S. (Ed). (2001a). *Kitchen Culture in America: Popular Representations of Food, Gender, and Race.* Philadelphia: University of Pennsylvania Press.

Inness, S. (Ed). (2001b). *Pilaf, Pozole, and Pad Thai: American Women and Ethnic Food.* Amherst: University of Massachusetts Press.

Jancovich, M., Faire L., & Stubbings, S. (2003). *The Place of the Audience: The Cultural Geographies of Film Consumption.* London: British Film Institute.

Jeffords, S. (1989). *The Remasculinization of America: Gender and the Vietnam War.* Indiana University Press, Bloomington.

Julier, A. & Lindenfeld, L. (2005). Mapping men onto the menu: masculinities and food. *Food and Foodways, 13,* 1 & 2, 1–16.

Kaufman, L. (1980). Prime-time Nutrition. *Journal of Communication, 30,* 3, 37–46.

Kimmel, M. (1996). *Manhood in America: A Cultural History.* New York: The Free Press.

Kimmel, M., Hearn, J., & Connell, R.W. (2005). *The Handbook of Studies on Men and Masculinities.* Thousand Oaks, CA: Sage.

Kirshenblatt-Gimblett, B. (1999). Playing to the Senses: Food as a Performance Medium. *Performance Research, 4,* 1, 1–30.

Kirshenblatt-Gimblett, B. (2006). Making Sense of Food in Performance: The Table and the Stage. In S. Banes & A. Lepecki (Eds.). *The Senses in Performance.* New York: Routledge.

Korr, J. (2008). Healthy Cartoons? A Content Analysis of Foods in Children's Animated Television Programs. *Food Culture & Society, 11,* 4, 449–462.

LeBesco, K. & Naccarato, P. (Eds.). (2008). *Edible Ideologies: Representing Food and Meaning.* New York: State University of New York Press.

Lindenfeld, L. (2003). *Feasting Our Eyes: Food Films, Gender, and American Identity* (unpublished dissertation). Davis: University of California.

Lutz, C. & Collins, J. (1993). *Reading National Geographic.* Chicago: The University of Chicago Press.

MacInnes, J. (1998). *The End of Masculinity.* Buckingham: Open University Press.

Marvasti, A. (2003). *Qualitative Research in Sociology: An Introduction.* London: Sage Publications.

Moore, R. & Gillette, D. (1990). *King, Warrior, Magician, Lover: Rediscovering the Archetypes of the Mature Masculine.* San Francisco: Harper Collins.

Parasecoli, F. (2005). Feeding Hard Bodies: Food and Masculinities in Men's Fitness Magazines. *Food & Foodways, 13,* 1–2, 17–37.

Parasecoli, F. (2008). *Bite Me: Food and Popular Culture.* Oxford: Berg.

Pfeil, F. (2002). Getting Up There with Tom: The Politics of American 'Nice.' In Gardiner, J. K (Ed.) *Masculinity Studies & Feminist Theory: New Directions* (pp. 119–140). New York: Columbia University Press.

Ray, K. (2007). Domesticating Cuisine. *Gastronomica, 7,* 1, 50–63.

Roberts, C. (2002). Content analysis. In Smelser, N. J. & Baltes, P. B. (Eds.), *International Encyclopedia of the Social and Behavioral Sciences.* Amsterdam: Elsevier.

Robinson, C. & Spivey, S. (2007). The Politics of Masculinity and the Ex-Gay Movement. *Gender & Society, 21,* 5, 650–675.

Roth, L. (2005). "Beef. It's What's for Dinner": Vegetarians, Meat-Eaters and the Negotiation of Familial Relationships. *Food, Culture & Society, 8,* 2, 181–200.

Sarpavaara, H. (2007). Dionysian and Apollonian in Advertising: The representations of Pleasure and Discipline in Finnish Television Advertisements. *Qualitative Sociology Review, 3,* 2, 202–220.

Sellaeg, K. & Chapman, G. E. (2008). Masculinity and food ideals of men who live alone. *Appetite, 15,* 1, 120–128.

Shapiro, L. (2001). *Perfection Salad: Women and Cooking at the Turn of the Century*. New York: The Modern Library.

Shapiro, L. (2004). *Something from the Oven: reinventing Dinner in 1950s America.* New York: Viking Penguin.

Simpson, M. (2002). Meet the Metrosexual in salon.com, July 22. Retrieved August 27, 2008, from http://dir.salon.com/story/ent/feature/2002/07/22/metrosexual/index.html

Stam, R. & Spence, L. (1983). Colonialism, Racism and Representation. *Screen, 24,* 2, 2–20.

Story, M. & Faulkner, P. (1990). The Prime Time Diet: A Content Analysis of Eating Behavior and Food Messages in Television Program Content and Commercials. *American Journal of Public Health, 80,* 6, 738–740.

Swenson, R. (2009). Domestic Divo? Televised Treatments of Masculinity, Femininity and Food. *Critical Studies in Media Communication, 26,* 1, 36–53.

Waller, G. (Ed.). (2002). *Moviegoing in America: A Sourcebook in the History of Film Exhibition*. Malden, MA: Blackwell.

Whitehead, S. (Ed.). (2006). *Men and Masculinities: Critical Concepts in Sociology*. New York: Routledge

Wilk, R. (2006). Serving or Helping Yourself at the Table. *Food, Culture and Society, 9,* 1 7–12.

Williams-Forson, P. (2006). *Building Houses out of Chicken Legs: Black Women, Food and Power*. Chapel Hill: University of North Carolina Press.

Section Three

Culture and Society: Food and the Communication of Social and Cultural Values

10

Dinner time discourse: Convenience foods and industrial society

John R. Thompson

Food allows social and cultural values to be communicated openly yet under a veneer of mundane everyday living. Society can communicate those values through the system of practices that insinuate certain forms of food into our everyday lives. Changes in the symbolic nature of food can also mark subtle changes in the values communicated. Consider two examples of food symbolism: one from 1980s cinema and a second from a 21st-century TV cooking show.

In the 1983 movie farce *Doctor Detroit*, a high-class prostitute prepares dinner for a group of stuffy college faculty at the home of an equally stuffy professor who somehow managed to become the prostitute's pimp. After a kitchen disaster destroys the haute cuisine she originally planned, she orders a delivery of fast food chicken. Confident that she can outwit those over-educated intellectuals, she dresses up the pedestrian chicken parts with a sauce and the faculty raves as you knew they would.

Fast forward to the early twenty-first century. Master French chef Jacques Pepin opens a recent series of public broadcasting cooking shows with a "one-minute recipe." In one of these episodes, he begins with a story of buying an already-cooked rotisserie chicken and a bag of pre-cut, pre-washed lettuce at the supermarket. At home, he combines melted butter, herbs and garlic and pours it over an attractive platter of the cut-up chicken and lettuce. Raising a glass of wine to the camera he proclaims: "Now it becomes your own chicken, Chicken Persillade. Make the supermarket work for you. I am Jacques Pepin. This is *Fast Food, My Way.*"

Clearly, much has happened in 25 years to turn an anti-establishment joke into haute cuisine. The two media examples underscore a shift in our relationship to food and its preparation—but Pepin barely nods to the increasing pace of life that drove the change. Pepin stakes a claim on a growing food phenomenon in American life—pre-packaged, often pre-cooked, food at the grocery store that maintains a relatively straightforward form (that is, no Styrofoam, no Happy Meals packaging) and has *not* been the subject of numerous books, documentaries, social movements and health reports telling consumers not to eat it. Yet, this food is still largely based on car culture and working consumers racing from one location to another. These foods can be purchased and consumed quickly, yet lend themselves to a traditional sit-down meal, at least in appearances. In short, convenience foods present themselves as genre-benders and thus are worthy of further investigation. They are neither fast nor slow, fish nor fowl, by the dominant discourses of food; they violate the fast/slow binary.

Stepping back to place these curious foods into a larger context, fast food and slow food frame a discursive battle over pace. These are tropes that link pace to the human condition through the bodily necessity of food. This chapter asks what we can learn about the struggle over pace by viewing this lowly roasted chicken (or the sushi, or the bagged lettuce, or the pre-cut fruit etc. now available in the local supermarket or the Wal-Mart supercenter) as a rhetorical artifact on the frontier of two discourses, one assailed because of its dominance (fast food) and the other struggling to recover a culture built around epochal moments (slow food).

The skeptical reader might already retort that it is just a chicken after all, a somewhat trivial subject of critique in a complex world. My response is that, as rhetorical artifacts, these foods are structured into the world for a reason. Because food is a part of the human condition, the structuring of food *commodities* into the world implies the structuring of food *consumers* into the world as well. Against that backdrop, this chapter claims that the emergence of these "convenience" foods aims to blur the lines between slow food/fast food discourses and keep the "home field advantage" within spaces controlled by the food industry—in this case, the grocery store. By offering wholesome food that promises to restore time with family, the food industry engages in an interplay of what de Certeau (1984) described as spatial strategies and temporal tactics arrayed throughout everyday life (p. xix). As discourses of resistance built around food grow in scope, these convenience foods offer concerned consumers a temporal tactic for managing life, while remaining articulated to industrial society. Through these commodities, the food industry co-opts the discourse of wholesome foods and effectively articulates three spaces through these commodities: the workplace, the grocery store, and the home kitchen. Yet, the pace-driven tropes of slow food and fast food haunt this meal, a haunting even present in the name of Pepin's show and book, *Fast Food My Way* (2004, followed up with a sequel in 2008), one of many such cookbooks forming a new genre within the popular cookbook category.

This chapter proceeds first to a discussion of time and society then links that discussion to food discourse and the tropes framing this project. From there, I borrow from de Certeau (1984) for a theoretical framework to consider these convenience foods and then a discussion of the foods themselves. I will close with some thoughts on where this food phenomenon might be leading us during a globalizing time in which job insecurity is on the rise and the future is not quite so stable as it might once have appeared.

Time for Dinner

To consider fast food and slow food is to consider temporal experience—specifically pace—in the context of the human condition. At the center of this fast/slow dialectic is the nature of industrial society. It is a conflict communicated by tropes of pace, yet it is a larger conflict of negotiating values against the backdrop of clock time and industrial society.

Bluedorn (2002) elaborated social and historical constructs of time such as the importance of the *time giver* (p. 150). Industry's temporal organization of clock time is now society's time giver, the central organizer of temporal experience. The time giver entrains other processes to its cycles. In agrarian society, the time giver was the sun. The sun's entraining power was marked by "epochal" moments in which events occurred, such as planting and harvest (p. 31). Industrial society, by contrast, works almost exclusively on "fungible" time or "clock time" in which time is organized into equal parts—whether minutes, hours or days—and then structured for greatest efficiency (p. 28). Bluedorn argued that fungible time was particularly adapted to capital's needs. Not only could fungible time be organized for efficiency, fungible time also provided the tool to colonize more of workers' available time by equating any minute with any other minute (p. 245). According to Thompson (1967), this dynamic created the separation of time into "the work day" and "my time" for laborers, with the work day being devoted to the discipline of task time. Thompson (1967) wrote:

> Those who are employed experience a distinction between their employer's time and their 'own' time. And the employer must use the time of his labor and see it is not wasted: not the task but the value of time when reduced to money is dominant. Time is now currency, it is not passed but spent. (p. 61)

This shift to an industrial society with its manufactured sense of time (manufactured, rather than set by cycles of nature) changed not just time spent working, but the internal experience of time writ large.

Glennie and Thrift (1996) reinterpreted Thompson's work to account for overall *time structuring*, a more flexible construct than Thompson's task time. While still built on the shift to industrial society, McGrath and Kelly (1992) extended the construct of time structuring to account for the multiple dimensions of time in everyday life and the human need to structure time so as to manage personal and economic demands of industrial society. This larger view of society *after* the shift Thompson highlighted provides fertile ground and is the terrain of this chapter. In plowing that ground, McGrath and Kelly (1992) took a social psychology approach to time structuring and argued that not just people and not just employers, but that entire *societies* structure time and when they do they are implementing value systems:

> [P]hilosophical issues about time represent a set of value orientation issues on which each culture must take some stand. Each culture must somehow resolve those issues for itself and its members in order to carry on day to day affairs. (McGrath & Kelly, 1992, p. 403)

Conflicts naturally arise over those values and temporal patterns develop over time to negotiate those tensions.

The advent of the lunch hour suggests one bit of negotiation between ultimate productivity and the conflict with basic human needs. In the movie *Modern Times*, Charlie Chaplin offered a view of industrial society in which productivity was so prized that industrial scientists invented a machine that would feed workers efficiently, refueling the human machine with as little productive down time as possible. Once again, the joke was not far removed from a future reality as fast food industrialized the very process of eating so it more closely matched the pace of industry. Ritzer (2008) critiqued the industrialization of everything in society and the uniformity and pace that industrialization engendered, using McDonald's as the archetype (a paradigm Ritzer argued also powered enterprises such as IKEA and Starbucks). Critiquing the subtleties of a McDonald's layout, he connected the limited menu to the uncomfortable chairs to the noisy environment to the drive-through window to show that the entire creation of the McDonald's experience is about pace—eat and leave or, better yet, *leave before you eat* in the case of the drive through window (p. 15). Ritzer (2008) observed:

> The fast-food restaurant also dehumanizes consumers. By eating on a sort of assembly line, diners are reduced to automatons rushing through a meal with little gratification derived from the dining experience or from the food itself. The best that can usually be said is that the meal is efficient and is over quickly. (p. 154)

Ritzer's analysis connects to Chaplin's meditation on industrial society through the construction of bodily needs—eating to sustain life—as an industrial problematic, an interruption in the productive rhythms of industrial society and thus something to be tolerated but minimized via technology. In the case of McDonald's, make the chairs uncomfortable and the environment annoying and the workforce will get back to work soon.

Fast food then serves the purpose of articulating bodily needs to the temporal structuring of the industrial system. The fact that fast food is an industry itself means it entrains others to *its* needs. Indeed, part of Ritzer's (2008) "dehumanizing" thesis centers on workers trained to do quite specific things repeatedly, with no variation tolerated. The system extends beyond the storefront as well to include industrial farming and thus armies of low-wage farmworkers are required to feed such a system. Such industrial regimes have forced small farmers off their land and turned them into wage earners in the industrial food system, as Barndt (2008) documented.

As fast food has spread beyond hamburgers and French fries, it has also commodified various cuisines, such as Mexican food where Taco Bell is, at best, an abstraction of the rich culinary heritage of Mexico. Taking a different view of Mexican wage earners than Barndt (2008), Pilcher (1997) argued that assembly line tortillas offered one of the few culturally-acceptable and affordable foods to Mexican wage laborers (p. 408). While they are not the hand-made, high-labor tortillas of their heritage, such tortillas are cheap and plentiful in a society vastly changed by globalization. On the other side of the world, Roden (2006) argued something similar about Moroccan couscous, once the product of a day-long process of rolling flour and now transformed into a just-add-water commodity (p. 25). In both of these instances, the industrial food system commodified a culinary staple of a given culture that was once made through a painstaking investment of time. Today, it is sold back to that society as a faster food.

By selling culturally-acceptable time-saving foods, industrial society recovered productive time from the process of cooking and eating and made a profit for the food system. Elsewhere, Rosenthal (2008) reported the opposite effect as the Mediterranean diet—fabled as quite healthy in the West—is dying out among the cultures that produced it as fast food has entered the region and marketed itself to youth (Rosenthal, 2008, para. 3). Against these backdrops, fast food can be thought of far more broadly than just McDonald's and the like. Fast food, as McGrath and Kelly argued, becomes a way of setting a "fast living" pace as a social value, whether it is *replacing* a culinary tradition or commodifying hand-made foodways *within* a given culinary tradition.

With values squarely in the picture, the growing backlash against the fast food industry becomes more complex. Certainly, some critics have linked fast food to growing rates of obesity and chronic diseases such as diabetes (Nestle, 2002; Schlosser, 2002). In popular literature, a growing genre of extensively-researched books by food advocates argue for a simple, personalized approach to food and cooking rather than relying on fast food and pre-packaged foodstuffs (see Bittman 2008 and Pollan 2006 as examples). Social movements also play a role in this food backlash. Carlo Petrini's Slow Food Movement was launched well before this current wave of resistance literature. The Slow Food Movement has created—in a bit of irony bordering on paradox—a *global* movement about *local* cultures. The movement offered "slow food" as a trope that now defines not just a way of eating and cooking, but also a critique of fast-paced industrial society. In telling the story of Slow Food, Andrews (2008) argued:

> Slow Food's critique is aimed essentially in the direction of contemporary global capitalism and its varying impact on the quality of life. It presents a critical engagement with contemporary lifestyles: representing not a simple contrast between "tradition" and "modern," but a response to contemporary ways of living, whereby concerns around food are rooted in wider issues over the effects of globalization, the disparity between obesity and famine, environmental crisis, the impoverishment of small farmers, and increasing global economic inequality. It reflects a desire on the part of quite different people for an alternative way of living, in which pleasure is central.... (p. 17)

This one passage channels many of the issues already mentioned in this chapter. Essentially, Slow Food argues that living at a pace by which simple pleasures and social moments such as eating are rendered inconvenient is actually damaging to social relations. Food's position as a bodily need has been colonized by a homogenizing industrial society that undermines long-held social graces and culture built around food and replaces it with fast living. Parkins (2004), using time as a lens to critique the Slow Food Movement, characterized Slow Food as promoting a discourse of the *ethics* of time (p. 368). Parkins (2004) tied this temporal ethics to an attempt to restore human agency to contemporary lifestyles stating:

> This desire to re-learn how to value or cultivate a certain sense of time is at the heart of movements which, since the late 1980s, have emerged to promote slow living as a way to restore meaning, authenticity, security or identity to time-deprived subjects. (p. 369)

As pace increases, according to Parkins, political subjects lose the ability to mindfully engage in the world around them, resorting to *mindless* refueling through fast food, rather than the *mindful* engagement of social relations that might attend a meaningful meal.

At the root of this discursive battle over pace is the concept of the time giver. Hassard (1991) argued that we are born in a natural time (that time in which the sun and bodily needs provide time orientations), but we grow to become acculturated into other socially-constructed times (p. 105). Physiological needs (food especially considering the elemental needs of the infant he describes) become structured into larger social patterns. As societies become more complex, work claims more of a person's time because of the social division of labor (p. 114). Hassard argued: "As functional specialization requires the synchronization of parts and activities, the more need there is for temporal coordination of the various activities among the various parts (Hassard 1991, p. 118)." In essence, as pace increases the society needs more of a given person's time to sustain itself, rendering these more "natural" aspects of living unproductive—and not just unproductive to the forces of capital alone, but also to the society at large.

Bluedorn and Waller (2006) pushed further this notion of a society-wide temporal relationship regarding industrial society, casting time as a shared public resource and borrowing the spatial concept of the "public commons" to construct a "temporal commons" defined as: "The shared conceptualization of time and the set of resultant values, beliefs, and behaviors regarding time as created and applied by members of a culture-carrying collectivity" (p. 367). The theorists argued that market forces, extending the concept of the private ownership of tangible assets, have *enclosed* the temporal commons for the purpose of developing the efficiency of time, much like real-estate developers are granted effective control over city blocks to develop the land (pp. 366–368).

Both enclosure movements, of tangible and intangible assets, have largely been accepted by the public. While critical of the status quo, Bluedorn and Waller (2006) do not claim a conspiracy afoot. Rather, they offer that the unintended consequences of enclosing the temporal commons have not been explored and that resistance movements occur where values conflict with the temporal ordering of society. They call out the Slow Food movement as one of those resistance movements and hypothesize that it will ultimately be constrained by this enclosure of the temporal commons and its "bounds and nesting structures" (p. 390).

Put another way, this discursive battle over pace actually tests *what is nested within what* when it comes to political economy and culture. The expansion of *the contained* will be limited by *the container* in which it resides. According to Bluedorn and Waller (2006), culture is contained within political economy (p. 370). Yet, even that outline uses a spatial metaphor. From a temporal perspective, the question is who or what is the timegiver.

So, the challenge in analyzing rhetorical artifacts on the frontier of this fast/slow pacing of society is multi-dimensional. The critic must apply a lens that inherently parses these nesting structures that Bluedorn and Waller (2006) saw as the ultimate determinants of victory. That lens also needs a fundamentally temporal component, an appreciation of contemporary society, and yet must recognize the everydayness of things such as food and eating. To establish such a theoretical lens, I turn to de Certeau (1984) and *The Practice of Everyday Life.*

Methodological Notes: Spatial Strategies, Temporal Tactics

In this section, I hope to accomplish two things: 1) briefly justify the apparent novelty of looking at a roasted chicken as a rhetorical artifact; and 2) outline an analytical framework to employ in such a study. Put another way, to understand the rhetorical work that a roasted chicken might perform, it is worth taking a moment to point out that I am not the first to argue that non-linguistic phenomena are structured into the world for rhetorical purposes, that is to say, for reasons of persuasion and creating identification. Other critics have looked at non-linguistic phenomena with powerful results. Hart (1999) critiqued the role of the TV (an artifact that channels linguistic discourse, but also sits as a physical object in most living rooms) in political discourse. Brummett (2008) outlined an entire rhetoric of style that deployed a broad look at clothing and other physical objects. The field of public memory often uses physical monuments as a critical object (see Phillips, 2004 for a broad look at the field).

These works stand out in part because of their selection of objects to be read as texts. At least since Aristotle, the study of rhetoric has been based largely—though not exclusively—on the study of language-based texts, and it is not my intention to undermine that study by looking at chickens. Yet even Aristotle (1991) did not define rhetoric as a linguistic phenomenon, but as the "ability [sometimes rendered as a "faculty"] in each particular case to see the available means of persuasion" (p. 36). Once we separate words from the rhetorical motive, and locate that motive within rhetors themselves, many more systems of signs present themselves as rhetorical media. In the twentieth century, even Kenneth Burke (1941)—while primarily focused on language as the basis of organizing the world—allowed that: "Words are aspects of a much wider communicative context, most of which is not verbal at all" (Burke, 1941, p. xvii). Elsewhere, Burke (1950) argued that the rhetorical motive could hide in the mundane nature of daily life:

> And often we must think of rhetoric not in terms of some one particular address, but as a general body of identifications that owe their convincingness much more to trivial repetition and dull daily reinforcement [sic] than to exceptional rhetorical skill. (p. 26)

I contend that food, cooking, and eating fall into this "general body of identifications" Burke described. Barthes (1997) said something quite similar when he argued that food constituted a system of communication not just within anthropological settings of exotic indigenous people but also within modernity (p. 29).

This system of communication, then, provides the means of doing things with food rhetorically. Unpacking the nature of those rhetorics requires more than just appreciating food as a system of signs. Food can be considered as both a category of physical objects and an array of practices (cooking, shopping, growing, consuming etc.). To capture this larger context of food, I turn to de Certeau.

De Certeau (1984) used rhetoric as a framework for analyzing the meanings of practices that constitute daily life. De Certeau's point of departure was that modernity formed the foundation of life, but that individuals chose from a template of practices by which to negotiate their roles in the modern world (p. xix). These practices make use of the bricolage of modern life, turning those components into "the discursiveness that combine these elements which are all in general circulation and rather drab" (de Certeau, 1984, p. xviii). This bricolage of rhetorical elements might range from commodities to certain ways of doing things that are combined with "artisan-like inventiveness" (de Certeau,

xviii) into a language of its own that can be enunciated for resistance, identity construction, or the negotiation of life in a world not of one's own making.

De Certeau (1984) put many such things under the umbrella of this everyday rhetoric including walking, talking, reading, cooking, and eating. He compared the specific usage of ways of "making do" with what was available to the inventiveness of language by observing:

Both rhetoric and everyday practices can be defined as internal manipulations of a system—that of language or that of an established order. "Turns" (or "tropes") inscribe in ordinary language the ruses, displacements, ellipses, etc. that scientific reason has eliminated from operational discourses in order to constitute "proper" meanings. (de Certeau, 1984, pp. 23–24)

So, forces of power (in the present project, industrial society) seek to eliminate things (such as epochal time) that do not fit the scientific reason (one might think of Taylorism or Fordism here) of the prevailing order. Yet, those concepts do not go away entirely, but become part of a vast storehouse of ideas, discursive moves and practices that can be drawn on by ordinary individuals as they manipulate the bricolage of their daily lives. Ordinary individuals "poach" things and "turn" them to their own uses (de Certeau p. xii).

De Certeau (1984) offered a framework for understanding the push and pull inherent in this process of poaching, turning, resisting and making do, and it is this framework that will animate the following ruminations on the lowly supermarket roasted chicken. He identified a system of spatially-oriented "strategies" and temporal "tactics" from which to analyze practices (pp. 35–39). Strategies specifically exteriorized certain phenomena from a given space. De Certeau claimed:

I call a *strategy* the calculation (or manipulation) of power relationships that becomes possible as soon as a subject with will and power (a business, an army, a city, a scientific institution) can be isolated. It postulates a *place* that can be delimited as its own and serve as the base from which relations with an *exteriority* composed of targets or threats…can be managed. (de Certeau, 1984, p. 36, emphasis in original)

A strategy involves a physical or even conceptual *space* where a certain logic of control reigns. It is a victory of space over time. The temporal is not necessarily a foreign concept on this terrain. However, it is managed in a manner similar to the way a commander on a hill can identify an approaching enemy. The commander can calculate the time to engagement and use that time to plan a strategy on a landscape he or she knows far better than the enemy.

Conversely, de Certeau identified temporally-oriented efforts as "tactics" that must be organized around time because they take place on someone else's terrain. A tactic, therefore, involves the greater proportion of poaching and turning as de Certeau (1984) explained:

> The space of a tactic is the space of the other. Thus it must play on and with a terrain imposed on it and organized by the law of a foreign power…It operates in isolated actions, blow by blow. It takes advantage of "opportunities"…What it wins it cannot keep. This nowhere gives a tactic mobility, to be sure, but a mobility that must accept the chance offerings of the moment, and seize…the possibilities that offer themselves at any given moment. (p. 37, emphasis in original)

So, a tactic is the seizing of a moment of opportunity. It can be a powerful moment, but it is fleeting. It has the advantage of mobility because it is not tied to a given space of its own power. However, it disappears as the instant of its achievement passes to the next moment. To sustain any momentum requires stringing together other such moments, each fading as the moment of victory passes because the terrain is still under someone else's control. A tactic is an opportunistic poaching of something discovered in the cracks of an organized terrain of power. De Certeau put it bluntly by writing: "In short, a tactic is an art of the weak" (p. 37). Industrial society renders any singular individual weak, in essence, since the individual does not own the terrain. Drawing on Hassard's (1991) idea of an infant existing in a natural time until it is acculturated into social time, one might think of everyone as an immigrant into industrial society and its temporal commons.

Ultimately, strategies and tactics present ways of contravening space and time depending on the distribution of power because:

> [S]trategies pin their hopes on the resistance that the *establishment of a place* offers to the erosion of time; tactics on a clever *utilization of time*, of the opportunities it presents and also of the play that it introduces into the foundations of power. (de Certeau, 1984, p. 39, emphasis in original)

As I turn to examining convenience foods, the nature of the bets on place and time become central to untangling what is happening from the perspective of the food industry and that of the temporally over-stretched consumer. This lens takes us beyond what might seem an easy conclusion that these roasted chickens are simply a "hybrid" between fast and slow food. I think de Certeau's framework can demonstrate that to be a simplistic and erroneous conclusion.

The Whole Chicken and Nothing But the Chicken

My claim is that convenience foods embody a ratio of strategy and tactic under de Certeau's framework. The net result is that those consumers remain articulated to industrial society, essentially *buying time* from the grocery store in an effort to provide the healthful benefits of wholesome foods to their families. Yet, time spent in the workplace is not sacrificed, thus consumers remain engaged in the fast living of industrial society.

Since tactics can only be used on someone else's strategic terrain, de Certeau's (1984) framework requires that we first identify the relevant spaces and who controls them. The *most* relevant space is the grocery store. The roasted chicken is not to be found at a farmer's market or a community garden, two other spaces—de Certeau's strategies—that also compete today for a role in consumer lifestyles and identity construction under the emerging food discourses of resistance. Yet, this lowly chicken arrays two other relevant spaces: the workplace and the home kitchen. As Thompson (1967) and others argued, the modern workplace is the locus of the temporal hegemony of industrial society as time giver. Discourses such as the Slow Food Movement challenge that hegemony and its reassignment of time (made easy by a fungible time paradigm) from economically unproductive tasks—such as cooking dinner—to economically productive uses at the workplace.

What might appear to be a victory of these newer discourses is not necessarily so when viewed through the lens of spatial strategies. By offering a relatively healthy (relative to traditional fast food) and traditional (no Styrofoam, it can go from store packaging to a serving platter in one move) pre-cooked alternative, the grocery store maintains a spatially-organized relationship between the consumer and food industry, and the worker and workplace. What is more, these relationships are maintained through offering a temporal tactic to time-starved consumers attempting to eat healthy and recover epochal moments as these newer food discourses encourage. Yet, that offer is made by the food industry, leveraging the terrain it controls within industrial society.

Convenience foods remain articulated to work schedules as the time giver. Yet, there is another space arrayed by this now quite powerful chicken: the home kitchen. Even the master chef, Pepin, turned cookbook author and public-TV celebrity still describes the process as starting "when I'm coming home from work" even though his version of "work" remains rather unique among jobs. We also see these convenience foods co-opting other aspects of a new media-driven food culture. Rachael Ray, for instance, has built an empire by prominently using food commodities such as pre-cut vegetables and encouraging a creative usage of processed foods. The advertising sponsors of these media programs, bakeoff contests, and other fare are part of the food industry. These time-saving foods are offered as a means of constructing identity in the kitchen and restoring a semblance of traditional family time within industrial society—that is, without sacrificing work time.

This linkage co-opts aspects of the new food movements and positions the consumer's kitchen as a space in which commodities can be transformed into works of art, a la Pepin's Chicken Persillade. As de Certeau (1984) indicated in defining the strategic nature of spaces, "it allows one to capitalize acquired advantages, to prepare future expansions, and thus to give oneself a certain independence with respect to the variability of circumstances. It is a mastery of time through the foundation of an autonomous place" (de Certeau, 1984, p. 36). New food discourses represent an example of the "variability of circumstances" for industrial society. Even as these discourses position the kitchen as a space to be leveraged for health and epochal moments, it is also now a site of "future expansions" for industrial society, and the chicken is a tool of colonization under these new circumstances.

As these new food discourses attempt to pry open Bluedorn and Waller's (2006) temporal commons, it is reasonable to believe that industrial society will attempt to bar the gate. So, while a bit whimsical to contemplate, de Certeau's (1984) analytical template combined with the literature of time scholarship indicates that industrial society is using a roasted chicken to wedge the gate shut. It is also worth noting that the pre-cooked chicken costs more than the chicken that still needs cooking from the store's refrigerated section. In effect, the grocery store is selling health-conscious consumers the extra time they are devoting to the workplace—and doing so at a premium price.

Conclusion

In Thompson's (1967) foundational piece on clock time and work discipline, he observed that labor patterns displayed a "characteristic irregularity" until the clock time paradigm diffused into society and the rigidity of time equating to wage labor took hold (p. 71). Until that point, laborers would come and go somewhat flexibly and perhaps pursue some personal projects while at the workplace, or they would fish or farm on the side as their forebears had done. Clock time so changed individual orientations to time that labor ultimately disciplined itself and industrial society moved forward under its own momentum. Other orientations and traditional occupations that workers previously attempted to keep alive on a part-time basis were stamped out. Once the *time equals money* equation-oriented society began to clock time and wage labor, these other pursuits were seen as *costing time* without economic productivity as a return on that investment.

In the ensuing generations, epochal time and Hassard's (1991) natural time have become irregular, certainly in the West. In a globalizing world, Bluedorn and Waller's (2006) temporal commons is a site of struggle. Using a different lexicon, Chatterjee (2004) noted this struggle over the temporal commons as it colors the march of industrial society—and clock time—around the world claiming:

> Within its domain, capital allows for no resistance to its free movement. When it encounters an impediment, it thinks it has encountered another time – something out of pre-capital, something that belongs to the pre-modern. Such resistances to capital (or to modernity) are therefore understood as coming out of humanity's past, something people should have left behind but somehow haven't. (p. 5)

New food discourses, such as the Slow Food Movement, are impediments to that free movement of industrial society and capital, and these discourses do, indeed, channel other time orientations. They remind us that fast living is a constructed sense of time, not a natural one. So, if Chatterjee (2004) is correct, perhaps it is not so whimsical to expect that industrial society would respond to these impediments by producing a chicken…and stuffing it with time so that others might speed up to its pace.

One thing this chapter does not address is just what time structures are being built around this lowly roasted chicken. Put another way, what we do with these chickens once we get them into our kitchens and our family and social dynamics is ultimately the most telling aspect of this food commodity and it might be too soon to truly understand those dimensions. Cooking shows from Jacques Pepin and Rachael Ray can show you what to do with the chicken up to the point it is served. After that, it is up to the consumer. For some, no doubt, the chicken is nothing more than fuel for the next dash on the strategic terrain of industrial society. For others, the chicken might be a true opportunity in de Certeau's (1984) framework of practices, a temporal tactic to wedge some epochal time back into the dinner hour. Only time will tell. Bon Appetit.

References

Andrews, G. (2008) *The Slow Food story: Politics and pleasure*. Montreal: McGill-Queen's University Press.

Aristotle. (1991) *On Rhetoric: A theory of civic discourse*. G. Kennedy (Ed.). Oxford University Press.

Barndt, D. (2008) *Tangled Routes: Women, Work, and Globalization on the Tomato Trail.* New York: Rowman & Littlefield.

Barthes, R. (1997) Toward a psychosociology of contemporary food consumption. In Carole Counihan and Penny Van Esterik (Eds.), *Food and Culture: A Reader (2nd ed).* (28–35). New York: Routledge.

Bittman, M. (2008) *Food matters: A guide to conscious eating with more than 75 recipes*. New York: Simon & Schuster.

Bluedorn, A. C. (2002) *The human organization of time: Temporal realities and experience*. Stanford: Stanford Business Books.

Bluedorn, A.C., Waller, M.J. The Stewardship of the Temporal Commons. *Research in Organizational Behavior. 27*, 355–396.

Brummett, B. (2008) *A Rhetoric of Style*. Carbondale: Southern Illinois University Press.

Burke, K. (1950) *A Rhetoric of Motives*. Berkeley: University of California Press.

Burke, K. (1941) *The Philosophy of Literary Form*. Berkeley: University of California Press.

Chatterjee, P. (2004) *The Politics of the Governed.* New York: Columbia University Press.

De Certeau, M. (1984) *The Practice of Everyday Life*. Berkeley: University of California Press.

Doctor Detroit. [Motion picture] (1983) Michael Pressman (Dir). Perf. Dan Aykroyd, Fran Drescher. Universal Pictures.

Glennie, P., Thrift. N. (1996) Reworking E.P. Thompson's 'Time, work-discipline and historiography'. *Time & Society, 5*, 275–299.

Hart, R. P. (1999) *Seducing America: How television charms the modern voter.* Thousand Oaks: Sage.

Hassard, J. (1991) Aspects of time in organizations. *Human Relations, 44,* 105–125.

McGrath, J.E., Kelly, J.R. (1992) Temporal context and temporal patterning: Toward a time-centered perspective for social psychology. *Time & Society, 1,* 399–420.

Nestle, M. (2002)_*Food politics*. Berkeley: University of California Press.

Parkins. W. (2004) Out of time: Fast subjects and slow living. *Time & Society, 13,* 363–382.

PBS. [Episode of cooking show] (2009) One minute recipe: Chicken persillade. *More Fast Food My Way*. Retrieved from www.jacquespepin.com

Pepin, J. (2004) *Fast Food My Way*. New York: Houghton Mifflin.

Pepin, J. (2008*)* *More Fast Food My Way*. New York: Houghton Mifflin.

Phillips, K. (2004) *Framing Public Memory*. Kendall Phillips (Ed.) Tuscaloosa: University of Alabama Press.

Pilcher, J. M. (1997) Taco Bell, maseca, and slow food: A postmodern apocalypse for Mexico's peasant cuisine. In Carole Counihan and Penny Van Esterik (Eds.), *Food and Culture: A Reader (2nd ed)*. (400–410). New York: Routledge.

Pollan, M. (2006) *The omnivore's dilemma: A natural history of four meals*. New York: Penguin Press.

Ritzer, G. (2008) *The McDonaldization of Society, (5th ed)*. Los Angeles: Pine Forge Press.

Roden, C. (2006) *Arabesque: A Taste of Morocco, Turkey, and Lebanon*. New York: Knopf.

Rosenthal, E. (2008 September 23) Fast food hits Mediterranean: A diet succumbs. *New York Times.* Retrieved from www.nytimes.com

Schlosser, E. (2002) *Fast Food Nation*. New York: Harper.

Thompson, E.P. (1967) Time, work-discipline and industrial capitalism. *Past and Present,. 38,* 56–97.

11

"A four-legged duck?" Chinese restaurant culture in the United States from a cross-cultural/inter-cultural communication perspective

Vincent (Tzu-Wen) Cheng

An old Chinese saying from *The Book of Han* (a Chinese classic of the history of the Western Han from 206 BCE to 25 CE) states, "for a king, his people are most sacred; for the people, food is most sacred." It not only underscores, from the Chinese perspective, the importance of food to the survival of individuals and to the construct of societies, but also connotes that one may gain insight into the complexities of social and cultural values observing their everyday practices of food production, preparation, and consumption. If we truly are what we eat, does going to a Chinese restaurant in United States say more about Chinese or American culture? Through a close examination of both *what* and *how* people eat at Chinese restaurants in the United States, this chapter offers analysis and reflection to this question.

Food and eating have played an integral part in Chinese culture for over 4,000 years. Growing up in rural Taiwan in the 1970s, where "Have you eaten yet?" was a common greeting, I experienced first-hand the Chinese culture's preoccupation with the preparation and eating of food from a very early age. One of my earliest childhood memories is listening to the sounds of my mother and grandmother (sometimes my father as well) cooking in the kitchen. To this day, the sounds of chopping and sizzling food comfort me. While other boys my age were busy playing dodge ball and spinning tops, I enjoyed accompanying my mother and grandmother to local markets, learning how to cook using various kitchen utensils, and, most of all, attending banquets with my parents that were held at fancy restaurants or outdoors in makeshift tents. Through many explicit and implicit lessons learned during these food-related events, I not only gained rich contextual information about how Chinese food is produced, prepared, cooked, served, and consumed, but also I developed strong familial, communal, social, and cultural ties to Taiwan that were associated with the culinary experience.

Coming to the United States in 1996, I began a new chapter in my life. Even though Taiwan at that time was considerably westernized on the surface—and was regarded as one of East Asia's Economic "Tigers" (or "Dragons") because of its high growth rate and its rapid industrialization between the 1960s and 1990s—at its core, Taiwan nonetheless remained traditionally and culturally Chinese. Therefore, the initial cultural shock when I first arrived in the United States was profound, and my process of acculturation thereafter has been fascinating, frustrating, thought-provoking, and rewarding. For the past decade, as an "outsider within" the United States, I have been studying law, speech communication, and international education at the same American university, teaching numerous communications-related courses at two different American universities, as well as living among Americans in the culturally and ethnically diverse city of New York, all while simultaneously observing cultural differences from an academic point of reference.

Among the many challenges I have had to face as an international student and scholar in the United States is finding "authentic" Chinese/Taiwanese restaurants that can assuage my inescapable homesickness. Although in New York City there are three well-established Chinatowns and Chinese restaurants or Chinese take-out places on almost every city block, the quest for "authentic" Chinese food has proven to be a formidable task. Chinese restaurants in the United States are, for the most part, as foreign to me as any other ethnic or national cuisine. To further complicate matters, I have had numerous encounters with local Americans of various ethnic backgrounds who have found my ignorance and lack of experience with the "Chinese" food that they have grown accustomed to surprising and perplexing. "You don't have fortune cookies in Taiwan? What about chop suey? No? Not even egg-rolls?" Their questions seem to dispute my "Chinese-ness" (as though my Taiwanese nationality invalidates my Chinese cultural heritage) and have made me feel like an "insider without"—someone who looks Chinese (and even speaks Mandarin), yet knows very little about "Chinese" food.

Intrigued by these Chinese food experiences in the United States—as both an "outsider within" and a perceived "insider without"—I intend to explore in this chapter Chinese restaurant culture in the United States and its implications for understanding Chinese American identity development, and I will use my personal experiences at New York City Chinese restaurants as a launching point for analysis. Through examination from a cross-cultural/inter-cultural communication perspective of both *what* and *how* people eat at these Chinese restaurants in New York City, this chapter will demonstrate that, contrary to many Americans' general perception, Chinese restaurant culture in the United States is essentially American. This study will suggest that a parallel of this perceptual inconsistency (that is, what Americans *think* Chinese food and foodways are versus what they *actually* are) can be drawn with how Chinese Americans are perceived as perpetual foreigners in the United States, when in fact they are long-standing Americans who have been in the United States for many generations.

The Globalization of Chinese Food

Before discussing Chinese restaurant culture in the United States, it is first necessary to briefly review the growing literature in the social sciences regarding the globalization of food in general, and about Chinese food in particular. Several comparative food studies in the past decade cite food as an example of globalization—one that connects cultures, peoples, and locations (Hannerz, 1996; Wilk, 1999; Plotnicov & Scaqlion, 2002). More recently, studies on food-related globalization can also be seen from the ongoing impact analyses regarding the introduction of "Western" fast-food giant McDonald's in East Asia (Watson, 1997; 2006). Using food as their medium, these studies represent a new line of inquiry into the cultural meanings of commodities, consumption, and modernization. By treating the "Third World" as modern, post-industrial, and capitalist—rather than as remote, exotic, and primitive—these studies suggest that the post-modern, post-colonial world must be understood within the context of consumption and global economy. However, as pointed out by Wu and Cheung (2002) in *The Globalization of Chinese Food*, the theoretical framework employed by these studies is fundamentally and ironically tied to the post-industrial Western world and is concerned primarily with the "western" impact on "peripheral" areas of the world. This paradigm requires further reconsideration in order to adequately explain the global spread of Chinese food, which began to take place much earlier than the nineteenth century. The examination of Chinese food as a global force should be conducted in the historical perspective of perhaps a millennium, rather than just within the modern era (Wu & Cheung, 2002).

Moreover, to many globalization theorists (Schiller, 1976; Hamelink, 1983; Tomlinson, 1991), globalization is often viewed as an ominous homogenization of the world—where sameness is ubiquitously imposed, and difference is steadily suppressed or eliminated. According to this view, since the nineteenth century advanced societies at the "center" (the First World) have been extracting labor and raw materials from poorer and weaker states at the "periphery" (the Third World) while simultaneously imposing upon these poorer and weaker states their dominant mode of production, which in turn prompted increasingly hegemonic values in response to these impositions. Wu (2002) challenges this theoretical framework by contesting that the development of Chinese cuisine overseas has *not* followed the assumed globalization pattern outlined above. He contends that researchers who draw on current Western theories associated with multinational capitalistic domination, commercialization, industrialization, and international trade have largely overlooked how Chinese cuisine overseas has developed. Using field data collected in Papua New Guinea and in Hawaii, Wu argues that Chinese cuisine overseas is neither the result of a direct flow of cultural traditions from the center to the periphery, nor the diffusion of a capitalized cooking industry powered by professional chefs and restaurateurs from China. Instead, Chinese cuisine overseas, especially in restaurants, demonstrates re-creation, invention, and representation of Chinese cooking by Chinese immigrants who were self-taught cooks. These Chinese immigrants not only improvise dishes using ingredients and cooking materials available to them locally, but they also improvise how they present their dishes, so as to satisfy the imagination of both Chinese migrants and their host populations (Wu, 2002).

Through re-creation, invention, and representation, Chinese cuisine has been improvised to suit its host culture(s) by waves of Chinese emigrants from China, Hong Kong, Taiwan, and Southeast Asian countries ever since the second half of the nineteenth century. As a result, Chinese cuisine in its various forms and manifestations has reached North America, Australia, Europe, and, more recently, Oceania—as well as Central and South America. In the following section, this study will narrow its scope of inquiry to Chinese restaurants in the United States, and examine the causes, practices, and consequences of the various forms and manifestations of improvised Chinese cuisine in the context of the United States.

The History of Chinese Restaurants in the United States

Restaurants have been central to the American experience since the 1850s, serving as eating establishments, important regional landmarks, community meeting spots, and cultural institutions. While restaurants have often served conservative social functions by preserving established foodways and cultural boundaries, they have also been innovative social agents that have exposed Americans to a variety of social groups that they may not otherwise have encountered. In search of cheaper, faster, and/or more exciting food options, Americans have often set their ethnic and cultural prejudices aside to experience other culinary traditions (Barbas, 2003). Among these options, since the mid-nineteenth century, have been Chinese restaurants. Considering the significance of history in discussing intercultural interactions and cultural identities from a cross-cultural/inter-cultural communication perspective, I will first explore the history of Chinese restaurants in the United States.

In 1848, the discovery of gold in the Sacramento Valley, California, prompted the first wave of migration from South China to the United States. Although most of the estimated 25,000 Chinese who arrived in California by 1851 were engaged in mining or in domestic or manual labor, due to a shortage of women domestics, some worked as cooks (Roberts, 2002). Regarded as a reliable workforce, these early Chinese immigrants were warmly welcomed by the Americans. It was in California Gold Rush mining towns in the mid-nineteenth century that the first Chinese restaurants in the United States, known as "Chow Chows," sprang up to serve a mixture of Chinese (mostly Cantonese) and non-Chinese laborers. Marked with triangular yellow silk flags, as was customary in China, Chinese restaurants were given a friendly reception and quickly spread eastward, as well as into metropolitan areas such as San Francisco and New York City where Chinatowns had been established (Jen, 2005).

By the 1870s, scores of non-Chinese Americans, mostly white working-class men, could be seen on the streets of Chinatown in both San Francisco and New York City. They were lured to Chinatown not only by its houses of gambling and prostitution, but also by the possibility of finding cheap meals. Accustomed to Chinese cooks who had worked with them in the mines and on the railroads, these working-class men would frequent Chinese restaurants and dine either on American dishes—such as black beans, steak and eggs, or hash—or on "Chinese" dishes such as egg foo yong (dubbed "Hangtown Fry"), rice casseroles, and fried noodles (Barbas, 2003).

America's initial welcoming attitude to its Chinese immigrants soon turned against them, fomenting into an anti-Chinese hostility that engendered racial tensions and prejudicial comments. Variously stigmatized as posing an economic threat, as being unable to comprehend the principles of democracy, and as bringing filth and disease with them (Roberts, 2002), Chinese communities were often abused in the press along with derogatory references made to their eating habits.

For example, an 1877 magazine cartoon entitled "Uncle Sam's Thanksgiving Dinner" stereotypically depicts various immigrants enjoying their respective national dishes: a Frenchman chews frogs' legs, while an African-American servant brings a turkey to Uncle Sam, and a Native Indian squats peaceably beside his fellow guests. All are in harmony, except for one figure who draws horror and disgust from the other diners—a Chinaman who is about to eat a rat (Jen, 2005). Another example is given in Wu's *The Yellow Peril: Chinese Americans in American Fiction 1850–1943* (1982), where a character in the novel *Almond-Eyed: The Great Agitator; a Story of the Day*, written by Atewell Whitney and published in San Francisco in 1878, says the following about the Chinese: "They follow our hard-working people close to their heels, steal their trades, cheapen labor, and then sit down to a dinner of rice and potato sprouts, such as a hearty white would starve on" (as cited in Wu, 1982, pp. 31–32).

In 1882, prejudice against the Chinese culminated in the passage of anti-Chinese legislation, the Chinese Exclusion Act, which introduced restrictions on Chinese immigration. By the early twentieth century, Chinese laborers had gone from playing a significant role in nearly every sector of the American economy since the mid-nineteenth century—including agriculture, mining, manufacturing, and transportation—to being forced out of the general labor market by hostile labor unions, exclusionary legal policies, and racial discrimination. The few employment opportunities left to Chinese Americans were mainly in the area of service industries, such as laundries and the restaurant business (Takaki, 1989).

The virulence of anti-Chinese prejudice in the late nineteenth century made it unlikely for non-Chinese Americans to patronize Chinatowns, where most Chinese restaurants were located. An 1893 guild, King's Handbook of New York, described the area around East Broadway and the Mott, Bowery, and Worth Streets as "a veritable Chinatown, with all the filth, immorality, and picturesque foreignness which that name implies" (as cited in Stokes, 1915–1928, vol.5, p.1617). There was also a popular belief held by many non-Chinese Americans that Chinese food incorporated all sorts of disgusting things

(Roberts, 2002). Chinese restaurants in the United States during this period faced threats on three different levels: first, due to a worsening public perception of Chinatowns and Chinese food, U.S. Chinese restaurants were rapidly losing their non-Chinese clientele and were patronized almost exclusively by Chinese; second, due to the passage of the Chinese Exclusion Act, the Chinese population in the United States fell significantly; and third, due to the lack of other job opportunities for immigrant Chinese, the U.S. Chinese restaurant business became extremely competitive.

Out of survival necessity, Chinese restaurateurs strove to overcome these threats in three ways; first, by joining the campaign to clean up Chinatowns; second, by transforming Chinese restaurants and the food they served into something that was "familiar-yet-exotic" to the average non-Chinese American; and third, by opening up Chinese restaurants catering to non-Chinese clientele outside Chinatowns.

By 1900, Chinese restaurateurs, as part of the "clean up Chinatown" campaign, refurbished their establishments with gaudy lanterns, colorful wall decorations, and bright red facades to match non-Chinese Americans' stereotypical image of the "Orient," and they scrubbed their floors and kitchens meticulously to avoid any rumors of poor sanitation. In the quest for a "familiar-yet-exotic" menu, Chinese restaurant cooks began inventing and serving a variety of ingeniously concocted "Chinese" dishes that used local ingredients and catered to American tastes. Among the new "Chinese" dishes that appeared during this period was "chop suey"—a concoction typically involving bean sprouts, celery, onions, water chestnuts, green peppers, soy sauce, and small pieces of either chopped pork or chicken (Barbas, 2003; Hsu, 2008).

There are many versions of the origin of "chop suey." One version argues that it was "invented" in New York City in 1896 by Chinese ambassador Li Hung-Chang's chef, who devised this dish to appeal to both American and Chinese tastes. Another version traces the dish back to California during the Gold Rush, when white gold miners frequented Chinese eating places and were given dishes composed of scraps of meat and vegetables (Burros, 1986; Yu, 1987; Roberts, 2002; Hsu, 2008; Coe, 2009; Liu, 2009). Regardless of its disputed origins, chop suey caught on like wildfire in the early twentieth century; it became a staple of Chinese restaurants, and chop suey houses soon mushroomed in cities across America. Americans' love affair with chop suey could also be observed in the popular culture of the time, with chop suey references made in films and songs such as "Cornet Chop Suey" and "Who'll Chop your Suey When I'm Gone?" (Luo, 2004).

Then, in the early twentieth century, amidst the success of chop suey, California saw the birth of the fortune cookie—an item that later became yet another staple and iconic symbol of Chinese restaurants in the United States. Both San Francisco and Los Angeles lay claim to the origin of the fortune cookie. Makoto Hagiwara, a Japanese-American and a member of Golden Gate Park's Japanese Tea Garden in San Francisco, is said to have first invented the cookies in 1909; others contend that David Jung, founder of the Hong Kong Noodle Company in Los Angeles, invented them in 1918. In 1983, San Francisco's Court of Historical Review ruled in favor of San Francisco being the cookie's official birthplace; the decision, however, was criticized as being less than serious and biased in favor of San Francisco. Whatever its true origin, the fortune cookie in its present form, with a cheerful prediction or affirmation folded inside a brittle beige carapace, is an indisputably American invention that became an indispensable part of Chinese restaurant culture in the United States soon after World War II (Borgna, 2005; Tompkins, 2005; Lee, 2008).

Between 1900 and 1920, even though the total number of Chinese employed had declined, the number of Chinese restaurants had doubled (Takaki, 1989). The tremendous expansion of the Chinese restaurant industry during this time was a result of the physical improvements made in many Chinatowns, as well as of the growing popularity of chop suey and other Americanized "hybrid" dishes, such as egg foo yong, egg rolls, and chow mein. Sensing the popularity of Americanized Chinese food, many first- and second-generation Chinese Americans decided to establish "chop suey parlors" and full-service Chinese restaurants outside the boundaries of Chinatown, expanding into ethnically-mixed urban and suburban neighborhoods. Their bold moves proved to be a great success (Barbas, 2003).

During World War II, Chinese restaurants in the United States experienced an upsurge in both numbers and reach (Roberts, 2002). Although the U.S. Chinese restaurant business suffered a reversal immediately after the Korean War due to anti-Chinese sentiment, by the 1950s and 60s, "going for Chinese" had become not only fashionable for urbanites, but also a part of the suburban vernacular. Menus from Chinese restaurants in the United States that date from this period can be seen to have been reaching out to the suburbs, and to other ethnic communities. Reaching out to the Jewish community were kosher Chinese restaurants in New York suburbs with names such as "*Glatt Wok*,"

"*Wok Tov*," and "*Shang-chai*," serving dishes like Matzoh Foo; reaching out to the Italian community was the *House of Lee* in Oakland, California, featuring "fried ravioli" (better known as "wontons"); there was also *Mon Lay Won*, a turn-of-the-century New York City restaurant that called itself "the Chinese Delmonico's." Outside these large metropolitan areas, there was *Jade Garden* in Bismarck, N.D. for example, which featured the local specialty "hot and spicy walleye," and there was also *Brillante*, a Mexican and Chinese spot in Paterson, N.J. which offered General Tso's Pollo. For many newly-arrived immigrants during and after the Second World War, eating at Chinese restaurants was a way of forging a new American identity and was an initiation into American culture (Luo, 2004; Jen, 2005).

The 1965 liberalization of immigration laws brought a new wave of Chinese immigrants and new food from many different regions of China. Until 1965, Cantonese-speaking immigrants—mainly from the county of Toisan—dominated the restaurant industry, and menus reflected a standard repertory of tasty (but Americanized) Cantonese dishes. A new influx of Chinese immigrants and Nixon's visit to China in 1972 inspired an "authenticity revolution" in the U.S. Chinese restaurant business. Rather than serving solely Americanized Cantonese dishes, some Chinese restaurants in the United States once again catered to newly-arrived Chinese immigrants with more authentic Chinese dishes from regions such as Sichuan, Hunan, and Shanghai, to name just a few (Luo, 2004; Jen, 2005).

By the early 1970s, luxurious and successful Chinese restaurants like Shun Lee Dynasty, the first New York City Chinese restaurant to receive a four-star review in *The New York Times*, began sprouting up in large U.S. metropolitan areas. Meanwhile, newly established Hunan and Sichuan restaurants quickly influenced U.S. Chinese restaurants everywhere, with dishes like "General Tso's Chicken," and "Crispy Orange Beef." However, just like their Cantonese predecessors, as they became mass-produced, these new dishes soon became Americanized and bore little resemblance to their authentic Chinese counterparts (Luo, 2004).

Today, Chinese restaurants in the United States are overwhelmingly run by Fujianese immigrants, many of whom were smuggled into this country illegally and flocked to the restaurant business because they had few other labor options. According to the latest statistics cited in a 2005 article published in the *Asian Reporter*, in addition to the more than 41,000 independent Chinese restaurants that currently exist in the United States, there has also been an increase in the number of Chinese chain restaurants, such as *P.F. Chang's* and

Panda Express ("Asian Cuisine Boasts Growing Popularity in U.S." 2005). In fact, the total number of Chinese restaurants in the United States has now surpassed the combined number of McDonald's, Wendy's, and Burger King franchises (Luo, 2004). These numbers don't lie—U.S. Chinese restaurants are surely an integral part of the American eating experience.

Chinese Restaurant Culture in the United States

Having placed U.S. Chinese restaurants in a historical context, this section will, from a cross-cultural/inter-cultural communication perspective, analyze both *what* people eat and *how* they eat at U.S. Chinese restaurants by drawing on the author's personal dining experiences in Taiwan, China, and the United States.

What People Eat at U.S. Chinese Restaurants

It can be observed from the history of Chinese restaurants in the United States that much of what people eat at U.S. Chinese restaurants these days is not "authentic" Chinese cooking that has been brought in by professional chefs and restaurateurs from China. Rather, as Wu has argued, it is the result of years of re-creation, invention, and representation of Chinese cooking by Chinese immigrants who are largely self-taught cooks. Given the hostile anti-Chinese legislation, prejudiced public imagination, and derogatory rhetoric of the past, there has been immense pressure for U.S. Chinese restaurants to acculturate in order to survive.

According to the model of acculturation proposed by Berry (2003) new immigrant minorities typically employ a variety of acculturation strategies. The term "acculturation strategies" refers to the type of plan or method that individuals use—voluntarily or involuntarily—in responding to new, stress-inducing cultural contexts. While traditional conceptualizations of acculturation take a one-dimensional approach—contending that individuals must lose their original cultural characteristics to take on characteristics from more dominant cultural groups in order to achieve cultural and social adaptation—Berry takes a multi-dimensional approach that places both cultures on parallel continuums, indicating an individual's ability to maintain his or her culture of origin while adopting characteristics from a more dominant cultural group. He identifies four alternative acculturation strategies: integration, assimilation, separation, and marginalization. In *integration,* some degree of cultural integrity is maintained while one moves to participate as an integral part of the dominant culture. In *assimilation,* original cultural features are given up completely in favor of those of the majority. In *separation,* no features of the majority culture are accepted, and only the original culture is valued. In *marginalization,* both the original and the dominant cultures are denied (Berry, 2003).

Applying Berry's model to identify how U.S. Chinese restaurants have acculturated to the more dominant American culture, we can, through a process of elimination, identify the strategy of *integration* as the most successful for the Chinese immigrant community in the context of the restaurant business.

Marginalization is a strategy that some Chinese immigrants have adopted when they open restaurants in America. There are numerous Japanese restaurants, Thai restaurants, Malaysian restaurants, and Mexican restaurants, and so on, owned and run by Chinese immigrants. While this is certainly an intriguing topic—and a legitimate strategy that some Chinese immigrants have used to acculturate into American society—it is not immediately relevant to this study's topic (i.e. Chinese restaurant culture in the United States), and remains a subject for future research.

As for the *separation* strategy, historically the number of Chinese immigrants as a demographic body was kept purposefully low (as has been discussed in relation to the Chinese Exclusion Act); therefore, there was not a large enough population to make separation a sustainable strategy—that is, it was not feasible to open a restaurant catering exclusively to a separate Chinese population that was not large enough to ensure the success of such a venture.

While some Chinese immigrants tried their hands at opening up "American" restaurants (based on the dominant European American culture) which offered familiar menu items served with familiar silverware and in "American" fashion and dress, the fierce competition from other European immigrant communities often made the *assimilation* strategy too risky and challenging for most Chinese immigrants.

For the majority of Chinese immigrants, then, *integration* as a strategy of acculturation has emerged as the most successful and desirable strategy, since in so doing they were able to capitalize on maintaining a certain degree of cultural integrity while also negotiating their culinary habits with the more dominant American community, developing a cuisine that was "familiar-yet-exotic" to the American palate.

The degree of integration of U.S. Chinese restaurants into American society can easily be observed by simply looking at the menu items of these restaurants from a Chinese or Taiwanese perspective. For instance, when I first came to the United States, many of the "Chinese" menu items at the local Chinese restaurants were completely foreign to me. Items such as "shrimp toast," "egg rolls," "crab rangoon," "Mongolian beef," "chop suey," and "fortune cookies" may strike the typical American as quintessential Chinese dishes, but in fact, to a native Chinese such as myself, these are entirely unknown, and just as "exotic" to the Chinese palate as they are designed to be for the American palate! The ingredients and preparation methods retain some loose affinity with other Chinese dishes (using julienned ingredients, for example, as well as similar-yet-toned-down spices and sauces), so there is some degree of cultural integrity being maintained. But in the final analysis, these dishes demonstrate how successfully U.S. Chinese restaurants have acculturated into the more dominant culture—masking their Chinese origins within their newly improvised "Chinese" food. Much of the Chinese cuisine in the United States is essentially American. In fact, according to a 1928 *New York Times* article, when chop suey was exported to China as an American fad, it met with resounding indifference and failed to appeal to the prevailing Chinese taste ("Chop Suey, Popular Here," 1928). Similarly, according to a 2004 *New York Press* article, in 1995 the company *Golden Bowl* tried, but failed, to sell fortune cookies in China (Gershenson, 2004). These examples are further evidence of the Americanized Chinese cuisine's *integrated* status with the dominant American culture; the improvised hybrid cuisine's innate American quality proved incompatible with the cuisine's ostensible Chinese origin.

It is not only the composition and ingredients of Americanized Chinese food that constitute the cuisine's *integrated* acculturation strategy; the manner in which the food is prepared also shows the degree to which Chinese immigrants compromised their cultural heritage to accommodate the more dominant culture's habits and expectations vis-a-vis the dining experience. As any son or daughter in Taiwan/China knows (and as my parents constantly exhorted me when I was a child), it is paramount in the Chinese tradition to make use of *all* parts of an animal that sacrifices its life for human consumption; anything less is considered a waste of food and a sign of utter disrespect. Some parents (my own included) even go as far as to warn their kids that if they throw away any part of an animal, in their next life they will be reincarnated as the animal they have wasted. Bones, eyes, brains, feet, intestines, tripe, stomach—all are considered to be not only edible parts of an animal, but are often considered choice parts which have an animistic quality to them. If you want to improve your eyesight, it is widely believed by people in Taiwan/China that you will benefit from eating eyeballs; analogous benefits can also be obtained from eating the heart, liver, brain, and penis.

U.S. Chinese restaurants rarely include any distinguishable body parts in the dishes they serve. In accordance with the dominant culture's preferences, meats are usually de-boned or filleted, and dishes are served without any sign of bones. This would strike most diners in Taiwan/China as unfortunate, because sucking the marrow from bone is considered good for the diner's own bones, and is an integral part of eating meat. Along with the preparation of meat, most U.S. Chinese restaurants, in accordance with the dominant culture's preferences, go out of their way to camouflage their food so as to ensure its presentation will not remind customers that they are about to eat the remains of a once-living animal. In contrast, in Taiwan/China, the presentation of the entire animal is regarded as a guarantee of freshness, an opportunity to appreciate the sacrificed animal, and a ritualistic part of the dining experience. Therefore, while serving meat in the animal's bodily form—and in its entirety—are the norms in Taiwan/China, serving meat in a non-animal "camouflaged" form—and in selected portions—are the norms for Chinese restaurants in the United States. In an U.S. Chinese restaurant it is rare to see the succulent eyes of a whole fish staring up from a dish, or to witness a chef right before your eyes skillfully carving meat off of a whole duck with its head and neck still attached. So while some Chinese dishes in the United States are more "authentic" and may correspond to dishes you could just as easily find in Taiwan or China, the careful and deliberate removal of body parts that American customers would typically blanch at is a telling result of an acculturation process based on the *integration* strategy.

Parallel to how meat is prepared and presented, Chinese food in the United States typically treats vegetables as a garnish rather than as a main ingredient. Thus, while dishes made exclusively of vegetables are common in Taiwan/China, they are rather unusual at U.S. Chinese restaurants. The difference in emphasis placed on vegetables can especially be seen in the use of carrots and tomatoes, which rarely make up single dishes at U.S. Chinese restaurants and are used more to add color to meat dishes than to add any significant flavor. Chinese cuisine in Taiwan/China makes frequent use of Asian leafy vegetables, such as Jie Lan (Chinese kale/broccoli), Jiu Cai (Chinese leek), and Kong Xin Cai (water spinach)—ingredients which one rarely finds here, and which in Americanized Chinese dishes are usually replaced with more available local ingredients, such as broccoli, string beans, bok choy, and snow peas. All of these aspects of Chinese food in the United States are further proof of the *integration* strategy employed by various waves of Chinese immigrants in order to acculturate into the more dominant U.S. culture.

Chinese immigrants are not the only immigrants who have successfully flourished by integrating their cuisine into the American cuisine; many so-called

"American" dishes have their roots in other lands and cultures. For example, apple pie, pizza, chowder, French fries, hot dogs, and hamburgers are all either identical to, or derived from, European dishes. Chinese food in the United States, however, seems to be unique in that many Americans do not realize just how American it actually is, and that it differs significantly from the cuisine of Taiwan/China; they still perceive it as "foreign" in spite of its immense popularity in the United States.

How People Eat at U.S. Chinese Restaurants

Not only many dishes served in U.S. Chinese restaurants are as American as apple pie, pizza, chowder, French fries, hot dogs, or hamburgers, the typical manner in which these dishes are served and consumed also reflects dominant American values, such as individualism and small power distance.

The concepts of individualism and power distance are discussed by Hofstede (1996), an influential Dutch expert on the interaction between national cultures and organizational cultures, in his foundational book, *Cultures and Organizations: Software of the Mind.* This landmark cross-cultural communication research was the result of a massive survey Hofstede conducted with IBM employees in 72 countries and regions in 1968 and again in 1972. Additional data collected later from other countries, and from other large companies besides IBM, were used to verify and enhance his original results.

Hofstede demonstrates in his study that there are persistent national and regional cultural dimensions affecting how people behave in any given organization. These dimensions are *collectivism* versus *individualism*; *large power distance* versus *small power distance*; *femininity* versus *masculinity*; and *strong uncertainty avoidance* versus *weak uncertainty avoidance*. Hofstede later added a fifth dimension, *long-term orientation* versus *short-term orientation* (Hofstede, G. & Hofstede, G. J., 2005; Hofstede, G. & Hofstede, G. J., & Minkov, M., 2010). For the purposes of this chapter, only the dimensions of *collectivism* versus *individualism* and *large power distance* versus *small power distance* will be discussed, because these are the two dimensions that show the sharpest behavioral contrasts between China and the United States.

Collectivism (China) versus individualism (United States). According to Hofstede, in *collectivist* societies, family structure is based on the extended family. The concept of the "we" group (or in-group) is the major source of an individual's identity, and social relationships are developed in terms of groups. Group dependency in this type of society is highly valued. In short, in collectivist societies the interest of the group prevails over the interest of the individual. In contrast, in *individualist* societies, family structure is based on the nuclear family and the concept of "I" is the major source of an individual's identity. A person's identity is distinct from other people's identities, and people are classified according to their individual characteristics rather than according to their group affiliations. Individual independence is highly valued in this type of society. In short, in individualist societies the interest of the individual prevails over the interest of the group.

To measure the degree of individualism in the different countries and regions that were surveyed, Hofstede developed a formula to calculate the individualism index (IDV) score of each country and region. His research shows that among the 74 countries and regions surveyed, China's IDV score tied with five other countries and regions, which received rankings ranging from 56–61; the United States' score ranked number 1 on the IDV index, indicating that the United States as a society was the most individualistic of those surveyed (Hofstede, G. & Hofstede, G. J., 2005).

The pronounced difference in the United States (as the most highly individualistic society) and China (as a markedly more collectivist society) is readily observed in the manner in which dishes are served and consumed at the contrasting societies' Chinese restaurants. At Chinese restaurants in the United States, prix-fixes menus for groups of different sizes are rarely seen. Most menus are written with the assumptions that an individually-sized portion will be ordered by each customer individually, that an ordered dish will subsequently be placed squarely in front of the customer who has ordered that dish, and that the dish will be eaten exclusively by that customer. Most waiters and waitresses at U.S. Chinese restaurants reinforce this highly individualistic manner of serving and consuming dishes by explicitly asking each and every person in a dinner party what they personally wish to order.

This contrasts sharply with the way in which food is ordered, served, and consumed at Chinese restaurants in Taiwan/China. In Taiwan/China, prix-fixes menus for groups of different sizes are common. Most menus are written with the assumption that the "family portion" size will be collectively shared and consumed by the entire party, and the dishes are therefore placed in the center—usually on a revolving "lazy-susan"—so that diners can more easily circulate them to one another. Moreover, when servers in Taiwan/China take a party's order, they usually defer to the host, who orders collectively for everyone, balancing the dishes between different food groups and flavors.

Of course, I am not arguing that Americans, due to their individualistic values, are incapable of sharing food. What I am trying to argue is that people in the United States and in Taiwan/China operate under very different default assumptions when it comes to group eating. Unless they explicitly express otherwise, people in the United States assume that they will be eating together *individually*, whereas people in Taiwan/China, unless they explicitly express otherwise, assume that they will be eating together *collectively*.

For someone such as myself coming from a highly collectivist society, it was (and continues to be) jarring to see multiple people in the same party order the same exact dish for individual consumption. In fact, my heart sinks a little each time I see this in a U.S. Chinese restaurant, because I feel sorry for the party's lost opportunity to consume more than one flavor and food group in the course of their meal, and thus achieve a more balanced and varied diet. For me, this phenomenon of eating together "separately"—which can be frequently observed at Chinese restaurants in the United States but very rarely in Taiwan/China—oxymoronically defeats the whole purpose of eating "together."

In addition, I recognize that some Americans, accustomed to the highly individualistic manner in which food is ordered and served, may find it equally jarring to go to a restaurant in Taiwan/China and try to modify a dish listed on the menu. U.S. Chinese restaurants have adapted themselves to a society that values individual tastes and styles, and will thus accommodate an individual customer's highly detailed specifications for a dish's ingredients or the way it is prepared. This sort of "have-it-your-way" individualistic approach to ordering food would be regarded as very odd and unreasonable in a collectivist society such as Taiwan/China.

These aforementioned observations are not discussed to place any value judgments on either the dining experience in the United States or in Taiwan/China; rather, they are used to reinforce Hofstede's findings regarding the differences between China as a collectivist society and the United States as a highly individualistic society. Furthermore, they demonstrate and confirm how Chinese restaurants in the United States have pursued an *integrated* strategy in order to acculturate into America through their development of a distinctive Americanized Chinese dining experience.

Large power distance (China) versus small power distance (United States). According to Hofstede, power distance is defined as the extent to which less powerful members of the society expect and accept that power is distributed unequally. In *large power distance* societies, inequalities of status, power, and wealth have been allowed to grow, and are respected. Therefore, people in these societies expect and accept a hierarchy in which everybody has a well-defined place that is rarely questioned. In contrast, *small power distance* societies de-emphasize the differences between people's status, power, and wealth. In these societies, equality and opportunity for everyone is stressed, and people strive for equality and demand justification for any perceived inequality.

To measure the degree of power distance in different countries and regions, Hofstede used formulated surveys to calculate a Power Distance Index (PDI). The higher a society's PDI score, the more it conforms to large power distance behaviors; the lower a society's PDI score, the more it conforms to small power distance behaviors. His research data show that among the 74 countries and regions surveyed, China's PDI score was in a three-way tie with two other countries and regions, whose rankings ranged from 12 to 14. In contrast, the United States' score was also in a three-way tie with two other countries and regions, but with rankings which ranged from 57 to 59 (Hofstede, G. & Hofstede, G. J., 2005). Thus, China is a country that anticipates and accepts inequalities of status, power, and wealth in its society, whereas the United States anticipates more egalitarianism. These differences in large power distance versus small power distance inform how food is served and consumed at U.S. Chinese restaurants, which can be illustrated with the following personal anecdote.

Shortly after arriving in America, I was treated to a dinner celebrating my birthday with three other American friends at an up-scale "authentic" Chinese restaurant in midtown Manhattan. After making it clear to the waiter that we wished to share our food "family style" we then ordered *as a group* a Peking Duck, among other things. To my great surprise (but not to the surprise of my three American friends), instead of being served in a big communal plate, all the ordered dishes were served on four individual plates one after another, with equal portions placed in front of each dinner guest. To my even greater surprise, after the Peking Duck was served, I noticed that amidst the equally distributed duck breast slices, there was one duck leg on each of our four plates. Since the legs were not presented as part of a whole duck, it did not strike any of my American friends as odd that *the one Peking Duck we had ordered came with four legs,* but I was utterly bewildered! The fact that each member of the dinner party was assured a choice leg portion of duck demonstrates this U.S. Chinese restaurant's rather implicit recognition of, and adaptation to, American small power distance values—which emphasize equality and de-emphasize status differences. Although the food at this restaurant was quite "authentic" in taste, by serving food equally, this "authentic" Chinese restaurant removed a huge part of the power distance dynamics that are evident in, and crucial for, the group eating experience in Taiwan/China.

In Taiwan/China, people with less power see group eating as an opportunity to show respect and gratitude by reinforcing existing power distance through the offering of limited and choice food portions to people with more power. At the same time, people with more power see group eating as an opportunity to show love and hospitality by breaking down existing power distance through the offering of limited and choice food options to people with less power. It is through these food-plying activities that power distance is negotiated and maintained.

Returning to the Peking Duck story: since all four of us were served equal portions of everything (including one duck leg each), the four people—of varying ages and job-statuses—were forced to dine without any opportunity for food-plying activity. This was the first time I realized just how profoundly my background in a large power distance society had shaped my identity. Sitting at a square table and eating equally-portioned food from my individual plate at a U.S. Chinese restaurant, I felt like a fish out of water—even though I was in an environment in which I was supposed to feel most at home. It was quite an alienating dining experience for me, albeit an informative and memorable one, and in many ways, it became the primary impetus for this study.

Conclusion

From the cross-cultural/intercultural analysis above regarding both *what* and *how* people eat at U.S. Chinese restaurants, it is apparent that Chinese restaurant culture in the United States has become an integral part of American culture. Nonetheless, based on my observations of, and my interactions with, U.S. citizens over the past decade, I firmly believe that there is a perceptual inconsistency between what many U.S. citizens *think* Chinese food and foodways are, and what Chinese food and foodways *actually* are.

I also believe that a parallel perceptual inconsistency exists in the context of Chinese American identity. Despite countless acculturation success stories enjoyed by Chinese Americans of many generations since the mid-nineteenth century, Chinese Americans in the United States are still frequently portrayed by the American mass media, and perceived in the American general public's eyes, as perpetual foreigners. Many of my Chinese American colleagues and students have shared with me their frequent encounters with questions such as "How did you get to speak English so well?" and "Where are you *really* from?" For me—an international student and scholar from Taiwan who aspires to become an acculturated Chinese American someday in the future—the struggles of my

Chinese American colleagues and students with this aforementioned perceptual inconsistency take on a personal quality and have in part inspired this study.

It is worth stressing that this chapter—which closely examines how U.S. Chinese restaurants originated historically, adapted to the dominant culture, and continue to thrive today—does not intend to label Chinese food in the United States in any way as "inauthentic." Nor does this chapter argue for the superiority of a static, "authentic" Chinese cuisine that can be geographically/culturally located in Taiwan/China, where some kind of essential Chinese quality is being preserved against the onslaught of global capitalism and fast-food culture.

Chinese cuisine in Taiwan/China, like Chinese cuisine in the United States, has a dynamic history that has adapted and changed over time, and it continues to do so. This study is not concerned with devising a measure of authenticity for Chinese cuisine. Rather, this chapter argues for a greater recognition of how *genuinely American* the Chinese food dining experience in the United States is. Engaging in an *integration* strategy of acculturation, Chinese restaurant culture in the United States has successfully adapted to a highly *individualistic* and *small power distance* society, with improvised ingredients and presentation techniques from the food of its original culture, China. This sometimes makes for strange anomalies, like a four-legged duck, but in the end it is a story that is as American as apple pie—or should I say, "as American as fortune cookies?"

Moreover, with the parallel acculturation process that can be drawn from Chinese Americans' identity development, this chapter also argues for a greater recognition of how *genuinely American* the experience of Chinese Americans is. In my view, when conceptualizing Chinese Americans, one should see them as neither perpetual foreigners, nor *"fake"* Chinese; rather, they are, and should be seen as, *genuine Chinese Americans* who have become an integrated part of America's diversity.

References

Asian Cuisine Boasts Growing Popularity in U.S. (2005, April 12). *Asian Reporter, 15,* 7.

Barbas, S. (2003, March). "I'll take chop suey": Restaurants as agents of culinary and cultural Change. *Journal of Popular Culture, 36,* 4, 669–686.

Berry, J. (2003). Conceptual approaches to acculturation. In K. M. Chun, P. B. Organista & G. Marín (Eds.), *Acculturation: Advances in theory, measurement, and applied research.* (pp. 17–37). Washington, DC: American Psychological Association.

Borgna, B. (2005). The history of the fortune cookie. *Infoplease.* Retrieved July 12, 2010, from http://www.infoplease.com/spot/fortunecookies.html.

Burros, M. (1986, August 30). De gustibus; chop suey, at 90, is still a mystery. *New York Times*, p. 46.

Chop suey, popular here, is hardly known in China (1928, November 11). *New York Times*, pp. 151.

Coe, A. (2009). Chop Suey: A Cultural History of Chinese Food in the United States. New York: Oxford University Press.

Gershenson, G. (2004, September 28). Flour, eggs, sugar, fortune: Inside the factory behind all these happy messages. New York Press. Retrieved July 12, 2010, from http://www.nypress.com/article-10205-flour-eggs-sugar-fortune.html.

Hamelink, C. J. (1983). *Cultural autonomy in global communications.* London: Longman Group UK Ltd.

Hannerz, U. (1996). *Transnational connections, culture, people, places.* London: Routledge.

Hofstede, G. (1996). *Cultures and organizations: Software of the mind* (1st ed.). New York: McGraw Hill.

Hofstede, G. & Hofstede, G. J. (2005). *Cultures and organizations: Software of the mind* (2nd ed.). New York: McGraw Hill.

Hofstede, G., Hofstede, G. J., & Minkov, M. (2010). *Cultures and organizations: Software of the mind* (3rd ed.). New York: McGraw Hill.

Hsu, M. Y. (2008). From chop suey to Mandarin cuisine: Fine dining and the refashioning of Chinese ethnicity during the cold war era. In S. Chan & M. Y. Hsu (Eds.), *Chinese Americans and the Politics of Race and Culture* (pp. 173–193). Philadelphia: Temple University Press.

Jen, G. (2005, April 27). A short history of the Chinese restaurant: From stir-fried buffalo to matzoh foo young. *Slate.* Retrieved July 12, 2010, from http://www.slate.com/id/2117567.

Lee, J. 8. (2008). *The fortune cookie chronicles: Adventures in the world of Chinese food.* New York: Twelve Books.

Liu, H. (2009). Chop suey as imagined authentic Chinese food: The culinary identity of Chinese restaurants in the United States. *Journal of Transnational American Studies.* Retrieved July 12, 2010, from http://escholarship.org/uc/item/2bc4k55r#.

Luo, M. (2004, September 22). As all-American as egg foo yong. *New York Times*, p. F1.

Plotnicov, L. & Scaqlion, R. (2002). *The globalization of food.* Long Grove, Illinois: Waveland Press, Inc.

Roberts, J.A.G. (2002). *China to Chinatown: Chinese food in the West.* London: Reaktion Books.

Schiller, H. I. (1976). *Communication and cultural domination.* Armonk, NY: M.E.Sharpe.

Stokes, I. N. P. (1915–1928). *The iconography of Manhattan island, 1498–1909: Compiled from original sources and illustrated by photo-intaglio reproductions of important maps, plans, views, and documents in public and private collections.* New York: Robert H. Dodd.

Takaki, R. (1989). *Strangers from a different shore: A history of Asian Americans.* Boston: Little, Brown & Co.

Tomlinson, J. (1991). *Cultural imperialism: A critical introduction.* Baltimore: The Johns Hopkins University Press.

Tompkins, J. (2005, February/March). Who invented the fortune cookie? *American Heritage, 56,* 1, 14–15.

Watson, L. J. (Ed.) (1997). *Golden arches east: McDonald's in East Asia.* Stanford: Stanford University Press.

Watson, L. J. (Ed.) (2006). *Golden arches east: McDonald's in East Asia* (2nd ed.). Stanford: Stanford University Press.

Wilk, R. R. (1999). Real Belizean food: Building local identity in the transnational Caribbean. *American Anthropology, 99,* 244–255.

Wu, D. Y. H. (2002). Improvising Chinese cuisine overseas. In D. Y. H. Wu & S. C. H. Cheung (Eds.), *The globalization of Chinese food* (pp. 56–66). Honolulu: University of Hawaii Press.

Wu, D. Y. H. & Cheung, S. C. H. (Eds.) (2002). *The globalization of Chinese food.* Honolulu: University of Hawaii Press.

Wu, W. F. (1982). *The yellow peril: Chinese Americans in American fiction 1850–1943.* Hamden, CT: Archon Books.

Yu, Renqiu (1987). Chop Suey: From Chinese food to Chinese American food. *Chinese America: History and Perspectives, 1,* 87–100.

12

The white farm imaginary: How one farmers market *re*fetishizes the production of food and limits food politics

Christie McCullen

The chapters in this section demonstrate how deeply food is embedded in social and cultural contexts. In Thompson's chapter, the discourse on food, specifically the discourse of fresh-roasted chickens, communicates competing social commentaries on the nature of social and economic relations. In Cheng's chapter, we see how Chinese restaurant culture in the United States communicates Chinese-American identity and experience with cultural exclusion. In Mudry's chapter, the discourse of science and quantification used in the 1917 United States Department of Agriculture food guide communicated not only dietary ideals, but also social ideals. In this chapter, I investigate the representation of food growers at a farmers market in California and what that image says about the racial politics of food production, consumption, and activism in the United States.

Scholars and activists of sustainability often use an analogy of a three-legged stool to describe this concept. Accordingly, sustainability is composed of concerns for the environment, economics, and equity. However, within conceptions and practices of sustainability, environmental and economic concerns often trump those for equity. To draw attention to the shadowed emphasis on equity, Agyeman (2005) coined the term "just sustainability" to emphasize and promote change that not only ensures wise use of natural resources but also ensures equitable distribution of environmental risks and benefits.

The alternative agrifood movement putatively strives for just sustainability. Specifically, it asserts that positive social and environmental outcomes will result from fostering direct relationships between producers and consumers (Kloppenburg, Hendrickson, & Stevenson, 1996). Farmers markets and community supported agriculture (CSA) are the two leading alternative agrifood institutions and they attempt to foster these relationships through direct marketing, a strategy wherein producers sell directly to consumers without the mediation of a supermarket or other middleman. While food sold through supermarkets typically renders food production invisible, farmers markets aim to "teach" through consumption—as customers buy food directly from farmers, they can meet and socialize with the grower, inquire about the whereabouts of the farm, and learn about the methods of production. In this way, farmers markets are often assumed to be transparent places where production/consumption relationships are visible and knowable, as opposed to the hidden relationships of the conventional food system. Logically, the movement posits that when these relationships are knowable to the general public, the exploitation and pollution afforded by that invisibility will not be tolerated.

Marx's (1976) concept of commodity fetishism is useful in understanding the alternative agrifood movement's imperative of direct producer/consumer relationships. According to Marx, the price of a particular commodity in capitalism is an abstract value that obscures the true value of that commodity (that is, the labor that created) and this obfuscation leads consumers to endow the commodity with a life of its own (a fetish) rather than seeing it as a product of someone's life and labor. Marx called this "commodity fetishism" and scholars since have adopted the verb "fetishize" to describe the process and mechanisms that conceal the value of labor inherent in products. Likewise, scholars use the term "defetishize" to describe any effort to reverse this concealment and make the conditions of production visible (Cook, Crang, & Thorpe, 2004). The alternative agrifood movement's imperative for direct producer/consumer relationships is such an effort to defetishize the production of food. I use this term to examine the role of the farmers market in this attempt. Likewise, I also use this term to show the process through which one farmers market continues to conceal the labor that produces food.

Despite their efforts, many farmers markets only partially defetishize the production of food. In this paper, I draw on 18 months of ethnographic research at the Davis Farmers Market in Davis, California, to describe who is included and excluded from the images of sustainable agriculture produced at this market. My research shows that through shopping at the market, customers develop a vision of farms that I call the "white farm imaginary." The term "imaginary" is used here to describe a shared set of symbols, narratives, values, and institutions that influence the consciousness and practices of a social group. Termed as such, this imaginary paints a scene of sustainable agriculture where white family farmers nobly work the land and Latino farm workers do not exist. In this way, the imaginary interpellates white farm owners as the main political subjects of the alternative agrifood movement. By also stripping Latino farm workers from political subjectivity in this movement, the white farm imaginary fails to fully defetishize the production of food in a way that could contribute to just sustainability. Instead, this farmers market and the imaginary it creates is a mechanism through which farm labor is again concealed. Unfortunately, this imaginary is just one example of the ways that whiteness operates in alternative agrifood systems. However, recognition and critique of the small ways in which whiteness is constructed in this context contributes to new visions of a food system that can foster just sustainability.

Whiteness in Alternative Agrifood Systems

My research builds on previous scholarship that describes and critiques the whiteness of the alternative agrifood movement. Much of this work argues that the movement's whiteness confines its potential to mobilize greater political action and drive food system transformation. It is commonly acknowledged that white people make up the majority of alternative agrifood movement followers, and the popular website "Stuff White People Like" satirically confirms this by listing organic food and farmers markets in its top ten list (Lander, 2008). Several scholars, in particular Rachel Slocum and Julie Guthman (2003), have set out to understand why white people are so animated by this movement, and also how that white prevalence often leads to the movement's racial exclusivity.

In a study on a farmers market in Minnesota, Slocum (2007) contributes to the critique of alternative food's whiteness by understanding it as something that is produced socio-spatially. Using Saldanha's (2006) idea of viscosity, Slocum describes farmers markets and other more expensive alternative food spaces as places where pale bodies hypervisibly display property privilege, thus coding the spaces as white, affluent, and exclusive. This research runs contrary to the popular belief among farmers market and CSA managers that markets are culturally neutral spaces (Allen, FitzSimmons, Goodman, & Warner, 2003).

Slocum (2007) also adds that whiteness is constructed discursively through the use of "white imaginaries" in alternative food spaces. She claims that these imaginaries entitle some and silence others, but she does not describe them in any detail. In an extension of Slocum's work, Guthman (2008a, 2008b) fills in these details to illustrate those imaginaries more. She argues that common alternative food discourses, such as the desire and aesthetic of all natural, organic food, the value of working with the land, and the desire for alternatives (Guthman, 2008a), as well as politics of conversion (2008b), reflect whitened cultural histories and values, and therefore disproportionately inspire white people as opposed to people of color. For example, the assumed universal value placed upon working with one's hands in the dirt ignores the fact that many African-Americans may associate such work with the legacy of slavery, especially when it is so emphatically promoted by whites (Guthman, 2008a).

Borrowing Slocum's term of white imaginary, the white farm imaginary that I describe at the Davis Farmers Market is a reflection of a larger ideology of the alternative agrifood movement called new agrarianism (Allen, 2004). New agrarianism—the valorization of a food system centered on small family farmers and the preservation of a so-called rural culture through direct marketing—also reflects a whitened cultural history. Assumed in this ideology is a universalized American identity based on romantic agrarian roots. It centers the American experience around a more European-American one and selectively deletes most people of color's agricultural history in the United States. For example, it ignores the justification of Native American displacement with white homesteaders, the enslavement of African-Americans, the exploitation of Asian immigrant labor in California's first factory farms, and the exploitation of Mexican farm laborers who harvest the majority of food grown in the United States today (Allen, 2004; Guthman, 2008a). The alternative agrifood movement's new agrarianism is a recent iteration of an agrarian populist ideology that, quoting Thomas Jefferson, touted small family farmers as ideal American citizens. Like the agrarian populist movement, the alternative agrifood movement garners support by drawing on this emotive narrative. The white farm imaginary created in some farmers markets today is therefore not a new phenomenon, but a contemporary iteration of a long-standing narrative around who grows food in the United States. What makes the whiteness of today's imaginary so stark is that it is created under circumstances that explicitly claim to tell the full story—farmers markets. Allen (2004) claims that the new agrarian ideology positions farm owners as the group most oppressed by the conventional food system. In an extension of her work,

I contribute to our collective understanding of the racial politics of agriculture by showing how the white farm imaginary of today's farmers markets reifies and reproduces that whitened ideology and excludes Latino farm workers from political subjectivity in the movement. In the next section, I will describe how the white farm imaginary is produced at the Davis Farmers Market, despite its intentions to defetishize the production of food.

Methods

The data below come from 18 months of ethnographic study of the Davis Farmers Market in Davis, California. In this study, I used a variety of participant observation techniques appropriate for the site including shopping, vending, shawdowing customers, and prolonged observing of several stands (one hour per stand). During the second half of my study, I spent most Saturdays as either a volunteer or a paid vendor at two different stands. Because this opportunity as a vendor allowed me to experience the customer-vendor relationships for the full duration of each market (five hours), I was able to confirm or complicate previous observations and note the most common patterns. I was also able to have more prolonged, casual conversations with the farmer who hired me and other farmers and vendors who visited our stand. When I was not vending, I took copious field notes and expanded those after leaving the site. Unfortunately, the hectic pace of market interactions did not afford me the time to take detailed notes while I worked as a vendor, but I would make quick notes while vending and expand those after the market.

I also strongly emphasized interviews in my data collection. I recruited interviewees as I shopped and vended, and interviewed anyone whose time availability lined up with mine. In total, I interviewed 28 market participants. Thirteen of these were in-depth, non-standardized interviews (averaging 49 minutes), and the remaining 15 were shorter non-scheduled standardized interviews (averaging five minutes). Because I was most interested in why customers chose to go to the market, I mostly interviewed customers. The in-depth interviews were with eight customers, one market manager, one farmer, one prepared food vendor, and two non-farmer volunteer vendors. The 15 shorter interviews were with customers only. I asked all interviewees about their motivations to participate in the market and the meanings they attached to that participation, recording and transcribing all their responses. I indexed all these interview transcripts and expanded field notes using the open and axial coding methods described by Strauss (1987).

Because I am generally interested in social justice, I was also very struck by what was absent in the themes that emerged organically from my data—mainly, little or no acknowledgement of or inquiry around farm labor—and coded that "missing data" as well (Ryan & Bernard, 2003, p. 92). Thus, my discovery of and insights into the white farm imaginary were greatly influenced by both presence and absence of information in interviews and field observations.

Findings

The customers I interviewed and observed at the Davis Farmers Market communicated a desire to buy directly from "the people who grow their food." Indeed, it is this desire that drives them to shop at farmers markets most. Not only do they want to ensure that farmers get a fair price for the food they grow, but customers also want to ask farmers questions about growing, get advice on cooking, and develop friendships with them. But the vendors selling food behind the stand at the market are not the only people who grow food at these farms, and, at times, they are not growers (that is, farmers or farm workers) at all. Customers tend to conflate vendors with growers at the market because of the common sense notion that farmers markets are places where farmers do the actual selling and the institutional verification of this notion that comes with a mark as a California Certified Farmers' Market. This conflation leads to an assumption that vendors are growers, and since most of the vendors at the market are white, this assumption gives customers a misleading image of the racial makeup of alternative agriculture, or what I call the white farm imaginary. The impact of this white farm imaginary concerns me since customers are often motivated to action (that is, shopping at the farmers market) because of their concern for farmers' livelihoods. I question how this motivation for action might be different if the image of grower more closely matched reality. First, I will explain these findings in more detail.

Desire to Defetishize

The construction of the white farm imaginary begins with customers' desire to buy food directly from the people who grow it. The customers I interviewed are dedicated to buying at farmers markets for a variety of reasons all related to the defetishization of the social and environmental relationships that go into producing and distributing food. To use a common phrase at the market, customers want "to know where their food comes from" As the following two excerpts illustrate:

> I guess it's nice buying directly from the people that…those farms that grow the food. So, I—I like that the Aboreal's family, watching their kids, they're grown ups now. (Shawnee[i], personal communication, November 14, 2007.)

> Just knowing who's growing it, like I can talk to those people and they can talk to me and tell me, I can ask them "oh do you use sprays" or "how long are you going to have these for"? (Audrey, personal communication, November 19, 2007.)

The first of these excerpts from Shawnee shows that customers like the way that the farmers market facilitates a defetishization of food by allowing them first, to know growers at all, and second, to know them as individuals, as friends, and/or as fellow parents. By shopping from the Aboreal's stand year after year, Shawnee and Mrs. Aboreal formed a friendship beyond a business relationship, and Shawnee mentioned that friendships like those have strengthened her commitment to shopping at the market because she understands her consumption as financially supporting friends, not just local business people. When asked about their motivations to shop at the farmers market, most of the other interviewees claimed that this experience of getting to know growers personally inspired them to continue shopping there. Through observations at stands, I found this to be common among customers. During times when the farm owner or regular vendor took a break from the stand, I overheard inquires or was asked about the whereabouts of the missing vendor. When I or another vendor explained where the missing person was, customers would commonly wait for their return or say something like, "Well tell him I came by and said hi."

Many customers also express a desire to buy directly from farmers so that they can learn more different varieties of produce, growing practices used on the farm, and cooking techniques. In the second of the interview excerpts above, Audrey expressed this desire. As someone really interested in particular varieties of foods and sustainable agriculture techniques, she values the opportunity that the farmers market offers to learn about these details. I have overheard hundreds of small conversations like these between customers and vendors at the market. Questions about growing practices are more common at conventional stands or stands that don the distinction "chemical-free," meaning that they are not certified organic, but use organic practices. At all the stands, especially those selling ethnically-specific or less common varieties, customers curiously ask questions about the particular varieties, such as their seasonality, their flavor, and their preparation.

Customers' desire to defetishize food also shows in their desire to—using a common farmers market refrain—"pay the true price of food." Customers want to ensure that growers get adequate compensation for their work, since farmers' wages are often invisible in traditional market relationships. The following excerpt exemplifies this reason:

> I appreciate the fact that my dollars are going to the people who are doing the work and not to three or four or ten layers of stuff in between me and the farmer. It's something – and I preach about fair trade too. That the people who are doing the growing, the work, can make a living at it. (Isabel, personal communication, December 4, 2007.)

In this excerpt, Isabel echoes a sentiment mentioned by each of my interviewees—that she wants to buy directly from the people who grow food to ensure that they get a fair and living wage for the work they do. With the rise of the conventional food system, and its ability to achieve economies of scale through industrial production and cheap labor costs from the global South, small-scale growers in the United States have increasingly lost competitive advantage in traditional markets. The alternative agrifood movement has advocated for greater compensation for small-scale farmers through direct marketing initiatives like farmers markets and CSA boxes[ii] where farmers set fair prices for their food, often above the average market value[iii]. Having face-to-face contact with a vendor at the market gives customers a sense that they are directly supporting farmers and that the money they exchange for produce goes directly to that person.

The excerpts above show that customers at the Davis Farmers Market defetishize food by building relationships with the vendors at the market by talking about growing practices, produce varieties, food preparation, vendors' lives, and by buying food at a price set by the farmer. However, in their quest to defetishize food, no one I interviewed mentioned that they had inquired about labor on the farm, nor did I overhear such questions. The customers I have interviewed and observed, as well as the alternative agrifood movement more generally (Allen, 2004), have positioned farmers (that is, farm owners) as the social subjects of agriculture, or in other words, as "the people who grow food." Farmers are believed to be the people most disadvantaged by the problematic conventional food system, reflecting new agrarian and farm-centric ideologies (Allen, 2004). Absent from these ideologies, and from the image of growers created through institutions like the Davis Farmers Market, are the thousands of Latino farm workers who actually do a majority of the growing of produce (planting, plowing, weeding, and harvesting) in California. In the next sections, I will explain how farm workers have become invisible in the image of "the people who grow food" at the Davis Farmers Market specifically and also in the alternative agrifood movement.

Partial Defetishization

I have witnessed patterned behavior at this farmers market that indicated that customers tend to believe that produce vendors (that is, the people working behind produce stands) are growers, and interviews often confirmed this conflation. I refer to the image that customers have of the people who grow their food as the 'white farm imaginary' because this image of growers includes the white vendors who customers see at the market and excludes the mostly Latino farm workers back at the farm. The imaginary's construction is both a product of the images at the Davis Farmers Market and the general, and deeply rooted, cultural narrative of the movement that imagines sustainable farmers as white, small-scale, family farmers (that is, those who rely solely on family labor).

Customers' conflation of grower and vendor begins with a common sense deduction—farmers markets are places where farmers sell produce. Moreover, the discourse of the alternative agrifood movement champions farmers markets as places where customers buy directly from the people who grow food. All my interviewees said that they go to the farmers market in order to buy food directly from growers. In some respects, the Davis Farmers Market is a place where direct marketing between producers and consumers happens. As a California Certified Farmers' Market, farmers are the only people sanctioned to sell produce and other farm products at the market, as opposed to wholesalers and other middlemen (California Federation of Certified Farmers' Markets, 2009, para. 1). At the Davis Farmers Market, many vendors post signs on the backs of their trucks and vans that read 'Certified California Farmer,' indicating that they are officially recognized as an actual farmer and allowed to sell at certified markets like the Davis market. While observing stands I noticed that these signs puzzled some customers. A comment from one customer exemplifies this common confusion: "What does that mean? Of course they're a farmer, we're at a farmers market." Another customer I overheard said, "California Certified Farmer. Duh." These comments demonstrate the common sense belief that farmers markets are indeed places where people buy directly from farmers. While this law does ensure that only actual farm *owners* collect the profits made at markets, it does not mean that farm owners are the people who actually work at the stand during the market hours. Furthermore, this law, and the idea of direct marketing that is so strongly promoted by the alternative agrifood movement, do not dictate that vendors must be growers. In fact, it is common for farmers to hire vendors to fulfill the market labor of bagging, weighing, and selling produce, especially if they sell at multiple markets a weekend, and most of these vendors do not work at the farm.

My discovery of the conflation between vendor and farmer came in part from my own experience working at the market. I was one of the hired vendors; I worked an occasional Saturday and helped a few farmers sell their produce, but I never worked on the site of any of those farms. Each time I worked I had several conversations with customers wherein they assumed that I was either the farmer, the farmer's daughter, or the farmer's wife. Other non-farmer vendors confirmed that this misidentification happened to them as well. For example, Seamus, a white volunteer vendor for Rich & Plenty Farms, told me that customers frequently assume that he is one of the family farmers at Rich & Plenty. These customers will ask him questions about the farm, such as how the crops are responding to various weather conditions, and then look surprised when he tells them that he is not familiar with the farm. Marcus, another white non-farmer vendor at Produce Galore Farms, seconded Seamus's observations, and added that customers even seem annoyed when they find out in conversation that he is not a farmer. Perhaps they feel cheated from the defetishizing experience of interacting directly with the people who grow the food.

The conflation between grower and vendor that happens at the Davis Farmers Market is a partial defetishization of food that paints a racially skewed image of growers. To illustrate, vendors at the market are most commonly farm owners or non-farm worker vendors, and most of these faces are white. Latino farm workers, for the most part, do not vend at the market. Most of the vendors who do participate in growing food are white farmer-farm owners (for instance, Mr. and Mrs. Santucci of Santucci Farms) and not farm workers. However, the farm owner is not the only person who grows the food. In fact, most farm owners do more managing and planning than actual growing. Farm workers in California, most of whom are Mexican, do 80% of the growing, dispassionately referred to as "farm labor," and outnumber farm owners, most of whom are white, 18 to 1 (Allen, 2004). Even on small- and medium-sized farms like many of those that tend to sell at farmers markets, farm workers outnumber the farm owner and his or her family members. For example, Rich & Plenty Farms, a farm that customers repeatedly refer to as a family farm, employs more farm workers than family members. Overall, whites make up about 58% of the produce vendors at the Davis Farmers Market, a number that is disproportionately high compared to the percentage of whites actually involved in growing food. In general, this leads customers to create a white farm imaginary, a disproportionately white picture of the subjects of California agriculture.

Moreover, this high white representation is especially the case with the organic stands since these farms tend to hire additional white volunteer or paid vendors from town to help at their stand, creating a white imagined subject of *sustainable* agriculture in California. There are vendors of color at the market, but they are more likely to work at the conventional stands or the prepared food stands. These demographic differences lead to a perceived racialized division of labor along agricultural technique lines where whites grow organically and Latinos grow conventionally. Since produce that is both organic and local is considered the more ethical (that is, sustainable) in terms of growing and distribution methods, the lack of Latinos at organic stands further strengthens the image of a white, ethical grower, rather than images of varying color.

This mostly white representation at organic stands sends a message that white people are most involved in growing ecologically sustainable food. This image equates Latinos with large-scale conventional agribusiness, and not small-scale sustainable agriculture. However, sustainable agricultural methods necessitate more manual labor (for instance, hand weeding) than conventional methods because of the lack of chemical inputs used in organic and other more sustainable techniques, and most of that manual labor on sustainable farms is done by Latino farm workers (Getz, Brown, & Shreck, 2008).

The whiteness presented by the erasure of farm workers does not go entirely uncontested. For example, Rich & Plenty Farms, a family-owned farm that employs several young white people from Davis to sell at the market, also shows more racially accurate images of their farm and who grows their food. On occasion, they bring in a large photograph of their farm and all of its employees. In this image, customers see that Latino farm workers largely outnumber the Aboreal family members, and that none of the regular vendors work on the farm. Also, the image of a white sustainable grower is not entirely pervasive. The market also hosts a Hmong family's "chemical-free" farm, a Latino family's "chemical-free" farm, and a recently added Latino-owned organic farm.

Refetishizing the Production of Food

My interviews with customers have confirmed that customers tend to assume that the vendors at the market are growers. Since I recruited most of them through working at a stand, several of the interviewees asked me questions before our interviews to ascertain whether or not I was a farmer and a graduate student at the same time. This customer image of vendors as farmers becomes further complicated, since most of those white vendors tend to live and work other jobs in Davis. Customers see these white vendors working in town and assume that they need to have a second job to survive as a farmer, adding to the common narrative of the struggling family farmer. For example, Shawnee, a long-time customer, told me that she felt bad every time she saw the vendor, Forrest, working at the Davis Food Co-op because it meant he could not make a living just farming. When I told her that he was not actually a farmer, she said:

> OK, I wasn't sure. So some of the people that are there, I'm not really sure if they're farmers or if the farmers pay them to sell their food. Which is understandable. Like oh my gosh, how can you work all week and then sell your food? So some of that you don't really know the whole connections, what's going on. (Shawnee, personal communication, November 14, 2007.)

All of the interviewees I talked with expressed a desire to defetishize food by buying directly from the people ostensibly growing the food. However, Shawnee's excerpt here, especially the line "So some of that you don't really know the whole connections," demonstrates that the vendor-customer interaction does not completely defetishize the relationships between production and consumption. In fact, in some ways it leads to alternative fetishizing, or at least an imaginary story of food production, for the customers at the market. Details included in some customers' imaginaries are that most farmers are white, families provide most of the labor on the farm, and farmers are struggling to make ends meet. This supposed struggle, that is both real and imagined, leads customers to pity farmers and thus to feel obligated to and satisfied by buying from farmers at the farmers market. The struggle factor also leads some customers to romanticize and heroicize farmers for the work they do, in turn leading to more compassion for farmers and dedication to buy directly from them. In this section, I will share some evidence for the pity and glory customers attach to farmers, and also discuss the implications this heroicization has when the image tied to the hero is a white family farmer, as opposed to other food system actors, especially the Latino farm workers who grow the food sold at the market.

The customers I interviewed all felt compassion for farmers because of the extremely challenging work they perceived that they did in order to make a living. The following excerpts, where customer interviewees explained why they chose to shop at the farmers market, exemplify the general compassion felt for farmers:

> Ummm, so I would say maybe first would be supporting those farmers like, seeing them you know like out there and thinking of like 'oh they must work so hard and then coming out here to sell and make a living.' Again, that goes back to my compassion for small farmers. (Audrey, November 19, 2007.)

> An awful lot of farming couples, one of them had a job in town, a day job. And for the insurance and some of those things and it also has steady income. Cause generally in farming there are times when you're harvesting and you get the money and there's times when you're spending it. It's hard work, very hard to make it. And you're at the mercy of…the weather. If the umm if it rains the wrong time – in fact right when the almonds are blooming – there's no crop. The bees don't fly, the flowers fall off, there's no crop, and if you grow almonds, well it's a really lean year for you. (Isabel, personal communication, December 4, 2007.)

Both of these excerpts illustrate the customers' compassion for farmers' work and lives. As Audrey said, "Oh they must work so hard and then coming out here to sell and make a living," emphasizing that farming itself was hard enough without the additional burden of selling at the market. Several of the interviewees used similar phrases such as "make a living" or "for survival" to emphasize the humility of farmers or perhaps to contrast them to other hard-working individuals who do so for high incomes and status symbols. Farmers ostensibly work hard just to get by.

Isabel's excerpt demonstrates sympathy for farmers' hard work for two other reasons. First, from her experience growing up in a farm town, she witnessed that some farming families needed to work off the farm in order to earn welfare benefits like health insurance. Isabel also pitied farmers for the risks they take. By being "at the mercy of" nature, even their hard work can make survival difficult or impossible for farmers during some years.

In addition to pitying farmers for their hard work, some customers romanticized and heroicized farmers for making the choice to farm despite the struggles. The following excerpts from Audrey show how some customers idolize farmers for their seeming self-sacrifice:

> Like, I have compassion for farmers everywhere, like people who are struggling to make a living, you know, they are who feed the population. (Audrey, personal communication, November 19, 2007.)

> It's like food is like…it's not just…it's not easy…in a way. So I appreciate farmers like…you know, not take the…more easy work like…cause farming's not an easy job, like they could easily go to like…do some other kind of work, you know office or something. But they decide to like use their hands and use their like physical labor to like feed us. (Audrey, personal communication, November 19, 2007.)

When Audrey uses the word "feed" in both of these excerpts, she attaches nurturance and selflessness to the occupation of farming. Furthermore, she elevates farmers to hero status by explaining that they choose these nurturing roles despite the financial struggle, hard work, and physical labor. Like all heroes, they sacrifice their own good for the good of others.

Most of these excerpts came in interviewees' immediate responses to my question of why they chose to shop at the farmers market, showing that customers' pity, compassion, and idolization of farmers motivates them to buy directly from farmers. Shawnee's excerpt below exemplifies this emotionally-motivated consumption. She responded to a question about how she felt after buying directly from farmers with:

> Well I guess I always just feel better after going there, so it's like emotionally, it's like it feeds me both emotionally and with food. It's just always fun to check in with people and even when it's gloomy weather, it's like somehow you're in this together. You may not hang out on those days, but then I feel bad, it's like 'oh gosh they made the effort to pick this food, I need to go buy it from them. It must have been miserable for them to stand there and sell it when it's so cold.' But umm, yeah, so even on rainy days, I always feel better having gone and just kinda, it's funny how that, that emotional connection is…it's a really positive thing. So, I always leave with a good feeling. (Shawnee, personal communication, November 14, 2007.)

Like the other interviewees, Shawnee was motivated to action (for instance, buying directly from farmers) because of her compassion for farmers' struggles. Her explanation of being "in this together" with farmers shows a sense of responsibility and interdependence that all the other customers I interviewed expressed. Even on the coldest and rainiest winter days, she would bike twenty minutes into town to buy from farmers at the market and be with them in solidarity.

The solidarity with farmers that my interviewees expressed is impressive. However, I am troubled that the people behind the stand—the imagined or real farmers, but by no means the only people who grow the food—are the sole or primary subjects to whom the customers' compassion, money, and energy are dedicated. In the previous excerpt shown, Shawnee's sympathy for farmers came partly from her imagined recognition of a vendor working a second job, but also from an understanding that farmers who sell at the market work additional hours in order to sell there. Since customers see the farmers working extra hours at the market, they become sympathetic with this image of who grows their food, and not with an image that includes the farm workers who are largely invisible at the market. Shawnee's earlier quotation "you don't really know the whole connections, what's going on" exemplifies this invisibility. The customers are motivated to support the farmers because of the struggle they witness at the market, but they do not see or consider the challenges farm workers face, and therefore exclude farm workers from the discourse that explains who they support.

Defetishizing Again: Toward Anti-Oppressive Food Politics

In his *New York Times* essay "Naturally," Pollan (2001) describes a genre of organic food advertising that he calls "supermarket pastoral." Pollan claims that this packaging tells a romantic story of the production of organic foods that rarely matches the reality of its production. The white farm imaginary that I have described above is akin to the supermarket pastoral in that it illustrates the dissonance between the real and imagined landscapes of sustainable agricultural production. Farmers markets act as agents in perpetuating whitened American cultural myths and narratives about agriculture in the United States. Their efforts to defetishize the production of food are only partial; they reveal the production methods of food and introduce customers to farm owners but still hide the contribution and exploitation of Latino labor. Most customers would be surprised to find that an English-Spanish pidgin is the common tongue of sustainable agriculture production.

So if farmers markets serve to inspire political action by educating consumers about how food is grown, what type of political action does this imaginary inspire or not? As I have described above, the white farm imaginary interpellates white farm owners as the foremost political subjects of the alternative agrifood movement. This process effectively reifies the farm-centric and new agrarian ideologies that position farm owners as the main victims of our conventional food system. Consumers respond to this by acting politically through their consumption—biking through the rain, as the customer Shawnee claims, to ensure a hardworking farmer's fair compensation. The policies advocated for by the alternative agrifood movement aim to improve the welfare of farm owners and the food choices of consumers. Such policy recommendations include increased funding for direct marketing infrastructure, investment into value-added entrepreneurial efforts, and increased assistance for new farmers (Allen 2004). These policy recommendations indicate that farmers markets are more than just a site of political *consumption*; they also serve as a gateway to broader politics. Even so, the policy recommendations listed above prove to only serve the movement subjects created at farmers markets—farm owners and ethical consumers.

I contend that the white farm imaginary created in farmers markets continues to limit the politics of the alternative agrifood movement. The erasure of farm workers from this image poses several questions regarding these politics. Most importantly, how would the movement's discourse and prescribed actions be different if customers saw Latino farm workers behind the stands or knew that they were the people who grow their food? Would farm workers be heroes of the movement too? Would customers still be as compassionate? Would the interactions between customers and vendors be as friendly? Would customers' energy be directed at pedaling through the rain to buy directly from the grower? Or would that energy also be used to rally for immigration policy that allows for permanent residency for farm workers? Might the movement have built stronger alliances with the United Farm Workers and migrant rights groups? Would customers demand different agricultural labor policy that defended minimum wage instead of sanctioning non-living wages for farm workers? Would the movement challenge the notion of private property laws that create class distinctions between farm owners and farm workers? I do not claim to know the answers to these questions, but I am curious how much broader the political project of the movement would be if the glorified subjects were more than the farm owner and the paying customer. I believe that it is possible that the presence of Latino farm workers at farmers markets would acknowledge their role in growing sustainable food and also draw attention to the trade policies that have both encouraged Mexican campesino migration and forced small farmers out of traditional markets in the United States. Contesting trade policy such as the North American Free Trade Agreement for these social justice implications is a politics that will contribute to just sustainability far more than the market-based solutions of direct sales to consumers.

Even as I advocate for more farm worker presence at farmers markets, I recognize that their erasure is not an innocent act, and therefore a move for more presence will likely be met with resistance. For example, I question whether customers truly want to defetishize food production. It seems quite possible to me that many customers *want* the white farm imaginary; afterall, it matches a long-standing white cultural narrative that is ignorantly blissful. As one friend reminded me, "No one wants to get preached at when they're buying tomatoes." The white farm imaginary allows farm owners and customers to celebrate a certain self-serving political action and reject politics that may draw attention to their comparative privilege. Therefore, it seems that the presence of Latino farm workers may dampen some consumers' reverence for the movement. Considering those circumstances, it seems plausible that many farm owners are invested in upholding this white farm imaginary because it helps their business. Perhaps they hire extra white non-farm worker employees to sell at the market for that very reason. This inquiry deserves empirical study to assess the potential intentionality of hiring white vendors.

I would not be surprised if that is the case for some. However, successful initiatives like Fair Trade certification, which demands improved labor standards, suggest that plenty of people want to ensure safe and fair labor conditions for workers. Furthermore, there is a growing movement for fair labor certification within the United States. Don Villarejo, one of the original founders of the California Institute of Rural Studies, explains that people often assume that fair labor standards are part of organic certification (personal communication, February 20, 2007). I agree with this suggestion, giving me confidence that many farmers market customers do not just want a feel-good experience, they also want to ensure social justice for those who grow food. I contend, therefore, that contesting the white farm imaginary at farmers markets will inspire broader food politics—a politics that demands a food system that is both just and sustainable.

Endnotes

[i] I used pseudonyms for all of the names of interviewees and farms.

[ii] Community Supported Agriculture (CSA) projects take on several forms, but the most common form is a subscription box. In this practice, consumers pay a price to the farm upfront (either weekly or at the beginning of the season) and receive a box full of a portion of the farm's harvest for that week.

[iii] Unfortunately, because the movement operates primarily through market-based solutions, its focus on economic justice for farmers can lead to an economic injustice for customers who cannot afford the price of produce that fairly compensates farmers. This is another example of

the movement's impediments to just sustainability for eaters. In this paper, I am focusing on impediments to just sustainability for farm laborers.

References

Agyeman, J. (2005). *Sustainable communities and the challenge of environmental justice*. NewYork: New York University Press.

Allen, P. (2004). *Together at the table: Sustainability and sustenance in the American agrifood system*. State College, PA: Pennsylvania State University Press.

Allen, P., FitzSimmons, M., Goodman M., & Warner, K. (2003). Shifting plates in the agrifood landscape: The tectonics of alternative agrifood initiatives in California. *Journal of Rural Studies, 19*, 1, 61–75.

California Federation of Certified Farmers' Markets. (2009). What's a CFM? Retrieved February 16, 2010, from California Federation of Certified Farmers' Markets website: http://www.cafarmersmarkets.com/whats-a-cfm.html

Cook, I., Crang, P., & Thorpe, M. (2004). Tropics of consumption: 'Getting with the fetish' of exotic fruit. In A. Hughes and S. Reimer (Eds.), *Geographies of commodiy chains* (pp. 173–192). New York: Taylor and Francis, Inc.

Getz, C., Brown, S. & Shreck, A. (2008). Class politics and agricultural exceptionalism in California's organic agricultural movement. *Politics & Society, 36,* 4, 478–507.

Guthman, J. (2003). Fast food/organic food: reflexive tastes and the making of 'yuppie chow'. *Social & Cultural Geography, 4,* 1, 45–58.

Guthman, J. (2008 A). Bringing good food to others: Investigating the subjects of alternative agrifood practices. *Cultural Geographies, 15,* 4, 431–447.

Guthman, J. (2008 B). "If they only knew": Colorblindness and universalism in alternative agrifood institutions. *The Professional Geographer, 60,* 3, 387–397.

Kloppenburg Jr., J., Hendrickson, J., & Stevenson, G.W. (1996). Coming in to the foodshed. *Agriculture and Human Values, 13,* 3, 33–42.

Lander, C. (2008, January 18). #5: Farmers markets. Retrieved February 1, 2008, from Stuff White People Like website: http://stuffwhitepeoplelike.com/2008/01/18/5-farmers-markets/

Marx, K. (1976). *Capital: Volume 1: A critique of political economy*. London: Penguin Books.

Pollan, M. (2001, May 13). Naturally. *New York Times Magazine*. 22–32.

Ryan, G.W. & Bernard, R. (2003). Techniques to identify themes. *Field Methods, 15,* 1, 85–109.

Saldanha, A. (2006). Re-ontologizing race. *Environment and Planning D Society and Space, 24,* 1, 9–24.

Slocum, R. (2007). Whiteness, space and alternative agrifood practice. *Geoforum, 38,* 3, 520–533.

Strauss, A.L. (1987). *Qualitative analysis for social scientists*. Cambridge, UK: Cambridge University Press.

13

Quantifying the American eater: USDA nutrition guidance and a language of numbers

Jessica Mudry

In a 1902 United States Department of Agriculture (USDA) Farmer's Bulletin, scientist Wilbur O. Atwater wrote:

> The information gathered from a study of the composition and nutritive value of foods may be turned to practical account by using it in planning diets for different individuals.... By comparing the results of many such investigations it is possible to learn about how much of each of the nutrients of common foods is needed by persons of different occupations and habits of life. (p.32)

Atwater, a nutritional chemist at the USDA, saw science, the "information gathered from a study" of food, as the grounds upon which an American public should learn to eat. Americans should learn about the "nutrients of common foods" and craft their diet based on categories of occupation and "habits of life." In 1902, America was a land in flux. Waves of immigrants entered the country to fill factories and plants, and to populate major urban centers. These immigrants did not live in the way the American government would have preferred. They lived in cramped houses, had rococo taste in home decoration, and ate strong smelling and tasting foods. In order to better "assimilate" these new Americans, Progressive reformers, under the aegis of both public and privately funded organizations, attempted to teach Americans how to live, dress, be tasteful consumers, and eat. They encouraged new urbanites to live more modern, efficient, "American" lives, lives defined by "a dust-, germ-, and disease-free scientific ideal" (Cohen, 1980, p. 756).

For the USDA, learning the constitution of the ideal daily diet was defined by scientific method and calculation. The USDA scientists used a calorimeter to quantify food and human activity, and they used scientific data to construct numeric boundaries for "good" and "bad" foods and eaters. Food guides published by the USDA used numbers to craft rational eating patterns that aimed to minimize financial and edible waste, and maximize nutrition and work output among Americans at the turn of the twentieth century. The USDA's policies and publications attempted to control the diet, and living patterns, of populations of Americans. In order to conform to governmental guidance one needed to speak the language of science and numbers, and assess themselves against charts of data and planned caloric intakes. The enumeration of food, eating, and eaters allowed for the USDA to define the American diet and a "good" American by constructing meals and people with data and numbers.

In this chapter, I describe how discourses of science and quantification were integrated into American nutrition policy, the technologies that abetted the integration of the discourses, and how these discourses aligned the USDA nutrition policy with the goals of Progressive reformers. In order to accomplish this I address three aspects of American food from 1880 to 1920. First, I address how the calorimeter was the fundamental technology that provided scientists with numeric data about food and eaters. During this time, scientists built machines with the intention of improving aspects of social life. Hospitals began using analytical methods to test urine, perform X-rays, and assess blood counts. Health faddists began selling machines to measure and improve strength, energy, and sexual performance. Americans were becoming aware of, and defined by data produced by machines. In the field of nutrition, data reframed the epistemological bases for how scientists understood food. The calorimeter generated sets of numbers about foods that allowed scientists to construct relative notions of how good a food was by how many calories it had, and at what cost. As the USDA relied on a language of science to describe food and eaters, this discourse became integrated into policies aimed at the public, and introduced them to an abstract, quantitative conception of food.

Second, I address how this quantified language became the discursive framework in USDA food guides for an ordered and rational approach to eating an approach that fit neatly into the *zeitgeist* of the Progressive Era. With the birth of the Home Economics department of the USDA, the home became the lexical domain of science and reason. Progressive reformers encouraged urbanites, often new immigrants to America, to be measured in their eating patterns, as well as their housekeeping and taste in home decoration. Quantified food provided the USDA nutrition guides with a normalized and ordered means for food selection. The guides used numbers to circumscribe what Americans ought to eat, and the guides encouraged Americans to calculate their fiscal and physical consumption of food.

Third, I will argue that the discourse of quantification acted to construct an enumerated American eater whose data could be manipulated by and through federal policy. Using scientific and numeric rationalization, the USDA invented categories of Americans by age, profession, household income and sex. The food guides used these categories to encourage Americans to identify with a defined group and to purchase and cook foods that conformed to their numerically derived social status. To highlight this categorization and control I use Toby Miller's ideas of the "cultural subject," and "ethical incompleteness." Groups of eaters created by the USDA that could be controlled, managed and governed through federal policy kinds of "cultural subjects," products of policy that are "governed through institutions and discourse" (Miller, 1993, p. ix). The USDA food guides created normalized populations and created groups of eaters using a discourse of quantification and nutrition policies that followed were written using a language that attempted to strip subjectivity from the eater.

The American Calorimeter: Enumerating Food

The creation of the American notion of "nutrition" relied on the USDA's embrace of science and scientific methods to frame and shape their policies. The calorimeter was a cornerstone technology that helped scientists construct new knowledge about food and integrate a statistical, normalizing language into public policy about food. At the turn of the twentieth century, there were two kinds of calorimeters used by the USDA. The first, and simpler, was a bomb calorimeter: a sealed vessel into which a scientist put foods, or human waste and then exposed that food or waste to high heat. As the matter inside the bomb calorimeter burned, the heat given off increased. A scientist measured this increase in heat in calories, assigned a caloric value to the matter that was burned, and analyzed the resulting ash for minerals and protein content. Before the calorimeter, an apple was a juicy red fruit. Using the calorimeter, a scientist identified the apple as 81 calories, 0.27 grams of protein and 228 mg of potassium. The bomb calorimeter created numbers out of food and made disparate foods comparable. A room calorimeter, the second and more complex version of the device, was a sealed, insulated chamber (large enough for a person) that measured changes in room temperature as the person performed activities. A person riding a stationary bicycle, studying, or sleeping increased the temperature of the calorimeter by different amounts as each activity created different amounts of heat. The room calorimeter allowed for the measurement of human action. Combining data from the room and bomb calorimeters, a scientist could determine how much energy one took in during the day, and how much they put out.

The first American calorimeter was at Wesleyan University in the lab of Wilbur Atwater, a USDA scientist often called the "Father of American Nutrition" (Carpenter, 1994, p. 1707S). Atwater had received his PhD in 1869 from Yale University, and completed a postdoctoral course of study in Europe at the universities of Leipzig and Berlin. Atwater's research with German chemists and physiologists focused his academic interests on the interactions among, and applications of, humans, science and food. In late 1886, Atwater returned to Germany, to the laboratory of Max Rubner. A central issue in nineteenth century German science was the determination of the chemical composition of food and the best foods to eat in order to maximize human output. The scientists conceived of the human body as a de-animated machine, whose physical performance they set to optimize.[i] Rubner's interest was in the science of energetics. He believed that calories were the human fuel, and he conceived the body as a combustion engine. This analogy allowed Rubner to extend the first law of thermodynamics, the law of conservation of energy, to people (Cravens, 1996).[ii] The room calorimeter fit Rubner's concept of the closed system body/machine. Rubner noticed that when fueled by fats, the human body gleaned double the caloric energy than when fueled by sugars or proteins. Together with determining how much energy the "human machine" expended, Rubner collected caloric data and chemical analyses of commonly consumed foods. The data of energy expenditure, along with the data of energy available in food gave birth to a simple mathematical equation.[iii] Calorimetry could determine how much you should put in to your body, based on how much you put out.

Atwater's experiences with the German calorimeter gave him insight into the quantitative technologies of nutritional science, and provided him with a discursive framework within which he could express the results of the technology. Human calorimetry impressed Atwater. In it he saw a leveling, rational and impartial approach to food with myriad applications to ameliorate America (True, 1937, p. 103). Atwater began to write about food, the American diet, and the importance of good nutrition in USDA publications, as well as in the public press.[iv] In 1887 he wrote a series of articles entitled "The Chemistry of Food and Nutrition" for *Century Magazine*, a magazine that circulated widely among the middle-class public. In this publication, Atwater stated that America was ignorant about their diet, they ate too much sugar, and they wasted money on expensive cuts of meat that had no nutritional benefits in comparison with cheaper cuts. He called for the public to better themselves through education in the science of nutrition:

> Among those who desire to economize there is great pecuniary loss from the selection of materials in which the nutrients are really, though not apparently, dearer than need be.... Our task is to learn how our food builds up our bodies, repairs their wastes, yields heat and energy, and how we may select and use our food-materials to the best advantage of health and purse. (Atwater, 1887, p. 59-60)

Atwater's audience for his piece in *Century* was clear. He saw the calorimeter, and the science of nutrition as a boon for middle-class America, which "desired to economize." In the coming years home economists would lobby for control of the teaching of the science of nutrition, and tout it as saving the health and economy of America. Their message of "New Nutrition" encouraged the consumption of food that was healthy and economical, a message that, by 1916, was standard in most middle-class cookbooks (Levenstein, 2003, p. 97).

For the fiscal year of 1895, Congress made an appropriation of $10,000 for investigations into the nutritive value of human foods, with "a view to determining ways in which the dietaries [sic] of our people might be made more wholesome and more economical" (Atwater, 1895, p. 387).[v] Atwater used a portion of the government money allotted to human nutrition research to complete, in 1897, the first US human respiration calorimeter based largely on the German design. With the help of Wesleyan physicist E.B. Rosa, Atwater perfected a room calorimeter that produced results of enviable accuracy. The calorimeter was a large copper-lined wooden box of about 170 cubic feet, large enough to accommodate a folding bed or table, or whatever athletic apparatus the experiment required. What was most amazing about the calorimeter, aside from the fact that it worked, was that the subjects appeared to remain reasonably well and comfortable during their calorimetric incarceration, which lasted, on average, four or five nights (Maynard, 1962 and Swann Harding, 1947).[vi]

The calorimeter was a social technology of measurement. Atwater could use the calorimeter to generate knowledge about food and eaters, and this knowledge facilitated his ability to justify and encourage particular eating behaviors, control social situations, and attempt to change cultural eating patterns. Historian Ted Porter (1996) calls this sort of social technology "a means of planning and of prediction" (p. 43). That is, these kinds of technologies "work best if the world they aim to describe can be remade in their image" (p. 43). The calorimetric data allowed the USDA to produce data about people and food, but also codify people and food with data. Food, and by extension eaters, became something to calculate, measure and empirically "know." The application of the calorimeter's data to life in America during the Progressive Era coincided with Progressives' hopes that technology could be used to eliminate injustices, and make American society more efficient in the face of waste. The calorimeter aimed to improve American life through scientized eating, but it stood as just one example of the technologies of the Progressive Era, which scientists thought could improve American life. Joel Howell, in *Technology in the Hospital* (1996), points out that between 1900 and 1925, a hospital visit changed markedly. By the 1920s patients were subjected to a battery of tests to analyze and quantify their blood, urine and skeleton. The tests and technologies abstracted health and healing but did so under the guise of the "efficiency movement" that defined the hospital's adoption of scientific ideals (p. 3). Patients were interpreted by and through doctors reading their data produced by machines, in a hospital setting. Only doctors with specialized knowledge and the ability to understand what a blood-examination or a urinalysis meant could diagnose and treat the patient. Howell writes that patient testing "could reinforce the ideas of Progressive era reformers" who "wanted a rational, numerical, graphic way to understand" the problem and how to fix it (Howell, p. 190).

While the means of technology to the ends of health were admirable, the Progressive Era saw technologies that were used in immoral and unfortunate ways. Some Progressive Era racists used science as a means to categorize and rank the quality of Americans based on the color of their skin and their physical features. The Progressive's intellectual commitments lie with social inquiry and science at the root of effective social control. Technologies of measurement like the craniometer, which measured the ratio of the skull width to skull length to infer brain size and, by proxy, intelligence were thought by some to indicate social order. Knowing this order, some Progressive Era racists feared a "race suicide" of the upper classes of light-skinned Europeans, where they would be "outbred by prolific, inferior immigrant stock" (Leonard, 2003, p. 693).

Whether the technology of measurement was used to abet noble or ignoble social causes, it was the way that the technology altered knowledge production that is important for this paper. Using a quantifying technology to measure human beings creates taxonomies defined and articulated by numbers, science and abstract thought. The person being measured, their experiences, their history or their knowledge became unimportant in the face of technologies that dictated, in a specialized and unfamiliar language, who and what one was. Economists, doctors, trained scientists and home economists who were comfortable with the specialized discourse of numbers, quantities, measurements and objectivity could then exert political and social control over those who they measured. As specialized knowledge informed public policy it demonstrated science's attempt to control American cultural life. Fecundity, sexual habits, and dinnertime all became the domain of science and all could be measured and controlled through scientific discourse. The subjects, whose lives were observed and categorized, came to be defined by these "cultural policies" as either good, or bad, weak or strong, dirty or clean, and superior or inferior. Public policy could then use science, rationality, and numbers to define what Toby Miller (1993) calls an "ethical incompleteness," a determinant, and often quantified, weakness or ambiguity, be it diet, skin color, or energy level, for which subjects needed to compensate by following particular policy guidelines, if they could.

The First Official USDA Food Guide: Counting Calories and Categorizing Eaters

The quantification of food, and Atwater's research with the calorimeter, were part of a larger cultural transformation occurring in America. Aiming to control and educate waves of immigrants, domestic science, the rational structure behind "Home Economics," aimed to "Americanize" immigrants and focus their attention on living in an efficient and effective manner: working hard, living frugally and being healthy (Gabaccia, 2000, 128–31). Scientific data about living conditions, nutrition and public activity made the Progressive Era's reform workers mandate to synthesize, organize and manage democratic life in America a much easier task. In *A Search for Order: 1877–1920*, Robert Wiebe (1967) examines the rise of bureaucratization and industrialization. Wiebe's normalized and standardized "order" was facilitated by an enumerated discourse that allowed for the generation of groups and types of people and cataloging them based on sets of nutritional numbers.[vii]

For Wilbur Atwater eating well meant learning which foods were both healthy and economical and eating the correct amount for your age, sex and profession. Atwater (1895) used his data from the calorimeter to define foods that were "healthful" and "economical," and he categorized good foods as the ones that yielded the most nutrients for the least money (p. 359). Distinguishing between good and bad food required an understanding of the scientific composition of various foods, the nutrients they furnished to the human body, and calculating a cost/nutrient ratio for each. In the USDA publication *Principles of Nutrition and Nutritive Values of Food* (1902) Atwater wrote:

> Ten cents spent for beef sirloin at 20 cents a pound buys 0.5 pounds of meat, which contains 0.08 pound of protein, 0.08 pound of fat, and 515 calories of energy, actually available to the body, while the same amount spent for oysters at 35 cents a quart would buy little over half a pound of oysters, containing 0.03 pound of protein, 0.01 pound of fat, 0.02 pound of carbohydrates, and 125 calories of energy; or if spent for cabbage, at 2 1/4 cents a pound, it would buy 4 pounds, containing 0.05 pound of protein, 0.01 pound of fat, 0.18 pound of carbohydrates, and 460 calories of energy, while of wheat flour at 3 cents a pound it would buy 3 1/2 pounds, containing 0.32 pound of protein, 0.03 pound of fat, 2.45 pounds of carbohydrates, and 5140 calories of energy. Comparing the various materials in this way, it becomes clear that the fresh vegetables are the dearest sources of protein, meats and fish somewhat cheaper, and cereals the cheapest of all; and that oysters and lobsters are the costliest sources of energy, followed by some of the green vegetables and fruits, then the majority of meats, next potatoes, and cheapest of all, the cereals. (p. 42)

Atwater (1887) saw science as the mechanism through which one could learn about what to eat "to the best advantage of health and purse" (pp. 59–60). Thus, Atwater, and by extension the USDA, assumed two things: that Americans were persuaded by arguments about nutrition that were founded on fundamental scientific principles and that they would make economical food choices based on those arguments. Atwater's quote aligns the science of nutrition with free-market economics. Both nutrition and economics are meant to implicate rational individuals whose task it is to evaluate relative quantities. The discourse of quantification makes the alignment of science and economics possible. For example, Atwater's reference to lobsters and oysters is not meant as a critique of class but rather it is meant to rationalize food choice and strip those choices of conspicuous cultural markers. This was, after all, a middle-class document designed to level and equalize otherwise divergent groups.

The remedy for the evil of overspending on food was to be found, according to the USDA, "in an understanding of the elementary facts regarding food and nutrition and in the acceptance of the doctrine that economy is not only respectable but honorable" (Atwater, 1902, p. 45). To respect and honor economy here demonstrates that one is simultaneously capable of acting rationally and being patriotic (by patriotic, I mean acting as a morally good

"American"). In *Embellishing a Life of Labor: An Interpretation of the Material Culture of American Working-Class Homes, 1885-1915*, Lizabeth Cohen (1980) points out that Progressive reformers, who were hired to encourage the middle-class aesthetic (efficient, clean, and dust- and germ-free) and patterns of consumption among workers, were often rebuffed. Working class people aspired to own their homes in order to ensure the future economic success of their immediate family and the traditions of their community. However, how they decorated and lived in their homes, and what and where they ate became points for modification for the reformers (p. 762). Immigrant workers wanted material goods, foods and furnishings that demonstrated status and taste in their home country or community. They felt that things like feather beds, collections of tchotchkes, or patterned wallpaper showed they were acculturated Americans rather than "unsanitary, tasteless, and un-American," as they were seen by the middle-class (Cohen, p. 770).

Food, too, was a point of reform for the USDA home economists who, after the passage of the Smith-Lever Act in 1914, were given the responsibility for distributing advice about what to eat, a responsibility transferred from the USDA farmer's bureau and Atwater's control (Levenstein, 2003, p. 96). The Home Economists of the Progressive Era used scientific rationale and discourse to encourage efficient, economical and "clean" food, meaning that food should not be overly sauced or spiced and should maximize daily calories and protein for the least amount of money. Immigrants, often pining for tastes of home, offended Progressive sensibilities by buying things like cheese (at $1.25 a pound) or olive oil, in lieu of less expensive milk and lard (Levenstein, 2003, p. 106). Food historian Donna Gabaccia (2000) writes that the domestic science movement developed alongside, and provided the scientific thrust for, the domestic science of home economics. The goal of home economists was "to Americanize foreigners" and it succeeding in creating a widespread program for culinary change among new immigrants, often the poorest Americans (pp. 125–128). At the turn of the twentieth century, cooking and cleaning had become the lexical domain of the discourse of quantification. Domesticity "expanded into an objective body of knowledge that had to be actively pursued" (Shapiro, 2001, p. 7).[viii]

Atwater argued that families could minimize poor food choices (either needlessly expensive or devoid of "nutriments") if they knew how much and what kind of food was essential for the day's diet, and if they knew the most economical foods to select to achieve that diet. The USDA encouraged families to calculate their energetic needs for the day. This required one to learn or at least care about calories, proteins and nutritional quantities. Advice to the woman of the house was that if she had "a husband who is engaged in moderately hard muscular work like that of a carpenter or mason or active day laborer," he should take in about 3,500 calories (Atwater, 1895, p. 362).[ix] According to the USDA, "The wife if busy at work with her hands about the house or otherwise, will need perhaps eight-tenths as much" and the four children would together equal three more "men" at moderately hard labor, thus the family requires 1.12 pounds of protein and a fuel value of 14,000 calories (p. 361). The task at hand for the fictional "wife" was to select foods that obtained, at the least cost, sufficient proteins, fats and carbohydrates needed to meet the physical demands of her family. If she could make wise selections and obtain "abundant nutriments at less cost," she could save a little money for "extra comforts for the family" or for the savings bank. The notions of "wife," "laborer" or "child," however, were quantitative constructs. A wife was counted by the USDA as eight-tenths of her husband. Members of a USDA-defined "family" were numeric objects not sentient subjects.

In 1917, Caroline Hunt, a specialist in Food Preparation and Use at the Bureau of Home Economics wrote the first USDA food buying guide entitled *How to Select Foods: What the Body Needs.* The stated goal of the guide was to "give a simple method of selecting and combining food materials to provide an adequate, attractive, and economical diet" (preface). The first official guide, published in 1917, relied on the discourse of quantification to direct America's eating practices.[x] Specifically, this guide saw the human body as a deficient vessel with nutritional "needs" that were to be filled by the eater: "Evidently what a person who plans meals ought to know is what things the body needs in its food and how these needs can be filled by the ordinary food materials" (p. 3).

The quantified trope of "need" arrived in a timely fashion as American troops headed to Europe to fight and a food shortage loomed at home. Using Atwater's framework of proteins, carbohydrates and fats, middle-class Americans were encouraged to eat simply and frugally cutting down on their butter, meat and wheat consumption and substituting carbohydrates from bread and protein from meat with fresh vegetables and milk (Levenstein, 2003, p. 141). The message, to conserve and substitute, likely had less of an impact among those in lower socioeconomic classes, and the government published literature in the native language of many immigrant groups that encouraged them to eat according to American nutritional standards. The pleas to eat less meat, and to conserve butter and bread, may have rung hollow on immigrants who, because they had little money, were used to conserving these ingredients, if they ate them at all (Levenstein, pp. 142–143).

The Bureau of Home Economics, always closely affiliated with the USDA because it was a "women's department within the agricultural college" of land-grant institutions, sought an efficient and simple way to teach the public about food (Shapiro, p. 176). Teaching people the *proper* way to eat was of great concern to USDA experiment stations and extension co-ops because they considered the dinner table a rapid way for reforming Americans' eating patterns and their relationship to food. This first food guide established the pragmatic value of food that was simple, clean, and wholesome. The food guide shows a photo of a bounty of eggs, milk, bread, fish, beef and a basket of fruits and vegetables. The guide outlines a sample meal for a sample family that is a man, woman and three children:

> Food materials such as those shown in the pictures may be combined into three meals in many ways. The following meals are given not because they are recommended above many others that might be used but simply to show that such foods can be combined into dishes that are commonly used in American homes. The meals here suggested would supply the following substances in about the right proportions to keep the family in healthful condition and to make the food taste good, providing they were well prepared. (Hunt, pp. 5–6)[xi]

The food guide is clear in its goals: eat in the prescribed, measured manner, in order to maximize your health and in order to make your home more American. Using the discourse of quantification, *How to Select Foods* employs "need" as the theme around which to structure the problem of filling human physiological requirements and the maintenance of human labor output. The guide

> tells very simply what the body needs to obtain from its food for building its tissues, keeping it in good working order, and providing it with fuel or energy for its muscular work. It shows in a general way how the different food materials meet these needs and groups them according to their uses in the body. (Hunt, preface)

The guide contrasted these "needs" for tissue building, strength and muscular work with the irrational appetite and the unreliability of hunger and personal tastes. The guide also warns that in determining what one ought to eat "appetite is not always a safe guide," and "neither can hunger and its satisfaction always be relied on" (Hunt, p. 3). Manual laborers, read immigrants working in steel mills, textile mills and meat-packing, had eating habits that offended home economists' sensibilities. Black coffee, cured meats, garlic, and homemade breads were heavily flavored and considered to feed an irrational appetite instead of a calculated physical need (Levenstein, pp. 106–108).

One of Hunt's main concerns in the food guide is that the nutritive demands of the hard laborer be met, and she took great pains to categorize what each type of laborer, woman and child need:

> The exact amount which each person needs depends upon age, sex, size, and amount of work done with the muscles. An elderly person, or one of quiet habits, needs less food than a vigorous young one; a large person more than a small one; a man more than a woman; grown persons more than children; and a farmer working in the hayfield, a mechanic, or a football player more than a man who sits at his desk all day. (p. 11)

By learning "how to select foods" according to the calculable physical output of this individual, and by cooking like they do in "American homes" the empirical needs of the family would be better met than if they followed an individual's "appetite," "hunger," or "satisfaction." For those families who did not follow the principles of the guide, Hunt was not optimistic:

> It is believed that it is impossible to plan the meals for a family wisely without at least as much knowledge of how different kinds of food serve the body as this bulletin has given and that the safest short cut to good planning lies in considering foods in the five groups here described. (p. 12)

Wisdom, as Hunt defined it, came from a body of knowledge—knowing the functions of food, quantities that defined food's functions, and human caloric requirements. Meeting the empirical needs of the family became the goal for the home cook. The cultural subjects defined by "age, sex, size, and amount of work done with muscles" ought not to be satisfied with the meal because it tasted good; rather because proper food selection met their needs.

The establishment of five food groups: fruits and vegetables, meat and meat substitutes, starches, sugars and fats, in the 1917 guide shows the influence of Wilbur Atwater, the father of Caroline Hunt's co-author, Helen Atwater. The 1917 guide used Atwater's nutrition research and shaped it for public consumption. Using Atwater's calorimetry research the authors group foods based on their known chemical composition and function in the body. The groups, Hunt claims,

> will be helpful for the housekeeper to form the habit of thinking of the many different kinds of food which she handles.... If the housekeeper will consult [the groups] in planning meals until she has learned where each kind of food belongs, she will have taken the first step toward providing a diet which will supply all the food needs of her family. (pp. 8–9)

Here, Hunt outlines the importance of method in meal planning and how the food guide fosters a particular understanding of good food. Following the method of food grouping for meal planning reassures the housekeeper that her meals will be simple, correct and nourishing. The food guide encourages the "wise" housekeeper to "think of foods according to their group" during meal planning, shopping, and curing and canning for the winter (pp. 10–11).

How to Select Foods recasts the dinner plate, food shopping and food preparation into a science experiment, foisting upon Americans a new epistemological framework with which to understand and talk about food. The food guide required assessment of the family's physical output (their "needs") in order to guide what they ought to eat, and required reconceptualizing food into groups based on its nutritive function. As science and nutrition became the epistemological foundation for these new food groups, and a theme for this first food guide, the food groups established an epistemology for the family meal and represented an ontological shift in food from a tasty pleasure to an apparatus of scientific method (Hunt, 1917, p. 8). Keeping an American house meant adopting a new approach to food, and eating what science and federal policy told you was needed.

Constructing and Controlling a Countable Eater

The discourse of science and quantification in the USDA food guides facilitates the construction, quantification and discursive control of American populations. The USDA's construction of eaters, and their attempts to use scientific reason to sway the eating patterns of populations, demonstrates how they rely on a language of science and numbers to communicate and rationalize public policy. Categorized by age, employment and sex, a subjective and malleable concept like "eater" becomes normalized through concepts like calorie intakes and daily protein requirements. This normalization and quantification allowed the federal policy to judge the quality of an eater based on how closely they followed the scientific recommendations. The enumeration of food, and the American eater, allowed subjective concepts like "quality" to be judged in terms of frugality, calories or nutritional bounty. A quantified food could be "good" or "bad" based on its cost, protein or calorie count, and "good" Americans ate the appropriate amount of food for their daily needs—food that was plain, nutritionally efficient, and economical. Harvey Levenstein (2003) points out that social workers often judged new immigrants' level of assimilation through their gastronomic choice, noting things like "still eating spaghetti, not yet assimilated" (p. 105).

Thus, underpinning the USDA's use of the discourse of quantification and the USDA food guides are imagined audiences, groups of Americans that become the targets of an enumerated discourse. "Laborers," "Wives," "Americans," or "eaters" are not actual samples of the population or even real people. Rather, these words, which represent sets of numbers and statistics, are discursive signifiers invented by the USDA. These signifiers avail themselves to numeric control by the discourse of quantification. The formation of these groups, and their numeric management by the USDA, represent kinds of "cultural subjects," produced and organized by policy and discourse. According to Toby Miller in *The Well-Tempered Self* (1993), the cultural subject is a fictional entity that is "governed through institutions and discourses" (p. ix). Cultural subjects are products of policy, dreamed up to represent populations whose behavior can be managed, remedied, trained or aligned by discourses. In this case the "American eater" is a cultural subject that is fabricated by the USDA to represent heterogeneous masses of the American population. The USDA food guides, and much of the early nutrition research performed in the USDA-sanctioned labs, parses out this eater by sex, age, race, caloric needs, geography and occupation. Eating, tastes, and pleasure derived from food are largely cultural, experiential and geographical, but the USDA can manage this disparity using quantification. If, as Miller argues, policies produce publics, then USDA defined "nutrition," food guides and Recommended Dietary Allowances create kinds of eaters.

A discourse of numbers, because it can be used to manage, group and control both information and individuals who are implicated by that information, acts as an ideal milieu for the production of cultural subjects. By inscribing "ethical incompleteness," or qualitative judgments upon people's character based on their adherence to policy initiatives, the USDA makes "Americans" and "eaters" a manipulable and assessable collective. This collective is manipulated through measurement and quantification and in the process individuals are stripped of their subjectivity and personal judgments. The argument is that individuals in this collective can see their "incompleteness" in federal policy and attempt to remedy it, or "complete" themselves using the discourse of the policy. The discourse of quantification makes achieving this completion easy because achievement is not contained in subjective, or hard-to-define, political ideals. "Completion" for the American eater comes from abiding by nutritional numbers and by measuring themselves against numeric standards. The "good" laborer, wife, or child (good being a normalized term) ate according to the USDA's specified numbers. The USDA's "good" wife ate 80 calories to her husband's 100, and four children equaled three moderately hard-working men and ate the same number of calories.

The USDA, through its early experimentation on food and human metabolism, its food guides and their messages, and through the creation of norms and standards attempted to manage publics by having them compare themselves to these externally generated numbers. Miller (1993) calls these guiding messages "technologies of governance" (p. xiii). These technologies, which may be everything from a calorimeter to a food guide to a pictorial representation of a good meal, help imprint ethical incompleteness upon the eater. By relying on the discourse of quantification to achieve the recognition of ethical incompleteness, the USDA encourages the use of that discourse, which circumscribes choices and conversations that follow. During the Progressive Era, the time of publication of the USDA first official food guide, the USDA's ideal, complete and normal eater is numerate and well versed in the discourse of quantification. Ideal eaters heed nutritional advice, read food labels and food guides, and compare their own food intake with what is "normal" for their USDA-delineated demographic. This eater does not say things like "broccoli isn't good" because the USDA eater's bases for judging broccoli are folic acid content, fiber, or vitamin C, not whether or not the eater likes the taste of broccoli. The "ethically complete" American eater of 1917 eschews borscht, *mortadella*, or homemade rye bread in favor of a supper of vegetable soufflé or orange shortcake, parts of the USDA's sample meals for a family in 1917 (Hunt, p. 6). The complete and normal eater, as defined by a discourse of quantification does not taste their food, or experience their meal and they do not care where or with whom they are eating.

Miller's concept is useful here because it helps point to the limits and inadequacies of the discourse of quantification—its inability to know, in all its fullness, the place of food in American culture. In fact, by inventing numerically defined and tempered Americans, the USDA illustrates its desire to strip away the human and subjective facets of food and eating. The USDA uses the discourse of quantification in its food policy to construct the ideal American eater. The eater becomes a fictional aggregate of numbers and statistics, and demonstrates the USDA's vain attempts to use science and mathematics to manage and control human activity. The caloric and nutrient intake circumscribed social conditions and the quality of life of the people in early USDA nutrition studies performed by Wilbur Atwater. The introduction of quantity as an inherent quality to American food and the human act of eating, normalized personal gastronomic preferences and allowed eaters, and their food, to be ranked, counted and measured. According to the USDA, while everyone differed in the amounts and proportions of food they needed to eat, in the actual practice of eating

> we are apt to be influenced too much by taste, that is, by the dictates of the palate; we are prone to let natural instinct be overruled by acquired appetite; and we neglect the teachings of experience. We need to observe our diet and its effects more carefully, and *regulate appetite by reason.* [Emphasis added] (Atwater, 1895, p. 368)

The establishment of USDA food guides was a fundamental first step in establishing a national, and normalized American diet. At the semantic level, enumerated food made gastronomic knowledge impersonal, and devoid of any social, cultural, or geographic influences. The definition of reason and rationality shifted the discourse of food and eating from taste and experience to calculation and equation. This shift still resonates with us today.

Applying quantification to food and the American eater, a process facilitated by the calorimeter's production of data, allowed the USDA to promote gastro-fiscal responsibility, morality, and rational consumer action dictated by numbers. Numbers became the basis for qualitative judgments about who should eat and buy what. After the development of the science of nutrition, moral terms like "good" and "bad" became enumerated and objectified in discussions of food. The virtue of numbers and, as Atwater puts it, "reason" in the American diet, as they pertain to the USDA's construction of the American eater, is that they have rigorous certainty, a rational formulaic approach to food, and the ability to reduce qualitative social patterns to data. The post-calorimeter applications of the quantification of food represent the American government's acceptance of the rules and language of science as the knowledge foundation for an American diet, the authority of the federal scientists as the arbiter of truths about food, and the integration of the language of quantity into qualitative, or subjective social discursive venues.

Endnotes

[1] For more on early German nutrition researchers, see Anson Rabinbach's *The Human Motor: Energy, Fatigue and the Origins of Modernity* (New York: Basic Books , 1990).

[ii] Both Rubner and Carl von Voit's ideas of the human machine had, according to Cravens, "large ideological import." Concurrent with the "hard science" approach to the human body by scientists like Rubner and Voit, there was an opposing view expounded by the vitalists. The vitalists maintained that the living and non-living forms of nature had qualitative differences. By arguing that the human body worked according to the same principles as a steam engine, the chemical nutritionists successfully challenged the theologians, clerics, poets and philosophers ideas regarding life and nature. pp. 130–131.

[iii] Rubner's calorimetric experimentation served as the foundation for isodynamic law, where he established that 100 grams of fat was equivalent to 211 grams of protein, and roughly 240 grams of starch or sugar. These findings led to the Rubner factors of "calories per gram" for protein, fats and carbohydrates: 4.1, 9.3 and 4.1 respectively. While these numbers were very similar to Atwater's later discovery of the 4, 9 and 4 calories/gram of protein, fats and carbohydrates, Rubner's data did not consider how digestion may affect the caloric energy available in certain foods. Thus Atwater, who did extensive work on the digestibility of foods in conjunction with calorimetry, is credited with the discovery. See Buford Nichols' "Atwater and USDA Nutrition Research and Service: A Prologue of the Past Century" *The Journal of Nutrition* 124 (1994): 1724S–1725S.

[iv] Between the years 1875 and 1881 Atwater published 69 articles in American Agriculturalist entitled "Science Applied to Farming" that encouraged the application of scientific knowledge to practical farming. He also published, in 1894 in the Farmers' Bulletin No. 23, an article entitled "Foods, nutritive value and cost" which was aimed at housewives, and served as perhaps the first federally issued food guide.

[v] This amount increased to $15000 in the fiscal year of 1897.

[vi] The calorimeter revealed precise measurements about human energy expenditure. By monitoring the change in temperature in the room during the human subject's various activities, the calorimeter determined the quantities of nutrients and energy that the human subject metabolized during different physical activities. It established the relationship between expended energy and metabolized energy, as well as the digestion and assimilation of foods. The Atwater-Rosa calorimeter could recover 99.8% of the carbon dioxide expelled by the subject during the experiment, and 99.9% of the heat produced by the human subject, as well as the substrates they metabolized. The system allowed them to measure the balance between food intake and energy output and to quantify the dynamics of human digestion. The room calorimeter was capable of amazingly precise measurement of human metabolism. It could record a change in room temperature if the human subject so much as wound his watch. By studying the digestibility and metabolization of foods and the energy produced in the human body, Atwater determined that

fats yield 9 calories of energy per gram, and carbohydrates and proteins 4 calories per gram each. These "Atwater Units" of metabolizable energy of foods based on the chemical composition became the linchpins in the study of American nutrition. See Jeanne Wiggen, "The room calorimeter: Atwater's "copper box" revisited." *Agricultural Research,* 41 (1993): 12–14.

vii Among popular health reformers of the Progressive Era, Horace Fletcher's health program best represents the *zeitgeist* of the time. Fletcher was convinced that chewing food morsels until they became a pulpy liquid would allow the body to better assimilate the food, and use it more efficiently, a Progressive Era goal. For Fletcher efficiency meant that there would be little or no food waste to linger in the intestine, and thus feces would be scant and infrequent. Earlier American health reformers like John Harvey Kellogg, Bronson Alcott and Sylvester Graham (namesake of the Graham cracker) used religious morality as reasons to follow their regimens. To deny oneself of pleasurable or piquant tastes, meat, caffeine, and sugars was to be moral and spiritually pure. Though self-denial was encouraged by these reformers as promoting godliness, and was in line with both a Puritan ethic and Victorian mores of suppression, Kellogg, Alcott, and Graham used science and medicine to buttress their religious messages. For more on religion and diet see James Whorton's *Crusaders for Fitness: The History of American Health Reformers* and Daniel Sack's book *Whitebread Protestants: Food and Religion in American Culture.*

viii For an extended discussion of the domestic science movement and its relationship to food see *Perfection Salad* by Laura Shapiro, and Hamilton Cravens' "Establishing the Science of Nutrition at the USDA: Ellen Swallow Richards and Her Allies." *Agricultural History* 64. (1990): 122–133. Also, see Roma Apple's article "Science Gendered: Nutrition in the United States, 1840–1940" in Harmke Kamminga and Andrew Cunningham's text *The Science and Culture of Nutrition 1840–1940* pgs 129–154 and Sue Ellen Hoy's *Chasing Dirt: The American Pursuit of Cleanliness* New York: Oxford University Press, 1995. In particular, Hoy's chapter "Public and private cleanliness in the Progressive Era," as well as Nancy Tomes' *The Gospel of Germs: Men Women and the Microbe in American Life*, Cambridge: Harvard University Press, 1998 are good resources. In Tomes' work the chapter entitled "Disciples in the Laboratory" invokes science as the thrust behind the home economics movement, and cleanliness as a scientific standard (Tomes, 91–113).

ix Atwater saw nutrition primarily in terms of its ability to improve the physical strength of laboring men. Because men were the wage earners, they were most in need of nutritious foods, and to consider them the prototype for his studies that determined "nutritional requirements per pound of body weight" was safe, and even generous to the nutritional needs of women and children, whose level of activity would be considerably less. See Atwater's "Food and Diet" in the *1894 Yearbook of Agriculture.*

x Hunt published a guide in 1916 entitled "Food For Young Children" but it did not address the nutrition needs of the whole family.

xi Caroline Hunt, *How to Select Foods,* 5–6. The use of the word "common" is ironic considering the USDA defined the family, the foods, and parameters under which one should eat.

"Commonly used foods," could be anything that the USDA wanted them to be, just as the definition of the "American home" was up to their discretion as well.

Acknowledgments

This chapter was previously published in *Food, Culture and Society* in the Fall 2006 issue volume 9, no. 1.

References

Atwater, W.O. (1887). The Chemistry of Food and Nutrition. *Century Magazine.* 34 May–Oct 1887: 59–60.

Atwater, W.O. (1895). Food and Diet. *1894 Yearbook of Agriculture.* U.S. Department of Agriculture. Washington DC: Government Printing Office.

Atwater, W.O. (1902). Principles of Nutrition and Nutritive Value of Food. *Farmers' Bulletin 142,* U.S. Department of Agriculture (Washington, DC: Government Printing Office.

Carpenter, K. J. (1994). The Life and Times of W. O. Atwater (1844–1907). *The Journal of Nutrition,* 124, 1707S–1714S.

Cohen, L. A. (1980). Embellishing a Life of Labor: An Interpretation of the Material Culture of American Working-Class Homes, 1885–1915. *Journal of American Culture, 3,* 752–775.

Cravens, H. (1996). The German-American Science of Racial Nutrition. In Hamilton Cravens, A. Marcus & D. Katzman (Eds.) *Technical Knowledge in American Culture: Science, Technology and Medicine Since the Early 1800's.* Tuscaloosa: University of Alabama Press. 127–145.

Gabaccia, D. (2000). *We Are What We Eat: Ethnic Food and the Making of Americans.* Cambridge: Harvard University Press.

Harding, T. S. (1947). *Two Blades of Grass: A History of Scientific Development in the U.S. Department of Agriculture.* Norman: University of Oklahoma Press.

Howell, J.D. (1996). *Technology in the Hospital: Transforming Patient Care in the Early Twentieth Century.* Baltimore: Johns Hopkins University Press.

Hunt, C. (1917). *How to Select Foods.* U.S. Department of Agriculture, Bulletin 808. Washington, DC: Government Printing Office.

Leonard, T.C. (2003). More Merciful and Not Less Effective: Eugenics and American Economics in the Progressive Era. *History of Political Economy 35*, 4, 693–712.

Levenstein, H. (2003). *Revolution at the Table: The Transformation of the American Diet.* Berkeley: University of California Press.

Maynard, J. (1962) Wilbur O. Atwater: A Biographical Sketch. *Journal of Nutrition, 78,* 1–9.

Miller, T. (1993). *The Well-Tempered Self: Citizenship, Culture, and the Postmodern Subject.* Baltimore: Johns Hopkins University Press.

Nichols, B. (1994). Atwater and USDA Nutrition Research and Service: A Prologue of the Past Century. *The Journal of Nutrition, 124,* 1724S–1725S.

Porter, T.M. (1996). *Trust in Numbers: The Pursuit of Objectivity in Science and Public Life*. Princeton: Princeton University Press.

Rabinbach, A. (1990) *The Human Motor: Energy, Fatigue and the Origins of Modernity.* New York: Basic Books.

Shapiro, S. (2001). *Perfection Salad: Women and Cooking at the Turn of the Century*. New York: Modern Library.

True, A. (1937). *A History of Agricultural Experimentation and Research in the United States 1607–1925*. Washington D.C.: Government Printing Office.

Whorton, J.C. (1984). *Crusaders For Fitness: The History of American Health Reformers*. Princeton: Princeton University Press.

Wiggen, J. (1993). The room calorimeter: Atwater's "copper box" revisited. *Agricultural Research, 41,* 12–14.

Section Four

Environmental Issues: Food Communication and the Natural World

14

Hunting, gardening, and the original work of art: A homological analysis

Barry Brummett

Politics and the table are no strangers to each other. In the United States we have a long history of dumping tea into harbors to protest taxes, boycotting grapes in support of Cesar Chavez, or renaming French fries Freedom fries in irritation at the French for correctly opposing our corrupt Iraq war. Recent engagements with "green" politics have created a new interest in what people eat. The works of Michael Pollan (2006; 2008) have drawn widespread interest as they ask us to think of going to McDonald's or Whole Foods to obtain dinner as politically charged acts.

Pollan and others I will mention below argue that growing (and in Pollan's case at least, hunting) your own food is a responsible practice of ecological politics. Or if one cannot do that, then careful choices of where one obtains one's food can have important "green" political consequences. Anyone who has ever debated whether to buy "wild" fish from far away or local, farm-raised fish understands the host of complicated political, ecological issues that go into this evening's poached salmon. This politics is woven into our everyday lives, since we must eat and as a result we must have practices and regimens for obtaining that food. Food is where most of us engage most directly in ecological politics.

Of course, there are wider politics in which we might engage, at the city, state, or national level, including electoral politics. Here I want to show what our practices of procuring food can teach us about the possibilities for those wider politics. I think how we obtain food can help us understand how to govern ourselves more broadly. To do that I will use a critical method called *homology*.

This chapter identifies homologies existing among the experiences of growing one's own vegetables in a garden—hunting animals for food—discourses about gardening and hunting—shopping for food in a supermarket—and Walter Benjamin's (1968) distinction between the work of art and the mechanical reproduction. From probing into this motley collection of texts and experiences, I will make some observations about how politics works for many of us today, and how it might work differently. The sense of "politics" I use here goes from the personal, local, ecologically implicated politics of where we obtain food to the wider levels, of city, state, or national politics, by which I mean broad, socially organized means of contesting and gaining power. Let me begin by explaining the critical method I will use here.

The Method of Homological Criticism

Form is a central component of our experience. Life follows patterns, and many patterns cut across different modes of experience. "Competition" describes a form of experience which we may see at work, while bowling, or in seeking time and attention from family members. We also experience texts of that pattern of competition on television, or while reading books. The "comic" pattern of making a foolish error, suffering the consequences, and being reinstated in a forgiving community may underlie much of what we do during the week, as well as what we see on television or hear about in songs.

A critical analyst using the method of rhetorical homologies identifies a number of texts and experiences that follow a formal pattern in significant ways (Brummett, 2004; 2006). The analyst chooses this method because texts and experiences that are formally similar can rhetorically influence one another on that level of form. The critic is then identifying paths of influence through formal means. When one identifies texts and experiences that are formally similar, probing into the characteristics of some texts and experiences in the set invites examination of other, homological texts and experiences in the set to see whether the same characteristics obtain. Sometimes they do not. But if they do, then a comparison of these texts and experiences guided by that logic of form can be a fruitful way to study the texts and experiences. The method also becomes a fruitful way to understand new dimensions of the form itself.

For instance, in life from time to time, one debases oneself in order to enter a special, protected place set aside for important purposes. This debasement may consist of surrendering oneself to close scrutiny or examination. It may involve the removal of potentially offensive clothing. It likely involves speaking just the right words while avoiding at all costs the utterance of the wrong words. Now, what is like that, in our world? Surely, entering a temple or place of worship. But also, entering the secured area of an airport. There are many discourses to instruct one as to how to enter the special place. But might there also be some discourses that themselves require abasement and a special vocabulary to enter? How about reading, understanding, and discussing the latest fashionable but impenetrable critical cultural theorist? Do we make our graduate students "go past security" to enter the temple of these authors? If one can see all these discursive and physical experiences arraying themselves in a homology, what might be understood about any one member of the formal set by probing into another member? Do people put up with the debasements of the security checkpoint or the graduate seminar room because we are trained in the debasements of the sacred place? Where do we "go" once we have entered the sacred place, in all manifestations of the form? Feel free to ring the changes on this homology yourself.[i]

I now want to establish a pair of homologies linking hunting, gardening, going to the supermarket, original works of art, and mechanical reproductions. To understand this homology, let me begin by turning to Walter Benjamin's (1968) explanation of the original work of art in contrast to the mechanical reproduction. We will see the form underlying this distinction reverberating homologically in the garden, the hunting field, the supermarket—and in politics.

Walter Benjamin

In the 1930s, the German critic Walter Benjamin (1968) proposed a distinction between the original work of art and the mechanical reproduction to explain in part the emergence of film and photography, replacing a world of painting and theatre (pp. 217–252). Benjamin's work has proven to be enormously provocative of scholarship and critique (e.g., Ferris, 1996; Gunn, 2001; McCole, 1993). I intend to avoid plunging into the depths of that commentary, which might rival the Talmud itself. Perhaps I am not yet ready to debase myself and enter that temple. Instead, I want to use the simple, broad outlines of Benjamin's distinction and, later, to return to some of the political ramifications he suggested for it.

The original work of art, Benjamin (1968) argues, has a *history* and *tradition* (p. 223). There are *stories* that may be told about it: This work was painted in this or that year by the artist, it has been held in these museums or by these noble folk. Here in the work you may find this encoded secret, joke, or political reference. No other object has been down quite the same narrative path as this one. Uniqueness is of the essence with the work of art. The original work of art also has an *aura*: it is special; one holds it in awe and stands a step back in homage and veneration (p. 221). Thus, we have some *distance* from the original (p. 233). The work of art has *authority* in several senses: it may be traced to a distinct author, but the work itself also has the power and presence of authority in the lives of those who encounter it (p. 221). One senses the work of art as distinct and special. The idea of *authenticity* often attaches to the original work of art (p. 220).

In contrast, the mechanical reproduction is identical to all other reproductions in its set. It has no special history or tradition. No story may be told of it. Its origins are likely unknown. The mechanical reproduction has no aura: one unit being much like another unit, the thing itself is not revered. Being not an object of veneration or awe, people absorb the reproduction without much thought into their lives, erasing distance through consumption. Mechanical reproductions are predictable, and the characteristics of them may be readily known. This means that the meanings of mechanical reproductions are also highly predictable and widely known. Since things are mechanically reproduced almost always to sell them, advertising makes sure we know what meanings attach to these reproductions so we might buy them for those meanings.

This logic of properties and distinctions between the original work of art and the mechanical reproduction is enormously suggestive in understanding our world today. The recurring contrast between the unique and the copy is the underlying form of this homology; it is likewise a discursive form, since in nature there are no totally original works of art nor truly identical copies. This tension between the unique and the copy is played out repeatedly in our lives and in our discourses.

Most of us are awash in mechanical reproductions, yet we long for the characteristics of the original work of art, often expressed as a yearning for authenticity. On the positive side, mechanical reproductions create a system of signs with predictable meanings that allow commodities to function as a kind of language, a system of communication. Through this system we know how to read others, and how we ourselves will be read, by our displays of mass produced stuff.

The logic behind this distinction is itself a formal pattern: the unique versus the copy. Since actual experience has very little that is either an exact copy or utterly unique, the unique/copy distinction is symbolic, discursive, and thus rhetorical. Might we learn more about how that form of the unique versus the copy works by examining other manifestations of the distinction? To answer yes to that question, let me turn to the matter of getting food to eat.

Hunting, Gardening, and the Supermarket

I propose that the practices of gardening and of hunting are homologous, or formally resonant, with the original work of art and its creation. Practices of buying food at supermarkets are homologous with the mechanical reproduction of mass produced copies. The small farmer's market or roadside stand, the local organic co-op grocery lie somewhere in between. The homology I propose is in line with increasingly widespread attention to the morality, ethics, and politics of food today. As George Will (2009) argues, "eating has become highly charged with moral judgments" (p. A19).

The formal resonance between mechanical reproduction and buying food in a supermarket will be easier for most to see, certainly given how few people grow their own food in gardens, while fewer still hunt their own food. Imagine yourself in the produce aisle staring at stacks of identical bags of carrots. Most of the carrots within a given bag will look alike. Open a bag of so-called "baby carrots" and these machined hunks of vegetable are even more identical. Pick up a potato, replace it, walk over to a neighboring aisle and back, and the odds of being able to recognize the original potato are slim. Go over to the meat aisle and notice the identical looking cuts of meat on the unvarying trays, wrapped in plastic. Admire the identical tubs of identical liver. Monitor in yourself what is likely a rather flat affective response: this stuff is alright, but nothing to write home about.

It is not just that this food all looks alike; it has the characteristics of the mechanical reproduction, especially when considered in contrast to the work of art. Where did the carrot come from? What is the story of the steer that became all this meat? Where is the aura or distinctiveness of vegetable or animal such that it becomes a presence, an entity, in relationship to which one can stand? There is no history, story, tradition, or aura to the stuff of the supermarket. One has so little distance from these copies that one consumes them without much thought, they are there largely to disappear through ingestion. Giving little thought to the mass reproduced copies of the supermarket is precisely the point: they are convenient, they serve a purpose, their own special features have vanished. A foodstuff may be branded, but in that case the brand is what attracts attention and veneration. Ah! This steak is certified Piggly Wiggly Organic Angus, we exclaim—which tells us nothing of the particular animal in which the steak began, nor of the journey of the steak itself.

The homology between the original work of art and hunting or gardening/gathering one's own food may be more difficult to see, especially given how little of our food comes from those activities. Perhaps more people will be familiar with gardening, so let us begin there. The land of the garden itself will be a work of art, a thing with a history that is constantly being written. The garden plot is a canvas, a palimpsest that is constantly reinscribed. Although the gardener may purchase mass distributed products to use in the garden—think of stacks of bagged peat moss, for instance—the garden itself is the product of a history of pains taken, of soil tilled, of compost dug in. Often the gardener will keep a history of the garden, knowing what has been planted where and when. One remembers when to plant, and when the season is coming to an end. Each plot is thus a unique creation with its own identity, history, and tradition. It is a work of art.

Each vegetable gathered from the garden is unique. They are not the identical looking products of the store. A freshly pulled carrot may be wonderfully knobby compared to its supermarket brethren, with long hairy roots still attached. An astonishing variety of sizes and shapes, of blemishes and scars, may be found on each fruit. Each one is picked at its own moment of ripeness, not on an industrial schedule.

To gaze upon a line of garden carrots is to gaze upon a history, as one knows when they were sown, when sprayed for insects, when thinned, and so forth. As one eats the food, the gardener has a sense of what it took to produce that foodstuff, an appreciation for each fruit as the culmination of a process of creation. One may feed the vegetables to friends with a sense of pride: "these were picked an hour ago" is a claim of a wholly different order from "I bought this at the Super Wal-Mart." In this sense, vegetables and fruits one has raised in the garden have a kind of aura. Thoreau said that every man looks upon his own woodpile with a kind of affection (2009, p. 135). Yes, if one chopped and stacked it. And one looks upon the sliced tomato on the plate, if one labored over it, with the same kind of relational regard.

Hunting for meat is, I think, even more homologous with the original work of art, although even more remote from most people's experience. The animal taken is special. One may harvest a dozen tomatoes, but likely only one deer, or a brace of pheasants, in an outing. The hunter has a relationship with the game, it is wooed and courted. What one hunts and brings in will have been chased or lain in wait for, for hours or days. Stratagems and skills are employed, even if sitting in a blind. Care is taken in preparing for the shot, or the flight of the arrow. Each animal taken has its own unique way of running, dying, and of being recovered by the hunter. The hunt thus makes a story, a history, and establishes that particular creature as a special being with whom the hunter has a relationship.

Bringing the results to the table requires a kind of involvement utterly unknown to the supermarket shopper. Gutting and butchering a deer is a great deal more involving than pulling and cleaning a carrot, never mind pulling a wrapped steak out of the grocery case. It is a tactile, physical, emotional experience not found in the meat aisle of the local Safeway. The affect is totally different from viewing pork chops in plastic. And when one sits down to consume a piece of meat that one has been responsible for putting there, the meal has an aura, a history and tradition, that can only come from this kind of involvement in the process of gathering meat. One can serve the meat to others and tell the story of how it got there, of how one pulled the trigger and cut the meat from the bone. And I think one is much less likely to waste meat that one has killed, since you know what it took on all sides to get the food to the plate.

There is a wide popular literature that replicates these characteristics of the mass reproduction and the original work of art. In discourse, we find the same themes echoed that I have suggested above may be found in the practical experience of the shopper, the gardener, and the hunter. Let me turn briefly to some examples of discourse about food that resonate with the homologies I have suggested here.

Michael Pollan is a widely read author, and the distinctions I am observing here may be found especially in his book *The Omnivore's Dilemma.* Pollan (2006) tracks the progress of four meals from the growing of the raw materials to the actual meal. He goes from a highly "industrial" (p. 71) meal at McDonald's to a meal he hunted and gathered himself. It is a progression from mechanical reproduction to the original work of art.

Pollan observes that "the American supermarket doesn't present itself as having very much to do with nature" (p. 15). He decries the predominance of corn both as an animal feed and an ingredient in manufactured food, corn from "genetically identical plants" that are "the biological equivalent of a patent," equating this kind of food with mechanical reproduction (p. 31). Planting this corn is mechanical, "stitching an interminable cloak" in the soil (p. 35). Such a farm is "managed on industrial principles, as a factory" (p. 45). The corn produced on the farm is mechanized in "a rhythmically chugging feed mill" (p. 66).

The meat offered in the market is described in mechanical terms as "boneless and bloodless geometrical cuts," the carrots "machine-lathed into neatly tapered torpedoes" (p. 16). The meat is produced in a feedlot, "the industrial way…as a most impressive machine for turning number 2 field corn into cuts of beef" (p. 80). The distinctiveness of the food is gone: "you come to regions of the supermarket where the very notion of species seems increasingly obscure: the canyons of breakfast cereals and condiments; the freezer cases stacked with 'home meal replacements' and bagged platonic peas" and so forth (p. 16). The connection of supermarket shopping to mechanical reproduction is made clear in his repeated references to "the industrial food chain" (p. 17). The shallowness of choice is clearly described in his accusation that "the food industry has done a good job of persuading us that the forty-five thousand different items…in the supermarket—seventeen thousand new ones every year—represent genuine variety rather than so many clever rearrangements of molecules extracted from the same plant" (p. 20).

In discussing the meal he himself hunted and gathered, he speaks in language resonant of the aura, of history and personal involvement, for this meal "gave me the opportunity, so rare in modern life, to eat in full consciousness of everything involved in feeding myself: For once, I was able to pay the full karmic price of a meal" (p. 9). Pollan with a gun in his hand in the field becomes an artist: "I am the alert man" (p. 335). When a wild pig is shot, it is decisive: "I felt I'd been party to something momentous, something that felt like a collision of worlds" (pp. 346–347). He feels "pride: I had actually done this thing I'd set out to do, had successfully shot a pig….And then there was this wholly unexpected feeling of gratitude….More than the product of any labor of mine (save receptiveness) the animal was a gift—from whom or what I couldn't say" (p. 353). Serving the pig "was the necessary closing act of that drama,…which meant making the best use of its meat by preparing it thoughtfully and feeding it to people who would appreciate it" (401)—all language of the original work of art. Narrative emerges at that table, in "the stories told by this little band of foragers,…stories, like the food that fed them, cast lines of relation to all these places and the creatures living (and dying) in them" (p. 407). A language of history, tradition, and narrative could not be clearer. Note how his language echoes Benjamin's discussion of our stance toward the work of art when he says that if we hunted for our meat "maybe when we did eat animals we'd eat them with the consciousness, ceremony, and respect they deserve" (p. 333).

One does not have to go far to find other parallel discourses. The Outdoor Channel of cable television is literally full of shows in which the story is told of a hunt, the individual animal shot is prized as singular and rare, and exclamations are consistently made over the beauty and wonder of the slain creature. Food writers such as Erin Ergenbright often speak in the mystical terms of the work of art, as when she writes, "I truly believe that a meal is the culmination of an entire journey from birth to death to table; a journey that includes and is colored by, every person involved—not least the person who eats it" (2006, p. 180). In an earlier age, the great philosopher and poet of hunting, Josè Ortega y Gassett (1995) would contrast the creativity and life connecting the activity of hunting with the dullness and stupidity of an industrial society.

So What?

A great advantage of homological criticism is that once a homology is established, drilling into the characteristics of one member of the homology may suggest further parallels in other members. Formal reverberation, once begun, may echo in unsuspected frequencies. I think we will find that to be true with the homology I have identified here. To begin this process of exploration, let me note that Benjamin locates mechanical reproductions in the realm of *politics*. What can he mean by this? As I (Brummett, 2006) and others have argued elsewhere, for Benjamin the work of art was resonant with the adoration of unique, fascist political figures of his time: Mussolini, Hitler, and so forth. He welcomed what he saw as a growing fascination with film and other mechanically reproduced art as a symptom of a shift in the collective psychology away from the one great idol.

What sort of politics is this, a politics aligned with mechanical reproduction? To enrich our understanding of that question I would return us to the homology with food. Each side of the homology embodies a different logic: the logic of *choice* or the logic of *decision*. Mechanical reproduction offers us a choice among identical copies. To understand the connection of decision to the original work of art, I want to push a distinction not highlighted in Benjamin, and that is the distinction between creating versus using, or being a spectator of, the original work of art. Decision is part of both sides of that distinction, but I think it resides even more so on the side of creating the work of art, which is, I believe, closely aligned with hunting and gardening (perhaps more so with hunting).

The supermarket, the site of mechanical reproduction, is governed by the logic of *choice*. One may choose this bag of carrots or that bag. One may choose both. One may choose one and then reverse one's choice and pick another or put the first one back. The consequences of choice are not enormous. Capitalism urges upon us a sense of vast choice in the market, because if one's choices are wide one's consumption may well increase. Faced with one kind of coffee, you might buy only one bag. Faced with a hundred varieties of coffee, you might buy a selection. Choice is also fostered precisely by a reduction in consequences for each choice made. If worlds turned or fell on selection of a bag of carrots, we would shop much differently than we do now.

The garden and the hunting field, on the other hand, are governed by the logic of *decision*. For the deer, worlds do turn or fall on somebody's decision to pull the trigger. I believe that for most hunters, and surely all responsible ones, the moment in which one decides to pull the trigger, to release the arrow, is a moment altogether different from the choice between buying this filet or that one. One is sharply aware of what will happen, irreversibly, if things go as planned. Decisions are, well, decisive. This applies although perhaps not as poignantly for the gardener as well. The carrot seed once sown cannot be unsown. The carrot once pulled cannot be stuck back in the ground. There is no catch and release hunting, nor gardening.

Decisiveness also necessarily involves consideration, the raising of questions and consideration of costs, benefits, and consequences. One may choose without considering the consequences of choice. But a decision requires thinking about the decision. Of course, capitalism encourages a regime of choice because mindless choice leads to more consumption. Careful decisions would likely reduce the amount of sheer "stuff" purchased, and is thus antithetical to the logic of capitalism.

Is it useful to see our current politics as a politics of choice, informed by this discussion? As the careless selection of this or that identical turnip? Is it helpful to consider that because of huge populations, lack of agency, a shift in power from the state to the corporation, or for whatever reason, political action now seems on the level of unremarkable choice? Certainly the dominance of corporate media elites in presenting most politics to the public seems like mechanical reproduction, as one middle aged white guy with a flag pin after another is reproduced in front of us. Can we read the declarations we hear every single election, that this is the most important decision the American people have ever had before them, as homologous with the market's desperate ploys to make the mechanically reproduced seem authentic and original? For elite media institutions, the politics conveyed to us is as much a product as are the supermarket's cereal boxes.

Let me note that one gradually moves from decisive hunting and gardening in the direction of choice and mechanical reproduction as one moves, toward the halfway world of the local, perhaps organic, farmer's market. There you find heirloom tomatoes, not far from original works of art but not *my* heirloom tomatoes. We find grass fed bison from local producers, but not the bison *I* raised and killed. Here we are closer to being spectators rather than creators of original works of art. We participate vicariously in decisions, having eliminated some food system middle men. Here we find the middle ground of green politics, which in preaching the local and the healthy to people who cannot or will not get their own food must cultivate *mindfulness*. Surely mindfulness in food or politics is desirable, even if a somewhat more tepid version of decisiveness. Perhaps the artistic cognate of mindfulness is *connoisseurship*. If we cannot all be artists in making politics, can we get a better politics by encouraging the public to become connoisseurs, just as one might be a connoisseur of the artistic stuff in the farmer's market?

The "green" movement may be understood as resisting the rush to mindless choice, and by its very nature it opposes capitalism's encouragement of overconsumption. Green is small, and often centered around personal decisions. But the mindfulness of being green can be seen writ large in politics on the broad scale.

I loop back through food in this way to pose the question of whether there is some way for us today to recover a more decisive, if not altogether singular politics. If we cannot all go plant and pluck our next Senator, can we at least find a good one at the local organic farmer's market? Murray Edelman suggestively argues that "art is worth attention as an antidote to political mystification because works of art depend for their power upon properties that contrast revealingly with the characteristics of political language. Art helps counter banal political forms," (1988, p. 126) and what can be more banal than mass reproduction?

I am not proposing a return to the politics of the Great Person decried by Benjamin. But where has a politics of the ordinary okra gotten us? Are there forms of politics homologously parallel to the farmer's market that are congenial for how we live today, and for the possibilities of politics in this world? Is there some way to understand Barack Obama's startlingly successful use of the Internet, for instance, as a politics halfway between choice and decision, a politics that is "mass" enough to avoid fascism but "artistic" enough to engage individual involvement and engrossment? Might this distinction help the political activist, or voting recruiter appeal to new or young voters by striking the right rhetorical tone?

It may be useful to think of the public as recruited to be artists in creating the candidate Obama. Certainly, email appeals invited the intimate and personal participation of the individual in sculpting The One. We might think about the ways in which Obama's heavy use of the Internet *both* reduced psychological distance for many voters but also made of him a "real" person—and thus something of an original work of art to keep at a respectful distance. Like so many works of art he was, after all, a "first." If Obama had more of a sheen of authenticity about him, is it because he edged closer to being the authentic work of art than did other candidates? Was his shibbolcth of "change" a rhetorical cousin of authenticity when so many of his fellow politicians are seen as mediated reproductions?

Perhaps the distinction between the original work of art and the mechanical reproduction gives us a speculative instrument for thinking about a politics that works and is attractive. As the fascination with mechanical reproduction of the early twentieth century fades in our era, might we see how an appeal to do your civic duty by voting—just like all those other units out there—might come to seem less persuasive than appeals to make a work of art? Are there creative ways to make politics creative in meaningful ways and not just for show?

The challenge is to replicate the sort of mindfulness and decision found in green politics, exemplified in the processes of gardening and hunting, on a broader political scale. But the micropolitics of ecological carefulness, like the microdecisions of what to eat and where to get it, are nevertheless formally connected to broader issues and practices of politics, and we may be coached on the micro scale for participation in the macro.

My purpose in this chapter has been to explore a homology that I believe obtains across these dimensions of hunting, gathering, and shopping in stores for food. If this discussion has led by strange and unexpected paths toward new politics, then perhaps I have also illustrated the generative power of homological methods as a kind of criticism.

Endnotes

[i] Why is a homology not a metaphor? I have no fundamental objection to seeing homologies as metaphorical, and if a language of metaphor can lead the critic to the same understanding, so be it. However, I would say they are different primarily because a homology is *discovered* while a metaphor is *proposed*. Homological criticism argues that a formal structure shapes

and, at least in part, generates the texts and experiences in the homology. The homology, being generative, is therefore prior and fundamental to the texts and experiences. To say "my love is a red rose," however, proposes that you see my love and a red rose in a particular way. No principle of generation is implied. Connected to this rationale is the fact that metaphors tend to be short, unless extended. Homologies are often extended beyond the range of even an "extended metaphor."

References

Benjamin, W. (1968) *Illuminations*. Trans. Ed. Harry Zohn and Hannah Arendt. New York: Schocken Books.

Brummett, B. (2004) *Rhetorical Homologies: Form, Culture, Experience*. Tuscaloosa: University of Alabama Press.

Brummett, B. (2006) Rhetorical Homologies in Walter Benjamin, *The Ring*, and Capital. *Rhetoric Society Quarterly, 36,* 449–469.

Edelman, M. (1988). *Constructing the Political Spectacle*. Chicago: University of Chicago Press.

Ergenbright, Erin. (2007) Table for One. In J. Ferrari-Adler (Ed.) , *Alone in the Kitchen With an Eggplant.* (pp. 179–186). New York: Riverhead Books.

Ferris, D. S. (1996) *Walter Benjamin: Theoretical Questions*. Stanford: Stanford University Press.

Gunn, J. (2001) Benjamin's magic. *Telos, 119,* 58-74.

McCole, J. (1993) *Walter Benjamin and the Antinomies of Tradition*. Ithaca: Cornell University Press.

Ortega y Gassett, J. (1995) *Meditations on Hunting.* H. B. Wescott, (Trans.). Belgrade, MT: Wilderness Adventures Press.

Pollan, M. (2006) *The Omnivore's Dilemma: A Natural History of Four Meals*. New York: Penguin.

Pollan, M. (2008) *In Defense of Food.* New York: Penguin.

Thoreau, H. D. (2009) *Walden*. Scotts Valley, CA: CreateSpace.

Will, G. (2009, 26 February) Prudes at Dinner, Gluttons in Bed. *The Washington Post*, A19.

15

A critical crisis rhetoric of seafood

Michael S. Bruner and Jason D. Meek

The world has been consuming more food than it produces. The world faces a perpetual food crisis. These stark claims were presented in a thirty–three page article in *National Geographic*, complete with fourteen full pages of color photos from China, Brazil, India, the Philippines, and Iowa (Bourne, 2009). The article argued that the first Green Revolution has ended, and that there simply is not enough food to go around.

In a similar vein, although this time with a focus on ocean ecosystems, a study by Worm, Barbier, Beaumont, Duffy, Folke, Halpern, et al. (2006), published in *Science*, indicated that the loss of biodiversity in the world's oceans was having a significant impact on marine populations and species. Commenting on this study, Stokstad (2006) wrote: "If a new analysis of marine ecosystems data is correct, commercial fish and seafood species may all crash by 2048" (p. 745). In other words, if current trends persist, there will be little seafood in 40-50 years.

These stark examples of public discourse about food, in general, and about seafood, in particular, indicate that contemporary communication about food is not a mundane topic. This chapter explores a range of contemporary public discourse concerning seafood, with a focus on the complicated environmental demands and nutrition demands faced by seafood consumers. Research on seafood discourse is not as fully developed as research on other discourses about food and merits further attention.

Seafood discourse is significant, because the stakes are high. In the United States alone, seafood is a $20 billion industry. According to a 2008 report from the National Oceanic and Atmospheric Administration (NOAA), U.S. citizens consume approximately sixteen pounds of seafood per year. Moreover, the United States is one of many seafood "giants." China, Japan, India, Brazil, Russia, and several other nations must be considered in any global view of seafood. But beyond the economic concerns of the marketplace, public discourse about seafood is a complex combination of communication, science, politics, ethics, material practices, nutrition, health, and globalization.

Not only is the arena complex and the discourse complicated, but also consumers are faced with ever-changing rhetoric. In *The Omnivore's Dilemma*, Michael Pollan (2006) commented on how consumers in the United States in the 1970s were warned to cut back on the consumption of red meat. Two decades later, "the blamelessness of steak was restored," according to Pollan's account. Now bread and pasta "acquired a moral stain" (p. 2). Pollan is correct that these swings of "the dietary pendulum" are confusing and may push consumers toward food neurosis. It is one thing to give up beef for seafood in a "heart healthy" diet (a phrase made popular by the American Heart Association). It is another thing to question the decision to eat more seafood so soon after the decision was made.

Communication about seafood, like communication about food, is ever-changing. Some of the changes are related to seafood and health. But seafood discourse has another urgent note, because it is connected to discourses about the environment, especially sustainability. Note the dual themes of health and sustainability in a January, 2009, press release about the market research report, *U.S. Market for Seafood*:

An increasingly health-conscious public eager for heart healthy "happy fat" and low calorie meals has made seafood one of the fastest-growing food categories. The United States represents one of the most important seafood markets in the world, both from a consumption and catch perspective. Many factors are influencing the growth and direction of the seafood market, not the least of which include a push toward sustainability in the production and retailing of fresh seafood and shellfish and an effort by the industry to educate consumers on the safety of seafood products and the ease of cooking and preparation.

Seafood discourse, then, is significant for health and environmental reasons, but it is complex and ever-changing. In an attempt to make sense of the sometimes contradictory discourses about seafood, the current chapter presents a critical crisis rhetoric of seafood.

This stance will be explained more fully below. Suffice it to say here that, in the following analysis, the critique of ideologies and power relations is central. As Ono and Sloop (1992) stated the case: "We encourage the critic to work to initiate new relationships, to imagine new ways of constructing the world, and to replace the logic of dichotomies with alternatives" (p. 50). Communication scholars already are familiar with Burke's *A Rhetoric of Motives* (1950) and the rhetoric of science (Campbell, 1996; Gross, 1990). This chapter combines a discussion of the persuasive elements in seafood discourse with the notion that consumers face a crisis and must act.

The plan of this chapter is briefly to review some relevant literature, to describe the method, and then to concentrate on the complicated environmental demands and nutrition demands faced by seafood consumers. In an attempt to ground this chapter in everyday life, many examples of contemporary seafood discourse are included, and practical considerations abound. The focus is on marine species as seafood, although it is obvious that species such as salmon blur the distinction between salt-water and fresh-water species. As a general rule, the examples of public discourse are drawn from sources that have a large audience. The analysis of discourse is divided, for ideological reasons and for the sake of clarity, into "Problems" (or "Opportunities," if one prefers) and "Solutions." The Problem-Solution format is well-known in communication studies. It must be acknowledged, nevertheless, that this format is a conscious choice among many options. The chapter concludes with implications and suggestions for further research.

Literature Review

Food currently is one of the most interesting and contested sites in public discourse. Several popular books have brought food issues directly into the public eye: *Fast Food Nation* by Eric Schlosser; *Omnivore's Dilemma* by Michael Pollan; and *The End of Food* by Paul Roberts. This study takes note of this interest in food issues, as well as the rhetorical complexity of the debate. The current chapter extends previous work on public discourse and food issues by communication scholars, including Retzinger (2009, 2007, 2005, 2003, 2001).

The literature on the world's oceans and sea creatures is vast. However, some of the literature is important for its emphasis on communication and the environment. For example, one could start with Rachel Carson's book, *The Sea Around Us* (Carson, 1961). This book is noteworthy, because it is rhetorical discourse by a scientist, influencing the reader to regard the sea with wonder and even reverence.

The work of Jacques Cousteau (1910–1997) must be mentioned, because of his long career and his success in interjecting his underwater endeavors into public discourse. His work took on many different forms, from books to film to TV. For example, the 1953 book, *Silent World*, later realized as a film with the same title, won an award at the Cannes Film Festival in 1956. Well into the

1990s, Cousteau's name was evident in mass media, including the TV series: *Cousteau's Rediscovery of the World I* (1985) and his book on *Madagascar* (1995). Cousteau was so much a part of international public discourse that his approach was awarded its own label—"divulgationism"—a simple way of sharing scientific concepts (see *Jacques Cousteau*, 2010).

Public discourse about environmental issues has taken many forms over the past three decades, but a combination of argumentation and visual rhetoric has some advantages in reaching diverse audiences. First, audience members have different learning styles, so multiple channels have an advantage. Second, the power of images seems to be increasing, as we become more and more accustomed to relying upon the three screens of contemporary life—the mobile phone, the TV, and the computer.

The extensive literature on aquaculture is important, not only for scientific readers, but for anyone interested in scientific perspectives on seafood. Aquaculture is the water-based counterpart of agriculture. As such, it faces many of the same challenges and opportunities. For example, global warming may have just as much impact on our oceans as on our continents. A useful collection of essays on aquaculture, edited by Barry Costa-Pierce (2003), is *Ecological Aquaculture: The Evolution of the Blue Revolution.* A second, recent, and quite readable sample of the aquaculture literature is *Farming Fish for the Future* by Brian Halweil, Worldwatch Report (2008, 176). The final chapter, "Toward Sustainable Aquaculture Standards," raises the contested issue of certification standards. Halweil's insights are quite relevant to this chapter:

> Just as buyers of meat and milk are becoming more vigilant, seafood shoppers will also begin to ask more questions about what the fish are fed, how they are raised, and where they are from—either because they wonder if it makes the fish less healthy to eat, or because they are concerned it harms the fish. (p. 36)

These dual concerns—about humans and about sea creatures—will resurface in several sections below.

This review of literature also includes other significant books on seafood that are aimed at a mass readership. These works combine science with a narrative appeal and, in many cases, have an agenda. Two books merit special mention. Trevor Corson's *The Secret Life of Lobsters* followed lobster "fishermen and scientists as they unravel the mysteries of our favorite crustacean" (Corson, 2004). The second book is titled, *Bottomfeeder: How to Eat Ethically in a World of Vanishing Seafood.* The author, Taras Grescoe (2008), argued that we need to eat near the bottom of the seafood chain. For example, he recommended mussels over salmon. This perspective will be examined below in the section on "Solutions."

One of the theoretical foundations of this chapter is the perspective developed by DeLuca and Peeples (2002) that today the traditional view of the "public sphere" as argumentation must be supplemented by the inclusion of the "public screen" (p. 131). In the current study, the phrase "public discourse" includes both the "public sphere" (traditional oral arguments, words, reasons, text) and the "public screen" (images, visual rhetoric). The next section explains the method in more detail.

Method

From Foucault (1972, 1970) comes the notion that every era has its own vocabulary, its own concepts, and its own complicated (but largely unconscious) manner of making sense. This foundation for what is accepted as knowledge is similar to what Kuhn (1996) called a "paradigm" in his well-known book *The Structure of Scientific Revolutions* (pp. 16–17). The paradigm might be grand in scale, such as "The Cold War." Within the Cold War paradigm, one was encouraged to think of the world as divided into East and West, totalitarian and free, and locked in a long struggle. A paradigm might be less grand in scale. For example, one's belief could be anchored in the sentence "Columbus discovered the New World" or, conversely, in the sentence "Columbus encountered the New World." The point here is that one resides, thinks, and acts within both some grand paradigms and some not-so grand paradigms such that it is very difficult to escape the paradigms of an era.

Critical rhetoric is a stance that encourages one to examine paradigms, ideologies, and power relations (McKerrow, 1989). The role of the critic is to debunk, to reveal, to expose, and to make the hidden clear. The critic, it seems, is committed to constant critique. As the critic explores the dimensions of domination and freedom, the critic may uncover new possibilities for making sense and for taking action, but the critic cannot rest.

From Biesecker's (1992) perspective, the task for critical rhetoric is not to enable a radical paradigm shift. The task is less ambitious and more practical—to offer points of resistance, to make possible transgressions against the current order, to find new ways of making sense, and to facilitate the emergence of new forms of community and coexistence. This work is ever-changing, because of the constant flux of the world. The critic is dealing with a moving target. But the critic, through style, may produce cleavages that lead to new formulations.

Critique, then, may be valuable but does not serve as its own end. From Charland (1991) came the idea that the critic must have some inkling of what the good might be. Although the postmodern critic largely has given up the concepts of the Truth and the Good in the absolute sense, Charland maintains that some contingent good for a time, a place, and a community must be part of the equation (p. 73). As noted above, Ono and Sloop (1992) share a similar perspective, when they urged the critic to acknowledge her/his place in society and to work toward envisioning new alternatives (p. 58).

In sum, one part of the method of this chapter is to present a critical rhetoric of seafood. Through the critique and deconstruction of contemporary public discourse about seafood, the analysis will attempt to expose and reveal paradigms and ideologies, while at the same time suggesting new ways of making sense. For example, so far the term "seafood" has been used uncritically, in its ordinary language sense. What if one questioned the term and interrogated its usage? Why do we think of marine species as "seaFOOD"? How is it that public discourse names and frames marine species primarily as human sustenance? What if audiences explored alternatives? Perhaps by making audiences aware of the largely unconscious seaFOOD paradigm, the critic could help audiences change the status quo in discourse.

The second part of the method of this chapter is drawn from Cox (2007) and Plec (2007). Cox argued that environmental communication is a "crisis discipline" similar to conservation biology, and could choose ethical norms (pp. 7–8). It is not enough to study a subject, when the subject itself is in peril. Plec attempted to forge a union between critical rhetoric and environmental communication as a crisis discipline. She argued that both are concerned with the examination of "regimes of representation" (p. 53). In the present chapter, these regimes are equivalent to the paradigms and ideologies found in public discourse. Plec also stated that both share "sustainability" as their *telos*. In the present chapter, *telos* is referred to as the good which the critic seeks to make clearer in each set of contingent circumstances. Finally, Plec asserted that both assume "engagement in a critical cultural politics" (p. 54). In this chapter, the equivalent point is that the critic is not above the fray. The critic is located in society. The critic's discourse is part of public discourse. Critical rhetoric *is* rhetoric. It is meant to influence and persuade.

Therefore, this chapter is not only a critique; it is advocacy. "Sustainability" certainly is a popular and seemingly admirable goal in the current era. However, one cannot offer a critical rhetoric of seafood without examining the discourse of sustainability, too. The second part of the method of this chapter is to advocate against some actions and for other actions. Therefore, the next two sections of the chapter are devoted, respectively, to an analysis of public discourse about Problems related to seafood and public discourse about Solutions.

Problems

Overfishing

Some types of seafood are being overfished, leading to aquatic candidates for the Endangered Species List. According to *Seafood WATCH*, overfishing is defined as "catching fish faster than they can reproduce." *Seafood WATCH* reports that Atlantic cod and blue fin tuna are among the many species that are suffering from overfishing (Monterey Bay Aquarium, "Seafood WATCH," n.d.). Another useful definition of overfishing is offered by Koster (2007): "The practice of commercial and non-commercial fishing which depletes a fishery by catching so many adult fish that not enough remain to breed and replenish the population. Overfishing exceeds the carrying capacity of a fishery." For example, in northern California the salmon fishing season depends upon the number of salmon returning to spawn in the Sacramento and Klamath Rivers.

The rhetoric of "sustainability" sometimes comes up when the topic of overfishing is raised. Fishing fleets obviously are materially engaged with the issue of sustainable seafood catches. To cite Koster, again, the world's fishing fleets are two to three times as large as necessary. Consumers also have a responsibility to grasp the "big picture" with respect to global seafood populations and to act accordingly. For example, large fishing fleets with large annual catches may mean lower prices for consumers in the current era. At the same time, large fishing enterprises may result in the demise of certain kinds of seafood.

The rhetorical critic may note that "overfishing" contains the stem word "over." A legitimate critical question is: "Over what?" The widespread technical definition of "overfishing" makes two assumptions. First, it assumes that commercial fishing is an acceptable practice. Second, it assumes that fish breeding rates are at the core of the definition of "overfishing." A critic could offer alternative ways of thinking. For instance, are indigenous peoples or peoples in poorer nations "overfishing" when they fish endangered species to survive? Do protein deficiencies, hunger, or starvation change one's perspective on overfishing?

A critic may offer another perspective on "overfishing." Is the definition of "overfishing" a global concept based on total populations, that is, all of the members of one marine species, no matter where they are located? Or, is overfishing defined one ocean at a time? Further, is the reproductive cycle subject to ups and downs, independent of commercial fishing? If so, can overfishing be determined by a single fishing season or by a succession of fishing seasons? Finally, does the concept of overfishing apply to marine species that take a long time to mature? If a fish takes thirty years to mature, capturing only one specimen might be "overfishing." The rhetorical challenge with respect to "overfishing," is to move beyond basic definitions to systemic perspectives. A simple vocabulary in public discourse, while useful at first, may not hold up well in the long run. Total catch, of course, is only one problem. Another problem has to do with waste, or what we have come to call collateral damage.

Bycatch

"Bycatch" is the current term for "unwanted" animals caught during the fishing process. *Seafood Watch* cites the United Nations when reporting that an astounding 25% of the world's catch is thrown away. According to the United Nations Food and Agriculture Organization, one in four animals caught in fishing gear dies as bycatch—unwanted or unintentional catch. Tons of fish are tossed out, dead or dying, because they're not the kind the fishermen wanted to catch. The discarded animals may have no market value, or there may be no room on the boat to bring them to shore. Or the bycatch may be a marketable species, but too small to sell. Sometimes, fish are discarded because the fishermen lack the proper permits to land them. Dolphins, sea turtles, seals and whales all get caught by accident in fishing gear and drown. Seabirds, including endangered albatrosses, drown when they snatch baited hooks and are pulled under water (Food and Agriculture Organization of the United Nations, 2010).

Bycatch may contribute to overfishing, directly or inadvertently. In the United States, one of the best-known bycatch case studies has to do with so-called "dolphin-safe tuna." According to an article by Bob Egelko in the *San Francisco Chronicle*, (2003, January 3): "Dolphins swim above schools of tuna in the eastern Pacific and were dying in the hundreds of thousands each year before U. S. conservation groups led a campaign to change fishing practices" (A–4). A 1972 law put limits on U.S. tuna boats' use of nets to encircle and kill dolphins. The case was reopened during the Bush administration. While consumers had grown accustomed to "dolphin-safe" labeling, the meaning of the label itself was in danger of being undermined. In addition, the rhetorical critic can see a bitter irony in the dolphin-safe label. Apparently, it is acceptable to kill tuna but not dolphins.

Public discourse in the United States seems to have warmer emotional overtones associated with certain animals. Among the more preferred animals are giant pandas, gorillas, koalas, baby seals, sea turtles, whales, and dolphins. Public discourse is less "warm and fuzzy" about wart hogs, skunks, rattle snakes, rock fish, and moray eels. Do the favored animals have better publicity mechanisms? Are humans judging and framing capriciously or based on scientific data? Why are some animals condemned and some protected? Speaking openly about these inequities may lead to opportunities for a new discourse about both land and sea creatures. Some sea creatures are wild. Other sea creatures are domesticated. In the next section, domesticated marine species are the subject.

Fish Farming

Humans hunt and gather. Humans also domesticate and grow their food stock on land or in the sea. Fish farms are a significant part of the contemporary seafood industry. Domesticated seafood offers humans more control over the supply chain. However, in the effort to control marine species, including their feeding and breeding, humans open a range of potential problems.

Worldwatch advised that consumers face two issues when addressing aquaculture: the conditions for the seafood and the treatment of the seafood, on the one hand, and the impact on humans, on the other hand. Seafood consumers are faced with the questions: "How was the seafood caught?" and "Where was the seafood obtained?" For wild fish, consumers may worry about "freshness," that is, time to market or time to table. For farmed fish, consumers might require another set of criteria to guide decision-making.

Some fish farms are being criticized for being "dirty," that is, they surround fish in filth and release some of that filth into the environment. A second criticism of fish farms is that they use inferior food, and that they might utilize chemicals, hormones, or pharmaceuticals. Another criticism of fish farms is that domesticated fish will escape into the oceans and interact with their wild cousins, to the detriment of the wild fish stock.

Advocates of fish farms voice arguments similar to those wielded by supporters of genetically-modified foods. Advocates claim that fish farms hold the promise of feeding the world. While it is problematic to take a possible food source away from developing nations, the critic must examine both the discourse of feeding the world and the fear appeals against fish farms, including the specter of unintended long-term consequences. One useful suggestion concerning fish farming is to have a reputable organization certify both the quality of the fish farm's practices and the quality of the seafood sent to market. Fish farms might cause environmental damage. But the subject of environmental damage goes far beyond fish farming.

Environmental Damage

Critics allege that some fishing techniques, such as ocean floor trawling, do serious damage to the environment. The damage, however, may be hidden under thousands of feet of water and may be visible only to divers, submarines, and underwater cameras. To date, the breadth and depth of visual rhetoric concerning undersea environmental damage is limited. An exception is a rare video published on *www.YouTube.com* by highseasmoratorium, entitled "Bottom–trawling video." As the footage rolls, the narrator explains how dragging the huge nets across the bottom destroys the ecosystems on the ocean's floor.

If DeLuca (1999) is correct about "image politics," then any progress in addressing seafood issues will contain an important visual component, such as the "Bottom-trawling video." To take another example of image politics, *Greenpeace* is the environmental organization most often associated with direct action and image politics in environmental advocacy. In fact, *Greenpeace International's* web site has links to many forms of visual rhetoric, including photo stories, video news releases, slide shows, and webcams (Greenpeace International, 2010). While direct action often is visible only to the participants, improved video technologies and the Internet today can disseminate images around the world, sometimes in real time broadcasts.

Bruner (2005) extended DeLuca's work by offering a typology of environmental image events, including "victimology" and "muckraking" (pp. 197–198). In addition, noting that Hoffner and LeVine (2005) and DeLuca and Peeples (2002) suggested that "the glance of habit is tactile," Bruner explored the possibility that audiences today do not "focus" on the visual, as one might have expected in previous eras. All of which led Bruner to suggest that the "tactile metaphor might liberate image politics from the tyranny of the visual!" (p. 198). It remains for future rhetorical critics to determine if a tactile metaphor is applicable to environmental advocacy vis-à-vis seafood.

Genetically Modified Seafood

Helvarg (2001) reported on the possible effects on blue crabs of research into molt-inhibiting hormone (MIH). Researchers at the University of Alabama at Birmingham cloned the gene for the blue crab's MIH. According to Helvarg's account, the hope was to "force crabs to molt on command, providing a year-round supply of softshell crabs for the seafood industry. The risk, according to critics of the biotech industry, is if such an MIH blocker gene got loose in the wild, it could turn blue crabs into soft targets for predators and disease, spelling disaster for the crabs, the ecosystems they inhabit, and the fisherman who depend on them" (p. 29). In the current era, examples abound of discourse about genetically modified foods. Such examples often show the tension between the almost miraculous capabilities of human science and the fear of unknown consequences.

Witte's (1992) work on fear appeals is relevant here. One can address a known threat, if one has a workable solution and self-efficacy (pp. 331–332). However, if the exact nature of the threat is unknown, then one may not be able to control either the threat or the fear. When Witte's model is applied to genetically modified seafood, one can see that the fear of long-term yet unknown consequences may compromise the ability: 1) to even know what the threat is and 2) to take action against the threat. The consequence is to be mired in fear. Nevertheless, this chapter does not end with the reader mired in fear. While, due attention has been given to Problems, the next section is devoted to Solutions.

Solutions

Sustainability

The term "sustainability" has become the mantra of the environment movement, and the term can be connected to seafood as well. The idea of "harvesting" at a rate that can be continued forever has tremendous appeal.

One potential problem with the current notion of sustainability is that it seems to necessitate a vast and complex calculus. When dealing with one species in one locale, such as in a timber harvest plan for redwood trees in northern California, sustainability could function effectively as a guide for logging. A timber company would cut only so many trees of a certain age, would plant additional trees, and would rotate cutting in a cycle of one hundred years or more. Consider now a similar set of calculations—but this time for all marine species in all of the world's oceans. The prospect is daunting to say the least.

Another issue with sustainability is that it is based on the paradigm of the gentle and wise human. Humans still are the stewards. Seafood still is food. The model implies that humans have the right to harvest other species. Further, humans have the wisdom to harvest intelligently, and humans have the foresight to plan for centuries into the future. All of this may be accurate. Sustainability is preferable to plunder. However, the critic must ask if there is another, even better, paradigm for the relationship between humans and marine species.

Peterson's (1997) approach to sustainability, which she phrased in terms of "sustainable development," called attention to the tensions between the two concepts. Drawing upon Kenneth Burke, Peterson argued that "Sustainable development offers a representation of environmental policy decisions as comic, rather than tragic, drama" (p. 53). Comic criticism, in the Burkean sense, focuses on symbolic representations and may not eliminate material conditions, such as depleted stocks of North Atlantic cod. Nevertheless, Burke and Peterson offered the critic a way to "call into question the cultural values that the current technological worldview emphasizes and create fresh possibilities for environmental policy" (p. 53). This endeavor fits well with the current chapter's view of a critical crisis rhetoric of seafood.

Limits

Historically, discourse and images about the world's oceans have been filled with a certain amount of awe and wonder, as evidenced in film adaptations of Jules Verne's *20,000 Leagues Under the Sea* (1870) and books and TV shows continuing through the era of Jacques Cousteau (1910–1997). Coupled with this discourse was the sense that the oceans were boundless, a realm akin to outer space. The "Blue Frontier," to borrow a phrase from Helvarg (2001), was almost limitless. The possibilities were virtually endless. The rhetoric of vastness and limitlessness made the sea appear infinite, not finite.

This rhetoric, as one can see in hindsight, masked material limits. One could argue that the world today needs a rhetoric of limits to counteract the effects on the sea of the rhetoric of limitlessness. Japan provides an example of environmental policy arising out of the recognition of limits: "alarming reports that up to 90% of the coral that surrounds many of Okinawa's islands has died off" raised a strong outcry from preservationists (Fackler, 2009, p. 8). The Japanese effort to solve the problem through coral transplants is more than interesting. But the main point here is the recognition that coral can die. Discourse about the sea today must contain the rhetoric of limits and even death if the world hopes to address the critical issues facing marine species.

The Color Blue

Another solution to the problems facing the world's oceans and marine species is to make better use of the symbolic dynamics of the color "blue." According to Livesey (2001), "Green talk" is helpful both to environmentalists and to corporations, as they engage in sense-making and discursive battles (pp. 60–61). This chapter encourages the development of "Blue talk" as a way of raising consciousness about the world's oceans and marine species.

Resources for the development of "Blue talk" already may be available in the famous view of earth from space—the Blue Planet photograph and the 2001 BBC broadcast, *Blue Planet.* If the earth is mostly water, then water, in general, and the oceans, in particular, need and deserve more emphasis in public discourse. Water could be represented by the color blue, or by the blue planet image. The challenge is to infuse blue with the same rhetorical power that green has achieved. This task is not straight-forward, nor easy. It is hard to make a term or an image symbolic, let alone iconic. It is hard to construct a social movement. Yet, a beginning point is to engage in discursive battles, to create meaning, by self-consciously featuring and promoting the color blue in public discourse about the oceans and about marine species.

A current example of the strategic use of blue may be seen on the web page of the Monterey Bay Aquarium (see *www.montereybayaquarium.org*). The deep blue found there is different than the lighter blue featured on the well-known site, *www.google.com*, and has the potential to be associated with ocean waters. A second example may be seen on the web page of Ocean Watch Australia (*Ocean Watch Australia*, 2010). The right hand of the page features dark, ocean blue. Even more provocative, however, are the fish symbols on the upper left-hand side of the page. One fish is green and the other fish is blue, suggesting that earth and ocean might be fused, and that green and blue can be linked.

Veganism

A vegan diet is a more strict form of a vegetarian diet. One does not eat animals or animal products. Similarly, one could give up eating seafood altogether, that is, all marine animals. Many people have adopted a vegan diet for health, spiritual, and environmental reasons. For instance, one could give up seafood because it involves cruelty to animals. Boiling a live lobster could be seen as abhorrent and unconscionable.

An interesting figure in public discourse about veganism is Erik Marcus. His 1998 book, *Vegan: The New Ethics of Eating*, situates a vegan diet as an *ethical* choice. Marcus decided to make the book available as a free download from *www.Vegan.com.* This decision also could be seen as another ethical choice, with respect to dissemination and access to information about the vegan way of life. His latest book, *The Ultimate Vegan Guide: Compassionate Living Without Sacrifice* (2009), encourages "ordinary citizens" to prevent the cruelty inflicted upon animals.

It might be fruitful to consider where and how discourses of veganism are taught and learned. One way is to read about the vegan option, as in the books by Marcus. Yet, one probably needs a prompt to become aware of the literature. College students, certainly, are exposed to the vegan option through coursework, readings, mentors, and peers. So, one solution to addressing the world's seafood problems is to expose college students to the issues.

Nevertheless, earlier life experiences also must be considered. For example, many children and teenagers have years of experience with school lunch programs. What do school lunch programs teach about seafood? It is clear that communication about food is controlled to some extent by the U. S. Department of Agriculture's National School Lunch Program (Huget, 2008, September 30). To what extent does low cost milk and cheese provided to schools undercut or even block learning about a vegan diet?

Food choices are also influenced by vendors, who provide rebates to school budgets. It is obvious to the critic, then, that education about food, seafood, or veganism has a strong structural component, in addition to the component of interpersonal and small group communication. Given that reality, addressing seafood problems through the vegan option will take institutional transformation as well as individual change.

"Watchdog" Organizations

In the United States, The Center for Science in the Public Interest (CSPI) has gained somewhat of a reputation for functioning as the "food police." CSPI sometimes has ventured into seafood issues, such as when the "Death on the Half Shell" report cautioned the public against shellfish that might be contaminated with the *vulnificus* bacteria. Bruner (2003) pointed out how CSPI campaigns used recognizable rhetorical strategies, including a graphic language, problem-causes-solutions pattern, and fear appeals (p. 355). It might be profitable to analyze other organizations' rhetoric, with a mind to seeing how current public discourse about seafood is constructed.

Fish Watch is a program under the umbrella of the U. S. National Oceanic and Atmospheric Administration (NOAA). *FishWatch* offers several perspectives on seafood, including "Seafood and Your Health" and "making informed decisions about the seafood you eat" (National Oceanographic and Atmospheric Administration, National Marine Fisheries Service, Fish Watch, 2008). The Center for Science in the Public Interest often has called for more regulations and more government intervention in food issues. NOAA provides news and education through *FishWatch*, but "works within the Magnuson Stevens Act, Marine Mammal Protection Act, and the Endangered Species Act to fulfill its mission of promoting healthy ecosystems." The rhetorical critic might note in this mission the combination of law and legislation with a systemic approach to seafood and marine habitats. Indeed, systems language is one of the prominent features of discourse about seafood.

The *Earth Island Institute* was founded in 1982 by environmentalist David R. Brower (Earth Island Institute, n.d.) The institute is associated with coastal protection projects and the Bluewater Network (Bluewater Network, n.d.). A relevant Bluewater project was an examination of the environmental effects of the two-stroke engine on fishing boats. Bluewater Network merged with Friends of the Earth in April 2005. According to their new web site, "This strategic move combined two of the country's most innovative and effective environmental organizations" (Friends of the Earth, n.d.). What is interesting for the critic is: (1) how partnerships between organizations create synergy and (2) how education is an important component of advocacy.

Earth Watch Institute, founded in 1971, emphasizes the connection between science and people (Earthwatch Institute, n.d.). Its ocean-related projects include reef monitoring and whale sharks. There are two relevant appeals that might strike the rhetorical critic. First, *Earth Watch*'s rhetoric contains an underlying appeal to scientific expertise. The rhetoric of expertise has been studied by communication scholars (Lyne & Howe, 1990), and its persuasive force is extenuated by the current dominance of scientific discourse as a ruling paradigm. The second emphasis of *Earth Watch* is a "participation" theme: "Join us in an expedition." Audiences may be persuaded by the appeal to *action*, to learn by *doing*, and to make a difference. Critics might want to analyze these appeals from several perspectives, including the extent to which whether the organization benefits itself by building a constituency.

The Food and Agriculture Organization of the United Nations could be one of the leading players in international public discourse about the world's oceans and seafood issues. Considering the potential global significance of the United Nations, a recent press release merits space and attention here:

> June 2009, Penang/Rome - Saying that vulnerable fishing and coastal communities around the world will bear the brunt of climate change's impacts, a group of 16 international organizations today have urged climate negotiators to ensure that fisheries and aquaculture are not neglected in ongoing discussions regarding a successor to the Kyoto Protocol. In a policy brief issued in advance of UNFCC talks in Bonn, Germany, the Food and Agriculture Organization of the United Nations (FAO), the Secretariat of the Pacific Community (SPC), the United Nations Environment Programme (UNEP), the World Bank, the World Fish Center and 11 other organizations warned that millions of fishers, fish farmers and coastal inhabitants will experience less stable livelihoods, changes in the availability and quality of fish for food, and heightened risks to their health, safety and homes as a result of climate change. (Food and Agriculture Administration of the United Nations, 2010)

The complicated press release begs further interpretation, but space permits only an examination of two of the main issues from the point of view of a critical crisis rhetoric. First, the critic may notice the rhetorical link to global warming or climate change. Climate change is an urgent issue in contemporary public discourse, and linking the oceans and fisheries to climate change is a powerful rhetorical move. Second, the critic may notice the appeal to international cooperation. Seafood issues almost by definition are global issues, and solutions to seafood issues require that many entities work together. Creating this cooperation will require persuasion both of the public and of insiders and elites in national governments and international organizations. A beginning point may be to exploit the rhetorical power of the term "collaboration."

Labeling, Certification Standards, Best Practices, and Recognizable Logos

DeLuca and Peeples (2002) urged critics to strive for a better understanding of "visual rhetoric" and the "public screen" (p. 131). Their insights suggested that "labels" and "logos" were a powerful force and, by extension, could be examined in public discourse about seafood. In addition to "dolphin-safe" labels on tuna, there are many other seafood labels and logos afloat in the global marketplace. For example, the Marine Stewardship Council (MSC) asserted on its web site: "The MSC meets the highest benchmarks for credible certification and ecolabelling programs, including the UN Food and Agriculture Organization guidelines and the ISEAL Code of Good Practice" (*Marine Stewardship Council, Certified Sustainable Seafood*, n.d.). Despite the up-beat tone of the MSC's claims, the rhetorical critic must ask some hard questions.

One of the most pernicious rhetorical practices that the critic can address is the co-optation of labels. For example, in the arena of agriculture, claims abound that foodstuffs are "organic" or do not contain genetically modified ingredients. Which set of definitions are operative? Who makes these certifications? How trustworthy are the labels? All of these critical questions can be applied to seafood, too.

According to *Seafood Watch*, many organizations around the world are advocating for seafood certification and labels. These forms of rhetoric have a tangible presence and a life of their own in public discourse, as can be seen from the ongoing discourse about "dolphin-safe" tuna labels. The concerned critic could invest effort in the labeling process for seafood. However, one must recognize that the process is long and arduous. The development of the "organic" label in the United States, for example, took ten years.

International Conferences

The role international conferences play in seafood discourse merits further attention. Environmental discourse at these conferences sometimes is directed toward the creation of public policy and even international law. The Kyoto Protocol, for example, is a heavily contested topic in public discourse. The current study suggests that rhetorical critics might play a useful role not only in studying but participating in international conferences on seafood issues.

A recent conference, called *Seafood & Health 2008,* held in Norway in May, 2008, connected seafood and health issues. Promotional materials for the conference stated:

> The effect of seafood consumption on human health is a constantly revisited subject, since seafood is reported to have both positive effects on human health and at the sametime contain compounds potentially detrimental to human health. Reports related to these subjects may affect governmental dietary advice and consumer's seafood intake. Our knowledge in the field of seafood and health is constantly evolving and at a conference in 2008 leading scientists in the field of seafood and health, in addition to policy makers and governmental representative will present the latest in this field. (National Institute of Nutrition and Seafood Research, 2008)

The emphasis on seafood and *health* at this conference demands attention from critics. Indeed, the growing field of Health Communication has much to offer to this dialogue. For example, to what extent are fear appeals an acceptable and potentially effective part of health promotion campaigns? (Witte, Meyer, & Martell, 2001).

Eat Simply

The central message of the book *Bottomfeeder* is that one should try to eat seafood that is low on the food chain. In other words, eat mussels or sardines instead of salmon. This discourse of simplicity is based on the argument that seafood that is low on the food chain does not use much total energy to produce or to reproduce. One is not wasting anything in eating a mussel. The argument is almost identical to the contention that it makes more sense to eat grain than to feed grain to cows and then to eat beef (Robbins, 1987).

Aquariums and Seafood

The 2004 annual meeting of the National Communication Association made the Shedd Aquarium the site of an interdisciplinary conference panel, entitled "Right Bite: Public Relations Outreach." Taking advantage of its Lake Michigan lakeside location, the Shedd Aquarium has emphasized the Great Lakes. The aquarium's web site declared:

> The Friday-night fish fry is a tradition in many Midwestern communities and a favorite for many Chicagoans, including members of the Right Bite team! But how sustainable are the Great Lakes fisheries? And is the Friday-night fish fry a good choice? (Shedd Aquarium, RIGHT BITE, 2004)

While the Great Lakes are not an ocean setting, the Shedd Aquarium nonetheless addresses issues similar to the ones that are central to this chapter. First, what can an aquarium do to educate the public about aquatic environments and species? Second, what can an aquarium do to advocate for more enlightened seafood practices?

The main embodiment of the Shedd Aquarium's efforts in education and social influence is the RIGHT BITE program. This program is noteworthy because it attempts to bring local restaurants into conversation with consumers about seafood choices:

> We promote the importance of sustainable seafood in our education programs, exhibits and special events… even in the food choices we make for the animals in our care. You can be sure that we serve only sustainable seafood in our own restaurants, Soundings and the Bubble Net. And we have enlisted many restaurants across Chicago to join our effort. We've also developed the Right Bite program to educate consumers, restaurant owners and seafood purveyors about the importance of choosing sustainable seafood. We've reached millions of people through media events, chef presentations and family programs. (Shedd Aquarium, RIGHT BITE, 2004)

By encouraging seafood consumers to interact with the aquarium, with restaurant owners, with purveyors, with culinary schools, with media leaders, and with chefs, the Shedd Aquarium has created a rather unique nexus. From the standpoint of critical rhetoric, it must be acknowledged that there is some danger of "elitism" in privileging seafood restaurants and an aquarium (whose admission ticket prices range from $11.95 on up). In fact, in ordinary language "fish" has les status than "seafood." However, RIGHT BITE at Shedd Aquarium is a significant voice in public discourse in the Midwest about seafood.

On the West Coast, the Monterey Bay Aquarium is a significant voice in public discourse about seafood. The Monterey Bay Aquarium's trademark program is called *Seafood Watch* (Monterey Bay Aquarium, Seafood Watch, n.d.). Seafood consumers can obtain a seafood guide to help them make appropriate seafood choices. For example, consumers are steered away from eating Orange Roughy. The seafood guide uses both visual rhetoric (a symbol and color labeling) and a narrative argument. Here is the entry about Orange Roughy:

> Orange Roughy, which don't mature until they're at least 20 years old and can live over 100 years, show dramatic population declines in some areas. They live in deep waters where they're caught with habitat-damaging trawl gear when they gather to feed or spawn around seamounts and oceanic cliffs. A number of deep-sea shark species caught as bycatch in orange roughy fisheries are threatened.

Notice that the guide contains three fairly sophisticated reasons for not consuming Orange Roughy: 1) the fish takes many years to mature; 2) the species is a deep water fish, which means that the trawling gear used to catch it damages the ocean habitat; and 3) threatened or endangered species may be caught as bycatch.

In addition, the Monterey Bay Aquarium is a leader in communication and technology with respect to seafood. The seafood guide is available to download on smart phones. The charge of "elitism" might be raised here, again, with respect to technology and seafood guides. However, the use of "smart phone" technology is one way to reach younger audiences, and to reach them at the point of decision-making about seafood.

Shock Ads

Aquariums, of course, are subject to many of the same criticisms leveled against zoos and "Sea World"-type parks. For example, the advocacy organization People for the Ethical Treatment of Animals (PETA) has lobbied against using animals for entertainment purposes. Its Media Center suggested that zoos are "pitiful prisons":

> Despite their professed concern for animals, zoos can more accurately be described as "collections" of interesting animals than as actual havens or homes. Even under the best of circumstances at the best of zoos, captivity cannot begin to replicate wild animals' habitats. Animals are often prevented from doing most of the things that are natural and important to them like running, roaming, flying, climbing, foraging, choosing a partner, and being with others of their own kind. Zoos teach people that it is acceptable to interfere with animals and keep them locked up in captivity, where they are bored, cramped, lonely, deprived of all control over their lives, and far from their natural homes. (People for the Ethical Treatment of Animals, n.d.)

This anti-zoo (or aquarium) discourse deserves serious consideration, as does PETA's startling use of visual rhetoric. PETA's billboard and print ads for vegetarianism, including one with a nude Alicia Silverstone, entitled *Vegetariana,* have stirred debate and controversy. PETA also encountered resistance to a proposed TV ad, "Veggie Love." According to the *Washington Post*: "NBC has nixed a new Super Bowl ad from the animal rights activist group People for the Ethical Treatment of Animals because the ad is too sexually explicit" (De Moraes, 2009, January 28). There are no easy answers for rhetorical critics who analyze this graphic, "in your face," Hollywood-style public discourse. Is publicity of any sort effective, simply because it is publicity? Are the causes urgent and the stakes high enough to warrant a violation of the usual norms of decorum?

The Collaborative Learning Approach

A fitting way to conclude the Solutions section of this chapter is to call favorable attention to The Collaborative Learning Approach outlined by Daniels and Walker (2001). They define Collaborative Learning as "a framework and set of techniques intended for multiparty decision situations" (p. 15). As a conceptual framework, Collaborative Learning redefines environmental conflict as an opportunity for all stakeholders to learn. As a practical guide, Collaborative Learning offers "a means of designing and implementing a series of events to promote creative thought, constructive debate, and the effective implementation of proposals" (p. 15). When applied to seafood issues, Collaborative Learning holds the promise of enabling stakeholders in very complex situations to work together.

In northern California and southern Oregon, elements of Collaborative Learning are evident in the process that led to the recent landmark decision to tear down four dams on the Klamath River (Sims, 2009). Stakeholders included farmers, Native American nations, scientists, government agencies, PacificCorp power company, those engaged in sport fishing, and related businesses. With respect to seafood, tearing down the four dams may improve the prospects for salmon in the Pacific Northwest.

One should not underestimate the time and energy that is required by The Collaborative Learning Approach. In the Klamath case, discussions have been ongoing for more than ten years. However, framing a situation in terms of *learning* may defuse some conflict and may provide space for creating solutions. Even when multiple parties offer individual perspectives and present scientists with competing views, the *learning* focus encourages thoughtfulness.

Conclusion

This chapter has offered a number of examples of seafood-related problems and solutions in contemporary public discourse. In keeping with McGee's (1990) insight that audiences create text out of fragments, this chapter takes public discourse quite seriously. The fragments analyzed throughout the chapter are a part of the complicated, contradictory, and ever-changing discourse faced by seafood consumers. Citizens and consumers must struggle constantly to create a coherent text, to make sense of the world of seafood.

This chapter is more than critical rhetoric, however; this chapter also presents a crisis rhetoric of seafood. Because communication about seafood is part of a crisis discipline, this chapter attempts to persuade readers that they have an urgent ethical obligation to act. From this point of view, public discourse about seafood shares many of the same rhetorical features of the "American Jeremiad" (Bercovitch, 1978).

Jeremiah was an Old Testament prophet, who brought an unwanted message of gloom and doom and, perhaps, redemption. Bercovitch saw a similar rhetorical form in the early American rhetoric of John Winthrop. For the present chapter, the relevant point is that current seafood rhetoric, in part, follows the form of the American Jeremiad: 1) The world's oceans and marine species are imperiled; 2) Human sins, such as lack of awareness, pride, avarice, and greed, are significant causes of the problem; 3) Humans must repent and change their ways; and 4) If humans repent and reform, then redemption is possible. Admittedly, this analysis is only one path that a critical crisis rhetoric of seafood can take. Yet the critic already is part of public discourse and already is committed to a path.

The implications of this chapter are that communication about seafood truly is significant and merits immediate, serious attention from scholars and the public. Further research would be illuminating on the many issues raised above, such as the basic seaFOOD paradigm, the "bottomfeeder" hypothesis, the *Seafood Watch* program, and the role of the local aquarium. This chapter has placed more emphasis on Solutions by devoting twice the number of pages to Solutions than to Problems. Guided initially by the principle that action must be tempered by analysis, the chapter concludes with the strong message that analysis must lead to action. Communication about seafood cannot ignore the 21st -century imperative of eating ethically.

References

American Heart Association (n.d.). Retrieved December 21, 2009, from www.americanheart.org.

Bercovitch, S. (1978). *The American jeremiad.* Madison, WI: The University of Wisconsin Press.

Biesecker, B. (1992). Michel Foucault and the question of rhetoric. *Philosophy and Rhetoric, 25,* 351–364.

Blue Planet (2001). BBC.

Blue Water Network/Friends of the Earth (n.d.) Retrieved June 1, 2010, from www.foe.org/bluewater-network

Bourne, J. K., Jr. (2009). The end of plenty: Special Report. The global food crisis. *National Geographic,* 215 (6), 26–59.

Bruner, M. S. (2003). Learning, knowing, and deciding about food: The case of the Center for Science in the Public Interest. In G. Walker & W. Kinsella (Eds.), *Finding our way(s) in environmental communication: Proceedings of the Seventh Biennial Conference on Communication and the Environment* (352–358). Corvallis, OR: Department of Speech Communication, Oregon State University.

Bruner, M. S. (2005). Economics, environmental advocacy, and image events. In L. Volkening et. al. (Eds.), *Wilderness, advocacy, and the media: Proceedings of the eighth biennial conference on communication and environment* (193–201). Athens, GA: University of Georgia, Department of Speech Communication.

Burke, K. (1950). *A rhetoric of motives.* New York: Prentice Hall.

Campbell, J. A. & Benson, K. (1996). The rhetorical turn in science studies. *Quarterly Journal of Speech, 82,* 1, 74–109.

Carson, R. (1961). *The sea around us.* New York: Oxford University Press.

Charland, M. (1991). Finding a horizon and *telos*: The challenge to critical rhetoric. *Quarterly Journal of Speech, 77,* 71–74.

Corson, T. (2004) *The secret life of lobsters: How fishermen and scientists are unraveling the mysteries of our favorite crustacean.* New York: HarperCollins.

Costa-Pierce, B. (Ed.) (2003). *Ecological aquaculture: The evolution of the blue revolution.* Oxford, UK: Blackwell.

Cousteau, J. (1956). *Silent World.* Motion picture released by Columbia Pictures Corp.

Cousteau, J. (1985). *Cousteau's Rediscovery of the World.* TV series premiered on PBS.

Cousteau, J. (1995). *L'ile des esprits: Madagascar.* Paris: Plon.

Cox, R. (2007). Nature's 'crisis disciplines': Does environmental communication have an ethical duty? *Environmental Communication, 1,* 1, 5–20.

Daniels, S.E. & Walker, G. B. (2001). *Working through environmental conflict: The collaborative learning approach.* Westport, CT: Praeger.

DeLuca, K. (1999). *Image politics.* New York: The Guilford Press.

DeLuca, K. & Peeples, J. (2002). From public sphere to public screen: Democracy, activism, and the 'violence' of Seattle. *Critical Studies in Media Communication, 19,* 2, 125–151.

De Moreas, L. (2009, January 28). Veggie tales, it's not: PETA's Super Bowl ad is too much for NBC to stomach. *Washington Post,* C7.

Earth Island Institute (n.d.). Retrieved June 1, 2010, from www.earthisland.org

Earthwatch Institute (n.d.). Retrieved June 1, 2010, from www.earthwatch.org

Egelko, B. (2003, January 3). Activists sue over relaxed tuna-label rules. *San Francisco Chronicle,* A–4.

Fackler, M. (2009, April 15). Coral transplant surgery prescribed for Japan's reefs. *New York Times,* section A, p. 8.

Fish Watch (n.d.). Retrieved December 1, 2009, from www.nmfs.noaa.gov/fishwatch/index

Food and Agriculture Organization of the United Nations (2010). Retrieved June 1, 2010, from www.fao.org

Foucault, M. (1970). *The order of things.* New York: Pantheon.

Foucault, M. (1972). *The archaeology of knowledge.* New York: Pantheon.

Friends of the Earth (n.d.). Retrieved June 1, 2010, from www.foe.org

Greenpeace International (2010). Retrieved June 1, 2010 from www.greenpeace.org/international

Grescoe, T. (2008). *Bottomfeeder: How to eat ethically in a world of vanishing seafood.* New York: Bloomsbury.

Gross, A. (1990). *The rhetoric of science.* Cambridge, MA: Harvard University Press.

Halweil, B. (2008). *Farming fish for the future: Worldwatch report 176.* Washington, D.C.: Worldwatch Institute.

Helvarg, D. (2001). *Blue frontier: Saving America's living seas.* New York: W. H. Freeman and Company.

Hoffner, C. & LeVine, K. J. (2005). Enjoyment of media fright and violence. *Media Psychology, 7,* 2, 207-237.

Huget, J. (2008, September 30). School lunches, making the grade? *Washington Post,* HE01.

Jacques Cousteau (14 June 2010). Retrieved June 19, 2010, from http://en.wikipedia.org/wiki/Jacque-Yves_Cousteau

Koster, P. (2007). Overfishing—A global disaster. Retrieved June 1, 2010, from http:overfishing.org

Kuhn, T. S. (1996). *The structure of scientific revolutions.* Chicago: University of Chicago Press.

Livesey, S. M. (2001). Eco-identity as discursive struggle. *Journal of Business Communication, 38,* 1, 58–91.

Lyne, J. & Howe, H. (1990). The rhetoric of expertise: E. O. Wilson and sociobiology. *Quarterly Journal of Speech, 76,* 2, 134-151

Marcus, E. (1998). *Vegan: The new ethics of eating.* Ithaca, NY: McBooks Press.

Marcus, E. (2009). *The ultimate vegan guide: Compassionate living without sacrifice.* Santa Cruz,CA: Vegan.com.

Marine Stewardship Council, Certified Sustainable Seafood (n.d.). Retrieved June 1, 2010, from www.msc.org

McGee, M. C. (1990). Text, context, and the fragmentation of contemporary culture. *Western Journal of Speech Communication, 54,* 3, 274–289.

McKerrow, R. (1989). Critical rhetoric: Theory and praxis. *Communication Monographs, 56,* 2, 91–112.

Monterey Bay Aquarium, Seafood Watch (n.d.). Retrieved June 1, 2010, from www.montereybay aquarium.org

National Institute of Nutrition and Seafood Research (2008). Seafood and health. Retrieved June 1, 2010, from www.nifes.no/seafoodhealth

National Oceanic and Atmospheric Administration, National Marine Fisheries Service, Fish Watch (2008). Retrieved June 1, 2010 from www.noaa.gov

Ocean Watch Australia (2010). Retrieved June 1, 2010 from, www.oceanwatch.org.au

Ono, K. A. & Sloop, J. M. (1992). Commitment to *telos*—a sustained critical rhetoric. *Communication Monographs*, 59 (1), 48–60.

People for the Ethical Treatment of Animals (PETA) (n.d.). Retrieved June 1, 2010, from www.peta.org/MC/factsheet

Peterson, T. (1997). *Sharing the earth: The rhetoric of sustainable development.* Columbia, SC: University of South Carolina Press.

Plec, E. (2007). Response to Cox: Crisis, coherence, and the promise of critical rhetoric. *Environmental Communication, 1,* 1, 49–57.

Pollan, M. (2006). *The omnivore's dilemma.* New York: Penguin.

Retzinger, J. P. (2001). Setting the agenda—and setting the table—for genetically modified foods in the press. In M.-F. Aepli, J. Delicath, and S. Depoe (EDS.), *Proceedings of the 6th Biennial Conference on Communication and Environment.* Cincinnati, OH: Center for Environmental Studies and Department of Communication.

Retzinger, J. P. (2003). Suitable to serve: Salad as a mode of environmental discourse. In G. Walker and W. Kinsella (Eds.), *Finding our Way(s) in Environmental Communication: Proceedings of the Seventh Biennial Conference on Communication and the Environment* (pp. 338–351). Corvallis, OR: Department of Speech Communication, Oregon State University.

Retzinger, J. (2005). The embodied rhetoric of 'health' from farm fields to salad bowls. In L. Volkening et. al. (Eds.), *Wilderness, Advocacy, and the Media: Proceedings of the Eighth Biennial Conference on Communication and Environment* (pp. 104–115). Athens, GA: University of Georgia, Department of Speech Communication.

Retzinger, J. P. (2007). A sociable movement: Nature and culture, city and country, producers and consumers together at farmers' markets. In B. Willard and C. Green (Eds.), *Proceedings of the Ninth Biennial Conference on Communication and Environment.* Chicago: DePaul University, Department of Communication.

Retzinger, J.P. (2009). Animal, vegetable, or mineral: Viewing food production through a TV screen. Paper presented at the 10th Biennial Conference on Communication and Environment. Portland, ME: University of Southern Maine.

Robbins, J. (1987). *Diet for a new America.* Walpole, NH: Stillpoint.

Shedd Aquarium, RIGHT BITE (2004). Retrieved December 1, 2009, from www.sheddaquarium.org/Right_Bite

Sims, H. (October 9, 2009). The Klamath Settlement. *The North Coast Journal.*

Stokstad, E. (2006). Global loss of biodiversity harming ocean bounty. *Science, 314,* 745.

U.S. Market for Seafood (January, 2009). Retrieved December 1, 2009, from www.marketresearch.com

Verne, J. (1870). *Twenty thousand leagues under the sea.* Popularized in a 1916 film directed by Stuart Paton; a 1954 Disney film, directed by Richard Fleischer; and a 1997 film directed by Ro Hardy.

Witte, K. (1992). Putting the fear back into fear appeals: The extended parallel process model. *Communication Monographs, 59,* 4, 329–349.

Witte, K.; Meyer, G.; & Martell, D. (2001). *Effective health risk messages.* Thousand Oaks, CA: Sage Publications.

Worm, B.; Barbier, E.; Beaumont, N.; Duffy, J.; Folke, C.; Halpern, B., et al. (2006). Impacts of biodiversity loss on ocean ecosystem services. *Science, 314,* 5800, 787–790.

16

Eating the view: Environmental aesthetics, national identity, and food activism

Anne Marie Todd

First Lady Michelle Obama made headlines when she planted a vegetable garden on the White House lawn in March 2009. Lauded by environmentalists and foodies alike, the White House garden symbolized an important transformation of America's relationship with food. The nation's food supply relies on high-intensity and high-yield industrial agriculture so the American diet consists largely of processed foods, and many Americans don't interrogate the origin or production process of what they eat. Yet, mounting environmental and health crises have recently focused America's attention on food production systems and consumption patterns. Pollan (2008) describes the modern food crisis: "The era of cheap and abundant food appears to be drawing to a close… [and] the health of a nation's food system is a critical issue of national security" (p. 62). Indeed, communication about America's food system has come to frame debates about environmental issues, with implications for the manifestation of our national identity.

In response to economic concerns, food contamination scandals, and the local-food movement, a modern victory garden movement has emerged (MacVean, 2009b; Meyer, 2009, p. 6; Severson, 2008). Seed companies and gardening stores report record sales. Burpee & Co., one of the country's largest seed sellers, saw a 40% sales increase from 2007–2008. The National Gardening Association estimates seven million more home gardens will be planted in 2009, a 19 % increase from 2008 (Murphy, 2009). Vegetable gardens in American backyards, or on the White House lawn, are not new. Victory gardens were an important part of the home front effort during World War II. Eleanor Roosevelt famously planted a vegetable garden at the White House and persuaded millions of Americans to do the same, with the result that Americans grew 40 % of their own food during World War II (MacVean, 2009a). Yet not since Jimmy Carter tended an herb garden has the President of the United States signaled any interest in gardening. Michelle Obama's planting of the White House vegetable garden is a symbolic action that represents more than America's interest in playing in the dirt: it reveals our changing relationship with food.

This chapter examines the "Eat the View" campaign that launched during the 2008 presidential election with the goal of persuading the next president to plant a vegetable garden on the White House lawn. This campaign began on February 6, 2008, when Roger Doiron, founder of Kitchen Gardeners International (KGI), submitted his idea about what the new president should do on his/her first day to an online contest hosted by OnDayOne.org. Doiron proposed that the next president should "Eat the View!" by planting a large organic kitchen garden on the White House lawn. He argued that the garden should be large enough to supply the White House kitchen with enough surplus for local food banks. The Eat the View! campaign grew quickly: Kitchen Gardeners International circulated an online petition, which gathered 100,000 signatures; and launched a dynamic website including two web videos, one of which played on national television by virtue of winning the "Climate Matters" video contest. The movement's activity gained headlines: It was featured in over five hundred newspapers, including *The New York Times, International Herald Tribune, The Washington Post,* and *Chicago Tribune.* The Eat the View! idea was voted grand prizewinner of the On Day One contest and was thus formally submitted to President Obama on inauguration day. Two months later, on March 20, 2009, First Lady Michelle Obama planted a large organic vegetable garden on the White House lawn.

Eat the View! contributes to our understanding of food communication in three ways: it changes America's food aesthetic, uses this new aesthetic to shape America's national identity, and provides a new model for food activism. These three dimensions of Eat the View! Campaign's discourse form the analysis section of this chapter, and my findings demonstrate the significance of a White House garden for America's response to global environmental issues. Before delving into this analysis, I first provide a brief theoretical framework to ground this analysis, and explain my methodology.

Food Symbolism and Public Discourse

Eat the View! is a symbolic campaign that aims to "plant high-impact food gardens in high-profile places" (Kitchen Gardeners International, 2009a). The campaign discourse highlights the iconic nature of the White House garden, and seizes on this symbol to invigorate the national imagination. "Public images operate as intermediate forms of symbolic action between the level of individual choice and structural determination. The image appears in the public media, acquires iconic status, and influences collective action" (Hariman & Lucaites, 2007, p. 47). Hariman and Lucaites (2007) argue that iconic images work because they "mediate the social, political and cultural contradictions in which a particular people find themselves to a degree that allows them to address common problems. This mediation is always contingent, provisional, and incomplete, and it always comes at a cost" (p. 48). In this way, these images are intermediaries, and impact public discourse by providing a way to communicate values that might seem in conflict with each other. An image synthesizes such feelings, and allows us to visualize the solution or approach to an issue.

Food functions symbolically as a system of communication, a series of images that marks cultural implications of the way we eat (Barthes, 1964). Food discourse reveals patterns of social relations and thus functions as social representation (de Certeau, Mayol, & Giard, 1998). Food production and consumption are practices that shape our identity. Cultural geographers Bell and Valentine (1997) aver the importance of food in the construction of space and place in identity formation. Throughout history, food production has connected people to the land; as humans have developed more sophisticated food production, the process has become more mechanized and altered our relationship to natural resources (see Marx, 2000). Global food production masks the origins and processes of food, perpetuating the myth of abundance on which America was founded (Mackin, 2006). In this way, food is an environmental symbol, because it represents humanity's fundamental relationship with the natural environment (DeLuca, 1999; Killingsworth & Palmer, 1992).

Gardening communication is an aspect of food discourse that remains unexplored by scholars of rhetoric. The language of gardening constructs the role of food production in American society and thus has implications for how we participate as consumers of food. Given that mediated representations of food communicate desire and consumption (Shugart, 2008), discursive strategies that link food with health and the environment demonstrate possibilities for social change (Cooks, 2009). The modern victory garden movement is part of America's emerging public discourse about food and thus influences practices of food production and consumption. Gardening is an example of what Cindy Spurlock calls "place-based, embodied experiences" and thus it has the qualities that she locates in food discourse as having "significant potential for challenging unsustainable discourses of consumerism" (Spurlock, 2009, p. 5). Eat the View!'s successful campaign for a presidential vegetable garden marks a shift in America's relationship with food. The "country's most emblematic landscape [is now] a symbol for health and sustainability" (Doiron, 2009b).

Eat the View! is a web and email campaign that offers a variety of new media for public consumption. In this chapter, I analyze the campaign's online discourse, including emails, websites, petitions, and animated and live videos. I look carefully at the images and texts used throughout all of these forms of media, establishing common themes and rhetorical strategies. I draw on Hariman and Lucaites' (2007) work in interpreting photographs and other iconic images, and DeLuca's (1999) concept of how images function in environmental activism.

Rhetorical analysis of this campaign reveals three rhetorically significant themes about America's relationship with food. First, I examine the aesthetics of gardening as an alternative vision of the American landscape, namely how the emphasis on edibility responds to America's entrenched lawn aesthetic. Second, I discuss how Eat the View! uses American cultural history to construct gardening as part of America's national identity. Specifically I examine how the campaign uses iconic images and democratic symbolism to establish the role of food in American democracy. Third, I explain how Eat the View!'s model of food activism offers a new model for online social movements, by using new media to persuade activists to engage their local environs. In the conclusion, I discuss the profound implications of this campaign for the study of food discourse and environmental rhetoric. This campaign demonstrates how aesthetics of place and national identity provide opportunities for Americans to reimagine their relationship with food and develop sustainable consumption practices.

Edible Landscapes and American Food Aesthetics

The motto of Eat the View! is "edible landscapes for all." This campaign evokes an environmental aesthetic that rethinks the modern connection between food and environment. The campaign questions the notion of edibility and offers a changing food aesthetic that upends America's deep-seated love affair with the sod lawn. While the meaning of aesthetics sparks enough debate to render an entire field, we may describe aesthetics broadly as sensuous knowledge and perception of beauty (Goldman, 2001). In *de Poetica,* Aristotle (ed. 1941) posited art as a means of representation and communication. Like ethical terms, aesthetic terms are invoked with the purpose of eliciting a certain response (Ayer, 1952). Aesthetic terms evoke an emotional reaction—we feel pleasure, optimism, or other sentimentality toward a concept represented in words or images.

Environmental aesthetics encompass a broad sense of the world at large (Carlson, 2001; 2002). Environmental aesthetics considers the role of place in how we interpret experience and rests on the assumption that the world's environments offer much to appreciate (Carlson, 2001; 2002; 2009). Therefore, an environmental aesthetic necessarily involves an ethical sense of beauty: a sense that one must act to preserve the value of the environment. Eat the View! establishes a new food aesthetic by first using the symbolic action of the White House vegetable garden to critique the aesthetic of the suburban lawn, and second, deconstructing current food systems to offer new aesthetic of edibility.

Edible Lawns and a New Landscape Aesthetic

America is defined by its environment. Throughout American history, one is confronted with the central role of nature in American identity. America is "nature's nation," a historical idea grounded in the land itself (Grusin, 2000). From the early days of American democracy, the nation's greatness was defined through the land itself; pride of country grew from nature. "The fertility of the American soil, the enormous variety and fecundity of its plant and animal life, the vast reaches and unlimited resources of its waters and woods, the salubrity and balance of its climate, all made the United States a mighty stage for new great developments in human history" (Nye, 1960, p. 44). Throughout America's history, love of the land has informed public discourse regarding the nation's future course. In the latter half of the twentieth century, the birth and growth of suburbia transformed America's love of the land as productive, to a manicured landscape, epitomized in the suburban lawn. Today there are 23 million acres of lawns in the United States (Doiron, 2008b); it is safe to say that lawn is the dominant residential landscape. Americans feel strongly about their grass: lawn maintenance requires thousands of hours of mowing time and millions of gallons of water each year.

The video "This Lawn is Your Lawn" chronicles Roger Doiron reclaiming his lawn. We first watch him destroy the sod: he cuts out squares of sod and digs it up. Close up shots of the layer of sod being lifted up reveal it to be an artificial layer of turf. He is removing the sod in order to make room for his vegetable garden, but this is also a symbolic act as we see him destroy sod—the essence of the suburban landscape. The video ends with a picture of the new garden sprouting up, replete with striking, vibrant colors of chard and the lush foliage of tomatoes. As we witness the transformation of Doiron's lawn, we can visualize the transformation of the American landscape: one not defined by neighborhood covenants on keeping one's lawn mowed and hedges trimmed but by a diverse, creative, and productive landscape filled with vibrant color of vitamins and nutrition. Pollan (2009) describes the impact of this new "lawn":

> As deeply as Americans feel about their lawns, the agrarian ideal runs deeper still, and making this particular plot of American land productive, especially if the First Family gets out there and pulls weeds now and again, will provide an image even more stirring than that of a pretty lawn: the image of stewardship of the land, of self-reliance and of making the most of local sunlight to feed one's family and community. (para 1)

Eat the View! presents a new landscape aesthetic visualized in Doiron's lawn in front of his anonymous white house in Maine. The ubiquity of Doiron's style of house means his could be any lawn in America. And by showing Americans how to do it, Eat the View! asks Americans to transform more lawns into productive, edible landscapes: "To make this happen, though, we need more people asking for and digging these landscapes" (Kitchen Gardeners International, 2009a) .

In this way, Eat the View! is a campaign to actively change the American landscape. In addition to demonstrating to Americans that it is possible to dig up their own lawns, Eat the View! asks Americans to identify "high-profile pieces of land that could be transformed into edible landscapes. Sprawling lawns around governors' residences, schoolyards, vacant urban lots, these are all views that should be eaten" (Doiron, 2009a). The campaign suggests a change in landscape aesthetics that supports healthy America. Here, iconic images and symbolic lands transform into productive, which is new symbolism that American identity is entwined with its land, and goes back to conservationists. Landscape maintenance is no longer about cutting blades of grass, but harvesting food. And so the landscape aesthetic extends beyond the turf itself into the kitchen table. This is an aesthetic of environmental responsibility, perhaps encapsulated best in an image from the end of "Garden of Eden" video: a view of White House vegetable garden from West Wing with the caption, "it makes sense" (Doiron, 2008a). The new landscape aesthetic emphasizes environmental responsibility and a new concept of edibility.

Freshness, Deliciousness and the Aesthetics of Edibility

The second tenet of Eat the View!'s environmental aesthetic is the reclaiming of freshness. Celebrating the movement's victory, the website proclaims the future is going to be "fresh juicy and delicious… good, clean food is on the way!" (Kitchen Gardeners International, 2009a). The campaign emphasizes an aesthetic appreciation of food that deepens our understanding of the process of food production. This is exemplified in the website's explanation of the concept of Kitchen Gardeners:

> Kitchen Gardeners love food, both product and process. They do not dream of eating a good tomato, but a true tomato, picked warm and juicy from the vine at the peak of its ripeness. Their love of food is a complete one that extends beyond the plate to the soil and the natural processes and cycles from which good food comes. Kitchen Gardeners are in tune with the natural world, the weather, and the seasons. They look for ways of working peacefully and harmoniously with nature, rather than fighting against her. They are stewards of the land, whether it be a farm or a window-box. (Kitchen Gardeners International, 2009b)

The fresh aesthetic emphasizes establishing a more intimate relationship with food. Eschewing processed food with unknown origins, Kitchen Gardeners seek a deeper understanding of the ecological process through more engagement. The environmental aesthetics of engagement espoused by Eat the View! establishes kitchen gardeners as knowledgeable consumers, and espouses a stewardship of the earth, an environmental ethic where Americans reject Trader Joe's cellophane-wrapped produce and grow their own.

The campaign's fresh aesthetics responds to the era of modern convenience with fast food delivering excessive calories through straws and in nugget-sized pieces. Eat the View! expresses "dissatisfaction with the nation's commercial food supply" (Damrosch, 2009, p. H07). The video "Garden of Eatin'" chronicles the increasingly processed nature of fast food: "As food travels farther, the president's diet features more processed foods and tasteless produce eaten out of season" (Doiron, 2008a). Eat the View! attacks the modern food production system on an aesthetic level, arguing that food tastes better if it is local. Kitchen Gardeners' "enjoyment of the fruit is a complete one because it is inextricably entwined with the memory of the plant in its various stages of development. They taste not only the fruit, but the care and honest labor that went into making it" (Kitchen Gardeners International, 2009b). Eat the View! argues for transparency of food production process, arguing that knowledge of food production is an important aspect of food enjoyment. The campaign's aesthetics emphasizes the importance of source in determining edibility.

The campaign's discourse offers images to support this new food aesthetic. The video "This Lawn is Your Lawn" offers beautiful images of a home garden harvest. We see crops poking out of the garden soil, radishes and onions in neat rows. The next image is of gleaming radishes on a table, gloriously pink and white, next to enormous onion bulbs with long green shoots. This visualization of food as beautiful from all parts of the process epitomizes, illustrates the concept "from field to table." The rhetoric of the campaign illustrates that the future will be juicy and delicious, and this food aesthetic promotes a healthy and sustainable living. Eat the View!'s environmental aesthetic is one of engagement. The campaign urges us to rethink long-held principles of suburban landscaping and embrace vegetable gardening as a new environmental aesthetic.

This Lawn is Your Lawn: Symbolic Action and American National Identity

Rhetoric is "a constitutive force and a source of national identity essential to the operation of the public sphere and the constitutional polity" (Ivie, 1996, p. 162). As communicators, citizens negotiate national identity through symbols and visual rhetoric. Citizenship is expressed through rhetorical practices grounded in patriotism, or love of one's homeland.

> Concepts such as citizenship, emotions such as love of country, acts such as public advocacy, and practices such as critical reflection can only be taken up by others if they also provide some basis for identification, some grounding in the positive content of lived experience. The abstract forms of civic life have to be filled in with vernacular signs of social membership. (Hariman & Lucaites, 2003, p. 35)

Images Reveal the Nation

The presidency and the White House have strong symbolism in American identity. Presidential rhetoric constructs political culture. Presidential rhetoric evokes a sense of American history and national identity and is important in passing policy, generating support, and promoting public discourse (Medhurst, 1996). Presidential rhetoric shapes America's environmental attitudes (Peterson, 2004). Perhaps most acutely obvious in Ronald Reagan's assignation of ketchup as a vegetable, presidential food rhetoric influences the way Americans eat.

A presidential garden is an important symbol in constructing food policy as Richard Heinberg, Senior Fellow, Post Carbon Institute explains: "Public education is a key aspect of the food and farming transition, and a garden on the White House lawn would provide a supremely public, symbolic statement about the importance of local, small-scale, sustainable food production" (Heinberg, 2009). Symbols educate and motivate a public by establishing both the possibility and desirability of an idea. Symbols and images evoke certain emotions and ideas that have common appeal to a public audience.

Iconic Images of the First Family and White House Lawn

Eat the View! employs the Obamas' personae to tap into broad popular support for the First Couple. To emphasize the symbolism, the campaign appropriates Obamas' images and places in Americana. The Obamas are "Eaters in Chief!" (Kitchen Gardeners International, 2009a) featuring the Obamas' altered image of the painting, *American Gothic*, by Grant Wood. Barack and Michelle Obama's faces are superimposed on the bodies of the quintessential pitchfork-wielding farmer and his wife. Instead of the dour farmer and wife whose faces are besotted with the hardship of toiling in the fields, Michelle and Barack Obama have optimistic expressions in their eyes and are each biting into a carrot. The orange carrot injects vibrant color into the painting, signaling a different outlook for farmers. With this alteration, the campaign takes an iconic image in American culture and communicates a different kind of farming experience. The campaign's alteration of this iconic image works to evoke American national identity and a new vision for the future.

In another altered image, the campaign transfers the symbolic action of the White House garden into actions by all Americans. In the lead photo of the campaign's website, Obama's face is affixed to an image of Roger Doiron, the leader of the campaign, jumping on a shovel. The original image was of Doiron digging up his own lawn, but the transformed image features a smiling Barack Obama digging up the White House lawn. Obama's image is used as an inspiration to Americans, and the caption draws on the President's successful campaign cry "yes we can" by proclaiming victory: "yes we did!" This cry strengthens the use of the Obamas as a symbol because it makes connections to the political fervor that surrounds him. Doiron asked that the garden should be "large enough to capture the imagination of American people and the world" (Doiron, 2009c).

By incorporating presidential images into American culture and capitalizing on Barack Obama as a motivating figure, the campaign taps into American national pride. In this way, the Obamas are leading by example. Thus the symbolic action is transferred to plain Americans who want to respond to the Obamas' call. Doiron (2009c) explains the effect of a more modest garden, writing that he and his family were able to:

> grow roughly half of the vegetables we need with a modest sized garden. So if we can do that as a busy family in Maine, on less than a third of an acre, with no fulltime gardening staff whatsoever. And with the challenges that go along with our climate, it just makes me think that this is something that a lot of other people can be doing.

A second way the campaign emphasizes American identity is by employing the White House as an important symbol of American history and national identity. Appealing to Americans' sense of democracy, the campaign lays claim to the White House lawn as the people's lawn. Upon moving into the White House, the Obamas emphasized that their new home belonged to the American people. Its symbolism as the house of government signifies the people as the foundation of society. Because of this history, the symbolism of the White House garden takes on special meaning as representative of the nation as a community. A nation suggests "a definite social space, a fairly well demarcated and bounded territory, with which the members identity and to which they feel they belong" (Smith, 1991, p. 9). The White House is a social space, one that symbolizes American democracy.

Eat the View! employs the symbolism of democracy to inspire Americans to sign the petition to call up on the President to plant a garden. The campaign videos, *This Lawn Is Your Lawn,* is set to the tune of "This Land Is Your Land" sung by Woody Guthrie. The folk tune invokes patriotic themes, noting "this land was made for you and me." The video opens with a picture of the White House lawn and the words "your land" in the vibrant green grass. We then see an ordinary suburban white clapboard house (in Maine, it turns out) with the words "my land" written on the sod lawn. Drawing on Guthrie's lyrics, the video shows an image of the White House, with the caption: "the White House is our house and the White House lawn is our lawn."

The campaign draws on American history, the story of the White House to provide an historical connection for a modern garden. The video "Garden of Eatin'" tells the story of White House lawn, how presidents John Adams, Thomas Jefferson and Andrew Jackson grew their own fruits and vegetables, brewed their own beer and built a greenhouse, respectively. A frequently used image on the website is a photograph of the White House with lawn and sheep from Woodrow Wilson's time in office. These images use historic images of the White House to help Americans visualize a new White House lawn. Eat the View! declares a White House garden to be a positive symbol of

> beauty, health, a sense of time and place, and a deep sense of self-reliance. The impact it would have on children, particularly on those who have garden programs in their schools, to see that yes, the president of our country, and his wife and children, eat from a vegetable garden! (Madison, 2009)

In this way, the first family and the White House are a way that the symbolism works to persuade Americans that it is patriotic to plant a garden. This helps inspire plain Americans to plant their own backyard gardens. Interviewed after winning the On Day One contest, Doiron cited President Obama's inaugural address and noted that

> the new era of responsibility can start at home and it should start at home. It can start on a very very simple level with simple actions and if those simple actions are done by hundreds of thousands if not millions of people they really do add up. (Doiron, 2009c)

Gardening and the Movement for Democracy

The second way that Eat the View! constructs American national identity is to demonstrate the White House garden as a symbol of democracy. Kitchen Gardeners International is a people's movement. Roger Doiron's use of Obama's images and as leaders of the movement is strategic, but really, he is the hero. Americans may want to imitate the president's actions, but they learn how by watching Doiron dig up his own lawn. The video *This Land is Your Land* tells the story of how he dug up his own lawn and planted a vegetable garden. We see him pulling up sod, see him raking and laying grass, and see his sons helping/playing in the garden. The video allows us to visualize how we might participate in the gardening movement.

The opening screen image from the video *This Lawn is Your Lawn* is a picture of Roger Doiron standing on a shovel, breaking ground on a White House vegetable garden. As we later learn in the video, this is actually a picture of him in his own lawn, superimposed so that he seems to be digging up the White House lawn. The cartoon bubbles read: "Hey, who's that and what does he think he's doing?" "It's that guy from Maine who's planting veggies on the 'First Lawn." "Can he really do that?" "No *he* can't, but *we* can, if we all pitch in." (Eattheview.org!). Here, Doiron leads by example, he is the leader of the movement, and it is his story, not President Obama's that inspires Americans.

Eat the View! capitalizes on the symbolism of the White House garden to explain the importance of food in American democracy. The message is that all Americans can eat well. A CNN story noted that the "White House garden will feed many" (White House garden will feed many, 2009). Food is a resource upon which American democracy is based. Alice Waters, founder of Chez Panisse, a Berkeley, California, restaurant that pioneered using only fresh, organic produce argues "local, affordable, nutritious food should be the birthright of all Americans, not just the privilege of a few." She continues that such a garden would demonstrate "to the world that the American presidency is dedicated to the good stewardship of the land. Supporting seasonal, ripe, delicious, American food would not only nourish the First Family, it would support our farmers and energize the nation" (Waters, 2009). In this way, the White House garden is a symbol for the right of all Americans to be healthy.

The Eat the View! campaign is to promote the reimagination of the American environment, making the connection between "the garden and the table" (White House garden will feed many, 2009). It connects the national symbol of the White House garden to the local landscape of Americans. The symbolism works because it reinvigorates the national imagination by drawing on our pride in democracy. The White House garden is a powerful message about the foundation of democracy: the equitable distribution of resources. Gardening becomes democratic, patriotic, and America becomes symbol of environmentalism. Through the images and icons of the garden, connect symbolic action with real engagement by real Americans. In the next section, we discuss how the aesthetics of the Eat the View! campaign changes our relationship to food and suggests that gardening is an important part of American democracy.

Planting Grassroots: Food Activism and Movement Success

By encouraging gardening as part of democratic participation, Eat the View! promotes a new brand of food activism—one characterized by a decidedly democratic message of inclusion. Victory gardens are symbols of healthy democracy: citizens participate in the food production process. Many have studied Internet activism in general and online environmentalism specifically (Johnston & Smith, 2002; Keck & Sikkink, 1998). Indeed, "technological and social changes have produced the public screen" (DeLuca & Peeples, 2002, p. 134). While many laud the Internet for increasing awareness, one common criticism of online petitions is they are merely armchair activism: that is, with the click of the button, people feel that they have done enough, and thus don't donate resources such as time or money to further the campaign.

Eat the View! offers a model of food activism. It reconsiders the Internet as a means for grassroots activism. Eat the View! demonstrates it is possible to transform Internet campaign into actual activism, as Internet activists literally put down roots as a result of communication among individuals. On one level, the campaign's goal is to collect signatures of an online petition. Whereas most campaigns might stop there, or send a follow-up email asking for money, Eat the View! works to establish a community support network for kitchen gardeners. Virtual communities tend to deemphasize place-centered discourse due to the dispersed nature of participants, but Eat the View! marks a new era in Internet activism by providing connections through activists in local places. In this section, I examine how Eat the View! uses new media to promote movement success, and how the campaign creates an active network that establishes local connections for online environmental activism.

New media and movement success. As an Internet campaign, Eat the View! uses new media to gain publicity and to engage Americans. The website is an example of diversified new media, using viral videos (the video of "This Land Is Your Land" was viewed nearly 14,000 times), and social networking services such as Facebook to "grow a large support base, attract international media attention and help inspire a larger grassroots effort" (Doiron, 2009a). The campaign uses new media to get the message out: in addition to the videos, the website makes available speeches and interviews by Roger Doiron, founder of the campaign, and asks garden writers and bloggers to freely republish movement discourse with links back to Eat the View!'s website. The website has 2, 260 supporters. It is a people-powered campaign, illustrated by photos of thousands of members and a list of "featured supporters" that help create connections (Kitchen Gardeners International, 2009a).

Eat the View! uses multiple tactics of new media to gain publicity. The campaign's website and email list and online petition are hallmarks of Internet activism. Eat the View! also used more innovative tactics. The campaign won two contests for its idea for a White House vegetable garden. "On Day One" and "Climate Matters" were both contests designed to call attention to issues important to Americans, determined by topical videos submitted and voted on by citizens. Eat the View! also used the online auction house Ebay to stage a clever publicity stunt. Doiron auctioned off one-square-foot plots of the White House lawn (virtual, of course) to raise money and awareness of the cause. The campaign used new media effectively, as demonstrated by the fact that over 100,000 people signed its petition and that it received coverage in over 500 newspapers. In his acceptance speech as recipient of a Heart of Green award (an award dedicated to environmentalist innovators), the founder of KGI, Roger Doiron, explicitly thanked the media for helping to spread the word about the campaign . Eat the View!'s reliance on diverse channels of new media to gain public support exemplifies the growing methods of communication available to today's activists.

Moreover, the campaign used these channels to claim success. While Michelle Obama did not explicitly acknowledge the campaign in her public rhetoric planting the garden, Eat the View! issued a press release noting that 100,000 people applauded her actions. In a victory letter to supporters, Doiron noted, "Michelle Obama heard our call!" (Doiron, 2009d). Doiron's message to supporters congratulates the Kitchen Gardeners International community for a successful long-term project: "Back in the middle of the presidential primary season when 99.9999% of the population was focused on who the next president was going to be, we were the .0001% of the population that was thinking about what his or her family was going to eat and where it would be grown" (Doiron, March 2009). By claiming success, the campaign encourages its supporters to take pride in the victory and continues to push for continued transformation of America's landscapes.

Online Networks and Local Activism

More than just an online campaign, Kitchen Gardeners International is an active network; tellingly, the campaign uses an exclamation point much as Earth First! does to emphasize action over words. Eat the View! is a how-to movement where members share gardening knowledge to encourage local action. In this way, Eat the View! and Kitchen Gardeners International are antidotes to armchair activism. Eat the View! demonstrates that online environmentalism can inspire local action to address global problems. The campaign brings the environmental movement into people's homes and back yards; people find inspiration for activism in the kitchen and garden.

Roger Doiron asks Americans to join him in persuading the president to "walk the talk" and plant a vegetable garden. Doiron, himself, decides that "talk is cheap" and decides to plant his own garden, thus embodying activism. Doiron's story forms an inspirational narrative for the campaign: he reports on his family's $2000 savings from their vegetable garden to explain the economic impact a home garden can have. He uses this to explain what is possible: "there are about 90 million households in the US that have some sort of yard, [and] factor in the thousands of community and school gardens we could be planting, this really could add up" (Doiron, March 2009). Doiron leads by example, and provides information for Americans to follow. A striking image on the campaign website depicts ten- and twenty-dollar bills sprouting from dirt. A simple image, this taps into people's personal economic worries, but in doing so, it connects gardening to a larger, global market system. The sprouts symbolize how gardening can help individuals to reestablish an economic foundation and control their own economic future.

This is a do-it-yourself movement. The videos provide more than images of activism, they are also a demonstration of how to participate in the movement's goal of creating edible American landscapes. In many ways, the website becomes a handbook for would-be kitchen gardeners. The website is built on the network of Kitchen Gardeners International and becomes a forum for gardeners to participate in the movement. The forums offer a place for members to offer advice on home economics or share a comment (Doiron, March 2009). Recent forum discussion topics include: the economics of home gardening (4 comments), Dog poop in the compost pile? (9 comments), Starting my seeds indoors today (because I am going insane) (16 comments), Helping a gardening newbie in TN (4 comments), Urban maple tappers? (20 comments). And the forum topic: How can the Internet help people plant gardens? (62 comments). The answers to this last question might seem obvious given the advice provided in other forums, but topic posts include links to other gardening forums, events, and more ways for gardeners to leave their computer screens.

It is in this way that this online movement embodies citizen involvement. Participation in this movement requires more than a click of the mouse, or the signing of a petition. Its goal is not to raise money, but to encourage Americans to take action by planting a kitchen garden because "responsibility begins at home!… We can choose to lead by example and can demand that our elected officials do the same" (Kitchen Gardeners International, 2009a). Eat the View! envisions all Americans as participating in democracy as food activists, and the campaign's online discourse creates the framework for local action. Kitchen gardeners have virtual communities for support and ideas, which they can take back for their local communities. In this way, Eat the View!'s online discourse makes the link between global and local environmental issues that is necessary to inspire sustainable living worldwide. The campaign offers a reconnection with place; the suasory discourse of the online community encourages people to act out of responsibility to their local communities.

Here is online discourse's potential for social change. For online environmental communication to be effective, activists must connect with their local communities to communicate wisdom learned in their online discussions. Just as activists forged connections in cyberspace based on a sense of obligation, so too can they connect with members of their local communities who are similarly motivated and inspired. Online activist communities will be most effective if they supplement rather than supplant local connections.

Conclusion: American Food Aesthetic and New Food Activism

Eat the View! campaign's discourse and the symbolic action of the planting of the White House vegetable garden offer a food aesthetic that promotes American democracy, encouraging citizens to participate in food production. This has three implications for the future study of food as political discourse.

First, Eat the View! offers an alternative discourse to globalized food production. In his early explanation of globalization, Giddens (1990) noted that public space is increasingly dislocated from place, as people network to other social contexts across the globe. Eat the View! responds to this feature of globalization by promoting reconnection and relocation with place. The gardening movement responds to globalization by establishing a new geography of power where people have control over their land. Eat the View! suggests that rather than addressing the world's problems at the global level, change can begin at home, in our backyards. This movement transforms the power of activism so that it is possible to make a local impact in a global world.

Eat the View! responds to international fears about the collapse of the global economy by providing a way for people to find economic stability. By gardening, citizens are taking matters into their own hands, wresting control of their food back from corporations and industrial agriculture. "In times of uncertainty… people cling to things they can control, like their own backyards and food supply" (Meyer, 2009, p. 6). By reasserting the importance of local action, Eat the View! reconnects Americans with their own backyards and offers a new model of grassroots activism that makes global connections between local communities. In this way, Kitchen Gardeners International creates a global community where gardeners around the world can address the challenges of globalization.

Second, Eat the View! demonstrates how rhetoric can transform our relationship with food. The discourse of the kitchen gardener transforms the way that we enjoy food: "Unlike mere foodies who flit from one trendy spot to another in search of instant culinary gratification, Kitchen Gardeners set out roots in a place and begin planning their pleasure months in advance" (Kitchen Gardeners International, 2009b). Kitchen gardeners are food activists; by participating in the local food production process, they change the global system. The website urges viewers to "grow some tomatoes. You're in charge" (Damrosch, 2009, p. H07). The campaign urges Americans to reject the passive consumption of fast-food meals and TV dinners. With elevated standards of fresh taste, kitchen gardeners are active eaters who plan and anticipate the fruits (and vegetables) of their labor.

Eat the View! urges a new food populism. An online newspaper devoted to environmental issues, *The Daily Green* dubs Doiron as a "populist foodie" (Shapley, 2009). Eat the View! expands the concept of foodie from white tablecloths to backyards and vacant lots. In this way, the campaign promotes a sense of equality in American lifestyles. Eat the View! promotes activism for food justice. The campaign opens the door to organic food for Americans who can't afford to shop at Whole Foods. Eat the View! presents a populist vision of American food systems and establishes gardening as a way to make fresh food a possibility for all Americans.

Finally, Eat the View! reaffirms food's place in sustainability discourse. With this participation in the environmental productivity, the campaign establishes the possibility for sustainable living. Through a critical questioning of the industrial food system, Eat the View! establishes the environmental impact of what we eat. The campaign's connection between gardening and cooking provides a way for consumers to green their lifestyles; by growing their own vegetables, Americans can reduce their food miles. The use of edible landscapes promotes an environmental ethic for Americans to take responsibility for local environments and be part of a movement for more sustainable practices worldwide. Eat the View! brings the environmental movement into the kitchen, and gets America back in the garden.

References

Aristotle. (1941). De poetica. In R. McKeon (Ed.), *The basic works of Aristotle* (pp. 1455–1487). New York: Random House.

Ayer, A. J. (1952). *Language, truth and logic.* New York: Dover.

Barthes, R. (1964). *Elements of semiology* (A. Lavers & C. Smith, Trans.). New York: Jonathan Cape.

Bell, D., & Valentine, G. (1997). *Consuming geographies: We are where we eat.* New York: Routledge.

Carlson, A. (2001). Environmental aesthetics. In B. Gaut & D. M. Lopes (Eds.), *Routledge companion to aesthetics* (pp. 423–436). London: Routledge.

Carlson, A. (2002). *Aesthetics and the environment: The appreciation of nature, art and architecture*. London: Routledge.

Carlson, A. (2009). *Nature and landscape: An introduction to environmental aesthetics*. New York: Columbia University Press.

Cooks, L. (2009). You are what you (don't) eat? Food, identity, and resistance. *Text & Performance Quarterly, 29,* 1, 94–110.

Damrosch, B. (2009). Don't let pesticide lobby scare you. *The Washington Post,* H07.

de Certeau, M., Mayol, P., & Giard, L. (Eds.). (1998). *Practices of everyday life, vol. 2.* Minneapolis: University of Minnesota.

DeLuca, K. (1999). *Image politics: The new rhetoric of environmental activism*. New York: Guilford Press.

DeLuca, K. M., & Peeples, J. (2002). From public sphere to public screen: Democracy, activism, and the "violence" of Seattle. *Critical Studies in Media Communication, 19,* 2, 125–151.

Doiron, R. (2008a). Garden of eatin': A history of America's garden: Kitchen Gardeners International. Retrieved February 28, 2010 from http://www.eattheview.org/videos

Doiron, R. (2008b). This lawn is your lawn: Kitchen Gardeners International. Retrieved February 28, 2010 from http://www.eattheview.org/videos

Doiron, R. (2009a, March 20). 100,000 applaud announcement of a new White House food garden. Retrieved May 13, 2009 from http://www.eattheview.org/page/press-release

Doiron, R. (2009b). Acceptance speech at the daily green's heart of green awards. New York City. Retrieved February 28, 2010 from http://www.thedailygreen.com/environmental-news/latest/roger-doiron-video

Doiron, R. (2009c). Interview. U.N Dispatch: Global News and Views. Retrieved, February 28, 2010 from http://www.undispatch.com/node/7889

Doiron, R. (2009d, March 19). It's official: The Obamas will "eat the view". Retrieved May 15, 2009 from http://www.eattheview.org

Doiron, R. (March 2009). Kitchen Gardeners International newsletter. Retrieved May 15, 2009 from http://www.eattheview.org

Giddens, A. (1990). *The consequences of modernity*. Stanford, California: Stanford University Press.

Goldman, A. (2001). The aesthetic. In B. Gaut & D. M. Lopes (Eds.), *Routledge companion to aesthetics* (pp. 181–192). London: Routledge.

Grusin, R. (2000). The reproduction of nature: Cultural origins of America's national parks. *Letters, 8,* 2.

Hariman, R., & Lucaites, J. L. (2003). Public identity and collective memory in U.S. Iconic photography: The image of "accidental napalm". *Quarterly Journal of Speech, 20,* 1, 35–66.

Hariman, R., & Lucaites, J. L. (2007). *No caption needed: Iconic photographs, public culture, and liberal democracy*. Chicago: University of Chicago Press.

Heinberg, R. (2009). Testimonial. Retrieved May 3, 2009, from http://www.eattheview.org/page/testimonials-1

Ivie, R. L. (1996). Tragic fear and the rhetorical presidency: Combating evil in the Persian gulf. In M. J. Medhurst (Ed.), *Beyond the rhetorical presidency* (pp. 153–178). College Station, TX: Texas A&M University Press.

Johnston, H., & Smith, J. (Eds.). (2002). *Globalization and resistance: Transnational dimensions of social movements*. New York: Rowman & Littlefield Publishers, Inc.

Keck, M., & Sikkink, K. (1998). *Activists beyond borders: Advocacy networks in international politics*. Ithaca, NY: Cornell University Press.

Killingsworth, M. J., & Palmer, J. S. (1992). Ecospeak: Rhetoric and environmental politics in America. Carbondale, IL: Southern Illinois University Press

Kitchen Gardeners International. (2009a). Eat the view! Retrieved May 30, 2009, from www.eattheview.org

Kitchen Gardeners International. (2009b). What is a kitchen gardener? Retrieved February 28, 2010, from www.eattheview.org

Mackin, A. (2006). *Americans and their land: The house built on abundance*. Ann Arbor: The University of Michigan Press.

MacVean, M. (2009a, January 19).Victory garden movement showing real growth. *San Francisco Chronicle,* p. F4.

MacVean, M. (2009b, January 10). Victory gardens sprout up again. *Los Angeles Times*.

Madison, D. (2009). Testimonial. Retrieved May 3, 2009, from http://www.eattheview.org/ page/ testimonials-1

Marx, L. (2000). *The machine in the garden: Technology and the pastoral idea in America* (2nd ed.). New York: Oxford University Press.

Medhurst, M. J. (Ed.). (1996). *Beyond the rhetorical presidency*. College Station, TX: Texas A&M University.

Meyer, S. (2009, May). Why garden? *Organic Gardening, 56,* 6.

Murphy, K. (2009, May 14). Lead is a concern for urban gardens. *The New York Times,* pp. D1 & D9.

Nye, R. B. (1960). *The cultural life of the new nation, 1776–1830*. New York: Harper & Row.

Peterson, T. R. (Ed.). (2004). *Green talk in the White House: The rhetorical presidency encounters ecology*. College Station, TX: Texas A&M University Press.

Pollan, M. (2008, October 12). Farmer in chief. *The New York Times Magazine,* 62–71, 92.

Pollan, M. (2009). Testimonial. Retrieved May 3, 2009, from http://www.eattheview.org/page/ testimonials-1

Severson, K. (2008, July 22). A locally grown diet with fuss but no muss. *The New York Times,* p. A1.

Shapley, D. (2009). 10 Food Visionaries Delivering Local, Organic and Healthy Foods to the American Mainstream. *The Daily Green*. Retrieved February 28, 2010 from http://www.thedailygreen.com/healthy-eating/eat-safe/heart-of-green-food-470301

Shugart, H. (2008). Sumptuous texts: Consuming "otherness" in the food film genre. *Critical Studies in Media Communication, 25*(1), 68–90.

Smith, A. D. (1991). *National identity*. London: Penguin Books.

Spurlock, C. M. (2009). Performing and sustaining (agri)culture and place: The cultivation of environmental subjectivity on the piedmont farm tour. *Text & Performance Quarterly, 29*(1), 5–21.

Waters, A. (2009). Testimonial. Retrieved May 3, 2009, from http://www.eattheview.org/ page/testimonials-1

White House garden will feed many. (2009). Atlanta: CNN. Retrieved February 28, 2010 from http://transcripts.cnn.com/TRANSCRIPTS/0904/11/cnr.09.html

17

Discourses of consumption and sustainability on the Food Network

Janet M. Cramer

As a manifestation of culture, food is one of the most potent media for conveying meanings related to identity, ethnicity, nationhood, gender, class, sexuality, and religion—in short, all those aspects of social, political, and relational life that convey who and what we are and what matters to us. As the chapters in this collection illustrate, food is laden with social and cultural values and ideals and has potent communication power. The focus here, however, is food as a product of the natural world and how it can serve to connect us to soil, water, sun, and creature. In this sense, food is both a symbol and a product of our environment and of humans' relationship with the natural world. As Hinrichs (2007) notes, "food can and should be connected to community vitality, cultural survival, economic development, social justice, environmental quality, ecological integrity, and human health" (Hinrichs, 2007, p. 1).

A link between sustainability and food has been well-established by scholars from various disciplines. Certainly, Michael Pollan (2006) in *The Omnivore's Dilemma* generated widespread interest in the ecological and political facets of food production and consumption, as did the Slow Food Movement in Italy and the United States. Scholars have focused on food politics and sustainability to encourage advancement on these topics in education (Corson, 1995), philosophy (Vanderheiden, 2006) agriculture (Foley, et al., 2005; Horrigan, Lawrence & Walker, 2002), economics (Partidário, Lambert & Evans, 2007) and medicine (Peters, 1997), as well as to consider how communication plays a role in consumer understandings and attitudes (Mühlhäusler, 2006; Parkins & Craig, 2009). A growing interest in food and culture has encouraged questions regarding how food choices define cultures and how changes may be made to view food and cultural values in different, more beneficial, ways.

The focus and purpose of these studies, in general, is to see how food production and consumption can be made more sustainable and how the choices humans make about what to eat (and where and how this happens) can have environmental consequences. And, certainly, "food as a rhetorical construct emphasizes its relationship to biological, environmental, and cultural factors," because, as Meister (2001) notes, "biologically, we require from food the energy, nutrition, and 'resources' necessary for maintaining a healthy existence" (pp. 168–169). So my focus in this chapter is to consider food and food discourse as the means through which humans establish, enjoy, and make enduring a mutual and respectful relationship with the natural world.

Discontinuity between and dominance of humans over the natural world is the "essential problem" facing our world today (Berry, 1999, pp. 4–5). In order for humans to rectify this essential problem, we must develop practices and ways of living that are mutually enhancing to both humans and the natural world (Franck, Roze, & Connolly, 2000). The starting point for this study is the assumption that a "right relationship" with food is a necessary foundation for developing such practices. The research in this chapter begins from the assumption that human relationships with food and, especially, the process of producing and preparing one's own food, are fundamental to understanding or reconceptualizing a relationship between humans and the earth that is more sustainable.

Emerging environmental, economic, and social concerns regarding the way food is grown, processed, and distributed make it essential to look at the effects of food choices on the long-term stability of the food system and the overall health of the planet. Central to these choices are the acts of producing, cooking, and consuming food. Simply put, the way in which we raise and eat our food reflects how we value ourselves, our communities, and the land. In this paper, I look specifically at the act of cooking and the way this act is constructed discursively in the programming of the Food Network. The purpose of research is to examine whether Food Network programming discourse promotes sustainability (defined here as the ability to sustain right relationships between humans and earth in a manner conducive to both) or consumption (defined here as an anthropocentric split between humans and nature in which the satisfaction of human desires is considered of highest value even if it means the degradation of natural resources).

Why the Food Network Matters

The specific research questions guiding this study focus on media discourse and how it promotes, constructs, and/or reproduces meanings and dominant ideas about food and cooking. Thus, it is motivated by the broader theoretical concerns of media studies, specifically cultural studies: How do media contribute to ideology? How are culture and media intertwined, both constituted by and constituting each other? What ideas, values, notions, concepts, beliefs, and so on are embedded in media discourse, thus contributing to various forms of ideological hegemony? Hall (1977) has written that "the mass media are more and more responsible for providing the basis on which groups and classes construct an 'image' of the lives, meanings, practices and values [that] can be coherently grasped as a 'whole'" (p. 340). This construction of what Hall (1991) refers to as "social knowledge" occurs within a mass-mediated cultural sphere through "systems of representation" that may be uncovered through an analysis of discursive practices, uncovering those ideas that we take for granted as common sense. Hall argues for empirical analysis of the observable evidence of cultural constructions: the various texts and images produced within a culture to describe itself to itself.

Media texts are thus considered constitutive of a given culture and should not be seen as passive nor as simply reflective of a culture's values and priorities. Since this research is focused on ideas and values embedded in the discourse of food, an appropriate media text would be one of the many cooking shows or networks devoted to lifestyle issues related to cooking. The Food Network is the only U.S. network devoted to food and cooking. According to Meister (2001), "since its inception in 1993, the Food Network has become one of cable's most successful and most watched networks" (p. 165). Founder Reese Schonfeld believed that a network focused on food would capitalize on the huge advertiser market for food and packaged goods, meshing programming and ads in "a seamless promotion of commodities" (Ketchum, 2005, p. 219). The early shows were focused specifically on cooking instruction, but by 1997, network executives expanded their target audiences and focused on "all things food" (cited in Ketchum, 2005, p. 219). By 2003, the network had an average of 727,000 viewers during prime time. In 2006, the Food Network was among the top five cable networks watched by women, ages 25–54, earning average ratings of .7. The evening lineup attracted a more diverse audience with ratings averaging .5 for shows such as *Throwdown with Bobby Flay*, *Ace of Cakes*, and *Dinner Impossible*. According to Brooke Johnson, the president of the Food

Network, the network "is all about making food fun and approachable to our viewers" ("Why advertise on the Food Network"). Such an approach has made the Food Network one of the top ten cable channels during the weekend, with an average of 316,000 viewers. Among women it is one of the top five cable channels with an average 216,000 viewers during the weekend daypart. Daytime and primetime audiences reached a peak in January, 2008, with overall audiences of 307,000 for daytime and 458,000 for primetime ("Food Network research information").

In February, 2008, I watched 30 hours of weekday daytime and primetime programming on the Food Network. I selected various shows to view spanning several days and weeks during the month. The primetime programming was randomly selected 3-hour blocks beginning at 5:00 p.m. and included such shows as *Paula's Party*; *Diners, Drive-ins and Dives*; *Throwdown with Bobby Flay*; *Unwrapped*; *Iron Chef America*; and *Good Eats*. Daytime programming was based on those programs that the Food Network identifies as their more popular offerings: *Easy Entertaining with Michael Chiarello*, *Barefoot Contessa*, *Paula's Home Cooking*, Tyler Florence's *Tyler's Ultimate* and *Food 911*, and *30-minute Meals with Rachael Ray*. In the method used here, one seeks to uncover the codes, constructions, cultural assumptions, connotations, values, and beliefs embedded in the text by noting recurring patterns, such as the repetition of certain themes, phrases, rhetoric, images, and so on in the discourse (Altheide, 1996; Christians and Carey, 1989; Grossberg, 1991; Pauly, 1991). As I watched the programs, I made various notes that enabled me to collect data on how "food" and "cooking" are portrayed in Food Network programming and how viewers are implicated in order to answer my research questions, which focused on: What are the overall themes that suggest sustainability? What are the overall themes that suggest consumption? What other themes are present in the discourse?

Sustainability Themes

As defined above, sustainability, for the purposes of this research, is defined as the ability to sustain right relationships between humans and earth in a manner conducive to both. Based on this definition, and existing literature that explores this concept, I identified four specific themes in Food Network discourse that suggest sustainability: civic agriculture, seasonality, vegetarianism, and sensuality. Each is defined below with examples from the programming on the Food Network.

Civic Agriculture

Civic agriculture, also termed "alternative food networks" (Parkins & Craig, 2009), is characterized by locally oriented farm production—that is, agriculture production with an emphasis on local markets rather than national or international mass markets. For instance, civic agriculture promotes farming and food production that is integrated into communities, where the emphasis is on the quality of a product not its quantity in terms of mass production. Usually, such agricultural operations are smaller than their mass-market cousins, and the markets are developed through local needs and consumption rather than indirect links through wholesalers, brokers and processors (Lyson, 2007). As a result, proponents of civic agriculture argue that agricultural development should be motivated by social needs and processes rather than purely by economics. According to Lyson (2007), farmer's markets are the first step for the creation and promotion of local food systems. Such a sustainable system requires that communities include "alternatives that enhance the local economy, adapt local food production and distribution to their region, and provide participants with more direct experiences within the food system" (Peters, 1997, p. 956). In other words, food production and consumption is conducted locally. Although some scholars have critiqued this "politics of localism" (e.g., DuPuis & Goodman, 2005) that civic agriculture posits, the cultural meanings around the local are still viable and political positions that motivate ideas around sustainability (Parkins & Craig, 2009).

All of the *daytime* programs viewed for this study featured some references to home gardens or showed the host traveling to their local town to purchase produce, seafood, or meat for that day's menu. In some cases, most notably *Easy Entertaining with Michael Chiarello* and the *Barefoot Contessa*, the hosts were shown going to their own gardens to harvest herbs, collect eggs, or pick lemons from a tree. On an episode of *Tyler's Ultimate*, host Tyler Florence suggested that "if you have some parsley or rosemary growing in your garden, that would be great to add here" (Tuchsman, 2008b). One episode of *Paula's Home Cooking* focused on preserving fruits and vegetables, an episode that both promoted seasonality (another identified sustainability theme, discussed below) and the value of growing one's own produce. Paula Deen told viewers, "if you're gonna preserve these foods, you might as well grow 'em too" and that one doesn't need a lot of space to produce a crop worth preserving. In this episode, she also asked her guest how he was able to plant and harvest such a "beautiful garden" without pesticides, which allowed her guest to extol the virtues of dish soap and water over harmful chemicals (Elliott, 2008b). In daytime programming with such images, I noted only one reference to "organic" produce, which was in an episode of *30-minute Meals with Rachael Ray*, where Rachael tells her viewers to "use a nice, cloudy organic apple cider to make this gravy" (Tuchsman, 2008j).

Although daytime programming featured several scenes that could be classified under the civic agriculture theme, none of the *primetime* shows had references to the civic agricultural virtues of farmer's markets or home gardens.

Seasonality

The existence of global food systems for production and distribution mean that most foods that were previously available only when "in season" are now available year-round. Most food sold in the United States travels an average of 1300 miles before it reaches the U.S. dinner table, burning large amounts of fossil fuels. This global food marketplace requires markups for transportation but also for storage, processing, distribution, marketing, and retailing of the product. Thus, references to seasonal produce are somewhat similar to the civic agriculture theme.

This theme was expressed less frequently in Food Network programming. The canning episode of *Paula's Home Cooking*, mentioned earlier, was a notable example. For instance, in this episode, Paula Deen said, "Take advantage of the things that are around you this time of year and are available... Sometimes it's really hard to say goodbye to summer's fruits and vegetables, so think about canning them." Host Ina Garten of *The Barefoot Contessa* said that some ingredients—such as beets—were available year-round, so viewers should use them fresh, rather than canned. In another episode Garten said, "When I was at the farm stand and saw all these pears and apples, I thought: I have to make a pear and apple crisp" (Tuchsman, 2008f). Other times the host would mention that if something was in season to use that particular ingredient or to prepare root vegetables, as Tyler Florence told his viewers, when the weather gets colder. All of these references occurred during daytime programming.

Vegetarianism

From John Robbins in *Diet for a New America* to Peter Singer's 1975 classic, *Animal Liberation*, the environmental and moral consequences of meat eating have been well documented. These and many other authors have argued that meat eating represents a waste of natural resources and that it leads to the suffering of animals, what Singer termed "speciesism," equating it with the equal rights movements that condemned sexism and racism. Given the operational definition of sustainability used in this chapter, vegetarianism was classified as a sustainability theme. Conversely, as described below, meat eating is classified as a consumption theme.

This theme is also included because it is notable in its absence from Food Network discourse. Of 46 shows watched, only three featured menus or topics that were vegetarian or that didn't center around meat in some way. Of these three shows, only one, *30-minute Meals with Rachael Ray*, constituted an entire vegetarian menu. The other two shows that focused on non-meat menus or topics were a *Good Eats* show that focused on doughnuts and an episode of *Paula's Home Cooking* that featured only desserts. The vegetarian show on *30-minute Meals* featured an "asian vegetarian feast" of noodle bowl, roast mushroom yakitori and cucumber salad. In addition to the menu, host Rachael Ray frequently asserted that vegetarian meals should be eaten more often, saying, "We could use a lot less meat in our diets; it wouldn't hurt us to have a vegetarian night a couple of nights a week." Vegetarian meals were presented as "guilt free": Rachael told her viewers, "you can eat the whole pan and feel good about it." It was also portrayed as a thoughtful thing to do for your vegetarian friends: "It's a meat eater's world, so it's really thoughtful to cook for your vegetarian friends," Ray proclaimed. Despite these positive assertions, Ray was careful to emphasize the quasi-meat aspects of her vegetarian menu, claiming that the roasted mushrooms were a wonderful meat substitute because "they get beefy when they roast up," and they're "meaty and satisfying." But she also acknowledged some anxiety over the protein content of such meals and told her viewers, "if you really wanted extra protein, you can add shrimp or chicken, but we're using edamame… soybeans" (Tuchsman, 2008a).

Certainly, vegetables are prepared on Food Network programming, even though some hosts, such as Ray, suggested adding bacon to "get your kids to eat [them]" (Tuchsman, 2008e). But hosts did emphasize, and prepare, balanced meals, and the use of fresh herbs was ubiquitous, even if vegetarian meals were not portrayed.

Sensuality

For this theme, I draw from a concept developed by Cramer & Foss (2009) that suggests that our communication practices have led to an epistemological split between earth and humans—a split that can be characterized by subject/object dualism and an absence of sensual intersubjectivity. The relationship between humans and the natural world is primarily encountered through the senses. Merleau-Ponty (1968) suggests that perception is the reciprocity between humans and the entities that surround them; that is, in our perceptions of the natural world, we are touched as much as we are touching, seeing, or hearing:

> Between the exploration and what it will teach me, between my movements and what I touch, there must exist some relationship by principle, some kinship, according to which they are not only…vague and ephemeral deformations of the corporeal space, but the initiation to and the opening upon a tactile world. This can happen only if my hand, while it is felt from within, is also accessible from without…if it takes its place among the things it touches, is in a sense of them, opens finally upon a tangible being of which it is also a part. (p. 133)

The notion of a "sensual subject," who is driven by receptivity and vulnerability, may be key to imagining a reinvented humanity that realizes and appreciates rather than denies and deprecates a deep affinity and interdependence with the natural world. Thus, sensuality is a theme that supports the definition of sustainability used here—that is, a mutual, beneficial interdependence.

By far, the most frequent theme in daytime and primetime programming was the one of sensuality. Obviously, taste is the sense most frequently glorified, with hosts often shown sampling their own, or another's, cooking accompanied by the "hmmmm" of a satisfied consumer—what Wiggins (2002) rightfully identifies as the "gustatory mmms" of pleasure. Tasting food was accompanied by rolling the eyes, closing the eyes, and exclamations of pleasure. But sensuality was also conveyed through references to the food being beautiful or gorgeous, to having a satisfying texture or color (as in crispy hash browns or the importance of peanuts sprinkled on top of a cupcake to provide not only flavor but texture), and to smells. If a connection with nature is established—and communicated—through a sensual connection with nature, then food and cooking is the premier vehicle for such a connection and the one most promoted by the Food Network.

The examples mentioned above illustrate the prevalence of sensuality in Food Network discourses. Also, for instance, when Ina Garten emphasizes "texture" in various recipes, she is promoting the activation of senses that occurs through food. "It's good to have flavor, texture, and also the color," Ina tells her viewers (Tuchsman, 2008d). "It's not just the flavor; it's the texture." Similarly, Tyler Florence refers to "fantastic" aromas and says, "I can taste everything: the herbs, the tomatoes, the beef broth, the aromatics" (Tuchsman, 2008f). Or, "The spices hit your tongue in a bunch of different places; the cinnamon is sweet, the paprika is a little spicy and smoky, the clove is rich, the chili is hot" (Tuchsman, 2008h)

Consumption Themes

Themes associated with sustainability were certainly present in the discourse of Food Network programming. Themes that could be identified as consumption—defined here as an anthropocentric split between humans and nature in which the satisfaction of human desires is considered of highest value even if it means the degradation of natural resources—were present as well. Meister (2001) argues that the Food Network promotes excessive consumption as a rhetorical device consistent with the "good life." This "good life science" is associated with excessivism and waste, thus promoting an anthropocentric attitude toward nature. Eating food—fatty food, in particular—is one of the hallmarks of enjoying life. Meister argues that the Food Network encourages eating to excess and uses food as a symbol of satisfying human desires rather than as something from nature. The themes identified here—food and gluttony, food as competition, and meat eating—conform to this assessment and are thus identified as consumption themes.

Food and Gluttony

Through portion sizes, full menus that nearly always include desserts, and food as entertainment and pleasure, the Food Network promotes excessive food consumption. In addition, the food consumed is usually prepared in high-fat ways. Butter, cream, deep-fried foods, meat, cheese, and lots of sugar are common ingredients and methods of preparation. The worst of these shows was *Diners, Drive-Ins and Dives*, in which the host visits small-town or out-of-the-way eateries known for gargantuan portions of such foods as chicken-fried lamb chops, cheese steaks, tater tot pizza, hot wings, chile rellenos, cinnamon roll French toast, and homemade pie. Customers and the host are shown continually throughout the show eating these creations. Nearly all of the shows included meals with 4 to 5 plates. In addition, quantities exceeded those recommended by most dietitians. One show, for instance, featured a restaurant that served two pounds of steak for two people. Daytime programming also promoted the use of butter and cheese. In one episode of *Paula's Home Cooking*, host Paula Deen suggested that doughnuts be used as hamburger rolls (Elliott, 2008a).

Food as Competition

More than daytime programming, primetime Food Network programming emphasizes the competition of preparing food with shows such as *Throwdown with Bobby Flay* and *Iron Chef America.* The latter features rhetoric such as, "Let the battle begin…," "The cooking continues as the action reaches a boiling point," and "the heat is on" (Seidel, 2008). These competition shows are popular among Food Network viewers and, though prevalent in primetime, are not restricted to those evening hours. Perhaps seeking to draw on the popularity of such a notion, an episode of *30-minute Meals* played on the competition theme, claiming that cooking a good meal could be equated with success. Host Rachael Ray told viewers:

> So your neighbor to the right just put in a swimming pool and your neighbors to the left are tooling around in a new sports car. Well, there's one way you can establish yourself as a force to be reckoned with in a highly competitive neighborhood: make an amazing meal for everybody. I've got the perfect menu for keeping us with the Joneses, and you'll be impressing those neighbors in under 30 minutes. (Tuchsman, 2008g)

Meat Eating

As mentioned above, the consumption theme portrayed most often in the discourse was that of meat eating. Beef and chicken were the most frequent items on the menu, but occasionally pork chops or lamb were prepared as well. Seafood, usually salmon or scallops, was the third most often cooked item. Prosciutto and bacon were frequently used as toppings for vegetables or stuffings. Bacon, especially, was lauded as an exceptional addition to most meals, even if those meals already included meat. Tyler Florence, for instance, told viewers that a "big fat juicy steak" was made even more delicious with the addition of bacon and onions (Tuchsman, 2008b). Paula Deen thought meat was so appealing that she told her viewers, "This hamburger already looks good and we haven't even started cooking it." Later, it would become a 5-inch patty that Deen would call the "most decadent burger you've ever laid your eyes on, y'all" (Elliott, 2008a)

Ambivalent Themes

In addition to themes that could be classified as either promoting sustainability or consumption, were themes best described as "ambivalent." In this sense, they neither promoted a connection with the natural world nor ignored such a relationship for the pursuit of solely human pleasure. These themes were prevalent enough, however, to warrant mention, as they indicate how Food

Network programming represents food and the act of cooking. These themes were: a) food as pleasure, or cooking as easy and simple, b) Food as a way to connect with others, and c) cooking as an inexpensive activity.

Food as Pleasure or Cooking as Easy and Simple

The portrayal of cooking on these shows—with the exception of 30-minute meals which purports to be real time—hides the amount of time the preparation and cooking can take. In addition to this visual device, the hosts frequently comment on how simple something is, how little time it takes, or how super easy it is to make. Ina Garten is often shown preparing a meal while also preparing for guests, working on her next cookbook, or meeting with publishers, telling her viewers, "Just because I have a really busy day doesn't mean I can't have friend over for an elegant dinner; it just takes a little planning and an easy menu I can make ahead" (Tuchsman, 2008d). Paula Deen says, "I love to cook; isn't it fun? It's like therapy" (Elliott, 2008c). Michael Chiarello's show has "easy" in its title, *Easy Entertaining*. On this show, host Chiarello demonstrates how effort a day before a party can result in a carefree party-preparation day, using rhetoric such as, "All I have left to do…," or "Super simple," and "Super easy to make." As mentioned, the standard format of "cooking montages" hides the amount of time something actually takes, and making a flourless chocolate cake, according to Tyler Florence, will take about five minutes. By presenting cooking in this way, Food Network programming presents the process as easy and the act of cooking and consuming food as extremely pleasurable.

Food as a Way to Connect with Others

Another ambivalent theme presented in Food Network programming was the preparation and consumption of food as a way to connect with others. For instance, every daytime episode viewed used some sort of party or event as the motivation for cooking, from Michael Chiarello's outdoor movie party (Chiarello, 2008a) to Ina Garten's dog's birthday or 20th anniversary party, to Paula's tea party. Later, Food Network executives would produce a show devoted to this concept, *Paula's Party*.

Beyond special occasions, though, some hosts said that cooking a meal was a way to reconnect with loved ones. Tyler Florence, for instance, said:

> Turn off the blackberry, shut off the e-mail and return to the pleasure of a family meal. The best day for that is Sunday… I can't think of a better night of the week to relax, enjoy your family, and end the week on a high note. (Tuchsman, 2008i)

And Rachael Ray guaranteed her viewers that they would get "a soulful payment back from cooking at home and sharing it with people you care about" (Tuchsman, 2008e).

Cooking as an Inexpensive Activity

The third ambivalent theme present in Food Network programming was that cooking was not an expensive choice—indeed, cooking at home was often presented as the inexpensive alternative. Although some evening programming, such as *Diners, Drive-ins, and Dives*, seemed to promote eating at restaurants, other Food Network programs implied or expressed outright that it would be more economical and preferable to prepare a tasty and satisfying meal at home. Still, such messages were sometimes coupled with the idea that food and one's cooking could convey images of wealth. For instance, host Michael Chiarello of *Easy Entertaining* told his viewers that the "budget party" he was demonstrating was a way to be "cheap but chic." He suggested that in order to "make a cheap meal look like a 5-star affair, set the table with some of your most exquisite tableware… and chill the wine glasses." With such techniques, he could look as if he had spent a lot on the meal, but in fact had done "this entire meal for $10 a person" (Chiarello, 2008b).

The message here presents viewers with two values: to appear high class but also to be budget conscious. Other scholars have discussed issues related to food and socioeconomic class (see Lucas & Buzzanell in this volume) that seem to be relevant here. Despite the assertions that meals can be, as Rachael Ray says, "super affordable" (Tuchsman, 2008j), the other message of some Food Network programming indicates that cooking at home can give a different appearance of being well-off or as belonging to a high socioeconomic class.

Conclusion

Motivated by environmental concerns and the imperative for humans to establish or reinforce a harmonious relationship with the natural world, this research considered food as a medium by which humans could create or foster such a mutually beneficial relationship. The assumption—or perhaps the hypothesis—was that human relationships with food and, especially, the process of producing and preparing one's own food, are fundamental to understanding or reconceptualizing a relationship between humans and the earth that is more sustainable. Thus, the purpose of research here was to examine whether Food Network programming discourse promoted sustainability—which was defined as the ability to sustain right relationships between humans and earth in a manner conducive to both—or consumption, which was defined as an anthropocentric split between humans and nature in which the satisfaction of human desires is considered of highest value even if it means the degradation of natural resources. The overarching research questions focused on whether, or to what extent, these themes were present in Food Network programming and to uncover other themes that might be in the discourse.

In general, daytime programming contained discourse and images that were more consistent with sustainability themes than nighttime programming on the Food Network. The evening programming contained more discourse that was consistent with the definition of consumption. Four themes were uncovered that suggested sustainability, as defined for the purposes of this research: civic agriculture, seasonality, vegetarianism, and sensuality. Three themes were found that related to consumption, as defined here: gluttony, food as competition, and meat eating. In addition to themes associated with sustainability and consumption, I also identified three "ambivalent" themes that were prevalent enough to worth mention: food as pleasure, food as a way to connect with others, and cooking as an inexpensive activity.

The presence of such a variety of themes suggests that Food Network programming can be read in a variety of ways. This research doesn't assume that popular culture texts are all-determining or that ideas and themes presented in this discourse have unmitigated influence or effects—ideological or otherwise. But, as discussed above, media texts are central to cultural meaning-making and ideological hegemony. This research is concerned, then, with the overall construction of meaning around a particular activity—in this case, cooking a product of the natural world for the purposes of the intimate act of eating. This intimate act, of course, is the taking of something into one's body for the purposes of sustenance, cultural practice, or pleasure.

In *The Raw v. The Cooked*, Levi-Strauss (1994) established a binary opposition between nature and culture that could be exemplified in the act of cooking:

> We thus begin to understand the truly essential place occupied by cooking in native thought: not only does cooking mark the transition from nature to culture, but through it and by means of it, the human state can be defined with all its attributes. (p. 164)

In other words, "cooked," or the process of cooking, is a cultural transformation of the raw. Despite some criticisms of Levi-Strauss' structural methodology, this opposition between nature and culture (or raw and cooked) is important in "terms of the way in which food is both thought about and represented" (Ashley, Hollows, Jones & Taylor, 2004, p. 36). When we eat, and when we cook the products of creation, we establish a relationship between ourselves and nature. The assumption guiding this study is that human relationships with food and, especially, the process of producing and preparing one's own food, are fundamental to understanding or reconceptualizing a relationship between humans and the earth that is more sustainable. Because the Food Network focuses specifically on the act of cooking (of the 46 shows watched for this study, only five featured raw foods of any kind), it provided a valuable medium by which to discover the meanings created about cooking in popular culture.

Overall, a love of food and of working with food, primarily as a means of building relationships with others—whether these are relations of love or competition—is the message conveyed through Food Network discourse. One's relationship with the natural world, however, is sacrificed in the discourse of these shows. Selected scenes from *Easy Entertaining with Michael Chiarello* or the *Barefoot Contessa*, for instance, that romanticize a connection with the natural world through one's garden or through the pleasures of seasonal eating cannot compete with an overall discourse that promotes meat eating and a general discourse of food availability—regardless of the season, where the food originates, and whether it is organically grown. In its emphasis on sensuality, the Food Network comes closest to circulating discourses of connection with the natural world. But returning to Levi-Strauss' argument regarding the raw and the cooked, our connection with the natural world is only through the mediation of human effort and the transformation of the natural into a cultural discourse. How we conduct that act, what materials we use in the process, and how we approach the final act of consummation will, in the end, be the most compelling evidence of a mutually beneficial relationship between humans and the natural world.

References

Althiede, D. (1996). *Qualitative media analysis*. Thousand Oaks, CA.: Sage.

Ashley, B., Hollows, J., Jones, S., & Taylor, B. (2004). *Food and cultural studies*. London and New York: Routledge.

Berry, T. (1999). *The great work: Our way into the future*. New York: Bell Tower.

Chiarello, M. (Producer) (2008a). (2008, February 4). *Easy Entertaining* [Television broadcast]. New York, NY: Food Network.

Chiarello, M. (Producer) (2008b). (2008, February 5). *Easy Entertaining* [Television broadcast]. New York, NY: Food Network.

Christians, C. G, & Carey, J. W. (1989). The logic and aims of qualitative research. In G. Stempel, & B. Westley (Eds.), *Research methods in mass communication, 2nd ed.* (pp. 354–374). Englewood Cliffs, NJ: Prentice Hall.

Corson, W. H. (1995). Priorities for a sustainable future: The role of education, the media, and tax reform. *Journal of Social Issues, 51,* 37–61.

Cramer, J., & Foss, K. A. (2009). Baudrillard and our destiny with the natural world: Fatal strategies for environmental communication. *Environmental Communication: A Journal of Nature and Culture, 3,* 298–316.

DuPuis, E. M., & Goodman, D. (2005). Should we go home to eat? Toward a reflexive politics of localism. *Journal of Rural Studies, 21,* 359–371.

Elliott, G. (Producer) (2008a). (2008, February 4). *Paula's Home Cooking* [Television broadcast]. New York, NY: Food Network.

Elliott, G. (Producer) (2008b). (2008, February 5). *Paula's Home Cooking* [Television broadcast]. New York, NY: Food Network.

Elliott, G. (Producer) (2008c). (2008, February 24). *Paula's Home Cooking* [Television broadcast]. New York, NY: Food Network.

Foley, J., DeFries, R., Asner, G. P., Barford, C., Bonan, G., Carpenter, S. R., et al. (2005). Global consequences of land use. *Science, 309,* 570–574

Food Network research information. Accessed March 18, 2008 from http:// foodnetworkadsales.com/ research/

Franck, F., Roze, J., & Connolly, R. (Eds.) (2000). *What does it mean to be human: Reverence for life reaffirmed by responses from around the world.* Boston, MA: St. Martin's Press.

Grossberg, L. (1991). Strategies for Marxist cultural interpretation. In R. K. Avery, & D. Eason (Eds.), *Critical perspectives on media and society* (pp. 126–159). New York: The Guilford Press.

Hall, S. (1977). Culture, media and the 'ideological effect.' In J. Curran, M. Gurevitch, & J. Woolacott (Eds.), *Mass communication and society* (pp. 315–348). Newbury Park, CA: Sage Publications.

Hall, S. (1991). Signification, representation, ideology: Althusser and the post-structuralist debates. In R. K. Avery, & D. Eason (Eds.), *Critical perspectives on media and society* (pp. 88–113). New York: The Guilford Press.

Hinrichs, C. C. (2007). Practice and place in remaking the food system. In C. C. Hinrichs, & T. A. Lyson (Eds.), *Remaking the North American food system: Strategies for sustainability* (pp. 1–15). Lincoln, NE: University of Nebraska Press.

Horrigan, L., Lawrence, R. S., & Walker, P. (2002). How sustainable agriculture can address the environment and human health harms of industrial agriculture. *Environmental Health Perspectives, 110,* 445–457.

Killingsworth, M. J., & Palmer, J. S. (1992). *Ecospeak.* Carbondale: Southern Illinois University Press.

Ketchum, C. (2005). The essence of cooking shows: How the Food Network constructs consumer fantasies. *Journal of Communication Inquiry,29,* 217–234.

Levi-Strauss, C. (1994). *The raw and the cooked (Introduction to a science of mythology: 1).* London: Pimlico.

Lyson, T. A. (2007). Civic agriculture and the North American food system. In C. C. Hinrichs, & T. A. Lyson, T. A. (Eds.), *Remaking the North American food system: Strategies for sustainability* (pp. 19–32). Lincoln, NE: University of Nebraska Press.

Meister, M. (2001). Cultural feeding, good life science, and the TV Food Network. *Mass Communication & Society, 4,* 165–182.

Merleau-Ponty, M. (1968). *The visible and the invisible* (C. Lefort, Ed.; A. Lingis, Trans.). Evanston, IL: Northwestern University Press.

Mühlhäusler, P. (2006). Environmental discourses. *Annual Review of Anthropology, 35,* 1: 457–479.

Parkins, W., & Craig, G. (2009). Culture and the politics of alternative food networks. *Food, Culture, and Society, 12* (1): 77–103.

Partidário, P., Lambert, J., & Evans, S. (2007). Building more sustainable solutions in production-consumption systems: the case of food for people with reduced access. *Journal of Cleaner Production, 15*(6): 513–524.

Peters, J. (1997). Community food systems: working toward a sustainable future. *Journal of the American Dietetic Association,97,* 955–957.

Pollan, M. (2006). *The ominivore's dilemma.* New York: The Penguin Press.

Robbins, J. (1987). *Diet for a new America: How your food choices affect your health, happiness, and the future of life on earth.* Walpole, NH: Stillpoint.

Seidel, B. (Producer). (2008, February 18). *Iron Chef America* [Television broadcast]. New York, NY: Food Network.

Singer, P. (1975). *Animal liberation.* New York: Harper Collins.

Tuchsman, B. (Producer) (2008a). (2008, February 5). *30-minute Meals with Rachael Ray* [Television broadcast]. New York, NY: Food Network.

Tuchsman, B. (Producer) (2008b). (2008, February 4). *Tyler's Ultimate* [Television broadcast]. New York, NY: Food Network.

Tuchsman, B. (Producer) (2008c). (2008, February 5). *Paula's Home Cooking* [Television broadcast]. New York, NY: Food Network.

Tuchsman, B. (Producer) (2008d). (2008, February 5). *Barefoot Contessa* [Television broadcast]. New York, NY: Food Network.

Tuchsman, B. (Producer) (2008e). (2008, February 5). *30-minute Meals with Rachael Ray* [Television broadcast]. New York, NY: Food Network.

Tuchsman, B. (Producer) (2008f). (2008, February 5). *Tyler's Ultimate* [Television broadcast]. New York, NY: Food Network.

Tuchsman, B. (Producer) (2008g). (2008, February 7). *30-minute Meals with Rachael Ray* [Television broadcast]. New York, NY: Food Network.

Tuchsman, B. (Producer) (2008h). (2008, February 7). *Food 911* [Television broadcast]. New York, NY: Food Network.

Tuchsman, B. (Producer) (2008i). (2008, February 25). *Tyler's Ultimate* [Television broadcast]. New York, NY: Food Network.

Tuchsman, B. (Producer) (2008j). (2008, February 28). *30-minute Meals with Rachael Ray* [Television broadcast]. New York, NY: Food Network.

Vanderheiden, S. (2006). Two shades of green: Food and environmental sustainability. *Environmental Ethics, 28,* 129–145.

Wiggins, S. (2002). Talking with your mouth full: Gustatory mmms and the embodiment of pleasure. *Research on Language and Social Interaction, 35,* 311–336.

Why advertise on the Food Network? Accessed March 18, 2008 from http://foodnetworkadsales.com/why_food/press_releases

Section Five

Food and Communication in Relationships: Organizational and Interpersonal Contexts

18

Youth empowerment in family conversations and decision-making about food

Matthew Kaplan, Lynn James, Frances Alloway, and Nancy Ellen Kiernan

An 11–year old boy and his grandmother who cares for him talk openly about how their family makes decisions about food:

> Usually, my grandma and me just sit down and make a list of the things we're going to make, like apple pie or mashed potatoes or something. And then we just go to the store and get the stuff that we're going to make and then we just make it. (Child)

> I started when they were little. You know, it's something that we prepare the meals together. And there are sometimes that they like to do that. I was laid up last year, I had surgery and my back was out, and I could not do anything. And they just took over everything. They did the cooking. I was really surprised. I knew they could cook, but I didn't think they could do it on their own without me being there. But they could. (Grandmother)

In the midst of growing social concerns about the eating competencies and practices of children and youth (Swidey, 2004; Piddock, 2004; Kant & Graubard, 2003), and the challenges that caregivers encounter when trying to influence the eating practices of children (Galloway, Lee, & Birch, 2003; Fisher & Mitchell, 2002; Golan & Weizman, 2001), this conversation is provocative and compelling. It provides an image of a child who is confident, positive, collaborative, and proactive in the realm of food selection and preparation. It also illustrates how food operates as a form of communication and how food-related behaviors are learned and reinforced in family contexts.

A large body of research shows how family members, especially parents, serve as the primary influence on children's eating practices (e.g., Mitchell,

Newell, & Shumm, 1987; Spruijt-Metz, Lindquist, Birch, Fisher, & Goran, 2002). Some common themes found in the literature include how parents model appropriate (and inappropriate) eating behavior (Birch, 1998; Forthun, 2008; Golan & Weisman, 2001) and how specific parenting practices contribute to the development of children's eating problems. For example, Birch, Davison, and Fisher (2003) note how restrictive feeding practices promote overeating in pre-adolescent girls. Satter (1988) emphasizes how inadequate parenting, particularly when there is excessive rigidity, negatively affects children's emotional development and how this, in turn, contributes to problematic eating patterns. When parents place enormous amounts of pressure on their children's eating behavior, this can make it less likely that children will pay attention to internal physiological cues that indicate hunger or satiety and hence develop patterns of over-eating or under-eating. Satter (1988) states:

> If a parent consistently overlooks, ignores, or overrules cues coming from the child, the child does not learn to experience, interpret, and trust his own reality. He does not know or respect his own signals of food regulation and learns to regulate feeding based on the interaction with his parent. (p. 7)

Nutrition scientists and educators realize the importance of being aware of the role of all family members, including grandparents,[i] and the need to be sensitive to the power of family dynamics for contributing to eating practices both healthy and unhealthy. However, most nutrition education programs are crafted to reach mono-generational audiences without the active participation of other family members who can influence each other's food-related attitudes and behaviors. Even when articulated as "family-focused," educational outreach campaigns tend to involve giving members of one generation information to give to the other. For example, the "Making the Family Connection" program, a USDA/FNS initiative under "Team Nutrition" (USDA Team Nutrition, 2005) has the parent take home information. Conversely, other nutrition education programs target children who are expected to take the information home to review with their parents and caregivers (Domel et al., 1996). Yet, there are certain limitations to nutrition education initiatives that target members of a single age population and work with them outside of their family context. Domel et al. (1996), for example, describe how children in a school program focused on choosing fruits and vegetables faced barriers in making better choices at home because it was their parents, non-participants of the program, who made decisions about what food was purchased.

One reason many programs only target one generation, such as children, is because they are a captive audience while in school. With the majority of mothers working outside the home, it is difficult to reach parents with their limited time schedules. Another factor that contributes to such age-segregated patterns of program delivery is inadequate attention to the multifaceted role of the child in the family dynamic for making decisions about food. In the nutrition education literature, the primary focus is on what parents, other caregivers, and nutrition educators can do to directly and effectively influence what and how children eat. The child is often portrayed as a passive entity, with nutrition-related information being *bestowed upon* them. How children eat tends to be characterized as being malleable as a function of parental and educator influence and manageable as a function of the "right" kinds of influence.

In this chapter, we attempt to go beyond looking at the parenting side of the equation and focus in on the role—and the voice—of children in food-related decision-making in order to understand how food operates as a more complete system of family communication. We describe a focus group study of how families discuss issues related to eating healthfully and unhealthfully (Kaplan, Kiernan, & James, 2006) and present a six-point "continuum of child involvement and empowerment" which we use to frame the wide range of comments made by focus group study participants in regard to their ideas about child involvement in family food-related decision-making. To provide a context for considering study results and issues raised in regard to how children influence family eating practices, we present findings about the communication dynamics underlying families' conversations about food.

Also in this chapter, we explore how our framework for understanding child involvement and empowerment relates to the broader youth participation literature and describe how our study team applied study findings to develop two family-based nutrition education programs, the national award winning Penn State Extension *Family Fitness Program* (James et al., 2006; and James, 2009) and the other FRIDGE (*Food-Related Intergenerational Discussion Group Experiences*) (Kaplan et al., 2007). We also note results from a pilot study of FRIDGE in regard to what was learned about designing activities to facilitate family conversation and egalitarian decision-making about matters related to food.

In the context of this book's theme of *Food as Communication/Communication as Food*, we examined the extent to which families communicate about food in positive or negative ways, and the extent to which children or parents dominate or share in that communication. The results had implications for the design of two new educational programs where family communication dynamics took center stage.

Overview of Focus Group Study

The conversation between a child and his grandmother noted at the opening of this chapter took place as part of a focus group study designed to examine how families discuss (and under what conditions they discuss) issues related to eating healthfully, and whether families perceive a need to improve the way they have such discussions. The study was conducted by a team of nutrition educators and social scientists at Penn State University who were concerned about the dearth of information available on how to design alternative, age-integrated approaches for nutrition education and child overweight prevention. The study was also intended to inform the development of intergenerational curricula aimed at helping family members communicate more effectively in their efforts to reach a healthier diet.

The research team conducted three intergenerational focus groups in geographically and culturally diverse low-income communities in Pennsylvania. Each focus group consisted of four to eight families that included 10–14 year-old children, their parents, and/or grandparents, recruited from nutrition education program sites. In total, 17 families, with 44 individual participants, took part. Representation from the different generations was balanced with 17 children, 20 parents and seven grandparents (all of whom prepare meals or snacks for their grandchildren at least three times a week).[ii]

The focus group questions stimulated participants to talk about the food and nutrition issues that they felt comfortable and uncomfortable discussing with one another and to share their ideas about how they might better communicate and cooperate in regard to their food selection, food preparation, and eating practices.

Study Findings

Whereas just about all of the parents and grandparents understood the consequences of poor diets for today's children (for instance, obesity and chronic disease), many expressed extensive anguish over their inability to help their children eat more healthfully. Most of the study participants noted that they found it hard to understand and negotiate other family members' food preferences, agree on appropriate food portions, collaborate on food selection decisions, and figure out ways to eat together. However, there were some families that seemed to effectively avoid conflict and misunderstanding when communicating with one another about matters related to food. One theme commonly noted by these families is that they made an intentional effort to involve children as partners in the process of meal planning, food shopping, and meal preparation. Below, we present results related to conflictual as well as harmonious patterns of family communication about food and focus in on issues of child involvement in decision-making. For a more extensive report on study findings, see Kaplan et al. (2006).

Communication Challenges Related to Food

Family communication difficulties noted in all three focus groups fit into two broad communication categories, *conflictual patterns* and *disengagement.* In regard to responses fitting into the former category, parents and grandparents were particularly outspoken about their inability to influence children's eating habits, and the children were relatively quiet. Realizing this, the moderator pointedly asked the children to share their views about what their parents were saying. In response, children could identify and plainly voice their disagreement with their parents on specific foods and the parents' manner. Regarding the second major communication difficulty, d*isengagement from communication*, which included instances in which children exhibited well-developed *escape strategies*, several parents expressed frustration and attempted to confront their children on this issue. Examples of responses alluding to both categories of family communication challenges are presented in Table 1.

It is also relevant to note that there was some variation in respondents' reported goals and expectations for food-related communication taking place within their families. For example, whereas some parents expressed a desire for less disagreement and conflict, there were other parents who did not consider ease or comfort of communication with children as the goal. One parent articulated the latter point of view, "See, I'm having a problem with this word 'comfortable' because as a parent I'm not concerned with comfort. I'm concerned with effective" (Parent).

Table 1: Examples of responses alluding to family communication difficulties.

Communication Theme	Examples of Responses	Generation (gp, p, c)
Conflictual patterns		
	"I usually cook and what I cook on the stove they may not eat. So they eat canned goods or boxed stuff or TV dinners. So I don't discuss anything with them because anytime I suggest something they don't want it and so then I don't cook it and that just makes them eat whatever they choose to eat in the refrigerator."	p
	"The discussion is 'I don't want to eat it, Mom.'"	p
	"Yes we do (discuss things). The fact she don't want to eat… The end."	gp
	"It's futile. It's not …. It's not always a pleasant conversation. Sometimes I'm to the point of crying because I think I'm doing all the right stuff and it's still not the right stuff."	p
	"And my husband and I try to talk healthfully to him and he, 'Yeah, yeah, yeah,' but as long if he doesn't feel full, then it's just not enough. It doesn't matter whether it's healthy or not."	p
Disengagement		
	"And you say [the parent pointing to the child], 'I don't like that Mom' and walk out of the room."	p
	"And then what happens? When he says, 'No you can't have another something.' What do you do? You cry. You go up to your room and shut the door."	p
	"…Usually when we have dinner, then I just walk upstairs and like if I don't see something I like I'll go back downstairs."	c
	"When there's a disagreement… they'll go to Grandma's to eat."	p

Harmonious Patterns of Communication about Food

When asked how, if at all, families communicate about eating healthfully, the participants revealed several intergenerational communication practices which contributed to a sense of family harmony. In two of the focus groups, respondents noted having *ongoing, frequent conversation about eating healthfully*. Here are some examples of their comments:

"I think it's just that we've always talked about it from the time they were little. About good food and what's good for them. It was instilled in them" (Grandparent).

"(We talk about healthy eating) every time we go to the store" (Parent).

"My family discusses health and food and weight a lot. And every time we have a family thing with extended family, we know… I know they're going to talk about it" (Parent).

"(We talk about healthy food) any time you mention the word food" (Child).

Parents set the rules for eating is another theme that came up in two of the focus groups as a good way to avoid conflict in family communication about food. As evident in the following example, for some parents at least, youth involvement in decision-making about food is a non-issue.

It's breakfast, lunch and dinner. And after dinner, about an hour and a half before bedtime, yes, they can have a snack. Sometimes before bed we'll just give them like little sugar cakes. But then it's go to bed. But other than that, no, it's very structured. Meal time is very structured. (Parent)

Several other strategies used by families in their efforts to establish harmonious intergenerational patterns of communication, each noted in only one focus group, include: talking casually to children (noted by children and parents), providing information in a simple, easy to understand way (noted by a child), and using humor (noted by a parent and a grandparent).

Child Involvement and Empowerment

Efforts to involve children in food-related activities. In all three of the focus group sessions, when asked to discuss what they do to help their families eat healthfully, some respondents noted that *involving children in food-related activities* was a goal and they provided examples of how this is done in their families. The following quotes reflect instances in which children help with meal planning, food shopping and meal preparation.

"My mom says if I cook breakfast that I can pick out the stuff I want to cook. If they want eggs, I'll choose the kind of eggs I want" (Child).

"When my dad makes like homemade mashed potatoes and stuff, I like help him with mashing them with the masher thing" (Child).

He cooks. And when I was working, I'm telling you, he would call and say, 'Hey mom, how do you make such and such a thing? Or how do you make…' And not thinking that he would literally do it, but when you came home and opened the door, you're like 'Man, what the heck is that smell?' It's something that you knew you always made. But he made. That's the way we did it. (Parent)

A "child involvement and empowerment continuum." Respondents articulated a wide range of ideas about the role children should play in how families make decisions about food. These notions can be placed along a six-point continuum of "child involvement and empowerment," with the categories reflecting qualitative distinctions in power relations—for instance, who has control in making decisions about food. Table 2, below, describes these categories and indicates the prevalence of responses for each category found in the focus group discussions and in the comments of participating family members. Table 3 provides examples of responses fitting into each of the six *child involvement and empowerment* response categories listed in Table 2.

The Importance of Family-to-Family Interaction and Mutual Support

We learned that the focus group setting provided a powerful dynamic for promoting intrafamilial as well as family-to-family sharing and support. Respondents were unanimously positive about their focus group experience for the following four reasons.

A comfortable venue for learning and self expression.

"It helped me to talk out loud and tell what I want to say to my mom and other people… without getting embarrassed or shy" (Child).

"I feel like I can open up and like say what I have to say" (Child).

The opportunity to reach and learn more from members within one's own family.

I think in this kind of venue it's a different feeling. It's a different sense of conversation I get and it doesn't seem to be such a hot topic. It doesn't touch my buttons the way it does when it's family. (Parent)

"Our conversations are normally stunted. This drew her out more" (Parent).

Table 2. Categories of child involvement and empowerment in food-related decision-making.

Categories of child involvement	Description of category	Number of focus groups in which one or more families noted category of child involvement	Number of families with members making responses fitting into category*	Generations attesting to this level of involvement. G P C
Child in control	Child takes lead role in making decisions. Tends to make decisions on his/her own or overrides parents'/caregivers' wishes or decisions. There are various ways and degrees to which children exert control over food decisions. [In extreme cases, child behaves in a domineering manner, leaving adult caregivers with little input; research team members labeled this phenomenon as "authoritarian childing."]	3	11	G P C
Full partnership	Child has an equal say (as adults) in making decision about food. He/She helps set parameters and is able to provide meaningful input.	3	3	G P C
Limited partnership	Parameters for making decisions are set by the adults, but the children are given some choice among options and have some influence in the decisions that are made; child functions as a "junior partner" in the family.	3	10	P
Consultation	Child is told of his/her choices, and has a chance to voice an opinion, but is unable to influence food-	3	7	G P C

	related decisions. All decision-making power is in the hands of the adults.			
Child is informed	Child is told about parents' food-related decisions and expectations; has no chance to give input or express his/her opinion.	2	4	P
Child is not informed	Child receives no information about food related decisions; has no chance to give input or express his/her opinion. [In some cases, there is reference to extenuating circumstances that make it difficult to involve children in food-related decisions, e.g., budget challenges and having a large family to feed.]	2	3	P

* Note: Some families made multiple comments, fitting into more than one category.

The opportunity to hear other people's ideas and perspectives.

"I thought it was helpful. I mean we heard things that you can kind of take back home and say, 'Okay, we're going to try this. And see if it works for our family" (Parent).

Learning that they are not alone in their food-related challenges.

Well I'm glad that I came. This way I see that others are having the same problem that I'm having as far as their eating, you know. And it's good to know that she's just like the rest of them. And I thought it was just her. (Grandparent)

These comments about the focus group experience suggest that the multi-family discussion group venue provided individuals with a neutral, nonjudgmental ground for expressing their own views about issues related to food.

Table 3. Respondents' comments about child involvement and empowerment in decision-making.

Level of Child Involvement/ Empowerment	Examples of Responses
Children in Control	"I try to tell them they have to eat it, that it's healthy for them. And it's like they'd rather not eat. And they won't eat. And they'll go to the refrigerator and find something else for them to eat." (parent)
	"When I come home, I drop off my bag, I wash my hands, I'll eat cereal and do my homework. And then later if they ask me if I'm hungry I'll say no. And then like maybe around 10:00 I'll eat some more cereal and I'll go to bed." (child)
	"Sometimes (my child) doesn't want what I'm making… He has something different. We have two different meals or else I'll just make what he wants for both of us." (parent)
	"Like this morning, I had made cream of wheat. And I had (packaged meat) and orange juice. She didn't stop in the kitchen. She kept going. And I'm calling her to come have breakfast and she's going to school." (grandparent)
Full Partnership	"Usually, my grandma and me just sit down and make a list of the things we're going to make, like apple pie or mashed potatoes or something. And then we just go to the store and get the stuff that we're going to make and then we just make it." (child)
	"She'll focus on my opinion and my little sister's opinion. And she'll pretty much go from there. Like if we like it, then she'll probably make more of it on a weekly basis and if we didn't like it too much, then she'll, you know, try to cut back on it." (child)
Limited Partnership	"I'm pretty well satisfied with how meals go. Because like I mentioned earlier, if she doesn't like something I made, then it's like, 'Alright, what are *you* going to make *yourself* in it's place.' And then I get veto power." (parent)
	"Well, for dinner I let my kids choose what they want to eat because there's only three kids and normally they choose the same thing. Or if I'm in a grouchy mood I'll say, 'Okay, we're having liver and onions for dinner' and that's pretty much the end of it. But most of the time I let them choose." (parent)
Consultation	"I ask, but then I cook whatever I want." (parent)
	"She doesn't talk about it (healthy eating) all the time. The only time is like when she's going shopping for food like she'll talk to me about it because like I want something and she says no. Like if I want something like pudding or something. She's like, 'No.' And then we'll start talking about it. And that'll be like the last thing we'll talk about." (child)
	"There's only one meal made in the house and that's not a bunch of different things for different people because it's not a restaurant, it's a kitchen. And that's what they eat." [Moderator: "Well, do you

	ever talk about these things?"] "Well, I ask them what they want to have. But it doesn't matter what they want to have." (grandparent)
Child is Informed	"…You know, when I learn things then I always explain to her what I've learned and then I try it on her. But it doesn't … it doesn't work." (parent)
	"At least I let them know first." (parent)
Child is Not Informed	"They usually just eat whatever I make… Usually most of the shopping I do is what's on sale. I coupon shop. And especially with the prepackaged stuff, that's how we make it affordable really. We have a large family. There's five children and my husband and myself in the house right now. So they'll eat anything I put on the table." (parent)
	"So I have my son, (my daughter who lives nearby), her son, her (my daughter who is here), her sister, she's 15, and then her (other daughter who is here) or my daughter's boyfriend. So it's many different stomachs. You know, so most of the time I just take charge and they eat whatever I cook. If they want to eat it's there… I don't give them that many choices you know." (parent)

Discussion

Whereas much of the nutrition education field is informed by learning theory and is focused on behavior influence strategies that parents and professionals can employ to promote desirable eating behaviors in children, our findings suggest that children take a proactive role, often with the encouragement of parents, in family decision-making on food-related matters. From an empowerment ideological orientation (as articulated by Rappaport, 1984, and Zimmerman, 2000), the education and behavior change process is more appropriately framed as something that is done *with* rather than *to* children, with children being viewed more as valued "partners" than solely as "targets" for behavior change. This is consistent with how some of the families that had success in eating healthfully in our study functioned; they managed to avoid conflict in their food-related discussions and decision-making process by involving children as partners in meal planning, food shopping, and meal preparation.

In developing our six categories of "child involvement and empowerment" (in decision-making about food), we drew upon Arnsteins's (1969) categorization system for describing variation in levels of citizen participation in community decision-making, and took into account Hart's (1992) broader use of Arnstein's "ladder of citizen participation" framework to address issues and obstacles related to youth participation in various community settings. Hart's

(1992) eight categories are: 1) manipulation; 2) decoration; 3) tokenism; 4) assigned but informed; 5) consulted and informed; 6) adult initiated, shared decisions with children; 7) child initiated and directed; and 8) child initiated, shared decisions with adults. The first three categories are considered non-participatory insofar as youth do not necessarily understand the goals of the projects in which they are involved nor are they provided with true choice with regard to whether they participate and the degree and manner in which they participate. At issue is the lack of power that many youth have in initiating and influencing important discussions and decisions that affect their lives.

Whereas Hart's category that reflects the highest level of youth participation—*child initiated, shared decisions with*—is desirable, the last category of our "child involvement and empowerment" continuum—*children in control*—is undesirable. The difference is that in Hart's final category, decision-making is shared between youth and adults whereas in our last category, the adults take no active role in decision-making.

Lansdowne (2001), who writes about the rights of children and youth, clearly articulates why such a lack of adult involvement is problematic. In examining the meaning of Article 12 of the Convention on the Rights of the Child, which says that children are entitled to participate in the decisions that affect them, Lansdowne states:

It is important to understand clearly what Article 12 does and does not say. It does not give children the right to autonomy. It does not give children the right to control over all decisions irrespective of their implications either for themselves or others. It does not give children the right to ride roughshod over the rights of their parents. However, it does introduce a radical and profound challenge to traditional attitudes, which assume that children should be seen and not heard. (p. 2)

Just as it is problematic when parents provide no openings for youth to have input on important decisions, youth need to be open to hearing adult views and allow for their input. Both sides have a right to self expression as well as a responsibility for listening to the views of other family members.

The families that participated in our focus group study indicated that they need and want help in finding ways to communicate more effectively across generations and work together to attain a healthier family diet. Interestingly, many respondents noted that they did not know how to have food-related conversations that are non-adversarial or how to value children as "partners" in making positive behavior changes.

Taking these findings into account, research team members expanded the team to include more nutrition educators and set out to develop two family-focused nutrition education programs designed to be delivered with multi-family, multi-generational groups. The first program, *Family Fitness*, is an overweight prevention program for all children ages 8–12. The Family Fitness team, which includes nutrition, physical activity, intergenerational, and family strengths educators and specialists, developed the curriculum and program materials for children ages 8–12 and their families. The curriculum is based on motivational interviewing and transtheoretical (Stages of Change) theory to actively engage families in hands-on activities and discussions for positive food, physical activity, and family communication changes. The Family Fitness Program has been found to significantly improve child diets, physical activity, family physical activity, and communication and agreement for improved diet and physical activity. The following quotes from participating children, parents, and grandparents speak to the improved communication and greater sense of family unity attributed to their program experience:

"Got a little bit closer, with cooking, Briana likes to make things herself now & helps me" (Parent).

"We've become an even closer family and we try more physical activities" (Parent).

"We learned a lot about making better choices. This class should be available for all kids and parents" (Child).

"Our family is having more open discussions about the importance of healthy eating and exercise. As a family, we are trying to watch less TV and eat more fruits and vegetables" (Parent).

"Opening communication diminishes shame and shows us we have a part in decision making about food and physical activity" (Parent).

"More aware of what he is eating, how much, how often, reminds his parents of what is good and not good to eat" (Grandparent).

"We are much more aware of what we eat. And how much we eat. She is more agreeable if I say no to a bad choice of snack" (Parent).

"We became closer and want to try new foods together" (Child).

"Better communication on food and activity, gave us a structured goals and objectives" (Parent).

"We all make a choice to eat at home instead of eating out and are having fun with what we eat at home. It is now more fun to eat at home instead of out. Also, my son likes to try the (WHOLE GRAIN Thing) that's what he calls it" (Parent).

"My granddaughter and I have been able to communicate more with each other and we enjoy doing more things together, such as expressing our views on certain subjects and meal planning and preparation" (Grandparent).

Sample lesson topics include family fitness values, using the food pyramid to make healthy food choices and meals, breakfast for all, eating out and fast foods, healthy snacking, healthy beverages, setting limits and sweets and fats, finding time for physical activity, family communication, overcoming resistance to change, and family time management. The curriculum includes nine youth lessons, five family meeting lessons, and four parent learn-at-home lessons. *Family Fitness* programs have been running for 5 years, and are currently offered in 30 counties in Pennsylvania. Extension educators in New York have been trained to run the program as well. (For more information about the Family Fitness program, including marketing and staff training materials, readers are encouraged to see the website, www.extension.psu.edu/familyfitness.)

In the next section, we describe the other Penn State initiative, FRIDGE, which was designed with a focus more exclusively centered on the family communication dimension of food-related decision-making. The overall goal is to make such communication easier, more fun, and more effective for program participants.

The FRIDGE Program

Structure of the Curriculum

Overview. The FRIDGE program is designed for groups of 4–8 families, with each family represented by one or more children 10–15 years of age, their parents, and, if available, their grandparents or other relatives in caregiving roles. FRIDGE has 17 activity modules that fit into three sections:

Enhancing family communication about food: Activities build family members' communication skills and encourage sharing about views and experiences related to food (selection, preparation, and consumption).

Learning together about food and nutrition: Activities provide information about nutrition, food portions, and healthy food preparation methods.

Working as a team to improve family eating practices: Activities encourage family members to use learned communication skills and nutrition knowledge to improve their family eating practices and set healthy eating goals.

The following components run through the entire curriculum:

Each section begins with an "ice breaker" (warm-up) activity.

At the end of each section, families are given a "take out" activity to encourage them to practice at home those skills learned during the session.

The activities utilize a range of media formats to promote learning and communication, including poetry, sketching, role playing, puzzle making, recipe searching, and photography.

The FRIDGE curriculum (Kaplan, 2007) is available online (see *http://intergenerational.cas.psu.edu/Docs/FRIDGECurriculum.pdf*) as well as in hard copy.

Emphasis on building communication skills: The FRIDGE curriculum development team paid close attention to the focus group study finding that many individuals (not just youth) have poor communication skills, and this can hinder an entire family's efforts to cooperate on efforts to eat more healthfully. Accordingly, an entire section of the FRIDGE curriculum is devoted to activities that help participants develop basic communication skills. Key communication principles emphasized through these activities are presented in the "RECIPE for Good Communication" skills handout provided to program facilitators and participating families. RECIPE stands for:

R = Reflective Listening
E = Encouragement
C = Compromise and cooperation
I = "I" Messages
P = Practice
E = Encouragement

Helping participants gain more insight into each other's lives: Each family member has a body of experience and knowledge that is unique to their situation. If they aren't knowledgeable about or understanding of the experiences of others in their family, they are more likely to have difficulty comprehending the views and ideas that emerge as a result of that experience. Accordingly, FRIDGE includes several structured activities designed to help participants understand more about what members of their families "know" about food as well as the pressures in their daily lives that influence what and how they eat.

The *Coolish or Foolish* activity was designed to help participants become more aware of the social pressures that influence others in their family to eat non-healthfully. In this activity, participants break into family groups and review several pieces of advice generally given out by nutrition educators, such as to eat 4–5 cups of fruits and vegetables each day. For each piece of advice, family members take turns answering some questions about how they (and their peers) view, and the degree to which they follow, this advice. This activity generates good conversations about social pressures that may come from friends, family members, food companies, restaurants or other sources, such as the Internet.

The *Think you Know Me* game is designed to help family members learn more about each other's food preferences and practices. The activity is patterned after the *Newlywed Game*, a long-running TV game show which took to the airwaves in 1966. The format is simple: A question is posed to one person in each family pair about some aspect of how the other person in the pair eats or feels about food. That person writes down their answer. Their partner also writes down the answer that they think their partner wrote down. A pair wins 1 point for each correct match. The family pair that wins the most points wins the game.

Some of the differences in family members' food preferences and sensibilities can be understood as a function of generational experiences. People growing up in different eras have been exposed to variations in readily available food, accepted food, methods of preparation within their family and cultural group, the latest scientific information about what is considered healthy and what is not, media messages aimed at influencing consumer food selection behavior, and food guidance recommendations from the government. Several FRIDGE activities involve creating a *dietary knowledge timeline* to help family members of different generations develop a better appreciation of the impact of historical food recommendations/guidelines on each other's eating habits. In one of these activities, called *Match the Food Guidance System to the Date*, each family gets a series of pictures (and descriptions) of the various historical food guidance systems along with a separate list of dates. They are then tasked with matching each food guidance system with the correct date—1940s, 1950s–60s, 1970s, 1990s, and 2005.

Another activity, *Back to the Future, Food Time Capsule,* has participants sort pictures of food and food preparation tools into eras and then discuss the values and life style of families in each era. Food and tools from earlier eras show a pride in "baked from scratch," family meals and more ethnocentric meals. Children are encouraged to compare their lifestyle with this past.

Several FRIDGE activities were designed to help family members express their views about food and family and to work together to develop a shared vision as to how, as a family, they can better communicate and cooperate to eat more healthfully. Through a series of *Sharing Visions* exercises, participating families generate common vision statements about *How We Communicate, How We Learn Together about Nutrition*, and *How We Work Together to Eat Healthfully*.

In the *Dinnertime: What Does It Mean to Eat Together?* activity, participants first read a humorous poem about one family's very hectic dinner time dynamics. In family groups, they then reflect upon what dinnertime is like in their own homes, discuss ways to improve family interactions during this important family time, and create poems that reflect shared visions about dinnertime.

The *Out with the Unhealthy and In with the Healthy* activity is designed to help families to make concrete plans to operationalize some of their visions for eating more healthfully. To assist them in moving from their old food behaviors to the new, recommended behaviors, each family group creates two "wardrobes" of food items. The "Out with the 'Unhealthy'" wardrobe consists of food items which represent the kinds of foods they used to eat (and which they might still be consuming). For the "In with the 'Healthy'" wardrobe, families place foods they plan to eat to improve their intake and meet the dietary recommendations. Each family takes home and puts up the "In with the Healthy" wardrobe as a reminder of their eating improvement vision and plans.

The Facilitator's Role

The FRIDGE program delivery requires staff with family communication facilitation skills as well as nutrition education skills. Whether the program is facilitated by one or two individuals, the facilitator plays a crucial role in stimulating and extending family dialogue. This "conversational" framework, which is woven throughout the curriculum, often takes the form of the facilitator asking participants a series of provocative food and nutrition-related questions, such as "What should be done to curtail harmful junk food?" "What is proper 'family meal' etiquette?" and "What can individual family members do to make meal time easier for other members in their family?" The facilitator also helps to generate discussion about social values, e.g., attitudes toward cooperating with, and displaying civility toward, family members.

Results from Pilot Study of FRIDGE

As part of a pilot study of FRIDGE, programs were conducted in five sites in different regions of Pennsylvania. Site selection decisions were made to include Cooperative Extension and non-Extension sites in urban, suburban, and rural areas. Programs were implemented in a range of community settings: YMCA (one site), community hospital (one site), and Cooperative Extension nutrition education sites (three sites). In total, 23 families participated in the pilot study. Of the 46 individual participants, 23 were adults and 23 were children.

Results from this pilot study of FRIDGE indicate that the program effectively encourages participants to share their views and feelings about food with other family members and helps them to establish family plans to adopt healthier food selection, preparation, and eating practices.

Below, we report on some of the findings that most closely relate to the topic of youth involvement in family conversations and decision-making about food (see also Kaplan, Alloway, & Middlemiss, 2009).

Most families in the pilot study enthusiastically welcomed the opportunity to talk about food-related issues as is evident in the following post-project comments.

"I really enjoyed hearing the young people talk about their food issues" (Grandmother).

"[What I liked most was] coming together as a family and discussing our recipe plans" (12-year old girl).

One program facilitator commented about the dearth of communication and mutual understanding between family members in regard to issues related to food:

> This game [the *Think you Know Me* activity] helped families realize how little they knew about each other. Even just basic things like their favorite snacks and their favorite dinner. They [parents] are assuming that they know what the kids want, and kids are assuming that parents know what they want. It just shocks me, as it shocked them, how little they really talk about these things. And they didn't realize it was happening till you put it right in front of them.

Participants made a number of comments at the end of the program that reflected the emergence of a more collaborative perspective about food-related decision-making.

"I learned that my children can help more when it comes to planning and preparing food and meals" (Mother).

"We need to work together planning meals as a family so we eat less sugary foods" (Grandmother).

"I learned to listen when making decisions on what to eat and plan [for our] menus" (Mother).

"[I learned] "to let them [the children] make more decisions about our meals" (Grandmother).

Another indication of the program's impact in terms of helping some families move toward a more collaborative framework for making decisions about food included an increase (from the pre- to post-program questionnaire responses) in the number of people in participating families who help with meal planning and in preparing grocery shopping lists.

Consistent with findings from the focus group study reported earlier in this chapter, some participants noted that they appreciated learning that they are not alone in their food-related challenges. An inter-family support dynamic was evident in some of the discussions that we observed, such as the following conversation about lowering high fat foods.

Mother: "Dairy Queen, I get a small cone. She [teenage daughter] gets 3,000 calorie dessert [with brownies]. Maybe I should stop going there."

Daughter: [Looks down and sad.]

Facilitator: "How about figuring out a trip to DQ that's occasional?"

Mother: "My family is awful with food."

Other mother: "It's *all* families."

Another theme that emerged from this pilot study of FRIDGE relates to the skills and knowledge that people need to contribute effectively and positively to family discussions about food. Here are two post-project comments about how participating youth were able to apply what they learned about food and nutrition:

"My daughter started reading food labels after attending the FRIDGE classes and requested that I purchase a healthier version of ice cream when we were grocery shopping" (Mother).

"My grandson asked me if we could prepare a stir fry recipe made in class instead of picking up take out food" (Grandmother).

Conclusion

Lansdowne (2001) notes that one of the arguments often used to challenge participation by children is that they lack competence or experience to participate effectively. To challenge this notion, she states:

> Provided they are given appropriate support, adequate information and allowed to express themselves in ways that are meaningful to them – pictures, poems, drama, photographs, as well as conventional discussions, interviews and group work – all children can participate in issues that are important to them. (p. 8)

For young people to be engaged and to have meaningful input in family decisions about food and nutrition, there needs to be more than good intentions. As we learned from our focus group study on how families communicate and make decisions about food, when youth have knowledge and skills, and there is a shared sense of legitimacy surrounding what they can contribute to families' efforts to eat more healthfully, they can and do make valuable contributions to family eating choices. In this context, it helps when there are nutrition education programs, such as FRIDGE and *Family Fitness*, that reach out to entire families, and work with them in a way that enables all family members—across generations—to be co-learners, collaborators, and partners for taking responsible action.

Endnotes

[i] With growing numbers of single parent families, families with working mothers (Galinsky, Aumann, & Bond, 2009), and families with grandparents and other relatives raising children (Simmons & Lawler Dye, 2003), grandparents play a vital caregiving role in many families and thus contribute to decisions made about food selection and preparation.

[ii] The majority of the study participants (N=27, 61%) were low income, having received or eligible to receive food assistance from SNAP (formerly food stamps) or Farmer's Market fruit and vegetable vouchers. In terms of racial background, 19 of the participants (41%) were Caucasian, 19 (41%) were Black/African American, and eight (17%) were Hispanic. In academic achievement, 20 of the adult participants (46%) went as far as grade school, two (5%) completed some high school, 10 (23%) completed high school, three (7%) attended technical, four (9%) attended college, and five (11%) were college graduates.

References

Arnstein, S.R. (1969). Eight rungs on the ladder of citizen participation. *Journal of the American Institute of Planners, 35,* 4, 216–224.

Birch, L. L. (1998). Psychological influences on the childhood diet on adult health and disease. *Journal of Nutrition, 128,* 2S, 407–410.

Birch, L. L., Davison, K. K., & Fisher, J. O. (2003). Learning to overeat: Maternal use of restrictive practices promotes girls' eating in the absence of hunger. *American Journal of Clinical Nutrition, 78,* 215–220.

Domel, S., Thompson W., Davis, H., Baranowski, T., Leonard, S., & Baranowski, J. (1996). Psychosocial predictors of fruit and vegetable consumption among elementary school children. *Health Education Research, 11,* 3, 299–308.

Fisher, J. O. & Mitchell, DC. (2002). Parental influences on young girls' fruit and vegetable, micronutrient, and fat intakes. *Journal of the American Dietetic Association, 102,* 1, January.

Forthun, L. F. (2008). *Family nutrition: Parenting and family life.* Gainesville, FL: Cooperative Extension Service, Institute of Food and Agricultural Sciences, University of Florida. Publication number: FCS8869. http://edis.ifas.ufl.edu/fy1059

Galinsky, E., Aumann, K., & Bond, J. T. 2009. *Times are changing: Gender and generation at work and at home.* New York: Families and Work Institute. Retrieved October 7, 2009, from http://familiesandwork.org/site/research/reports/Times_Are_Changing.pdf

Galloway A. T., Lee, Y. & Birch, L. L. (2003). Predictors and consequences of food neophobia and pickiness in young girls. *Journal of the American Dietetic Association, 103,* 6, June, 692–698.

Golan, M. & Weizman, A. (2001). Familial approach to the treatment of childhood obesity: Conceptual model. *Journal of Nutrition Education, 33,* 2, Mar/Apr, 102–107.

Hart, R. (1992). Children's participation: From tokenism to citizenship. UNICEF Innocenti Essays, No. 4., UNICEF/ International Child Development Centre, Florence, Italy.

James, L., Ehret, M., Malehorn, M., Routch, N., Packer, S. et al. (2006). The Family Fitness Program. College of Agricultural Sciences, The Pennsylvania State University.

James, L. (2009). The Family Fitness Program, *Networking News, Nutrition Education for the Public*, American Dietetic Association, Summer, 4–5, 9.

Kant, A. K., & Graubard, B. I. (2003). Predictors of reported consumption of low-nutrient-density foods in a 24-h recall by 8–16 year old U.S. children and adolescents. *Appetite, 41,* 2, 175.

Kaplan, M., Alloway, F., Crago, N., Herzog, F., James, L., Kiernan, N., Middlemiss, W., Nolte, T., & Weinreb-Welch, L. (2007). *FRIDGE* (Food-Related Intergenerational Discussion Group Experiences). Curriculum guidebook (137 pages). Penn State University, University Park, PA. [Available online: http://intergenerational.cas.psu.edu/Docs/FRIDGECurriculum.pdf.]

Kaplan, M., Alloway, F., & Middlemiss, C. (2009). A Feasibility Study of FRIDGE – An Intergenerational Nutrition Education Program. *Journal of the National Extension Association of Family and Consumer Sciences, 4,* 55–61. [Available online: http://www.neafcs.org/assets/Journal/2009-Journal.pdf

Kaplan, M., Kiernan, N. E., & James, L. (2006). Intergenerational family conversations and decision-making about eating healthfully. *Journal of Nutrition Education and Behavior, 38,* 5, 298–306.

Lansdowne, J. (2001). Promoting children's participation in democratic decision-making. Retrieved May 3, 2009, from http://www.unicef-irc.org/publications/pdf/insight6.pdf

Mitchell, S.E.; Newell, G.K., & Shumm, W.R. (1987). Dietary quality and family environment. *Psychological Reports, 61* (3), 791.

Piddock, C. (2004). "Snack attacks." *Current Health, 1*, Oct., 1, 16–18.

Rappaport, J. (1984). Studies in empowerment: Introduction to the issue. *Prevention in Human Services, 3*, 1–7.

Satter, E. (1988). Feeding in the family context. In K.L. Clark, R.B. Parr, and W.P. Castelli (Eds.). *Evaluation and management of eating disorders: Anorexia, bulimia, and obesity*, pp. 3–15. Champaign, IL: Life Enhancement Publications.

Simmons, T. & Lawler Dye, J. (2003). *Grandparents Living With Grandchildren: 2000–Census 2000 Brief.* Washington, DC: U.S. Bureau of the Census.

Spruijt-Metz, D., Lindquist, C.H., Birch, L.L., Fisher, J.O., & Goran, M.I. (2002). Relation between mothers' child-feeding practices and children's adiposity. *American Journal of Clinical Nutrition, 75*, 581–586.

Swidey, N. (2004). "All talked out: Some negotiating with your kids is good. But spending 20 minutes debating your 4-year old on why it's time to leave the park is not. Children's mouths can keep up, but as research is showing, their brains cannot." *Boston Globe*, Nov. 17, BGM 23.

USDA Team Nutrition flyer—"Are You on the Team?" Retrieved January 13, 2005, from http://www.fns.usda.gov/tn/Resources/ontheteam.pdf.

Zimmerman, M. (2000). Empowerment theory: Psychological, organizational, and community levels of analysis. In J. Rappaport & E. Seidman (Eds.), *Handbook of community psychology*, 43–63. New York, NY: Kluwer Academic-Plenum.

19

"Mama thinks I'm feeding you": Using food rules to restructure school meal programs

Marianne LeGreco

Conversations about food open up a space for individuals and institutions to consider some of our most routine practices. At the same time, the discursive spaces surrounding food also enable those same individuals and institutions to pursue creative changes with regard to our everyday eating habits. This chapter examines the relationship between food and communication by focusing on the routine practices and creative changes that are enacted in school meal programs.

In his best-selling critique of the food service industry, Schlosser (2001) investigated the pitfalls of America's transformation into a *Fast Food Nation.* Simply put, our reliance on convenience foods, such as fast food entrees from McDonald's or reheated fish sticks from the freezer, is having detrimental effects on our health. Early in his exposé, Schlosser turned his lens on foods sold at school. More specifically, he demonstrated how commercial organizations including Coca-Cola, Pepsi, McDonald's, and Pizza Hut had crept into school food service. Many schools rely on lucrative contracts with major food and beverage companies to fund extra-curricular activities and other needs that stretch outside their budgets. What makes this trend particularly troubling for Schlosser and other critics is that "the primary mission of food companies is to sell products. Food companies are not health or social service agencies, and nutrition becomes a factor in corporate thinking only when it can help sell food" (Nestle, 2002, p. 2).

In an effort to address the precarious and sometimes problematic relationships between school meal stakeholders and the food service industry, a number of states and local school districts have used policy initiatives to institute significant changes to the way students are fed in schools. For example, the state of Arizona implemented two such policies in 2006—the Arizona Nutrition Standards and the local wellness policy initiative. These policies limited students' access to sodas and most snack foods, while increasing access to fresh fruits and vegetables and other whole foods. In doing so, the policies created a unique opportunity to examine the communication practices surrounding school meal programs.

School meal programs provide a context for many activities. The lunch hour gives students a chance to take a break, catch up on homework, socialize with their friends, and get something to eat. Meal programs also provide job opportunities, as managers, cooks, and dishwashers are all required to serve each breakfast and lunch. For the purposes of this project, the most important context that school meals provide is that of organizing everyday eating practices. Students eat as many as two meals a day at school, making it one of the most routine structures that they encounter as they learn how to create their own eating practices. Moreover, school meals are often produced using institutional methods, such as reheating chicken nuggets or deep-frying French fries.

In addition to a context for organizing, meal programs also provide a context for researching activities including policy, communication, transformation, and dialogue. With regard to the relationship between food as communication and communication as food, I argue that a variety of school meal stakeholders use food as a means to communicate agency. Students, in particular, make use of food rules to communicate their agency as consumers, and they often show a diverse application of the food and nutrition resources that have been made available to them.

This chapter illustrates how the dominant discourses that organize eating enable and constrain the ways in which school meal programs are organized and students' food rules are enacted. Using Counihan's (1992) notion of food rules, I illustrate a case study[i] of policy changes and school meal programs in Arizona. To do so, I first outline three dominant discourses that organize eating. Following this description, I use these discourses to position how food rules were structured and restructured during significant food policy changes in Arizona school meal programs.

Dominant Discourses that Organize Eating

Practices and policies surrounding food provide an interesting lens through which to view the intersections between symbolic communication and material consumption. In one of his famous aphorisms, Brillat-Savarin (1925) proclaimed that "the fate of nations hangs upon their choice of food" (p. 3). As individuals living within a larger culture, we organize our eating amidst a range of institutions, prescriptions, and values that shape, and are shaped by, our food choices. The key to optimizing those choices lies in our discourse or the various ways in which we talk about food, construct texts and symbols to communicate nutrition information, and create institutions to help us manage our eating habits. More specifically, nutritionist Marion Nestle (2002) argued in *Food Politics* that discourses tell us how much to eat, which foods to eat, who decides what we should eat, and where to get what we want to eat. In other words, discourses enable and constrain our food choices. These discourses are produced and reproduced by individuals, state institutions like the United States Department of Agriculture (USDA), and commercial organizations in the food service industry. As such, they play an important role in organizing our eating practices.

Similar to the notion that discourse plays a significant role in our choice of food, Counihan (1992) developed a concept that she called "food rules" to illustrate the rules that we construct to organize our eating. She argued that "rules about food consumption are an important means through which human beings construct reality" (p. 55). The search for sustenance, selection of food, and fulfillment of physiological needs constitute a few of our most basic routines. At the same time, the concerns of our cultures, our access to nourishing foods, and the limits of our nutritional needs make our food choices considerably more complicated. As Counihan clarified:

> In different cultures, people endow food with meaning on the basis of its primary qualities such as color, taste, texture, or smell; according to its method of preparation or presentation; or by the manner and order in which it is served. It may also take on the attributes of those who contributed to its preparation or production. In addition, food has meaning according to what it does to the body in terms of weight gain or loss, or feelings of strength or weakness. (p. 56)

Food serves as a vehicle of power, whereby individuals can express autonomy through their food choices; however, those choices cannot escape the social relations that influence their emergence. School meal programs are situated within these larger discourses and food rules; therefore, this section clarifies three dominant discourses and food rules that organize eating in most contemporary Western societies.

Eat More versus Eat Less

The discourses of "Eat More" and "Eat Less" serve as a critical point of departure for understanding the organization of eating practices. Nestle (2002) first interrogated these opposing discourses in her critique of the food industry. She argued that when the USDA gained jurisdiction over American dietary advice in 1862, malnutrition ran rampant throughout the country. Thus, the USDA began an aggressive campaign to encourage citizens to "eat more of a variety of foods." This statement was incorporated strategically into a number of guidelines including the *Dietary Goals for the United States* and the *USDA Food Guide Pyramid* (Nestle, 2002). At the same time, this government initiative to promote consumption enabled the emergence of an industry devoted to eating more. A complex network of supermarkets, fast food and fine dining restaurants, cookbooks, television shows, licensed dieticians and nutritionists, advertisements, and public service announcements were carefully deployed with a mission of making people eat. Furthermore, Brownell and Horgen (2004) noted the change that federal efforts to encourage eating had on our food language. Tiny, petite, enough, and moderate are words that are rarely part of our lexicon; rather, we use language that implies size and value such as super, large, extra, and monster (p. 180).

While the USDA achieved great success in their campaigns to Eat More, perhaps their initiative enjoyed too much success as overeating soon eclipsed malnutrition as our primary dietary concern. As early as the 1960s, doctors encouraged the USDA to change their policy to persuade Americans to Eat Less; however, the USDA remained skeptical about adopting such a stance, opting instead to let individuals take more personal responsibility for their food choices. Efforts to capitalize on the discourses of Eat Less have produced two interesting consequences. Initially, Nestle (2002) argued that the food industry routinely ignores efforts to curb consumption and "uses its substantial resources, political skills, and emotional appeals to discourage attempts to introduce 'eat less' messages into public discussion of dietary issues and, instead, to encourage people to eat more" (p. 359). In other words, the food industry spends great time and money to ensure that Americans do not Eat Less, thereby securing their profitable position in American food culture. At the same time, new industries have emerged to help individuals manage their problems with eating. Organizations such as Weight Watchers, fitness centers, and Overeater's Anonymous have surfaced to aid us in carrying the personal responsibility that many institutions, economists, and politicians believe is necessary to overcome overeating (Lockford, 1996; Martin, 2002).

Although discourses that encourage us to Eat More have mobilized a number of individuals and institutions to offer resources for constructing a healthy diet, they have also obscured the food rules that guide our nutritional limits. Human bodies are designed to process only so many calories over the course of the day. Calories refer to the energy within foods that our bodies use to breathe, walk, grow, think, and live in general. The recommended daily calorie intake varies per person; however, most state health institutions and dieticians suggest that schoolchildren take in anywhere from 1600 calories/day for children ages 4–6, to 2200 calories/day for most children over age 6, to 2800 calories/day for teenage boys (Cooper & Holmes, 2006). These calorie recommendations are basic food rules in place to communicate nutrition information; however, many cultures eat for more than just nutrition and treat food as more than just fuel for the body (Fisher, 1937; Henderson, 1970; Meister, 2001).

Food as a Democratic Choice

Another dominant discourse that organizes eating encourages consumers to cling tightly to values of individual choice and freedom. Griffiths and Wallace (1998) argued that "food has traditionally been seen as one of the most democratic and freely available aspects of our daily lives, demanded in surplus as a right by the consumer of the developed world" (p. 5). Simply put, very few individuals and institutions tell consumers what to eat. Only a small number of policies dictate which food choices we can and cannot make in a given situation, and most of those policies relate to food safety or childhood nutrition. As such, the majority of consumers rely on *Recommended Daily Allowances* from organizations like the USDA and the Food and Drug Administration (FDA) in making food choices, but we are still free to decide which foods we actually eat.

In the United States, especially, reverence for freedom and democracy is reflected directly in the cultural construction of food rules. As Henderson (1970) explained, "The consumption of food in America today is not an art and not a necessity. In its simplest interpretation, it is part of the American birthright" (p. 5). The very idea that we have a choice when it comes to what we eat is a food rule that falls in line with American values, including individual freedom, consumer sovereignty, and personal responsibility. If a consumer wants to eat healthy foods, that choice is hers to make; if she wants to consume only junk food, that choice is hers as well. Like the discourses that direct us to eat more, however, the discourses that frame food as a free choice also contribute to confusion about eating for optimal health. Consumers face consequences for exercising their freedom to choose junk food all of the time, namely in the form of increased risk for heart disease, diabetes, and obesity. At the same time, the discourses that encourage us to restrict our choices in order to avoid those health consequences are not nearly as strong as those discourses that position food as our last great democratic freedom.

Institutional critiques of food service have questioned just how free and democratic our food choices actually are. For example, both Nestle's (2002) and Schlosser's (2001) analyses of the food service industry have argued that government institutions might not tell us what to eat, but pervasive advertising and strategic marketing from the food service industry directs us to make certain choices. When Oscar Meyer and Kraft urge kids to "make lunch fun again" in advertisements for their Lunchables product line, they also suggest that their cold pizza and fake cheese is more desirable than other choices, such as hot pizza with real cheese and some vegetables. The persistence of such advertising techniques has a strong influence on how consumers, children in particular, view the food choices available to them (Goldberg, Gorn, & Gibson, 1978; Signorielli & Staples, 1997). Children begin to value a fun, brightly colored lunch that they can assemble on their own, as opposed to one that is nutritionally balanced and probably better tasting. Thus, the food service industry allows consumers to believe that we are free to choose the foods we want, as long as we choose their product. Foucault (1978) noted that "power is tolerable only on condition that it mask a substantial part of itself" (p. 86). When we, as consumers, believe that we have the power to demand our food, we fail to interrogate our dependence on an industry that promotes certain foods over others, markets particular foods to specific groups, and ignores repeated claims to curb consumption in the name of consumer freedom.

Critical commentaries on social class have also questioned the freedom of our food choices in terms of health disparities among lower and working class families. Obesity rates are significantly higher across working classes where less healthy, processed and fast foods are marketed heavily (Ehrenreich, 2002), and as Counihan and Kaplan (1998) noted, "class, caste, race and gender hierarchies are maintained, in part, through differential control over and access to food. Different consumption patterns are one of the ways the rich distinguish themselves from the poor" (p. 2). Simply put, working classes have less access and opportunity to adopt a health-conscious diet, yet they are denounced for eating the foods most readily available and financially feasible for them (Guttman & Ressler, 2001). The production of eating practices and the choices that individuals make with their food also reproduces structural and practical differences between social classes. As a consequence, working class individuals tend to gravitate toward cheaper foods purchased in large quantity, while dominant classes have the resources that enable a greater sense of food security.

Although individuals are quick to protect the freedom allotted to their food choices, particularly when a government institution suggests a change in those choices, critiques of class disparities in health practice illustrate how food choices might not always be so free (e.g., Guttman & Ressler, 2001). At the same time, food choices continue to be praised as democratic practices that demonstrate our sovereignty as consumers (Griffiths & Wallace, 1998). Therefore, freedom and choice continue to operate as dominant discourses that we use to construct and defend our eating practices.

Constructing a Balanced Diet

The final dominant discourse that organizes eating involves the institutional advice to construct a "balanced" diet. Federal institutions and organizations, the USDA included, often remain neutral in their advice on what foods to consume. Many Registered Dieticians also take a similar approach, claiming that all foods can have a place in a healthy diet when eaten in moderation. These stakeholders stress the concepts of "variety" and "no such thing as a bad food" in their messages. In doing so, they also reproduce several benefits of balance in a healthy diet. For example, one of the reasons that dieticians and nutritionists encourage their clients to learn how to incorporate their favorite foods into a balanced diet is to reduce the likelihood that an individual will develop an eating disorder or a problematic relationship with food. Moreover, the symbolic discourses that support a balanced diet also achieve the material benefits of getting the necessary vitamins and minerals that make a body work better. In other words, vitamins and minerals come to us from a variety of different sources from fish to leafy green vegetables to whole grains and so on. As such, constructing a diet that balances different foods also increases the likelihood that an individual has access to the variety of nutrients in those foods.

Beyond its nutritional merits, some food and nutrition critics (e.g., Nestle, 2002; Brownell & Horgan, 2004) believe that the mantra "there is no such thing as a bad food" is in place to support the interests of the food industry. As Nestle (2002) clarified:

> It is in the interest of food companies to have people believe that there is no such thing as a "good" food (except when it is theirs); that there is no such thing as a "bad" food (especially not theirs); that all foods (especially theirs) can be incorporated into a healthful diet; and that balance, variety, and moderation are the keys to healthful diets. (p. 21)

If there are no bad foods, then all products have a potential place in a healthy diet. Nestle is quick to note the contradictory position in this statement, however, because some food rules demonstrate that certain foods are *better* and *worse* than others. For example, the USDA's My Pyramid works to ensure that foods like whole grains, fruits, and vegetables are eaten in greater abundance than foods like meat/protein or fats and sweets. Therefore, the notion of balance also serves the interests of the food service industry as they attempt to market a wide range of food products.

Although the advice to construct a "balanced" diet might seem like a sound suggestion, a disparity exists between the advice and the actual practices of constructing a balanced diet. More specifically, most Americans are severely out of balance when it comes to their actual eating practices. When it comes to fats and sweets, for example, the Food Pyramid and the USDA suggest that we consume these foods sparingly. However, the average American consumes about 3.7 servings of fats and sweets a day (Nestle, 2002). Thus, the notion of "balance" in a diet is a relatively contested concept. In other words, the recommendation to eat a balanced diet does not give us complete freedom to eat whatever we want whenever we want. Rather, eating a balanced diet means actually incorporating a lot of different types of foods onto our menus. Nonetheless, balance remains a dominant discourse that a number of individuals and institutions produce and reproduce across a variety of food rules.

In her analysis of food, sex, and identity, Probyn (2000) argued that when we eat food we taste power. The three dominant discourses outlined above illustrate some of the instances of power that individuals and institutions taste in the production and reproduction of food practices. These discourses are often implicated in the food rules associated with school meal programs. The following section focuses on meal programs more specifically and illustrates how some of these dominant discourses were made meaningful through food and nutrition policies.

A Case Study of School Meal Programs

School meal programs offer an intriguing illustration of both food rules and the dominant discourses that organize eating. Meal programs are characterized by a precarious balance between managing a kitchen and preparing food for children. Most lunchroom workers are expected to feed anywhere from 30 to 3000 students in just under two hours, sometimes less. The organization of such a feat, especially one that keeps food costs down and follows all of the appropriate guidelines, presents school meal stakeholders with a daunting task. Moreover, school meal programs that receive public funds are accountable to the federal government for reimbursements through the National School Lunch Program (NSLP), state government, and the local school board for additional funding and structure, the individual school for adherence to its policies, and parents and students for providing food that is both healthy and desirable.

In addition to the complex organization of individuals and institutions, the constitution of school meal programs also requires stakeholders to negotiate specific food rules as they structure food choices for students. For example, schools are not required to participate in the NSLP; however, if they want to receive federal reimbursements to subsidize their meal program, they must apply to the NSLP and follow specific guidelines about the construction of their program meals. Specifically, every meal for which a school receives a reimbursement must offer a balance of different foods, including protein/meat, fruits and vegetables, grains, and milk. Moreover, schools may not sell Foods of Minimal Nutritional Value (FMNV) in competition with the meal program. FMNV are that special class of foods that provide primarily empty calories. Sugary candies and chewing gum would be considered a food of minimal nutritional value; however, a Snicker's bar would not because its peanuts give it some nutritional value. Simply put, the NSLP reproduces the food rules generated by the USDA, the Department of Health and Human Services (DHHS), and the advice that they give in the Dietary Guidelines for Americans.

This case study emphasizes the communication practices of three school districts in the Arizona Public School System: Marketplace, Campustown, and Westfield.[ii] Several stakeholders who worked within these districts attempted to restructure their food rules and school meal programs in light of significant policy changes. Each of these districts took a different approach to meal service, and all three have found some level of success in promoting healthier eating habits for their students. Moreover, Marketplace, Campustown, and Westfield demonstrated some of the most improved financial reports after the implementation of their new school meal structures and discursive practices. For instance, Marketplace High went from making $3000/day in gross sales to $5000/day because of their approach. The school now goes through 40 pounds of cantaloupe, 20 pounds of honeydew, and a case of grapes/day. Additionally, Campustown Elementary's efforts have also resulted in an increase in service from 280 meals/day to 408 meals/day. Finally, the Westfield district was cited regularly as having some of the lowest food costs in the state. By focusing on the ways in which Marketplace, Campustown, and Westfield changed their communication practices and food rules, this section traces how students in these districts ate more, exercised their freedom to choose, and attempted to balance their diets.

Eating More of What?

School meal programs have a history of outlining what students should eat more or less of through food and nutrition policies. The first formal policy that organized school meal programs in the United States was instituted in 1946 by President Harry Truman. The National School Lunch Act (Public Law 396) included a two-fold mission: to assist with the health of the nation's children and ensure a market for U.S. farmers. Before this act, disparate individuals and institutions had organized themselves to provide meals for students as far back as 1890, when Ellen H.S. Richards started the New England Kitchen. This program provided meals and nutrition education to working class families in Boston and provided the model for the National School Lunch Program (Cooper & Holmes, 2006). These policies ultimately serve as food rules that ensure schools have the resources that they need to feed their students.

As mentioned previously, this case study focuses on two food and nutrition policies in Arizona schools. On April 26, 2005, then-Arizona Governor Janet Napolitano signed House Bill 2544. This bill effectively established the Arizona Nutrition Standards as the primary guideline for foods sold on campus across Arizona schools. Affectionately dubbed the "junk food bill," the Arizona Nutrition Standards required K-8 schools to remove all sodas and most snack foods from school grounds.

Similar to both House Bill 2544 and the Arizona Nutrition Standards, part of the federal Child Nutrition and WIC Reauthorization Act of 2004 asked schools that receive federal funding to create their own local wellness policy. These local wellness policies needed to address specific subjects, such as foods sold and served on campus, physical activity, and nutrition education; however, schools were encouraged to assemble their own group of stakeholders to craft the actual policy texts.

Both the Arizona Nutrition Standards and the local wellness policy initiative went into effect on the same day. As of July 1, 2006, these policies have put the focus on improving school meal programs and other activities that promote healthier students. Not only do these two policies share similar topic matter and timelines, they also serve as food rules that attempted to re-organize the eating practices of students attending school in the Arizona public system. For example, the policy text of HB 2544 established calls for the state-level nutrition agency to clarify the foods of which students should eat more and/or eat less. The text calls for the state-level nutrition agency to "develop minimum nutrition standards that meet at least federal guidelines and regulations for foods and beverages sold or served on the school grounds of elementary schools, middle schools and junior high schools during the normal school day" (Arizona House Bill 2544, 2005, ln. 5–8).

The three school districts that provide the illustrations for this case each instituted new food rules and communication practices in order to fulfill the demands of these policies. For example, the Marketplace district has transformed the main cafeterias in their junior high and high schools to resemble a healthier version of a shopping mall food court. At Marketplace High, students have their choice between one of five cuisines. Options include an Asian Line, a Mexican Line, an All-American Line, an Italian Line, and a Sandwich and Salad Line. In an effort to encourage students to eat more fruits and vegetables, each entree in the main cafeteria is served as a combo meal with a side salad or vegetable, fruit, and beverage.

In addition to Marketplace, significant changes were also initiated at Campustown Elementary. The Campustown district chose one of their elementary schools as a test school to implement their new approach to meal service. In short, Campustown moved from a "heat and serve" system to offering three options made with fresher ingredients. Rather than re-heating food that has been heavily processed, Campustown wanted their students to eat more fresh and whole foods. To facilitate this change, students could choose between one hot meal option (e.g., spaghetti) *or* one of two cold options (e.g., a fruit and yogurt pack *or* a salad made with fresh vegetables).

Finally, the Westfield district took an approach that encouraged students to eat more fresh fruits and vegetables, without necessarily eating less of traditionally popular foods. Students could choose from a rotating hot lunch option (e.g., baked chicken) or express entrees (e.g., pizza, chicken sandwiches, and burgers). All meals are served with an expansive salad bar of fresh fruits and vegetables produced primarily by local farmers. The food service director for Westfield was particularly committed to teaching students to incorporate a lot of different types of foods into their daily routines.

Across the two policies and the three districts, the food rules and communication practices were placed squarely on increasing students' intake of fruits, vegetables, and whole foods, while limiting their access to foods of minimal nutritional value. At the same time, some stakeholders noted the difficulties of health promotion efforts that emphasized eating more whole foods and less processed foods. A supervisor responsible for many re-designs within the Marketplace district explained:

> I think it's very difficult to get in the calories that kids need without having some of those products that you now can't have. If you put all fresh, all natural foods on a plate, it's very hard to meet the calorie requirements [established by the USDA and the NSLP]. And that kid's gonna look at that plate and wonder if it's enough to fill their stomach.

Although the Arizona Nutrition Standards (AZNS) and local wellness policies operated as food rules that attempted to reorganize students' eating practices, these rules alone cannot guarantee that students will consume foods in the ways the policies intended. More specifically, students often found ways to work around the food rules. The AZNS and some local wellness policies set parameters for portion sizes on certain foods; however, the policy texts did not limit how many items a single student can buy. During one of my observations at Marketplace High, I watched one student purchase three bottles of Powerade, two burritos, and two individual pizzas for his lunch. Further down the line, I noticed students exiting the cafeteria with fistfuls of chocolate chip cookies. As one of the food service managers at Westfield middle school explained:

> We want to put the emphasis on kids and nutrition, but they can still take doubles and we can't stop them. There might be a note that pops up on our computer system that says 'mom says no doubles,' but beyond that they take seconds a lot.

Because the policy texts of the AZNS and most local wellness policies stopped at the nutritional content and portion sizes for the foods sold on campus, some stakeholders, students in particular, searched for ways to resist the rules simply through buying more.

In working around these rules, students ultimately demonstrated how their food choices operated as a way to communicate their agency to eat more or eat less of certain items. Food and nutrition policies can offer recommendations and institute structural changes, but students still have the final say about eating more or less of the foods they want. While Marketplace, Campustown, and Westfield all recorded an increase in the number of students who bought full meals through their lunch programs, a student could still find ways to construct a meal solely out of cookies. This notion of choice is illustrated further in the following section.

Structuring Food Choices at School

Some of the most explicit commentary on using food rules to structure food choices came from Campustown Elementary. At first, the new format at Campustown Elementary proved problematic for some students. The K-5 graders were sometimes overwhelmed by their new ability to choose between three meal options, and the food service manager noted how some students had never heard of a few of their new dishes. "We had kids crying because they didn't know what rice almandine was" the manager quipped. "So, I substituted it with the noodles from the oriental salad." She stressed the need to have a program that gave students lots of choices, but was flexible enough to work with kids who would rather cry in front of all of their friends than eat rice almandine. Other stakeholders emphasized how students enjoyed having variety and choice. I asked one of the lunchroom workers if she had noticed a change in the students since Campustown had implemented their new program. She replied, "they like to see the hot lunch getting served. They like to see fresh mashed potatoes in front of them. They also like to have their choices, especially the Smucker's sandwiches and the salads." The immediacy of food and the opportunities for choice illustrate a key point that has made food service changes at Campustown possible. Meal programs operate as a space where students learn to make choices; therefore, communication practices need to consider how students learn to move through this process.

Although some stakeholders were worried that the AZNS and local wellness policies would ultimately limit choices available to students, several schools used these policy opportunities as a chance to offer students a wider variety of healthy choices. The importance of choices was also evident in my conversation with the supervisor from the Marketplace district. With regard to the decision to offer five different meal lines, she stated candidly, "we don't want to treat them like babies. They are old enough to make decisions about food." Simply put, students do need an opportunity to learn *how* to make choices, and the school meal program is one venue for them to learn how to make *healthy* choices.

One of the ways in which schools have contended with the communication practices surrounding choice is through the process of branding. Although branding has been critiqued for its negative influence on society in general (Klein, 2002; Schol, 1999) and school meal programs in particular (Schlosser, 2001), some schools have re-imagined branding as a way to communicate more effectively with students about healthy eating options. A former food supervisor for the Marketplace district explained the rationale behind branding school lunch:

> If you go to the food court in the mall, how many different choices do you have? Why should [school lunch] be any different? Kids today are so overly exposed to all of those kinds of things, that if you can't meet what they're doing, then you're not going to get anywhere. You have to mimic what's actually going on in the real world.

Simply put, stakeholders who want to promote healthy eating changes need to examine the different messages and structures to which students are exposed both inside and outside of school. Because branding and consumer identities have become such a significant part of contemporary societies (du Gay, 1996; Twitchell, 2000; Schol, 1999), this supervisor suggests that schools find healthier ways to use such organizational and health communication practices.

The Marketplace district hopes to have found an appropriate balance between food and fun by creating a healthier version of a branded food court. When I spoke with a supervisor and a manager who played integral roles in the transformation of Marketplace's meal program, the supervisor stated, "Kids have such a sophisticated taste these days. They have so many options outside of school. So, we decided to mimic some of the popular hot chains." Food service stakeholders at Marketplace looked at chains such as Panda Express, Fazzoli's, Chipotle, McDonald's, and Subway in order to study the rules and resources that structured their food service. The supervisor also claimed that "we wanted to make healthier versions of these products that tasted just as good." Marketplace developed their five cuisines and named them South of the Border, Little Italy, [Marketplace] Grill, Subs & Salads, and The Asian Line. Menu options are healthier in that Marketplace uses whole grain products, does not fry any of their food, and includes their entrées in combo meals with sides like fruit and water. Moreover, each line has its own menu board complete with individual and combo items, prices, and beverages. By borrowing from another meal-time structure, the fast food restaurants with which students were familiar, Marketplace was able to develop a presentation-style for their healthier options that made students want to buy their brand.

Similar to their use of branding, Marketplace also attempted to redefine the ways in which vending was discursively positioned in their schools. Simply put, they enabled a switch to "healthy vending." When I asked Marketplace's food service supervisor what exactly "healthy" vending included, she described choices of baked chips, nuts, trail mixes, 100% fruit juice, pretzels, and fruit snacks. In other words, the switch to healthy vending makes snacks of a higher nutritional value available to students throughout the day.

The Marketplace's food service supervisor also explained the implementation of healthy vending in her district. She recounted a conversation that she had with Marketplace High's on-site food service manager. The manager was shocked to report that she regularly filled her vending machines twice a day. The supervisor recalled:

> Her sales didn't drop at all when we only had healthy stuff in there. One day, we watched this girl walk up. And she gets this super snotty look on her face and says "oh, everything in here is healthy, oh what are we going to eat. I can't believe they did this to us." And then she puts $1 in the machine and gets some baked chips.

This example suggests that when students want something to eat and have the money to buy products from the vending machine, they will still buy the healthy options that have been made available. Some stakeholders have explained this phenomenon as having more to do with the students' need to express their agency as consumers as opposed to their need for a snack. The food service director from Westfield offered the following observation: "Kids like to use vending machines, because it's like a slot machine. They see their money go in, and they see something come out."

In a way, some schools provided students with a way to exercise their agency as consumers by offering them choices through branding efforts and vending programs. Rather than using local policies to outlaw these practices, stakeholders re-imagined ways to use branding and vending as a way to help students learn to make healthy food choices. What is particularly interesting about these food rules, however, is how the illustrations *both* affirm the use of branding and healthy vending as a way to encourage choice *and* demonstrate how these communication practices often distance consumers from the food itself. For example, the use of vending has the potential to reduce the notion of choice to mindless consumer behaviors such as putting a coin in a slot. At the same time, the switch to *healthy* vending has some innovative potential in terms of reinforcing the need for balance in one's diet. The following section expands upon this third dominant discourse that organizes eating in school meal programs.

Emphasizing Balance in Students' Diets

As mentioned previously, the discourse of balance is a dominant set of texts and communication practices that extend across nutritional contexts—from USDA literature to individual food rules used by the schools in this case study. For example, the food service director for the Westfield district worked to ensure balance by increasing his students' access to fresh foods. More specifically, their program teaches students that they can eat a piece of pizza, as long as they also pair that entrée with fresh fruits and vegetables. As Westfield's director explained, "[students] get a salad bar *and* a fruit bar, you know watermelon, kiwis, cantaloupe. Every day, year-round, strawberries and kiwi." Rather than just limit the junk food, these schools also re-invented the ways that they organized the foods on their lunch line.

Another of the ways in which the food service director for Westfield also enforced the notion of balance is by avoiding food labels such as "healthy" and "junk food," as well as "good foods" and "bad foods." Most federal and state discourses about nutrition, as well as most advice from Registered Dieticians, intentionally avoid labeling foods as good or bad. They do so because individuals need to get their nutrients from a variety of sources, and these stakeholders do not want individuals to develop a disordered relationship with a "bad" food. The food service director for Westfield clarified this discourse, claiming that "in moderation, all foods are pretty good. I don't buy that line that there are no bad foods, though. I think there are bad foods." At the same time, he also urged adults to be careful when using these words when communicating with students about food. He went on to explain that labeling food as good or bad is more like propaganda than good nutrition promotion. When we can teach children that *all* foods *can* have a place in a healthy diet, but *some* foods are *better* for your body than others, this director feels like the right message is being communicated to students.

The challenge that multiple stakeholders face is managing a structure that actually enables balance and moderation. Some individuals have taken the advice that *all* foods *can* be a part of a healthy diet to mean that *favorite* foods should *always* have a place on the menu. Marion Nestle problematized this approach to eating in *Food Politics* (2002), claiming that most Americans eat more than three servings of fats and sweets a day even though the Food Pyramid says to consume these items sparingly. Moreover, policies and other food rules can only do so much to ensure that students have access to a balanced diet; these communication practices cannot always ensure that students will actually eat the food that has been made available.

At every school whose lunch service I observed, I spent a day by the garbage cans. In an effort to illustrate how students actually consumed food after the institution of healthier policy texts, I thought it pertinent to watch what ended up in the trash. Food waste has become a big concern for schools, in terms of both the financial stability of their programs and the nutritional stability of their students. Simply put, students do not always eat what they put on their tray or pack in their lunchbox. I even saw one middle school boy throw away his entire meal—tray and all. At Campustown Elementary, for example, a young boy who sat close to the garbage can took one bite of his hot dog and launched it toward the trash. Fortunately, he hit his mark. An impromptu game of hot dog basketball then broke out among the boys at the table. This first boy looked at me with a grin and said, "this is much more fun."

Similar to the ways in which they worked around the rules that encouraged them to eat more or eat less, students also worked around the rules that attempted to ensure balance in their diets. For example, during one of my observations at Marketplace High, I noticed that several students in the food court would pay $3.50 for an individual pizza and a bottle of water. If they bought the combo meal, they could spend $3.00 for an individual pizza, an apple or side salad, and the bottle of water along with juice and milk. When I asked Marketplace's food service supervisor about this, she said, "We would tell them 'if you walk back over there and pick up an apple you can get this for so much less.'" Yet, students at Marketplace would spend more money simply to have the foods that they wanted and nothing more. Others would return to the line, pick up the additional items, and immediately throw away the side salad and the milk once they reached the nearest garbage can.

The food service manager at Campustown Elementary also noted the various ways that students enacted food practices in ways that worked around the goals of the AZNS and local wellness policies. She recounted the story of a group of young boys who consistently picked the salad pack. The staff was surprised that the boys had taken such a liking to the salad, until they realized that the boys chose the salads for the pudding cup that was included in the pack. They ate the pudding and threw the rest away.

With the rise in obesity rates in young people, public health research has pointed to myriad ways in which students' eating practices are out of balance (Kubik, Lytle, Hannan, Perry, & Story, 2003; see also Cullen & Zakeri, 2004). When students are given the freedom to make their own food choices among options such as French fries, pizza, chicken nuggets, mixed green salads, fresh fruit, and other whole foods, many of them seem incapable of enacting the "balance" that is recommended by most dieticians and federal institutions. As a consequence, students are consuming too much of the pizza and French fry calories and not enough of the fruit and vegetable calories. Even when food rules and communication practices increased students' access to fresh foods to balance out the overabundance of processed foods in their diets, some of those students would rather waste the food than eat a few vegetables (or in a few cases, spend more money NOT to eat those whole foods in the first place).

In some ways, these examples illustrate how students continue to use their food choices to communicate their agency as consumers. If students do not want to eat a salad or a piece of fruit, you can make them buy it, but you can't make them eat it. As one of the Westfield lunchroom workers clarified, "kids here love the kiwi; although, some kids do have two bags of baked chips and a slushy. You can give them the resources, but you can't make them use it." At the same time, these examples suggest that stakeholders must search for savvier ways than simply increasing access to fresh foods if they actually want to persuade students to change their personal food rules.

Food Rules at School

In response to the problematic eating habits of students at school, several discourses have emerged to encourage the restructuring of food choices at school. This chapter has focused on three of those discourses and the ways in which students were expected to eat more or eat less, restructure their food choices, and learn how to incorporate balance and moderation in their diets. In this final section, I address some of the implications that extend from the case of Arizona schools. More specifically, I focus on the implications of branding and policymaking as communication practices that can restructure food rules.

Although the freedom to make one's own food choices and balance one's own diet reinforces a sense of agency and consumer sovereignty, these discourses are not wholly unproblematic. For example, when students are exposed to options in addition to the NSLP program meal, their consumption of fruits, vegetables, and other whole foods tends to decline (Cullen & Zakeri, 2004). School meal programs have changed over time to reflect food choices that are more appealing to their student consumers. When students reach middle school, they often find vending machines, a la carte menu options, and a host of foods that are sold outside of the NSLP. These foods are not Foods of Minimal Nutritional Value (FMNV), per se; however, they are the types of foods that many critics identify as the culprits in poor eating practices (see Schlosser, 2001).

A communication practice that deserves particular attention involves the branding of school meal programs. Schools such as Marketplace High have found great success branding their lunch programs to mimic popular fast food chains. This practice allows stakeholders to build a sense of connection between students and the school meal program, while they also serve healthier versions of their products. Moreover, branding also enables students an opportunity to use food to communicate their identity as consumers. Branding has been conceptualized as a process that can enable consumer participation in some fairly compelling ways (Twitchell, 2000). Yet, the critiques of branding remind us that this process can also reproduce mindless consumer practices (e.g., Klein, 2002; Schol, 1999). When a parent suggests that students only want to drop a quarter in a vending machine and do not care what they buy, for example, that parent's comment demonstrates the dangers of desensitizing students through too much branding. In addition to branding, public health and communication research have placed the emphasis on policy as a way to promote healthier eating practices for students. For example, research has suggested that "healthy food choices and school policies that require healthier foods at school snack bars should be promoted" (Cullen & Zakeri, 2004, p. 463). Additionally, Kubik and her co-authors (2003) identified "meaningful policy initiatives at both an organizational and a legislative level" as an ideal strategy for enabling healthier practices (p. 1168). Moreover, Salisbury (2004) reviewed several federal initiatives and state policies from California, Texas, and Maine, claiming that policies held the most potential for transforming eating practices at school and beyond. By emphasizing policy and the restructuring of school meal programs, these recommendations also highlight the need for more sophisticated communication strategies for working with policy and promoting healthy eating practices. This need for greater attention to communication practices across the life of a policy initiative was also illustrated in this case study of school meal programs.

This case study suggested that the communication practices and food rules of most interest in the restructuring of school meal programs should be the practices of the students who eat at school. Adult stakeholders drew upon the structures of the AZNS and their local wellness policies to mobilize those policy texts and transform their meal programs; however, *students'* use of the meal program and other wellness-related structures illustrate whether or not healthy eating is being practiced. Just as school meal stakeholders consumed various aspects of the AZNS and their local wellness policies to restructure their meal programs, so too do students consume the resources made available through those meal programs. Individuals always encounter some sort of disjuncture between dominant readings of a text and the more local interpretations of meaning (Mumby, 1987; see also Hardy, 2004; Hardy & Phillips, 2004). As such, there is much to be said about how individual students both embraced and worked around the changes that were enabled and constrained by Arizona nutrition policies. Stakeholders must pay close attention to how students consume the resources to which they are given access and how they (re)construct their food rules in relationship to policy changes.

Conclusion

During one of my observations at Campustown Elementary, the food service manager suddenly tore through the cafeteria shouting, "Come on kids, eat up. Mama thinks I'm feeding you!" She bustled around the room, repeating this line as she encouraged students to eat at least half of everything that was in their lunch. The Campustown manager had consistently told me that part of her job was to teach kids how to eat. She often mentioned how some students, particularly the younger ones, would just sit there and stare at each other with a tray of food in front of them if you did not give them a little guidance about how they needed to eat. The phrase "Mama thinks I'm feeding you" captures several complex levels involved with school food service. Initially, there is the assumption that schools actually feed students while they are away from home. Also, this statement highlights the partnership between parents—mothers in particular—and schools in making sure that children learn how to eat. Often, these assumptions require food rules, like the AZNS or local wellness policies, in order to provide a documented posture about school food service and ensure multiple stakeholders that student needs are being met.

Now that the Arizona Nutrition Standards and local wellness policies are in place to restructure meal service, the relationship between policy, communication, and food rules can be examined more thoroughly. Having addressed school meal programs as a context for organizing, this chapter has described both the dominant discourses that structure eating practices as well as some of the unique changes that have surfaced in relation to the AZNS and local wellness policies. School meal programs have become a popular topic of social discourse across many contexts, and these programs could benefit from more refined practices of communication and more meaningful and practical policy initiatives.

Endnotes

[i] This chapter is part of a larger project that examined school meal program changes in Arizona between 2004 and 2007. The project used a qualitative method of research called as Discourse Tracing (LeGreco & Tracy, 2009) to examine how discursive practices, such as food rules and policy changes, were instituted across different school meal contexts.

[ii] All schools are referred to by pseudonyms, and all individual research participants are labeled according to their professional relationship to a particular school or its meal program.

References

Arizona House Bill 2544. (2005). Retrieved October 17, 2006 from http://www.azleg.state.az.us/legtext/47leg/1r/bills/hb2544h.pdf.

Brillat-Savarin, J. A. (1925). *The physiology of taste.* New York: Doubleday and Company.

Brownell, K. & Horgen, K. (2004). *Food fight: The inside story of the food industry, America's obesity crisis, and what we can do about it.* New York: McGraw-Hill.

Cooper, A & Holmes, L. M (2006). *Lunch lessons: Changing the way we feed our children.* New York: HarperCollins.

Counihan, C. (1992). Food rules in the United States: Individualism, control and hierarchy. *Anthropological Quarterly, 61*, 51–62.

Counihan, C., & Kaplan, S. L. (1998). *Food and gender: Identity and power.* Amsterdam: Harwood Academic Publishers.

Cullen, K. W., & Zakeri, I. (2004). Fruits, vegetables, milk, and sweetened beverage consumption and access to a la carte/snack bar meals at school. *American Journal of Public Health, 94,* 463–467.

du Gay, P. (1996). *Consumption and identity at work.* London: Sage.

Ehrenreich, B. (2002) *Nickel and dimed: On not getting by in America.* New York: Holt.

Fisher, M. F. K. (1937). *The art of eating.* New York: Hungry Minds, Inc.

Foucault, M. (1978). *The history of sexuality: An introduction* (Vol. 1). New York: Vintage Books.

Goldberg, M.E., Gorn, G., & Gibson, W. (1978). Some unintended consequences of TV advertising. *The Journal of Consumer Research, 5,* 73–81.

Griffiths, S., & Wallace, J. (1998). *Consuming passions: Food in the age of anxiety.* New York: St. Martin's Press.

Guttman, N., & Ressler, W. (2001). On being responsible: Ethical issues in appeals to personal responsibility in health campaigns. *Journal of Health Communication, 6*, 117–136.

Hardy, C. (2004). Scaling up and bearing down in discourse analysis: Questions regarding textual agencies and their context. *Organization, 11,* 415–425.

Hardy, C. & Phillips, N. (2004). Discourse and power. In D. Grant, C. Hardy, C. Oswick, & L. L. Putnam (Eds.), *The Handbook of Organizational Discourse* (pp. 299–316). London: Sage.

Henderson, M. C. (1970). Food as communication in American culture. *Today's Speech, 18,* 3, 3–8.

Klein, N. (2002). *No Logo.* New York: Picador.

Kubik, M. Y, Lytle, L. A. Hannan, P. J., Perry, C. L., & Story, M. (2003). The association of the school food environment with dietary behaviors of young adolescents. *American Journal of Public Health, 93,* 1168–1173.

LeGreco, M. & Tracy, S.J. (2009). Discourse tracing as qualitative practice. *Qualitative Inquiry, 15,* 1516–1543.

Lockford, L. (1996). Social drama in the spectacle of femininity: The performance of weight loss in the Weight Watchers' program. *Women's Studies in Communication, 19,* 291–312.

Martin, D. D. (2002). From appearance tales to oppression tales: Frame alignment and organizational identity. *Journal of Contemporary Ethnography, 31,* 158–206.

Meister, M. (2001). Cultural feeding, good life science, and the TV Food Network. *Mass Communication and Society, 4,* 165–182.

Mumby, D. K. (1987). The political function of narrative in organizations. *Communication Monographs, 54,* 113–127.

Nestle, M. (2002). *Food politics: How the food industry influences nutrition and health.* Berkeley: University of California Press.

Probyn, E. (2000). *Carnal appetites: Food sex identities.* New York: Routledge.

Salisbury, C. G. (2004). Make an investment in our school children: Increase the nutritional value of school lunch programs. *BYU Law Journal,* 331–352.

Schlosser, E. (2001). *Fast food nation.* New York: Perennial.

Schol, J. (1999). *The overspent American.* New York: Harper.

Signorielli, N., & Staples, J. (1997). Television and children's conceptions of nutrition. *Health Communication, 9,* 289–301.

Twitchell, J. (2000). Two cheers for materialism. In J. B. Schor & D. B. Holt (Eds.), *The consumer society reader* (pp. 281–290). New York: The New Press.

20

Food bank culture: Food and nutrition communication in a hunger-relief organization

Tara J. Schuwerk

Hunger relief organizations are an integral part of the discussion of the food as communication/communication as food paradigm for the populations they serve and those that support them. We must continue to build our understanding of this paradigm by researching and discussing multiple areas of food and communication, including hunger relief organizations, so that we can more fully understand how food demonstrates social, cultural, and political phenomena and, ultimately, the role of food and communication in our lives. The study presented in this chapter is situated within the section on Food and Communication Relationships due to its focus on the intersection of a food bank, food, nutrition, individuals and the relationships maintained by food and communication.

Communication scholars are pursuing research in a number of areas related to food, nutrition, and communication, varying from the relationship between food, culture, and communication through practices of consumption (LeGreco, 2005) to the investigations into the appearance of racial minorities in television advertisements for low-nutrition products (Henderson & Baldsty, 2003). Studies have also been conducted involving various relationships between children and nutrition (Harrison, 2005; Signorielli & Staples, 1997; Signorielli & Lears, 1992; Rasnake, Laub, Lewis, & Linscheid, 2005) and child feeding practices and the process of receiving and transmitting messages (Bruss, Morris, Dannison, Orbe, Quitugua, & Palacios, 2005). There is also developing interest in the training of journalists assigned to cover the ever increasing news topic of food and nutrition (Hampl, 2004). Chew, Palmer, and Kim (1998) have examined nutrition behavior mediated through health motivation and salience and Meister

(2001) has studied the critical implications of "cultural feeding." In addition, Aldoory secured two grants to study public perceptions of food bioterrorism in the news and to study effects of conflicting news and information about food safety (NCA, 2004). Although these scholars have contributed worthwhile research to expand the health communication field, there is a lack of communication research in the area of nutrition and hunger-relief. This study involving food and hunger-relief seeks to narrow this gap.

Data indicate that between 36 and 49 million Americans are "food insecure," meaning that they are in need of food assistance, and/or do not have an adequate quality or sufficient quantity of food (United States Department of Agriculture [USDA], 2008; Feeding America, 2009). Likewise, according to the Food Research and Action Center (2008), "food insecurity refers to the lack of access to enough food to fully meet basic needs at all times due to lack of financial resources" (p. 5). This number represents approximately eleven percent of the population of the United States.

Many programs are currently functioning to help alleviate food insecurity in the United States, such as the Supplemental Nutritional Assistance Program (SNAP) and the Special Supplemental Nutrition Program for Women, Infants, and Children (WIC). Food bank and food pantry organizations, such as Feeding America, the largest private, domestic, hunger-relief organization in the United States, also exist to aid in hunger-relief. All of these organizations and programs work to provide access to food through various means. For example, the programs may provide canned goods, financial assistance, and/or allowances for specified foods. However, despite these established programs, malnutrition presents another significant problem beyond the identified food insecurity issue. Research suggests that users of these and equivalent programs and services in the United States and Canada are at risk of malnutrition (Bell, Wilbur, & Smith, 1998; Tarasuk & Eakin, 2003). Studies conducted on nutrient intake and food consumed by those individuals in a state of food poverty indicate a diet poorer in nutritional quality than the general population (Bell et al., 1998), a diet significantly different from the USDA Food Guide Pyramid recommendations (Wadsworth & Fellers, 2001), and a diet lacking in specific nutrients such as fiber, vitamin A, folate, carotene, potassium, and magnesium (Verpy, Smith, & Reicks, 2003; Connell, Yadrick, & Hinton, 2001; Briley, Padget, Gillham, Wilson, & Roberts-Gray, 2001; Koch, 2000; Starkey, Gray-Donald, & Kuhnlein, 1999).

Bell et al. (1998) reported that several studies have previously addressed food bank organizational structure, user profile, and funding. Homeless and nontransient users of the system, food availability, and nutritional status of users have also been studied. However, very little to no research on communication has been conducted in hunger-relief organizations relating specifically to nutrition and health messages. It is clear that there is a gap in the research concerning health and nutrition messages being communicated in hunger-relief settings. As a public problem, a study of nutrition communication in a hunger-relief setting would "enable socially invisible or silenced groups to be seen and heard" as well as to "perhaps point to 'problems' where none were thought to exist" (Lindlof & Taylor, 2002, p. 72) while concurrently investigating a "communication phenomenon … yet to be described" (p. 86).

With Feeding America (2009) providing food assistance to over 25 million people each year, investigating the communication in a hunger-relief setting, such as food and nutrition messages, could provide valuable information for the organization, those that the organization serves, and the community at large. Such information might address safety, effective communication with staff, clients, food donors, and sponsors, cultural patterns, and increased awareness.

In addition, with an increase in media coverage of recent natural disasters and the plight of the survivors (e.g., Hurricane Katrina in 2005, the Pakistan Earthquake in 2005, and the Asian Tsunami in 2004), the need for, and awareness of, emergency food providers has risen. Compounding needs created by these natural disasters is the current economic situation now facing many individuals. As the recession continues, food banks and food pantries are seeing more and more people in need (Ritter, 2009; Orr, 2009; Contenta, 2009; Monsebraaten, 2009). This increased demand will not disappear overnight, and therefore, hunger-relief organizations will be at the forefront, supporting these individuals as they get re-settled and "back on their feet." In light of this increase in hunger-relief efforts, understanding the communication in this context of hunger-relief organizations, food insecurity, and nutrition is vital considering the aforementioned malnutrition of those relying on hunger-relief organizations. Identifying nutrition messages and how they are expressed at the organizational level would be valuable to many hunger-relief organizations by illuminating areas for more effective communication and better quality service. On a societal level, investigating food and nutrition messages being disseminated through a hunger-relief organization could help to not only improve the nutrition of the food bank clients but also could help to re-define societal perspectives on poverty-level food and nutrition issues. This research also serves to help us understand food as communication within a context often overlooked.

Food Insecurity and Hunger Relief in the United States

In a study conducted by Bell et al. (1998), clients in an emergency food relief service consumed inadequate amounts of calcium, folate, iron, protein, zinc, and vitamins A, C, D, and E. This malnutrition can be directly linked to the food clients do or do not consume as supplied by a hunger-relief service. The nutritional needs of millions of people that are food insecure and/or utilizing food assistance programs are not being met.

Federal hunger-relief assistance programs exist, along with food banks, food pantries, and soup kitchens. Each of these programs is set up differently, but seeks to achieve a similar goal of providing the means to supply nutritious food to those that are food insecure.

"Food bank" is a term that originally referred to a collection hub and distribution center that functioned as a provider of bulk food to local hunger-relief assistance programs, such as a church food pantry. The food pantry distributed the food to those directly in need. However, the term food bank has now evolved through use by the clients, community workers, and the media (Starkey et al., 1999) to refer to local food assistance sites as well. The term food bank, in this study, is used in its initial context as a regional collection and distribution center. The terms "food pantry" and "food shelves" are used to refer to the local food-relief context. Because of the decrease in the number of low-income households using federal benefits and the increased use of food pantries (Koch, 2000), and the resources of food banks, as well as the unique responsibility of the food bank to provide actual food in comparison to the aforementioned food assistance programs, I chose to focus on a food bank in this study.

The food bank is distinctive in this framework because of the constraints of client choice. For example, WIC and the SNAP program provide participants with a way to purchase food. WIC provides checks to purchase food that is rich in one or more of the following nutrients: calcium, iron, protein, vitamin A and vitamin C with new foods being phased in during 2009 (USDA, 2009a). SNAP provides electronic debit cards to purchase only food and plants or seeds to grow food, excluding alcohol, vitamins, hot foods, or any food to be eaten in the store (USDA, 2009b). These programs allow the clients to choose, with some restrictions, what items to purchase for their consumption. In contrast, food banks rarely allow customer choice in specific foods, as they typically sort donated food and then ship it out to other agencies, such as food pantries. The food pantry may request a box of canned meat, but have little to no say in what types of canned meat they receive; nor do the food banks generally work with the clients directly. Therefore, the food that gets distributed to the local hunger-relief organizations is largely determined by the food bank, eliminating customer choice for both food pantry and client.

Organizational Culture: Schein

While examining the data gathered, Schein's (1992) work on organizational culture became a useful lens through which to view themes that emerged. This review aids in the understanding of the analysis of the data even though I did not enter the field with this framework in mind. Schein (1992) defines organizational culture as

> a pattern of shared basic assumptions that the group learned as it solved its problems of external adaptation and internal integration, that has worked well enough to be considered valid and therefore, to be taught to new members as the correct way to perceive, think, and feel in relation to these problems. (p. 12)

With this definition, Schein (1992) outlines three specific levels of organizational culture. At the surface level are artifacts, or the "visible organizational structures and processes" (p. 17). This is the most visible and tangible level. Artifacts are the physical and social environment. This level of culture also encompasses behavior, rituals, customs, technology, and language. In this research, the artifact level will also include the organizational processes that make behavior routine.

Another level is espoused values (Schein, 1992), or the goals, strategies, and philosophies of the organization. These are slightly less visible than artifacts and tend to be complex. Espoused values develop from the success of decision making within a group in the organization. When decisions about a problem produce a solution that the group sees as reliable, the group accepts the decision and it becomes a reality. They no longer question the decision; the solution becomes an espoused value (Schein, 1992).

The last level consists of basic underlying assumptions and is considered the deepest level of culture (Schein, 1992). These assumptions are unconscious, usually taken for granted beliefs, perceptions, and thoughts. Underlying assumptions guide behavior and are the source of values and action.

Organizational Culture and Nutrition

Taking into account the organizational elements Schein outlines and applying them to the food bank, it is important to note that as a third party food provider, the food bank assumes part of the responsibility for providing food. The current supply of food from food banks has led to complaints from food pantries and clients about nutritional value in foods provided, including specific health needs and age and health-appropriate foods (Verpy et al., 2003; Tarasuk & Eakin, 2002; Briley et al., 2001). Verpy et al. (2003) also identified concerns by pantries over the safety and quality of food, such as expired items. A primary issue that emerges is this: do food banks consider what quality and nutritious food is being provided to the clients and, if so, is this apparent throughout the culture of the organization? If the culture of the food bank organization is structured with communicated values of nutrition, as noted in many food bank mission statements, is it apparent in their communication throughout the food redistribution process?

It is necessary to understand what nutrition messages are being communicated in relation to the values and structures within a food bank because the organization's culture may dictate basic organizational functioning. "An organization's culture influences all aspects of organizational life" (Fitzgerald & Desjardins, 2004, p. 122) and this culture is often communicated through values (O'Reilly, Chatman, & Caldwell, 1991). The organizational culture of the food bank impacts communication related to the food bank itself, member agencies (such as food pantries), those receiving food from these organizations, and the community.

The available supply of distributable food is almost entirely dependent on donations, so the quantity, selection, and quality of food vary. Verpy et al. (2003) note that most donors do not "consciously consider nutrition when deciding which foods to donate" (p. 12). Studying the communication within a food bank organization may identify why this happens and/or how to encourage more nutrient-dense food donations. Briley et al. (2001) suggest that a registered dietician working in conjunction with the food bank could significantly improve/affect the selection of nutrient-dense foods and the re-distribution process, but this is not a common practice in the United States. Both of these factors significantly limit the quantity of nutritious food available to re-distribute. If supplying nutritious food is a priority, what do food banks communicate when they accept donations of foods low in nutrients, such as cookies or high-sodium foods such as boxed soup? What is communicated when the food bank then re-distributes these foods? What effect does it have on those associated with the hunger-relief effort and society in general? To begin answering these questions, it is necessary to understand the communication structures within food banks and how communication is expressed.

Background, Data Sources, and Analysis Procedures

Reflecting on current problems in society (Lindlof & Taylor, 2002), including malnutrition among the food insecure, I conducted a preliminary literature review. This review found a dearth of literature on communication in food banks, specifically communication related to nutrition messages, and messages about hunger-relief. Since the provision of food services to community members in need is an important ongoing process, it makes practical sense to focus this research on nutrition messages being exchanged and the overall health communication regarding hunger-relief within the food bank.

My primary research purpose in entering the hunger-relief setting was to improve understanding of nutrition messages and health communication connected to an organization providing services to those who are food insecure. Investigating this communication from an interpretive perspective provides an in-depth understanding of human actions, motives, and feelings (Lindlof & Taylor, 2002), making sense of human experience and communication phenomena in context, and providing 'thick description" (Geertz, 1973) about a relatively unexplored area.

The "Western Food Bank" (W.F.B.) is located in the Southwest United States and was the primary site of investigation. This food bank is a community-based non-profit organization established over twenty years ago that provides hunger-relief in various ways, including supplying food and related commodities and services to people in need through a network of partner agencies, providing a system for the distribution of food and related commodities, partnering with emergency food programs and other non-profit organizations that meet the critical needs of low-income hungry and food insecure families and individuals, and educating the public about hunger and food insecurity. The W.F.B. collects, acquires, stores, and distributes almost 14,000,000 pounds of food and related items each year through a network of partners and agencies in a region stretching over approximately 25,000 square miles. The W.F.B. is engaged in a number of programs and therefore provides several volunteer opportunities, including sorting donated food and packing food boxes.

Data Sources

I entered the field with a known investigative purpose as a "participant-as-observer" (Lindlof & Taylor, 2002). To understand how the food bank works and to understand some of the messages being exchanged, participant observation and informal on-the-spot "ethnographic interviews" were extremely valuable (Lindlof & Taylor, 2002). Through 21 hours of field observations at the W.F.B., I gained insight into various issues of nutrition, health, and food safety resulting in 70 pages of single-spaced typewritten text. "Jottings" (Emerson, Fretz, & Shaw, 1995) were made and my fieldnotes were developed through an "active process" of construction generally within 36 hours after the observations. The majority of my participant-observation took place during the 8 a.m. to 2 p.m. set volunteer time schedule in the food bank's sorting room, an area where donated food is sorted into categories. This context provided the most appropriate data for my research questions because of the need to observe communication in practice within the organization.

For most of my visits to the food bank, I actively sorted food in order to gain a better understanding of the organization and to place myself in communication interactions directly involving the food to be redistributed. These hours of observation and participation illustrated "how cultural symbol systems are used to attribute meaning to existence and activity" (Lindlof & Taylor, 2002, p. 11) and helped create the familiarity with the social practices desirable for later explanations.

An additional source of data was four interviews conducted with two food bank volunteers, one member of management, and one independent nutrition expert. These interviews helped to provide depth, reinforce and/or clarify my observations, and provide important participant perspectives. Participants were recruited through conversations with food bank employees and food bank volunteers. The expert on nutrition was solicited through a local university health center.

The interviews were conducted at places convenient and safe for both the participant and researcher, such as the W.F.B., the university, or over the telephone. The questions varied slightly depending on participant's specialized role within the organization. Some of the questions included "Is there a registered dietician or nutritionist employed by the food bank?" and "What is the perfect food to be donated to the food bank?" and "How is the food the food bank receives different from what the food bank would like to receive?" Nevertheless, a loose organization of questions was maintained to allow for comparison and cross-referencing during data analysis. These interviews were important because they provided information about "key features and processes of the scene" (Lindlof & Taylor, 2002, p. 176) such as establishment of the food sorting categories, programs run by the food bank, types of food donated and redistributed, and nutrition. The interviews also aided in understanding formed opinions, motivations to act, and complex attitudes (Lindlof & Taylor, 2002). For instance, baby food that is expired or will expire in two weeks is to be discarded, while "adult" food is not inspected for expiration dates. Interviewing the nutrition expert and food bank management about the expiration dates revealed attitudes about adult choice and responsibility that could not be discovered by simply observing the scene.

Each of these interviews was recorded on audio-tape and was transcribed no later than one week after the interview. The interviews were semi-structured and resulted in 30 pages of single-spaced typewritten text. I was able to obtain specific language forms used in the natural setting of the food bank as well as explore and understand the Lindlof & Taylor (2002) term "native conceptualizations of communication" (p. 174).

A third source of data was documentation provided by the W.F.B. These documents included statistical summaries released to the public, information posted on their official website, and internal memos/papers. This data supplied valuable information on the organization's background, policies and procedures, partnerships, and other institutional related matters.

Analysis Procedures

The data were analyzed using a modified grounded theory approach, or constant-comparative method, based on the work of Glaser and Straus (1967). This is an iterative process that involves collecting data, identifying themes that have emerged, reviewing and comparing data, collecting additional data, and refining themes (Charmaz, 2001). Initially, the data was read to identify health communication and nutrition messages expressed within the W.F.B. among volunteers, staff, and management. The data was first categorized using open line-by-line coding, in which the data was broken down into categories by closely examining and comparing similarities and differences among the underlying meanings of the identified categories (Charmaz, 2001). My own commentaries, or elaborate reflections (Emerson et al., 1995), were included throughout the fieldnote writing process and were considered in the coding process. Theoretical memos (Charmaz, 2001), considered to be summaries of major findings and/or interpretations of specific areas, were used to help expound emerging themes.

Secondarily, I turned to axial coding, which involved the reconstruction of the data by assessing the context of and the connections among the categories (Strauss & Corbin, 1998). During this process, the categories were mutable and frequently compared and contrasted and, if needed, adjusted to include new experiences and/or discrepant cases. Once new observations began yielding less valuable information, I realized the categories and themes were "theoretically saturated" (Glaser & Strauss, 1967) and I began to taper off my participation in the scene.

Nutrition Messages and the Food Bank

An examination of the data led to several explications of food and nutrition messages being communicated within the W.F.B. I will present those explanations in the following discussion. The first section involves the expression of messages, including message construction, origin of the message, and means of transmission. This section, which helps explain the groundwork of the communication within the organization, sets the stage for the following discussion on the communication of food safety and the priority of nutrition.

Expression of Messages

My analysis of the data leads me to believe that food and nutrition messages are expressed at the W.F.B. in a variety of ways. After participating in this scene for four months and analyzing the data, it made sense to classify the messages into two large categories. These two umbrella categories are explicit and implicit messages, and under these categories are several more refined categories of messages. Table 1 displays the categories.

An explicit message is communication that is clearly expressed or readily observable. Through analysis of the data, I have sorted the explicit messages at the W.F.B. into verbal, written, and/or symbolic communication messages. These messages are constructed in a variety of forms, such as through training, giving tours, and asking and answering questions.

Table 1.

Message construction	Transmission means	Origin of message	Form of message	Detailed form of message
Explicit	Verbal	Program Manager	Training of volunteers	Items to discard
				Sorting instructions
			Warehouse tour (volunteers & public)	Explanation of after-school program
		Volunteer(s)	Asking questions to other volunteers	Food sorting questions
			Asking questions to staff	Food sorting questions
				Operation questions
		Staff	Answering staff & volunteer questions	Food sorting answers
				Operation answers
				Negotiating answers
	Written	W.F.B.	Mission Statement	Posted on website
		Feeding America & W.F.B.	Posted Instructions	Box labels
				Items to discard
				Sorting box instructions
	Symbols	W.F.B.	Pictures	Specific items to discard
Implicit	N.A.	Feeding America	Pre-determined food categories	Shelves full of empty boxes to be filled
	N.A.	W.F.B.	External acceptance of all items	Donations
	N.A.	W.F.B.	Internal rejection of items	Donations

The verbal messages are communicated through words and seem to have three distinct origins. The first source is the program manager. The program manager, Mika, gave several other new volunteers and me a tour of the facility and trained us on sorting the donated food. For example, when I was being trained, I was told that any baby food items, like rice cereal or formula, that had expired or would expire in the next two weeks were to be discarded. This was a verbally expressed, explicit instruction.

Other explicit, verbal messages originate with Karl, a staff member who works primarily in the sorting room. Throughout my observations, he continually answered volunteers' questions about where to place specific items and also provided instructions and clarification, such as, "If the rice has a spice in it, then it goes in the boxed-meal box" or that "Marshmallows go into the snack box." On occasion, Karl also answered operation-type questions that were related to food and nutrition, such as, "Should we worry about ensuring a variety of food within a specific sorting box?"

The third source of explicit, verbal messages is the volunteers themselves. The volunteers in the sorting room communicate with each other and often figure things out themselves if needed. An example of this is a conversation recorded in my fieldnotes between another volunteer (V2) and me about where to place a can of pumpkin.

I spent a few minutes explaining to V2 why the can of pumpkin he had in his hand went into the vegetable box and why the can of pumpkin I had went into the dessert box. The cans had the same picture on the front of them, but mine had the word, "filling" in light blue italics off to the side, indicating that it was a product to be used as pie filling. In contrast, the regular can of pumpkin he was holding would get counted as a vegetable. After this explanation, anytime V2 was unsure of a food categorization he would come ask me instead of Karl or the other volunteers.

As mentioned previously, explicit messages at the food bank are also written and/or in the form of a symbol. These two types of explicit messages primarily originate from the W.F.B. itself or from Feeding America. These written messages are disseminated on the website, through posting of the organization's mission statement, as well as through posted instructions within the sorting room. Examples of these instructions are the documents attached to the wall above the sorting boxes. These instructions list what food items are to be placed into which sorting box. An example of an explicit message expressed through a symbol is the photographs of food items that are to be discarded. While these photographs represent a symbolic message, for instance that discolored ketchup should be thrown away, it is still a message that is readily observable, and therefore, explicit.

The implicit messages at the W.F.B. are those that are implied though not directly expressed. This knowledge remains embodied in key employees making it difficult for me to discern the precise origin or constructor of the messages. For instance, when I asked Mika who came up with the sorting box food categories, she replied, "I honestly can't even tell you. They probably came through standards through [Feeding America] and we adapted it to our needs. They have changed over the years a little bit."

Because these messages are not directly expressed they cannot be categorized in the same way as explicit messages. However, this doesn't make the messages any less significant because the messages are often still sent and received, and also communicated through both the artifact and values level of organizational culture. The implicit messages did take on specific forms that could be identified. One such form is the pre-determined food categories set in place to classify donated items. Another is the food bank's visible acceptance of all donated items. Another form is the food bank's internal rejection of specific donated non-food items, such as aspirin.

Much of this communication is not unique to the W.F.B. Nevertheless, it is valuable to be able to explore and identify how food and nutrition messages are communicated in a hunger-relief organization. What we see here of particular significance is that at the W.F.B., the administration, volunteers, and staff create a structure that communicates messages of food and nutrition to other volunteers and staff, and the larger community. Specifically, this information helps us to understand the construction, transmission, and origin of nutrition messages and in what forms they are expressed within the food bank. This understanding allows for a more concentrated look at health communication in the focused setting of food and food banking. This knowledge aids in understanding the communication of organizational values related to food and nutrition.

Messages Expressed—Food Safety

Identifying what food and nutrition messages are being expressed and how they are expressed is vitally important. The data illustrates two main messages regarding food and nutrition. The first is that food safety is important. During my volunteer training I received explicit information on food safety as illustrated through my fieldnotes:

She explained to us what food was to be thrown away. Any baby food items like rice cereal or formula that had expired or would expire in the next two weeks were to be thrown away. Any discolored food items, like brown funny-colored ketchup, were to be tossed as well. Any cans that were severely dented also were to be discarded. The dented cans that looked OK were to go in a separate box for someone else that was specially trained to inspect later. We also were supposed to trash any item that was open, unsealed, or "sampled." Any can that was missing a label was also to be discarded, as well as items that "looked old," like someone had "cleared out their pantry for the first time since 1980."

The recognition of possible "bad" food is significant in regard to health concerns. The food bank does not want to pass on any food that may be hazardous to someone's health. If the food has been damaged, compromised, or contaminated and is passed on to those people in need, someone could become ill. Therefore, food safety seems to be an espoused value of the W.F.B. By having verbal, written, and symbolic food safety messages explicitly communicated, the importance of food safety is apparent at this cultural level of the organization.

Unfortunately, adherence to these guidelines for food safety is not always followed in the sorting room. On occasion, the volunteers, as well as Karl, the worker in the sorting room, seemed to form their own discard guidelines. For instance, I never saw the indicated separate box where moderately dented cans were to be placed for later inspection. And when I asked Karl about it, he said that he rarely throws any dented can into the trash. Just put the dented can in the sorting box, and if someone down the line, presumably the receiving food pantry or food-insecure people, thinks it is too dented to eat out of, they can throw it away themselves. "If I would eat out of it, then I sort it into the boxes to get shipped out."

This quote typifies the fact that the espoused value of food safety is not always congruent with food safety messages being expressed and acted upon. On another occasion, food safety rules were violated regarding product labels and sorting guidelines. According to the verbal instructions I received during training, items without the original label are to be discarded. The following excerpt from my fieldnotes illustrates a food safety violation.

> I was placing sorted food items into their appropriate boxes. Upon doing so, I came across a can that did not have a manufacturer label attached. I picked the can out of the box and saw that it had the words 'chicken noodle soup' written on it in purple marker. I asked Karl why the can had been sorted into a food item box since it did not have a label and was supposed to have been thrown in the trash. His response was that he had put the can in there because it didn't make sense to throw out perfectly fine food and that I should put the can back into the box and not to worry about it.

The preceding data suggest that the organizational espoused value of food safety may not be clearly communicated to the staff of the food bank itself. The purple marking indicating that the can contained soup is clear evidence that the can may have undergone some level of tampering and/or that the food could be old, since the label may have fallen off due to age. The food bank's organizational intention is to not take the risk of redistributing food items that have been tampered with or are old because they may not be safe. If food safety is not clearly communicated, the structures and processes of the organization may not function in coordination with the espoused value. This ultimately means that it is possible for unsafe food to be redistributed, creating problems for the food pantries and for those that are food insecure.

Volunteers finding themselves in a position where they can't remember and cannot find a specific photograph or written instruction have no other option but to rely on their own decisions or ask other volunteers and/or Karl. I was told by the program manager during training that it would not be a big deal if we forgot what she told us because Karl would be in the room and we could ask him or could look at the notes posted on the wall above the shelves or at the pictures posted above the trash cans. Considering the aforementioned episodes when Karl gave contrary instructions coupled with the possibility of a volunteer being in a situation where she relies on herself or Karl for instructions, it is clear to see how the value of food safety could again be in opposition to the organizational culture and processes in operation (Schein, 1992).

The real possibility of these situations, ensuing from a communication exchange, makes it clear that food safety, as an espoused value, is not necessarily practiced in the organizational structure. This may be due to a lack of communication. It may also be because on the food sorting level, food safety may, in actuality, be inconsistent with the sorter's feelings toward food waste. Reexamining Karl's response that it doesn't "make sense to throw out perfectly fine food" it is easy to see how he may believe that canned food missing a manufacturer's label poses no risk, and that there is nothing inherently wrong with redistributing it. This creates some confusion for other volunteers who may be looking at it from a health standpoint, where they're not really sure what is in the unlabeled can. From an outsider perspective, it also calls the food bank's dedication to food safety into question, as redistributing potentially unsafe food does not demonstrate adherence to an espoused value of food safety.

Situations like these illustrate how important examining health communication is in a hunger-relief setting. If Karl is more worried about wasting food and acts on that worry, this may eventually cause problems for the larger organizational culture since it is in opposition to the espoused food safety value. The food bank's levels of culture (Schein, 1992) are left in disharmony. Explicitly discussing the organizational culture and dedication to food safety issues in regards to health could help alleviate the contradiction of values, and in turn strengthen the overall culture of the food bank.

Messages Expressed—Nutrition as a Priority

Providing nutritious food to those who are food insecure is another espoused value of the W.F.B. It is explicitly written in part of their mission statement, "to provide acccss to nutritious food for those who are without." It was also explicitly stated by the program manager during an interview. I asked Mika, "What are the food bank's goals?" She replied,

> To alleviate hunger in our community. And also to provide nutrition education. Being able to provide not just food to fill the bellies but also nutritious food to be able to feed the mind as well.

This value is so important to the culture of the W.F.B. that they have entered into a partnership with the department of nutrition at a local university to develop a nutrient tracking database, funded by a grant supported by two other institutions, one for-profit and one not-for profit. Mika stated:

> They are coming in and analyzing our food donations for nutrient content. They let us know… what we're high on and what we are low on nutrient-wise so we can tailor our food purchases and food drives to those items that we're low on. So, for instance, they take all the donations and figure out that we are low in carotene and folate. So we start doing targeted food drives and purchases for … carrots and spinach and things like that.

This nutrient tracking program is fairly new, only having begun about six months ago, and in my four months of volunteering, it was never mentioned, and I never observed any program close to what Mika described. This is not to say that the nutrient tracking project is not taking place as Mika indicated, only that it is not yet detectable by volunteers in the food donation sorting room.

However, as an espoused value, nutrition as a priority is in conflict with the artifact level of the organizational culture (Schein, 1992). In order to understand the implications to be discussed, it is essential to understand how the food bank works. According to the organizational document, "How Food Banking Works," the food bank receives food from food drives, grocers, growers, individual donations, and state, regional, and industry sources. They then inspect, categorize, inventory, and store this food in the food warehouse. The W.F.B. then provides a shopping list of available products to all member agencies. The member agency creates its own food order, and the W.F.B. packages each individual order for the agency to pick up or to be delivered. The member agencies maintain their own food pantries or on-site feeding programs and distribute the groceries or prepared meals through shelters, soup kitchens, and other feeding programs to individuals and families in their service area.

First, it is imperative to take note that in this explanation of the process of receiving donated food and redistributing it, summarized from a W.F.B. document, nutrition is not explicitly stated or referenced. This omission points toward a conflict between levels of culture. The espoused value of nutrition is at odds with the structure of the organization and the process of food banking.

The next example that illustrates the contradictory values of nutrition in the food bank is the organizational procedure that all donated food is accepted. The W.F.B. does not refuse acceptance of any food item. Mika commented during an interview that the best food to be donated is dry beans, "nature's perfect food," because of the nutritional value and dry beans is the top food the W.F.B. would like to have donated. However, the most often donated food is "ramen noodles." According to Mika, ramen noodles are wonderful "cost wise for the people doing the food drives, but not so good for us because there is nothing really in there that's good for you. It's wonderful filler, but there is nothing but sodium and fat in it." The food bank receives donations of all types of food, including potato chips, cookies, candy bars, macaroni and cheese, instant mashed potatoes, peanuts, marshmallows, canned meat, and canned vegetables, just to name a few. What the community and member agencies see is that the food bank accepts all donated items, so they may believe that all food is equally "good" to donate, when in fact, nutrient-dense food would be preferable.

If nutrition is a priority, what does the organizational practice of accepting all donated food say about the W.F.B.'s dedication to providing nutritious food? What it might say is that the food bank wants to provide nutritious food to those in need, but nutrition takes a proverbial back seat to making the donors feel like they are being generous and helpful. It is easier to accept the food that is donated than to reject the donation on the grounds of low nutrient content, since the food bank depends on food donations for the majority of the food they redistribute, yet it is problematic because it sends a message that any donated food is acceptable. This may leave the food bank with a smaller supply of nutrient-dense food and quite possibly contribute to the larger problem of malnutrition among those that depend on hunger-relief agencies for their food.

According to the nutritionist interviewed for the study, however, it is important to note that no one particular food is really bad for you; it depends on the quantity and how the rest of your food intake is balanced. However, if the majority of food that is being donated is not nutrient-dense, but the food bank continues to accept and redistribute it, this balance is generally not possible for those dependent on the food bank for their food. In addition, the donors seem rarely to learn otherwise.

The fact that the food bank does not formally educate the community unless requested is another practice at odds with, or at least unsupportive of, nutrition as a priority. During an interview with Mika, she talked a little about nutrition education.

> Interviewer: Since the top foods that are donated aren't exactly the same as the top three foods that the W.F.B. would like, how would you get people to donate less ramen noodles and more dry beans or peanut butter?
>
> Mika: It's going to be the community education piece. It's um, not just sitting here hoping that someone knows to give the nutritional food. It's getting out there and speaking to the community and telling them what our needs are. Um, you know, if we don't educate people, we can't assume they know.
>
> Interviewer: Does the food bank do that? Do you do community education pieces?
>
> Mika: Yea, we have um, two of our staff that go out and do community education.
>
> Interviewer: And where do they do that at?
>
> Mika: Anywhere that asks.
>
> Interviewer: Like schools, or…
>
> Mika: Actually right now we are doing more civic organizations. But we're happy to go out to schools. Schools would be wonderful. I don't know that we have a marketing plan for that, but I think that is something that we need to start focusing on.

In addition to general community education, Mika also indicated that they tell donors about the new nutrient database project when donors call:

> When a school calls us and asks us or tells us they want to do a food drive, and they say "so what are we looking for?" and so we'll say, or we explain the nutrient tracking system that we've got established and tell them to focus on a certain item.

The key in both of these discussions is that the donors have to specifically ask about nutritious foods and the community has to ask for nutrition education. It is not automatically communicated by the food bank. The organizational espoused value of nutrition needs to permeate all cultural levels of the organization, and then extend to include those donating the food. Communication could ease some of the disharmony among the levels of culture, enabling the food bank to become a stronger organization. Taking the effort and dedication necessary to change the culture of the communication within the organization may be difficult and time consuming. However, with the strength of communicative effectiveness, the W.F.B. could place nutrition as a top priority at all levels of their culture. The priority of nutrition within all cultural levels of the food bank could help to create the communication needed to become proactive in educating the community, as indicated by the program manager herself. This would aid in debunking certain myths about food insecurity in the community, help provide more nutrient-dense food options to those needing hunger relief, and work toward changing overall perceptions about food and nutrition.

Conclusion

On an organizational level, the highest effectiveness is reached when the espoused values are shared and infuse the other cultural levels of the institution (Schein, 1992). My recommendations for the W.F.B., in consideration of the explicit and implicit food and nutrition messages being shared among volunteers and staff, and by extension with the immediate community, would be to engage in an in-depth analysis of the three cultural levels of the organization (Schein, 1992). In particular, the food bank may want managers to be more involved in the communication transactions of the sorting room. Even the brief analysis provided in this study reveals the disjuncture between cultural levels and how aligning them would benefit both the food bank and the agencies and people they serve. Examining artifacts, espoused values, and basic underlying assumptions of the organization and its workers would provide a better understanding of the organizational culture and how it relates to food safety and nutrition.

The nutrition priority of the food bank is not directly visible in the sorting room, and appears to be not directly visible to the community either. Improving the communication with both of these groups would help to educate the public and, therefore, bring in more nutritious donations. Volunteers would see how important it is to have nutritious food donated and would also be able to act as sources of information out in the community in their daily interactions and discussions about the food bank.

For instance, an article was published in a local newspaper about a food bank not used in this study. The article, while indicating several places for people to take food donations, did not discuss nutrition or types of food to donate. The food bank in the article was concerned about declining donations. This prompted someone at my university to send an email stating that a donation box was being placed in the main office of our department to collect food to be taken to the food bank. Of the food donated by my colleagues, there were no items that would fit into one of the W.F.B.'s four most valued categories. Knowing what I have learned during this study, I could have posted a sign near the box or sent an additional email indicating the best nutritional foods to donate. Yet, the only reason I knew which foods might be best to donate was because I had asked during data collection for this study. Imagine the difference in donations being made if other volunteers took similar information into the community or if the food bank made direct, explicit efforts to request these foods.

I also believe that the nutrition program that has been started in partnership with the local university is a worthwhile project. The information in this nutrient database is vital. However, I believe the possible communication outcomes are even more important. Explicit communication with food bank workers, volunteers, and the community about this database and the information gathered can help assist in the (re)education of the population about food and health.

People depending on food banks and pantries to supply the majority of their food are often malnourished. Receipt of nutrient-dense foods depends largely on food banks and the donations made. A change needs to be made in the communicative practices of food banking to help ensure the availability of nutritious foods. Commitment to this change means that the food bank makes a change on a cultural level. If the culture, at all levels, of the food bank is food safety and nutrient-dense foods then we are one step closer to rightly serving those in need.

There are several limitations to this study that should be noted. This research focused on only one hunger-relief organization. The addition of several other food banks as research sites would be beneficial in the examination of a larger hunger-relief organizational culture. It may have also been valuable to include member agencies' perspectives on the food bank, as well as the perspectives of donors and clients, but due to access and time constraints, these were not the main focus of this research.

This investigation into a hunger-relief setting provides information about food and nutrition messages that are communicated when levels of organizational culture do not seem to be in harmony. The field of communication now has one starting place for future research in a hunger-relief setting. Future research may include food safety and nutrition messages at other levels of the hunger-relief effort, such as food pantries or soup kitchens, health-campaigns in relation to food donations, or even a follow-up investigation into the communication messages of a food bank that has recently employed a new system to ensure the provision of nutrient-dense food. Any of these future endeavors would help us better understand food as communication and communication as food.

References

Bell, M., Wilbur, L., & Smith, C. (1998). Nutritional status of persons using a local emergency food system program in middle America. *Journal of the American Dietetic Association, 98,* 9, 1031–1033.

Briley, M. E., Padget, A. M., Gillham, M. B., Wilson, K., & Roberts-Gray, C. (2001). Nutrition education for organizations supported by food banks. *Topics in Clinical Nutrition, 16,* 4, 21–27.

Bruss, M. B., Morris, J. R., Dannison, L. L., Orbe, M. P., Quitugua, J. A., & Palacios, R. T. (2005). Food, culture, and family: Exploring the coordinated management of meaning regarding childhood obesity. *Health Communication, 18,* 2, 155–175.

Charmaz, K. (2001). Grounded theory. In R. M. Emerson (Ed.), *Contemporary field research*, (pp. 335–352). Prospect Heights, IL: Waveland Press.

Chew, F., Palmer, S., & Kim, S. (1998). Testing the influencc of the health belief model and a television program on nutrition behavior. *Health Communication, 10,* 227–245.

Connell, C. L., Yadrick, M. K., & Hinton, A. (2001). Nutrient intakes of food insufficient adults who use food assistance programs in the southern region of the United States. *Journal of the American Dietetic Association, 101,* 9, A–78.

Contenta, S. (2009, Feb). Food bank use jumps as economy worsens. Retrieved May 29, 2009, from http://www.thestar.com/News/World/article/587649

Emerson, R. M., Fretz, R. I., & Shaw, L. (1995). *Writing ethnographic fieldnotes.* Chicago, IL: University of Chicago Press.

Fitzgerald, G. A., & Desjardins, N. M. (2004). Organizational values and their relation to organizational performance outcomes. *Atlantic Journal of Communication, 12,* 3, 121–145.

Feeding America (2009). Hunger and poverty statistics. Retrieved May 26, 2009, from http://feedingamerica.org/faces-of-hunger/hunger-101/hunger-and-poverty-statistics.aspx

Food Research and Action Center. (2008, Nov). Hunger and food insecurity in the United States. Retrieved May 22, 2009, from http://www.frac.org/html/hunger_in_the_us/hunger_index.html

Geertz, C. (1973). Thick description: Toward an interpretive theory of culture. In *The interpretation of cultures*, (pp. 3–30). New York: Basic Books.

Glaser, B. G., & Strauss, A. L. (1967). *The discovery of grounded theory: Strategies for qualitative research.* Chicago, IL: Aldine.

Hampl, J. S. (2004). Conflicts of interest and hyperbole: Nutrition in the media. *Journalism & Mass Communication Educator, 58,* 364–372.

Harrison, K. (2005). Is "fat-free" good for me? A panel study of television viewing and children's nutritional knowledge and reasoning. *Health Communication, 17,* 2, 117–132.

Henderson, J. J., & Baldasty, G. J. (2003). Race advertising, and prime time television. *Howard Journal of Communication, 14,* 2, 97–113.

Koch, K. (2000). *Hunger in America. CQ Researcher, 10,* 44, 1033–1056.

LeGreco, M. (2005, February). *Playing with our food: Consumption as communication in the constitution of culture.* Paper presented at the annual meeting of the Western States Communication Association, San Francisco, CA.

Lindlof, T. R., & Taylor, B. C. (2002). *Qualitative communication research methods* (2nd ed.). Thousand Oaks, CA: Sage.

Meister, M. (2001). Cultural feeding, good life science, and the TV Food Network. *Mass Communication and Society, 4,* 165–182.

Monsebraaten, L. (2009, April). Welfare cuts drive up food bank use, study confirms. Retrieved May 29, 2009, from http://www.thestar.com/News/Canada/article/626671

National Communication Association (NCA). (2004). News and notes: Grants. Spectra, 40(7), 12. (Available from the National Communication Association, 1765 N Street, NW, Washington, DC 20036.)

O'Reilly, C., Chatman, J., & Caldwell, D. (1991). People and organizational culture: A profile comparison approach to assessing person-organization fit. *Academy of Management Journal, 14,* 487–516.

Orr, K. (2009, April). Recession sparks increased demand at food banks. Retrieved May 29, 2009, from http://www.kpbs.org/news/2009/apr/22/recession-sparks-increased-demand-food-banks/

Rasnake, L. K., Laub, E., Lewis, M., & Linscheid, T. R. (2005). Children's nutritional judgments: Relations to eating attitudes and body image. *Health Communication, 18,* 3, 275–289.

Ritter, K. (2009, Jan.). Press Release: Extraordinary demand for food hits St. Mary's Food Bank Alliance. Retrieved May 29, 2009, from http://www.firstfoodbank.org/pressroom/DemandForFood011108.pdf

Schein, E. (1992). *Organizational culture and leadership* (2nd ed.). San Francisco, CA: Jossey-Bass.

Signorielli, N., & Lears, M. (1992). Television and children's conceptions of nutrition: Unhealthy messages. *Health Communication, 4,* 245–257.

Signorielli, N., & Staples, J. (1997). Television and children's conceptions of nutrition. *Health Communication, 9,* 289–301.

Starkey, L. J., Gray-Donald, K., & Kuhnlein, H. V. (1999). Nutrient intake of food bank users is related to frequency of food bank use, household size, smoking, education and country of birth. *Journal of Nutrition, 129,* 4, 883–889.

Strauss, A. & Corbin, J. (1998). *Basics of qualitative research: Grounded theory procedures and techniques.* Beverly Hills, CA: Sage.

Tarasuk, V., & Eakin, J. M. (2003). Charitable food assistance as symbolic gesture: An ethnographic study of food banks in Ontario. *Social Science & Medicine, 56,* 7, 1505–1515.

United States Department of Agriculture [USDA]. (2008). Food security in the United States: Key statistics and graphs. Retrieved May 26, 2009, from http://www.ers.usda.gov/Briefing/FoodSecurity/stats_graphs.htm

United States Department of Agriculture [USDA]. (2009a, March). Frequently asked questions: What food benefits do WIC participants receive? Retrieved May 22, 2009, from http://www.fns.usda.gov/wic/FAQs/FAQ.HTM

United States Department of Agriculture [USDA]. (2009b, May). Eligible food items list. Retrieved May 22, 2009, from http://www.fns.usda.gov/SNAP/retailers/pdfs/eligible_list.pdf

Verpy, H., Smith, C., & Reicks, M. (2003). Attitudes and behaviors of food donors and perceived needs and wants of food shelf clients. *Journal of Nutrition Education and Behaviors, 35,* 1, 6–15.

Wadsworth, T. L., & Fellers, R. B. (2001). Assessing the nutritive quality of food distributed from a food bank: Implications for nutrition education. *Journal of the American Dietetic Association, 101,* 9, A–78.

21

The corporate colonization of communication about global hunger: Development, biotechnology, and discursive closure in the Monsanto pledge

Ross Singer

Like other chapters in this section, this chapter highlights organizational themes of empowerment, constraint, hunger relief, and stakeholder participation. My specific contribution is a global and critical theory perspective from which food-related practices are seen primarily as an effect of corporate power. As I will show, among other places the story of the corporate takeover of the food supply can be found in corporate social responsibility (CSR) reporting, which over the past decade has become an institution in the United States agricultural industry and broader global economy. In what have become heated debates on the ethics of corporate science, particularly in the arena of biotechnological or genetically modified (GM) food (Rudy, Coppin, Konefal, Shaw, Eyck, Harris, & Busch, 2007), CSR reporting has allowed agricultural companies to "speak for themselves." More than arguments over a single moral issue, competing discourses of biotechnology surface deeper philosophical questions about the role of democracy in science and conversely, the role of science in democratic organizing against global hunger and poverty (Jasanoff, 2005). As a result, communication studies on the biotechnology debate confront complex and interconnected discourses of development, risk, and sustainability.

Although communication scholars have given significant attention to public perceptions, scientists' views, media coverage, and activist discourse on food biotechnology (e.g., Durham, 2005; Gamble & Kassardjian, 2008; Gunter, Kinderlerer, & Beyleveld, 1999; Henderson, 2005; Hornig-Priest, 1995; Motion

& Weaver, 2005; Munro & Schurman, 2007; Nisbet & Lewenstein, 2002; Schurman, 2004), there is comparatively little work on how pro-biotechnology groups have been able to institutionalize their point of view into regulatory policy. In particular, few studies examine how corporations and industry strategically negotiate the meaning of biotechnology (Henderson, Weaver, & Cheney, 2007; Kleinman & Kloppenburg, 1991; Sorj & Wilkinson, 1994). Following Henderson, Weaver, and Cheney (2007), this chapter contributes to an organizational communication perspective. I focus on corporate narratives of biotechnology and how their meaning promotes the formation of certain identities through an ideological understanding of the material experience of hunger.

Through a case analysis of Monsanto, the U.S.-based multinational firm currently holding sway over the global biotechnology market, this chapter advances a critical organizational perspective on CSR in the agricultural industry. The case of Monsanto, I propose, illuminates the utility of Deetz's (1992) corporate colonization theory for understanding the role of agricultural corporations in what Escobar (1995) calls today's myth of "professionalized development." This myth, which reflects an ideology of techno-scientific progress, envisions non-Western poor populations as potential consumers. Monsanto's corporate narrative of biotechnology appropriates Western ideological assumptions in a way that unethically suppresses inclusive stakeholder participation in the debate over biotechnology. As I will illuminate, close consideration of the company's narrative helps extend a currently limited scholarly understanding of how actual organizations engage in systematically distorted communication (Leonardi & Jackson, 2004; Lyon, 2007; Thackaberry, 2004).

Following a critical approach to CSR (Kuhn & Deetz, 2008), the intent of this chapter is to expose unarticulated assumptions and control mechanisms embedded within the underlying institutional order of Western agriculture. The goal is to create "discursive openings" (Thackaberry, 2004) for inclusion of stakeholder values in corporate and state decisions. Given that Monsanto is one of the world's most profitable corporations, its sheer size and growing influence invite a close reading of power in terms of a "discourse of suspicion" sensitive to "interest-driven discursive strategies that lurk beneath ostensibly consensual meaning systems" (Mumby, 2004, p. 237). Despite decades of activist scrutiny, the current exacerbation of a world food crisis has only bolstered Monsanto's profitability, which is currently growing at a faster pace than ever before (Friends of the Earth, 2009). From 2005 to 2008, the firm's annual gross profit rose 111% to just under $6.2 billion, with 54% of net sales from North America. In the fiscal year of 2008, Monsanto invested more than $980 million in agricultural research and development—what it describes as "researching new tools for farmers." The majority of this research focuses on biotechnology traits, elite germplasm, breeding, new variety and hybrid development, and genomics (Monsanto, 2008). With an overview and rationale for this chapter in order, I will now foreground my analysis by situating Monsanto's biotechnology program within a global context of poverty and hunger.

Food Insecurity and Corporate Biotechnology

According to the Food and Agriculture Organization of the United Nations (2009) (FAO) the great irony of global hunger is that the majority of undernourished people live in rural regions. As a result, organizing local agricultural economies is central to managing this problem and achieving a minimum standard referred to by involved organizations as "food security." The FAO defines food security as a condition in which "all people, at all times, have physical, social and economic access to sufficient, safe and nutritious food that meets their dietary needs and food preferences for an active and healthy life" (p. 8). Davis, Thomas, and Amponsah (2001) suggest that through a series of stages tracing back to the early 1970s, food security theory and practice has given rise to public and private organizational efforts around three hubs: (1) direct "relief" development, (2) global transformations of legal and institutional frameworks in relation to increased food trade, and (3) research and development of biotechnological crops in the form of micro nutrient-dense staples. In this chapter, I focus primarily on the third hub, which is receiving increasing attention because of new recognition of the food supply as inherently connected to nutrition, environmental issues, cultural practices, education, and personal health (Davis et al., 2001). As I explain in detail below, biotechnology research and development has also become a popular topic of the questions it raises about the social responsibilities of private interests that fund it.

Although I will use the term "biotechnology" in this chapter, more precisely I am referring to agricultural genetic modification as a specific branch of the field of biotechnology. Genetic modification entails gene splicing through recombinant DNA technology. GM food combines traditional plant breeding with new methods of gene alteration. Proponents such as Monsanto (2009a) have claimed that GM crops increase food production and pest resistance, and in the near future will be used to improve drought defense and nutrient content. The World Health Organization (n.d.) (WHO) continues to support the use of GM seed to fight global hunger and poverty and has helped validate its use in development organizing. However, WHO discourse also reveals the contentious nature of the biotechnology issue. While the WHO confirms that "GM foods currently available on the international market have passed risk assessments," it also stresses the need for additional research into several possible latent and long-term risks of GM crops (p. 3). As I elaborate upon below, it is these risks that continue to stir controversy and criticism.

There are several major criticisms of agricultural biotechnology that together comprise what is commonly described as the "precautionary" perspective. One criticism, which has been put forth by ecologists and entomologists, is that the biology of GM crops and their toxins lead to earlier development of insect resistances as well as new and stronger resistances than found in non-biotechnological crops. That is, any attempt to control pests through such technology may actually increase pesticide use while worsening pest problems (Friends of the Earth, 2009; Gould, 1998; Jenkins, 1998; Sasu, Ferrari, Du, Winsor, & Stephenson, 2009). For farmers, this means continuously buying new, better, and more expensive "stacked trait" seed from companies such as Monsanto. Contributing to a critique along these lines, a longitudinal study by U.S. Department of Agriculture researchers Fernandez-Cornejo and Caswell (2006) suggests that while biotechnological traits can prevent crop yield loss from pests, biotechnology does not increase crop yield potential and may even decrease yields. Other researchers also focus on the question of who benefits from biotechnology. Cummings (2008) and Friends of the Earth International (2009) note that rather than being used for feeding the world's impoverished people, most biotechnological crops are used for animal feed, biofuels, or highly processed food in economically advantaged countries. This research underscores that hunger is fundamentally attributable to poverty, which is a political problem and not a technological one. Poverty is a product of the politics of food distribution, farmers' lack of credit and land, and declining governmental investment in agriculture. Another charge against biotechnology has been leveled by the Institute for Responsible Technology (2007). According to the Institute, biotechnological crops include biological properties that contain human allergens, which may result in illness upon consumption. A related investigation by Charman (2005) questions why U.S.-based corporations commercializing biotechnology conduct their own safety tests over tests potentially administered by the Food and Drug Administration. As past investigations by Schurman (2004) and Mendick and Sawer (2009) confirm, a majority of U.S. supermarket food has been manipulated using biotechnology but with few labels to indicate it. This makes for a starkly different situation than that found across a cadre of European countries that have largely pulled biotechnological food off the shelves of their grocery stores. Finally, recent studies by Cluis (2009) and the World Health Organization (n.d.) promote attention to potentially catastrophic effects of unintentional cross-pollination between biotechnological and non-biotechnological crops from field to field. While the most important potential effect is the loss of natural biodiversity, other implications for farmers include charges of corporate property rights infringement and contamination of the food supply with non-edible varieties of biotechnological crops. This issue has become more prominent in the wake of an actual and widely publicized instance of cross-pollination represented in the Canadian Supreme Court case *Monsanto v. Schmeiser* (Cluis, 2009).

To make proper sense of how critical voices have positioned Monsanto's narrative of biotechnology, it is necessary to place the issue within the broader history of the company. Long before the biotechnology debate, Monsanto came under fire for the environmental effects of the industrial coolant PCB. After enjoying a four-decade long monopoly on PCB sales, a 2002 court case turned up studies conducted in the 1960s revealing that the company knew about and concealed grave dangers of PCBs, as well as related company waste-dumping (Grunwald, 2002; Vidal, 2007). During this same period, Monsanto was a leading producer of dioxins. Dioxins in Agent Orange, a chemical airdropped to defoliate jungle cover during the Vietnam War, created a major controversy for Monsanto, one of the companies producing it. In 1984, after 291,000 American Vietnam veterans began reporting health problems ranging from infertility to cancer, Monsanto and several other companies completed a $180 million settlement (Beder, 1997; Steinglass, 2005). Despite the debacle with Agent Orange, today Monsanto continues to generate major profits from dioxin-containing products such as the herbicide Roundup. Although the company continues to receive criticism for dioxins, in the 1980s activists began turning their attention to Monsanto's early forays into biotechnology. Specifically, Monsanto was attacked for marketing the bovine growth hormone, also called bovine somatotropin (BST) or the product Posilac. The company touted this product as enhancing milk production and therefore fighting global hunger. However, recovered documents later revealed that Monsanto knew BST caused pain, infection, and suffering in milk-producing cattle. Additionally, Monsanto concealed its knowledge that the product led to the contamination of milk and promoted the formation of antibiotic resistant bacteria in animals and humans. Given that many governments were paying farmers subsidies to produce less milk because of overproduction, Monsanto's claim that it was fighting hunger also proved deceptive (Achbar & Simpson, 2004).

Although the negative publicity that such products generated for Monsanto affected its attempt to market biotechnological seed, aggressive public relations and lobbying helped the company's profits to continue to grow exponentially. Considering that 24 countries including the United States now allow farmers to grow biotechnological seed and grocery vendors to sell biotechnological food (Monsanto, 2009b), Monsanto's historical persistence has proven effective. Below, in an attempt to generate insight into some of the discursive conditions of possibility for this success, I probe how Monsanto has legitimized the development and commercialization of biotechnology during the past decade. To set up this analysis, I will first provide an overview of the theoretical framework used.

Theoretical Framework

The case study developed in this chapter takes a critical organizational discourse analysis (Mumby, 2004) perspective informed by Deetz's (1992) theory of corporate colonization. Grounded in philosophical contributions from Habermas and Foucault, among others, Deetz's (1992) theory explains changes in everyday communication generated by the homogenization of identities made possible by the modern capitalist organization. By the term "colonization," Deetz means the invasion and usurpation of individual and group meanings, as well as functions of traditional institutions such as religion, family, and community. Fundamental to corporate colonization theory are "discursive closure" practices exhibited by the modern corporation. These communicative techniques help (re)produce the appearance of consensus and the asymmetrical distribution of benefits across stakeholder groups. As "rather quiet, repetitive micropractices, done for innumerable reasons, which function to maintain normalized, conflict-free experience and social relations," discursive closing practices "close off" discussion and critical self-reflection (p. 189). The phrase "done for innumerable reasons" is important because it suggests that deception may be strategically manipulative or unknowingly accomplished. Drawing from Habermas, Deetz recognizes that there is no guarantee that organizational actors or their stakeholders will recognize ideological communication pathologies steering their practices. As such, the intentional and unintentional practices of multiple parties contribute to systematic distortions manifesting in taken-for-granted organizational discourses and routines.

According to Deetz's theory, distorted systems are often dominated by "discourses of managerialism" (p. 221). Managerialism is an institutionalized "discursive genre" with real structures of rewards as well as "a set of discursive moves that interpellates a particular type of subject and produces a particular world." Under managerialism, the primary mode of everyday reasoning becomes "cognitive-instrumental"—based on value-standards such as efficiency, predictability, and complete control. The "favored expressive modality is money; and its favored site of reproduction is the *formal* organization" (pp. 222–223, emphasis in original). Importantly, Deetz postulates that the modern corporate form does not require managerialism and could be based on other, more democratic models of thought and decision making.

Deetz (1992) identifies several commonly used discursive closing practices that conceal the production of identities and often support managerialist ends. Deetz attempts not to derive a comprehensive list of practices, but rather to address some particularly common ones. For the purpose of this chapter, the following discursive closing practices that Deetz discusses prove instructive: *naturalization*, *legitimation*, and *disqualification.* Naturalization refers to communication about a socially produced phenomenon as if it were "given in nature." This process turns social configurations of meaning into transparently observable, fixed, trans-historical, and external facts. Legitimation, Deetz states, "appears in the rationalization of decisions and practices through the invocation of higher order explanatory devices" such as cultural myth. Myths allow for transcending conflict and glossing over contradictions. Disqualification refers to a clear "determination of who has the right to have a genuine say" on a given topic (p. 189) based on professional qualification, expertise, and specialization. With this overview in place, I now turn to Monsanto's corporate narrative on biotechnology and how Deetz's theory informs a critique of its ideological functions.

Discursive Closure in Monsanto's CSR Reporting

Understanding the role of Monsanto's Pledge in the company's CSR reporting is the first step in coming to terms with how Monsanto's narrative of biotechnology configures its relationship with stakeholders. Presented at the beginning of the company's CSR reports, the Pledge provides the guiding vocabulary and moral vision for each document. Monsanto's reports explicitly attempt to illustrate how the Pledge translates into programs, policies, goals, and a positive corporate culture. As the 2005 report summarizes, "The Pledge values apply to all of our work at Monsanto" (p. 34). In the 2001–2 report, Monsanto explains,

> The Monsanto Pledge was announced two years ago. It was based on interviews with hundreds of stakeholders…Their feedback helped us to better understand public expectations and suggested to us what corporate social responsibility might look like for a company solely focused on leading-edge agriculture. (Monsanto, 2003, p. 3)

The report elaborates, "The Pledge represents our stake-in-the-ground. It shows what we stand for as a company" in a list of eight core commitments: Dialogue, Transparency, Sharing, Benefits, Respect, Act as Owners to Achieve Results, Create a Great Place to Work, and Integrity. Dialogue refers to listening carefully to diverse stakeholders. Transparency means ensuring that information is available and understandable. On Sharing, the company states, "We will share knowledge and technology to advance scientific understanding, to improve agriculture and the environment, to improve crops, and to help farmers in developing countries." The company's commitment to Benefits is a promise to deliver high-quality products. Respect means sensitivity toward "religious, cultural, and ethical concerns of people throughout the world," as well as the safety of employees, customers, consumers, and the environment. Act as Owners to Achieve Results suggests that Monsanto will pursue a clear direction in a socially accountable manner. Create a Great Place to Work refers to supporting diverse people and thought, as well as innovation, learning, teamwork, and recognition among employees (Monsanto, 2003, pp. 1–2). Finally, Monsanto deems Integrity "the foundation for all that we do" and consists of "honesty, decency, consistency, and courage" (Monsanto, 2009b, p. 4).

Monsanto's 2001–2 report, like the company's other CSR reports, states that in addition to demonstrating practices by which the company is carrying out its Pledge, the reports would place significant emphasis on controversies, dilemmas, and feedback from stakeholders pertaining to the company's products. A letter from Chief Executive Officer Hugh Grant, a regular feature in the reports, reads, "Stakeholders candidly told us that, while they liked reading about the good things we were doing, they also know some controversies still surround our products and that we should discuss those too" (Monsanto, 2003, pp. 3–4). In this discourse, Monsanto clarifies that its CSR reporting is driven by an interest in advancing dialogue with stakeholders. In the close textual reading that follows, my purpose is to explicate and assess the degree to which the company reports actually engage in socially responsible communication. Guided by an interest in how Monsanto has narrated corporate social responsibility and issues of power in relation to biotechnology over time, I examined every CSR report that has been released by the company as of mid-2009. These reports span approximately a decade, with the first report (2001–2) and the most recent report (2008–9) covering biennial periods, and all others appearing annually. Although I initially approached the text with the critical scholar's general interest in power, I considered Deetz's (1992) theory among several possible frameworks after first synthesizing and reconstructing Monsanto's narrative. I present this narrative here using Deetz's concepts of legitimation, naturalization, and disqualification to organize and explain its implications for inclusive stakeholder participation in the debate over biotechnology.

Legitimizing/Universalizing corporate interests

Appeals to higher-order explanations, or techniques of legitimacy, undergird how Monsanto rationalizes its commitment to CSR in the realm of global hunger. Both the 2004 and 2006 reports open with two-page spreads asserting global food needs as the company's top commitment. The former features a section heading that reads, "Meeting the World's Food Needs Sustainability" and in large font draws attention to "800 million people" in Asia and Africa "who remain chronically undernourished." The text elaborates, "As the global population grows, the challenge to feed the increasing numbers becomes more difficult." Monsanto also suggests that increasing the amount of crop production per acre is the *only* option but that currently "productivity is being held back by the realities of soil degradation, insufficient fresh water, biological competition, and limited quantities of arable land" (Monsanto, 2004, pp. i–2). Likewise, the 2006 report states, "Despite advances over the past century, many people cannot earn enough money to purchase food, and they do not have the resources to grow enough food of their families" (Monsanto, 2006, p. 4). Similar statements can be found across every CSR report examined. The company positions its corporate science mission as driven by two intertwined and universal crises of our time: population growth and environmental degradation.

Although a general connection has been established between population growth and environmental degradation, Monsanto's claim at the specific level that a sole commitment to increasing crop yields will solve both crises remains highly contentious. From the perspective of Deetz's (1992) theory, evidence of distortion appears not in what is present in Monsanto's easily understood narrative of crisis, but in what is missing. Among alternative knowledge claims precluded by Monsanto's reports through discursive closure, perhaps foremost is that as shown by over two decades of scholarship, the rate of world food production growth continues to outpace the rate of population growth (Holt-Giménez, 2008; U.S. Working Group, 2009). Monsanto's avoidance of this claim highlights that the discourse of professionalized development depends on highly reductive and unstable attempts to convert the political problems of population growth and global poverty into issues of scientific and economic growth (Escobar, 1995). Monsanto (2007) continuously appeals to the "growth of modern agricultural practices and crops that generate ever-increasing yields" and statements such as "Farm income increased by $5 billion in 2005" (pp. i, 41). However, these assertions distort the actual historical effects of increased crop volume. Alternative knowledge claims suggest that current policies encouraging corporate consolidation, overproduction of food, and the global sale of food below the cost of production exacerbate poverty and hunger. Increased production under agricultural modernization has forced farmers to operate larger farms, but this has made them worse off financially, ultimately reducing the number of full-time farms (Knight, 2006; U.S. Working Group, 2009). This effect is only one component of what Colander (1998) describes as the "good/bad paradox" of economics generated by Westernized farming. From this view, past success in finding ways to grow more crops per acre is therefore the very condition upon which expansion of acres and corporate power have become imperatives.

Success Stories

Success stories manifesting a Western agricultural myth of success serve as another device through which Monsanto practices legitimation. These stories celebrate emancipation in developing countries in the form of corporate agri-science and an individualist ethic of entrepreneurialism. Foregrounding selected stories, Monsanto (2006) depicts its goal as "poverty alleviation/food-self-sufficiency" (p. 5) and suggests that biotechnology can "help farmers meet challenges and manage risks so that they can achieve self-sufficiency and even prosperity" (Monsanto 2007, p. 6). Across an array of success stories featured in the reports, Monsanto describes the company's fight against global hunger through descriptions of its philanthropic wing—the Monsanto Fund—and its participation in global development programs. Reports describe these programs through the lens of the basic Pledge commitments. For example, in one report, Monsanto tells its readers,

> In developing countries, as part of our Pledge sharing commitment, a dedicated team of Monsanto employees reviews the humanitarian needs of resource-poor farmers and looks for ways that we can help, either through granting access to our patents, sharing our technologies, or working with local people and organizations to enable them to improve their crop yields. This sharing is our long-term interest since once they become successful, these same farmers may become satisfied customers. (Monsanto, 2003, p. 18)

In this statement, a layer of ambiguity obscures possible details on exactly what is meant by "sharing our technologies" or how impoverished farmers would be able to afford the high price of the company's seed.

Even across rather elaborate descriptions of success stories, ambiguity contributes to discursive closure. To illustrate, the 2001–2 report describes the Monsanto Humsafar Program—"humsafar" meaning "companion on an eternal journey"—organized in India's largest corn-growing region. Monsanto explains that although the region historically "has abysmally low yields," its Humsafar Program, which was started just two years earlier, is making a difference. In April 2001, 12 Humsafar personnel began an experiment with 14 villages. These personnel—all "university experts"—stayed in the villages and "trained the chosen 700 farmers to use correct farm practices." In addition to doubling corn yields through introduction of hybrid seed, weed control, and other techniques, "Humsafar partners worked to make sure middlemen didn't squeeze out their usual hefty margins. Group buying power was established" (Monsanto, 2003, p. 17). These excerpts define the program as a living example of CSR in the fight against poverty and hunger, reminding readers that "it all begins with better seed" (2006, p. 9). By exclusively emphasizing increases in crop production and the estimated number of beneficiaries, these stories work to transcend criticisms of the Western colonization of culture and questions about the future implications of biotechnology. Indeed, such programs implicitly place farmers in "underdeveloped" countries on the same path of Western farmers who adopted hybrid seed decades ago before shifting to biotechnology.

Naturalization

Marketing as human generosity. At a deeper level, Monsanto's appeal to global hunger takes the form of a device of legitimation grounded upon other naturalized discourses of certain causes, constraints, and solutions. The reports represent population growth and environmental degradation as part of an objective, external, and unavoidable reality encompassing the problem of global hunger. Monsanto describes this reality as consisting of urgent threat and opportunity that can only be managed through technology. In Monsanto's CSR reports, discursive structuring through naturalization manifests through the notion that the marketing of technology and professionalization of development is made possible by human generosity in the form of technological sharing. To illustrate, the 2004 CSR report, which announces food security as one of its top priorities, features a column by Robert B. Horsh, Ph.D., titled "Why We Share." Horsh writes,

> It is a natural human value to want to share with others—to touch them in ways that make a positive difference in their lives. It is a privilege to be in a position to share—to have the resources, time, and expertise. (Monsanto, 2004, p. 9)

In Horsh's statement, sharing becomes a universal standard of moral judgment and a natural part of what it means to be human. Horsh's words, however, conflate and hide additional, potentially conflicting motives behind Monsanto's discourse on global hunger and sustainability. Monsanto's continuous reaffirmation of the value of generosity in its biotechnology narrative results in the misleading appearance of a consensus on the solution to global hunger. In this way, naturalization helps the CSR reports de-politicize Monsanto's interests and downplay its dominance.

Biotechnology as a tool. Across the CSR reports, Monsanto naturalizes biotechnology as an "agricultural tool." This label portrays biotechnology as external, transparent, and real, rather than discursively produced and manifesting unknown effects. The company features ambiguous statements about agricultural tools that when situated in the larger text, specifically allude to biotechnology. A statement in enlarged text atop one of the opening pages of the 2006 report is an example: "We, at Monsanto, are in unique position to help growers increase food production with modern agricultural tools." The report adds, "We are working to deliver the benefits of these tools to Africa…which has great potential to reduce poverty and become self-sufficient in agriculture" (Monsanto, 2006, p. 5). Only a few pages later, after describing several development programs and partnerships in Africa involving the dissemination of hybrid seed, a section titled "Beyond Hybrids" explains that Monsanto is conducting several biotechnological "field trials" in Africa. Monsanto adds that partnerships will be needed to ensure that African nations are able "to keep pace with improved trait crops in the next decade." The report notes current technical obstacles and elaborates on Monsanto's desire to foster a natural progression from traditional hybrid seed to biotechnological crops in developing regions. This discourse is significant because it shows how naturalization of biotechnology may elide differences between various forms of agri-science to distort risks and render genetic modification as just another agricultural tool.

In descriptions of biotechnology as tool, naturalization also makes possible the appearance of a shift in the locus of socio-political agency from corporate actors to disadvantaged farmers and local-level interests. A 2004 report statement on "Reaching the Poor" by Ruth Oniang'o, Ph.D., founder of the Rural Outreach Program in Nairobi illustrates this technique: "**Food security is not just a matter of better food distribution, but rather a factor of giving people the tools to better feed themselves.** Biotechnology is but one of the tools available" (p. 11, bold in original). In iterations like this one, the farmer is in full control of his or her destiny. The naturalized assumptions are that humans are entitled to and able to dominate nature, and that technology is a primary means of human autonomy. In Monsanto's reports, these assumptions are especially prevalent in the annual feature of "issue discussion" sections on controversial topics such as corporate control of the seed supply. In its 2005 report, Monsanto responds to its critics on this topic by asserting, "Farmers have a choice about whether to buy Monsanto seed," adding, "Given the chance to grow biotech crops, many farmers choose to…not because they lack alternatives, but because they recognize value" (Monsanto, 2005, p. 28). Here, discursive closure is a function of Monsanto again downplaying its own dominance. Similar renderings of agency appear in Monsanto's description of its involvement in public-private development program partnerships. The 2006 report reads, "Monsanto is just one player among many whose contributions and talents will be needed…we create synergy out of the pieces that each party brings to the table" (p. 9). One ethical problem with these statements is that they latently promote naturalization through what Deetz (1992) dubs "misrecognition of self-determination" in which managerial discourse positions the individual as rational, unified, and transparent. Positioning farmers and other stakeholders as rational allows for suggesting that they are openly subordinating themselves to the social contract of the corporation to reap the advantages of "having choices based on self-interest" (p. 292). The locus of misrecognition in this particular naturalizing discourse is the point of definition at which Monsanto fails to distinguish between agrarian independence and Western capitalistic individualism. As underscored earlier in the chapter, the latter has only fostered farmers' subordination to corporate paternalism.

Genetic reengineering as organic evolution. Another way that Monsanto contributes to discursive closure on biotechnology is its positioning of this social experiment in genetic science as if it were part of the earth's natural biological system. Across its reports, Monsanto discusses the issue of "adventitious presence"—unintentional trait formation in (often non-GM) seed, grain, or feed, and food products. In the 2001–2 report, Monsanto states, "natural biological factors such as dissemination of pollen and seeds, as well as mechanical mixing of seeds and grain and human error can all play a role in adventitious presence." Here, adventitious presence—a consequence that critics warn may result in the contamination of edible crops with non-edible varieties—is reinterpreted as trans-historical, normal, and transparently observable across the biological whole of the agricultural ecology. The same report reads, "Regardless of production system—conventional, organic, or biotech—the practical nature of a dynamic biological system demonstrates that '100 percent purity' is not, and never has been feasible in production agriculture" (p. 12). This excerpt reiterates that unintentional breeding between biotechnological crops with non-biotechnological crops is synonymous with everyday biological processes organically evolving in earth's ecological system.

A section in one report titled "Grower's Perspective: Adventitious Presence is Part of the Natural Order" captures the role of careful discursive definition in the naturalization of biotechnology:

> Many natural systems make up 'the system' that makes up our world…The system has always challenged the human mind. We think, dream, and explore within it. Many new ideas, experiments, and technologies, have been accommodated by the system. It has accepted, many times over, the interaction and integration of technologies. 'What was' often turns into 'the improved.' (Monsanto, 2003, p. 13)

The section leverages this imagery toward strategic issue management by adding: "Current concern about adventitious presence is a result of new technologies…Adventitious presence has always been part of the natural order…The natural systems air, wind, water, soil, and the mobility of living things support continuous mixing and alternation" (Monsanto, 2003, p. 13). Monsanto's use of the term "concern" in this discourse—which replaces more formidable and conflict-laden terms such as "counterargument"—is consistent with other reports' discourse on controversy surrounding biotechnology. An illustration of how this word choice naturalizes biotechnology appears in the 2005 report, which states, "Some people have voiced concerns about whether pollen from biotech crops might be picked up by non-biotech varieties on neighboring fields and affect the marketability of those crops." Monsanto then attempts to resolve the issue by appealing to an already-existing consensus:

> The good news is that practical experience clearly demonstrates that the coexistence of biotech, conventional, and organic systems is not only possible, but is peacefully occurring around the world where farmers have a choice among different production methods. (Monsanto, 2005, p. 30)

By suppressing conflict through such statements, Monsanto universalizes its claims about biotechnology as a corrective to problems of global hunger and sustainability. Positioning biotechnology as natural and harmonious subverts valid public concerns about risks that cannot be known, even through modern science.

Disqualification

Producing corporate expertise. As theorized by Deetz (1992), disqualification assists in the reproduction of a distorted presumption that decision making participants enjoy equal opportunity to select and employ different speech acts, and have access to various forums. I turn now to three key devices through which Monsanto's CSR discourse on global hunger proposes who has the right to a genuine say: expert testimonials, fear appeals, and self-aggrandizement.

Through its reports, Monsanto publicly circulates statements such as, "We listen to our customers and other stakeholders to understand their needs and expectations" (2009b, p. 33). These announcements stage the appearance of open discussion and equitable distribution of benefits. However, as underscored below, when examined in relation to the larger text and its ideological assumptions, these announcements exclude stakeholders who would define problems and solutions to global hunger differently. In this way, CSR reporting defines whose voices are credible and what stakeholder claims are worthwhile.

One way Monsanto practices disqualification in its corporate narrative of biotechnology is by exclusively appealing to expert voices supporting biotechnology. Monsanto's discourse of corporate expertise emphasizes perspectives, experiences, and elite credentials of selected supporters such as those on its "Biotech Advisory Council," and depicts critics as misinformed and fearful. For example, the 2005 report notes that in 1999 "some stakeholders expressed fears" that Monsanto's development of "sterile" seed technology might lead to corporate dependence among smallholder farmers. Monsanto developed the seed, which was labeled by critics as "terminator technology," to prevent farmers from saving Monsanto's patented seed from the previous year's crop for the next year. Some varieties would render sterile seeds generated from a crop or in other cases by deactivating only the biotechnological traits. In the 2005 report, Monsanto notes that as a result of stakeholder fear, it decided not to pursue commercialization, but that its experts constantly reevaluate that stance. The company adds that given the possible benefits, "the responsible approach" is to evaluate "appropriate applications." The report goes on, "To that end, Monsanto is engaged in dialogue with experts and interested parties to learn what technological applications might be available" (Monsanto, 2005, p. 29). These excerpts stress the commitment to dialogue in Monsanto's Pledge commitment, but through two acts of disqualification violate this commitment as well as the commitment to mutual respect. First, critics are rendered fearful and as subordinate to Monsanto, which is linked to expertise and responsible action. Second, this hierarchy seems to discredit critics and eliminate them from future discussion. Monsanto's reference to ongoing engagement appeals only to "experts" and "interested parties," which are presumably those stakeholders *supporting* commercialization of sterile seed through "appropriate applications."

Expert testimonials on biotechnology offer evidence of a more aggressive variation of the practice of creating the appearance of socially responsible corporate science in the face of misguided criticism. An excerpt from the 2004 report asserts, "this issue is dogged by misinformation and fear, which tends to camouflage the options that are available to address the whole issue of food insecurity" (Monsanto, 2004, p. 11). In a similar statement found in the 2006 report, Kinyua M'Mbijjewe, Monsanto's African public and government affairs representative, reports that there is "still some fear of the unknown where misinformation about biotech crops exists," but "the more farmers see what the tools of modern agriculture can do for them…the more they want them" (Monsanto, 2006, p. 9). These excerpts position critics as fearful and in need of an expert point of view. These statements go further than the previous examples offered, however, by dismissing critics outright. The suggestion is that it is biotechnology's critics that promulgate systematic distortion about its potential role in resolving problems of global hunger and sustainability.

Further evidence of Monsanto's reports accusing critics as a group of enabling systematic distortion appears across other reports' expert testimonials. In the 2005 report, Robert Paarlberg, professor of political science and government, interjects, "In open meetings on biotechnology policy at which Monsanto scientists came under sharp attack from hostile and poorly informed critics, I was impressed by the tolerant, calm, and nonjudgmental manner used…in responding to their critics" (Monsanto, 2005, p. 33). Paarlberg's full testimony suggests that even before the Pledge was created, the company displayed a commitment to transparency, dialogue, and respect. Not unlike the quotations provided above, this statement juxtaposes the responsible and rational corporation against an irrational opposition. From an alternative view, the "us" versus "them" moral binary found in this discourse helps rationalize disqualification while inviting stakeholder consent to biotechnology. Producing corporate expertise in this way results in an ethical contradiction in which Monsanto practices discursive closure in the name of open dialogue and mutual respect. As detailed below, the company's use of its *own* fear appeals as well as self-aggrandizement contribute to this contradiction.

Inspiring fear. Even though Monsanto disqualifies critics of biotechnology as fearful and irrational, the reports themselves use fear to deflect and suppress alternative viewpoints. Fear appeals appear most prominently in Monsanto's description of the need for increased farm production to counter population growth. Monsanto (2004) opens one report with a two-page heading that reads, "Meeting the World's **Food Needs** Sustainability" (bold in original, pp. i–1). The report discusses key societal exigencies the company plans to address with its products. In this discussion, fear manifests in the articulation of an ultimatum:

> It has been predicted that if ways aren't found to grow more per acre, over the next 50 years a third of all remaining natural tropical and temperate ecosystems could be lost to clearing for farming purposes. Such forest loss and fragmentation of natural habit would severely affect global biodiversity. (Monsanto, 2004, p. 2)

Extending this discourse, a later Monsanto report warns that there may be an extremely negative future in store should solutions in the form of agricultural technology not be identified and adopted. Monsanto proposes that if mankind is to escape what is widely known as the "Malthusian nightmare" of population growth outpacing the food supply, a technological vision of "sustainable yield" is required:

> Although the challenge is daunting, it is not new. More than 200 years ago, the Rev. Thomas Malthus wrote that the power of populations is greater than the power in the earth to produce subsistence for man. Since his time, numerous people have argued that population growth would increase the demand for food faster than agricultural production could keep pace. (Monsanto, 2009b, p. 8)

Monsanto elaborates, "so far, they have been wrong," but even with the "great hope" that technology provides, "our success is by no means guaranteed." A key reason for this, according to Monsanto, is that "some people oppose…technological advances that have allowed the world to maintain a readily available and reasonably affordable food supply." In this statement, society is left with few options for survival and biotechnology is one of them. Monsanto's conclusion that "[t]he facts are simple and sobering" leaves little room for alternative knowledge claims about the problems undergirding global hunger and the possible solutions (Monsanto, 2009b, p. 8).

Self-aggrandizement. As another device of disqualification, self-aggrandizement works in close conjunction with the inducement of fear insofar as it relies on the perceived need for an ultimate technological solution. This device resonates with Deetz's (1992) conjecture that it is the self-producing, self-referential nature of much of today's corporate discourse that generates systematic distortion in the name of enhanced rationality. In Monsanto's CSR reporting, self-aggrandizement is the means by which the company evokes a problem-solution narrative structure. Self-aggrandizement allows Monsanto to propose a technological solution—sustainable yield—to the fundamental problems that *the company* defines as underlying global hunger. Monsanto (2004) repetitiously asserts that it is "in a unique position to help overcome many of the obstacles of sustainability" (p. 4). In addition to noting its current elite industry position, the company boasts of its pioneering past: "Over the years, Monsanto has provided products…which have favorable environmental characteristics, and crops improved through biotechnology that help farmers increase yields and reduce impacts on farmland." The company adds, "Monsanto is now a leader in the sciences of genomics and genetic modification" (p. 4). Other statements proudly appeal to the company's history and the vast beneficiaries it has served over time: "Beginning in the early 1980s, we believed that biological solutions were the future for agriculture. They would meet the world's growing food needs." Monsanto then announces, "After nine years of commercial experience, 7 million growers now use biotech products on more than 150 million acres in 18 countries worldwide" (p. i). Through statements like these, Monsanto elevates its own solutions to the scale of the world's grandest problems and proactively sets its own standards, expectations, and assumptions about sustainable agriculture. Hence, in this discourse, the disqualifying function of self-aggrandizement precludes discussion on the added burden that corporate biotechnology brought to the environment, the agro-food industry, diverse stakeholders, and the company itself.

Discussion

From a theoretical perspective, this critical analysis of Monsanto's CSR reporting re-positions agricultural biotechnology as an articulation of a corporate system of meaning that colonizes identities and distorts the material experience of global hunger. In this way, the chapter demonstrates the promise of a critical organizational communication perspective for identifying and contesting how agri-science companies narrate the commercialization of biotechnology as symbolic of their commitment to CSR in the fight against global hunger. The narrative constructed through a close reading of official corporate texts highlights the instability of today's Western agricultural myth of development celebrating individual progress and scientific consensus. The case of Monsanto suggests that CSR reporting functions as an ideological vehicle for continuously re-adapting this myth, re-securing stakeholders in a subordinate position, and closing the debate over biotechnology. Although Monsanto addresses stakeholders, especially disadvantaged farmers and undernourished people, through a narrative of self-determination and local empowerment, this narrative's managerial assumption of a consensus on cultural values paradoxically blocks inclusive stakeholder participation. Monsanto contributes to the professionalization of development and the colonization of identity in a way that reproduces what Escobar (1995) describes as a "politics of poverty." The aims of such a politics are "not only to create consumers but to transform society by turning the poor into objects of knowledge and management" for the purpose of optimizing life (p. 22). This does not mean that the poor are trapped, but rather that as Deetz (1992) explains, the discourse of managerial ideology reserves a role for everyone.

Several practical insights derived in this chapter deserve attention as well. First, although Monsanto has the legal right to market its biotechnological seed and other products, this right should only be as stable as the company's ability to ethically defend the product's moral and pragmatic legitimacy in open public forums. As I have shown, the company's discourse on biotechnology as a solution to problems of global hunger and development is deceptive. Yet at the same time Monsanto itself must be recognized as part of a historically and ideologically reproduced system of distorted norms in which corporate science and public-private development partnerships become post-political institutions of free market discourse. Hence, because a preventive, precautious, and system-wide understanding of the failed regulation of corporate agri-science is necessary, it would be remiss to place exclusive blame on Monsanto. In the project of producing democratic accountability, I argue that communication research can help policymakers and activists ethically contest the ways in which corporations—as well as their proxies—uphold unethical norms. Second, as the corporate sale of seed and food constituted through biotechnology continues to expand, at a very minimum, corporations such as Monsanto should show how their local programs promote real accountability for possible risks and the livelihoods of undernourished and poor communities. Third, activists, policymakers, and non-profit organizations might use studies such as this one not only to enhance their argumentation strategies in public discussion, but also to carve out new discursive openings for an alternative agricultural system. Recent survey research on farming strategies successfully used to fight hunger and foster environmental sustainability across a host of developing countries lists use of "locally appropriate seed" as only one of several strategies actually in use. Examples of other strategies include intensifying a single component of a farm operation or enhancing farm diversity by introducing a new component such as fish ponds or dairy cattle. Other farmers are using natural resources more carefully through techniques such as water harvesting and irrigation scheduling (Pretty, Morison, & Hine, 2005). Indeed, the promotion of such alternatives will be of utmost importance if agricultural institutions are to enable rather than constrain the formation of a pluralistic, decolonizing, and hunger-free society.

References

Achbar, M., & Simpson, B. (Producers). (2004). *The corporation* [Motion picture]. Canada: Zeitgeist Video.

Beder, S. (1997). *Global spin: The corporate assault on environmentalism.* Totnes, UK: Green Books Ltd.

Charman, K. (2005). Genetically modified food has great potential for harm. In S. A. Kallen (Ed.), *Food safety* (pp. 41–51). Detroit: Greenhaven.

Cluis, C. (2009). Rounding up the Schmeiser case: Benefit and liability issues of transgenic crops. *The Science Creative Quarterly*, *4*. Retrieved October 3, 2009, from http://www.scq.ubc.ca/rounding-up-the-schmeiser-case-benefit-and-liability-issues-of-transgenic-crops/

Colander, D. C. (1998). *Economics* (3rd ed.). Boston: Irwin McGraw-Hill.

Cummings, C. H. (2008). *Uncertain peril: Genetic engineering and the future of seeds.* Boston, MA: Beacon Press.

Davis, C. G., Thomas, C. Y., & Amponsah, W. A. (2001). Globalization and poverty: Lessons from the theory and practice of food security. *American Journal of Agricultural Economics*, *83*, 714–721.

Deetz, S. (1992). *Democracy in an age of corporate colonization: Developments in communication and the politics of everyday life.* Albany: State University of New York Press.

Durham, F. (2005). Public relations as structuration: A prescriptive critique of the StarLink global food contamination case. *Journal of Public Relations Research, 17*, 29–47.

Escobar, A. (1995). *Encountering development: The making and unmaking of the Third World.* Princeton, NJ: Princeton University Press.

Fernandez-Cornejo, J., & Caswell, M. (2006, April). *The first decade of genetically engineered crops in the United States.* Economic Information Bulletin Number 11, Economic Research Service, the U.S. Department of Agriculture. Retrieved September 23, 2007, from http://www.ers.usda.gov /publications/eib11/eib11.pdf

Food and Agriculture Organization of the United Nations. (2009). *The state of food insecurity in the world: Economic crises—impacts and lessons learned.* Retrieved October 3, 2009, from http://www.fao.org/ publications/en/

Friends of the Earth International. (2009, February). *Who benefits from GM crops? Feeding the biotech giants, not the world's poor.* Retrieved May 1, 2009, from http://www.foei.org/en/media/archive/2009/ gm-crops-feed-biotech-giants-only

Gamble, J., & Kassardjian, E. (2008). The use of selected community groups to elicit and understand the values underlying attitudes towards biotechnology. *Public Understanding of Science, 17*, 245–259.

Gould, F. (1998). Evolutionary biology and genetically engineered crops. *BioScience, 38*, 26–33.

Grunwald, M. (2002, January 1). Monsanto hid decades of pollution: PCBs drenched Ala. Town, but no one was ever told. *Washington Post.* Retrieved May 1, 2009, from http:// www.lexisnexis.com/universe

Gunter, B., Kinderlerer, J., & Beyleveld, D. (1999). The media and public understanding of biotechnology: A survey of scientists and journalists. *Science Communication, 20*, 373–394.

Henderson, A. (2005). Activism in "paradise": Identity management in a public relations campaign against genetic engineering. *Journal of Public Relations Research, 17*, 117–137.

Henderson, A., Weaver, C. K., & Cheney, G. (2007). Talking 'facts': Identity and rationality in industry perspectives on genetic modification. *Discourse Studies, 9*, 9–41.

Holt-Giménez, E. (2008, October). *The world food crisis: What's behind it and what we can do about it.* Food First: Institute for Food and Development Policy, Policy Brief no. 16, October 2008, 2–3, Retrieved June 20, 2009, from http://usfoodcrisisgroup.org/files/ food_crisis_policy_brief.pdf.

Hornig-Priest, S. (1995). Information equity, public understanding of science, and the biotechnology debate. *Journal of Communication, 45*, 39–55.

Institute for Responsible Technology. (2007, May). *Genetic engineering foods may cause rising food allergies.* Retrieved May 1, 2009, from http://www.organicconsumers.org/articles/ article_5296.cfm

Jasanoff, S. (2005). *Designs on nature: Science and democracy in Europe and the United States.* Princeton, NJ: Princeton University Press.

Jenkins, R. (1998). BT in the hot seat. *Seedling, 15*, 13–21.

Kleinman, D. L., & Kloppenburg, J., Jr. (1991). Aiming for the discursive high ground: Monsanto and the biotechnology controversy. *Sociological Forum, 6*, 427–447.

Knight, A.J. (2006). Supersizing farms: The McDonaldization of agriculture. In G. Ritzer (Ed.), *McDonaldization: The reader* (pp. 183–195). Thousand Oaks, CA: Pine Forge Press.

Kuhn, T., & Deetz, S. (2008). Critical theory and corporate social responsibility: Can/should we get beyond cynical reasoning? In A. Crane, A. McWilliams, D. Matten, J. Moon, & D.S. Siegel (Eds.), *The Oxford handbook of corporate social responsibility* (pp. 173–196). New York: Oxford University Press.

Leonardi, P. M., & Jackson, M. H. (2004). Technological determinism and discursive closure in organizational mergers. *Journal of Organizational Change Management*, *17*, 615–631.

Lyon, A. (2007). "Putting patients first": Systematically distorted communication and Merck's marketing of Vioxx. *Journal of Applied Communication Research*, *35*, 376–398.

Mendick, R., & Sawer, P. (2009, October 18). Britain will starve without GM crops, says major report. *The Daily Telegraph*. Retrieved October 25, 2009, from http://www.telegraph.co.uk/

Monsanto. (2003). *Commitments to our stakeholders: 2001–2002 Monsanto pledge report*. Retrieved October 2, 2008, from http://www.monsanto.com/pdf/pubs/2002/2001–2002PledgeReport.pdf

Monsanto. (2004). *Growing options: Monsanto company 2004 pledge report*. Retrieved October 6, 2005, from http://www.monsanto.com/monsanto/layout/our_pledge/default.asp

Monsanto. (2005). *Seeding values: Monsanto 2005 pledge report*. Retrieved October 2, 2008, from http://www.monsanto.com/pdf/pubs/2005/fullfilling_the_pledge.pdf

Monsanto. (2006). *The sum of our commitments: '06 pledge report*. Retrieved October 2, 2008, from http://www.monsanto.es/files/pledge_report.pdf

Monsanto. (2007). *Growth for a better world: 2007 pledge report*. Retrieved October 2, 2008, from http://www.monsanto.com/responsibility/our_pledge.asp

Monsanto. (2008). *Monsanto 2008 annual report*. Retrieved August 4, 2009, from http://www.monsanto.com/investors/financial_reports/annual_report/2008/default.asp

Monsanto. (2009a). *Conversations about biotechnology: Glossary*. Retrieved October 12, 2009, from http://www.monsanto.com/biotech-gmo/asp/glossary.asp

Monsanto. (2009b). *Grown for the future: Monsanto company 2008–2009 corporate social responsibility report*. Retrieved September 23, 2009, from http://www.monsanto.com/responsibility/default.asp

Motion, J., & Weaver, C. K. (2005). A discourse perspective for critical public relations research: Life Sciences Network and the battle for truth. *Journal of Public Relations Research*, *17*, 49–67.

Mumby, D. K. (2004). Discourse, power, and ideology: Unpacking the critical approach. In D. Grant, C. Hardy, C. Oswick, & L. Putnam (Eds.), *The Sage handbook of organizational discourse* (pp. 237–258). London: Sage.

Munro, W. A., & Schurman, R. A. (2007). Sustaining outrage: Cultural capital, strategic location and motivating sensibilities in the U.S. anti-genetic movement. In W. Wright & G. Middendorf (Eds.), *The fight over food: Producers, consumers, and activists challenge the global food system* (pp. 145–176). University Park: The Pennsylvania State University Press.

Nisbet, M. C., & Lewenstein, B. V. (2002). Biotechnology and the American media: The policy press and the elite press, 1970–1999. *Science Communication*, *23*, 359–391.

Pretty, J., Morison, J., & Hine, R. (2005). Reducing food poverty by increasing agricultural sustainability in developing countries. In J. Pretty (Ed.), *The Earthscan reader in sustainable agriculture* (pp. 375–398). London: Earthscan.

Rudy, A. P., Coppin, D., Konefal, J., Shaw, B. T., Eyck, T. T., Harris, C., & Busch, L. (2007). *Universities in the age of corporate science: The UC Berkeley-Novartis controversy*. Philadelphia: Temple University Press.

Sasu, M. A., Ferrari, M. J., Du, D., Winsor, J. A., & Stephenson, A. G. (2009). Indirect costs of a nontarget pathogen mitigate the direct benefits of a virus-resistant transgene in wild *Curcurbita. Proceedings of National Academy of Sciences*, *106*(45). Retrieved November 14, 2009, from http://www.pnas.org/cgi/doi/10.1073/pnas.0905106106

Schurman, R. (2004). Fighting 'frankenfoods': Industry opportunity structures and the efficacy of the anti-biotech movement in western Europe. *Social Problems*, *51*, 243–268.

Sorj, B., & Wilkinson, J. (1994). Biotechnologies, multinationals, and the agrofood systems of developing countries. In A. Bonnano, L. Busch, W. H. Friedland, L. Gouveia, & E. Mingione (Eds.), *From Columbus to ConAgra: The globalization of agriculture and food* (pp. 85–101). Lawrence: University Press of Kansas.

Steinglass, M. (2005, February 27). Vietnamese seeking redress from US in Agent Orange suit. *Boston Globe*. Retrieved May 1, 2009, from http://www.lexisnexis.com/universe

Thackaberry, J. A. (2004). 'Discursive opening' and closing in organizational self-study: Culture as trap and tool in wildland firefighting safety. *Management Communication Quarterly*, *17*, 319–359.

U.S. Working Group on the Food Crisis. (2009). *Backgrounder on the global food crisis*. Retrieved June 20, 2009, from http://www.usfoodcrisisgroup.org/

Vidal, J. (2007, February 12). The wasteland: How years of secret chemical dumping left a toxic legacy. *The Guardian*. Retrieved May 1, 2009, from http://www.guardian.co.uk/environment/2007/fed/ 12/uknews.pollution1

World Health Organization. (n.d.). *20 questions on genetically modified (GM) foods*. Retrieved November 12, 2009, from http://www.who.int/foodsafety/publications/biotech/20questions/en/index.html.

22

High school students' perceptions of environmental and communicative influences on eating behavior

Lynn M. Walters

Food is power. Pundits have long proclaimed that food is one of the elements that can support progress along a spiritual path. Food contains the essential nutrients required for life, and it evokes memory and delight. Fields are fought over and orchards burned in times of war. Whereas there are many in the Western world who obsess over myriad food choices or how to burn calories faster, famine and poverty claim growing multitudes. This paradox of abundance and scarcity in the world grows daily.

In the United States, we are living in a "complex food choice environment" (Contento, 2007, p. 3). Before 1900, people ate mostly food that grew near where they lived, with a maximum variety of about 200 different foods. During the late twentieth century, typical supermarkets in the United States stocked about 12,000 items, chosen from a supply of 60,000 foods and food products (Molitor, 1980). A multitude of food choices are also available from vending machines, fast food restaurants, and a growing number of super-sized food centers. The food industry is blamed for its greed in creating products without concern for the health of consumers and impact on society (Nestle, 2002).

One result of so many food choices is the obesity crisis now being seen in many industrialized nations. The Centers for Disease Control (CDC) has identified unhealthy dietary practices as one of six risky behaviors in youth resulting in chronic illnesses and premature morbidity and mortality (1996), as obesity has been found to be a significant risk factor for the development and progression of a number of chronic diseases—including coronary heart disease, diabetes and certain types of cancer (United States Department of Health and Human Services, 1988, 2001). The costs associated with annual obesity-related health care in the United States include expenditures estimated at $117,000,000 (Sibbald, 2002). These costs are rising and do not include societal impact and personal suffering. The consequences of overweight and obesity reveal that dietary choices have an impact far beyond the individual.

Myriad factors influence individual choice, including availability and access, prior experience, perceived preferences, food preparation skills, perceived health benefits, family and social support, and direct and indirect messages. Preferences may be as simple as, "the hungrier you are, the more direct and uncluttered is your relationship with food" (Keeling, 2001, p. 153). This statement is not meant to minimize issues of starvation or eating disorders but is intended to remind us that food is necessary for survival in a world where frivolous, disordered, wasteful, and obsessive behaviors related to food and eating may appear commonplace.

The purpose of this study is to investigate high school students' perceptions of the influences on their eating behavior.[i] High school students give voice to the current generation; they have developed food preferences and possess the cognitive skills to consider and articulate the development of their food choices and eating habits. Three research questions are posed:

What cultural conditions influence high school students' dietary attitudes and behavior?

What do high school students perceive as the most influential sources of information about dietary behavior?

How do high school students make sense of the interface between messages received and their lived experiences surrounding food choice?

The significance of this study is to test assumptions about how high school students view their food choices, especially against common perceptions that children and youth are easy prey of the media and the environment. This study investigates the multiple meanings of food perceived through direct experience of the individual and through the interplay among individuals, families, and society.

The Changing Foodscape

Interpretive communication theories may be useful to understand the intricacies and nuances of human interaction (Miller, 2005). Symbolic interactionism is an interpretive theoretical framework that may be used to investigate multiple manifestations of human conduct and interaction (Littlejohn, 1983). Along with hermeneutics and phenomenology, symbolic interactionism emphasizes the importance of "intersubjective creation of meaning" (Miller, 2005, p. 57). Although he did not name this theory, George Herbert Mead's posthumous publication, *Mind, Self, and Society* (1934) postulated "shared meaning of symbols as the binding factor in society" (as cited in Littlejohn, 1983, p. 46). Critical concepts of symbolic interactionism include that human thought and social interaction mediate the context of society, and that mind and self are constructed within the social context. Furthermore, this interweaving between individual experience and society create meaning, thus producing culture, societal norms, and beliefs (Miller, 2005), including norms and beliefs about food, a vital element needed to sustain life.

People eat in a social context. Direct and indirect messages delivered by role models, including parents, peers, siblings, and others may promote or discourage development of healthful dietary patterns (Birch and Fisher, 1998; Birch, 1999). Key environmental factors in dietary patterns include exposure to and accessibility of foods, social context of food experiences, and interactions with adults (Birch and Fisher, 1998; Birch, 1999). In 1938, Karl Drucker conducted a study that demonstrated that children were more apt to follow other children's food choices than adult food choices. Drucker hypothesized that although adults were perceived as authority figures, peer influence was more highly valued, due to identification (as cited in Berenda, 1950).

Social norms around food have changed dramatically over the last twenty years, as restaurants have taken over a major portion of the role of food preparation and with children and their families eating out more frequently than ever before (Dyson, 2001; Frazao, 1999). In 1977–78, foods eaten at home accounted for 80% of total calories consumed by children but declined steadily to 68% in 1994–96 (Lin, Guthrie, and Frazao, 2001). In 2001, Americans spent more than $110 billion on fast food, a dramatic increase from the approximately $6 billion spent in 1970 (Schlosser, 2001). We eat while watching television, driving cars, talking on the phone, and reading the news of the day. American children watch at least 21 hours of television per week (American Academy of Pediatrics Committee on Public Education, 1999). They are exposed to a plethora of food advertisements, mainly focused on energy-dense, low-nutrient foods. It is estimated that by the time American teenagers have graduated from high school, they have viewed, on average, 360,000 television advertisements (Dalmeny, Hanne, and Lobstein, 2003). We have, perhaps unwittingly, transformed the value of food from family-centered and shared nourishment to commodified consumption.

One of the consequences of this shift in social norms related to food is that the number of overweight American children and adolescents has doubled during the past two decades, with at least 25% of children and youth in the United States estimated to be overweight. The prevalence of overweight and obese individuals in the United States is continuing to rise, especially among minorities and low-income populations (Ogden, Flegal, Carroll, and Johnson, 2002). The number of overweight non-Hispanic black and Mexican-American adolescents increased more than 10 percentage points between 1988–1994 and 1999–2000 (Story, Evans, Fabsitz, Clay, Holy Rock, and Broussard, 1999). The CDC (2002) reports that between 1990 and 2002, obesity in New Mexico (where this research took place) increased from approximately 10% to 20%, with 61% of the adult population currently overweight or obese. Looking toward the future, there is convincing evidence that overweight children and adolescents often become overweight adults (Serdula, Ivery, Coates, Freedman, Williamson, and Byers, 1993).

Research to date has focused largely on how media and environmental influences create barriers to healthy eating, especially physical and psychological reinforcement, contradictory social pressures related to food, and conflicting perceptions of healthy eating (Stevenson, Doherty, Barnett, Muldoon, and Trew, 2007). This research, however, suggests that, while media may pose a significant threat to healthy eating practices, health behaviors are shaped and nurtured by the home environment, and interaction between adults and children may mediate the direct effects of both advertising and public health information campaigns (Rimal and Flora, 1998).

Focus group studies about eating behavior have been conducted with adults, adolescents, and children. One recent adult study investigated perceptions of factors that influence healthful food consumption. Nine focus groups in the Lower Mississippi Delta looked at perceptions of food choices that either contribute to or detract from individual health. Results indicated that health concerns played an important role in considering dietary change. Participants acknowledged the influences of family and cultural norms that emphasized the importance of practicing healthy eating when young, saying:

> If you eat unhealthy when you're young, you're going to be sick when you get old. I know a lot of kids that just overeat, and that's bad for them because the weight is there then. They'll get high blood pressure later, they're obese. (McGee, Richardson, Johnson, S., Thornton, Johnson, C., Yadrick et al., 2008, p.105)

In contrast to adults, children and adolescents are not motivated strongly by health concerns (Story, Neumark-Sztainer, and French, 2002). Recent studies have investigated adolescents' attitudes and behaviors about food through inquiries into the effects of advertisements and health messages (Adams and Geuens, 2007; Stevenson et al., 2007). Adams and Geuens hypothesized that adolescents may interpret and evaluate products advertised as "healthy" versus "unhealthy" in a different manner than adults. In an experimental study with 15-year-old Belgian adolescents exposed to one of four conditions: 1) healthy product with healthy slogan, 2) healthy product with unhealthy slogan, 3) unhealthy product with healthy slogan, and 4) unhealthy product with unhealthy slogan, Adams and Geuens found that the adolescents as a whole were vulnerable to commercial messages, labeling them a "fragile age group," (p. 182) subject to persuasion by misleading marketing tactics that often promote high-profit, high-calorie, low-nutrient foods.

A study that sought "to map out the variety of understandings of healthy eating among adolescents" (Stevenson et al., 2007, p. 420) utilized focus groups with Irish adolescents from 12 to 15 years old to investigate topics ranging from fast food and healthy eating, to the Atkins Diet, vegetarianism, organic foods, and processed and genetically modified foods. This study underscored findings from adult studies that knowledge about nutrition and health does not necessarily motivate healthy eating behavior (Brown, McIlveen, and Strugnell, 2000; Story et al., 2002). Stevenson et al. (2007) sought to investigate the impact of healthy versus unhealthy messages, with some lip service to taste. Although not the direct focus of the study, results revealed multiple factors influencing adolescents' eating behavior. In addition, cooking, as described by several "self-identifying 'healthy eaters,'" (p. 430) was identified as providing perceived control and self-efficacy, factors which may encourage high school students to engage in exploring a variety of healthy foods.

A large body of literature is concerned with the effect of media on children and young people, examining the unequal number and relative quality of messages produced through the vast resources of corporations compared with the limited resources devoted to nutrition education (e.g., Dalmeny et al., 2003, and Contento, 2007). However, this view does not take into account natural intelligence and the potential impact that families and educators may have on students' personal belief systems. A number of researchers are convinced that "the *experience* of eating in a specific environment may have more bearing on consumption patterns and behavior than any supposed influence of food-related messages children receive" (Haden, 2006, p. 269).

In a comprehensive review of individual and environmental influences on adolescent eating behaviors, Story et al. (2002) found four levels of influence on eating behaviors, including individual or intrapersonal influences, the social environment, the physical environment, and society. This research acknowledged the complexity of factors that influence adolescent eating behavior. Using an ecological perspective, the study utilized Social Cognitive Theory as a framework within which to examine the importance of reciprocal determinism and the complex interrelationships that influence adolescents' food choices.

Although research has revealed a variety of factors that influence adolescents' food choices, the approach that has largely been taken is to investigate how to fix the problem of poor dietary patterns. Story et al. (2002) argue for further qualitative study to expand the understanding of relationships between and among the varied influences on adolescents' eating behavior and to identify and improve measurement of predictive and outcome variables.

As exploratory research concerned with bringing to light perceived influences on high school students' food choices, this study seeks to understand the interplay between food and culture, individual and family, including mediating factors which may affect sensory perceptions of various foods. From a communication perspective, food is a symbol positioned squarely in the center of human interaction. Using an interpretive approach to examine how high school students construct meaning through interaction with food and the environment, this project will expand understanding about the influences on the dietary patterns of this population.

Focus Group Process

Focus group methodology was used to engage high school seniors in discussion with the aim of learning about students' perceptions of the influences on their dietary behavior. Participants were a convenience sample of students at a charter high school in Santa Fe, New Mexico, with a diverse school population representative of the larger community: 60% Anglo; 40% Hispanic or from other ethnic backgrounds; and 30% from low-income families, as defined by qualification for free or reduced-price school meals. The school supported the concept of this study, as it was aligned with initiatives in the school related to food, including cooking, gardening, and a healthy school meals program. The particular classes from which participants were chosen were 12th-grade students enrolled in government and economics classes that focused on social issues, including food and agriculture.

The focus groups were conducted in a classroom setting in spring 2008. Participants were 17 or 18 years old, with eight students participating in each of three focus groups. The study population included 24 participants, all 17 or 18 year-old high school seniors enrolled in a government and economics class in a charter high school. Twelve of the participants were male and 12 female. Each of the three focus groups included eight participants, though gender distribution was not equal in each focus group.

Each focus group met for 30 to 40 minutes during the school day and discussed questions ranging from the general to the specific (see Appendix A for Focus Group Discussion Guide). Discussions were digitally recorded, with field notes taken by both the researcher and one non-participating student in each focus group. Recordings were subsequently transcribed, and the transcriptions were checked against recordings to ensure validity of the data. Using the transcripts and field notes, I reviewed the data in order to identify recurring trends and patterns. These data were then sorted into thematic units using the organizing framework of the focus group discussion guide. The most relevant quotes were included in each thematic section and a descriptive summary was compiled that included dominant and minor themes from the focus groups.

Student Voices

Upon analyzing the data, I found that the students displayed a remarkable breadth of understanding about the factors that influenced their food choices. These factors included family and culture; hunger and the senses; body intelligence; influences of media messages, education, and peers; perceived body image; and food access and the environment. In addition, participants noted that tastes may change over time and discussed eating disorders as a known phenomenon in their world. One group delved into meat eating versus vegetarian practices, with boys overwhelmingly enthusiastic about eating meat and girls expressing concern for animals as well as expressing some squeamishness about killing animals.

Family and Culture

Although long considered to be the primary nurturing influence on eating behavior, given current trends of fast food consumption, prevalence of meals eaten away from home, and strength of peer influence, it could not be assumed that families would be seen by participants as relevant to their food choices. However, family and culture emerged as strong themes throughout the focus group discussions. Participants saw their families as having the first, and often most important, impact on their eating behavior. Students mentioned how food "just brings everyone together," and expressed fond memories of growing up with good food:

> I think to me the food that my mom makes no matter where she gets it, to me is just the healthiest food. It just makes me feel very special and stuff. Like if a family member cooks for you I think that that's what I would call cooking with love.

A number of students referred to uniquely valued foods prepared by their family, especially grandmothers' special dishes:

> One of my memories is I always remember going to my great grandmother's house, it was this tiny little place, and she made the best Cuban food ever. She's this sweet little old lady from Cuba and there'd be chicken and rice and platanos and fried yucca. And all these different things that are like my favorite things on the planet and her flan: our family, I just remember ever since I was little, our family would fight over her flan. She'd make a huge like pizza-sized thing of flan and we all would over who got it, or who got the last piece. I've never found flan as good as hers, ever. She's really particular about who she gives her recipe to, but she said that she would only tell either me or my aunt Cynthia.

One student remarked that the meaning of home was the smell of "fresh-made flour tortillas from your grandmother." This prompted an expression of longing for an idealized family by another student who said, "I wish my grandma made flour tortillas." However, memories of family meals did not always evoke positive emotions. Several students recalled unpleasant times at the family table:

> My earliest memory was probably, I don't know how old I was. I was really young. My mom would always, like for breakfast, even for lunch, she'd make me a bunch of scrambled eggs and put milk in them, and I'm like "Ugggghhh!" I'd just sit there at the table for like an hour or just staring at them, while she was trying to get me to eat them.

Culture was perceived as a vital influence by a number of participants. Students discussed how the foods they grew up with varied among the group, depending upon ethnicity and cultural background. One boy suggested:

> It really depends on what culture you're raised into. Like ever since I was little I was always taught to eat at home rather than to eat out or go any other place than besides at home. I was always taught certain things, (for example) what not to drink, all the time.

A number of the students exhibited a remarkable maturity and understanding about how the conditions in which they had grown up influenced how they have constructed meaning around food:

> I think it's definitely how you're raised because if you've grown up eating a certain thing, then that's considered the normal thing to eat and traditional. It makes you feel comfortable. It just brings back good memories. And even when I'm away from home here in Santa Fe I go through like green chile withdrawals. And then I finally get home and have a huge plate of green chile chicken enchiladas and it's awesome.

Hunger and the Senses

It is not surprising that the interplay between hunger and the senses emerged as a strong factor of influence. Students expressed appreciation for enjoyment through their senses with some understanding the interplay between what tastes delicious and what makes the body feel good. Students easily distinguished between natural hunger, cravings, and sensual pleasure, with some integrating instinct and knowledge related to consequences of food choices. Most students were aware that memories and context influenced their sensual experiences with food.

Participants described the impact of visual cues in determining the appeal of foods, expressed by one student as, "If it looks good you're like, 'Oh wow, that looks like it could be really tasty, I really want to try it.'" Food smells were mentioned in memories of home-cooked meals: "Ever since I was little my house was…everyone was always cooking. So there's always that smell when you walk in." How food smells was also described as an important cue to predict how food will taste: "If something smells good usually it will taste good."

The pleasure of eating led to a discussion of the effects of being led by one's senses. One student remarked, "Isn't it like exercise, sex, and food that release endorphins? I'm sure there's a huge relationship between enjoyment and eating." Students commented on being seduced by purely sensory desires: "I know for some people eating McDonald's can be like drinking, in the sense of you eat it and really enjoy it, but then you feel awful." Yet other students asked, "Just because it doesn't taste good doesn't mean it's not good for you?" "But if it tastes good does that mean it's not good for you?" These comments exemplify some of the confusion that adolescents and others face in making food choices.

Body Intelligence

Anderson (2006) defines body intelligence "as the awareness and use of bodily sensations to (a) support health and well-being, (b) supply information about environmental safety and comfort, and (c) enhance personal and spiritual development over a lifetime" (p. 359). A number of female students brought up the idea of the body knowing what is good for it through an integration of instinct and intelligence.

Related to food choices guided by body intelligence, comments ranged from, "Probably you feel it right after you eat it" to "I don't think this is good for me." Another student noted:

> We have taste buds and we find some foods pleasurable and I think that it's good to eat flavorful and also I think my diet is really like very healthy and it's also very good tasting to me. So I think they go hand-in-hand. You just have to find the right balance.

Influences of Media Messages, Education, and Peers

The focus groups revealed how students made sense of the interface between messages about food and their lived experiences with food. Students discussed the impact of messages received through different types of media, education, and peers, and consequent social and individual responsibilities.

It was apparent that the educational experience of students in this high school class had a strong impact on many of the students' views about food. Although they noted possible effects from varying types of media, including the Internet and television, movies such as "Fast Food Nation" and "Supersize Me," which were shown in class, provided a differing point of view with a powerful emotional punch. Other educational experiences in school, information shared by peers, and visiting farmers' markets were also mentioned. One student concluded, "If you can't pronounce the ingredients, don't eat it." For many of the students, facts and opinions merged:

> You can read anywhere about organic and I don't think necessarily going to Whole Foods and spending $6 on a pound of apples is so much better for you than going to Albertson's and paying $2 for a pound of apples. In like raw fruits and vegetables and that sort of matter I don't see the difference but I do understand like hormone-injected meat versus natural.

Discussions revealed perceptions of social and personal responsibility, colored by societal and cultural norms and values. Students' knowledge of current controversies about food advertising and the parallel to tobacco ads that influenced an earlier generation were striking:

> I remember they took off cigarette commercials on TV a long time ago. They regulated that. That's making a statement about trying to make people more healthy by not telling them to smoke on TV. And I think with regulations they should also start…they should regulate commercials: alcohol commercials shouldn't be on TV, and fast food commercials should not be on TV because they are not supporting healthy habits. The government should be a part of teaching healthy habits.

The need for government to act responsibly was mentioned by many students, with suggestions ranging from subsidies for healthy foods to educational programs to teach "people how to eat healthy." One student concluded, "You need to teach kids when they're young in order to eat healthy because unhealthy eating habits start when you're little." In addition, economic and class issues were not overlooked. As one student said:

> I realize that a lot of the cheapest foods are the worst for us and also the worst for the environment and socially, because of the conditions of the workers and of the food itself. So I think there's a big divide, like class divide.

Students also possessed an awareness of the impact that farming practices may have on environmental and human health, with one student commenting:

> Buying locally makes things healthier because you know where it's coming from. You know if that farm wherever it was grown was not using pesticides or anything. When it's farther away your home or your community, it's harder to know whether they're using preservatives or pesticides or GMOs.

There was considerable conversation about how and where students learned (or didn't learn) personal responsibility and the impact of personal food and lifestyle choices. Although students continued to emphasize family and culture as primary influences, the school environment, perhaps particularly for this class, was key: "Unless you go to this school I think you kind of have to be self-sufficient in finding that information yourself 'cause I don't feel like it's really provided for you very often." One group in particular, composed of five boys and three girls, emphasized the power of peer influence. The following is an interchange taken from that conversation:

> You can't always stay in the rut that you are. Eating like white pasta with no butter and no oil and cover it with cheese, you can't do that your whole life.
>
> Why not?

> Because friends are going to want you to try something different. If you don't your friends will say, "Oh you know, he's boring. He eats the same stuff over and over!"
>
> Or, "All the cool kids are doing it."
>
> Exactly!

Perceived Body Image

Emotion and body image were barely touched on as influential factors. It is possible that students didn't feel comfortable talking about their own food issues or self-soothing eating behaviors, but that is unknown. One student observed:

> I think that today so many people are concerned about the way that they look and so therefore they're resorting to Slim Fast and all these protein bars and things like that aren't always as healthy as just eating regular food. I think in today's society people need to be comfortable with who they are.

Food Access and the Environment

The students understood that food access issues include geographical and financial factors, which impact nutritional sufficiency and, as a result, health status.

Comments ranged from, "It's also about the availability too. A lot of people can only shop at gas stations and it's the expense;" to "Or if our fast food restaurants were relatively healthy. Like if you could get food fast that wasn't going to clog your arteries."

They also expressed an understanding that their environment offered healthy and tasty choices: "I think we're lucky here because there's a lot of local places where you can get a really somewhat healthy meal that's cheap and it's quick."

The impact that a recently implemented healthy school lunch program at the school had on student views was notable:

> We just need to do what our school's doing on a larger scale. Like our new lunch program is awesome and our garden. Basically the only relatively unhealthy thing we sell at lunch are chips, and how many chips are you going to eat that's going to kill you? But if we do that on a larger scale I think that would help.

Conclusion

The purpose of this study was to investigate high school students' perceptions of influences on their eating behavior. Themes that emerged from the focus group discussions revealed food as a symbol of importance in interaction among families, culture, and society. Cultural conditions described by students showed strong emotional connections with families that influenced their food preferences. Even those students who appeared less connected through food to their family or culture expressed preferences for and opinions about the consequences of food choices. The students acknowledged hunger and the senses as important influences on eating behavior. Although students mentioned various media as sources of information, the direct educational experience of their classroom and school environment appeared to carry more weight than mediated messages. And, though peer influence was brought up and discussed, participating students on the whole seemed confident in using their own discriminatory powers to determine food choices. Perceived body image was acknowledged, but not discussed in depth. Students were aware of and concerned about the interrelation of food access and social justice, concluding that influence and responsibility related to food choice is shared among society, the family, and the individual.

This study shares limitations common to most focus group research. Both the site and the sample were not randomly selected therefore generalization of the results is not advisable. A second limitation common to focus group methodology was that participants may have experienced peer pressure that influenced participant discussion (Krueger, 2000). A third limitation may have been created by use of questions about healthy or unhealthy foods, as this line of inquiry might have encouraged socially desirable responses.

Despite these limitations, the research presented here provides a glimpse into the complexity of influences around food choice as understood by young people. Participating students were poised to graduate from high school, with many about to go out on their own for the first time. They articulated and appreciated many aspects of food, including the positive emotions generated when eating with good friends and family. These young people are creating the future; they will determine how food will be grown, processed, distributed, and consumed. They will emerge from their families and cultures into a society that is challenged and burdened by the paradox of food excess and hunger, but that still carries diverse and rich traditions that value delicious, nourishing food. These students and their peers will determine the direction that we take in the production, processing, distribution, and consumption of food, whether we continue down the path of the commodification and desecration of our planet's riches or reawaken a joyful responsibility for the nourishment of all.

Appendix A

Focus Group Discussion Questions

1. What is one of your earliest memories about food?
2. What are some of your favorite foods?
3. Why do you eat the foods that you do?
4. What do you think makes food healthy?
5. Where do you get information about healthy food?
6. What do you think makes food unhealthy?
7. Where do you get information about unhealthy food?
8. What do you think makes food taste good?
9. What or who motivates you to try new food items?
10. What messages would you give to other students about eating healthy foods?
11. Could you talk about how you see the relationship between the messages you receive about food and the actual choices you make in your diet?
12. We have talked a lot and you have shared some very useful information. Is there anything else anyone would like to add?

Acknowledgments

I would like to thank the students who participated in this study and the school faculty and staff that supported this work. My appreciation goes to Ilia Rodriguez, Ph.D., for her direction and encouragement during this project, and Janet M. Cramer, Ph.D., for her expert review and continued guidance.

References

Adams, L., & Geuens, M. (2007). Healthy or Unhealthy Slogans: That's the Question. *Journal of Health Communication, 12,* 2, 173–185.

American Academy of Pediatrics Committee on Public Education. (1999). Media education. *Pediatrics, 104*, 341–343.

Anderson, R. (2006). Body intelligence scale: Defining and measuring the intelligence of the body. *The Humanistic Psychologist*, *34*,4, 357–367.

Berenda, R.W. (1950). *The Influence of the Group on the Judgments of Children*. New York: Columbia University Press.

Birch L.L, Fisher J.O. (1998). Development of eating behaviors among children and adolescents. *Pediatrics, 101,* 3, 539–549.

Birch L.L. (1999). Development of food preferences. *Annual Review of Nutrition, 19,* 41–62.

Brown, K., McIlveen, H., & Strugnell, C. (2000). Nutritional awareness and food preferences of young consumers. *Nutrition and Food Science, 30,* 230–235.

Centers for Disease Control and Prevention. (1996). Guidelines for school health programs to promote lifelong healthy eating. *Morbidity and Mortality Weekly Report, 45,*(RR–9), 1–47.

Centers for Disease Control and Prevention. (2002). *Chronic Disease Prevention Health Youth: An Investment in Our Nation's Future.* U.S. Senate Appropriations Committee Senate Report 107–84.

Contento, I.R. (2007). *Nutrition Education: Linking Research, Theory, and Practice.* Sudbury, MA: Jones and Bartlett Publishers.

Dalmeny, K., Hanne, E., Lobstein, T. (2003). *Broadcasting bad health: Why food marketing to children needs to be controlled.* A report by the International Association of Consumer Food Organizations for the World Health Organization consultation on a global strategy for diet and health. International Association of Consumer Food Organizations.

Dyson, L.K. (2001). American cuisine in the 20th century. *Food Review Magazine*, Economic Research Service *23,* 1, 2–7.

Frazao, E. (Ed.). (1999). America's eating habits: changes & consequences. U.S. Department of Agriculture, Economic Research Service, Food and Rural Economics Division. *Agriculture Information Bulletin,* No. 750.

Haden, R. (2006). Pandora's lunchbox: On esthetic education, children, and food. *Food Culture & Society, 9,* 3, 265–274.

Keeling, R. P. (2001). Food: Sustenance and Symbol. *Journal of American College Health, 49,* 4, 153–156.

Krueger, R.A. (2000). *Focus Groups: A Practical Guide for Applied Research* (3rd ed.). Thousand Oaks, CA: Sage Publications.

Lin, B., Guthrie, J., Frazao, E. (2001). American children's diets not making the grade. *Food Review, 24*(2), 8–17.

Littlejohn, S.W. (1983). *Theories of Human Communication* (2nd ed.). Belmont, CA: Wadsworth Publishing Company.

McGee, B. B., Richardson, V., Johnson, G. S., Thornton, A., Johnson, C., Yadrick, K., et al. (2008). Perceptions of factors influencing healthful food consumption behavior in the lower Mississippi Delta: Focus group findings. *Journal of Nutrition Education & Behavior, 40,* 2, 102–109.

Mead, G.H. (1934). *Mind, Self, and Society.* Chicago: University of Chicago Press.

Miller, K. (2005). *Communication Theories: Perspectives, Processes, and Contexts* (2nd ed.). Boston: McGraw Hill.

Moliter, G.T.T. (1980). The food system in the 1980s. *Journal of Nutrition Education, 12,* 103–111.

Nestle, M. (2002). *Food Politics: How the Food Industry Influences Nutrition and Health.* Berkeley: University of California Press.

Ogden, C.L., Flegal, K.M., Carroll, M.D., & Johnson, C.L. (2002). Prevalence and trends in overweight among US children and adolescents, 1999–2000. *Journal of the American Medical Association,* 288(14),1728–1732.

Rimal, R.N. & Flora, J.A. (1998). Bidirectional Familial Influences in Dietary Behavior. Test of a Model of Campaign Influences. *Human Communication Research*, *24*, 4, 610–634.

Schlosser, E. (2001). *Fast Food Nation*. New York: Houghton Mifflin.

Serdula M.K., Ivery D., Coates R.J., Freedman D.S., Williamson D.F., Byers T. (1993). Do obese children become obese adults? A review of the literature. *Preventive Medicine, 22,* 2:167–177.

Sibbald, B. (2002). Obesity may soon be leading cause of preventable death in U.S.. *Canadian Medical Association Journal. 166*, 642.

Stevenson, C., Doherty, G., Barnett, J., Muldoon, O. T., & Trew, K. (2007). Adolescents' views of food and eating: Identifying barriers to healthy eating. *Journal of Adolescence, 30,* 3, 417–434.

Story, M., Evans M., Fabsitz, R.R., Clay, T.E., Holy Rock, B., Broussard, B. (1999). The epidemic of obesity in American Indian communities and the need for childhood obesity-prevention programs. *American Journal of Clinical Nutrition. 69,* (4S),747S–754S.

Story, M., Neumark-Sztainer, D., & French, S. (2002). Individual and Environmental Influences on Adolescent Eating Behaviors. *Journal of the American Dietetic Association, 102*, S40–S51.

United States Department of Health and Human Services. (1988). *The Surgeon General's Report on Nutrition and Health.* Rockville, MD: U.S. Department of Health and Human Services, Public Health Service, Office of the Surgeon General. U.S. GPO, Washington.

United States Department of Health and Human Services. (2001). *The Surgeon General's Call To Action To Prevent and Decrease Overweight and Obesity*. Rockville, MD: U.S. Department of Health and Human Services, Public Health Service, Office of the Surgeon General. U.S. GPO, Washington.

Contributors

Frances Alloway is a Nutrition and Family Living Educator for Penn State Cooperative Extension in Southeast PA. She is a registered and licensed dietitian and manages two federal nutrition education programs for low income families, SNAP-Ed and EFNEP (Expanded Food and Nutrition Education Program). She has a B.S. from the University of Delaware and M.A. in Nutrition Education from Immaculata University. As one of the developers of the *FRIDGE* curriculum and coordinator of one of the pilot sites, she has seen the value of the intergenerational approach to nutrition education and is a recipient of healthy eating guidance from her senior family members.

Barry Brummett is the Charles Sapp Centennial Professor in Communication and Department Chair in the Department of Communication Studies at the University of Texas-Austin. He received his PhD from the University of Minnesota and has taught at Purdue University and at the University of Wisconsin at Milwaukee. He has published several essays and books, including most recently *A Rhetoric of Style* (Southern Illinois University Press).

Michael S. Bruner is a Professor in the Department of Communication at Humboldt State University. His interest areas include applied communication, as well as communication and the environment. Dr. Bruner's work appears in *Landmark Essays on Rhetoric and the Environment* and in *Enviropop: Studies in Environmental Rhetoric and Popular Culture*. His research on food issues includes "Learning, Knowing, and Deciding About Food: The Case of The Center for Science in the Public Interest."

Patrice M. Buzzanell is Professor and the W. Charles & Ann Redding Faculty Fellow in the Department of Communication at Purdue University, where she also received her Ph.D. Her research focuses on gendered workplace processes and structures, particularly as they relate to career.

Vincent (Tzu-Wen) Cheng is a full-time instructor in the Speech, Communications, and Theatre Arts Department at Borough of Manhattan Community College, which he joined in 2005. He also teaches in the Media, Culture, and Communication Department at New York University since 1999. Among the courses Mr. Cheng has taught are Speech

Communication, Cross-Cultural Communication, Conflict Management, Fundamentals of Speech, and Introduction to Human Communication and Culture. Currently a Ph.D. candidate in the International Education program at New York University, Mr. Cheng received two Master's degrees from NYU – an M.C.J. from the School of Law in 1997 and an M.A. from Speech and Interpersonal Communication program in 1999.

Kevin-Khristián Cosgriff-Hernández is a doctoral student in the Department of Communication at Texas A&M University. He earned a B.A. from the University of Chicago with an emphasis in Public Policy and an M.A. in Communication Management from John Carroll University. His doctoral research explores the construction and performance of identity in organizational and cultural contexts. He teaches classes in Small Group Communication, Negotiation, and Intercultural Communication.

Janet M. Cramer is an Associate Professor in the Communication and Journalism Department at the University of New Mexico, where she teaches a variety of courses in media studies, journalism, and communication at the undergraduate and graduate level. Her research focuses on the cultural studies of media, including food, gender studies and media history. She has written a history of media focusing on the cultural and intellectual traditions that have guided media development in the United States, titled *Media/History/Society: A Cultural History of U.S. Media* (Wiley Blackwell, Inc., 2009).

Kathleen M. German is currently a Full Professor in the Department of Communication at Miami University, Oxford, Ohio. Dr. German received her Ph.D. degree in Rhetoric from the University of Iowa. Her teaching and research interests are in the areas of rhetorical criticism, political communication, and documentary film with an emphasis on minority representations. She has also published work on American Indian and African American images in film as well as co-authored a leading textbook on public speaking.

Carlnita P. Greene is an Assistant Professor & Director of the Communication & Rhetoric program at Nazareth College of Rochester. Her research can be broadly defined as the intersection of rhetorical theory and popular culture. She has previously published on subjects as diverse as food culture and the media, identity and social style, rhetorical theory in the 21st century, and popular culture and pedagogy. Some of her recent publications include: "Towards a Rhetoric of Nostalgia and Cultural Memory: 'Silver League Base Ball' and the Performance of the Past" in *Sporting Rhetoric: Performance, Games, and Politics* (Peter Lang Publishing, 2009), "Shopping for What Never Was: The Rhetoric of Food, Social Style, and Nostalgia" in *Food for Thought: Essays on Eating and Culture* (McFarland Press, 2008), and "The 'Domestic Goddess': Postfeminist Representation in the Televisual Kitchen: A Media Ecological Analysis of Nigella Bites" in *Explorations in Media Ecology*, 4.3/4 (2005).

Lynn James has been an Extension Educator at Penn State University since 1998 and Co-Chair of the Penn State Extension Nutrition & Health work group since 2004. She provides program leadership for the state in diet, nutrition and health programs and offers direct programming in eight central PA counties. She is lead author of the *Family Fitness* curriculum, an award-winning nutrition education program which is now run in 30 Pennsylvania counties and in New York state, and principal investigator of a 5 year child overweight prevention study.

Andrew Jones is an Associate Lecturer in the School of Arts and Social Sciences at Southern Cross University. He teaches Media Studies and is also engaged in a doctorate titled: In/appropriating Sainthood—the Unbecoming Cause: Melancholy Wonder and Colonial Experiences.

Matthew Kaplan is Professor of Intergenerational Programs and Aging in the Department of Agricultural and Extension Education at Penn State University. In this position, he develops resources, provides training support, and provides statewide leadership in the development and evaluation of intergenerational programs implemented in a range of community settings. He has published several books including two that explore the international dimension of intergenerational work and one on intergenerational strategies for promoting community participation. He has a Ph.D. in Environmental Psychology from the City University of New York Graduate Center.

Defne Karaosmanoglu is an Assistant Professor of Communication in the Department of Journalism at Bahçeşehir University, Istanbul. She obtained her Ph.D. in Communication Studies from McGill University. Her research interests include narratives of history; spaces of nostalgia in the city; globalization and changing discourses around food and cuisine; theories of cosmopolitanism. She recently published an article entitled "Eating the past: Multiple Spaces, Multiple Times: Performing Ottomanness in Istanbul" in *International Journal of Cultural Studies*, 2009, Volume 12 (4).

Nancy Ellen Kiernan, Ph.D., Program Evaluator, works with other faculty to evaluate Penn State Extension programs. The research appears in *Evaluation Review, Evaluation and Program Planning, American Journal of Evaluation, Journal of Nutrition Education and Behavior, Preventive Veterinary Medicine, Journal of Extension* and received awards from the National Institute for Farm Safety for Research Leading to Prevention Programs; Penn State's Commission for Women for innovative evaluations; American Evaluation Association (EEE) for Sustained Excellence in Extension Evaluation and National Association of Family and Consumer Sciences' (NEAFCS) for Program Excellence through Research. Her program of research focuses on the implementation problems of evaluation.

Marianne LeGreco is an Assistant Professor in the Department of Communication Studies at the University of North Carolina at Greensboro. She earned her Ph.D. from the Hugh Downs School of Human Communication at Arizona State University. Her primary interests include the study of food policy and promotion, organizational and health communication, and qualitative research methods involving discourse. In her current research, she focuses on community-based food practices, healthy eating on a budget, and the need for kitchen literacy.

Laura A. Lindenfeld is an Associate Professor at the University of Maine in the Department of Communication and Journalism and the Margaret Chase Smith Policy Center. Dr. Lindenfeld's research focuses on media studies and cultural studies. She is particularly interested in the relationship between multiculturalism, media literacy, civic engagement, and education. Her current research project is an examination of the discourses and policies of food in the United States and their relationship to the proliferation of "food films" from the early 1990s to the present. She holds a Ph.D. in Cultural Studies from the University of California, Davis, 2001.

Kristen Lucas is an Assistant Professor in the Department of Communication Studies at the University of Nebraska-Lincoln. Dr. Lucas received her Ph.D. from Purdue University. Her current research investigates workplace dignity, blue-collar careers, and the ways working-class children negotiate intergenerational career discontinuities.

Amanda R. Martinez is a doctoral student in the Department of Communication at Texas A&M University. She earned her B.A. in Multinational Organization Studies with a minor in Communication, and a concentration in Spanish from St. Mary's University, and an M.A. from the University of Houston in Mass Communication with a Women's Studies Graduate Certificate. Her doctoral research focuses on the areas of health communication and mass media, with particular emphasis on race/ethnicity, culture, and identity. She teaches a variety of classes including Intercultural, Media, and Gendered Communication.

Christie McCullen is a Ph.D. student in Sociology at the University of California Santa Cruz and a graduate of the master's program in Community Development at the University of California Davis. Her master's research focused on the construction of whiteness at a farmers market in California's Central Valley. More broadly, Christie is interested in the race and class politics of social movements engaged in both social and environmental change.

Jason D. Meek is an alumnus of Humboldt State University, where he majored in History and completed advanced studies in the Department of Communication. His relevant work includes research on the history of Coca Cola advertising.

Jessica Mudry is an Assistant Professor of Technical Communication in the Faculty of Engineering at Concordia University in Montreal. Dr. Mudry obtained her Ph.D. in Communication from the University of Pittsburgh, where she was a Mellon Fellow. Dr. Mudry's research interests include: the rhetoric of science and technology, discourses of nutrition and food studies. Her past research project culminated in the book *Measured Meals: Nutrition in America*, published by SUNY Press. Her current project examines the rhetorical history of the calorie.

Fabio Parasecoli lives in Rome and New York City, where he is Associate Professor and Coordinator of Food Studies at the New School. His research focuses on the intersections of food, media, and politics. Among his recent publications are *Food Culture in Italy* (2004), *The Introduction to Culinary Cultures of Europe* (The Council of Europe, 2005), and *Bite me! Food in Popular Culture* (2008).

Tara J. Schuwerk is a Visiting Assistant Professor of Communication in the Department of Communication Studies and Theatre Arts at Stetson University. She earned her Ph.D. in Communication from the Hugh Downs School of Human Communication at Arizona State University with specializations in health and intercultural communication, using qualitative research methods. She explores the intersection of culture, health, and communication with emphasis on hunger relief, nutrition, and food. She also has interests in the communication experiences of women and their health and communication involving and surrounding international and transracial child adoptions.

Barbara F. Sharf is Professor in the Department of Communication at Texas A&M University. Her research has included studies of physician-patient communication; health and illness portrayed in popular media; patients' illness experiences, and qualitative research ethics. She has conducted many projects involving both clinical and public health communication as it intersects with ethnocultural complexities and racial and ethnic disparities. Dr. Sharf has served as a co-principal investigator to several funded (e.g., AHRQ, NIH, DHHS) projects. She teaches classes in Health Communication, Culture and Health, Narrative Inquiry, Interpretive Research, and Medical Ethics.

Joseph R. Sharkey is Professor of Social and Behavioral Health, School of Rural Public Health, Texas A&M Health Sciences Center in College Station, Texas; Director of CDC-funded Texas Healthy Aging Research Network Collaborating Center; Director of the CDC-funded Texas Nutrition and Obesity Policy Research and Evaluation Network Collaborating Center; and Director of the Program for Research in Nutrition and Health Disparities. Dr. Sharkey is Principal Investigator on three interdisciplinary research programs that examine complex, place-based factors that may either enable or constrain rural and underserved families from achieving and maintaining good nutritional health. Dr. Sharkey's main areas of interest include measurement of household and neighborhood food environments, nutritional assessment, and mixed-methods research.

Ross Singer is an Assistant Professor in the Department of Speech Communication at Southern Illinois University Carbondale. His interests include corporate social responsibility and sustainability discourses, discourses of agriculture, food and the environment and rhetoric and critical-cultural studies. Dr. Singer has been recognized for his work on various occasions, including a Top Paper Award from the Media Studies Interest Group, Central States Communication Association and a Non-Service Dissertation Fellowship from the School of Communication Studies at Bowling Green State University. He has also had several publications in professional journals, including *Environmental Communication.*

John R. Thompson is a Ph.D. candidate at the University of Texas at Austin, beginning his dissertation on the topic of *Food and the Rhetoric of Globalization.* Thompson's research agenda is shaped by globalization and its impact on rhetorics of constitution, identity and political economy. Thompson also asks questions of how underlying constructs of rhetorical theory—such as audience, ethos, topoi—might change when the landscape is global. In addition to studying food, Thompson is a home chef, cooking for his wife and two children in Austin, and a food blogger.

Deborah Morrison Thomson is an Assistant Professor in the School of Communication at East Carolina University where she teaches courses in rhetoric, media and health communication. She received her Ph.D. in Communication Studies from UNC-Chapel Hill. Her current research focuses a critical lens on food industry marketing practices that support childhood obesity. Recent work can be seen in *Text and Performance Quarterly* and *Critical Studies in Media Communication.*

Anne Marie Todd is an Associate Professor of Public Communication in the Department of Communication Studies at San José State University. She received her Ph.D. in Rhetoric and Cultural Studies from the University of Southern California's Annenberg School for Communication. Dr. Todd's research areas are environmental and social movement communication with particular emphasis on media activism, popular culture, and environmental rhetoric. An ongoing focus of her teaching and research is public understanding of climate change.

Lynn M. Walters is founder and Executive Director of *Cooking with Kids, Inc.*, an award-winning non-profit organization that engages elementary school children in hands-on experience with fresh, affordable foods from diverse cultures. A former restaurateur with fifteen years of nutrition education program experience, Ms. Walters brings her passion for cooking and gardening to her writing, research, and work with children. Her research interests focus on the behavioral effects of experiential learning with food; family, peer, and environmental influences on cooking and food choice; and the connections between pleasure and health.

Adele Wessell is a historian in the School of Arts and Social Sciences at Southern Cross University, Lismore, where she teaches environmental and cultural history. Her research is concentrated on food and the intersections between production and consumption where meanings are negotiated and impact on place.

Index